MASS MEDIA PROCESSES

Second Edition

Leo W. Jeffres
Cleveland State University

WAVELAND
PRESS, INC.

Prospect Heights, Illinois

For information about this book, write or call:

Waveland Press, Inc.
P.O. Box 400
Prospect Heights, Illinois 60070
(708) 634-0081

Dedication

To:
my parents,
Laurence and Edna Jeffres,
for their support all these years

Table of Contents

CHAPTER 7

Processing Print and Broadcast Messages— What Do We Do?

CHAPTER 8

Patterns of Media Content

Preface

M ass Media Processes, Second Edition began as the revision of Mass Media Processes and Effects published in 1986. The literature had grown so much since that time that we decided two volumes were necessary to cover the topics adequately. Mass Media Effects will be published later.

This text addresses the constantly evolving means by which film, print, and broadcast media attempt to entertain, inform, educate, or otherwise communicate with audiences—which also are changing continually. The interaction between the media and the audience is influenced by historical, political, economic and cultural factors. The channel chosen creates both constraints and possibilities. In short, mass media processes offer countless opportunities to explore how messages are formed and how audiences react to media presentations. How did the media develop as institutions for constructing messages? How are media messages and media systems similar or different around the world? How are media industries changing? What processes are used to construct newspaper articles, TV programs and films? Why do people adopt their unique patterns of media use? How do characteristics of films, TV formats and other messages affect the ways audiences understand them? Do media messages reflect the culture? This text will highlight numerous issues such as these in order to alert readers to the countless elements necessary for evaluating the mass media.

Comprehensive, up-to-date summaries of mass communication theory and research are difficult to write. The focus shifts constantly. What seems elementary at one level requires elaboration at another. The purpose of one reader may differ significantly from that of another. The "process" of writing this text mirrors the complexity of the field it attempts to profile. This revision includes a new chapter recognizing the important, growing literature on message processing. The first chapter has been expanded to accommodate a substantial discussion of the "currents" mentioned in the first edition but not treated at length. The literature on media industries is treated separately from the work on media organizations and message construction. Audience behaviors are the subject of two chapters: one focuses on exposure; the other looks at origins and influences. One of the themes of this book is derived from the last topic. Media behaviors deserve examination in their own right, without having to justify their impact on other disciplines. Endnotes accompany each chapter in order to incorporate references to the current literature. Any readers interested in pursuing specific topics should find ample sources to consult.

The text is designed to provide students with a comprehensive summary of the social science literature on mass communication processes. It explains how the media operate—as industries, organizations, and centers of message construction by professionals; the relationship between media and the social context in which they operate; the audiences exposed to media symbols; decoding processes used by audiences in making sense of media messages; and the pattern of media content that permeates our lives. *Mass Media Effects* will focus exclusively on the various political, social, economic and cultural effects attributed to mass media.

Although I began the revision with a basic framework of chapters, the new edition emerged from an inductive search of the literature, allowing the available research to determine the final structure and content. More than a decade and a half of social science journals have been sifted for research on mass communication and mass media. These were combined with the findings and perspectives elaborated in papers and manuscripts.

The summaries that follow, tentative or otherwise, are my own conclusions based on the literature. Certainly, other scholars may arrive at different conclusions. I hope the outline of my logic and evidence is sufficiently clear for students and scholars to make their own judgments. Since critical assessments are open-ended processes that produce only tentative results, the book is not a "final statement" but necessarily represents a slice of time ending with the publication of this text.

Finally, there are many people to thank for their direct and indirect contributions along the way. First, my work began with a co-author, Marilyn Jackson-Beeck, who started the project in 1979 and asked me to join her. "Pun's" contribution survives in the opening pages of the introductory chapter and the basic structure of the book. Several others helped along the way, including Dennis Davis and Jack Suvak, whose efforts made the preliminary edition possible. My co-author, Rick Perloff, provided an excellent chapter on social effects in the first edition and provided useful comments in the more recent writing. *Mass Media Processes, Second Edition* has benefitted greatly from various critiques. I thank Philip Allen, David Atkin, Benjamin Bates, Sharon Dunwoody, W. James Potter and others for generously providing their comments. None of these people are responsible, however, for any mistakes or final conclusions. The editors at Waveland Press were most helpful and cooperative, and the final manuscript benefited greatly from the careful editing of Carol S. Rowe. Finally, I want to thank two graduate assistants, Annie Sifford, Richard Griffin and Sylvia Fields, for checking the list of final references.

   My current work is certainly not an achievement isolated in time. Rather, it is a product of my own interactions with others along the way, including my colleagues and students at Cleveland State University. Furthermore, I am constantly amazed to find how useful past associations as a graduate student—at the University of Minnesota and the University of Washington—are. My interest in mass media began with Bert Cross at the University of Idaho many years ago. That interest was given practical form at the *Lewiston Morning Tribune*, which was a classroom filled with a host of talented journalists who had a high set of standards and a broad perspective about their work. To all these people, named and unnamed, I extend my thanks.

Leo W. Jeffres
Cleveland, Ohio

1

Studying the Mass Media of Communication
Philosophies, Models and Theories

  I. Introduction to mass communication
 II. Media characteristics
    A. Qualities of each medium—visual, sight and sound, permanence, indexability, scope, method of distribution
    B. Changing characteristics
III. Defining communication
    A. Communication discipline—focus, scope, coherence
    B. Perspectives on communication
        1. Mechanistic model
        2. Psychological perspective
        3. Symbolic interaction
        4. Pragmatic perspective
 IV. Analyzing the mass media of communication
    A. Perspectives on communication
        1. Idealism vs. realism
        2. Postmodernism
        3. Social/sciences vs. humanities and methods of investigation
        4. Foundations and starting points
        5. Paradigms, models and discipline goals
    B. Aspects of mass communication subject to research
        1. Encoding processes—processes of message construction
        2. Channels and behavior—natural sensory envelope
        3. Content of encoding/decoding activities
        4. Decoding processes
           a. Uses and gratifications
           b. Message processing
        5. Mass Media Effects
  V. Summary

magine what life would be like without mass media—without TV, radio, newspapers, magazines, books, and movies. Without mass media you would have to rely on face-to-face contact. You would be bound in space, geographically. And your communication would be bound in time—you could talk with people only while they lived, while they were physically present.

The telephone, bulletin boards, and other devices that carry messages between people may be viewed as media, but what makes a medium a mass medium is its ability to carry messages not just from one person to another but from one person to thousands or millions of others. For example, the president of the United States now can address the entire nation when he delivers a speech carried by TV. Whether he is in St. Louis or New York, people everywhere can watch and listen to him simultaneously. The fascination of the mass media is that they have liberated people from the normal constraints of time and space.

Recently, the definitions of media themselves have become blurred as new technologies integrate computers with television and telephones, and data bases or information services blur the relationship between "mass" and "point-to-point" communication. In general, mass media refer to electronic media— TV, cable, videocassettes, radio, films, and related technologies—and three types of print media—newspapers, magazines, and books—each of which is attended to by millions of people. Our focus is on mass communication, not just media as industries or institutions.

Most people grow up using several mass media daily. A good chunk of what we accept as "reality" today is a "mediated reality." The major distinction between the two is the relationship between the source (who constructs messages) and the receiver (who translates messages from the source). In face-to-face (interpersonal) situations, both parties immediately influence each other. People interact. Specifically-chosen words are delivered to you while you are prepared to interact at a pace that is more or less comfortable. You constantly provide feedback to the source, including nonverbal cues such as nods and questioning looks. Typically, you alternate roles. Contrast this with what happens when you watch TV. The relationship between you and the news anchor is impersonal. When you turn the set on, the messages are not designed for you alone. If you don't like or can't understand messages from TV, you can talk back to the set all you want, but there is no exchange and the program goes on. This makes you the receiver and only the receiver in most situations. On the other hand, you have a lot of freedom when you use mass media like TV. There is no obligation to pay attention, you can "tune out" whenever you wish, and you can choose various stories and programs. It is much more difficult to be so selective in your face-to-face discussions with friends, family, and associates.

Sources in mass communication are numerous and diverse. Consider, for example, the many sources involved in an edition of the *Reader's Digest*. Most of its articles are condensed by editors who work with material selected from other magazines and books. The original source, meanwhile, incorporated additional sources and material. The edi'ed articles are processed further by artists who illustrate and make the text fit small pages. Later, technicians and craftspeople run the presses, pour the ink, and bind the magazine. Multiple participants constitute the "source" in this example. Later chapters will explain in detail how sources encode media messages.

If source behavior is more complex than the simple reflections of the work of a single individual, receiver behaviors also are a complex bundle of personal interests, media uses and gratifications, and information processing. Later chapters will describe the audiences of mass media in greater detail. Briefly, people use the media for a variety of reasons. Books generally are chosen with considerable reflection, while much TV viewing begins with the intention of "passing time." People who live alone often find the radio or TV set a "noisy companion" that drowns out the silence, while others avoid TV except for an occasional planned viewing of a documentary. Some people read the daily newspaper only for the sports content. Others use opinion magazines and newspaper editorials as voter guidance at election time.

The feedback which occurs in mass communication—letters to the editor or Nielsen ratings, for example—generally is delayed and of lesser "magnitude" than in interpersonal communication. Many mass communication messages have "lives" of their own once they are created, while the fleeting comments of interpersonal conversations have no such permanence. By definition, the audience in mass communication is more diverse because size ensures that people of varying interests and backgrounds are included.

Media Characteristics

Each mass medium has particular attributes. Print media are strictly **visual**. Magazines and newspapers are designed to catch the eye through color, pictures, headlines, drawings, and typefaces. Messages transmitted by radio involve sound alone, while TV and movies are based on both **sight** and **sound**. Radio uses a barrage of music and sound effects to hold our aural attention, while television and the cinema employ action-packed, visual film images accompanied by music and speech. Sometimes the media have an effect we might not consciously notice. The next time you are watching a movie in a theater, notice how the audience is bathed in light. Noted media guru Marshall McLuhan goes so far as to say that TV and movies are tactile media producing a pleasant sense of all-over body stimulation.

A major difference between print and electronic media until quite recently was **permanence**. Messages in print media can be saved whereas those transmitted by the electronic media must be consumed during their fleeting lifespan. This characteristic relates directly to another feature of print media which is **indexability** by titles, headlines, and captions so you can decide if and when to read specific material. Typically, electronic media are nonindexable. Unless you have an audio or video recorder, messages transmitted by electronic media are impossible to review. Until you've seen or heard something, you don't know what it is about and then it's too late to make a choice. In addition to indexability, permanence allows the consumer to control the speed of message reception by altering reading rate. With electronic media, one receives messages at the transmission speed.

Scope is another distinguishing feature. Does a medium send messages to a national, regional, or local audience? This factor also affects the types of messages sent and is affected by the means used to distribute mass media. Each of the media can have either wide or narrow scope, but they tend to specialize. National media generally include television, movies, books, and magazines. TV reaches the largest audience. Most of its prime time programs are intended to appeal to everyone—all age groups, geographic areas, and socioeconomic groups. Books, movies, and magazines exclude many potential consumers—for example, the illiterate and indigent—although they also tend to concentrate on the national audience. In contrast, most newspaper and radio content is directed at the local audience.

Another way to classify mass media is by **method of distribution**. Basically, there are two ways to reach large, diverse audiences. Messages can be mass produced in multiple copies, or those messages can be presented once or a few times to large numbers of people simultaneously. Print media (books, magazines, newspapers) typically produce multiples of the same product; movies are shown in theaters to many people cumulatively. In contrast, radio and TV are broadcast media, which means that they seldom duplicate their messages but reach many when they transmit. Distribution and the element of permanence are obviously tied together. Videotapes and discs now parallel print media in producing multiple copies of the same product, previously available only in limited broadcasts.

When you decide to watch TV, read a book, or listen to the radio, much of the time your decision will center around content. Although the themes or topics in a medium may change somewhat, depending on audience receptivity, there are basic content structures that tend to reappear through time. For example, there are fiction, non-fiction, biography, science fiction, and reference books. Film offers various genre—horror movies, comedies, westerns, mysteries, and dramas. Radio formats range from Top 40, jazz, and talk to country and all-news. Newspapers may be general, business, urban, or suburban. Magazines run the gamut from general interest to photography and from fiction to special interests that include politics, jogging, and crafts. TV formats include situational comedies, soap operas, game shows, and police detective shows.

There is an amazing variety in the topics and themes presented in the mass media, but we also see these themes repeated across the different media. If a particular theme proves commercially successful, it probably will be adapted in a number of media. Books frequently become movies, which may become TV series. Recently, news stories have supplied the plot line for TV and cinema. Recording artists appear on MTV and other TV programs. Generally, the mass media exist symbiotically, which is to say that they operate to the benefit of each other.

Commercial messages comprise a major portion of some media content. Although books and films usually are not interrupted by commercial messages, some may appear at the beginning or the end. In contrast, consider that commercial radio and most TV stations include a minimum of nine and a half minutes of commercials per hour. About half of all newspaper and magazine content is advertising. Your choice of medium likely is to be influenced by your interest or disinterest in commercial messages almost as much as by articles, stories, or programs. In some cases, the commercial messages are the main attraction for consumers. For example, homemakers turn to the food ads in daily newspapers before the weekly shopping trip, and many people turn to magazine coupons to save money. On the other hand, commercial messages also constitute an annoyance. The VCR offers a way to avoid TV commercials, as does public TV. There also are noncommercial public radio and TV stations and some newspapers and magazines without ads.

In the United States and much of the world, mass media generally are run as businesses. They make money by selling either time or space. Electronic media such as TV and radio sell time to advertisers who hope that their commercials will be seen or heard when the audience tunes in to the programming. Print media sell space to advertisers hoping that their advertisements will be seen and read while receivers turn pages reading stories. The larger the audience, or the more "distinguished" the audience, the more money media can charge advertisers. In a sense, the mass media must deliver an audience to advertisers to remain in business themselves. This is a far cry from the interpersonal communication described earlier.

This has been a very general overview of the elements of mass media. As technology advances, even the definitions of mass media and interpersonal communication may change as different forms of communication converge.[1] For example, CD Rom discs permit individuals to use computers to access information previously available only in print. The new media technologies allow a single member of the audience to integrate a number of electronic and print media and to access and manipulate them to meet his or her needs. What previously required numerous participants in mass communication has been greatly reduced.[2]

Consequences of the new hybrid media must be considered. We have already discussed the capability of the mass media to release us from the boundaries of time and geography. The speed at which information now travels may further blur our perceptions. Meyrowitz (1985) sees the media as blurring boundaries between childhood and adulthood, between masculinity and femininity, and between the politician and citizenry. Thompson (1990) suggests that modern media have redefined the boundaries of public and private spaces. Ball-Rokeach and Reardon (1988) argue that forms of new media technologies are less important than how they are transformed by societies for communication purposes. We will address new media forms and how they fit into mass communication processes in subsequent chapters.

Defining Communication

As we stated at the start of this chapter, we are most concerned with examining mass communication. A brief look at what we mean by communication is helpful before we begin analyzing mass communication processes. Cronkhite (1986: 232) argues that communication is the "discipline whose focus is directly upon human symbolic activity, whose scope in practice includes little if anything that is not related to such activity, and whose coherence can be achieved by recognition of the study of human symbolic activity as its defining characteristic."[3] Thus, we will focus on such symbolic activities as encoding and decoding processes, the primary building blocks of mass communication. We will elaborate on these later in this chapter.

Despite efforts such as Cronkhite's (1986) to locate a focus for the discipline, a plurality of perspectives exists. The most familiar model of communication has been called the "information model" or **mechanistic model** (Fisher, 1978). An individual encodes a message that flows through a channel to another individual who decodes the message and may respond with feedback; the fidelity of the entire transmission is open to extraneous influence called noise. This model has produced an impressive display of studies which match components of the model or relationships between them. Though disparaged by some, this view of communication has been modernized and elaborated so that it continues to demonstrate a conceptual and research vitality. This is also the model most often assumed by other social science disciplines and the humanities.

However, this is not the only perspective of communication in use today. Scholars also are applying other perspectives in their study of both mass and interpersonal communication. Fisher's (1978) outline is a useful one. In addition to the mechanistic perspective, he describes three others: the psychological, the interactional, and the pragmatic. We will briefly discuss these and how they fit into analyses of the mass media of communication.

The **psychological perspective** on communication probably has been the second most important source of inspiration for mass and interpersonal communication research. It emphasizes the intrapersonal level and conceptual filters that affect the process of interpretation during encoding and decoding of a structured set of stimuli (such as media messages). Using this model, we can look at how people selectively scan incoming messages for relevant cultural content, how attitudes affect both encoding and decoding of messages on such topics as politics, and how media credibility affects an individual's consumption of media content. This perspective is favored by those inclined to emphasize the behavior of individuals and how they react in complex environments. It is almost totally ignored by those who focus on macro levels of research. Those working from this perspective point out that the operation of macro-level systems rests on assumptions about human behavior and interaction. The evidence of questioning those assumptions is gathered by looking at the communication behavior of people individually and in groups, including media consumption, people's perceptions of media, individual uses of the media, human processing of media content, and the impact of media on individuals.

A third perspective is a view of human communication which developed from **symbolic interaction**. In this view, the "self" is seen as arising through communication. The perspective is based on the view that people act toward objects on the basis of meanings the things have for them. Those meanings are derived from communication; the meanings are created, maintained, and modified through communication. The locus of this perspective is "role taking," in which people align their behavior with others. We can use this perspective to look at how people's self-concepts are developed through communication. A particularly important example for mass communication is the external images distributed by the media. In chapter 8, we will review media images and stereotypes. People see much of their personal identity captured by their involvement in occupations or professions, as well as ethnic, religious and other group membership. Consistent with this perspective, many argue that the media have an impact on their personal identities by presenting negative or insensitive images that subsequently feed into interpersonal channels and evaluations.

The **pragmatic perspective** conceptualizes communication as a system of human behaviors observed as a pattern of sequential interaction. The most important unit is the interact (for example, I ask a question and you answer equals one interact) or double interact, and the focus is on the system, not the individual. The interacts contain two kinds of information: one pertaining to content and one pertaining to relationship. The pragmatic perspective directs us to concentrate on the sequential behaviors that link people to each other

(Millar and Rogers, 1976). For example, what patterns of acts and interacts reflect escalating conflict or harmonious relationships? Observing people's interaction with the mass media, we might seek similar behavioral patterns reflecting sustained media credibility. The pragmatic perspective has had little impact on mass communication research. However, that might change as new technologies make mass communication more interactive and stimulate researchers to conceive of mass communication in pragmatic terms. Contemplating the various approaches available should sensitize communication researchers to use more complete models in their studies rather than focusing on individual components (see Jeffres and Hur, 1983; Hur and Jeffres, 1985).

Analyzing the Mass Media of Communication

If you and a friend walked into the CBS headquarters in New York City or the newsroom of your local paper, you probably would agree on what you saw and perhaps even on the significance of it. Scholars would probably have widely differing viewpoints. One might point to CBS as merely a vehicle for the reproduction of "mass culture," the place where the symbols of American society are turned into cultural artifacts that mold the conscious thoughts of Americans. Another might identify CBS as simply a reflection of the capitalistic system, its TV programs reflecting the beliefs and values of the dominant ruling class represented by CBS stockholders and their representatives in management. A third observer might see CBS as a group of coalitions jockeying for position in an uncertain environment where no single person or group has control; CBS itself would be but one source of symbols in a "pluralistic society." A fourth person might see the network as an institution and pattern of professional encoders molded by the long-term consequences of audience behaviors tapped by such measures as Nielsen ratings. If these four individuals were together, they might also disagree over what evidence would be acceptable for verifying their statements or settling arguments over which one best represented reality.

Perspectives on Communication

How one evaluates the mass media of communication would vary according to the communication perspective being used as well as the overall philosophical perspective employed. According to **idealism**, reality is the creation of the mind or spirit and reason itself is a superior source of knowledge. Following this tradition, critical scholars analyze texts and present rational models to explain mass communication as they seek "meanings" and values represented in human behavior. According to **realism**, objects perceived through our senses exist independently of the mind, and universals exist outside the mind; thus, we rely on our power of perception and the senses for learning about reality. Following this tradition, social scientists rely on experiments, surveys, content analyses, and information gained through the senses to test their models explaining mass communication. Here the goal is to understand patterns and origins of human behavior and arrangements valid across time and context.

By some accounts, there has been a blurring between the disciplines as scholars have borrowed each other's methods of inquiry and challenged each other's goals. **Postmodernism** is the phrase often used to refer to the pluralism of approaches to knowledge today. Although there is controversy over the use of the term, it refers to a loss of authority of styles, grand theory,[4] and, particularly, methods for ascertaining knowledge.[5]

Here we can only provide brief descriptions of the two major approaches to methods. A basic outline of the **scientific method** includes clear conceptual definitions of concepts, precise measurements that are open to inspection, critique, and reuse, and a reliance on techniques that gather information through the senses (e.g., surveys that ask questions about human intentions or observations of journalists' news-gathering strategies). Statistics are employed for precision but are not necessary, and over time, results are challenged by subsequent studies as theories are supported, modified, or discarded. Admission of knowledge is subject to debate within the relevant scientific community which has access to the methods and results.[6] Though there are differences in views about what "theory" should look like and how models or paradigms or perspectives should be constructed, there is consensus among particular scientific communities that empirical findings[7] should form the basis for making decisions about the admission of scientific "truth" or knowledge.

Critical and "idealist" scholars argue for the use of rational methods, or "empirical" methods which take into account the interpretive processes employed by scholars themselves. These include ethnomethodology, interpretive sociology, and phenomenology—"the study of how consciousness orients experience to produce knowledge in everyday life" (Traudt, Anderson and Meyer, 1987: 302; Bovone, 1989).[8] Methods employed by "idealists" focus on human interpretation and devalue the reliance on empirical data gathered through the senses. Inquiry is achieved through interpretive processes referred to as sense-making or reading. "Reading is a process through which a historically situated subject makes sense of the way her culture represents itself and produces 'pictures of (acceptable) reality'" (Ebert, 1986: 894).

Debates over the utility of methods often seem to consist of the creation and destruction of "straw men," with one perspective portraying the other's method in terms that are dated and appear absurd (Cronkhite, 1986), but the value of a method and a perspective will be based on the research and knowledge it generates, not shrill arguments.[9] Charges levied against the model of scientific inquiry argue that social scientific knowledge does not rely on an absolute foundation but is contingent and relative because of human involvement in applying methods or in the origins of those methods.[10] Attacks on critical methods note that the same charges can be levied against critical research. They also question the ideological/political base of these methods and the vagueness of their implementation.[11]

Debates over methods represent a search for secure foundations and a starting point for scholarly inquiry. This task is an effort to separate the knowing from the known. Realist scholars find origins in the physical world, which is assumed to exist independent of our senses. Chaffee and Berger (1987) note that the key to scientific theory is seeking and explaining by developing general principles that can be used to account for specific events or classes of events. **Testability**[12] within a community of scholars is the basis for a claim of validity. Although often ignored by critics, social science as process has always represented a form of relativity in that knowledge/research findings today are contingent, dependent upon continued verification tomorrow.

Although "idealist" scholars also attend to empirical phenomena such as human conversations and TV programs, their own methods of rational or interpretive analysis are based on human symbol use and communication. If symbol systems are the key to human inquiry, then communication processes themselves become the foundation. Penman (1988: 408) notes that in studying communication "we are in fact studying a process of which we are a part" and thus "we need to incorporate the fundamental qualities of the communication process into our research process." Habermas (1985) places communication in a central role in society.[13] Habermas's most important insight is that the specific structure of human communication is irreducible—"human beings can have dealings with one another without making each other into means for achieving individually predetermined ends, without closing themselves to the implicit or explicit demands of their fellow human beings for true knowledge, correct conduct, and authentic 'self-presentation'" (Joas, 1988: 36).[14]

Paradigms, Models and Discipline Goals. Scholars have used a variety of frameworks or perspectives for examining mass communication. Some of these have focused on mass media or communication as part of society, thus linking disciplines. In general, these have dominated empirical research in the area because of the relatively short history of our efforts. Other frameworks, of a more recent vintage in many cases, are restricted to communication or mass communication phenomena, thus serving purposes of the discipline itself.

Frameworks, perspectives, models, paradigms—though distinctions can be made—all refer to sets of assumptions, a preferred structure or form, or an explanatory goal. The concept of "theory" itself is often thrown into the hopper as well. A paradigm refers to a way of understanding, a model for studying or representing reality. Thus, we see literatures in communication that lay their foundation on one perspective rather than another, or which attack a research tradition on the basis that it follows an outdated paradigm—which generally refers to one they oppose, often presented as a straw man. To account for this, such critics argue for grander "perspectives" within which theorizing must be done. Within mass communication, several streams of research probably would merit the title of paradigm, or at least shared consensus among a set of scholars. "Within the brief span of about a half century, communication as a field has evolved with increasing maturity and clarity of purpose. [It] has seen the overthrow of linear models, the bullet theory, the limited or no effects perspective, and the classical diffusion theory, among others. Following each overthrow of the dominant view, the field has emerged stronger, both theoretically and methodologically. . . . This view is also consistent with Dewey (1948/1967: xvii), who said that 'science is a pursuit, not a coming into possession of the immutable'" (Gonzalez, 1988: 306-307). We will discuss the use or popularity of particular paradigms, models, or theories as we move through the literature.

Aspects of Mass Communication Subject to Research

In this section, we will examine particular symbolic activities—encoding processes, decoding processes, channel structure and usage, and content.

Encoding Processes. "Encoding" refers to **processes of message construction**. In mass communication, some encoding activities are journalistic news gathering, writing/acting/producing TV programs and films, and editing radio or TV commercials. Encoding behaviors occur from the individual level to their patterning in organizations. One line of research attempts to identify patterns of message construction, while a second looks at these processes in context.

An example of work on patterns of message construction is found in work on news-gathering activities by journalists. Some of this work is descriptive—determining the number of journalists filling particular roles. Other research attempts to explain relationships among professional encoders and how they construct messages. How do journalists define their roles—as public "watchdogs," as good citizens, as neutral observers? Definitions of professionalism also are important because encoding behaviors are tied to the guidelines established for the profession. For example, journalists who believe in some form of "objectivity" tend to attribute more information to sources. One growing body of work focuses on the information-gathering routines and structures used in constructing such diverse content as journalistic news stories and films. Journalists' definitions of news also are crucial in identifying features for encoding. We also see the construction of "factory models" and others that describe encoding processes within media units such as TV stations.

Other work relates encoders and encoding activities to their larger context and other disciplines. Profiles of journalists describe their ethnic and social background, education, and gender. Although again largely descriptive, we see some attention to sociological theories on professions in general. The larger media organization which "houses" or "represents" encoding activities also has been linked to context, and the best example of work here is that by Phil Tichenor and his colleagues at Minnesota. Traditionally sociologists have seen people's behaviors as shaped by the social structure and meanings of a society; Tichenor and his colleagues (1980) look at how a town's newspapers and other media reflect the size and diversity of its population. Papers in larger towns, for example are seen as distributing more conflict information than those in smaller towns because it is functional for such diverse communities.[15]

Efforts to describe encoding activities or relate them to context often are grouped with studies on the "production of culture" (Mukerji and Schudson, 1986), which have examined television and newspaper news,[16] television entertainment,[17] and works on publishing.[18]

Encoding activities and organizations have been linked to economic contexts more often than any other. For many, commercial TV is "first" an economic medium, and, thus, scholars need to look at where the money goes and for what.[19] "The socioeconomic analysis doesn't explain everything, but it does explain a lot. The flow of commercial television, the seemingly unrelated sequence of commercials, program segments, and promotional materials, can be usefully defamiliarized once we understand how everything is part of a marketing system. Form responds to function" (Budd, Entman, and Steinman, 1990: 172). However, while the economic links may be significant, alternative views note its limitations in explaining encoding behaviors (see Fiske, 1989). There is even diversity among those following the Marxist/radical traditions (Curran, 1990). For example, Peter Golding, a leading political economist, stresses the importance of ideological management and the individualist values of reporters rather than economic ownership of the press in accounting for a British tabloid crusade against welfare claimants (Golding and Middleton, 1982).

Encoding behaviors also have been linked to the political system. Research linking political beliefs of encoders with their encoding activities is meager but worthwhile; impact of chain ownership on encoding behaviors is one example. Gonzalez (1988: 303) claims the contrary, that research in communication has "increase[d] our understanding and practice of the 'democratic ideal,' including studies on public information campaigns, news gathering and gatekeeping, propaganda and persuasion, public opinion formation, political participation, diffusion of innovations, flow of information within and across countries, agenda setting processes and development in the Third World."

Channels and Behavior.   The concept of "channel" itself is a slippery
one, often used interchangeably with media. Each of the media can be
characterized as a channel—a means to convey information or link encoders
with particular audiences (Blake and Haroldsen, 1975; Connors, 1982). In
some perspectives on communication, the concept doesn't even exist, but it
is particularly useful in describing mass communication phenomena. As Lin
(1973: 41) notes, the concept of channel is linked to characteristics of the
encoding and decoding processes, in particular, the nature of activity and the
capacity or number of messages which can be conveyed efficiently. Print media,
for example, are better at transmitting large volumes of detail that audiences
can examine at their leisure. Pfau (1990) notes the need for investigating the
media as distinct variables, pointing out that TV resembles interpersonal
communication in the manner in which it exercises influence, placing greater
emphasis on relational as opposed to content messages, source as opposed
to content factors, and a warmer, more casual communication style.

The concept of **channel** is closely tied to technology, and it is here that
researchers have focused their attentions. As noted earlier, new technologies
have blurred distinctions between media and between mass and non-mass
communication. The new technologies and mass media in general alter the
relationship between people and their environment. Concerns about this
relationship are often centered on our understanding of reality.[20] Until the 19th
century, most people's actual experience was limited to events occurring within
the **"natural sensory envelope**—the limits of the human nervous system
to detect physical stimuli governed by natural, physical processes" (Funkhouser
and Shaw, 1990: 78).[21] The development of symbolic communication
(language and drawings, then writing, then printing) permitted access to
information without firsthand experience. Individuals thus could learn about
events that occurred outside their sensory envelope, "but this constituted
symbolic information, not experience."

Twentieth century communication innovations, particularly TV, films, and
computers differ crucially from all previous media and forms of communication.
The sight/sound media manipulate and rearrange not only the content but
the process of decoding experiences, shaping how the audience perceives and
interprets physical and social reality. "Introduced into one's sensory envelope,
they appear to extend it beyond its natural limits. Unlike speech, writing,
drawing, painting, and even photography, they let mass audiences perceive,
as quasi-eyewitnesses, events that happened in other times or in other places,
or that never really happened at all," producing "synthetic experiences"
(Funkhouser and Shaw, 1990: 78). The creation of new technologies also
affects encoding processes. For example, the news-gathering routines and
editing processes in film changed with the appearance of "special effects."

Magic window (Hawkins, 1977) is one of the concepts that links audience members to the channels. Potter (1988) says that perceived reality should be regarded as a multidimensional construct composed of three elements: magic window, utility, and identity. Magic window is concerned with how much a viewer believes television content is an unaltered, accurate representation of actual life. Utility addresses viewers' feelings that TV augments and expands direct experiences. Identity focuses on the similarity between television characters and situations, and the people and situations experienced in real life (Potter, 1988: 26).

Content of Encoding/Decoding Activities.   Content itself must be linked with encoding or decoding activities to fall within symbolic activity. Otherwise, discussion of media content would be limited to "cultural artifacts" linked to society in general or particular subcultures.

As mentioned earlier, content structures are identified by such terms as genre and format; these forms recur over time and link both encoders and decoders. Examples of genre are westerns and science fiction, and examples of TV formats are situation comedies and news magazines. Audiences (decoders) recognize examples of these and watch them with a set of expectations. Encoders use particular routines and strategies to create a particular structure (dialogue appropriate for characters in a specific genre, special effects, period costumes, or pertinent soundtrack), which may be modified through time. Content structures have been examined in all encoding organizations—from newspapers to radio stations and film producers. Some research has sought to relate content structures to decoding activities; credibility associated with content and its impact on learning or public understanding of the encoding activities associated with particular content are two examples.

Content also has been linked to other disciplines and domains, often with virtually no attention to the encoding or decoding processes themselves. For example, critical scholars have looked at film genres and linked them to society or culture in general. Some have examined films as "representative" of ideologies ranging from anti-women to "class interests." The concept of "stereotype" has probably received the bulk of the attention from empirical scholars, with many studies examining the distribution of women or minorities in media content vs. their actual representation in the country or society.

Decoding Processes.   Decoding activities are important in almost every theoretical focus used in the discipline today. In mass communication, "audience analysis" is a major subfield and a commercially viable research concentration. Decoding processes include two major "paradigms" or research concentrations, one focusing on **uses and gratifications** and one examining **message processing**.[22] Uses and gratifications researchers study the sustaining link of audience members to their media behavior patterns. People are seen as engaging in media behaviors to ascertain particular gratifications or to pursue particular uses; if those uses and gratifications are not forthcoming over time, the pattern will change. Chapter 6 elaborates on this research tradition.

Empirical scholars examine message processing, which emphasizes cognitive concepts in decoding activities. For example, how do people process articles written in chronological order as opposed to other forms? Critical scholars use "interpretive" methods for examining how audiences decode media symbols. All of these traditions—uses and gratifications, message processing, and interpretivism—see the individual as capable of generating meaning, and the individual's subjective experience is seen as the primary subject for analysis.[23]

Interpretive media theory is typified by assumptions of a) an active audience and b) media content which is open to individual interpretation by people "creating meaning in the process of consumption" (Evans, 1990: 147).[24] Critical scholars look at **patterns of interpretations**. Grossberg (1989: 257) notes, for example, that "television is never passively received and its texts are as open to different interpretations as any rock and roll song." The ability of audience members to use different filters and selectively perceive images has long been established in the empirical literature. Recently, critical scholars have noted a similar activity using an interpretive framework.[25] Thus, members of the audience—"lay theorists"—are at the mercy of their senses just as are researchers, but no more so.

The concept of "interpretive community" has been championed as an innovative and useful way to reconceptualize the media audience.[26] In this view, although individual interpretations may vary, differences in interpretation could arise from differences in the assumptions that underlie different interpretive communities rather than from differences between individuals (Allen, 1987); this conceptualization parallels the social background similarities of decoders examined by empirical scholars. The interpretive community may be an increasingly utilized concept but its usefulness and its distinctiveness from other more traditional conceptions of the media audience—as ethnic groups, gender groups, or age groups—are far from clear (Evans, 1990).

Often decoding is linked with the "effects" literature, but increasingly it is differentiated so that processing of media content receives its own due. Since audiences are "targets" for not only mass communication researchers but also those interested in politics, economics, marketing, and other disciplines, much research links decoding processes with other domains. It is the concept of the audience member's activity and ability to "resist" media that links decoding activities to other domains.[27]

Mass Media Effects. At one point, virtually the entire mass communication literature would have fallen into this area, and it remains the major question for many scholars. The issue of what constitutes effects is certainly important, but it has come to mean different things. "Effects" may refer to the relationship between encoding and decoding activities within mass communication. The concept also links mass communication processes with other systems and the larger society. Here we will merely note the area, which will be examined separately in a second book.

Summary

In this chapter we identified modern mass media of communication and their characteristics. Mass communication was defined and contrasted with interpersonal communication, with attention to how new technologies are blurring differences between different forms of communication. We briefly defined communication and described perspectives used by researchers. We then looked at paradigms, models, and goals of those who analyze the mass media. Aspects of mass communication which are the objects of inquiry also were examined, including: encoding processes, channels, content, decoding processes, and effects.

Chapter One Footnotes

1. See Reardon and Rogers (1988), Chaffee and Mutz (1988), Berger and Chaffee (1988) and Olson (1988).
2. Merging computer interactivity with the storage capability of books and visual impact of television, "hybrid" media allow smaller and more specialized audiences (Webster, 1986), communication with anyone virtually anywhere at anytime (Kobayashi, 1982), and programming controlled by the receiver (Olson, 1988). New media technologies allow access when and where the individual wants (Kobayashi, 1982), and the material can be manipulated to suit one's needs (Brand, 1987; Bylinsky, 1988). Examples of such new media technologies range from the Sony Walkman, the computer-as-book (Brand, 1987), self-programmed newspapers (Brand, 1987; Nace, 1986), interactive television such as "Captain Power," a syndicated TV program that allows viewers to interact with the videotaped characters through toys purchased and used at home (Kaye, 1987), and even more futuristic three-dimensional media environments (Olson, 1988).
3. Since the study of human symbolic activity often is central to disciplines that comprise the humanities and social sciences, we need to distinguish communication from other disciplines. Cronkhite (1986: 231) offers guidelines. Communication scholars look at symbols (a more general class of signs) rather than signs (anything that "stands for" something else, its significate), the fodder for linguistic analyses. In other words, while linguist focus on language construction, its use and development as a system, communication scholars look at how people use symbols to "communicate"—convey meanings and ascertain what's in the mind of others. Differentiating the symbolic behaviors of communication from "nonsymbolic" behavior studied by psychologists and sociologists, among others, is another task. Cognitive psychologists study the cognitive processing of symbols, but they study other types of cognitive activity as well. While social psychologists and sociologists may study the functions of symbolic activity in human social relations, this is not the focus of their domain. Cronkhite (1986: 236) distinguishes between "interpretation of nonsymbolic behavior, or nonsymbolic aspects of behavior, and the

communication achieved by symbols and symbolic aspects of rituals." He argues against accepting the popular statement by Watzlawick, Beavin and Jackson (1967), "You Cannot Not Communicate," as a definition of the discipline. The Watzlawick et al. chain of reasoning is as follows: one cannot not behave; all behavior is communication; ergo, one cannot not communicate. While not quarreling with the first premise, Cronkhite's emphasis on symbolic behavior constitutes a rejection of the second generalization that all behavior is communication. Thus, communication scholars may not be the only scholars studying symbolic phenomena nor claim to study all symbolic phenomena, but symbolic activity is their primary focus.

4. The "blurring of genres" (Geertz, 1980) and loss of "grand theory" have affected all disciplines (Fiske and Shweder, 1986). We also see an apparent erosion of older distinctions between high and low culture, between popular and elite forms, e.g., television and cinema (Petro, 1986: 16), between politics and humanities, and between science/art and historical and linguistic processes (Clifford, 1986).

5. The concept of "postmodernism" has a long and controversial history (Chabot, 1988; Collins, 1989; Feher, 1987; Glassner, 1989; Harvey, 1989; Hutcheon, 1989; Jameson, 1984; Ross, 1989; Sloan, 1987). Hall (1990: 339) notes that postmodernism is marked by the "collapse of the distinction between scientific and humanistic thought." By some accounts, the distinction between the sciences and humanities was clear earlier in this century, and philosophers had sorted out the bases for contributions from each. It is arguable whether the distinction was ever as clear as now portrayed, but there is no doubt that the lines have blurred further. Postmodernism is invariably defined vis-á-vis modernism but there is little agreement about the nature of modernism (Barzun, 1961; Bell, 1976; Bradbury and McFarlane, 1976; Chabot, 1988; Gluck, 1986; Kramer, 1973; Lukacs, 1950; Poggioli,1968; Read, 1953; Richardson, 1988; Sampson, 1989; Singal, 1987; Woolf, 1967). However, modernism is associated with a challenging of old relationships, a break with the past, the liberation of the individual from ties that bound one to the community, an acceptance of knowledge achieved through scientific methods, and a welcome to new forms of artistic expression. If the origins of modernism are controversial, the date of its demise is even more hotly contested (Gluck, 1986: 847), being located in the 1930s with the rise of fascism and totalitarianism (Willett, 1978), or in the 1960s with the disappearance of a "true adversary culture" (Trilling, 1965; Levin, 1966; Howe, 1970; Wolfe, 1975; Stark, 1974; Hassan, 1967; Steiner, 1967). Singal (1987: 21) sees American modernism culminating in the 1960s with its quest for spontaneity and the breaking down of cultural and social barriers. Or is modernism still with us today? Chabot (1988: 1, 18) notes little agreement about the timing of a modern-postmodern break and concludes it is "doubtful that a rupture of such magnitude has occurred."

6. Rorty (1979: 361,321) notes that the collapse of epistemology as a general theory of knowledge means that "objectivity" is redefined as involving "conformity to the norms for justification" of knowledge of "agreed-upon practices of inquiry." Thus, by reconciling objectivism and relativism, we end up with a scientific relativism ("conventionalism," Halfpenny, 1982) that depends on shared assumptions of investigators, which short-circuits logical problems and turns science into something of an "intellectual wrestling match." This is not far from Nagel's community of scholars. This works if researchers couple it with a realistic belief in a world that exists independently of our knowledge (Popper, 1979, 1983). For most mass communication and other social science researchers, this is a small leap to make. In fact, it represents what passes as "standard" scientific method today, despite characterizations by some theorists that paint a rigid, dated view.

7. Most research falling under the category of empiricism today probably would fit more comfortably under the label of "dualism," a philosophical system that tries to explain phenomena in terms of both mind-and-matter principles (e.g., Immanual Kant). Empiricism accounts for the bulk of contemporary American mass communication research and is the basis for the scientific method and its constituent requirements that evidence allow for testability

and rejection of hypotheses generated by critics and observers. In the view of some humanists, science has lost the human scope and perspective. They argue that particular sciences ask only questions permissible through their particular framework of thought and soluble only by available methods. They argue that only humanists keep their attention on basic human issues. But there is nothing wrong with asking particular questions and one might argue there is nothing else left than to ask particular questions. Science is the function of the increase of rationalization and sophistication. Though this may be a historical phenomenon in the long run, at present "it is about the best that we can do in mastering the world, and we can do it without practical respect for our particular subcultural ideologies" (Holub, 1987).

8. Phenomenologists studying communication "understand the knowledge others possess only as the meanings that they create from their confrontations between direct experience and the semiotic frame in which they live (reflexivity); we can understand others' meanings only after they are displayed through actions and discourse; and scholarship makes that understanding explicit and public through ordered analysis" (Traudt, Anderson and Meyer, 1987: 302-303).

9. Cronkhite (1986: 237) adds that "one most effectively advances a paradigm to which one is committed, not by arguing its superiority, but by providing 'examples' of its superiority." Communication scholars would best serve the discipline by resolving differences with dispatch, or momentarily agreeing to disagree and getting on with the business of doing research."

10. However, the attacks are generally against a particular conception of science, specifically **logical positivism**, the philosophical view that all meaningful statements are either verifiable or confirmable by empirical observation/experiment and that metaphysical (purely rational) theories are not meaningful. Though most empirical social scientists accept other forms of "truth" and the "received view" is only one acceptable form of theories today, critics of empirical science often use them as "straw men" representing all practicing scholars following social scientific methods (Bryant, 1985; Collins, 1989). Most philosophers make room for theoretical preconceptions ("perspectives," "paradigms") and for pragmatics in both theory formulation and research (Dummett, 1978; Putnam, 1983; Quine, 1969). There is a loosening up of what constitutes knowledge today. Whether one accepts the notion of "cause" or not does not dismiss the aim of testable, generalized explanatory principles (Collins, 1989: 134). "That there is more than one form of Truth does not necessarily entail the demise of all truth" (Barber, 1989: 171).

11. Until recently, empirical researchers have been reactive, seldom critiquing the "idealist" critics and their approaches or responding to the criticism. However, as Jacobson (1990: 6-7) notes, in abandoning objective foundations "the baby may have been thrown out with the bathwater." This is unnecessary. "For example, the fact that observation is an interpretive process . . . does not mean that all communication research should be designed as an attempt to reveal the grounds of understanding, even if it does deepen our self-understanding in profound ways." Furthermore, when left to defend the value and utility of interpretive processes without reference to science, interpretive and rational analysis has often been less than successful, and it remains to be seen whether such research will ever constitute a basis for human decision-making and social actions. Pointing to the inadequacies of scientific cause-and-effect research does not mean that interpretive and "idealistic" methodologies will fill the void by providing acceptable answers to how audiences process information, how components of mass communication systems are related to each other, or how media affect particular groups of people. There also is no consensus among "idealist" scholars on criteria for validity or reliability in judging the fruits of such rational methods, particularly in avoiding the political agendas which use research solely to advance personal and ideological interests, not the pursuit of knowledge.

12. This may occur within a single study (e.g., hypothesis testing) or across time as a general scientific process (e.g., generalizations inductively arrived at from the data are subject to testing by the same scholar or critics at later points in time).

13. Habermas argues that there are at least two forms of communication—communicative action and discourse. The latter is a form of "pure communication," via which we can search for objective validity. Called the "last great rationalist," Habermas insists that we need more, not less rationality; this seems to mean we should be able to give reasons for one's behavior or preferences, reasons that are understandable/meaningful within a given social context. Habermas's theory is erected on the premise that argumentation provides the key to significant knowledge about social relations.

14. Habermas's theory is erected on the premise that argumentation provides the key to significant knowledge about social relations. Habermas's theory of communicative action consists of a system of three types of action: the instrumental, the strategic, and the communicative. "Communication creates our social world, just as causality could be said to generate a physical one" (Penman, 1988: 398; Harre, 1983). Communication here is seen as a "self-generating" process rather than one determined by material factors. Meaning is brought about in the interaction between people, and knowledge emerges in the communication process, i.e., knowledge is meaning.

15. Also operating at this level, classical Marxists see media operations as determined essentially by economic forces (Murdock and Golding, 1977). Some variants of Marxism focus on how media in capitalist nations support the ruling class (Garnham, 1983; White, 1983; Hall, 1977).

16. See Epstein (1973), Fishman (1980), Gans (1979), Gitlin (1980), Golding (1981), Schudson (1983), Turow (1984), and Tuchman (1972).

17. See Cantor and Pingree (1983), Gitlin (1983), and Intintoli (1984).

18. See Coser, Kadushin and Powell (1982), Griswold (1981), Powell (1985), and Tuchman (1982).

19. See Budd, Entman, and Steinman (1990), Budd and Steinman (1989), Entman (1989), Gomery (1989), Livant (1979), Meehan (1986), Murdock (1978), and Smythe (1977).

20. Funkhouser and Shaw (1990: 75) note, "concern about the representation of reality is an ancient one." As early as 400 B.C. Plato doubted the social usefulness of art and poetry "because reality was the essence of the nature of things and art and poetry were a step removed."

21. Steuer (1992) notes that the highly publicized "virtual reality" experience rests on several technologies and can best be defined through the concept of "presence," one's experience or sense of being in a physical environment. The term "telepresence" is used to refer to media-induced sense of presence, and technologies vary in terms of their "vividness" and "interactivity." Vividness refers to the representational richness of the mediated environment as defined by its formal features, i.e., the way an environment presents information to the senses. Interactivity is the extent to which one can participate in modifying the content and form of a mediated environment in real time.

22. Both also are significant for the "media effects" literature, though that linkage is not necessarily part of the theories themselves.

23. "Interpretivists speak of individual interpretations of media content as being, in part, a product of 'social situation,' and gratifications claim to investigate the 'social character' of media use" (Evans, 1990: 152). In the final analysis, both remain psycho- rather than sociologistic because "the individual is seen both as creating meaning and as the most appropriate (or only) level of analysis."

24. Evans (1990: 147) describes the interpretive approach in mass communication as including reader-oriented scholarship (e.g., Allen, 1985, 1987; Lindlof, 1988; Radway, 1984a, 1984b), British cultural studies and its offshoots (e.g., Fiske, 1987a, 1987b; Morley, 1980), and media criticism of Newcomb (1984, 1988; Newcomb and Hirsch, 1984) and others (e.g., Dahlgren, 1985; Grossberg and Treichler, 1987). These approaches are said to introduce radically different models of media processes (Anderson and Avery, 1988).

25. Fiske (1987b: 302-308), for example, examines "oppositional viewing," whereby audiences frequently and actively resist "hegemonic content" when decoding television news. In other words, audience members arrive at conclusions that are contrary to the more popular view "represented" by the media messages. Examining the "autonomy of the audience," Morgenstern (1992) describes people as struggling for meaning in an effort to maintain a theory system sufficiently stable for knowledge to accumulate over time but responsive enough to accommodate change from the environment.
26. See Jensen (1987), Lindlof (1988), and Radway (1984a).
27. For the interpretivists, the activity of media consumers is conscious, rational, and frequently anti-establishment (Evans, 1990: 150). American scholars like Lawrence Grossberg and John Fiske "affirm that people habitually use the content of dominant media against itself, to empower themselves" (Budd, Entman and Steinman, 1990; Fiske, 1987b; Grossberg, 1984, 1989). This lack of solidarity with European scholars following a materialist/Marxist position has been the subject of disappointment for some who work under the rubric of "cultural studies" (Budd, Entman and Steinman, 1990: 170).

2

Media and Society

24   Chapter Two

I. Factors affecting development of the media—
   A. Literacy, education, religion, economic factors,
   B. Technology and natural sensory envelope, political
   C. Factors, urbanization, immigration
II. Emergence of the media—a brief history
   A. Booksmedia for posterity
   B. Newspapers—changing audiences
      1. First newspapers
      2. Colonial press
      3. Revolutionary war
      4. Penny press
      5. Civil war
      6. Forces of industrial revolution
      7. Yellow journalism
      8. Muckrakers
      9. Jazz journalism
      10. Interpretive reporting
   C. Magazines—specialize to serve diversity
   D. Film—adaptation of several media to a new form
   E. Radio—from simple to complex
   F. Television—learning from the past
   G. Advertising—both the bread and the wrapper
III. Relationships among the media—shifting forms and functions
   A. Changing characteristics
   B. Principle of relative constancy
IV. Mass media around the world
   A. Print media
   B. Broadcasting
   C. Cultural and linguistic features of media systems
      1. Linguistic factors
      2. Public perceptions
   D. Media's relation to governments
V. Challenging concepts of social control
   A. Four normative philosophies revised—authoritarian, libertarian, Marxist/communist, social responsibility
   B. What is freedom?
   C. Measuring freedom
VI. Summary

T he history of human communication stretches back to the beginning of human history. Our ability to engage in symbolic activity is the basis for our development as human beings and our ability to exist in communities. Over time, new systems of communication have emerged, as people have sought new ways to express themselves or to learn what was in the minds of fellow human beings. In his account of the history of human communication, Schramm (1988) starts with the prehistoric pictures on cave walls that preceded the invention of language and then writing itself. Institutions such as families, cities, schools, and churches played significant roles in the advancement of communication. The appearance of the first "mass medium" required the invention of paper and printing technologies, which were in place by the fifteenth century when books were produced. Mass media do not appear overnight, of their own volition, for no good reason; the media evolve for a variety of reasons. Newspapers, radio, and television have long histories of development and are the result of a convergence of many factors. Numerous economic, political, and social circumstances will be detailed in this chapter. With the appearance of each new medium, existing media have had to adapt during periods of uncertainty, yet each one has managed to persist. Schramm (1988) notes that mass media never seem to die, although single units within the media may cease to exist. All of the media available in the seventeenth through the twentieth centuries are still with us.

Factors Affecting Development of the Media

As far as print media are concerned, **literacy** is necessary before they can become popular. Although today literacy is recognized as an asset, at one time the Greek philosopher Plato attacked literacy for undermining people's memory and rhetorical abilities (Back, 1989). How has literacy affected the development of print media? Which came first? Why should people learn to read unless they have interesting materials available? We know that some books, magazines, and newspapers must be available to stimulate people to read or to learn to read. We also know that newspaper circulation will be quite small unless the pool of literate people is large. Economically advanced countries with high literacy rates have near saturation of newspapers while poorer countries encourage literacy programs with weekly papers, pamphlets, and wall sheets in an effort to catch up.

Education is the handmaiden of literacy; it stimulates the growth of print media. In the United States, as elsewhere, the spread of mass education fed large numbers of readers into the audiences of print media. Inspired by the philosophy of Thomas Jefferson, this country introduced a mass education system (beginning in 1830) to prepare the population to become responsible citizens capable of selecting wisely from the media and equally capable of contributing to a "free marketplace of ideas."

The growth of popular fiction and newspaper journalism had a profound impact, but Nord (1984) points out that **religion** also had a part to play. The missionary impulse lay at the foundation of this growing interest among the masses in learning how to read (Luke, 1989). Evangelical Christians dreamed of a genuinely mass medium that would deliver the same printed message to everyone in the nation. The church played a pioneering role in the introduction of print technology in Africa (Tomaselli, 1988) and continues to influence publishing there (Riddle, 1989). Religion also affects regulation of the media. For instance, Confucianism has influenced Korea's general acceptance of governmental restrictions on the press (Youm, 1986).

Economic factors also are important to media growth, sometimes in unpredictable ways. Not surprisingly, the wealthier people and countries tend to have and to use the greatest number of mass media. Contrary to expectations, movies flourished and radio boomed during the Great Depression of the 1930s. Often the radio was one of the last things Americans gave up as their standard of living fell. Inexpensive entertainment and news bulletins help people through hard times.

Another factor affecting media growth is **technology**. The printing press clearly had to develop for books and newspapers to be widespread, and the telegraph stimulated the growth of newspapers in the western United States (Scharlott, 1989). The components that go into a radio or TV set had to be invented before radio and TV could be used by more than a few tinkerers. Technology need not be complicated or directly linked to the new medium. For example, Dreyfus (1988) discusses the contribution of the invention of spectacles to printing and literacy. Technology is a response to social needs as well as a phenomenon that stimulates other social developments like mass media. Aitken (1985: 14) calls technology "one form of organized information" and sees inventions as simply new combinations of already-existing knowledge that result from specific communication networks. Although technology is a necessary ingredient in the development of media, it is not always sufficient. Printing can be traced back a thousand years to Asia, and Johann Gutenberg introduced movable type to Europe around 1440, but the first newspapers were not successful until more than a hundred years later (McIntyre, 1987). Clearly, technology works in combination with other factors.

Political factors wield enormous influence. Sometimes the influence is coincidental, sometimes it is invited, at other times it is imposed and resented. Radio, the first broadcast medium, represented a technological thicket during its early years. Almost every component of radio was separately patented in more than one country, making it almost impossible to put the parts together without ending up in court. Radio was stymied until World War I when urgent military needs for improved radio systems led to the suspension of all patent disputes. After the war many patent disputes remained; no one had sufficient patents to make a complete system. Within a three-year period (1919-1922) a series of cross-licensing agreements were made and, finally, the new medium took off. The chaos in radio also provoked a generally reluctant private sector to seek government intervention. This led to the formation of the Federal Communication Commission and licensing of radio stations. The most recent media technologies have faced a similar situation. Initially, cassette or video discs employed several technologies. Beta cassettes would not play on VHS machines and vice versa. Competition determined which system would survive. Such competition can create reluctance on the part of a public not wishing to be caught with obsolete technology. VCRs moved beyond this stage and grew rapidly but the newest technologies continue to face this dilemma (Laser Disks, DAT cassettes, computer software packages, high definition TV, AM stereo radio, etc.). New technologies, such as low-power transmitters, have helped the diffusion of media in developing countries (Singhal et al., 1988). The infrastructure often taken for granted must be in place before the media can progress.

   Urbanization and **immigration** contribute to the development of mass media. Back (1989) notes that similar changes through history have affected rhetoric and interpersonal communication. As cities increased their autonomy in the Middle Ages, the ability to sway crowds grew in importance. Large numbers of people are necessary to support a TV station or a daily newspaper. Urbanization promotes the growth of mass media so that countries and regions which are most heavily populated tend to have more newspapers, radio stations, TV stations, and movie theaters.[1] As immigrant groups move into various regions, they tend to develop mass media in their own languages.

The Emergence of the Media—A Brief History

Books—Media for Posterity

   The earliest book was "published" (actually, written by hand) on leathery, dried animal skins by Saxons living in what we now call England. The oldest printed book still surviving today was printed in 868, in China, letter by letter. Efforts at book production continued at a slow pace until the development of the printing press centuries later. With the printing press came mass production and a chance for a profitable new industry. In America early book publishing was quite limited, most of it consisting of Bibles, blank ledgers, account books, and custom-ordered books. Diversity of content and book distribution increased after independence.

The growth of libraries and mass education in the United States gave a big boost to book publishing. The *McGuffey Reader* was an illustrative case. The reader was published as a series of elementary school texts in the nineteenth century; it eventually had a circulation of more than 120 million copies. Today educational books still account for a significant portion of total book sales, with textbooks alone accounting for more than 30% of sales (Grannis, 1990). Shortly after mass education began in the United States, libraries also began. The first public library was founded in Peterborough, New Hampshire, in 1833. Further stimulation came from Andrew Carnegie, who gave more than $50 million for library buildings across the country in the early 1900s.

By the mid-nineteenth century, a New York publisher started selling song books for 10 cents and then ventured into dime novels which became very popular. The dime novels told tales of adventure about American pioneers. During the 1870s and 1880s salesmen sold books door-to-door. The salesmen searched out newly urbanized, literate city dwellers, offering books with plots featuring adventure, romance, scandal, and crime. Fiction also got a boost from newspapers which serialized dime novels and stories by such famous writers as Charles Dickens.

One of the most significant developments in the book publishing industry was the distribution of paperbacks along with magazines shortly after World War II. Virtually overnight, the number of potential purchasers for a book was increased ten to twenty times as books appeared at newsstands, drug stores, supermarkets, and variety stores throughout the United States. Today this is taken for granted, along with the numerous book stores and book clubs. This brief history of the book illustrates the interconnections between social and economic factors which were instrumental in the development of other media.

Newspapers—Changing Audiences

Before there were newspapers in the form seen today, there were attempts to provide similar content through other means. In early Rome, there were daily written records of the Senate called Acta Diurna. Centuries later, there were town criers calling out the news—"Ten o'clock and all's well." Actual news gathering appears to have first occurred in China during the Tang dynasty (618-907) when an official gazette was circulated among members of the court. McCusker (1986) describes an explosion of business newspapers in Europe— including Amsterdam, Hamburg, Frankfurt, and Venice—after about 1530, with one set of papers focusing on marine lists. By some accounts, the birth of the modern newspaper probably occurred between 1605 and 1610. These were single-page papers, printed on one side (Schramm, 1988). In late eighteenth century Europe a network of independent gazettes not subject to prior censorship had an impact on current events of the day, circulating in several countries. The French-language paper, *Gazette de Leyde*, which Thomas Jefferson called the best in Europe, was required reading for diplomats (Popkin, 1985, 1989).

In the United States, the first continuously-published newspaper was the *Boston News-Letter* dating from April 1704.[2] Most of the early colonial newspapers contained news that was hardly exciting by today's standards. Mainly, it consisted of clippings from London newspapers published second-hand. There were no photographs or large headlines. Items included sermon notices, obituaries, and commercial news. Circulation was limited since people were reluctant to pay for newspapers; the audience of literate, educated people was small. Benjamin Franklin altered that situation rapidly. He started the first chain of American newspapers, owned a series of printing plants, proposed the first magazine for the colonies, and was the first to suggest that advertising be sold to support papers.

Generally, the period before the Revolutionary War saw intense political struggles between the colonial press and the British government (Smith, 1988). There also were some Tory (pro-British) newspapers such as the *Lion Gazette*, which was eventually mobbed and later moved to British-held territory. New England printers generally supported the American side in the quarrel with Great Britain and used their newspapers to further the goals of the American Revolution. Printers often went on to hold political office, generally at the local level (Humphrey, 1987). The war had several consequences for the press: more readers, less government control, and increased frequency (semiweekly papers). From the beginning, newspapers discussed politics and covered government. The newspapers of Philadelphia covered the constitutional convention of 1787, discussing the qualifications of delegates, hopes for the meeting's results, and the decision to meet in secret (Humphrey, 1988).

The next decade saw an extremely partisan press where mud slinging was common and criticism intensely personal. Even George Washington, though supportive of an independent press, failed to escape criticism. Some believe he declined to run for a third term because of vicious attacks during his second term. Sloan (1988), however, examined party newspapers in the 1789-1816 period, finding more varied and better reasoned articles than the extensive use of personal attack many have cited. Editors opened their columns to reader contributions, making the partisan press a vigorous "marketplace" for ideas. Presidents often begin their terms with harmonious press relations, but the honeymoon usually turns to skepticism if not antagonism. Honeymoons have become increasingly shorter in recent years. Recent presidents were not the first to change their views once they had been subjected to criticism. Witness the following quotes from Thomas Jefferson who is widely cited for the comment that he would prefer a press without a government to a government without a press.

. . . our liberty depends on the freedom of the press, and that cannot be limited without being lost. (1786)

No government ought to be without censors; and where the press is free, no one ever will. If virtuous, it need not fear the fair operation of attack and defense. Nature has given to man no other means of sifting out the truth, either in religion, law or politics. (1792)

Indeed, the abuses of the freedom of the press here have been carried to a length never before known or borne by a civilized nation. But it is so difficult to draw a clear line of separation between the abuse and the wholesome use of the press, that as yet we have found it better to trust the public judgment, rather than the magistrate, with the discrimination between truth and falsehood. (1803)

Were I the publisher of a paper, instead of the usual division of Foreign, Domestic, etc., I think I should distribute everything under the following heads: 1. True 2. Probable. 3. Wanting Confirmation. 4. Lies . . . at present it is disputable to state a fact on a newspaper authority; and the newspapers of our country by their abandoned spirit of falsehood, have more effectively destroyed the utility of the press than all the shackles devised by Bonapart. (1813)

I deplore . . . the putrid state into which our newspapers have passed, and the malignity, the vulgarity and the mendacious spirit of those who write them. . . . These ordures are rapidly depraving the public taste. (1814)

Jefferson became president in 1801 and was returned to office in 1804; note the corresponding change in views. It should be pointed out that he never advocated government control despite personal reservations about press performance during his term in office. Press support often was linked to political patronage, which came in the form of government subsidies to editors for publishing local laws or through direct payments from the friends of politicians to editors. Stewart (1989) notes that when personal appeals to one editor failed, economic leverage and political exile followed. Economic leverage was a most effective means by which parties could control political communication (Dyer, 1989). By the end of the century, the proportion of newspapers with a declared party affiliation had declined markedly as the number characterizing themselves independent increased. This occurred nationwide (Baldasty and Rutenbeck, 1988; Lacy, Folkerts, and Dravis, 1990). As the fledgling nation grew, newspaper content shifted. Foreign relations constituted 49.6% of the news in 1809 but only 22.5% by 1812, as papers became more "American" (Avery, 1984, 1986). The government also encouraged the growth of the press across the country with the inauguration of the postal express in 1825 and lower postage for papers (Kielbowicz and Lawson, 1988).

By 1833, newspaper costs were cut to a penny, and the "penny press" was born. Benjamin Day's newspaper, the *New York Sun*, was the first such paper (the motto: It shines for all). Its low price attracted a large audience that included immigrants and the growing number of city dwellers. The *Sun* was such a success that it amassed a circulation of thirty thousand in just two years. Not only did the penny press reflect a change in the nature of the audience, it also meant a change in the definition of news. Instead of dry notices, it featured: police activity, sex, and vice.[3] The penny press also started to crusade with repeated attempts to influence the public on controversial public issues, including the question of slavery (Whitby, 1990). As street sales generated more income, papers hired more professional staff members. With a larger audience and advertising, reliance on political support declined. Baldasty and Rutenbeck (1988) examined newspaper industry trade journals and other sources from the 1800s and concluded that: partisanship declined during the nineteenth century, business concerns spurred that decline, many believed that newspapers would increase their circulation only if they emphasized topics other than politics, and rural editors were warned by trade journals to downplay partisanship to avoid bankruptcy. However, though partisanship declined, it did not disappear, and special interest newspapers existed with varying fortunes (Bekken, 1988).

Two important editors with very strong and influential perspectives were James Gordon Bennett of the *New York Herald* and Horace Greeley of the *New York Tribune*. Bennett founded his own state, national, and international news bureaus and succeeded in opening the galleries of Congress to journalists. He was one of the first to use the telegraph to speed up news gathering, and he began the first successful Sunday newspaper. Greeley was something of a radical who supported the Westward movement, serious news reporting, and specialization (for example, hospital news, fire news, military news). Among Greeley's famous correspondents were the author Charles Dickens and political philosopher Karl Marx. Greeley made the editorial page what it is today. He publicly supported women's rights, socialism, abolition of polygamy, liquor control, and the death penalty. He was also the first to develop what has now become a major means of news gathering—the interview. It is difficult today to imagine how news could be gathered without an interview; prior to Greeley's innovation, most news was based on reporters' personal observations and clippings from other papers.

With the Civil War in the 1860s, newspapers faced the problem of how to keep the public informed without giving aid and comfort to the enemy—which was difficult to define in a civil war. Large elements of the population from both sides were opposed to the war; thus, there was continuous, outspoken criticism of both the North and the South. Pro-South New York newspaper editors sometimes had to flee mobs whipped up by returning war veterans. The headline of one Wisconsin newspaper article on the draft said "Lincoln Has Called for 500,000 More Victims." President Lincoln also was accused of outright treason by some journalists (Becker, 1990).

For the first time, news collected by journalists could be transmitted so quickly by telegraph that it might affect the war, since battles often continued for days. This meant that some news releases were censored. Today's style of newswriting can be traced to the telegraph. Until its use, journalists tended to write long essays like novelists or narrate events in order of occurrence as historians do. However, since telegraph lines often were cut (specifically to prevent the transmission of news), important items would miss publication if they were contained in the last part of the story. To reduce the possibility of losing transmission of the most important facts, some journalists started putting the most important ideas in the first paragraph, structuring the remaining information in order of declining importance. This style, still popular, is known as the inverted pyramid. The style of newswriting coincidentally made it easy to cut stories too long for newspapers' strict space requirements. Readers today take for granted that they will learn the most important features of a news story first—through the headline and the lead (first paragraph). The inverted pyramid is convenient for readers as well as writers and publishers. With the Civil War, news—rather than editorial opinion—was firmly established as the primary purpose of newspapers (Hughes, 1989).

Great new forces affected newspapers after the Civil War. Changes introduced by the penny press and Civil War continued but newspapers were most affected by their new operating environments. Mechanization revolutionized the printing process and permitted newspapers to grow both in size (number of pages) and circulation (number of readers). Industrialization brought more advertising and improved transportation systems which helped get urban newspapers to people living in distant areas. Literacy increased rapidly since mass education had been in existence a number of years. Between 1870 and 1900, illiteracy declined from 20% to 11% of the population. The percentage of children in public schools rose from 57% to 72% during the same period. Competition between newspapers increased. The most intense competition was in New York City, although other cities also had more than one paper vying for the same audience. This led to the rise of evening newspapers, which attempted to reach a slightly different audience than morning papers. The competition also inspired the use of gimmicks to boost circulation at least temporarily. Nellie Bly's famous trip around the world to see if she could beat the eighty days suggested by Jules Verne in his novel was one such gimmick.

Editors tended to sensationalize in the heat of competition, culminating in the era called "Yellow Journalism"—named after a comic strip character. Audiences were offered a heavy diet of sin, sex, and violence. This format would be similar to supermarket tabloids today. Hearst is the name most often associated with Yellow Journalism; you may see his actions characterized by Orson Welles in the classic movie *Citizen Kane*. Although sensationalism often is used to characterize the press of this period, complaints about sensationalism date to ancient Rome (Stevens, 1985, 1991).

In the latter half of the nineteenth century, concentration of economic power by a few men and corporate excesses attracted the attention of civic-minded journalists. Editors strongly protested the accumulation of so much wealth by John D. Rockefeller, J.P. Morgan, Andrew Carnegie, and others. The journalists who investigated these men and their fortunes came to be known as **muckrakers**. Ida Tarbell's series on Rockefeller's company (Standard Oil) ran for two years in *McClure's* magazine. Lincoln Steffens wrote "The Shame of the Cities," attacking corruption in city and state government. Evensen (1989) finds evangelical origins in the muckrakers' battles against social ills (Bennion, 1986; Beasley, 1982-1983; Miraldi, 1990).

The years 1910-1914 mark the high point in the number of newspapers published in the United States—2,600 dailies and 14,000 weeklies. Economic pressures brought on by World War I led to a period of consolidation. Following the war, newspapers began using two techniques in New York City—the tabloid style format (smaller size) and extensive use of photography. The 1920s are called a period of "Jazz Journalism." They also represent a continuation of the emphasis on sex, crime, and entertainment from the Yellow Journalism period, plus some of the crusading from the Muckraking period. Prohibition provided sensational copy as socialites were caught in speakeasy raids. Photo-journalism focused on the glamorous and sexy Hollywood stars from the new medium of motion pictures. However, the 1920s were not all sex and sensationalism. By then Hearst had toned down his version of yellow journalism, the *New York Times* was establishing a reputation as a quality newspaper, and readers had access to the wit and criticism of such figures as H. L. Mencken and Walter Lippmann.

The 1930s and 1940s saw the rise of interpretive reporting. Two explanations are commonly offered. With the election of Franklin D. Roosevelt and the growth of government programs, people's lives were increasingly affected by external events which needed interpreting and more context for understanding. With the rise of modern scientific technology, journalists attempted to add "why" to their traditional questions of "who-what-when-where-how." The view that difficult subjects such as science and economics couldn't be made interesting also was discarded. This led to more specialization and better editorial backgrounds for journalists. The second factor here was the appearance of a competing medium, radio, which could deliver the news faster than newspapers could, even with "special, midday editions." Losing this "newness," newspapers turned to greater depth in their reporting.

Wire services appeared in the early nineteenth century and continue to affect the development of newspapers (plus radio and other media) today. Wire services made news less local and provided the same news to media across the country. One wire service is the Associated Press (AP), a cooperative news-gathering organization owned by member news organizations (mainly newspapers). The second major wire service for many years was the United

Press International (UPI), a commercial news service stemming from the 1958 merger of old wire services owned by Scripps (United Press) and Hearst (International News Service). In the last century the wire services influenced news writing by promoting the summary lead, inverted pyramid style, and political neutrality. Today, their decision as to whether a story deserves coverage is crucial because local editors tend to follow their lead. In daily newspapers, wire service news is typically the common denominator supplemented by news and features from various other sources (see Emery and Emery, 1992). Prior to the growth of wire services, printers exchanged their papers postage free through the mails, a custom dating to the early 1700s, and borrowed stories they found interesting. In this process, the major papers in New York and Washington achieved a stature out of proportion to their modest circulations (Kielbowicz, 1982).[4]

Magazines Specialize to Serve Diversity

Magazines are a relatively new mass medium compared to books and newspapers, yet today they far outnumber the older print media. In the United States alone there are more than twelve thousand magazines with a total circulation of several hundred million copies (Koek and Winklepleck, 1991). One of the first American periodicals was Benjamin Franklin's *General Magazine* and *Historical Chronicle*, which appeared only ten years after the first such publication in England. Shevelow (1989) notes that the development of magazines in the eighteenth century provided opportunities for women, who assumed an unprecedented place in print culture as both readers and writers.

In the latter half of the nineteenth century, modern national magazines multiplied. Congress helped to spur the growth of magazines by providing low-cost mailing privileges. The last decade of the nineteenth century witnessed a wide range of new magazines representing specialized markets (audiences), including *Popular Science*, *Scientific American*, *Home Arts*, and *Babyhood*. Employee publications and "house organs" also developed as advertising vehicles and specialized publications (Badaracco, 1990). Later, the muckrakers stimulated magazine readership with their exposés serialized in *McClure's*, *Colliers*, *Everybody's*, and other magazines.[5] News magazines began with *Time*, founded by Henry Luce in 1923. The huge circulations reached by general interest magazines such as *Life*, *Look*, and the *Saturday Evening Post* were in jeopardy by the 1950s. Compared to the cost of reaching the same size and type of audience by television, magazine ads were expensive. The magazine production process was too expensive to maintain by increased subscription and newsstand prices alone.

For the past two decades the trend has generally been towards specialized publications aimed at audiences ranging from apartment dwellers to joggers and antique collectors. Today one of the magazines with the largest circulation, *TV Guide*, concerns another medium.[6]

Film—Adaptation of Several Media to a New Form

The beginnings of film as a medium can be traced to a number of discoveries and inventions, including early photography. Capturing sight on film was envisioned long before the achievement itself was realized. One of the devices that stopped just short of this goal was the camera obscura, a design envisioned by Leonardo da Vinci in which light was admitted through a single small hole into a dark chamber. The invention of photography owes much to the Frenchman, Louis Daguerre, who worked on developing a photographic process using various chemicals in the 1830s. He sold the process to the French government in 1839. **Daguerreotypes** were the first photographs. Later in the nineteenthth century, George Eastman invented celluloid roll film, which made it possible to record a series of consecutive pictures on the same strip. Thomas Edison's lab then developed a motion picture camera using this film strip. In the 1890s, filmstrips were very short and consisted of dancing girls or comedic scenes. An American, Edwin S. Porter, created the first narrative film, "The Great Train Robbery," in 1903.

Before World War I, the public rapidly was introduced to the first film star, the first noted directors, the first picture palaces, and the growth of Hollywood. The early history of film also includes a struggle between producers and theatrical workers, many of whom were displaced as the younger industry expanded (Nielsen, 1988). World War I strengthened America's position in the international film market because almost all European film industries were shut down or their production cut severely. Hollywood studios grew in size and power as they produced large numbers of popular films and built chains of theaters. When the Roaring '20s ended, the motion picture industry was suffering from a series of major scandals, with Warner Brothers on the verge of bankruptcy. Then sound arrived to save the day. Al Jolson's musical, "The Jazz Singer," in 1927 was the first sound film to attract popular attention. Films flourished in the 1930s, when attendance grew despite the depression. The 1930s also were a golden age of the studio system, with most production centered in seven dominant companies: MGM, Paramount, Warner Brothers, RKO, Universal, Columbia, and 20th Century Fox. Each studio had its own stars and style. When World War II arrived, Hollywood turned to patriotic films, with stereotypes of Japanese and German villains. Studios enjoyed great success and earned high profits during this period.

After the war, the film industry went into a decline that was due in large part to competition with a new medium, television. When television arrived in the 1950s, attendance dropped to nearly half what it had been. The industry also was shaped by a 1948 decision which forced Paramount and the film studios to divest themselves of theaters that exhibited films to audiences (Edgerton and Pratt, 1983). Since television followed a radio model for generating revenues, not a motion picture model, film studios failed to enter the television industry successfully as radio networks would (Gomery, 1984).

Hollywood fought back with larger screens, film spectacles, and more adult themes. In the 1960s, a new cinema emerged to reflect a changing society, with emphasis on relevance and what had been experimental themes. In the 1970s and 1980s new genre or new definitions of old ones emerged—the disaster films in the mid-1970s, and the Star Wars saga in the latter part of the decade. With growing costs of filmmaking in the 1980s and 1990s, small films faced a difficult situation. The economics of the industry changed, with an increasing percentage of film revenues coming from videocassettes rather than box office receipts. This will be discussed further in the next chapter.[7]

Radio—From Simple to Complex

Today few people could build their own TV set, but most could easily put together a radio receiver as many hobbyists did in the early 1900s. In fact, both the telegraph and radio were developed much at the hand of non-scientists who recognized their commercial and practical value. A literature professor, Samuel Morse, was responsible for the first telegraph line strung between Washington, D.C. and Baltimore (a distance of about forty miles). On May 24, 1844, the first telegraph message was sent in dots and dashes. It asked, "What hath God wrought?" Although the government had financed the line, it threw away its opportunity to control the patents and relinquished all its rights, which became the property of private corporations.

The medium was left to private enterprise—a precedent that would be followed in the United States with the telephone, wireless telegraph, and home broadcasting. Sound escaped from the wire when Guglielmo Marconi, another imaginative tinkerer, modified lab equipment he had seen and strengthened it to the point where he could send dot-dash messages up to about a mile through the air without the help of telegraph wires. Transmission of the human voice was the next step and that occurred on Christmas eve in 1906. A decade of refinements that included invention of the vacuum tube prepared the way for radio broadcasting.

Early radio stations were set up by radio set manufacturers who needed to maintain a market for radio tubes and equipment after World War I ended heavy military usage. Westinghouse was the first to start regular programming with radio station KDKA, in Pittsburgh. What was then called the "radio music box" caught on and the number of stations grew so fast that the manufacturers shortly fell behind on orders. United States broadcasting in the mid-1920s was far different from the system installed only a few years later. Several hundred nonprofit broadcasters had begun operations in the first half of the decade, a majority affiliated with educational institutions. More than two hundred remained on the air in 1925 (McChesney, 1990).

Without government regulation or private agreements, however, the airwaves became a jumble of competing voices. Stations competed for the same spot on the dial, overpowering each other with stronger and stronger signals. As a consumer, you wouldn't necessarily know where to tune your radio to hear your favorite station because its frequency might change. Because of this, many stations failed entirely, especially small stations. Technical arrangements were so confused that the radio industry itself pressured the federal government to initiate regulation. Finally, in 1927, Congress passed the Federal Radio Act and created the Federal Radio Commission (FRC, later changed to the Federal Communication Commission, FCC).[8] Besides licensing uses of radio frequencies, Congress also stipulated that radio stations should serve the public interest, convenience, and necessity in return for using the public airways. Congress decided that broadcasters would be given licenses renewable every three years in order to review whether or not the station was fulfilling its role.

How to support radio broadcasting was still in question, at the time. A few radio listeners sent money to radio stations, but people preferred to listen to what they could find rather than pay for specific radio content. As late as 1929, few if any private broadcasters were thought to be earning profits from broadcasting (Codel, 1929). McChesney (1990, 1992) notes that public discussion before 1927 showed agreement that nonprofit broadcasting would play a significant or dominant role in the United States. The FRC pitted licensees against each other so that those with the most resources—commercial broadcasters and those with network affiliations—succeeded and the number of nonprofit broadcasters declined dramatically (McChesney, 1987, 1990). Eventually, advertising was used to support most radio broadcasting but not without extended public debate (Brown, 1989). Some labor leaders and newspapers supported development of nonprofit radio, and few academics supported the status quo. Even the Secretary of Commerce, Herbert Hoover, opposed commercials on radio saying: "It's inconceivable that we should allow so great a possibility for services, for news, [and] for entertainment to be drowned in advertising chatter." Nonetheless, the first commercial was aired in 1922 on station WEAF in New York (Long, 1987).

Radio networks soon began in order to cut programming costs for local stations. As network affiliates, the stations were in a position to receive and transmit high-quality live radio dramas. The first radio network (now also a TV network) was NBC, which managed two systems of interconnections between local radio stations (the red and blue networks). CBS was the second major radio network which began in 1927 as part of the Paley family's effort to sell La Palina cigars. CBS, under the direction of William Paley, successfully competed with the more established NBC, luring away big-name personalities such as Bing Crosby and Kate Smith. ABC came into being when the government insisted that NBC divest itself of one of its two networks; the blue network was sold to Edward Nobel who enjoyed a fortune based on sales of Lifesavers candy. Other networks also were in existence, some still today, such as the Mutual Broadcasting System. The newest radio network is NPR (National Public Radio), an organization linking non-commercial radio stations.

With the arrival of television, radio lost its prime-time entertainment function and reinvented itself by providing mobile audiences with a steady diet of music and news. Now a medium catering increasingly to commuters and the young, radio stations have proliferated formats to find the right combination of content to attract audiences.[9]

Television—Learning from the Past

A regular schedule of television programming was provided by the British Broadcasting Corporation (BBC) to London residents by late 1936 (Hubell, 1942). Television also was introduced in Russia on an experimental basis by 1937, and the Japanese government had planned to spend $1.5 million on TV research before 1938. France was readying installation of a TV transmitter on top of the Eiffel Tower in the late 1930s, and the Fascist Italian government was planning to introduce regular TV service in Rome in 1939 (Berkman, 1988).

Most of the European efforts followed traditions of government involvement. In the United States, tradition dictated private initiative. Television did not suffer the growth pangs that radio did in the United States. By the time TV sets were placed on the market, the technology was quite sophisticated. TV also borrowed its financial base since people were already accustomed to commercials from radio. The regulatory structure of the FCC was adaptable to the new medium. Even the visual quality was not novel since motion pictures provided the audience with some "visual literacy."

The first TV transmissions had taken place in 1931, about twenty years before television became widely available as a mass medium. The Second World War stymied television's development, since the war effort required parts and labor which would have gone into TV sets. In the United States, the FCC approved home televisions in 1941 but when station license applications came pouring in, a freeze was put into effect. Station construction was banned from 1948 to 1952 while a master plan was worked out to avoid technical problems. The plan involved an option of one standard system for color TV transmission and allocation of both UHF (ultra high frequency) and VHF (very high frequency) signals across the country.[10] The same networks which dominated radio also came to dominate television programming, though ABC did not fully enter the competition until the 1970s. Since it had started later than the other networks, it had fewer affiliates and thus a smaller audience and less advertising income to use in program production and development.

At first television productions were live, but "I Love Lucy"—which you can still see as reruns today—was recorded. The 1950s has been called the "golden age of television" because it brought audiences great comedians such as Milton Berle, Jack Benny, and Sid Caesar, as well as a string of dramatic productions such as Playhouse 90 that received critical acclaim (Baughman, 1985). By the mid-1950s, TV networks either produced or licensed programs themselves. Previously, the advertiser developed the programs they sponsored (Boddy, 1987).

In the early 1960s, network news expanded from fifteen minutes to a half-hour format that symbolized the growth of public affairs programming during a decade of racial unrest, spectacular space coverage, and Vietnam War protests. Both the 1960s and 1970s saw TV programs focusing on social themes, ranging from feminism to homosexuality, ecology, and government corruption. Although television's five decades have been characterized as a "vast wasteland" of light entertainment, they've also given us broadcasts of the McCarthy hearings that first cast doubt on the legitimacy of the senator's "red scare," children's programming such as "Sesame Street" and "Mister Rogers' Neighborhood," "live broadcasts" which brought American and Russian audiences together in exchanges in the 1980s, the Watergate hearings that unveiled the Nixon coverup in the 1970s, and almost instant news reports on "Desert Storm" and the Iraqi war in the 1990s.[11]

Cable TV has proliferated and new cable channels threaten the hold on prime-time programming by the three major networks—ABC, CBS and NBC. Cable News Network demonstrated its worldwide reach in covering the "Desert Storm" war in the Middle East, and several international news organizations began plans for their own cross-national TV news broadcasting. Video rental stores stocked with movies and a variety of other material combine with VCRs to make a formidable opponent in the competition for the audience's attention.

Advertising—Both the Bread and the Wrapper

Advertising has the dual quality of being both communication content and major financial support for many mass media. It has had this distinction almost from the start. Publications of the seventeenth century regarded the desire to buy or sell something just as much news as other events of the week, such as reports from a battle. Among the early advertisements were handbills, first distributed in early sixteenth century England and achieving enormous popularity with advertisers such as sellers of patent medicines (Burnby, 1988). By the middle of the nineteenth century, England was entering a period of economic growth accompanied by an expanding middle class pursued by retail advertisers offering all the symbols characteristic of social status (Tudor, 1986). Literacy stimulated the development of advertising as well as print media. The lettered sign and advertising came into being as the literate audience grew.

Outdoor advertising in the United States was introduced by circus operators. Owners of theaters or opera houses soon adopted the practice. Eventually the special structures holding outdoor advertisements became known as billboards (Hendon and Muhs, 1986).

Most United States advertising was local until national markets developed along with improved transportation and growing industrialization. Advertising agencies in the latter half of the nineteenth century simply purchased space from newspapers and then resold it to various clients. That role expanded as agencies took over planning functions as well as actual writing and illustration. Advertising appeared on the front page of newspapers when they consisted of only four pages, but with the expansion of newspaper size to eight pages in the penny press era, advertising volume grew and more ads were moved inside the paper. Advertisers sought outlets besides newspapers, and in the early part of this century, postcards were successfully used (Williams, 1988).

Along with the growth of advertising that accompanied the appearance of the consumer society came questions about the ethics of some advertising and its potential influence. Some magazines told readers that patent medicines they were giving to their children contained cocaine, morphine, and alcohol. To combat mounting public criticism, the Associated Advertising Clubs of America was organized in 1905 to campaign for "truth in advertising." As late as 1931, however, the Raladam case showed that the prevailing principle was "let the buyer beware." The Raladam Co. manufactured Marmola as a cure for obesity; the product contained an ingredient that produced harmful side effects in some consumers. However, the U.S. Supreme Court said that the Federal Trade Commission could not stop the product from being advertised because the 1914 FTC act did not forbid the deception of consumers unless the advertising injured competing business. Not until the passage of the Wheeler-Lee Amendment in 1938 were consumers put on a par with business.

Advertising on radio and television has long generated concerns. In 1945, the *St. Louis Post-Dispatch* started an editorial campaign advocating the elimination of all commercials in the middle of radio programs, beginning a national debate over commercialism in radio news (Murray, 1989). This was an apparent last-ditch effort, since another medium, TV, was beginning, and it too adopted advertising as a support base.

A number of other ethical questions have been raised through the years: Does/should advertising cause people to buy things they do not need? Does advertising unfairly influence journalists' professional decisions? Does advertising create conformity or influence elections? In any case, advertising has become an important institution that is evaluated not just for its commercial value but also its aesthetic content, popular acceptance, and professional standards. The Clio awards honoring the best in advertising attract more than 10,000 entries from over 40 countries, and annual ad revenues exceed $130 billion.[12]

Relationships Among the Media—Shifting Forms and Functions

The arrival of each new mass medium does more than simply enlarge the number of people who can be reached. As discussed in chapter 1, each contributes a different characteristic, forcing existing media to find some strategy for competing with the newcomer. The permanence and indexability of print media confront the mobility and immediacy of radio. Television combined radio's immediacy with the visual quality of film. Cable TV is less a new medium than a technological improvement on an old one; it expands volume (potential number of channels) and targets specific audiences—specialization. Cable systems "de-massify" the audience in some instances by targeting certain programming to a particular geographic audience while another area receives different content.

How do these peculiar qualities of mass media figure in their relationships with each other? As noted earlier, the introduction of a new mass medium does not mean that existing media will be replaced. Each new medium tends to supplement rather than supplant existing media. However, the survival means that older media must change their form and functions to continue. Some thought that radio would destroy the daily press and if not radio, then surely TV. The wire services initially refused to provide radio stations with news because they were viewed as competitors. Eventually, the print media recognized they had lost the "immediacy" quality but still had permanence and greater detail. Thus, the daily press moved to provide more indepth news, more description, more background, and more analysis.[13]

Radio was subjected to competition when television started to spread throughout the United States. Having been supplanted as evening entertainment, radio was forced to change both its format and its function. Radio dramas were replaced by music and news. Radio competed for its audience by becoming a musical companion that could follow people everywhere, particularly in the automobile. Radio stopped trying to capture the entire family and concentrated on particular audiences. Like magazines, radio specialized in terms of both content and target audiences. The "all-news" and "all-talk" stations of the 1970s aimed for a different audience than middle-of-the-road musical formats or hard rock music.

Television had its most direct impact not on radio, which managed to retool fairly quickly, but on the cinema, which saw two decades of downturn before recouping somewhat in the 1970s. Television has the quality of privacy more so than the social cinema (or "live theater"), which requires viewing among an audience of strangers. TV also was cheaper, at least in terms of direct costs. Motion pictures have tried several strategies: specializing (black films, the youth market) and "demassifying" the audience by aiming not at whole families but at segments which would be attracted by such things as pornography, wilderness films, and graphic violence. Special effects which draw repeat visits from younger people also have proven to be an effective strategy. Television's impact on newspapers is more recent than on film, in part perhaps because TV actually provided little news until the 1960s. There is some concern that TV news has now expanded to the point where it is decreasing the amount of time spent reading newspapers. What will the newer media technologies bring? Newer technologies seem to be spreading more quickly through the American audience; thus, we have relatively little time to consider what we want from new media and how some of the potentially negative consequences may be avoided.

The latest media technologies merge characteristics of interpersonal communication with those of mass communication. One of these is the **interactive** nature of some media technologies; electronic mail and computer conferencing are two examples. Interactive media are marked by two characteristics: widespread usage creating universal access as a public good and reciprocal interdependence where each person's access to the system is important to other users. The utility of the phone system to each of us is dependent upon everyone else's access; if access is not universal, the utility of the system itself decreases for users (Markus, 1987).

The **principle of relative constancy** first enunciated by McCombs (1972) says that the pattern of economic support for mass media is relatively constant, and the media of mass communication are staples in modern societies much like food, clothing, and shelter. The principle states that a relatively constant proportion of available wealth is devoted to mass media. In this scenario, the appearance of a new medium means further division of the pie, with other media losing some of their share. With a growing pie—a growing economy—there is room for new media and new technologies, but the debut of a new medium during a stable economy means that existing media suffer. The theory is useful for examining the introduction of new media. The complementary nature of print and audio/visual media is supported by the analysis of spending for each over time. The relative decline in spending on print is matched by relative growth for the audio/visual media (Fullerton, 1988). Even within the print media, tradeoffs are noted, with a decline in spending on books complemented by a sharp increase in spending on magazines and newspapers during limited periods.[14]

In the short run, new money may be attracted to the marketplace, allowing a new media innovation to establish a foothold. McCombs and Son (1986) concluded that cable TV and video-cassette recorders attracted new money to the marketplace and were not constrained by existing media when they first began to spread through the population. The question is at what point equilibrium is achieved among the media. Given the speed with which new technologies are developed and efforts to compete in the marketplace, the situation is likely to remain "stable" only on the surface.

One way the new media and existing ones survive is by finding their "niche" in the marketplace (Dimmick and Rothenbuhler, 1984). In the process of competing for audiences, advertising, and other resources, a specific medium survives by distinguishing itself from others, finding its niche on a series of dimensions. While two media may compete fiercely on one dimension, they differ on others which allow them to survive. Dimmick, Patterson and Albarran (1992) look at the "niche superiority" of TV, cable, and radio, concluding that TV is no longer the vastly superior competitor, but any displacement by cable is likely to be a slow process.

Although there are common themes in the development of mass media around the world, many unique forms and patterns also have emerged. Media organizations and practices vary from nation to nation. Differences often are linked to social, political, and cultural systems. The next section briefly notes unique features and widespread aspects of media systems. The intricate relationship between media systems and social, political, and economic factors is then examined.

Mass Media Around the World

Today almost no part of the globe is free from mass media. Except for a few island nations, every country has newspapers or magazines. Radio was the growth medium of the 1950s and 1960s world-wide. TV antennas are now popping up in developing nations, and cable TV has made greater inroads in Canada and some Western European nations than in the United States. Desktop publishing, made possible by computer technologies, has allowed entrepreneurs to start small newspapers in remote or difficult situations.

Print Media

The number of newspapers and newspaper readers varies greatly around the world. The highest circulations for individual papers are found in Great Britain and Japan, while Sweden and Norway have among the highest newspaper readership rates. Japan prints 584 newspapers per 1,000 people every day, compared with 268 in the United States (Hiatt, 1990; Self, 1990). The city-nation of Hong Kong has an amazing number of papers, offering readers more than 50 different titles (Chan, 1988). Despite poverty and illiteracy, India has seen its total number of newspapers climb to more than 25,000 (Yadava, 1991). In contrast, Botswana and Benin, two small countries in Africa, have only one daily newspaper.

The U.S. press system is very local, with few newspapers that are national in scope. This also is the situation in Switzerland and in Germany, where a strong regional press is based on individual cities. Although recently the provincial press has increased in importance, most Western European countries have been dominated by national daily papers. An example is Britain, which has seventeen national dailies divided into the prestige press and the "tube press," papers resembling supermarket tabloids in the United States.[15] Another trend found on many continents is the concentration of ownership of major newspapers into chains (Dunnett, 1988; Hiatt, 1990; Servaes, 1989). Countries emerging from decades of communist rule in Eastern Europe and the former Soviet Union are slowly evolving from centralized systems dominated by governments and the Communist party to more diverse media systems.

Broadcasting

Today radio is a universal medium, and over 190 countries have radio broadcast systems. However, television is rapidly catching up; fewer than 37 countries do not yet have their own TV service. The Pacific Island nation of Vanuatu got its first TV in 1992 in time to watch the Olympics. There also are more than 1.5 billion radio sets and close to three quarters of a billion TV sets around the world. The bulk of those sets are found in the industrial countries of North America and Europe, with the United States having more than a fourth of all TV sets.

Broadcasting systems around the world are being refashioned by powerful forces for change, including decreased regulation and increased privatization of broadcasting and telecommunication services, the impact of new technologies (such as satellite TV), the growth of international systems of ownership, financing and production (Ferguson, 1987), and a decrease in centralization as local media have grown.[16] Changes in the political systems are intensifying these trends, although many began before the fall of communism in Eastern Europe. For a couple decades, broadcasting has felt pressure from various groups, some demanding more public participation, others wanting more local programs, and some seeking more or less advertising. There also has been a growth in the exchange of TV programs between countries—accompanied by rising fears about the impact of foreign programming on national beliefs, values, and images.[17] Minority ethnic groups within countries worry about their ability to withstand the dominance of national media systems.

In the 1970s, Western Europe was a bastion for nonprofit public broadcasting, but by the mid 1980s, private TV was sweeping that continent and the rest of the world. McQuail (1990) summarizes the dramatic changes in Western European broadcasting: 1) a loss of legitimacy for monopolies by public broadcasting systems and less support for expansion of the public sector; 2) increased interest in market solutions and deregulation in communication, combined with consumer dissatisfaction with a restricted supply of TV; 3) moves to harmonize rules for broadcasting within the European Common Market and Europe; 4) widespread desire to gain national and European profit from developing industries based on new technologies; and 5) popular dissatisfaction with old "official" cultural regulations, which were not being surrendered willingly by the establishment. Similar trends have been noted on other continents.[18]

Cultural and Linguistic Features of Media Systems

Many features of media systems that are unique to specific countries reflect the local culture and language. Mass media often have been integrated with interpersonal communication and local customs. For example, in Nigeria, "New Masquerade," a media comedy, first is presented live on stage, then as a television program, and finally on gramophone records for villagers without other access. The Masquerade in African tradition is an oracle who utters profound truths in rather uncommon circumstances and is supposed to be a re-incarnation of the dead (Ebeogu, 1987). In Africa, the "bush telegraph," or communication drums, paved the way for the spread of radio (Ellis, 1989). The Chinese have contributed what may be considered a print medium with the personal touch—the "tatzepao," or wall poster. Although less significant today, it once provided an inexpensive means for the public to distribute their views by slapping a poster on a wall.

Construction of messages is not always left to professionals. In Sweden's community radio plan, voluntary groups produce programs and share transmitter time (McCain and Lowe, 1990). In China, media attempt to involve audiences and a Canton TV station trained amateur filmmakers to fill a third of the station's requirements (Hollstein, 1989). In Italy, independent radio stations with small budgets have appeared. Unable to afford correspondents, they have used the so-called "token reporter," a private citizen who simply proceeds to the closest phone booth to call the station. Clandestine radio broadcasting has emerged in Asia, operated by both communist and non-communist dissident groups (Soley and O'Brien, 1987). Differences in news-gathering styles also are found; in Japan reporters who do not belong to press clubs have little access to officials at government ministries.

Distinctive forms of media content are found in print and broadcast media. In Austria, radio is widely used for passing on messages about such things as lost or stolen property, meetings, personal greetings, and similar items. Novel TV formats also have emerged in numerous countries. Japanese TV features "hard-hitting" dramas in which the characters are frantically concerned about reaching ambitious goals—businessmen trying to succeed, schoolboys attempting to win a football match, students racking their brains to pass an exam. The soap opera is an internationally accepted TV format. However, the "telenovela" version popular in Latin America differs from the Anglo-American soap opera; though continuous serials, the story-lines or plots are not as open-ended and generally consist of 150–250 episodes. They also are more likely to have a happy ending (Frey-Vor, 1990). In Finland, an effort to create distinctive TV programming emerged as "messages loosely enclosed in videoplays," a form of theater that emphasized the techniques of alienation and distance rather than the visual capabilities of TV (Slade and Barchak, 1989). In China, a popular news-feature program was a 5-minute show called "This Day in History," designed to introduce Chinese audiences to world historical events and figures (Hollstein, 1989). In what was once East Germany, a series on TV called "The Black Channel" was aired every Monday evening presenting selected extracts from West German TV as examples of misleading propaganda or illustrations of the inequities of capitalism.[19]

Linguistic Factors.   Linguistic divisions are a major factor in determining the form of mass media. The entire media system of Belgium is duplicated in Flemish and in French. In Switzerland, some 75% of newspapers appear in German, 20% in French, and 5% in Italian, with less than 1% in Romansch. The canton of Grisons provides an extreme example of Swiss pluralism; school books must be published in six different languages. In Switzerland, there has been a question in German-speaking areas about whether standard German or Swiss German should be used in broadcasting. In the former Soviet Union, Russian is uniquely strong but more than 70 other languages are used in books, newspapers and magazines; 14 are particularly significant. The size of the speech community (number of speakers) is a major predictor of language use in the media (Rogers, 1987). Trying to revive the Irish language, Ireland's Radio Na Gaeltachta has served Gallic speakers throughout the island since the 1970s. In many other Western European nations, there are radio programs for foreign workers from Turkey, Spain, Greece, etc.

The white population of South Africa is split between the English and Afrikaan press, as well as languages spoken by the black and other ethnic communities (Van Wyk, 1989). Many developing nations of Africa and Asia have several languages. Some rely on the use of English and French at the national level. Thus, we find strong English-language newspapers in India (a former British colony) and the Philippines (previously a U.S. colony), and French-language papers in the Ivory Coast and Algeria (former French colonies). Malaysian newspapers historically have been patterned along linguistic and political party lines serving Malay, Chinese and Tamil groups. Singapore's concern with language takes two directions: one is a campaign to get people to speak Mandarin rather than other Chinese dialects (Hachten, 1989; Kuo, 1984), and the other is to encourage the use of English for economic reasons.

Language and religion play both a divisive and a unifying function in societies. For example, the Arab press has had strong ties to Arab culture, being closely bound to the Arabic language. The version used in papers is a modified form of classical Arabic universally understood by educated Arabs. The press is still heavily cultural and most of its content is not created by professional journalists but rather by educated Arabs who write poetry, plays, and stories. Iran emphasizes the Arabic language and religious programming, devoting a third of radio broadcasting to religious content (Skeikh, 1988). A London-based TV network in 1992 received nasty notes from Muslim traditionalists because women anchors didn't wear head coverings. Malaysia's media are conditioned by national policies on morality, belief in God, and respect for the constitution. Regulations stipulate that no alcoholic beverages or food with pork content be allowed on the air because Islam is the national religion, and all commercials must be produced in Malaysia and carry Bahasa Malaysia subtitles if in another language (Adnan, 1987; Frith and Hashim, 1988).[20] India's media culture seems to emphasize rites and ceremonies of various religions (Vilanilam, 1989). Many of India's films have distinctive connections to mythology, which refers not to fairy tales but to a process of humanizing the unknown (Rao, 1989).

Public Perceptions.   Attitudes toward particular media content and what constitutes news vary considerably around the world. In France there has always been more public distrust toward display advertising (as opposed to classified ads). In Norway there is much concern for culture and history and support for the view that newspapers should educate the public on such matters. Finnish papers devote much space to foreign news but also maintain a local, small-town character. They give almost no space to such things as crimes, divorces, and sex scandals, the last a staple of the "tube" press of Great Britain. The Swedes traditionally have had a deeper interest in current history and theology than people of other countries. This content is reflected in newspapers while stories of crime, trials, divorce, and suicide are considered more personal matters that are not the public's business. The Mediterranean countries of Western Europe have tended to place more emphasis on literary events and used a style of writing more akin to the "essay format."

Media's Relation to Governments

How are the media related to society and governments? Siebert suggests that restraints on the press increase as stress on the government and social structures increases (Dilts, 1986). In traditional communist nations the press system is tightly centralized through governmental and party controls and an absence of private ownership. However, media control generally is accomplished through a maze of laws and regulations. Most of them are restrictive, although some laws were enacted with the intention of preserving diversity in the press and others focus on potential effects of the media or aspects of news-gathering processes.

Who actually runs the day-to-day operations of TV and radio stations, and who is in charge of broadcast programming? The answer varies. Even among countries with the same system of ownership or financial support, actual control and organization often differ considerably. In the United States, the private broadcasting sector is regulated by the Federal Communication Commission which assigns frequencies and implements some controls to see that the stations operate in the public interest, convenience and necessity. Actual programming decisions are centered within the three TV networks at the national level and individual stations at the local level. Public broadcasting in the United States is kept at arms length from national political influence with most programming emerging from a few large stations or state-wide broadcast systems. We'll discuss the United States system more in the next chapter.

The structure of broadcast systems represents a clear statement of the relationship between media and government. For example, in China all broadcasting and film are controlled by a ministry under the highest executive body of government (Hollstein, 1989). Britain's famous BBC (British Broad-casting Corp.) is publically funded while commercial TV and radio are franchised and supervised by the Independent Broadcasting Authority (Madge, 1988). Germany has self-regulating regional broadcasters operating independently of central government supervision but with policies set by state governments and operated by councils representing segments of German society (Hirose, 1988; Hoffman-Riem, 1988; LeDuc, 1987). In Italy the government owned most of the stock in the broadcasting system and held a monopoly until the mid-1970s when private, local TV was allowed (Grandi, 1988; Noam, 1987). Japan's broadcasting system includes both commercial, privately owned stations and a national system that is a strange amalgam of public and private enterprise—a "private, juridical person" operating under a national honor system of sorts and run by an independent board of governors with a budget approved by parliament (Katz, 1989). The Dutch TV, called the "ultimate in pluralism," consists of government-owned facilities and air-time split among thirty social, political, and religious groups that qualify on the basis of membership.

While broadcasting systems often have direct government involvement and regulation, newspapers traditionally have had fewer government ties except in communist and other countries with authoritarian regimes.[21] However, the press and politics still maintain strong relations in some areas. The press of Western Europe has always been politically partisan—more so than the American press in recent years. In France, for example, journalists ally them-selves with one of the six unions which most closely reflects their political outlook. French readers also expect politics in journalism as a national phenomenon. However, the partisan press in recent years has tended to decline. In Belgium, the Socialist party press is all but dead (Servaes, 1989). In Sweden, since state press subsidies are designed to sustain diversity, the most widely distributed newspaper in any market niche is excluded from the subsidy program (Ekeecrantz, 1988). In Norway, the press is independent and there are few commercial chains. Most large papers are owned by corporations with shares divided among individuals and political parties (Ostbye, 1991).

Laws aimed at encouraging diversity have been common in Europe. In Belgium, direct and indirect state subsidies are given to newspapers to maintain "diversity in opinion newspapers" (Servaes, 1989), and France provides tax exemptions and newsprint subsidies (Dunnett, 1988). In Sweden there is a long tradition of press freedom and newspapers not only have the right but the duty to furnish the public with papers. Stoppage of publication through strikes or lockouts is a violation of law. Disputes are settled by negotiation or arbitration. Other laws have focused on media practices, using fines and legal threats (Chan, 1988; McLean, 1990), limits on newsprint or the size of newspapers (Lay and Schweitzer, 1990; Ryan, 1988), or requirements that journalists join particular organizations such as the National Islamic Front in Sudan or "colegios" in Latin America.

The issue of media independence ultimately is tied to economic support. Thus, government-sponsored systems depend more on public fees and taxes, while commercial operations depend on advertising and subscriptions. With the former come government regulation, while the latter operate more independently. Taken as a whole, media systems today are supported by a variety of resources but with widespread reliance on advertising. In 1987, fifty-one countries collected license fees from owners of TV sets (Signitzer and Luger, 1988). Other diverse sources include voluntary contributions for TV in Japan[22] and radio bingo in Denmark (McCain and Lowe, 1990).

Eastern Europe and the former Soviet Union are providing a vivid illustration of the importance of economic and political ties to media operations. Almost complete dependence on government support is being replaced by a shift to market systems and audience dependence. In what was East Germany, the media system is being reshaped in the image of former West Germany; a tense struggle over objectivity and what is newsworthy continues as journalists adjust to their new environment (Boyle, 1992). Sparks (1992) says Eastern European nations almost certainly will develop a press based on the market. Many Eastern European countries are still struggling with laws dealing with press ownership, including how to privatize the press and how much foreign investment to allow. These media systems face more changes as their political and economic systems are transformed (Kowalski, 1988; Wellman, 1990).[23]

Challenging Concepts of Social Control

Our survey of media systems around the world illustrates how the media draw from, react to, and contribute to the social, political, economic, and cultural situation in which they are found. Whether the media are viewed as a reflection of society—"the reflection hypothesis"—or as active contributors to the shape and form of daily life, there is no question that examining them will contribute to our self-knowledge. The potential of the media to exert influence creates a multitude of views about whether social control is necessary to define the relationship of media to society. Four major philosophies have traditionally been used to describe this relationship (Siebert, Peterson and Schramm, 1956).

Authoritarian: The oldest philosophy of mass media, the authoritarian view places the media in the position of supporting policies of the state. The media still function as private enterprise, although controlled by the government through licenses or patents, for example. When printing first emerged it was viewed as a threatening development and the government acted. In sixteenth century England Henry VIII declared all printing would be under crown control and used to support and advance the interests of the crown. Even the front pages of colonial newspapers such as Benjamin Franklin's *Public Occurrences*, carried the phrase "Published by Authority," which recognized the relationship between government and the mass media of that day. However, long before the appearance of colonial newspapers, people were fighting to loosen official restrictions.

Libertarian: This philosophy is rooted in the ideas of Milton, Locke, and others that people have the right to pursue truth which is best advanced when there is an "open marketplace of ideas." Libertarian philosophy values diversity and pluralism within society. This means that contrasting views should be allowed to emerge when they are present in a city, a nation, or other social context. It does not mean that each individual should entertain a pluralism of views. Emphasis is on the "potential" for individual expression and the absence of legal constraints and sanctions by the state. One of the first of many eloquent appeals against government restriction on communication was John Milton's *Areopagitica*. Protesting vehemently against the "chains that bind," Milton argued: "Give me the liberty to know, to utter and to argue freely according to conscience, above all liberties . . . who ever knew truth put to the worse, in a free and open encounter?" In Milton's arguments are clues as to what America's founding fathers had in mind when they drafted the first amendment to the U.S. Constitution, open discussion and debate, or open channels of communication. The First Amendment (still in effect today) says:

> Congress shall make no law . . . abridging the freedom of speech, or of the press; or the right of the people peaceably to assemble, and to petition the Government for a redress of grievances.

One month before the U.S. Congress adopted the Bill of Rights, another document was adopted to form support for the Libertarian philosophy. The Declaration of the Rights of Man and Citizens in France asserted equality of all people, sovereignty of the people, and the inalienable rights of the individual to liberty, property, and security. The libertarian press is regulated by members of society when they decide to support magazines or newspapers, for example. The media serve as the informational link between the government and the people.[24] Thus, if information is restricted, then the people's right to be informed is denied. Today the media of many Western nations are largely based on this philosophy, though there have been constant challenges and revisions. Media themselves have not always been consistent in their support of the First Amendment.[25] When the Libertarian philosophy was formally added to the U.S. Constitution, mass media technology and distribution were very limited. There was no photography, no telephone, no TV, and no radio. Few but the elite were able to read. As time went on the media became more accessible and literacy increased, but so did the size of media empires and the concentration of media ownership. Through the addition of new media there was increased diversity of voices, but many media outlets were owned by the same company or individual. Diversity of ideas was limited by the rise of broadcast networks, newspaper chains, and syndicates. Some of the challenges to mass media center on media responsibilities rather than media rights, which is the major concern of the fourth philosophy.

Marxist/Communist: The mass media reflect social arrangements determined by economic forces. History is a succession of dominant economic groups that exploit workers, with an inevitable revolution of the working class and eventual rule by the Communist party. Throughout history, media organizations and their content reflect the ideas of the dominant class. In communist countries, media are instruments of the government and are owned and used by the state. Freedom means that the working class operating through society owns the means to produce or operate TV, newspapers, etc. The mass media—viewed as agitators, teachers, and mobilizers of the public—are part of the "consciousness-raising industry" (D'Agostino, 1985; Mukerji and Schudson, 1986). The Marxist emphasis on ownership is translated into a network of controls and links between government officials, the Communist party, and media organizations.

Social Responsibility: This philosophy places many ethical and moral restrictions on the mass media, stressing responsibility instead of freedom. Media today are major economic institutions, and few people can afford to start their own newspaper or TV station as an outlet for their opinions. The Social Responsibility philosophy requires media to offer opportunities for people's opinions to be heard. This philosophy emerged in a report of the Hutchins Commission on Freedom of the Press in 1947 (McIntyre, 1987), although Bovee (1986) notes that New York Tribune editor Horace Greeley had anticipated the theory a century earlier. The commission set out to answer the question of whether freedom of the press was in danger. It concluded press freedom indeed was endangered for three reasons: 1) the press had grown as a mass medium while the percentage of people able to express their ideas through the press had decreased; 2) the few people able to use the press had not adequately served the needs of society; and 3) those directly in charge have at times engaged in practices the public condemned. This mid-twentieth century view of the relationship between mass media and the government puts less faith in the libertarian idea that truth will arise from the clash of ideas. The commission cited five main requirements for a socially responsible press:

1. The press must give a truthful, comprehensive, and intelligent account of the day's events in a context which gives them meaning.
2. The press must provide a forum for the exchange of comment and criticism.
3. The press must project a representative picture of the constituent groups in the society.
4. The press must represent and clarify the goals and values of the society.
5. The press must provide full access to the day's news.

These normative philosophies remain the cornerstones of many mass communication systems. However, the four philosophies are too restrictive for many observers (Blanchard, 1986; Brod, 1987; Johnson, 1986). Critiques come from several directions. Many, like Altschull (1984) for example, argue that independent media cannot exist because they necessarily reflect the larger social order. He argues for a schema with an economic base and provisions for three types of environments: the market economy, the Marxist society, and "advancing" countries (for economically developing countries in the Third World). From Marxists come challenges that private control has produced private monopolies where few citizens have any access to the channels of mass communication in capitalist countries. For example, most televised air time in the United States is accounted for by only three network organizations, though this has been declining in the face of competition from cable TV. A single newspaper, Axel Springer's *BZ*, took 25% of the market in Germany (Dunnett, 1988). Other criticism comes from Europe's "New Philosophers," who assert that nineteenth century philosophical systems are out of date and Marxism is an obsolete ideology that inevitably leads to totalitarianism.[26]

Objections also come from the Third World, where leaders and intellectuals in some developing countries argue that the Western concepts of "freedom," private ownership, and national development don't go together as the major philosophies suggest. Emerging nations in Latin America, Africa and Asia do not have the political stability of the United States or European nations, nor the traditions of civil liberties developed over centuries. At the same time they are faced with the need to plan and to mobilize the population for national economic and social goals. One such goal is unity among ethnic and racial groups often related only by conflict and past differences. If "freedom" of the media and free speech mean that this unity will not be achieved and critics will scuttle development programs, then such freedom is an unaffordable luxury. The view of leaders in some developing nations is that the mass media must be harnessed to work as a partner in national development. The "harness" represents a different definition of the relationship between the mass media and society (See Hachten and Hachten, 1987).

One proposal to describe media systems would alter the four major philosophies to account for the differences in developing nations. Ralph Lowenstein offers a two-tiered system that separates ownership and philosophy of a given press system (Merrill and Lowenstein, 1971). Three types of press ownership are offered:

1. **Private**—ownership by individuals or nongovernment corporations; supported primarily by advertising or subscriptions;
2. **Multiparty**—ownership by competitive political parties; subsidized by party or party members;
3. **Government**—owned by government or dominant government party; subsidized primarily by government funds or government-collected license fees.

The characteristic separating the three types of ownership is the source of financial support which Lowenstein believes indicates important operational characteristics of the press. For example, a privately owned media system most likely gets its financial support from advertising and subscriptions. Thus, we would expect such a system to be at least partially responsive to the needs of those chief sources of revenue.

The second tier is philosophies. Here, Lowenstein retains the authoritarian and libertarian philosophies in the same basic form given earlier. However, the Marxist-Communist philosophy has been abandoned to make way for "Social-Authoritarian." Examples of authoritarian governmental activities continue around the world. In one African nation, for example, the government has banned films, postcards, and even card games (Riddle, 1989).

1. **Authoritarian**—government licensing and censorship to stifle criticism and maintain the ruling elite;
2. **Libertarian**—absence of governmental controls, except for minimal libel and obscenity laws, assuring a free marketplace of ideas and operation of the self-righting process (Wuliger, 1991);
3. **Social-Authoritarian**—government and government-party ownership to harness the press for national economic and philosophical goals;
4. **Social-Libertarian**—minimal governmental controls to unclog channels of communication and assure the operational spirit of the Libertarian philosophy;
5. **Social-Centralist**—positive governmental controls to harness the press for national economic and philosophical goals, but without the ownership found in Social-Authoritarian philosophy.

The "social responsibility" term has been abandoned as ambiguous. In its place are two new concepts of philosophy which pay some allegiance to the spirit of libertarianism but recognize that modern society and technology have restricted the marketplace of ideas (Schwarzlose, 1989) and that some societal interference is necessary to unclog the "choked" channels (e.g., regulations of the U.S. airwaves by the Federal Communication Commission). Lowenstein moves a step further to suggest applying his typology by medium within each country. Thus, one philosophy may relate newspapers to society, while two philosophies are needed to describe the situation for broadcast media.

Lowenstein believes that his typology helps describe movements of national media systems. If a nation moves in the direction of Social-Libertarianism, for example, it attempts to maintain the idea of a privately owned media system while assuring the operational spirit of Libertarianism via self-regulation and government regulation. The aim of both Social-Centralism and Social-Libertarianism is to assure pluralism of voices although there is a limited number of channels. Emphasis on government control of information reflects movement towards Social-Authoritarianism.

Lowenstein's revision of the original four theories of the press is one of many, and new ones seem to appear with increasing regularity. Picard (1982/83) suggests aligning the approaches along a Libertarian-Authoritarian continuum rather than devising descriptive categories. He also suggests that the Libertarian model is dated, in part because of growing concentration of media ownership, and he offers the Democratic-Socialist model as a solution, a concept much like Lowenstein's Social-Centralist model (Picard, 1985). In this model, journalists are required to "open avenues for the expression of diverse ideas and opinions." Akhavan-Majid and Wolf (1991) argue that the U.S. mass media system today is best described in terms of an "elite power group model," which says the industry is organized as an elite power group which is concentrated, integrated with other elites, and able to influence the government but also be influenced and controlled by the government in return.

One of the most useful efforts is provided by Hachten and Hachten (1987), who look at media philosophies as clashing ideologies that represent differing perceptions about the nature and role of news. Their five concepts of the media include:

1. The **Authoritarian concept**—where the media exist to support the state or authority, and diversity is wasteful or irresponsible[27];
2. The **Western concept**—found in a handful of Western nations sharing such characteristics as protection of individual civil liberties, high economic and educational levels, a competitive democratic political system, sufficient private capital for media support, and an established tradition of independent journalism;

3. The **Communist concept**—similar to the Marxist system described previously) is still championed in some Western countries as well as Cuba, Vietnam, and China[28];

4. The **Revolutionary concept**—where the media are used to subvert the government or wrest control from alien rulers; and

5. The **Developmental concept**—where the mass media are seen as important instruments for nation building.

The latter two concepts are particularly useful when separated from the others. The Revolutionary concept of the media is a relatively short-lived one because it addresses what is inherently an unstable situation. Holstein (1992) compares the revolutionary power of the press in 1848 France and 1917 Russia. It applies equally to such situations as clandestine "self-publishing" that occurred before Glasnost in the Soviet Union, the use of audio cassettes in the Iranian revolution of Ayatollah Khomeni, the use of pamphlets urging opposition to colonial rule in the American colonies, or mobile radio stations sponsoring revolutions to overthrow governments of the left or right. The concept also may apply to civil war situations (Knudson, 1988). Once independence or power is achieved, however, the revolutionary philosophy is found wanting because it addresses a situation that no longer exists.

At that point, the Developmental concept is brought to the foreground. This concept holds that all instruments of mass communication should be mobilized by the central government to aid in the great tasks of nation building: fighting illiteracy and poverty, building a political consciousness, and assisting in economic development. When the private sector is unable to provide adequate media service, the government has the responsibility. For some, the developmental concept is a rejection of the Western concept, but the debate is likely to continue for some time.

Describing the philosophical foundations of national media systems is not an idle task. Indeed, the characterization of governments and social systems is part of the continuing world-wide struggle between different philosophies and ideologies. This intrudes upon the American system as well, for developing nations are dissatisfied with the pictures of their countries that appear in Western media. Essentially, the objections are an extension of the logic for the Social-Authoritarian philosophies. Local newspapers and radio stations are operated in a program of "development journalism." Yet the media of the United States and other nations contain little of this "good news" about development in Africa, Asia, and Latin America. Thus, since this may hamper progress, international news media also must be made to serve developmental objectives. Certainly this view assumes that mass media can have major effects on social, economic, and cultural development.

What is Freedom?

All media philosophies are based on notions of freedom, one of the most popular ideas in the world today (Paraschos, 1989). In some places, it refers to government ownership (Tannsjo, 1985), in others it means citizens can say what they want without being thrown in jail, and in all places, freedom has limits. Mass media are crucial to the exercise of power and the expression of ideas. Thus, the notions of freedom, democracy, and mass communication are intertwined. Recent debate has emphasized "media responsibilities to society." Merrill (1974) notes that the stress on responsibility naturally leads toward control and restrictions on media. He believes that pluralism should be the objective of American society and that means diversity of information and ideas but not necessarily the "number" of media units operating. When a government "forces" libertarianism to work by producing pluralism, the country no longer has libertarianism but control (Lichtenberg, 1987). The problem is how to define "responsibility."

What do we "want" from free speech and a free press? Though most of the goals are linked to government, others are equally important. Philosophers Immanuel Kant and John Stuart Mill stressed the role of freedom of expression in human self-realization or self-development (Lichtenberg, 1987). People want free speech because they value truth, value tolerance, wish to protect interests of other people, want to avoid disadvantages of suppressing speech, and believe in individual autonomy and the ability to think for oneself. Furthermore, the "accepted wisdom" in any society is never complete, and truth is only ascertained through unrestricted clash of ideas. This is a restatement of the "marketplace of ideas" concept used since the eighteenth century to justify freedom of expression (Smith, 1988, 1989). Truth also takes many forms— religious truth, scientific truth, artistic truth—and cannot always be proved, so the jury is the court of public opinion (Levy, 1985). Freedom of speech also is essential to the development of people as rational beings—capable of social interaction and self-government. Many of the characteristics associated with democracy depend on free access of all groups to the channels of communication—as both senders and receivers. One of these is the nonviolent competition for political power. Communication also is essential for the government's reliance on persuasion rather than force to accomplish its policies. Access to media channels is essential for those outside the government who want to influence its actions (Davison, 1965). All these goals are interconnected and linked to democratic processes.

Society has three chief instruments which can be used to encourage or to prod the mass media to responsible performance (Lichtenberg, 1987; Schramm, 1973). One is the government and its various regulatory bodies at the national, state, and local levels. The U. S. Federal Trade Commission, for example, is responsible for examining fraudulent advertising appearing on television. Local ordinances may affect the distribution of sexually explicit films. Second, the media themselves, their personnel and associations, engage in activities that lead to self-regulation. Journalists band together in professional associations and other groups that affect media performance. Third, the general public, individually through pressure and collectively in organizations like media councils, influence the mass media.[29]

Measuring Freedom

Several efforts have been made to measure press freedom and to classify nations' media systems according to normative categories. Most quantitative studies have relied on perceptions of press freedom by observers, socio-economic factors such as the literacy rate, or industry statistics representing the number of newspapers.[30] Weaver (1977), for example, looked for relationships between press freedom and development, concluding that mass media development was related to increased accountability of the government in some parts of the world.[31] Weaver, Buddenbaum and Fair (1985) found that an emphasis on education rather than economic productivity in less-developed countries contributed to stability, democracy, media growth, and press freedom from government control. Picard (1987) looked at the relationship between a group of political, economic, demographic, and media use variables and levels of state intervention in the press economies of 16 Western nations. The best single predictor of intervention was press tradition. High levels of intervention were related to a political press tradition and low levels associated with a commercial press tradition. Recently, strong support was found around the world for restrictions on journalists (Merrill, 1987).[32]

Ultimately, our attention to normative philosophies must extend from the media to entire communication systems. Mulgan (1991) looks at communication and control, shifting the focus away from political power to communication and technologies. New communication technologies are challenging political ideas of Western thought. Control is seen as a social resource which can be both liberating and oppressive. Mulgan (1991) says control is never simple or one-dimensional and we need to look at the structure and operation of increasingly complex communication networks.

Summary

Mass media do not appear overnight but have long histories that illustrate the impact of a variety of factors—growth of education and literacy, economic variables, technology, urbanization and immigration. In this chapter, we looked at the growth and development of newspapers, magazines, film, radio, television, and advertising. We identified the ways that existing media are affected by each new arrival on the scene. New media force those in existence to change their form and function to survive, but they do not supplant them. We also surveyed mass media systems around the world, witnessing the interaction of economic, political, social, and cultural factors. Finally, we reviewed historical interpretations of the relationship between mass media and society and new approaches to defining that relationship.

Chapter Two Footnotes

1. Tarr, Finholt, and Goodman (1987) note that "urban scholars generally agree that cities evolved in order to facilitate human communications [sic]." The importance of population also has been documented in recent studies (Hagner, 1983; Niebauer, Lacy, Bernstein and Lau, 1988).
2. There are a variety of approaches to dividing up the history of newspapers and other media. The chronology followed here reflects the traditional divisions, which are still useful. Other divisions are: dialectic and ecological models of social change, Kaul and McKerns (1985); business history divisions, Smith and Dyer (1992); ethnic group divisions, Nerone (1990). Shaw and Zack (1987) note a broadening of journalism history. Nord (1988) argues for an emphasis on the institutional structure of mass media.
3. Many of these topics appeared before this period. Oldham (1987) examined London newspapers from 1756 to 1786, finding considerable law reporting that included features of courtroom activity as well as serious legal and constitutional questions. Shaw and Slater (1985) found that American newspapers in the 1820-1860 period were not particularly "sensational" in their content and the style consisted of leisurely long paragraphs.
4. For more on the history of newspapers see Emery and Emery (1992), Folkerts and Teeter (1989), Harris (1987), and Stephens (1988).
5. Riley and Selnow (1988) analyzed 700 magazine titles published in the South from 1764 to 1984, finding few started prior to 1800 and only 109 from 1792 to 1816. Growth spurted in 1818 and again in 1833 but slowed with the Civil War. The Spanish-American War stimulated magazine starts but World War II had little impact on numbers.
6. For more on the history and background of magazines see Mott (1968), Peterson (1964), Riley and Selnow (1988), Stein (1990), Stevens and Johnson (1990), Wolseley (1973), and Wood (1956).
7. See Giannetti (1987) and Gomery (1990) for more on the cinema.
8. See Paglin (1990) for a history of the legislative activity associated with the Communications Act of 1934.
9. See Bilby (1986), Douglas (1987), Head and Sterling (1990), Hilliard (1985), Long (1987), McChesney (1990), Paper (1987), and Sterling and Kittross (1978) for more on radio's development.
10. O'Rourke (1982-83) notes that it took American industry more than two decades to develop a workable color TV system and bring it to the marketplace. RCA and CBS invested millions of research dollars for a system which would provide a good color picture, a reasonable number of broadcast channels, and a compatible signal that could be received by existing black-and-white sets. It was the competitive nature of the free enterprise system that eventually determined what system would be adopted.
11. See Head and Sterling (1990), Nmungwun (1989), and Sterling and Kittross (1978) for more on the development of television.
12. See Boorstin (1972), Wicke (1988), and Wright and Mertes (1974) for more on advertising.

13. Lacy (1987) found that the development of radio had little effect on declining newspaper competition during the 1929-1948 period.
14. Support for the principle has been found in the United States (McCombs, 1972) and other countries (Werner, 1986). However, McCombs and Eyal (1980) found a negative trend for the period 1968-1972 when controls were introduced for real economic growth, inflation, and population growth. Wood (1986) and colleagues (Wood and O'Hare, 1991) found mixed results using the concept of "share of income constancy" and other historic periods. Also see McCombs and Eyal (1980) and McCombs and Nolan (1992).
15. For recent trends and changes, see Dunnett (1988), Jenkins (1987), Morais (1987), Mazur (1987), and Self (1990).
16. Local broadcasting has developed in Luxembourg, Great Britain, Ireland, Finland (McCain and Lowe, 1990), and Denmark (Cheesman and Kyhn, 1991; Keirstead and Keirstead, 1987).
17. For years Finland's laws made it an offense to endanger the country's relations with its neighbors, a reference to the Soviet Union. Switzerland had a similar law.
18. Examples of these changes have been found in Belgium (Servaes, 1989), Sweden (Tomlinson, 1988; Weibull and Anshelm, 1991), and elsewhere. Also see Blumler (1992), LeDuc (1987), and Porter (1989).
19. See Head (1985), Martin and Chaudhary (1983), and Merrill (1991) for more on other countries' media systems.
20. Malaysian TV reduced air time for violent Hong Kong films to 5 hours per week because of complaints from the Chinese community that such films had bad effects and gave the Chinese a bad name. "Malaysia to Reduce Air Time for Violent Films," *Asian Mass Communication Bulletin* (March-April, 1992) 22(2): 16.
21. Examples from the recent past and present are Saudia Arabia, Egypt, Turkey, South Africa, Nigeria (Agbese and Ogbondah, 1990), China (Lent, 1989), Indonesia (Feldman, 1986), India (Ryan, 1988), Singapore (Hachten, 1989), and many other countries in Asia (Lent, 1989), Peru, Brazil (Garrison and Salwen, 1990), Bolivia, Ecuador (O'Connor, 1990), Mexico (Montgomery, 1985). Also see *Attacks on the Press: A Comprehensive Worldwide Survey* (1992).
22. For more on Japan see: Hattori (1989), Komatsubara (1989), Omori (1989), Shimizu (1986), and Tamura (1987).
23. For more on developments in Eastern Europe and the former Soviet Union see: Bohlen (1990), Gardner (1989), Goban-Klas (1989), Gollin (1990), Jakab (1989), Jakubowicz (1989, 1990), Manaev (1989), Mathewson (1990), McNair (1989), Mickiewicz (1988), Perlmutter and Perlmutter (1990), Petrescu (1990), Shlapentokh (1990), Szekfu (1989), and Zhou (1988).
24. Sloan (1987) questions the historical assumption that Americans held a broad libertarian philosophy in the early 1800s, arguing that even into the 1800s Americans believed in a limited concept of freedom of expression.
25. Bowles (1989) looked at newspaper editorial page support for free speech issues in the period from 1919-1969, finding general support when attention was forthcoming but silence in many cases.
26. With the collapse of communism in Eastern Europe, we have both objective critiques of Marxism as well as new voices arguing in favor of democracy and notions of the "marketplace of ideas." South America and Africa also have been changing, with only one "President for Life" ruling on the African continent in 1989.
27. In England, when the crown saw that the printing press was the source of potentially upsetting power, it licensed the press and brought it under greater government control. The licensing system didn't stop until the latter part of the seventeenth century, and then only as a result of political and economic pressures. Public opinion had become a force to be reckoned with, due to the growth of libertarian political philosophy. The monarch began to be ruled by public

consent which could be influenced by printers and publishers. This forced the crown to be more respectful of publishers.

28. Less than a month after the aborted coup in Moscow which led to the fall of the Communist party there, the annual festival of the French Communist party in Paris attracted as many as half a million people (Alan Riding, "If the Old Party's Dying, There's Life in the Fair," *New York Times*, Sept. 16, 1991, p. 7A). Also, though Marx would appear to be one of the most discredited thinkers of our time, his ideas continue to find currency even among those who abhor the Marxist/communist system of control built on them around the world. One observer notes that the fall of communism largely represented the collapse of public ownership of the means of production and crude economic determinism; it did not discredit all of Marx's observations about social welfare, the environment, wide-open competition, child labor, etc. (Henry F. Myers, "Das Kapital. His Statues Topple, His Shadow Persists: Marx Can't Be Ignored," *Wall Street Journal*, Nov. 25, 1991, p. 1.)

29. History is rich with incidents of violence directed against media and their personnel in the United States and around the world. Journalists once were intimidated and assaulted by the Ku Klux Klan (Scharlott, 1988). Some eighty-three journalists were killed on assignment in 1991 and abuses were recorded around the world. There are three types of such violence, the most pervasive being personal assault by people feeling a sense of personal outrage (Nerone, 1990; Sherer, 1991). Fights between editors themselves were common in the last century. Struggles over press performance have changed remarkably little over time.

30. Studies have been conducted by Nixon (1960), Greenberg (1961), Lowenstein (1970), Kent (1972), and Weaver (1977). The United Nations Development Program reported results of a study that used 40 indicators to measure freedom, using data from 1985. The report rated Sweden the freest and Iraq the least free, with the United States 13th among 18 countries judged to enjoy a high degree of freedom; 32 nations had medium freedom and 38 low freedom (Jerome R. Watson, "UN Exec Plugs Aid for Poor Nations," *Chicago Sun-Times*, May 24, 1991. p. 28).

31. Burrowes (1989) argues that we need studies that measure real-world restrictions rather than perceptions of press freedom. When a government is under stress, it can either restrict the press or change itself and give in to public demands for greater freedom (Belbase, 1981).

32. Government information/press officials from six regions of the world were interviewed to collect information for a control index that included national and international licensing, identification cards or accreditation, university education, and national and international codes of ethics. Twice as many countries favored in-country licensing of journalists as did not. Most said licensing was good if done by journalistic associations themselves, and a few favored government licensing. There also was strong support for journalistic identification or accreditation; only the United States and Mexico were not "in favor" of IDs, and they were "neutral." Though many said journalists should have a university education, few thought it should be required. Finally, only a few Western nations such as the United States, the United Kingdom, Germany, Netherlands and Greece were opposed to in-country codes of ethics for journalists, and strong support was found for international codes (Merrill, 1988a,b).

3

Inside Media Industries
Structure, Growth and Concentration

  I. Introduction
 II. Industries of the media institution
     A. Media as part of other industries
        1. The knowledge industry/information age
III. Growth of mass media industries
     A. The film industry
     B. Broadcasting—TV, cable and radio
        1. TV production industry
        2. Local TV operations
        3. Low-power TV stations
        4. Cable TV
        5. Radio
     C. Print media—newspapers, magazines and books
        1. Newspapers—dailies, neighborhood and community papers, alternative papers, weeklies, ethnic and foreign-language press
        2. Magazines—specialization
        3. Books
     D. New forms and media relationships
 IV. The economic support structure
     A. Ownership and the support structure
     B. Diversity and concentration of ownership
     C. Reasons for growth and change
        1. Organizational aging
        2. Social differentiation
        3. Competition
     D. Concentration among film and entertainment media
     E. Concentration in cable and TV networks
        1. Producing TV programming
        2. Ties between film and TV
        3. Cable becomes a major player
     F. Concentration in the print industry
        1. Growth of chains
        2. Umbrella model of competition
        3. Joint operating agreements
        4. Magazines—pure competition
        5. Book publishing
     G. Cross-Ownership of Media
     H. Impact of ownership and concentration
        1. Impact on the editorial page
        2. Impact on news coverage
        3. Impact of competition
        4. Translating ownership into content
  V. Summary

Mass media are important ingredients in the communication "cement" binding together social units ranging from families to ethnic groups, organizations, and countries. Any form of interdependence—the distinguishing characteristic of social units—requires communication in the "formative" stage as well as subsequent periods of maintenance. Without communication, we have aggregates with common interests or shared characteristics who do not form a social unit.

Much of the "communication cement" that connects (or disconnects) us occurs in patterns that represent mass media. In the last chapter we examined media and society. We now shift levels to look at the "patterns of encoding activity" that occur in mass communication. We begin with mass media industries and their relationship with other industries; economic functions are a defining force in the shape of mass media. Then we will consider central economic issues that interface with communication issues—concentration of encoding activity into a few hands and consequences of this development.

The mass communication institution is complex. Scholars thus find a wealth of material when they look at media institutions. Some find significance in the media as cultural industries (Miege, 1987); others view news media as a set of loosely interlocking political organizations (Cook, 1991). Clearly, we cannot review all potential patterns relating to mass communication, but we will look at some of the most meaningful and examine the evidence describing relationships.

Industries of the Media Institution

When Peter Jennings delivers a one-minute story about crime in America, he is supported by an entire system of people as well as a vast collection of microphones, cables, and other hardware. It is not just a short one-way conversation with the celebrated broadcaster. Jennings represents a number of complex organizations—ABC, the journalistic profession, and a far-flung industry of mass media. Broadcasting isn't the exception, either. The romantic image of the solitary artist seldom applies today because most message construction is a collaborative production (Ryan and Peterson, 1982). Mass communication is characterized by the cooperative efforts of organizations, professions, and groups of skillful people integrated into loosely defined industries. Contributions of individuals are significant, often paramount, but we need to look at the context in which media people encode messages.

Media perform four major functions for society—providing entertainment, passing on traditions, coordinating activities (for example, providing information that allows different branches of government to coordinate their policies), and acting as a watchdog over the government and larger environment. Some of these functions are shared by other institutions. New generations learn about their heritage not only from the mass media but also from their parents, schools, and churches. Since media serve such diverse functions, they often are classified as belonging to more than a single industry. For example, they produce revenue (an economic enterprise), provide recreation (leisure industry), and are operated by people whose product is "information" (knowledge industry).

Media as Part of Other Industries

Taking a long view, Beniger (1986) sees the media as part of the **control** revolution. Historically, people have gained control over their lives by collecting, storing, processing, and communicating information. The idea of an **information age** has been linked to Daniel Bell's (1976) concept of "post industrialism," which emphasized the view that agrarian-based activities once were replaced by industry as the dominant economic emphasis and now the latter is being challenged by the service industry (Lyon, 1986; Williams, 1988).[1] Bell (1989) argues that there has been a decisive change in the character of knowledge, with communication beginning to replace transportation as the major means of connecting people. Bell (1976, 1980) forecasts the emergence of a social framework based on new technologies of telecommunication.

Efforts to measure the information society emphasize people who "produce" information. This "knowledge class" in the labor force—tied to shifts in educational qualifications and skills—includes not only mass media encoders but also other professional encoders, including public relations experts, stock brokers, consultants, and librarians (Gouldner, 1979). Some measures of the information society are more expansive, including the "distribution" and "consumption" of information as well as encoding activity. Machlup (1962) was a pioneer in defining knowledge production as a complex economic activity.[2] Others have built on his work.[3] Viewing the information industry as being made up of those who create, move, and use information, Raphael (1989) identifies forty submarkets. Creators include printers and print media, information movers include phone companies and broadcast media, and users include consumer electronics, computers, and software. Current estimates of the size of the "information economy" vary (in part because of varying definitions about what to include); generally it is thought to be about 40-50% of the workforce in the United States.[4] The information industry in the United States—estimated at $400 billion (Raphael, 1989)—is concentrated geographically and has grown rapidly—from a low of 5% of the labor force in 1860 to about 50% today (Drennan, 1989; Hepworth and Robins, 1988).[5] In fact, the United States is the dominant supplier of information resources to the world, particularly to developing nations.

At least three innovations in the past created similar information explosions— language, writing, and printing. In each case, the lack of these inventions prevented the development of particular forms of civilization (Robertson, 1990). The current information revolution created by computer technology and new capabilities to communicate could have far-reaching consequences for human organization.[6] Bates (1989, 1990) points out that new information technologies and communication systems are being developed faster than many believe society has the capacity to assimilate. Fears about the impact of communication technologies focus on whether workers will benefit or suffer (Anderson and Harris, 1989; Kumar, 1978; Lyon, 1986; Meunier and Volle, 1986; Schiller, 1981). Furthermore, there are questions about what the final "information grid" will look like and issues of who will have access and control.

The information society or knowledge industry is significant for the mass media in several ways. First, the information society is based on new technologies which affect how media and other encoding organizations operate in collecting information and constructing messages. Second, the new technologies affect media audiences, their access to information, and how they process media messages. Third, the value of information is tenuous, and this has consequences for media as competing delivery systems or alternatives to other technologies.[7] Plans promoting development of new technologies have been developed in numerous countries and in areas of the United States (Lee and Gomez, 1992; Lyon, 1986; Strover, 1988; Williams, 1988).[8]

Growth of Mass Media Industries

How big are the mass media? A study by Sterling (1975) found that the number of media outlets had increased by nearly 270% in the preceding half century, and the figures have grown even more since then. Increases are due primarily to a growth in the number of broadcast stations while the daily press has dropped in units. Since 1950 media outlets and voices have increased at a rate faster than the population because of the introduction of FM radio, network affiliates and independent TV stations, low-power television, and cable services.

The Film Industry

Despite fluctuations, the U.S. film industry generally has prospered in the face of competition from other media and activities. In 1987, Hollywood turned out 515 new movies, an outpouring greater than any year since 1970 (Harmetz,

1988; Cronin and Litman, 1990). In that same year, the National Association of Theater Owners said there were more movie theaters in the United States than at any time since they began keeping track in 1948: 22,721 movie screens. Ticket sales reached $4.2 billion, the best in Hollywood's history (Harmetz, 1988).

In recent years, theater owners have been building more screens[9] but also trying to heighten the film-going experience by installing pleasant surroundings and more comfortable seats (Zehr, 1987). Film exhibitors make a considerable portion of their revenues from the sale of food (23% of revenue) as well as admission (Guback, 1987).[10] Another source of revenue for exhibitors is advertising, though that has met some resistance.[11] Ultimately, technological changes in film exhibition may attract audiences from other media, and there are plans currently to open experimental theaters presenting films using an audience-participation technique called artificial reality; audiences would wear goggles and earphones to create the sensation of moving through space, and lightweight gloves would allow each person to make things happen in the "collective fantasy world."

Traditionally, the film industry has been broken into film producers (major Hollywood film studios), film distributors (who send films across the country and around the world) and film exhibitors (today mostly chains of multi-screen complexes). Lines have become increasingly blurred through the years and interests of the three often conflict. In 1987, for the first time since the early days of Hollywood, an exhibitor—Cineplex Odeon—announced it would finance a program of independent film production directly (Harmetz, 1987), thus merging the three traditional functions of producing, distributing, and exhibiting films.

Links to other media also affect film production and exhibition. Film producers face escalating costs in making movies. The average price of 169 movies released by major American film companies in 1990 leaped 14% to $26.8 million, then dropped slightly the following year (Horn, 1991). Only 3 out of 10 films produced make money from exhibition alone (Dutka, 1989), but accounting methods and sales to other media (videocassettes, TV, cable) increase this percentage. While film producers gained another market for their products, exhibitors faced new competitors. Hollywood has adjusted as revenue from videos, cable, and over-the-air TV surpassed first-run exhibition (Gomery, 1989). In the 5 years from 1983 to 1988, the video industry increased 500%, with revenue from sales and rentals surpassing box office in 1985 (Prince, 1992).

Hollywood uses other media to promote films. A prime example is the publicity surrounding the annual Academy Awards. The Best Picture Academy Award can add $10-$40 million to the box office (Landro and Akst, 1988). The selling of movies to American audiences began to change in the mid-1970s, when Universal became the first major studio to skillfully employ saturation advertising on network TV to promote "Jaws." **Release patterns** are essential to a film's success. As Litman and Kohl (1989) note, summertime, Christmas, and Easter are the peak viewing periods, but competition at Christmas is so intense that release at that time no longer guarantees financial success. The rapidly growing market for American films abroad has led Hollywood studios to pay closer attention to foreign markets. In 1989, foreign revenues constituted about 38% of total industry revenues, up from 30% in 1980. Foreign theaters accounted for 42% of all worldwide box office rentals in 1988, up from 34% six years earlier (Arundel, 1990; Fabrikant, 1991).

Broadcasting—TV, Cable and Radio

Broadcasting outlets have grown dramatically in the past couple decades. In early 1993, there were 11,275 radio stations on the air (4,963 commercial AM stations, 4,742 commercial FM stations, and 1,570 educational/public stations) and another 1,410 authorized; 1,505 TV stations on the air and 183 more authorized; 1,291 low-power TV stations on the air and 1,061 more authorized; and some 11,254 cable TV systems.[12] Table 3-1 (page 86) provides figures that sketch changes in media industries.

Financial pressures are affecting the relationships between the TV networks and local affiliates. Like other media in the late 1980s to the early 1990s, broadcasters suffered from a decline in the growth rate of advertising as competition grew and the economy faltered (Powers, 1990; Lipman, 1991).[13] Reflecting the declining fortunes of the networks, CBS, NBC, and ABC formed a new organization, the Network Television Association, to promote network TV to advertisers and agencies in 1990. For years the major TV networks compensated their local affiliates on the basis of market size alone, but that system lacked incentives to promote network shows and increase audience share. NBC began plans to link affiliates' pay to performance as well as audience size,[14] and CBS later announced plans to charge stations' fees to carry certain programs. The average network affiliate earns about 5% of its gross revenue from network compensation, though small-market stations depend much more on it (Cox, 1989; Goldman, 1990).

The same financial pressures are starting to reshape the television production industry (Stevenson, 1987). Financial issues increasingly dominate production decisions. Independent producers have been squeezed out as suppliers of prime-time series programming to the major TV networks. Independents commanded about 14% of the prime-time schedule in 1990-1991, a large decline from 57% only two years earlier. Hollywood's major studios accounted for about 70% of the fall 1990 lineup. Studios bid up the price of key talent, making it harder for new competitors to break in. Critics say the trend could worsen, with a potential loss of diversity of voices contributing to broadcast TV (Koch, 1990). Major studios and some independents are producing not just inexpensive game shows but such slick dramas as "Star Trek: The Next Generation" and the late-night "Arsenio Hall Show."

Producers of TV programming depend on **syndication sales** because they generally charge the major networks below cost for first-run shows. Actual rates charged for syndication of specific shows depend on the size of the market served by a TV station. In one sale, the "Cosby Show" commanded $4.4 million per episode when the market was at its peak, but a flood of sitcoms entering the market at the beginning of the 1990s led analysts to predict prices of $500,000-$900,000 per episode for situation comedies (Goldman, 1990).

Film and radio-television industries share many features and are integrated in many ways, but they differ significantly in several respects. The exhibition component is largely missing for TV since "exhibition" occurs in the home. Furthermore, the local "distribution" component also is a center of production, making television a "local" medium unlike film. Most of the local "production" represents news rather than entertainment programming.

In the early 1990s, **local TV news operations** were retrenching after the free spending of the 1980s, when local news programming expanded aggressively. A survey of radio and TV stations without news operations found that half of the TV stations said they couldn't afford to do news, which was unprofitable (McKean and Stone, 1992).[15] Smaller local TV stations are re-examining costs of the late-night news program and at least four network affiliates recently cancelled theirs. West Coast affiliates favor finishing network programming by 10 P.M. so they can move up their nightly news shows to make them more profitable. Prime-time programs are broadcast 8-11 P.M. on the coasts and 7-10 P.M. in the Central and Mountain time zones. The latter often are more profitable (Connor, 1991).

Local TV news markets have been defined as oligopolies, markets with stability and a few sellers producing somewhat different products (Litman, 1979). With the advent of cable and low-power TV stations (LPTV), the number of competitors is no longer limited and viewer options expand the potential for competition. By 1990 the number of stations in the top twenty markets had increased dramatically and stations had to face less revenue growth, increasing program costs, and relentless competition (Powers, 1990).

Low-power TV stations have weaker signals, so they can only serve smaller towns and neighborhoods of metro areas rather than entire cities or regions as do regular over-the-air broadcasters. They began spreading across the country once the licensing process was laid out in the early 1980s. The FCC eventually plans to license about 4,000 low-power TV stations (Saddler, 1984) and has received more than 32,000 applications for low power television stations from community, minority and commercial interest groups (Atkin, 1987). By 1990, licensing reached a 35% annual growth rate. One purpose was to serve smaller communities and rural areas not reached by larger stations and to diversify the types of owners and operators. A national survey of LPTV stations found 76% privately owned, 21% publicly owned, and 3.2% owned by local government; minority ownership existed in 8.3% of the stations. The stations served the following types of communities: rural, 35%; urban, 32%; suburban, 16%. More than a third said they served specific demographic populations with their programming—25% Hispanic or black populations, 25% religious audiences, 40% age groups, and 5% agricultural audiences. Almost two-thirds produced local programs (Banks and Titus, 1990).[16] Except for the major national TV networks, no restriction was placed on the number of LPTV stations which could be owned by one company or person (30% of the owners had more than one LPTV station) until the FCC started enforcing a fifteen-station ceiling in 1982 (Atkin, 1987). With limited resources, there is some question whether LPTV stations can offer much original local programming and remain economically profitable.

Cable TV has grown dramatically in the past couple decades. Cable systems reach 53 million subscribers (57.1% of the nation's TV households), and more than 4,000 communities have granted cable TV franchises (Glass and Ammons, 1989). Cable News Network, which broadcasts news programming 24 hours a day, reaches more than 50 million households in the United States. Other major cable networks include the USA Network, with more than 46 million subscribers, MTV with 45 million, Nickelodeon with 44 million, and the Entertainment and Sports Programming Network (ESPN) with more than 50 million. Black Entertainment TV (BET) reaches 25 million viewers (Barchak, 1992). California has the most subscribers and Texas the most systems. The largest system—in Oyster Bay, N.Y.—has 500,000 subscribers, while some small ones have as few as 100. The largest multiple-system-operator (MSO) is Tele-Communications, Inc., which has more than 8.4 million subscribers. Most systems have more than 20 channels, the minimum required for systems built after March, 1972. The average monthly fee for basic services was $18 in 1991. About 4,400 systems originate programming, offering an average of 23 hours weekly. Most cable systems receive less than 5% of their revenues from advertising. Pay cable channels reach over 50 million subscribers.[17] Considerable money is being spent to expand the capacity and reach of cable systems (Fabrikant, 1991). Early in 1993, Telecommunications announced plans to expand its systems tenfold to 500 channels, with a schedule organized by TV format and genre as much as by channel.[18]

Cable operators also are investing more money in programming. The mix of cable programming continues to change as cable networks come and go. In 1991, FNN (Financial News Network) was acquired by CNBC (Consumer News and Business Channel), which is owned by NBC (Goldman, 1991). Courtroom Television Network now offers coverage of American trials, legal news, and commentary. The Sci-Fi Channel offers a mix of science fiction, fantasy, and horror programming (Sharbutt, 1991), and MTV announced it will begin programming three MTV channels starting in mid-1993. Significant local programming also is being offered by large cable systems. In 1992, a New York system began a twenty-four-hour local news channel modeled on CNN. Wirth (1990) argues that the cable industry is having an increasingly negative impact on broadcast TV as its power in advertising and programming increase.

Reports of the demise of radio clearly are premature.[19] Though the popularity of specific radio formats fluctuates rapidly, the medium continues to attract youthful audiences and commuters with a diet of music and news. Radio continues as the most "local" of the broadcast and cable media. Community-oriented radio stations have emerged in the past couple decades as a distinct form of broadcasting. Roots of such stations go back to the end of the Second World War, when urban commercial stations without network affiliations sold blocks of airtime to ethnic broadcasters. The emergence of politically conscious radio stations, such as those supported by the Pacifica foundation in California and New York, are a second source. The heyday of such formats coincided with the height of the Vietnam War protests in the late 1960s and early 1970s. Experimentation also was seen at college radio stations, which often became outlets for National Public Radio. The 1980s saw cutbacks in federal funding, which hurt National Public Radio and the community radio movement but led to more cooperation among advocates (Barlow, 1988).

The Print Media—Newspapers, Magazines, and Books

Observers have worried for years that growth of broadcasting and video would hurt the print media. The continuing decline in the number of dailies often has been taken as a barometer of the industry's health but the industry is much more complex than that.

Newspapers.   In general, newspapers have held up well in competition with radio, TV, videotex, and other media (Udell, 1990).[20] Using advertising as a measure, newspapers expanded 279% from 1975 to 1988, while the Gross National Product increased only 205%. Three factors are favorable for newspapers' growth: audience demographics are becoming more favorable as the population ages (older people read newspapers more often); papers are improving services to advertisers; and management's attitude toward competition has improved. Udell (1990) concludes that U.S. newspapers are adequately positioned to enjoy economic growth if the nation's economy grows.

The number of daily newspapers in 1992 was 1,570, including 974 evening, 576 morning, and 20 all-day newspapers. National newspaper circulation rose from about 40 million in 1930 to a peak of 63 million in 1973 but dropped to about 60 million in the early 1990s.[21] Daily circulation has failed to keep pace with the growing population. The total circulation is split so morning papers have about twice that for evening papers. While the total number of dailies has dropped continuously in recent years, the number of morning and Sunday papers has grown, the latter reaching 875 in 1991. The number of cities in the United States with a daily paper has actually increased, though the number of cities with two or more separately owned dailies has declined. Most cities have a local daily newspaper monopoly.

While the daily newspaper industry is profitable and generally healthy, it still suffers with the economic business cycle and accompanying declines in advertising (Reilly, 1990),[22] rising costs of newsprint and problems faced by some metropolitan afternoon dailies (Schwenk, 1988; Stanley and Tharp, 1992).[23] Newspapers continue to be the largest advertising medium. Compared to other industries, newspapers have done quite well. Tharp and Stanley (1990, 1992) looked at trends in profitability of daily U.S. papers from 1978 to 1988, finding papers of all sizes had a higher profit margin than manufacturing companies with comparable revenue. The smallest papers, those with circulations under 15,000, had significantly lower profit margins than the larger papers and the difference was growing larger over time (Blankenburg, 1989). Many publishers have changed the content and appearance of their papers to attract new readers while others have tried to cut costs, turning to lighter-weight paper and trimming page sizes (Freeman, 1988). Newspapers used to resist "marketing" themselves, but that has changed dramatically, and nine out of ten use some type of readership study (Fleener, 1986; Soley and Reid, 1985). The two largest daily papers in the United States are national papers, the *Wall Street Journal* and *USA Today*, followed by dailies in the largest metro areas, the *Los Angeles Times* and *New York Times* (both with circulations of a million or more).

A modest but important trend has occurred at the other end of the press spectrum, the neighborhood and small community press. Typically couples in their twenties and thirties have poured everything into small, workable community papers with intensely local, even personal coverage. In 1979 the editors of such a paper, the *Point Reyes Light* in northern California, received the Pulitzer Prize (Eisendrath, 1979). Estimates of the number of local papers range from dozens to scores. Neighborhood papers also are appearing in many large cities, including New York City, Boston, Cleveland, and Minneapolis-St. Paul. The prices of computers and printers have dropped substantially, allowing start-up ventures to enter the market inexpensively (Gaziano and Ward, 1978). Alternative papers also have grown in number (Patner, 1990).[24] These include the *Chicago Reader*, *Boston Phoenix*, and *New Times* (Phoenix, Arizonia), which focus on younger, up-scale markets. Abbott (1988) notes that a decline in the rural weekly press has been accompanied by a rise in the urban weekly press.

The weekly newspaper has been an important part of American history since colonial times. Circulation increases have occurred as free distribution newspapers and shoppers have proliferated. One estimate put the number of free papers at 11,000 in 1980, compared to 8,000 paid weekly newspapers (Rambo, 1980). Weeklies also are emerging as increasingly important advertising vehicles. While their numbers have declined, their circulation has grown consistently (Sharkey, 1989).

The black press has traditionally been a weekly press (Cassara, 1991; Johnson, 1988). Its roots go back 150 years to Cornish and Russwurms *Freedom Journal*, begun in 1827. From 1866 to 1905 the black press saw more than 1,200 papers begin, 70% in the South. Most had small circulations. The black press united with black churches to campaign for social justice. Another growth period occurred from 1905 to 1976 with the migration of blacks from the South to northern industrial cities. Recently African-American newspapers have faced growing problems in their struggles to survive. Some metro newspapers also are trying to reach ethnic audiences with special sections; the *Los Angeles Times* published a sixteen-page tabloid section in English and Spanish in cooperation with the city's largest Spanish-language newspaper.[25] The past quarter century has seen a sharp increase in Spanish-language publications and other media (Blumenthal, 1991). The first American Indian newspaper, the *Cherokee Phoenix*, was published in 1828. One of the primary tasks of the early native American papers was educational. With small markets, native American newspapers have struggled to survive. The *Navajo Times Today* was forced to reduce the frequency of publication to a weekly (Trahant, 1987; Ghiglione, 1987).

Foreign-language papers continue to flourish in the United States and a recent sample illustrates this: Czech, Portuguese, Slovene, Lithuanian, Urdu, Yiddish, Korean, and Arabic. The Chinese-language press is quite vigorous, including 19 Chinese-language dailies in New York City and 15 in Los Angeles and San Francisco (Lau, 1989). The United States also has a diverse religious press; American Catholicism has a membership of 50 million and a press circulation of 25 million.

Magazines.   In 1741, two magazines debuted in colonial British America. Today, hundreds of magazines come and go each year. Almost 500 new magazine titles are launched each year, and by 1990 there were more than 12,000 in the United States.[26] The growth in that figure slowed down in the late 1980s as advertising revenue slumped (Lipman, 1990; Reilly, 1989).[27] New magazines usually need at least four years to break even in terms of revenues and expenses, with a 20% survival rate after about four years (Husni, 1988). Most magazines have relatively small circulations. There are five magazines with circulations of 10 million or more in the United States, including *Reader's Digest* and *TV Guide*. The 79 magazines with a million or more circulation represent only 14% of the total for magazines audited by the Audit Bureau of Circulation.

The magazine industry has become very specialized.[28] Production of so-called specialty magazines has jumped dramatically as publishers divide their marketplace into small, lucrative pieces. Efforts to achieve volume have been replaced by focusing on audience segments appealing to advertisers, and wealthy readers have never been more popular (Fabrikant, 1987). A tabulation of magazines launched in one year shows the following most popular categories—sex (46 new titles); sports (42); lifestyle and service (37); automotive (29); metropolitan, regional, and state (27); computers (25); and home service/home (24).[29] While some targets focus on content, such as the entertainment market (Landro, 1987) and sports (Akst, 1987), others focus on audience characteristics, such as African-Americans (Sipchen, 1990) or women (Abrahamson, 1992). The specialized business press also has developed since World War II, with a spurt in the 1970s (Endres, 1988). There has been a growing number of regional magazines (Riley and Selnow, 1989), with a trend toward more narrow and focused audiences even at this level; examples include the *Las Vegan* and *Albuquerque Senior Scene Magazine*.

Books.   Book publishing has grown enormously in this century, from 13,470 titles published in 1910 to more than 46,000 in 1990 (Powell, 1982; Karp, 1992). The U.S. publishing industry generated $42.981 billion in shipments in four distinct categories in 1988: book publishing, $12.775 billion; periodicals, $18 billion; miscellaneous publishing, $5.96 billion; and electronic databases, $6.2 billion.[30] During the 1980s mass-market paperback sales grew at a modest rate while adult hardbacks saw a 12.4% annual increase from 1982 to 1989. However, by 1990, paperbacks were seeing a comeback as consumers in a recession moved to cheaper books (Cohen, 1991). Fiction represents about two-thirds of trade books sold, a ratio that may not have changed since Charles Dickens's day (Bogart, 1991). The number of retail bookstores in the United States grew from less than 10,000 in 1950 to some 25,000 in 1991.[31] One trend is towards "superstores," which usually stock over 50,000 titles rather than the 10,000 available in the average chain store (Cohen, 1991).

The debate over consequences of the book publishing industry's increasing integration into the entertainment industry has raged for many years as book publishers have become part of firms whose holdings span television, films, and newspapers. Book tie-ins with other media and merchandising and an emphasis on blockbusters have worried those concerned with creativity and the small press. Publishers themselves are affected by literacy levels, book purchasing habits, libraries, copyright regulations, and bookstores that operate on exceedingly narrow margins; a bookstore grossing $100,000 a year has an inventory of 8-10,000 books worth $30-35,000 and receives net profits of $15,000. Though small publishers often can make a profit on as few as 1,000 books sold, they have a serious problem persuading the bookstore chains to open accounts. The 15,000 small publishers stay afloat by catering to limited interests and pursuing every last sale as they compete with the 300 or so big trade-book publishing houses that produce about 60% of the 50,000 new titles appearing yearly in the United States (Jacobs, 1987).

New Forms and Media Relationships

A host of new media technologies are either in development or struggling to secure their place within the industry. The interactive videotext system in France has attracted large numbers of users (Tempest, 1987).[32] In the United States, the IBM-Sears computer services venture, Prodigy, offers news along with electronic mail, banking, shopping, and dozens of other services to those who have home computers (Hughes, 1989; Roberts, 1988). Even the fax has become a mini-mass medium for specialized purposes (Poore, 1989).[33] Direct broadcast TV (using satellite dishes), already a reality in Europe,[34] also may come to the United States, though most efforts so far have been unsuccessful in competing with cable (Landro, 1990). However, satellite dishes do dot the U.S. countryside, where cable is unavailable. In Japan, direct broadcast satellites offer a high-definition signal.

Interactive TV also is being watched closely in the United States, and several experiments are underway. In one, viewers could participate in game shows, choose different camera angles while watching live sports events, and select an exercise program personalized by age. The company's technology permits the viewer to personalize programming by using a special remote control (Alexander, 1990). In 1990, CNN viewers of a midnight newscast voted for news stories they wanted to watch by dialing a 900 number, producing a so-called viewer-interactive newscast, though it wasn't tailored for the individual but the majority (Barlow, 1988; Burns, 1988; McCarthy, 1990).

Newspapers are branching out and considering facsimile editions, stock quotes by phone, and newspapers for the home computer. The *Hartford Courant*, the nation's oldest continuously published newspaper, has been putting out a "Fax Paper," a one-page news summary it faxes just before 5 P.M. to a group of subscribers who want a glimpse of the next day's paper.

Technologies are redefining media and increasing links between them. A partnership between a Simon and Schuster subsidiary and Cable News Network allows the former to videotape business programs each weekend to accompany teaching guides faxed to teachers with cross-references between the news program and the company's textbooks (Cox, 1991). The publisher itself is owned by Paramount Communication. A Cleveland network TV affiliate produces brief reports that run every half hour on a local cable system; the station's 6 P.M. newscast is simulcast weekdays on a local AM radio station (Feran, 1991). A newspaper uses a cable channel several times each night to tell audiences what stories will be in the morning paper. In Santa Barbara, a local Spanish-language AM station simulcasts the local TV news in Spanish. In San Antonio, a local TV station has leased a channel on the local cable system and is filling it with old series and movies. A pharmaceutical company, Johnson & Johnson, produces a regular video news show distributed to employees at its branches by satellite and tape.[35]

New technologies also can threaten old relationships among media organizations. The use of satellites to gather news by local TV stations has altered the relationship between TV affiliates and their networks. Local stations using satellites are more apt to share news video with stations associated with competing networks and to give their own networks lower priority when sharing video on breaking news stories (Niekamp, 1990).

The emergence of technologies such as fiber optics, microwave distribution, VCRs, direct broadcast satellites, videotext, and high-definition TV challenge the status quo and contribute to an increasingly competitive communication industry. The speed with which technologies grow is dependent on several factors, including setting standards and allowing markets to develop (Ducey and Fratrik, 1989; Klopfenstein and Sedman, 1990). Each player has constituencies with an interest in the selection of particular standards; thus, broadcasters could lose if an incompatible high-definition TV standard is selected (Schaefer and Atkin, 1990). Just as important as standards are policies promoting or delaying development of products for which demand exists and economic factors that affect the ability of audiences to use new technologies.

The Economic Support Structure

The economic support structure for mass media tends to be where all controversies over media performance ultimately end. Some critics fear what growing chain ownership of newspapers and TV stations will mean for "diversity of voices" in the media. Some argue that more economic resources could improve media performance. Others note that only a weak connection exists between ownership and what appears in the media.

We can describe the economic support of the mass media as falling along a continuum ranging from direct to indirect consumer support. Figure 3-1 shows one end as 100% direct support through consumer purchases. Here we find the book industry which derives most of its revenues from public purchases at stores or through book clubs. At the other end is the broadcasting industry where most of the support is indirect through either advertising (mediated through businesses that add advertising costs to the product purchase price) or institutional support such as that given by private foundations or the government.

Government regulation is strongest at the "indirect" end of the continuum. Legal ownership of mass media varies along the continuum. Most media units on the direct end are held in the private, profit-making sector. Most books, magazines, and newspapers are commercial enterprises that must maintain

---

Figure 3-1

Media Support Continum

	Films			TV	
100%	Books	Magazines	Newspapers	Radio	100%
Direct	★	★	★	★	Indirect

Direct support comes in the form of subscriptions or purchases, while indirect support comes either through advertising or foundations, etc. Magazines, for example, get about half of their support from subscriptions/retail sales and half from advertising, while newspapers get about two-thirds of their revenue from advertising. The new technologies (e.g., cable, VCRs) are changing the continuum and will continue to do so.

---

a profit to continue publishing. There are exceptions; university presses are sometimes subsidized to permit the publication of scholarly works, and the government publishes books and magazines through the huge U.S. Government Printing Office. Some small neighborhood newspapers in large cities operate largely on the basis of volunteer efforts aided marginally by funds received from foundations and other donations. Moving toward the indirect end, we find that most TV and radio stations are profit-making concerns owned by private individuals or corporations. Furthermore, the major TV and radio networks, cable TV systems, and TV/film production companies are commercial enterprises (Bates, 1988; Fournier, 1986). However, there also is a substantial non-commercial segment.

The Public Broadcasting Service in the United States began in 1967 when there were 112 educational TV stations and several hundred unrelated radio stations licensed primarily to universities and other nonprofit entities. The TV stations were served by National Educational TV (NET), a national production center funded by the Ford Foundation. It provided five hours of nationally distributed programming weekly. The system has grown. Today approximately 360 educational TV stations are on the air, serving all major markets and the bulk of the population through the Public Broadcasting Service (PBS), which provides more than 25 hours of programs weekly. Stations are licensed to many different institutions, including state agencies, universities, community nonprofit corporations, school boards, and libraries. Financing comes from many sources (White, 1987). National Public Radio serves a network of more than 200 public radio stations with about 40 hours of nationally distributed programs weekly. Over half of these stations are licensed to universities, with sizeable percentages licensed to communities, public schools, libraries, and state and local municipalities.

Three national institutions with responsibility for public broadcasting have been established: the Corporation for Public Broadcasting, the statutory body through which congressional appropriations to licenses are administered; the Public Broadcasting Service (PBS) organized by CPB in 1970 to operate the interconnection service to all public TV licenses; and National Public Radio, set up to initiate programs and to serve the interconnection facility for public radio licenses. PBS has grown from solely an engineering organization to a significant role in programming and planning the system through which programs are selected and funded by stations via the Station Program Cooperative (SPC). Local public TV stations depend on viewer subscription campaigns to generate revenue, but the growth of public stations has produced competition in this area as well. About 40 public TV stations compete in the same cities and PBS has overseen discussions among local TV executives to avoid the overcrowding (Arnold, 1989; Phillips, Griffiths, and Tarbox, 1991).

Most support for media at the indirect end comes from advertising. A ranking of advertising by nations shows that U.S. advertisers spent more than advertisers in the next 57 nations combined. American advertisers paid 3.5 times more for ads than those in second-ranking Japan. Advertising in the United States accounts for about 2.4% of the gross national product. In 1990, 25.1% of advertising expenditures went to newspapers, while television received 22.1%, direct mail 18.2%, radio 6.8%, magazines 5.3%, yellow pages 6.9%, outdoor and miscellaneous the remainder.[36]

In every medium the consumer contributes to the cost of information dissemination through the purchase of a stamp, magazine, newspaper, radio, or TV set. How important is advertising as a "subsidy"? Do TV commercials or newspaper ads pay their own way? Although there are questions about how to measure advertising and non-advertising content, several studies have been conducted to examine subsidies (Soley and Krishnan, 1987). Callahan (1978) compared revenue sources and content for print and broadcast media and direct mail, finding electronic media offer far more non-commercial information as a percentage when compared with newspapers. While about 60% of newspaper space is advertising, 12% of TV time is commercials.[37] In one study, advertising accounted for 77% of total newspaper revenue, the remaining 23% being the price to consumers via subscriptions and newsstand sales. Editorial content consumed 38% of newspaper space compared to 62% for advertising. Advertising subsidizes information dissemination in newspapers, magazines, and over the radio if we assume production costs for the two types of content are roughly equivalent (Soley, 1989).

Another way to look at advertising as subsidy was taken by Lees and Yang (1966). They note that costs of TV are shifted to consumers via higher prices for advertised goods and services. If government taxes generated the same support for the TV system without advertising, some families would benefit and others lose because families differ in their purchases of advertised goods and services, the volume of their TV viewing, and taxes paid. The result is a redistribution of income. In their study, the largest gainers are families in the lowest income bracket, who gain about half of the net subsidy from advertising. The two highest income groups are chief losers in this redistribution. Thus, commercial TV in the United States generates a "substantial welfare effect" through the redistribution of income.

Diversity and Concentration of Ownership

Diversity is a goal of those who believe that American society should strive for diversity of ideas on issues. Though we might find general support for diversity and tolerance in the American public, how that is achieved is another matter. The battle over what ideas and images should appear in the media is ultimately a battle over control, often characterized as a struggle between independent owners and large corporate chains, between competing social, political or interest groups, or between large organizations and small individuals.

Private owners argue that efforts by intellectual elites to impose a "balanced picture" on media producers undermines the independence from governmental interference that is the basis for that diversity.[38] Social critics point out that newspapers owned by the same corporation represent fewer views and ignore less powerful segments of society such as minorities and women. Still other critics note that efforts by intellectuals or government to promote "cultural" fare and other images would reduce the satisfaction of the mass consuming audience if implemented. Owen (1978) argues that diversity as a government regulatory goal may be irrelevant for consumer interests. Who defines diversity is the key. The major force behind diversity and fairness as broadcasting goals has been the desire of groups who want more of their preferred programming or programming they think people ought to see. Thus, debates over diversity are debates over control.

The concept of the marketplace of ideas helps us to understand current and past status of the freedom of expression in the United States (Schwarzlose, 1989). In three centuries, the marketplace has evolved from: individual rights as a cornerstone, to majoritarian rights in a functioning democracy, to group or citizen rights in a social welfare setting. Concern at first centered on the rights of the individual vs. the government, then moved to a concern over whether the majority would trample on the rights of individuals (as Tocqueville feared), and finally to issues of whether the media were being irresponsible in providing the robust public discussion needed in a democracy. Three components help define current freedom of expression: 1) the nature of prevailing communication technology—which can change the size of the marketplace plus the speed and opportunity for communication; 2) the extent of the legal right of expression—interpreted in specific constitutional and court decisions; and 3) the number and diversity of marketplace participants—the mix of individual and institutional voices over time. Schwarzlose (1989: 34) argues that the dominant trend in the history of American mass communication is that media institutions have grown to monopolize the marketplace, gradually forcing out the individual's voice.

Market economics and social value approaches represent two ways of achieving diversity (Entman and Wildman, 1992). Both view diversity as a goal of communication policy but they differ on what diversity is, can be, or should be. The market school argues that economic efficiency promotes desirable goals, including diversity of ideas. It stresses competition and is deeply skeptical that government intervention is superior to an imperfect market. The market school's primary objective is to maximize the efficiency of media markets in satisfying audience preferences, but it has little to say about other values, such as spreading human knowledge or encouraging democracy, values often given equal importance by the social values school. The social school argues that economic efficiency is not a primary concern and unfettered competition may have undesirable effects. It assumes government intervention is potentially beneficial in achieving diversity. Three types of diversity may be examined: product diversity—the range of product attributes or messages available; idea diversity—referring to distinct thoughts or criticisms available on social and political issues; and access diversity—the extent to which all ideas are given the emphasis they deserve or are available in the media.

Busterna (1989) notes that antitrust laws are designed to deal with the economic marketplace, not the marketplace of ideas. The Supreme Court has clearly stated that the U.S. Constitution guarantees the freedom to publish but not the freedom to combine (form chains or monopolies) to keep others from publishing. Though some commentators believe that antitrust laws are powerless to prevent anti-competitive activities by daily newspaper chains, Busterna (1989) suggests two grounds for antitrust intervention: to prevent economic activities that detract from consumer welfare and to protect small competitors and maintain a higher degree of industrial fragmentation.[39]

Ideas enter social discussions from many sources, but the mass media are chief among these. Many fear that the diversity of ideas will be reduced if there is concentration of economic power. Concern over media ownership stems from a fear that those who own, if not control, the media's activities also will be among the other economic and political elites of society. A pluralist elite structure is thought to require media elites to be sufficiently autonomous from other elites (business, government, education, religion) to provide a detached perspective on activities and a critical account of behaviors.[40] More than a decade ago, Bagdikian (1979) outlined the dimensions of control of information organizations in the United States by a relatively small number of national and transnational corporations. Concentration has continued in communication industries, and studies show widespread connections among elites in institutions covered by and including the media. For example, newspaper company directors often are on the boards of the local United Way or Chamber of Commerce. Media and other elites also share socioeconomic characteristics. However, actual overlap of media and other economic elites is due in part to ownership of media units by larger firms (Dimmick, 1986; Dreier and Weinberg, 1979; Han, 1988; Winter, 1988).

Diversity of ownership depends on two trends—growth in the number of units and new media, and concentration of media in chains. Sterling (1975) looked at trends in daily newspaper and broadcast ownership from 1922 to 1970, finding a 270% increase in the number of outlets and voices because of the growth of broadcasting. Media voices—the number of different owners of stations and newspapers—increased by 185%.[41] Since that study, we have seen a continuing increase in the number of broadcast and cable outlets, along with low-power TV, and a small drop in the number of daily newspapers. Extending this analysis from 1977 to 1987, Waterman (1989) found a substantial increase in chain ownership in cable, movie theaters, and to a lesser extent newspapers but a slight decline in chain ownership of TV stations.[42]

Reasons for Growth and Change

When analysts say the media are fundamentally economic institutions, they are seeking explanations for growth, direction, and change in economic terms. Husni (1984) studied 234 new magazines started between 1979 and 1983, finding that only cover price and frequency of publication among the twenty-six factors had any impact on survival. Others have found that quality (Sumner, 1992) and magazine size are factors, with thick magazines and those winning prizes being more successful (Hall, 1976; Krishnan and Soley, 1987). Gomery (1989) uses the industrial organization model for economic analysis, but he reaches outside economics to identify powerful long-range influences for change: technology (coming of home video), politics (Department of Justice enabling the major film studios to purchase chains of theaters), and fundamental social and demographic changes (the graying or aging of America). Though the motive for media development may be political, religious, cultural, or economic, each new venture must overcome barriers that include such economic factors as lack of markets, skilled labor, capital, and technology or political barriers such as foreign exchange restrictions, censorship, or licensing. In a study of determinants of newspaper circulation in the United States from 1850 to 1970, Bishop, Sharma, and Brazee (1980) found competition from other media unimportant and suggest that population and other factors are more important.[43]

Organizational aging is another theory offered to explain the growth and decline of mass media and other organizations. Carroll and Hannan (1989) point to a common pattern in the evolution of diverse types of organizations (including newspapers, unions, and banks): they emerge in small numbers, increase rapidly, and then stabilize or decline. The cycle is explained by these factors: scarce resources are exploited and eventually decline, new technologies challenge old forms, and organizations face opposing processes of legitimation (political and social factors) and competition. An examination of nine newspaper populations that include American cities of various sizes and two foreign countries from their nineteenth century beginnings supported this model (Carroll and Hannan, 1989).

Social differentiation is another explanation for changes in demand for media (Demers, 1990). This model says that chain ownership increases as demand for newspapers declines. Declining demand occurs as society becomes more diverse. Social and occupational roles become more specialized, and audiences turn to specialized sources rather than general sources such as daily papers. In one analysis, Demers found that community diversity (measured as pluralism using population characteristics) was linked to lower newspaper circulation, as expected, but chain ownership did not grow with a decline in circulation.[44] Demers's model introduces communication concepts by pointing to information-seeking and decoding patterns, shifting the explanation to audiences and consumers.[45]

The issues of competition and concentration are not simple ideas. Applying the theory of the niche, Dimmick and Rothenbuhler (1984) show how media coexist by identifying their niche in competing for audiences and resources. Across time, a medium's niche may grow or shrink as new media technologies capture resources. Bates (1990) notes that media markets are no longer "neatly defined" and new media have produced new competition as boundaries between media break down and geographic boundaries overlap on a number of levels. This calls for new approaches to concentration, examining media for their distinctive ability to operate simultaneously in several markets— audiences, advertising, geography, and content-product substitutes. Thus, we could group the same "owners" in terms of audience share or the advertising market. Looking at local TV markets, Bates demonstrates that the market for audience in 1987 was generally less concentrated than the market for advertising.

Competition among the media for audiences and advertisers is intense and growing. Krugman and Rust (1987) found a direct relationship between cable penetration and network TV ratings; their results suggested that every 10% cable penetration resulted in a 3% drop in revenue and a 10% drop in audience share for the major networks (Katz and Lancaster, 1989). Theater owners are worried about the window between exhibition of first-run films and their appearance on network TV. In the early 1970s, a film would not appear on network TV until three years after it played in movie houses. Pay-TV cut that period in half and home video cut it in half again, while pay-per-view has provided further reductions. In some instances, the release is simultaneous (Guback, 1987).

Competition among media makes concerns for concentration within single media less important. Audience fragmentation has drastically reduced the national TV network ratings and there has been a dramatic increase in film and video program production in Western Europe (Luyken, 1987). Technology also has increased the possibilities for diversity, with more television channels via cable and more content diversity through VCRs. Bates (1989) notes that measuring diversity in any context is difficult.[46] A comparison of cable and newspaper ownership patterns shows that the top eight newspaper chain owners accounted for almost 39% of the total daily circulation in 1987, a figure close to the 35.3% concentration ratio reached by the cable industry the next year (Chan-Olmsted and Litman, 1988).

Concentration among Film and Entertainment Media

Hollywood has probably been the subject of more antitrust cases than any other industry in the United States (Hammond and Melamed, 1989). The Supreme Court's 1948 decision in *U.S. v. Paramount et al.* was the culmination of a series of antitrust cases that changed practices through which the major film companies controlled the movie industry up to that time. In 1947, the court found that the five major studios controlled 17% of United States motion picture theaters and 70% of the first-run theaters in the largest cities. The ruling took the movie studios out of the exhibition business, breaking up vertical control of the industry, which occurs when the same owner controls production, distribution, and exhibition. In the 1950s and 1960s, network TV supplanted theatrical film viewing as a dominant entertainment medium, and antitrust efforts shifted to television. As mentioned earlier, production-distribution companies have re-entered the theater business, resurrecting vertical integration of the industry. By 1987, the five largest domestic theater circuits—United Artists, AMC, General Cinema, Cineplex Odeon, and Carmike Cinemas—controlled about 25% of all screens, in contrast to the 17% of all theaters operated by the five major studios in 1945 before the antitrust action (Guback, 1987). The national share of the number of screens owned by the top nine movie theater chains rose from about 22% in 1977 to more than 42% in 1987 (Waterman, 1989). The increase in chain ownership parallels the growth in construction of multiscreen cinemas.

Concentration in Cable and TV Networks

The U.S. Federal Communication Commission, fearing the major TV networks would wield too much influence in the marketplace of ideas, restricted the number of local stations each network could own. The networks are among the most prominent chains (group owners), but others have emerged and even swallowed a network in one instance. The FCC's attention to the TV networks came as they were gaining power vis-á-vis Hollywood producers. In 1957, 41% of prime-time entertainment programs on ABC were advertiser-supplied, a figure that dropped to 4% by 1967. In a series of network antitrust cases the networks were given quotas on the amount of entertainment programming they could produce themselves and syndicate after network airing. Later in the 1980s the Justice Department abandoned its view of network power as cable TV gained audience share and challenged the networks as producers and distributors of TV programs (Hammond and Melamed, 1989). Thus, government concerns, along with public concerns, focus on power (Besen et al., 1984).

Concentration levels in the TV station industry have been compared with those in other U.S. industries. Larson (1980) examined the largest twenty owners in TV, viewing TV stations as sellers (of air time) and advertisers as buyers.[47] For most measures of concentration, the TV industry was less concentrated than most selected industries, especially as sellers, but when consideration was given to the networks and additional factors, the industry was highly concentrated. Others have questioned the networks' market share of programming and broadcast revenues. Howard (1983) found that about 79% of all TV stations were licensed to group owners. When the FCC established its multiple-ownership rules in the early 1950s, they were designed to restrict the size of individual groups; limits were 7 TV stations, including no more than 5 VHF. In 1985 the limit was raised to 12 stations as long as the group didn't reach more than 25% of the nation's TV homes. The local stations owned by networks are important economically. In 1992, the ceilings were raised again, so networks could own 24 TV stations (with a 35% audience reach), 30 AM radio stations and 30 FM radio stations.[48]

The number of groups owning TV stations increased from 158 in 1982 to 205 in 1989, and 5 groups reached the limit of 12 TV stations, while 24 groups held licenses to more than the former limit of 7 stations. Rule changes continue as the FCC reconsiders limits on the number of stations a group can own. Group ownership predominates at each level within the top 100 markets for both VHF and UHF stations. In 1992, only four groups reached more than 20% of the nation's TV households: ABC, CBS, NBC, and the Tribune Co.; of the remaining 189 group owners, 92% reached fewer than 5% of the nation's TV homes. Ted Turner's Atlanta super station reached 18.5% of the nation's households (Howard, 1989).

Looking at program markets and syndication, we find that the networks and local producers are dominated by Hollywood—the complex of about a dozen important production and distribution companies. These companies have supplied the networks with most prime-time TV series since the early 1960s, in part because of restrictive reuse fees charged by the American Federation of Television and Radio Artists (AFTRA) for taped programs. With the declining fortunes of the major TV networks, in 1991 the FCC reexamined regulations restricting networks from acquiring independently produced TV programs and participating in the syndication market.[49] However, Chan-Olmsted (1992) found little change in producers' share of prime-time programming; the networks produced 12% in 1988–1989, 15.1% in 1989–1990 and 13.7% in 1990–1991.[50] Matching audience ratings with suppliers, Chan-Olmsted (1992) found that the major studios seemed to supply the most popular programs, followed by the minors and independents, and last the networks.

Ties Between Film and TV.   There is a long history between the film and TV industries in the United States. In the mid 1970s, ABC owned 278 theaters in 11 southern states. Cable TV systems also have been acquired by film companies. "Hollywood" gets half of what the U.S. TV industry pays others to provide programs. Film producers in Europe have turned to the TV industry for support via production of feature films. Networks contribute to national film aid funds and co-produce films with private film companies. Public service broadcasting has kept the European film heritage alive.

Cable Becomes a Major Player.   Cable has become a significant player in the television industry, reducing the concentration in local TV markets (Bates, 1990, 1991). Concentration of ownership in cable accelerated in the early 1980s, as the percentage of cable households served by the top 10 operators rose to 42.5% in 1985 (Howard, 1986). Two years later, transactions reached $10 billion (Landro, 1988). Despite the growth in concentration, no single organization commands enough market share to dominate, so the industry remains competitive (Chan-Olmsted and Litman, 1988). However, the largest cable owner, Tele-Communications Inc. (TCI) also has invested in such cable programming companies as American Movie Classics, Black Entertainment Television, the Discovery Channel, and the Fashion Channel. The cost advantages of size come not from the technical distribution network of cable systems but by the larger operator's greater ability to package and sell services more effectively to potential subscribers. With growing strength, cable companies also face regulatory threats. As in the past, requests for regulation come from media adversaries, in this case, motion picture studios and independent broadcasters which depend on cable to carry their programs (Landro, 1987; Wirth, 1989).

Concentration in the Print Industry

Faced with economic pressures brought on by changing technologies, increasing competition for the advertising dollar and other factors, papers' profit margins are stagnant and the number of papers has dropped. The disappearance of newspaper competition has been going on since the nineteenth century; in 1880 about 62% of all U.S. cities had two or more separately owned and operated daily newspapers.[51] By 1940, however, 87% of the cities in the United States had only one paper (Nixon and Ward, 1961). The number of daily papers remained relatively constant until the early 1980s when a considerable number of papers stopped publishing. At the start of 1985, there were 1,688 daily newspapers in the United States, a figure that dropped to 1,586 in 1991 (see Table 3-1). The declining numbers reflect the extinction of most remaining competing newspapers (Anderson, 1990).[52]

Growth of Chains.   The number of newspaper chains went from 55 in 1930 to 127 in 1986, and the pace of concentration continues. The number of papers owned by Gannett (86) doubled from 1971 to 1984 (Pierce, 1983). Busterna (1988) reports that 127 newspaper chains accounted for 1,158 papers (average of 9.1 per chain) out of a total of 1,657; the remaining 499 independent newspapers represented only 30% of the total. In terms of circulation, the top 12 chains in 1987 accounted for 50% of daily circulation in the United States, an increase from 39% of the circulation 10 years earlier.[53] Chains with the most papers include Gannett, Thomson, Donrey, and American Publishing, each with 40 or more papers.[54] Antitrust laws have failed to slow the accumulation of newspapers by chains. As long as chains avoid acquiring a paper in competition with one they already own, they are safe because the courts focus on competition for advertising rather than circulation (Browning, Grierson, and Howard, 1984). Evidence of the market power of chains is illustrated in a study by Busterna (1991), who found that the Gannett group charged a national advertising markup of about 10% more than did independent newspapers.

Courts, legislators, and newspaper economists have wrestled with whether daily newspapers are natural monopolies because of economies of scale.[55] Daily papers operate in two product markets: selling information to readers and audience access to advertisers. Sentman (1986) found that when newspapers go out of business, advertisers shifted their ads to the surviving metro paper or to other papers about two-thirds of the time, while 20% shifted to other media and 10% disappeared. Picard and Lacy (1990) suggest shifting to the notion of a monopoly process by which power is exerted in markets. Newspapers have interactive monopoly power, a combination of market forces and product characteristics. While dailies may face no single paper that is a close substitute, they still face competition from other local media (Lacy and Picard, 1990).[56] Simon, Primeaux, and Rice (1986) looked at how monopoly ownership of morning and evening papers in a city influenced advertising rates. They found it 8-9% more expensive to advertise in one paper in a one-owner town, but it was considerably cheaper to advertise in both papers where both are owned by the same firm due to production economies of scale or pricing schemes.

Table 3-1

The Mass Media Industries: Numbers and Sizes

Newspapers

Daily and Sunday Newspapers in the U.S. (1991)

	Number	Circulation (millions)
morning	544	41.4
evening	1,015	19.2
all-day	27	
total	1,586	60.7
Sunday	875	62.1

No. of Daily Papers	1945	1950	1960	1970	1980	1984	1990
Total No.	1,749	1,772	1,763	1,748	1,745	1,688	1,586*
Morning Dailies		322	312	334		458	544*
Afternoon Dailies		1,450	1,459	1,429		1,257	1,015*
Sunday newspapers		549	563	586		783	875

(Sources: Editor & Publisher Yearbook (1984, 1985, 1992); ANPA Facts About Newspapers (1985); *Total no. includes 27 all-day papers not included in morning or afternoon tallies).

Magazines

No. of magazines published in U.S. (1992)	12,157
Daily magazines	29
Semiweekly magazines	23
Weekly	512
Biweekly	185
Semimonthly	210
Monthly	4,688
Bimonthly	2,377
Quarterly	3,248
Variant	885

(Source: Gale Directory of Publications and Broadcast Media 1992)

Television

No. of TV stations:	1950	1960	1970	1980	1990
on-the-air	97	573	872	1,013	1,436
authorized	111	673	1,038	1,094	1,684

(Broadcasting Yearbook 1990, p. H-55)

Radio

No. of radio stations:		1950	1960	1970	1980	1990
AM stations	on the air	2,086	3,398	4,269	4,558	4,966
	authorized	2,234	3,527	4,344	4,651	5,223
FM stations	on the air	733	688	2,476	4,190	5,665
	authorized	788	838	2,651	4,463	6,705

(Broadcasting Yearbook 1990, p. H-55)

Film	**1979**	**1981**	**1985**	**1987**	**1990**
No. of screens	17,095	18,144	21,097	22,721	23,000
No. of tickets sold (in millions)	1,121	1,067	1,056	1,086	
Avg. per-screen admissions	651,575	58,422	49,936	47,797	
Capital expenditures (in millions of $)	$19.0	$57.4	$164.0	$55.7	
Operating profit margin	9.3%	9.1%	11.6%	8.8%	

(Waldman, 1989; data sources, Natl. Assoc. of Theatre Owners; Merrill Lynch; Bremner and DeGeorge, 1990)

Umbrella Model of Competition. The umbrella model of competition divides newspapers into four layers, each acting as an umbrella that covers towns and cities in layers below it.[57] Papers compete with papers in layers above and below them. The first layer consists of large metropolitan dailies that cover an entire state or region, followed by a second layer of satellite city dailies that are more local than metro dailies but cover news occurring outside the originating city. The third layer papers are suburban dailies with largely local content, and the fourth layer is made up of weekly papers and shoppers. The final layer might include neighborhood/community newspapers that serve geographic neighborhoods in many metro areas. Examining the Boston area, Devey (1989) found readership of the metro dailies declining and satellite and suburb circulation rising over the 40 years studied, with some inter-layer competition between suburban dailies and satellite city circulation. Lacy (1985) found some support for circulation competition under the umbrella model but not for advertising competition (Tillinghast, 1988). Lacy and Dalmia (1991) found support for intercity competition among newspapers but also discovered intralayer competition not predicted by the model. In another study, Lacy and Dalmia (1992) found competition greatest between satellite dailies and weeklies during the week, followed by competition between Sunday editions of metro and satellite dailies and competition between weekday editions of metro and satellite dailies. Satellite dailies faced more intense umbrella competition than other types of papers because of competition from layers above and below.[58] Local newspapers in recent years have been less successful in employing the market niche strategy than have magazines, though the strategy was employed by Edward Scripps in the nineteenth century (Baldasty and Jordan, 1990).

Joint Operating Agreements.   The Newspaper Preservation Act of 1970 allowed two newspapers under separate ownerships to share non-editorial facilities to reduce costs while avoiding antitrust action (Adams, 1992). Although such papers may charge higher prices for advertising, a barrier to other papers entering the market, few cities can support more than one paper (Lacy, 1988). Journalists working for newspapers in joint operating agreements agree (91%) that the arrangement provides greater diversity of news and editorial opinions than single papers could provide and higher quality local news coverage than monopoly papers offer (Coulson, 1992).

Initially independent, today's weekly also is likely to be part of a group of publications owned by a small corporation. The one-family owner of a single paper increasingly has been replaced by individuals and families owning groups of publications; small corporations and a national chain now own more than half of weeklies (Guenther, 1987).

Magazines—Pure Competition.   Magazines represent perhaps the closest approximation possible to "pure competition" if viewed in terms of titles seeking audiences. Many are separately owned; editorial and creative processes do not benefit from economies of scale or significant fixed costs; and there is specialization of taste among consumers. However, looking at concentration of publishing in the hands of a few owners, Compaigne (1979) found that periodical publishing was somewhat more concentrated than newspaper and book publishing.

Book Publishing.   For years the U.S. book publishing industry has been highly decentralized, operating in an unpredictable market and organized along craft rather than bureaucratic lines. However, the book industry also has faced consolidation, and some industry analysts have predicted it eventually will end up looking like the movie industry with five or six major companies producing and distributing their own products as well as those of smaller independent firms. In the 1980s there was a sizable increase in the number of mergers and acquisitions, especially by foreign corporations (Greco, 1989; Landro, 1987). In 1987 four firms accounted for 40% of all general interest books sold (Lillienstein, 1987). However, technology makes it possible for even individuals or small businesses to begin publishing and there is a large and growing number of active publishers in the industry (Bekken, 1989). Concentration also is occurring at the retail end in the book publishing industry. Three major chains were expected to account for 45% of bookstore sales in the United States in 1987; one-store firms accounted for nearly 80% of book sales in 1958 (Bekken, 1989).

Cross-Ownership of Media

A wave of mergers has integrated media and entertainment organizations—linking print media, film producers, TV stations, theaters, and pay-TV services. The "magazine" company, Time, Inc., was owner of Home Box Office, the pay-TV service, when it merged with Warner Communications, Inc., a film producer. Many of the new multinational owners of American media are from other countries (Carveth, 1992; Chan-Olmsted, 1991). Sony Corp. purchased CBS Records in 1987 and Columbia Pictures in 1989. Matsushita Electric purchased MCA in 1990.

Strategic partnerships provide synergy as practiced by the Disney organization, which now weaves together TV and film production, theme parks, record and video divisions, and book publishing units, all helping each other (Turow, 1992). Dimmick (1986) points to economies of "multiformity"— ownership by a parent corporation of firms with two or more organizational forms. The operation of companies in more than one communication industry can result in lower costs, higher revenues, or both.[59]

In 1975, the FCC barred new cross-ownership of TV stations and newspapers in the same markets (Compaine, 1979; Loevinger, 1979). Companies can own broadcast and newspaper properties in separate markets. Howard (1989) found a steady increase in the affiliation of TV stations with newspaper publishers, with 43 of 205 TV station groups having ties with newspaper companies. Because the number of new UHF stations in the top markets increased substantially, the percentage of newspaper-affiliated UHF stations actually declined 8% between 1982 and 1989. The top 30 media companies in cable all have significant holdings in other media (Katz, 1989).[60]

Another way to look at concentration of media voices is to examine how many different voices or media outlets are available in a particular area. Since 1922 the total number of media outlets has increased much faster than the population. In a 1970 survey of 204 metropolitan areas of the country, the largest market was New York City, in which 610 media were available, with 519 of them originating in the market. There were 372 different owners. The smallest market was Glendive, Montana, with 36 media available to the public owned by 30 different owners (Loevinger, 1979). The increase in media product diversity and changes in technology soften the consequences of growing chain ownership (Waterman, 1988). Alvin Toffler (1971) suggests that America faces not a concentration of mass media voices but confusion arising from growing fragmentation and diversity.

90   Chapter Three

Impact of Ownership and Concentration

How does ownership and concentration affect media performance or content? A growing body of evidence helps us answer this question.

Impact on the Editorial Page.   The impact of ownership on editorial page content is central to the debate over diversity and political discussion. Some studies have found little impact of chain ownership on editorial pages (Borstel, 1956), while others have found non-group papers less likely to endorse a candidate and chain papers more homogenous in endorsing presidential candidates (Wackman et al, 1975; Gaziano, 1989[61]). Chain papers are no more likely to endorse Republicans than are non-chain papers (Busterna and Hansen, 1990).[62]

Studies also have linked chain ownership to ideas on editorial pages. Herman (1991) argues that market competition limits free expression by marginalizing dissent and making it difficult for dissidents to reach large numbers. Studies have found: conflicting evidence over whether papers become less aggressive in their editorials after being purchased by chains (Hale, 1988; Romanow and Soderlund, 1988; Thrift, 1977); chain papers are more homogeneous in their editorial positions than other papers (Adams, 1992; Akhavan-Majid, 1990; Akhavan-Majid, Rife, and Gopinath, 1991); editors at chain papers are more likely to be Republican, and non-chain editors more evenly divided among Republicans, Independents, and Democrats (Dizier, 1986).

Impact on News Coverage.   Does ownership affect news coverage or other newspaper content? Evidence on chain-independent differences is mixed, though on balance it suggests other factors may be more important. Lacy and Fico (1990) compared chain and non-chain papers in terms of a news quality index that included many factors.[63] Whether a paper was group owned or independent had no effect on news quality. Other studies of the effect of chain ownership or joint operating agreements also have found little impact on news coverage.[64]

However, some differences have been linked to ownership patterns; thus, editors at corporate-owned papers are more likely to favor coverage of business news (Olien, Tichenor, and Donohue (1988), and chain-ownership has been linked to heavier use of visuals (Pasadeos and Renfro, 1988), more frequent polling (Demers, 1988), increased "boosterism" (Browning and Howard, 1984), an increase in the space devoted to news, increases in photographs and feature news and a decrease in hard news (Hansen and Coulson, 1992), more news than music on radio (Riffe and Shaw, 1990), and more emphasis on profits (Demers, 1991). Gormley (1976) found that common ownership situations restrict the variety of news available to the public, particularly in smaller cities, because reporters in close situations tend to cover similar stories. Lewenstein and Rosse (1988) note that joint-operating-agreement papers usually act more like fully independent two-paper competitors than like a single dominant paper (Lacy, 1986). Busterna (1988) found TV-newspaper cross-ownership was negatively related to issue diversity in broadcast news.

Impact of Competition. How is competition related to media perform-ance? Lacy (1992) lays out a sequence of relationships leading from intensity of competition among media to financial commitment, to content quality, to audience utility, to market performance. Thus, as competition increases, the amount of money committed to news content increases. Then, the quality of content increases. With better content, audiences find media messages more useful and gratifying. With an increase in overall utility of the media to audiences, the media organization's position in the market improves.

Studies link competition among newspapers to the following: greater space for local city news (Lacy, 1988), increased diversity of messages (Johnson and Wanta, 1992), greater likelihood that a paper will win a Pulitzer Prize (White and Andsager, 1990), and higher use of color and graphics (Kenney and Lacy, 1987; Utt and Pasternack (1985).[65] Other studies of newspaper content before and after the demise of competitors have found a smaller newshole without competition (Candussi and Winter, 1988) but few content differences (McCombs, 1987; Wanta, 1990), suggesting other factors are more important. Similarly, competition between TV stations is related to higher audience ratings and more time devoted to local news (Powers, 1992).

In Lacy's model, competition can lead to the allocation of more resources for news gathering. Several studies have examined this possibility. Intensity of competition between TV stations has been related to size of news staff (Lacy, Atwater, and Qin, 1989) and the allocation of more resources for covering news (Lacy and Bernstein, 1992), but other studies show no relationship (Dominick, 1988; Powers, 1992). Intensity of competition between newspapers was related to the number of press services carried by newspapers in one study (Lacy, 1990), but no differences were found on staff size, wire services, or other resources between competitive papers and others in another study (Busterna, Hansen, and Ward, 1991). Competition also occurs between print and broadcast media. Lacy (1988) found that broadcast and cable competition had no impact on newspapers' allocation of resources, but Gladney (1992) found that newspapers adopted such innovations as more use of color, graphics, weather coverage, and shorter stories to compete with local TV news and to attract more advertising.

Translating Ownership into Content. How is ownership or legal control translated into policy and content? Certainly, intervention by owners in daily activities varies[66] and generally is limited to major decisions (Guback, 1986). However, the potential for interference is illustrated by the "Panax incident." The head of the Panax chain fired two editors who refused to run a shoddy article laced with insinuations that President Jimmy Carter had encouraged staff members to sexual promiscuity. The National News Council censured Panax; thus, there also are limits on owners, who face pressure from the public and professional groups.

Journalists learn about management's policies over time. The longer a staffer's employment, the better his or her prediction of those policies (Kapoor, 1979). A national survey of TV journalists found that those at independent and group-owned stations held positive attitudes toward their station's local news coverage but managers in group-owned stations held the most positive views (Coulson and Macdonald, 1991, 1992). Two-thirds of TV journalists at group-owned stations disagreed that such ownership inhibited diversity of news and editorial opinion. Coulson (1991) found that a plurality of print journalists in a national survey felt group ownership inhibited diversity of news and editorial opinion, and reporters at independently owned newspapers were more skeptical and critical of group ownership.

Several studies have examined issues about how ownership affects professional encoders and their content. Beam (1990) found no difference between group and independent papers in seven of eight indicators of organizational professionalism, but Soloski (1979) found group ownership associated with various influences on news processing. Busterna (1989) found that owner-managers placed less emphasis on profits and more on quality and ethics than did non-owners, suggesting that a personal stake in the enterprise meant that value was placed on non-economic factors. This contrasts with a finding by Olien, Tichenor, and Donohue (1988) that editors of individually owned papers are more prone to profit concerns than editors of chain newspapers. Demers (1991) found no difference between the amount of autonomy editors had at chain and independently owned newspapers. In Sweden, where the press has been subsidized by the government since shortly after World War II, none of the publishers surveyed said they had experienced direct government interference, and almost all felt their editorial content was not influenced by subsidies (Hilliard, 1992). Another example of ownership control is found in the network-owned and operated TV stations, which accept a higher percentage of network programming than do those stations independently owned (Litman, 1978).

The impact of legal ownership is not limited to commercial media. A survey of 125 public broadcast managers found that those who conduct on-air fund raising were least likely to want to editorialize, apparently out of fear of offending potential contributors (Handberg and Meeske, 1978). Similar actions by management are suggested in a case that involved Stan Freberg who produced a satirical show deriding welfare and budgeting policies for the Public Broadcasting Service in 1980. PBS did not accept Freberg's program, and a censor chopped out the offending segment and cut the program substantially (Lashley, 1992).

Summary

In this chapter we examined the media industries. The media are part of larger information and leisure industries which have assumed growing importance. Advertising is the major form of economic support for American media; it subsidizes the delivery of information and entertainment. The number of media units has grown tremendously in this century, but there also has been a growing concentration of ownership across the media. However, in terms of individual markets, the number of potential voices is enormous in most cases. Ownership can and does have an impact on the operation of media organizations and the encoding activity within them, sometimes illustrating the conflict between demands of the organization and those of professional encoding roles.

Chapter Three Footnotes

1. Bell (1989) identifies three technological revolutions, the first based on the introduction of steam power, the second on electricity and chemistry, and the third based on computers and telecommunication and related technologies. Bates (1988) points to two basic trends. First, the rapid development and diffusion of microelectronics and other information technologies is having an impact on industrial societies and information, and information products are increasingly important to Western economies.
2. He included: message multipliers—mass media; message carriers—telecommunication, postal service; information suppliers for individual needs—libraries, data banks, computer service; manufacturers and maintainers—printers, media, electronic and printing technicians and manufacturers; special service suppliers—news agencies, writers, artists; economic support agencies—advertising agencies; administrative support agencies—legal counsel, public relations, financial services; personnel support—unions, trade groups, training services; data-gathering services—audience, opinion research centers; education—schools and colleges.
3. Strover (1988) emphasizes the "information economy," which she says hold in common three ideas: that the information economy is weighted toward the service sector; productivity gains are realized from research and development in control technologies such as computers and robotics; and people in many jobs will experience greater need for, access to and use of information. Hudson and Leung (1988) used Porat's (1977) definition of the primary information sector to measure the growth of the knowledge or information industry in five subsectors that include: 1) research and development; 2) information services, which include advertising agencies, private information services, search and nonspeculative brokerage industries, nonmarket coordinating institutions, insurance industries, and speculative brokers; 3) media, including mass media as well as theatrical producers; 4) information technology, including "software" such as tapes and CDs as well as hardware; and 5) information trade, which includes retail stores trading in radio and TV sets, cameras, books, and papers, and film theaters.
4. See Barron and Curnow (1979), Hepworth (1990), Hepworth, Green and Gillespie (1987), Porat (1977), Schement and Lievrouw (1984). Viewing the knowledge industry as consisting of five kinds of information activities, e.g., education, media communication, and information machines and services, Rubin and Huber (1986) note an increase in the share of GNP devoted to knowledge production in the late 1970s and Hudson and Leung (1988) found an increase

in the United States from 1973 to 1983. Hepworth (1990) notes data showing that information occupations in the labor force accounted for 45.8% of employees in the United States in 1981, compared to 41% for the United Kingdom, 36.1% Sweden, 33.5% Germany, 41.5% Australia, 30.4% Denmark and 22.9% Norway. Hepworth concludes that data show advanced industrialized economies are growing more information intensive.

5. In 1991, spending on the "communication industry" totaled $188.91 billion, with the fastest growing segment being cable TV—up 10.4%. Spending by advertisers and consumers on products ranging from TV and magazines to records, books and films was expected to rise at a 7.1% annual compound rate over a five year period, reaching $266.3 billion by 1996 (Andrea Gerlin, "Spending on Communications Industry To Rise in Next 5 Years, Forecast Predicts," *Wall Street Journal*, June 29, 1992, p. B8A. Also see Dennis (1991) and *Information Industry Factbook*. Stamford, CT: Digital Information Group, 1989/1990 Edition).

6. See Fincham (1987), Lyon (1986, 1987), Robertson (1990), Salvaggio (1989), Schement (1989).

7. Bates (1988) discusses the point that the value of information is seen as independent of the technology, noting several basic issues: the indeterminacy of the value of information (information goods cannot be given a concrete value prior to their use and may be used more than once); the dichotomy between the value of information per se and the value of the physical embodiment of the information; and the incompleteness of considerations of the valuation of information goods.

8. Japan was among the first to produce a futuristic proposal, "The Plan for Information Society: A National Goal toward the Year 2000" (1972), which laid out technological goals which would in effect create a modern matrix linking Japan's citizens and cities.

9. Not sharing in this growth were drive-in theaters. Though the nostalgia for drive-in theaters has grown, their numbers have shrunk continually through the years. The first drive-in theater apparently opened in 1933 but the real boom in construction began following the Second World War and continuing to 1954. After 1970, more drive-ins closed than opened in any given year (Giles, 1982).

10. Out of $10 spent on a pair of tickets, the theater owner keeps $5, while $2.50 goes to pay the cost of the movie, $1.50 pays for distribution, and $1 goes for prints and advertising (Harmetz, 1987). In 1939 the admission price was 23 cents, compared to an average of $3.91 in 1987 and about $5 in 1992, with top prices of $7.50 in some metro areas (Bremner and DeGeorge, 1990). During the same period, the price of popcorn went from a nickel or dime in 1939 to an average of $2.37 in 1987.

11. Walt Disney said it would not allow theaters to run commercials before any Disney film (Lipman and Hughes, 1990).

12. "Summary of Broadcasting & Cable," *Broadcasting*, Jan. 18, 1993, p. 114.

13. One observer said mass media had been in a recession since 1985; in inflation-adjusted dollars, network TV ad revenue actually dropped 5%-6% in 1989 (Lipman, 1990). Network daytime programming was to be cut an hour the fall of 1991 (Connor, 1991).

14. Fifty percent for how much the station's audience watches non-network shows 4-8 P.M. daily and 50% on how many adults in the key advertising target group—age 25-54—watch network shows through the day.

15. The chief focus cited by TV stations without news were: alternative programming, 44%; evangelism, 26%; community service, 24%; and other, 6%. Evangelism was the prime focus of larger percentages of public (42%) and commercial radio (46%) stations. In the United States, some 50% of independent TV stations have no news operations, compared to 1.2% of network affiliates, 20.3% of non-commercial radio stations and 3.4% commercial radio.

16. Program types produced and the percentage of stations producing them were: sports, 24%; news, 20%; pubic affairs, 19%; religious, 14%; magazine shows, 9%; children's, 4%; variety, 1.5%; civic, 1.5%; instructional, minority, situation comedies, auctions, financial markets,

exercise and interview shows, 1% or less each. The study excluded a network of some 240 state-owned and operated LPTV stations in Alaska.

17. "Year in Review: Broadcasting and Cable 1991," *Broadcasting & Cable MarketPlace* 1992, New Providence, N.J.: R.R. Bowker, 1992.

18. Elizabeth Kolbert, "Deciding What to Watch When 500 Channels Await," *New York Times*, Jan. 4, 1993, p. 1.12

19. One report in early 1992 noted that most radio stations were losing money and hundreds of broadcasters unable to turn a profit or sell their stations had simply shut down, with 287 stations in the United States closed, 153 in the preceding 12 months. This was attributed to competition for advertising from other media and the government awarding hundreds of new AM and FM licenses during the 1980s ("F.C.C. Staff Seeks to Ease Radio Rule," *New York Times*, Feb. 27, 1992, p. 3C). In mid 1992, the FCC reported that 315 radio stations had gone off the air, including 75 FM and 240 Am stations. ("FCC Calls Halt to Rules Affecting Radio Ownership," *Wall Street Journal*, July 31, 1992, p. 17C).

20. From 1976 to 1984, newsprint consumption grew faster than the U.S. economy as a whole, though the rate of growth has declined somewhat since then. Udell says the newsprint consumption measure taps changes in both size and circulation and is a more superior measure of newspaper growth than other measures. Schwenk (1988) reports that the average household spent $89 annually on newspapers in 1984, and $134 on all reading material.

21. *Facts About Newspapers 93* Reston, VA: Newspaper Association of America, 1993.

22. Through the 1980s, major dailies were able to maintain operating profit margins of 15%-20% but ad linage has slumped. Classified advertising—40% of most newspaper advertising— has shown virtually no growth in most major markets (Lipman, 1990). Also, since the mid-1980s, at least 15 metro Sunday magazines in newspapers have folded and those remaining have lost large amounts of advertising (Patrick M. Reilly, "Parade USA Weekend Defy Ad Slump," *Wall Street Journal*, Nov. 19, 1991, p. 8B).

23. Stanley and Tharp analyzed costs and revenues for daily newspapers by circulation size from 1978 to 1990, finding advertising costs climbing but circulation costs declining for all sizes of newspapers. Papers with circulations under 10,000 were least responsive to economic cycles and were becoming less profitable over time, while those with circulations of 25,000-50,000 were least affected by economic cycles. Circulation made up a greater share of revenue for smaller papers and the real cost per inch of advertising was rising over time for all papers.

24. The 68 papers belonging to the Association of Alternative Newsweeklies reaped $100 million in combined revenue while serving a 3.5 million total circulation.

25. See "Newspapers Reach Area Immigrants with Spanish-Language Translations," *Minorities in the Newspaper Business* (May/June, 1987) 3(3): 1-2.

26. The figures vary slightly: more than 11,500 in *The Magazine Handbook* (1990-1991) New York: Magazine Publishers of America; and 12,157 in *Gale Directory of Publications and Broadcast Media*, ed. Julie Winklepleck. Detroit: Gale Research, Inc., 1992. In 1987, 477 magazines were launched (El Nasser, 1988), bringing the total to 11,593 magazines in the U.S.

27. Magazine circulation still grew faster than the U.S. population. With a per-issue circulation of 275,036,829 in 1980 and 363,194,636 in 1989; circulation per 100 adults grew from 171.7 in 1980 to 199.6 in 1989, according to the *The Magazine Handbook*, 1990-1991. New York: Magazine Publishers of America, p. 7.

28. Prior-Miller (1992) notes that scholars, advertisers, and others differ on what categories are used to describe magazines. Her analysis identified four common-used approaches to classifying magazines, with seven primary dimensions embedded in them. She offers a typology with four categories describing information functions, or how the information in the magazines is designed to serve audiences (lifestyle, occupation, scholarly, organization) and five other categories (primary audience, audience size, audience scope, editorial scope, and interest area).

29. Tabulation of 491 magazines launched in 1988 by interest category. Source: Samir Husni's *Guide to New Magazines*, 1989, Vol. 4. Also see *The Magazine Handbook*, 1990-1991. New York: Magazine Publishers of America, p. 4; *Gale Directory of Publications and Broadcast Media*, ed. Julie Winklepleck. Detroit: Gale Research, Inc., 1992 lists the following magazines by category for 1992: 2560 general circulation, 7678 trade/technical/professional, 471 agricultural, 61 Black, 245 college, 216 foreign language, 79 fraternal, 88 Hispanic, 59 Jewish, 554 religious and 159 women's publications.

30. See *1989 U.S. Industrial Outlook*.

31. "Books by the Number," compiled by Charles Barber, *Media Studies Journal* (Summer, 1992) 6(3): 15-22.

32. More than 8,000 services are offered on the Minitel, including a 25-million-entry electronic national phone book, horoscopes, and pari-mutuel betting. One of the most successful services involves erotic messages and sexual graphics. The system is the largest network of telephone-linked home computers in the world.

33. The fax may be one of several factors responsible for heavier telephone use. One telephone poll reported the amount of time spent on the telephone grew 24% from 1980 to 1987 while the population grew only 7%, according to the Federal Communication Commission (Hall, 1989).

34. Direct broadcast satellite services in Europe tend to be more comparable to SMATV in the United States, distributing signals to large dishes and systems that redistribute TV signals throughout a residential complex, hotel, etc.

35. These final three examples come from Benjamin Bates, personal communication, December, 1992-January, 1993.

36. *Key Facts 1991: Newspapers, Advertising & Marketing*, p. 9.

37. The number of prime-time commercial minutes per hour varies by channel and network. The average for the three major TV networks (ABC, CBS, NBC) was 9 minutes, 12 seconds in 1991, while the average was 11 minutes, 21 seconds for independent stations, 11 minutes, 12 seconds for all cable TV networks and 13 minutes, 21 seconds for syndicated programming. On cable, CNN had a high of 13 minutes, 22 seconds, while Arts & Entertainment had a low of 9 minutes, 35 seconds (Joanne Lipman, "Commercials Are Cluttering Cable Shows," *Wall Street Journal*, April 29, 1992, p. 1B).

38. Zolf and Taylor (1989) note that requirements to provide balance and diversity in Canadian broadcasting prohibit religious broadcasters from replicating American-style religions stations in that country.

39. Busterna (1988) notes evidence that chains can and do exploit their market power to charge higher advertising rates. However, mergers between chains and media corporations should not be equated directly with concentration. Mergers among the largest owners may further concentration but mergers among smaller firms can make them more competitive and decrease concentrated power. Mergers with non-media, non-communication firms may affect overall size but have no impact on concentration within the media industry. In communication, there has been a tradition of breaking up mergers among the largest firms and a tendency for most mergers to occur among smaller media enterprises.

40. Bernstein and Lacy (1992) found that about 30% of all stories in a sample of local TV newscasts dealt with issues and events about some government entity, and commentaries were infrequently aired.

41. Increases were due to a 1,000% increase in the number of broadcast stations, since the daily press dropped nearly 20%. Concentration of print media ownership increased but, with the introduction of FM and TV services, there was no increase in concentration of media ownership up to that period.

42. Daily newspaper circulation remained fairly constant while the number of theater screens grew 36%, weekly circulation of TV stations increased 56% and the number of cable subscribers

rose 244%; in the latter three industries, concentration trends obscure a higher absolute growth of larger chains. Weekly circulation of the top four broadcast groups rose 29%, while screens owned by the top four theater chains grew by 191% and the top four cable owners' number of subscribers rose by 344%. Considerable evidence suggests that various noncompetitive situations result in higher prices for newspaper advertisers and consumers (Picard, 1988; Thompson, 1984). However, evidence is contradictory whether group and independent papers differ on advertising and subscription prices (Beam, 1990; Blankenburg, 1983; Busterna, 1988).

43. A city or market's size and ability to support newspapers is a factor (Blankenburg, 1985). Economies of scale give some advantage to larger papers (Dimmick, 1986). Picard (1988) found that the amount of economic concentration in the newspaper industry increases rapidly as the size of the market decreases. A survivor analysis for daily papers from 1964 to 1981 suggests that papers with 5,000 or less circulation are withering away, those in the 100,000-500,000 circulation range have failed to gain market share and those in the 10,000-100,000 have seen increases in both number and market share (Norton and Norton, 1986). Of the 21 cities with two or more daily papers published under separate ownership, nine are in major metropolitan areas but 12 are in small or mid-size places that include Green Bay, Wis., Lincoln, Neb. and Anchorage, Alaska (Anderson, 1990). Weekly newspapers also face competition; one recent analysis suggests that small weeklies around major cities face competition from other metro media for advertising, as well as from more narrowly focused community papers.

44. Demers notes that chains can increase profits despite declining demand because they generate economies of scale and have greater resources. Chain ownership did increase as community pluralism increased.

45. Demers used data on newspaper ownership, advertising expenditures and population characteristics from 1910-1980. Household newspaper circulation did not mediate the effects of community pluralism on chain ownership.

46. Following Levin (1971), he measured the number of different channel types divided by the channel capacity of the cable system to provide a measure of cable system diversity. Looking at a national sample of cable systems during three different time periods, he charts increased channel capacity and increasing diversity from 1976 to 1981 and 1986.

47. He notes that the TV industry is often labeled an oligopoly where the largest 20 owners produce or control 75% of the product while the 8 largest have a share that either exceeds one-third or one-half, depending on high or low concentration.

48. UHF stations are counted at half circulation and VHF stations full circulation in computing audience figures.

49. The original FIS (Financial Interests and Syndication) Rules prohibited the networks from acquiring any financial interest in independently produced TV programs or from domestic syndication of foreign syndication programs. The new rules went into effect in June, 1991, eliminating the old restrictions but requiring that any programs acquired or produced be syndicated in the United States through independent third-party distributors. The rule changes are being contested (Chan-Olmsted, 1992).

50. The major Hollywood studios produced 53% in 1988-1989, 56.1% the following year and 58% in 1990-1991. Minors and independent studios accounted for the remainder, 35% in 1988-1989, 28.8% in 1989-1990 and 28.3% in 1990-1991.

51. See Busterna (1988), Lacy (1987), Neurath (1944), and Nixon (1968).

52. These include: *Tulsa Tribune* (1992), *Knoxville Journal* (1991), *Dallas Times Herald* (1991), *Los Angeles Herald-Examiner* (1989), *The Miami News*, Florida (1988), *The Globe Democrat*, St. Louis, Mo. (1986); *The News America*, Baltimore, Md. (1985); *The Cleveland Press* (1982), the *Citizen Journal*, Columbus, Ohio (1982). See: Brannigan (1988), Guy (1988), Lisby (1986), Turner and Yoshihashi (1989). In late 1991 the merger of two San Diego papers

98   Chapter Three

was announced, and Pittsburgh was slated to lose a paper in late 1992. In 1985 only 62 cities had competing dailies, and half were jointly owned or jointly operated, with only 28 cities having competing papers with no joint affiliation (Blankenburg, 1985; Brown, 1989). Readers in more than 670 cities have seen direct competition among dailies disappear in this century.

53. See Lisby (1986), Reilly (1990a,b), Servaes (1989), and Waterman (1989).

54. Editors of both independent papers (91%) and group-owned newspapers (62%) say chains are more interested in profits than in the communities they serve ("Absentee Owners Put Profits First, Editors Say," *Plain Dealer*, April 4, 1990, p. 5A. Associated Press Dispatch reporting results of a survey of editors of 234 newspapers, half group owned, for the American Society of Newspaper Editors).

55. Wirth (1985) found support for the proposition that the economic barriers to starting a daily newspaper are higher than those for starting a radio or television station.

56. For more discussions on economic models of concentration see Busterna (1988) on the industrial organization model and Litman (1988) on market structures.

57. See: Compaine (1979), Devey (1989), Kaniss (1991), Lacy and Sohn (1990), and Rosse (1975).

58. Miller (1992) applied the umbrella model to radio stations, finding that stations may compete between layers but there is also sizable competition within layers.

59. Factors favoring this trend are increased audience fractionalization and consequent uncertainty over the survival of old media and success of new ones, and the trend toward deregulation of media and business.

60. Only 7 companies were restricted to cable, while 16 also had newspaper interests, 8 had magazine interests, 9 owned radio stations, 14 owned TV stations, 4 had distributorships of films in theaters or by videocassette, and two were also book publishers.

61. Larger chains tended to be more diverse in their presidential endorsements, suggesting that size reduced constraints somewhat.

62. Large national chains had a more heterogeneous endorsement pattern than the smaller regional chains. However, Dizier (1986) found independent papers split their endorsements in 1984 while chain-owner papers endorsed Ronald Reagan by a 3-1 margin.

63. These included the ratio of staff-written copy to wire copy, size of newshole, ratio of illustrations to text, number of wire services (Hale, 1990, 1991), story length, and reporter workload. Lacy and Fico (1991) did find newspaper quality predicting circulation.

64. See: Browning, Grierson, and Howard (1984), Kenney and Lacy (1987), Meyer and Wearden (1984), Romanow and Soderlund (1978), and Wagenberg and Soderlund (1976).

65. Examining coverage of a riot by competing papers in Louisiana, Sylvie (1989) found differences on several measures but not on the intensity of the coverage.

66. Chain policies can be dramatic. In 1985, Gannett experimented with a Florida newspaper they owned, encouraging readers to subscribe to the national USA Today for national and international news and shifting content in the community newspaper to a local and national level (Smith, Tumlin, and Henning, 1988).

4
Encoding Activity and Media People

I. Introduction to media organizations

II. Film studios and organizations
   A. Studio development
   B. Filmmaking process
   C. Film encoding patterns—work routines and conventions

III. Newspaper organizations—organizational structure, management, communication in newsrooms, policies

IV. Broadcast organizations
   A. National TV entertainment
      1. Creativity in TV entertainment
      2. Production process for TV shows
      3. Styles and changes in encoding TV entertainment
   B. Radio organizations
   C. Pressures on creative processes

V. News-gathering and news-making—values and activities
   A. News and news values
      1. Comparing media menus
      2. Comparing TV newscasts
      3. Comparing newspapers
      4. Origins of news values
   B. Beyond values to news frames
      1. Professional and process frames
      2. Political-ideological frames
      3. Social frames
   C. Objectivity—origins, criticism, implementation

VI. Views and evidence on message construction—news-gathering and news-making processes
   A. Tools for gathering news—routine channels and initiative
   B. The beat system
   C. Editorial views
   D. Sources—selection and relationships
      1. Relations with sources
      2. Relations among reporters
   E. Gatekeeping
   F. Writing routines and conventions
   G. Producing broadcast news
      1. News management
      2. On-air conventions
      3. Development of TV news encoding patterns
   H. Judging accuracy
   I. Constraints on news-gathering and news-making processes

Mass media organizations comprise some of the most important institutions of modern nations. Institutional processes are organized,
systematized, and stable (Whitney, 1991). In organizations, roles[1]
are specified and relations between them delineated; for example, reporters
and editors occupy roles with certain expectations of their behaviors and
relationships. The relevant tasks to be performed in media organizations are
specified, and the media remain in existence beyond the life of any individual
participant.

We will look at several mass media organizations—their roles, policies, and
control[2]—and examine the media work that occurs in organizations—the
patterns of encoding activity that result in TV shows, newspaper articles, and
films.

Film Studios and Organizations

Film "encoding" organizations include both production houses and distribution networks. The organization which has emerged to accommodate the
actual encoding is the film studio, but it shares the honors with independents.

Studio Development

Four major historical eras describe the development of film organizations
(Balio, 1985). In the "novelty stage" (1894-1908), film evolved from its origins
as an amusement park novelty in arcades to one-reel stories in nickelodeons,
the first theaters. In the "struggle for control" stage (1908-1930), the industry
matured as a business and saw the development of technological (sound),
physical (bigger theaters), content (feature films), and organizational features
(star system). This was the period in which a half-dozen fully integrated motion
picture companies—the studios—emerged. In the "mature oligopoly" (1930-
1948) stage, the studios coordinated their behaviors under auspices of the
National Industrial Recovery Act, which was designed to encourage industrial
growth and combat unemployment. The studios established the star system
through exclusive long-term contracts. In the fourth period, "retrenchment,
reappraisal, and reorganization" (1948-present), the industry has adjusted and
reorganized following the impact of forced divestiture from the Paramount court
decision (separating studio production from exhibition in movie theaters), the
arrival of TV and subsequent cable, VCR and satellite technologies.

The "studio" emerged as the organization for producing films. The Hollywood studios have been called many things—from factories to families, dynasties, and empires, each expressing a perception of how studios are organized and operate. Each studio has a complex genealogy (Langford and Gomery, 1989), but they also share characteristics. Several decades ago, the studios had stables of producers, directors, writers, and stars, as well as the studio facilities and executives who approved projects and controlled the financing. The crew has been reduced and the stars let go, but the coordinating functions remain.

Filmmaking Process

Filmmaking is a process involving producers, directors, screenwriters, actors, cinematographers, film editors, and others. This process often begins when the producers-directors-writers try to pique the interest of studio executives with a rudimentary movie concept (Schickel, 1989; Turner, 1989). The pitch may take only a moment, and the movie's creators receive their first money to develop a more detailed version. If accepted, it can lead to the first draft of a screenplay and subsequent revisions.[3] Next the producer pulls together the cast and crew and finally begins shooting. Film editing, scoring, and previewing begin. When the picture is finished, the marketing department develops a plan to sell the movie to audiences, and detailed plans for distribution and advertising follow.

Filmmaking is a **collaborative process** in which professional encoders acting in a variety of specialized roles have an impact on the final product (Chase, 1975). Initially, directors like D. W. Griffith were their own producers. When the studio system evolved, studio heads began a system of supervision. Eventually the supervisors gained power and influence, becoming known as producers. Their job was to watch the money. Today, studios function more as financing and distribution than as production companies (Chase, 1975), but the potential control of the producer as deal-maker and coordinator remains. Some producers find a book, hire a director, and expect the director to do everything else—work with the writer on getting the script, do the casting, and secure other creative personnel as needed, according to producer Albert Ruddy (Chase, 1975). Some producers sit in their offices during production while others spend considerable time on the set; interaction depends on the personalities involved. In some cases directors are "cast," much like actors; others initiate projects themselves. In any case, directors are in charge once production begins, subject to intervention by the producer (Lloyd, 1976). The director's freedom has increased since the 1960s, but all roles and prerogatives are subject to negotiation.

In the early days, directors often wrote their own scripts or developed them from a writer's outline, but the functions eventually shifted to the formal role of screenwriter (Stempel, 1988). When sound was introduced, large numbers of playwrights and novelists were employed to supply the words, and they often functioned as "factory employees" whose output was revamped to fit studio specifications (Chase, 1975). Historically, the screenwriter had been a studio employee who worked with the director in developing material—always under obligation to the money people. When "auteur" theory (the director as author) was introduced in the 1960s, it shifted notions of authorship from the writer to the director. The screenwriter increasingly is asked to collaborate with the director rather than just provide material. Screenwriter Leigh Brackett notes that "no director worth his salt wants some writer telling him where to put his camera" so the writer's job varies, depending on control assumed by the director (Chase, 1975).

Actors are the most visible participants in this collaborative process, and they have been characterized as diversely as puppets, pawns, artists, and the centers of the film (Naremore, 1988). Which characterization is most appropriate depends on the film, the director, and the actor. The star system was founded on the notion that the actor is central. Under the old star system of the 1930s, writers often created or tailored scenes for particular stars who were thought to guarantee the box office. Today, the range of an actor's opportunities is defined by the material, since the actor's capabilities are known at the point of casting. Relations between actors and the director vary. Decades ago, Jean Renoir decided where to place the camera after the actors had finished rehearsing, but other directors run several cameras at the same time from different angles (Chase, 1975). When actors talk about their work (Caine, 1990), they are most apt to remember the way the director communicated with them. Peters and Cantor (1982) note that the three areas where screen actors work—TV, films, and TV commercials—provide limited job opportunities compared to the numbers seeking them. Thus, actors spend much time looking for work, and most rely on agents (who get 10% commissions) for casting interviews. Only the major actors have any control over roles they'll be hired to play, and jobs acquired often last a matter of days or weeks. On the job, actors face long periods between takes so there is much idle time (Peters and Cantor, 1982).

There are many other important creative participants in the filmmaking process. The director of photography (cinematographer) lights the scene, and the cameraman actually "films" it. A director's familiarity with the technology of filmmaking influences how he interacts with the cameraman (Sterling, 1987). The latter has to interact with the director, actors, the art director, and other creative personnel on artistic concerns as well as matters of time and money (Chase, 1975). The production designer (art director) designs studio sets and is responsible for the "look" of a film (Heisner, 1990). In the early days, art directors designed and built sets in the studio and then went with directors to find locations. Today more shooting takes place on locations, shifting the functions of the art director, who must work closely with the director of photography and the cameraman. A role seldom explored is script supervisor, the person who acts as liaison between the director and the editor and keeps a series of logs relating to the technical and administrative aspects of the process (Chase, 1975).

The film editor's role shifted when sound was added to film because it constrained the editing process. The film editor is responsible for selecting the pieces that make up the whole and assembling them into a final film (Ash, 1974), but editors get involved before production begins, often critiquing scripts and noting problems that may emerge later in the cutting room. Once shooting begins, the editor begins selecting and assembling pieces of film, sometimes suggesting to the director that scenes be deleted, compressed, or expanded. Whether the length of scenes backed by music is determined by the musical pieces or vice versa depends on the function performed by music in the scene. In most cases, the composer begins with the rough cut of the film and then fits music to the footage. Other creative roles in the production process are costume director and special effects artists; the latter role has expanded with new technologies (DeLauretis and Heath, 1980; Oumano, 1985).

Before court decisions abolished multiyear contracts, Hollywood studios operated a star system with players under long-term contracts that obligated them to appear in specific films. When the old studio system broke down and stars became independent agents, the balance of power in production was altered and major actors took more control of creative processes. The "narrative logic" of films lessened and they became vehicles for the stars. As the structure and organization of movie studios changes, creative directors lose or gain control. Schickel (1989: 13) notes that "despite the claims of some directors, most movies have many authors, none of whom has absolute authority over the finished work."

Competition with the major film studios has made life difficult for independents.[4] Cronin and Litman (1990) suggest that independent filmmakers reached their zenith in 1985. Encouraged by a few high-grossing films and Oscars for *A Trip to Bountiful* and *Kiss of the Spider Woman*, many independent studios increased their production. By 1989 the bloom had faded and the major studios regained their dominance, accounting for 95% of total U.S. box office receipts. Dominick (1987) found that the major film studios in Hollywood had less diversity in the films they released than did independent filmmakers. Independents also rely on video sales more than do the majors because they have depended on preselling videocassette and foreign rights for money to produce their films (Cronin and Litman, 1990). Many independents began making films released directly to videocassettes and bypassing theatrical exhibition. This phenomenon rose from fewer than 40 films per year in 1985 to more than 100 per year a couple years later. Independents also benefited from the rapid growth in the number of theater screens, which needed films to show.

Depending on shoe-string budgets, independents have developed an internal structure that is a "streamlined version of the majors' operations with more responsible financing" (Cronin and Litman, 1990: 12). Executives often double as directors, offices are in lower-rent districts outside Hollywood, production staffs are smaller, more filming is done on location, non-union workers are used, and marketing and promotion costs are tightly controlled. The success of independents rests on three major factors: creativity in an environment where the term is constantly being redefined, releasing films during slack periods,[5] and getting more out of their marketing and promotion by linking those efforts more closely to release dates (Cronin and Litman, 1990).

Scholars and film studios have long sought to identify the factors that make a film economically successful.[6] Litman and Kohl (1989) looked at many factors, finding that access to a large number of screens, summer release time, size of the budget, nomination for an Oscar, having top stars and directors, getting positive ratings by movie critics, making films which were sequels and of a particular film genre (science fiction) were all predictors of film rentals. Many studios campaign for Academy Award nominations because an Oscar increases a film's box office potential. Dodd and Holbrook (1988) found that an Oscar for best picture contributes to a film's revenues, while awards for best actress and best actor and nominations in all three categories make some difference.[7]

Film Encoding Patterns—Work Routines and Conventions

Each creative role is responsible for work routines and conventions that affect the final product—the feature film. The director has been identified as having the unifying vision and control. Salt (1983) claims that **style** can be considered as a set of decisions—number and types of camera setups, shot length, number and types of camera movements, color versus black and white, and so forth. Thus, we can look at changes in styles across time and compare filmmakers on these factors. For example, Howard Hawks keeps the camera at eye level. When the film medium first began the average shot length varied as new directors came on the scene and experimented. Some emphasized close shots, others medium or long shots. Early American films (1920s) used faster cutting rates in comparison with the Europeans, whose slow cutting matched the slow pace of their narratives and acting. In the 1920s and 1930s, European filmmakers also used a "medium shot style," while Americans used close shots consistently. Methods criss-crossed the oceans as filmmakers borrowed techniques and routines from each other.

New technologies—in film, lighting, and cameras—made new techniques possible; for example, the first zoom lenses of modern design became available in the 1940s. Reverse-angle cutting (cuts within a scene which change the camera angle by more than 90 degrees) is a stylistic feature that varied by period and director. An example is cuts between a watcher and his or her "point of view," a technique that Alfred Hitchcock used more often than other directors. Point of view shots are taken with the camera pointing along the direction of view of a character shown in the previous shot, so the viewer sees what is seen by that character. Salt (1983) suggests that Hitchcock used the "point-of-view" shot because of the "voyeuristic strain in his personality," and as a good way of securing audience involvement.

The major formal development in American filmmaking during the 1940s was a trend toward filming which used shots of longer duration (long-take shots). In the 1950s, the "jump cut" came into its full glory. In jump cuts, the camera moves directly from one shot to another taking place at a later time. By the 1960s, almost any technique seemed possible, and European film techniques had considerable influence on American cinema. Changes in film and other technology continued. Editing styles also changed, and the average shot length speeded up as the 1960s wore on, although the origins of this change are obscure (Salt, 1983). This trend toward the use of short shots continued into the 1970s in the U.S. while the long take continued to be the standard in European art films. The use of wide-angle lenses also emerged in the 1970s. The growth of special effects and computer-aided production techniques are major features of the 1970s, 1980s, and 1990s.

Message creators often elicit audience participation in telling their stories. Neuendorf and Sparks (1988) found that objects like chainsaws and tombstones caused viewers of horror movies to react with fright because they were associated with past horror movies. This is a cuing process, in which message encoders use skeletal material to tell stories that are meaningful and complete when decoded by audiences. Messages leave room for the audience to "complete the message" using various cues, but this also means that different decoders will come up with different understandings (Reynolds, 1991).

Newspaper Organizations

Large and small newspapers are organized in different ways, but the basic structure is similar, with five major departments: editorial, advertising, production, circulation, and business. The chart in Figure 4-1 shows that ultimate authority and legal responsibility lie with the publisher and, in large organizations, a board of directors answerable to stockholders. Most news is provided by staff reporters through the city editor, by national news agencies (AP) through the wire editor, and by out-of-town correspondents through the state news editor. Sometimes sports and social/living styles editors and their assistants or reporters are subordinate to the city editor. Editorials are written by the editor and editorial writers. The stories written by reporters are edited by copyreaders and eventually sent to the composing room. A makeup editor plans the

Figure 4-1

Example of Newspaper Organization

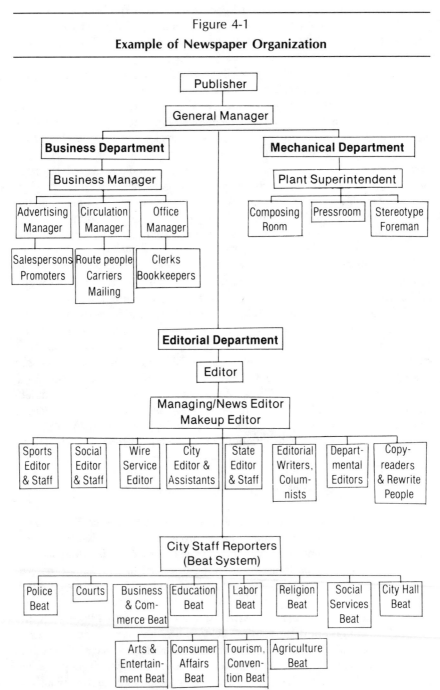

newspaper layout, determining what pictures and stories go on page one and elsewhere. On some papers the makeup editor also is the managing or news editor. On large papers a board headed by the managing or news editor may make some of these decisions.

As Figure 4-1 notes, there is a hierarchy in which editors supervise particular territory. Editors/managers perform two major tasks: coordinating activities and resolving disputes within their units. The chart also shows how influence is brought to bear from the inside or outside. At large newspapers, advertising and news editorial groups are physically separate and traditionally have had virtually no contact. If a large advertiser wants to affect news coverage via its perceived advertising leverage, the influence may either be an informal contact outside channels (between the advertising department representative and reporter) or it can follow the organizational chart, in which case actual influence receives the approval or rejection of management.[8]

The breakdown of personnel varies by newspaper size. A national U.S. survey of daily newspaper journalists in 1988 found that 47% were reporters, 16% copy editors, 15% news executives, 6% photographers, 3% editorial writers, and 13% others, with similar distributions for men and women.[9] Personnel in a newspaper represent investments in the organization.[10]

The chief functions of newspaper managers are: planning, organizing work and technology, financial management, leadership, and working with people. Newspaper managers spend 20-30% of their time supervising, 15-20% planning, 15-18% coordinating, 10-14% evaluating, and 11-13% investigating situations (Lavine and Wackman, 1988). Chief executive officers of newspapers and other media recognize the need for better managers, three-fourths of whom come from promotions within the newspaper (Lavrakas and Holley, 1989). Management includes advertising and marketing, finances, unions and other personnel,[11] production and distribution, as well as the management of editorial personnel—those involved in writing and editing stories. Increasingly, editors are participating in management training, which is related to professional commitment and an intention to stay in journalism (Senat, 1992).[12]

Management styles have been characterized in a variety of ways.[13] Journalists have tended to need more participation and autonomy than many people (Johnstone et al., 1976; Joseph, 1982, 1985; Petersen, 1992). Studies have shown that dissatisfaction among journalists is related to personal autonomy. Reporters want more control over their activities and the final editorial product. They want to pursue a story to its logical conclusion even if it embarrasses local elites in business, politics, or labor; influential individuals from these and other areas may try to put pressure on media management when they dislike the way they are treated in the media. Journalists expect some guidance from supervisors and a chance to participate in decision making.[14]

Publishers also want editors to consult with reporters but expect the former to make the final decision. Publishers accept reporter participation in decisions about how to cover stories, story suggestions, time needed to cover a story, and art suggestions, but they are less likely to think reporters should be involved in issues of salary, budget, or hiring. A national study of newspaper editors found that integrity and impartiality were the most important organizational standards, followed by editorial independence, staff enterprise, editorial courage, community leadership, staff professionalism, decency, and influence (Gladney, 1990).[15]

Management styles can affect the content of newspapers. According to one study, excellent papers are more likely to give reporters more independence (Connery, 1989). Top papers[16] gave their reporters time to work on long-range projects and independence in covering their beats. All sent reporters to workshops and seminars, and all had regular critiques of performance by the reporters, editors, publishers, and papers themselves. Community coverage was listed as the most important factor leading to excellence.[17] Communication with managers has been identified as a major problem in newsrooms. A national survey of daily newspaper journalists in 1988 found that the three major weaknesses of managers all were communication problems—poor at staff encouragement and feedback, poor at making assignments or decisions, and working poorly with people (Stinnett, 1989). High uncertainty because of communication styles can lead to misunderstandings and other problems within the newsroom.[18] Since the mental health of an individual is highly related to one's ability to communicate effectively within the organization, more attention needs to be placed on reducing uncertainty in newsrooms.[19]

A newspaper's policies govern how its reporters and editors operate in the newsroom and in the field. More than a third of newsrooms have a written code of ethics.[20] Plagiarism, using unpublished information for financial gain, and accepting financial discounts for personal use are serious violations. Other activities governed by codes include teaching, unpaid appearances on TV, participating in charitable activities, campaigning for politicians or officials, financial interests, and potential conflicts of interest (Davenport and Izard, 1985).[21] Non-monetary conflicts of interest are handled on a personal, individual basis (McAdams, 1986). A majority of journalists believe they should be involved in the community, but the actual level of public contact appeared to be considerably less (Burgoon, Burgoon, Buller and Atkin, 1987). Some policies deal with mistakes and public complaints, and some newspapers have ombudsmen to mediate between the paper and the public.[22] Most papers also publish corrections, but few have a written correction policy, and errors corrected most often are publication of wrong names, omissions of facts, incorrect figures, and wrong dates (Fowler and Mumert, 1988). Newspapers have the legal right to reject ads and a fifth have policies specifically prohibiting ads that range from fortune tellers to hair restorers, but most reject fewer than 10 ads a month (Pasternack and Utt, 1988).[23] One analysis of newsroom policies concluded that papers are becoming more market-driven and reader-oriented (Underwood and Stamm, 1992).

Broadcast Organizations

Newspapers and local TV stations share many similarities. Both "turn out a product" for public consumption, both have sales or business departments, and both have technical departments, but there are many differences too. While news departments of papers originate 40-50% of the content for papers, news is only a small percentage of the content of a TV station.[24] Thus, TV stations have more directors and managers competing with news directors for the station's scarce resources. An example of a TV station organization is found in Figure 4-2. Stations also select entertainment programs from national networks and distributors and produce local programming which is not news.[25]

National TV Entertainment

At the national level, TV organizations either commission or produce a variety of "entertainment formats" that are largely fiction—dramatic programs, situation comedies, and so forth. A TV production team includes executive producers, the producer, director, story editor, and assistant director. The executive producers administer the company and are responsible for selling an idea to the network, haggling over the license fee, mediating union quarrels on the set, and coordinating activities of the producer. The producer is assigned to each series by the studio and is answerable to the executive producer. The producer is responsible for a particular series and guarantees continuity of characterization, setting, and plot. The director ordinarily is hired on a one-time basis and is a free-lance artist. A director analyzes the script for serious production problems, suggests actors to the producer, contributes to rewriting the script when necessary, and controls the actual filming. The story editor rewrites the original script to accommodate changes in character or locale dictated by the producer, increased or decreased budgets or network time periods, or errors in dramatic construction. He or she may author an entirely new script based on the screen treatment. The assistant director is the lowest in the hierarchy of the production scheme. Duties involve blocking out the sequence of filming, arranging for extras and minor characters, directing background action, and making up cast-calls for shooting. Investigators have tried to explain popular drama as either a reflection of the creators' personalities or as a reflection of the economic values held by those controlling the communication channels. Both approaches provide only partial explanations of the complexities of the situation.

Everyone in the TV networks is in the **program department** in his or

---

Figure 4-2
TV Station Organizational Chart

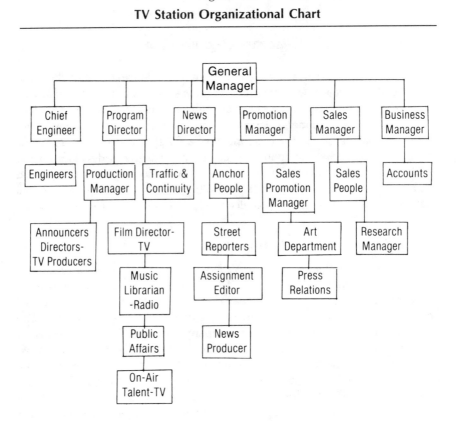

her heart (Shanks, 1976). "Wake the cleaning lady at 7 A.M. and she will tell you what to put in the schedule at 8 P.M. Saturday night or who to cast in the leads in a made-for-TV movie." Every TV show is at least indirectly affected by the planning, sales, research, and affiliates areas of a network—even though direct contact may not be there. Each network has several layers of bureaucracy. Deal making is so complicated that series often go on and off the air before formal contracts are even signed. Oral agreements and handshakes follow often lengthy negotiations. A fourth of all TV-movie deals fall through, not because of disagreements over creative content but over differences between lawyers for both sides. Of 100 presentations to a network, 30 pilot scripts are commissioned and 10 get orders, with one series ending up on the air.

Most American commercial TV drama is produced by a few major Hollywood production houses under contract to one of the major TV networks. Earlier in TV's history, the low prices paid by the networks for producing TV programs discouraged Hollywood studios from entering the business until the mid-1950s, leaving production to the independent telefilm producer and the networks themselves (Boddy, 1985). In 1960 control shifted from the advertisers, program producers, and stations to the networks. Previously, advertisers and entrepreneurs made pilot films for series sold to individual agencies which then purchased TV time. One producer interviewed in 1967 complained that he had only three potential buyers for his productions, while in the early days of TV there had been 30 or 40 possible buyers. By the mid-1960s, the networks had secured control of dramatic TV films. Because of a 1972 antitrust action against ABC, CBS, and NBC, Hollywood program suppliers have regained some power vis-á-vis the networks, and cable has opened the market even more. Networks claim that they are as dependent on the program suppliers as the suppliers are on them. With mutual dependency, each party blames the other for program content when criticism arises. Independent producers also have achieved some access to public TV.[26]

Creativity in TV Entertainment.   Creativity has been associated with all aspects of production, as well as artistic freedom and excellence in one's craft. Gitlin (1983) points out that TV shows are "packaged more than written," and the process is more political than artistic, with network standards departments and others acting as political brokerages testing the winds for trends, opportunities, and threats. Blumler and Spicer (1990: 86) note that domination of the U.S. TV industry by the three network buyers limited producers, writers, and directors. With an expansion of outlets (Fox, cable networks, first-run syndication, and home video), they interviewed 150 people in Hollywood and the TV industry to see whether this would change prospects for creativity. They found that the expansion of outlets has increased options for material which might be rejected in a particular market. The new marketplace also has increased opportunities for "imaginative, innovative, and thought-provoking television." However, originality is still limited by the need to reach mass markets, feelings that particular kinds of programs are more risky, budgetary concerns, emphasis on bottom-line management, and restrictive images of the audience.

Turow (1982) found that the TV networks were more receptive to unconventional programming during times of competitive pressures or unusual changes. Furthermore, conventional shows tend to be developed by people or production firms enjoying comfortable success in the TV industry, while unconventional shows emerge from those at low points in their careers.

The Production Process for TV Shows.   The producer is more important in filming TV series than in making feature films. He or she has both creative and executive authority, hiring the cast, directors, and writers and acting as coordinator between the parent film company and TV network for whom the show is being produced (Cantor, 1971/1988). Many of the tasks assigned to the film director are assumed by the TV producer, who works "on the line" and is responsible for day-to-day decisions. As observers have noted, "the feature film is a director's medium while television is a producer's medium" (Cantor, 1971/1988: 8).[27]

Three of the major creative parts of TV series production are under the producer's control—story, casting, and editing. The director shoots the film and is in control on the set but turns to the producer for final decisions. The producer also holds power over the scriptwriters, though it is not complete. Newcomb and Alley (1982) note that control is central to the concept of the self-conscious artistic producer. For most producers, the main job is to hire writers and develop stories with them to see that the story idea is carried through to the final TV show. Some shows have two producers, one for stories and the other for such production aspects as casts, sets, and administration of funds.

In her original study, Cantor (1971/1988) characterized TV producers as falling into three major categories, each with different backgrounds and views of the TV-show production process: filmmakers, writers-producers, and old-line producers. The "filmmakers" have the least control over the material presented because they have little to do with the original idea for a TV series and seldom rewrite material received from writers. They have few conflicts with the networks or production company and see themselves as honing their skills for a move toward feature films. The "writers-producers" were free-lance writers before they moved into producing to gain control over their work. Most come with background in various other print and broadcast media. They are more involved with the material in every way and have the most conflicts with networks and others involved. The "old-line producers," most now retired or deceased, were closer to the classic Hollywood producer who started with humble origins and a work orientation that made them successful and more highly paid. The new "baby boom" or "yuppie" generation of producers grew up on TV as their principal entertainment medium and see it rather than film as their destiny. Many started out as writers, and they want to work as producers of TV, whether commercials, sitcoms, or dramatic series.

Cantor (1971/1988) describes the process through which a TV show emerges. Ideas for series, closely guarded, are presented to a network executive, usually someone in charge of programming. A pilot script is commissioned, and the result becomes the property of the network, which has the option of contracting for rewrites. If the pilot show is made, it is shown to potential advertisers. If the network executives think the series will appeal to audiences and advertising agencies want to buy spots for the program, the network places an order with the production company or independent producer for a specified number of scripts to be produced. Unsold pilots often appear during the summer.

Many individuals play important creative[28] and technical roles in making TV programs, some of them parallel to those described under filmmaking. In addition to the producer, three of the most important are the writer, director, and actor. After a specific storyline is created and a writer selected, the writing continues. Writers become "stale" or too busy with other assignments, so others are added over time. Free-lance writers can talk over script ideas with a producer, but the Writers Guild of America restricts the number of talks to two, after which the writer must be hired for at least a story presentation. Many producers build up a cadre of writers that work on several scripts a season. When the producer initiates a topic, the "story conference" is arranged to discuss the story outline. After rewrites and discussions, the final script may be totally different from the original idea. The relationship between the producer and writer is one of conflict and interdependence (Cantor, 1971/1988). The relationship between the producer and the director is more conflict-free because the latter cannot change scripts and has limited power over the process. Directors do their work with minimal interference. They help select actors for supporting roles and have a say in selecting sets, costumes, and music. Most editing is done by directors or editors selected by them. Generally, the main actors have been cast before production begins. Important stars have consultation rights over scripts. The more popular or crucial the actor for the series, the greater his or her ability to influence scripts. Producers and directors also work with TV networks, which may introduce conflict because of disputes over content of the TV show or audience ratings.

Styles and Changes in Encoding TV Entertainment.   Barker (1991) looks at the emergence of television's encoding patterns, what he calls repertoire of representation. This refers to the aural and visual codes of TV, including sound effects, music, camera and performer blocking, editing patterns, lighting, and set design. Initially, the TV "shot" was viewed in terms of image quality, but once that improved, concern shifted to forms of presentation. The low resolution of early TV and the size of the screen made the "close-up" the only type of shot TV provided successfully. Barker (1991) adds that the close-up also fit well with TV's effort to be a more intimate medium for the home and efforts to convey drama through facial nuance rather than grand gestures. Early fixation on close-ups also explains why early TV programs consisted of single static shots with little movement by subjects. The development of equipment that allowed the use of multiple cameras and the ability to switch among them offered flexibility and the potential of using a variety of close-ups, long shots, and angles from different positions. Continuity editing, blocking, expanded depth of field, and instantaneous switching added to the forms used on TV.

Styles of encoding vary widely. Co-production of a TV series by Japanese and German TV organizations provides an interesting example (Tsuchiya, 1988). The programs introduced historic gardens in both countries to their respective audiences. The Japanese version used more camera movements and more shooting locations to cover the subject. Movements of the photographed subjects occurred more often in the German version. While the German segments varied in length, the Japanese versions were all exactly five minutes long. Images shown in both versions of the TV show were the same but the two sets of producers agreed on only 30% of the material shown to viewers. German producers showed more mobility in camera work and more zoom-ins than the Japanese, who used more upward movements.[29] Beginning and ending titles of the Japanese programs are always superimposed over photographic images, while the German version had no subtitles at all. Japanese used both classic and modern music throughout, while the German version used less music. All of the German programs used sound effects, while most Japanese programs used none. In a comparison of two different directors of a major TV drama, differences were found in editing, staging within the frame, and camera movement, suggesting that directors of TV series are more actively involved in the production process than traditionally acknowledged (Porter, 1987). Though TV may appear as the "seamless unfolding" of content (Williams, 1974, 1981), some argue that TV is organized by relatively autonomous, self-coherent segments that often follow one another with no particular connection (Naficy, 1989).

Radio Organizations

Radio personnel handle two types of content: music and talk-news. The three principal decision-makers in popular music radio are the program director, music director and the consultant (Rothenbuhler, 1985). The universe of records is defined for the station programmers by record distribution promoters, industry data in the trade sheets, and playlists of similar stations. Program directors choose some records simply because everyone else is playing the "cut."

The other key role on radio is the talk show host or personality. A study of on-air exchanges between radio talk-show hosts and callers found hosts were "directive" in their verbal style, offering guidance and information. Almost three quarters of the hosts' statements were social support. Thus, talk radio hosts provide moderate on-air support for both callers and the listening audience (Levy, 1989; Tramer and Jeffres, 1983).[30] When radio newspeople read the copy for advertisements, it creates confusion about roles and credibility. Griffiths and Goodman (1989) found a majority of radio news directors in the largest U.S. markets object to newspeople participating in on-the-air advertisements.

Pressures on Creative Processes

Many different kinds of citizen and pressure groups and even governmental agencies try to gain access to broadcast outlets to present their point of view. Pressures on creative people and the networks are constant. Those concerned with TV violence have been the most active in pressuring for change in TV drama. Groups concerned with the portrayal of women and minorities from 1970 to the present also have been making a concentrated effort to obtain the attention of the networks, Congress, and the Federal Communication Commission.

Although public opinion polls have shown a concern over the power of commercial TV, this power is not wielded by a few owners or creative professionals. TV, for example, does not necessarily reflect the tastes and ideology of either the creators or those who control the channels of communication, but represents a negotiated struggle between a number of participants that includes: networks, the advertisers, the government—Congress and the FCC, the courts and Justice Department, social critics and citizen groups, and program suppliers. Montgomery (1989) charts the influences of advocacy groups trying to affect TV content, noting that the TV industry has managed to protect itself, and interest groups have gradually accepted more limited goals and have learned to work with the system.

The struggle over TV content is not between the audience (which may be satisfied with dramatic content) and the creators, but among elites who value access for both economic and social reasons. Herbert Gans (1974) notes that pluralistic societies have an ongoing struggle between "diverse groups and aggregates over the allocation of resources which is not limited to strictly economic and political issues but also extends to cultural issues."[31]

News-gathering and News-making—Values and Activities

We have given a brief synopsis of types of encoding activity in mass media organizations. We will now take an in-depth look at the encoding of news by journalists. We have chosen this particular topic because we encounter it daily and because there are not empirical data available for the other media. Newspapers and newscasts reach a massive audience and serve as a link to most aspects of our culture. Learning how journalists encode the news adds a new dimension to what we learn from all the media.

The boundary between "news" and other media content has become fuzzier as the number of media has multiplied and the volume of media content mushroomed. Entertainment to one reader or viewer may be "news" to another. "Reality" content is probably a better label for the news and other content often grouped together today. The distinguishing feature of news is its presentation as an effort to represent reality rather than fiction. Whatever the sins of omission or concerns about balance or fairness, news is collected, written, filmed, or recorded to allow media audiences to participate in concrete events and situations and to see trends they could otherwise see on their own if they had the time and were present.

News and News Values

"No news is good news," "All the news that's fit to print," "That's news to me." We have a plethora of clichés and slogans dealing with news, but seldom do we actually define what it means. News is the consequence of the human desire to know the state of the surrounding social and physical environment. News existed long before the mass media were created to disseminate it. In the fifth century B.C., Sophocles wrote, "No man delights in the bearer of bad news." News is a valuable commodity of social exchange, and the urgent need for news arises in all social organizations, from the family to complex bureaucracies. Recent information may be essential for maintaining social cohesion. For example, conflict or cooperation between groups may depend on news of the attitudes and behavior of interacting groups.

All news has some basis in reality. In one sense, the raw material of news is limitless, unpredictable, and infinitely variable. Tuchman (1978) looks at how organizational routines make news. She starts with the glut of occurrences, or everyday happenings, which journalists recognize as news events by applying various criteria. However, assuming that life consists of occurrences doesn't help us get from reality to news.[32]

Efforts to define news often tend to dissolve into lists of events. Perhaps the best-known definition describes what is alleged to be an unmistakable news event: "When a dog bites a man, that is not news, but when a man bites a dog, that's news." If you made a list of occurrences that make the news, this novel situation might be on the list somewhere. List making is a useful beginning in our attempt to move from "reality," or "occurrences," to "news." The journalist looks for various criteria in deciding if occurrences merit the title of news, although the actual implementation often appears instinctive to reporters and observers.[33] These characteristics are dimensions linking events and situations to members of the audience. The more characteristics contained in a single occurrence, the stronger the connection with the audience.[34] Table 4-1 provides a list of such characteristics and evidence that they are applied in the news media. The list is not exhaustive, but it highlights common aspects of news stories.

Journalists have a dilemma. Professional values argue that some news should be disseminated because people "need" it—to become informed voters, for example. How large a role should audience interests play? Critics and special interest groups will second-guess, depending on their own values, but the

Table 4-1
News Values and Evidence of Their Use

Timeliness and Proximity	Recency and proximity are important values for identifying news, e.g., a distant two-car accident with four dead is not news but the same accident in your hometown is news to you. Burdach (1988) found a direct link between distance from an event and its publication; a fatal event 1,000 km away required 6.5 deaths for reporting to occur.[35]
Progress and Disaster	Examples are triumph, defeat, inventions, natural disasters, rapid changes; Wilkins (1985) notes that media emphasize crises, powerlessness, and individual helplessness in reporting on a blizzard; Singer, Endreny, and Glassman (1991) found the number of deaths in natural disasters affects the amount of coverage given.[36]
Eminence and Prominence	Big names make big news, even when what they do is trivial (Bridges, 1989). Squire (1988) and Wafai (1989) found powerful senators generating more news than less powerful ones. Prominence often is achieved or magnified by size.[37]
Conflict	Most conflicts are newsworthy, especially public ones, but size of the event and importance of the people also are factors (Straughan, 1989). Smith (1987) found a steady increase in newspaper articles reporting conflict from 1945 to 1985. Conflict takes many forms—physical, political, ideological.[38]
Novelty	The old adage about the "man biting dog" fits here, along with coincidences, unusual habits, novel ways of making a living, superstitions, and deviance.[39] How unusual, or atypical something is can be applied to all of the other news values as well.[40]
Consequences	Examples are effects of government actions, inflation, expected results of other occurrences (Harmon, 1989).[41]
Human Interest	These stories are viewed as having interest because they affect people emotionally, for example, the blind helping the blind. Chang and Lee (1990) found U.S. editors use human interest to determine the newsworthiness of international events.

dilemma persists. How well do journalists know their audiences and is that knowledge based on averages or diverse segments? In a survey of local residents in one city, Wulfmeyer (1984) compared audience responses to questions with predictions made by journalists at three TV stations. TV journalists did quite well in identifying types of stories viewers were interested in, with a perfect rank ordering of sports topics and entertainment features and minor discrepancies for news content categories and issues.[42] More recently, some newspapers have begun to use survey techniques to identify audience interests.[43]

Which characteristics are more important to you personally? Changes have occurred through the years. Recently, there has been greater interest in "people," and the characteristic of prominence has taken on greater significance. There also are differences between the media, so recency is more important for broadcast media. The list of characteristics in Table 4-1 is supplemented by a second list of factors that help promote occurrences to the rank of news.

> **intensity**—the greater the intensity of the event, the more likely it will be reported. Wolverton and Vance (1987) found the size of electric rate increases (a measure of intensity or magnitude) related to the amount of newspaper coverage.
>
> **ambiguity**—the less ambiguous the event, the more likely it will be noticed. Kleinnijenhuis (1989) and Peterson (1979) found support for this notion.
>
> **consonance**—this links expectations to the event; if a person predicts something will happen, he or she will more easily accept it. If one wants an event to occur, the same applies. Galtung and Ruge (1965) hypothesized that the more consonant an event is with the mental image of what journalists expect to find, the more likely it will be deemed newsworthy; Kleinnijenhuis (1989) found support for the concept.[44]
>
> **unexpectedness**—the unexpected and rare make good news. Sudden, violent risks get more coverage than chronic risks of equal consequence (Greenberg, Sachsman, Sandmann, and Salomone, 1989; Hetherington, 1989).
>
> **continuity**—once an event is news, it will continue even if its intensity decreases.
>
> **composition**—if an incoming story contrasts with other stories incoming, it more likely will be selected for balance.
>
> **meaningful**—based on cultural proximity (familiarity), and relevance (to audience). Chang, Shoemaker, and Brendlinger (1987) found that significance to the U.S. increased the likelihood an event would be covered by U.S. news media.[45]

elite countries—events concerning elite nations (Larson, McAnany, and Storey, 1986; Clarke, 1990; Yu and Riffe, 1989) and major areas within nations (Clarke, 1990; Whitney, Fritzler, Jones, Mazzarella, and Rakow, 1989) get more attention.[46] Stevenson and Straughan (1991) note a study showing that U.S. young adults' interest in and knowledge of news and events is less than any other generation of the past 50 years. Interest in foreign news is tied to whether people know about, like, or have traveled to the country (McNelly and Izcaray, 1986; Straughan, 1989).

personal terms—events that can be seen in personal terms or the results of individual actions are more likely to become news.[47]

negative consequences—the more negative its consequences, the more probable an event becomes news.[48]

sensationalism—the more sensational the event, the greater the likelihood of its coverage. Sensationalism has always been a basic element of the popular press, and sensational events such as violence, crime, and sex were staples in folktales and ballads centuries before there were newspapers (Stevens, 1991). Little attention is given to "the distinction between material which is made sensational by its manner of display and material that is inherently sensational," such as sex crimes (Stevens, 1985). Hofstetter and Dozier (1986) found TV news at one station was not dominated by sensational coverage but included a lot of what could be considered sensationalism.[49]

Time is probably the one thing we would all use to distinguish which occurrences are news and which aren't. The idea of time is hardly a simple one, as Roshco (1975) notes. For an item of information to be timely, it requires the conjunction of three things: recency, immediacy, and currency. **Recency**, or recent disclosure, refers to the fact that "it was just learned" rather than "it just occurred." An example is the Dead Sea Scrolls which made news two millennia after they were written because they had just been discovered. Also, with the opening of files in Russia, historical events have made news decades later. **Immediacy** depends on the interplay of communication technology and institutional practices of the media. It refers to "publication with minimal delay." For all-news radio and TV, delay is much shorter than it is for newspapers. In times past, when a single messenger might be the sole news medium for a report affecting the entire nation, immediacy was a matter of the time required for the courier to convey the message. In our age of multiple news media, much of the news is gathered by open exchanges between a news source and assembled reporters, so the immediacy with which news is reported depends upon the interplay between communication technology and the institutional practices of the media. **Currency** refers to whether the information is relevant to present concerns. News is not an absolute. Currency is as relative as the other aspects of timeliness. When editors and reporters exercise "news judgment" in assessing the "news value" of a report, they are applying their criteria of currency to the available items of recent information from which news is constructed. Immediacy links recent events and the media reporting them, while currency links these events to segments of the public. Recency makes an item of information into an item of news; currency, which is based on audience interest, gives the news item its **news value**. So news as timely information implies the existence and interaction of a news source, a news medium, and a news audience. The time concepts employed by news people in the production of news are central to their occupation. Broadcasters emphasize events that occur within a given day and highly value those occurring within the most recent few hours while daily newspaper journalists deal with material that appears as "yesterday's news." Language also features the notion of immediacy; stories contain such words as upheaval, suddenness, unpredictability. News stories which are still changing and unfolding are talked of as "breaking" stories. The general public and journalists tend to agree that one of the most important functions of newspapers is to provide a thorough and timely account of significant events (Burgoon, Bernstein, and Burgoon, 1983).

Journalists traditionally look for answers to the open-ended "**who, what, when, where, why,** and **how**" questions. One study analyzed the extent to which these traditional news elements, plus the larger **context**, were included in network TV news coverage of different categories of news (Graber, 1992). Over all, the who, what, when, and where questions were covered well by all types of stories, with adequate information in 90% of the stories. The weakest information was found for why and how questions; only 53% of the stories explained why the situation was occurring, and only 34% supplied information about how the situation occurred. The meaningfulness of stories is enhanced when they are placed into context—situations are related to other events or their significance to the audience examined. An average of 65% of the stories supplied contextual information.

Comparing Media Menus.   Application of news values can produce quite different newscasts or news menus. Stempel (1985) analyzed nine national news media, including newspapers and TV newscasts, finding substantial agreement on the mix of various news topics but disagreement on which stories should be used. The data confirmed the widely held notion that TV network newscasts were highly similar, but it also found that news selection patterns for newspapers are quite different from the networks. Another study also found relatively little sharing of stories among TV stations and newspapers (Welch (1991).[50]

Comparing TV Newscasts. Many of the same news items appear in competing newscasts at the local and national level. Ramaprasad (1991) found that each of the three U.S. TV networks shared 54-87% of its news segments with one of the other networks in an 1989 sample. In another study, two of three national networks agreed on the same lead story 91% of the time, while all three agreed 43% of the time. When all three networks featured different lead stories (9% of the time), all three usually carried leads of their competitors in the top six stories (Foote and Steele, 1986).[51] Strong similarities also have been found among local TV newscasts (Atwater, 1986; Davie, 1992), though that seems to vary by topic.[52]

Comparing Newspapers. A study of news use on the front pages of a sample of American daily newspapers found three news-use patterns that tend to support the earlier discussion of news values. Front pages of the papers devoted almost 85% of their space to news, averaging 54 stories per week. Looking at story characteristics, Bridges (1989) found that stories with the characteristic "timeliness" accounted for 63% of the page one space and prominence 61%; proximity was present in stories occupying half of the space, while conflict accounted for 38%, magnitude/intensity/size 35%, and consequences 26%. Further analysis showed that "hard news" was the major dimension characterizing stories on page one, while "interpretation" and "prominence" seemed to explain other dimensions.

News stories can be sorted on the basis of the prominence of particular news values. Corrigan (1990) content analyzed more than 900 stories from two national and two regional newspapers, finding that general news values can account for about 98% of the leads (the first paragraphs) of the front page stories. Since leads represent what journalists think are the most important or significant aspects of the story for readers, leads are an appropriate sample for reflecting overall news values. In terms of frequency of news values in lead sentences, the most frequent were: prominence (54.5%), vitality/conflict (51.9%), timeliness (45.4%), proximity (24.7%), significance[53] (24%), human interest (19.2%), and consequences (3.6%). Most leads contain multiple news values.[54]

What are the origins of what has been described as "newsworthiness." Reisner (1989) points to different traditions as providing explanations. The cultural studies perspective sees news as reproducing the dominant social codes and thematic representations of the most powerful groups in society. In this "hegemonic" perspective, news values or characteristics exist because they "reflect" the power structure.[55] A second conceptualization sees news as a product of various factors. In this view, news values change through time. In his personal analysis of enduring news values held by American journalists, Gans (1979) identifies eight clusters: ethnocentrism, altruistic democracy, responsible capitalism, small-town pastoralism, individualism, moderatism, social order, and national leadership. Wilke (1984) found that German newspapers covered increasingly diverse themes across three centuries, with less reporting about the social elite and more news concerned with non-elites.[56]

Efforts that tie newsworthiness directly to the social structure or political ideology provide no help in explaining how audience interests might change. News values used by journalists before and after glasnost in the Soviet Union may have changed "because" of major changes in the economic and political structure, but that doesn't explain why we would expect changes in audience news values—what they find interesting. Indeed, the extent to which news values are common across ethnic groups, nations, and cultures is an empirical question open to research. Galtung and Ruge (1965) say there are universal news values such as impact, unusualness, and cultural similarity of the event with an audience, and these are used by journalists in determining what is news. Western news values also are identified, including conflict, personally meaningful (event or situation), prominence and eliteness of a country.

Communication researchers have begun to compile a series of studies which support the Galtung and Ruge notion of **universal news values**. Haque (1986), for example, found a remarkable similarity in news judgment of national editors in India despite its size and cultural diversity, while Priyadarsini (1984) found crime news coverage in India resembling patterns found in Western countries.[57] Ito (1990) concluded that "components of 'news values' are basically universal" after finding similarities between current news stories and what constituted news in precursors of modern newspapers in Japan in the 17th century, before access to modern Western journalism. Stories included civil war, riots, murder, satire, suicide, seduction and rape. Within Sweden, Ekecrantz (1988) found a trend towards uniformity in the coverage of international affairs and less diversity, and in the United States Bramlett (1987) found both Northern and Southern journalists employed similar news values in covering desegregation, despite perceived social and political ideological differences. Reisner's (1989) study found that the traditional news values— conflict, consequences, size, and geographical area—are not simply artifacts of the media organization or reporters' justifications for their work. They represent systematic devices used to define and place stories. Starck and Yu (1988) describe the various ways in which news values are defined in China: interest/timeliness/importance; a concern with possible social effects; and six categories that include political, policymaking, timeliness, educational, social, and appreciative.[58] Straughan (1989) found the presence of traditional news values such as conflict and proximity had an impact on reader interest in news stories.

Implementation of these news values occurs through journalists. Here, individual differences will occur, depending on the situation.[59] Few studies actually look at the personal background and characteristics of journalists as factors affecting news judgment processes. Olasky (1986) looked at coverage of the Scopes "monkey trial," finding reporters from most major papers had an antipathy toward fundamentalist Christianity. Most spent as little time with the local people and the clergy as they could manage. Bertazzoni (1991) found in a study comparing editors with similar backgrounds and experiences that there were differences in the way male and female editors ranked the importance of particular stories. Women gave higher rankings to stories about education, family values, and abortion issues, while men ranked sports, conflict, and government higher. Lee and Kang (1986) compared news-value judgments of journalists in South Korea and the U.S., finding that Korean professionals were more interested in the Third World and American professionals more concerned with U.S. actions and policies. Student journalists from both countries were more concerned with development news than the professionals. Since "news gathering" is not a solitary process but involves a difficult environment and many different reporters, editors, and technical people, differences also are likely in the implementation of news values by editors and other gatekeepers involved.[60]

Beyond Values to News Frames

If implementation of news values was executed in precisely the same manner by all journalists, then journalism would be a technical routine with no human judgment or creativity. Clearly, that's not the case, and we expect diversity on many dimensions. We need to separate the concept of news values from codes, frames, and cognitive structures. News values are distinguished from other mental structures or **frames** used by journalists in constructing news stories. If news values represent the basis for selecting certain occurrences (events, situations) as candidates for news, then frames represent mental strategies for collecting information and constructing messages as the process of news making continues.

Professional and Process Frames.   If timely occurrences with particular characteristics are candidates for daily news, journalists still must make choices. Professional and process frames provide shortcuts in defining and identifying news. Journalists classify events as hard vs. soft news,[61] spot vs. developing news, and continuing news. **Hard news** refers to concrete, public events where reporters can amass significant facts about topics of interest and consequence to audiences. **Soft news** refers to features which are generally less timely, often less concrete, and usually not immediately important to media consumers. Tuchman (1978) says that journalists typify events as news according to how they happen. Events are classified according to how they fit in with practical tasks, e.g., soft news is usually controlled and seldom pertains to unscheduled events. Berkowitz (1990, 1992) found that TV newsworkers typify stories to quickly assess resource commitment and potential problems.

By routinizing the unexpected, journalists have guides for organizational behavior and evaluating performance.

Spot news refers to one-shot events while **developing news** refers to stories where facts are still emerging and the story is not complete. **Continuing news** refers to series of stories on the same subject based on events occurring over time. These definitions decrease the variability of events as raw material. Emphasis on reporting specific events has been criticized by many observers[62] in the U.S. (Wilkins and Patterson, 1987) and Britain (Kristiansen and Harding, 1984). Focusing on "concrete" occurrences that can be classified as "events" rather than treating ongoing processes or trends can lead to a fragmented view of society (Rositi, 1977). Dicken-Garcia (1989) argues that news categories have changed over time in response to journalistic and social developments.[63] Carroll (1988) examined network TV news coverage in 1969, 1977, and 1984, finding an emphasis on hard news but also a trend toward emphasizing situations rather than simply reporting the most recent occurrences—a shift from event-orientation.

Fishman (1982) says that reporters on beats rely on schemes of interpretation—called **phase structures**—to find out what's going on. For example, a reporter covering the courts would use arrests, plea bargains, and arraignments to formulate such activities as events. These schemes allow reporters to know when something new is happening and to distinguish between important and trivial events.

Political-Ideological Frames.   For years, neo-Marxist researchers have argued that news content routinely supports and extends the dominant ideology. Gitlin (1980: 7), for example, argues that news media portrayed the 1960s-1970s student protest movement as deviant and extremist, using frames that trivialized it. Frames here refer to "patterns of cognition, interpretation, and presentation, of selection, emphasis, and exclusion by which symbol-handlers routinely organize discourse." Content analyses done by the Glasgow University Media Group (1976, 1980) have supported this view; they found the British TV news covering industrial disputes stressed the views of management and the British government and cast a negative light on the strikers and unions. Others have looked at Cold War frames in coverage of foreign policy and conflicts (Anderson, 1988; Hallin, 1987). Entman (1991) shows that several national U.S. media emphasized the victims in the Soviet downing of a Korean jet, presenting it as a moral outrage, while the U.S. downing of an Iranian plane was framed as a technical problem.[64]

The concept of hegemony has become popular in describing the degree to which media encoders and media content "reflect" the ruling classes or status quo. Gramsci (1971, 1983) used this concept in his argument that the ruling groups shape popular consent through the production and diffusion of beliefs, values, and meanings by major institutions in a society. However, the argument has been applied in different ways with varying results.[65] Parenti (1986) made a case that the major American media create a coherent and unified worldview in which American capitalism is always the best possible social order, the ex-Soviet system is axiomatically bad, and right-wing governments are preferable to socialist alternatives. Lin and Salwen (1986) looked at how three press systems viewed Sino-U.S. normalization, finding 78% of the *New York Times* stories neutral in contrast to 69% positive in the *People's Daily* and 59% negative in the *Central Daily News* of the Republic of China/Taiwan. Campbell and Reeves (1989) note that clusters of stories with similar themes are linked in newscasts—for example, frames such as foreign intrigue or the Cold War. Yang, Schweitzer, and Harmon (1992) found that three American newsmagazines' coverage of Gorbachev and Deng reflected U.S. national interests.

Countering the Marxist view, others have found American media providing a multitude of views (Harrison, 1986; Newcomb and Hirsch, 1984). Barkin and Gurevitch (1987) found a mixture of themes in American news stories on unemployment. Carragee (1990) conducted a textual analysis of the *New York Times* coverage of the leftist, environmental Green Party in Germany, concluding that the paper gave the movement extensive coverage and also portrayed the party's positions on domestic politics in a manner not consistent with the "media hegemony thesis." According to that thesis, the *Times* would either have ignored the group or presented a negative, distorted picture.[66] Schiff (1991) compiled indexes reflecting news characteristics and political ideology of stories in 14 daily papers in Ohio. He found no difference in the extent to which editors relied on traditional news values to pick stories, but there were differences in terms of ideology. The big city papers reflected a more liberal bias and the dominant ideology.[67]

Social Frames.   Although some would define "everything" as political, we make distinctions between frames expressing power relationships and others that try to make sense out of human activity and the environment. Journalists must observe and make sense out of complex events and situations. The more they know, the better they are able to distinguish between events and people individually and the "same" phenomena socially or culturally. Anything can be political or social, but the likelihood that the audience will arrive at the same assessments is greater when journalists use symbols[68] that emphasize cultural or political aspects rather than the uniqueness of the individual or event. Focusing on interpersonal communication, Miller and Sunnafrank (1982) note there are three kinds of information: cultural information—knowledge about another person's culture, language, values, beliefs, prevailing ideology; sociological information—knowledge of an individual's membership groups and reference groups; and psychological information, which directs attention to another person's prior learning history.

We can extend these concepts to reporting about people and the environment. For a journalist, the goal is to provide sufficient information to know people in the news as individuals or to place events and situations in the most relevant context for the audience. Given the time and space constraints, journalists have difficulty providing background for assessing the uniqueness of phenomena. For example, Jensen (1986) found network TV news economic coverage presented a particular vision of society in which the state was responsible for protecting the economic system against major disruptions, but industries and communities have to work out their own solutions. Coverage of economic fluctuations was separated from coverage of the political institutions that are supposed to control those fluctuations. Barkin and Gurevitch (1987) found network TV stories offering few direct explanations of unemployment—consistent with professional practices of dispensing objective information—but providing many implicit reasons in broader statements about society. Daley and O'Neill (1991) found that mainstream newspapers and native Alaskan press had two different concepts of nature in their coverage of the Valdez oil spill.

What frames are used to describe people, events, and situations as unique phenomena or place them in a social context? Bailey and Sage (1988) found sportscasters framing sports events in terms of individualism and achievement, and Levine (1986) found the hard news of local newscasts of three network affiliates focusing on "helplessness" (things out of control, unpredictable, in chaos) in 71% of news stories. Vincent, Crow, and Davis (1989) looked at TV accounts of major airline crashes, finding three overall themes: tragic intervention of fate into daily life, the mystery of what caused the crash, and the work of legitimate authority to restore normalcy. Campbell and Reeves (1989) found that the TV show "60 Minutes" framed a homeless controversy in terms of class conflict, while network news accounts attributed homelessness to personal circumstances rather than the general economic system. Kress (1986) argues that the media address audiences in interpersonal terms that confirm their powerlessness.

Critics have often pointed to the media's emphasis on bad news rather than good news. Stone and Jensen (1987) found that three TV affiliates reported more bad news (56%) than good news (44%). Coon and Tse (1991) found a similar percentage of bad news at three TV affiliates, and more visual techniques were used for negative than neutral or positive news items.[69] Katz (1987) argued that crime stories selected by the media all tend to fit classic forms of moral problems. In an experiment with journalists at two daily papers, Bohle (1986) found negativism played a part in news selection, but it was not as strong as expected.

Objectivity

The concept of objectivity is still probably the most commonly accepted statement of the role journalists are expected to adopt.[70] Although no society of journalists ever formally adopted "objective reporting" as a canon of their craft, it has become the accepted term for designating allegiance to the nonpartisan pursuit of factual accuracy and is a prime example of a process frame.

If you selected a dozen people at random in the United States, a majority would probably tell you they want journalists to be fair and objective in their reporting of the news. Yet this concept of objectivity is one of the most controversial ideas not only in the newsrooms of TV stations and newspapers, but also in film production, academia, and the offices of elites who want to influence the media. Is the objectivity of documentary filmmakers the same as that of news journalists or that of social scientists? Reese (1990) notes that objectivity has been called the emblem of American journalism. Journalists who have concluded that they are not "wholly objective" have fallen back on accuracy, balance, and fairness as more defensible standards.

Objectivity has been examined as a sifting process to see whether violations of accepted norms of objectivity result from personal biases[71] of journalists, the news organizations' self-interests,[72] self-interest of society's elites, or from human error (McManus, 1991).[73] Objectivity is conceptualized as having two components, factuality and impartiality (Westerstahl, 1983). Stories are factual if they are true and relevant, and they are impartial if all sides to the issue are balanced (to the extent that there are different sides to an issue) and the presentation is neutral. Ettema (1987) argues that journalistic accounts are "justifiably factual" if professional standards of care with facts are taken. This approximates a legal approach to objectivity; the courts have used similar criteria in assessing negligence in libel cases. Koch (1990) argues that contemporary journalism flaws are rooted in the structure of the narrative style reporters use to describe specific events. Thus, even when all the facts are accurate, a story may be seen as slanted or incomplete in its selection of facts or inaccurate in the style of presentation.

An important distinction is between objectivity as intention and as outcome. Media philosopher John Merrill (1974) argues that objectivity has nothing to do with the actual performance but with the intention of journalists not to let their personal feelings affect their reporting. Objectivity here is a goal one should strive for. In another view, objectivity refers to the ability to interpret or view phenomena without having those views or interpretations unduly distorted by personal feelings; this view looks at the outcome. In this scenario, all news reports are incomplete and, thus, cannot be fair or accurate (Altschull, 1974), a scenario that condemns the journalist to failure.[74]

Origins of Objectivity.   The origins of objectivity in journalism are at best unclear. Journalists did not begin to use the word objective to describe their work until the 1920s, and the term originally was seen as an antidote to the emotionalism and jingoism of the conservative American press (Streckfuss, 1990). The roots of objective reporting are thought to be lodged in 19th century technology, industrialization, and urbanization (Blankenburg and Walden, 1977). Wire services are particularly credited with developing the notion. Objectivity was consistent with providing concise, interesting, nonpartisan news accounts that reduced transmission costs and attracted readers. Schiller (1981), traces objectivity's development in tandem with the commercial newspaper's assumption of a crucial political function—surveillance. The commercial newspaper's presence as a new social institution was justified because news objectivity was grounded in the paper's defense of public good in a world of fact. Objectivity drew from the belief that the new technology—photography— afforded an exact, accurate copy of reality. Stensaas (1986/1987) found that objective news reports increased progressively from the middle of the 19th century into this century. Nonobjective reports apparently were the norm in the 1865-1874 period, but objective reporting gained momentum before and during the 1905-1914 period and was firmly established by the 1920s, when 80% of the stories examined in New York City papers were objective. There was a strong relationship between objectivity, use of the inverted pyramid, and use of authoritative sources.

Since World War I, journalists have increasingly come to consider themselves professionals and have searched for an appropriate model (Janowitz, 1975). The model selected can best be called the gatekeeper model which sought to apply the canons of the scientific method to increase objectivity and to enhance one's effective performance. This model emphasizes the sharp separation of reporting fact and disseminating opinion. Objectivity became the keystone of journalistic morality during the 1930s. Explicit codification by professionals of techniques of journalistic objectivity occurred during the period leading up to the Second World War. The Canons of Journalism adopted by the American Society of Newspaper Editors in April, 1923, did not contain the word "objectivity" but did use "impartiality."[75] The distinction between news and opinion, or interpretation, in the Canons provides some support for the view that objectivity is tied to intention rather than outcome. At the very least, the professional norm of objectivity among journalists separated intentional news gathering and reporting from all the other activities of the media. It should be noted too that the Canons spoke to newspaper journalists, and later radio and TV. It did not include magazine journalism, opinion media, or explicitly political media.

After World War II, **media criticism** of an obsessively objective journalism grew along with a debate between advocates of objective detachment and those in favor of social responsibility in journalism.[76] Objective reporting has generally meant a constrained style that emphasizes concrete, obtrusive, and finite events rather than trends or other topics. However, reporters can "breach these structures in work labeled 'analysis,' 'investigation,' or 'interpretation.' Today you often see interpretation, where the reporter offers reasoned opinions based on facts. The exact boundary is hazy, yet tangible enough to press critics who call for interpretation as a needed alternative, and to devotees of objectivity who fear interpretation as a kind of creeping advocacy" (Blankenburg and Walden, 1977).

Two phenomena following World War II stimulated the reappraisal of standard reportorial methods and news content: one technological and the other political. Television's arrival and McCarthyism worked jointly to demonstrate the necessity to respond to the increasingly complex world. By the early 1950s Senator Joseph McCarthy's escalating accusations about the presence of communists in government were reported in glaring media accounts. This made at least some newsmen dissatisfied with what Elmer Davis labeled "dead-pan objectivity." Journalists were walking a tightrope between two great gulfs—on one side the false objectivity that takes everything at face value and on the other, the interpretive reporting which fails to draw the line between a reasonably well established fact and what the reporter or editor wishes were the fact. By the 1960s, the gatekeeper model of journalistic professionalism was questioned by some working journalists who recommended replacing the scientific method with the concept of the journalist as critic and interpreter.

Objectivity has been criticized in various intellectual quarters (Christians, 1977). Outspoken academic social scientists became doubtful about their ability to be objective and claimed that the search for objective reality led to a retreat from personal and political responsibility. Some journalists also proclaimed that the task of the journalist was to represent the interests of competing groups, especially those of excluded and underprivileged groups. Some, like Rivet (1976) in France, argue that journalism is a medium of action, and the journalist is a political protagonist. Another way of changing the role avoided personal preferences and values, but assigned to reporters role-obligations comparable to those of scientific researchers. Journalists would be responsible for indicating the validity of the information they reported and for assuring the accuracy of the material attributed.

Implementing Objectivity. The debate over reportorial objectivity raised the question of what constitutes adequate role-performance. Thus, we're faced with how objectivity is actually carried out. The prime writing form used to implement objectivity has been "attribution"—"he said," "she stated," "the president told reporters." All statements of opinion, preferences, assessments, predictions, etc., are supposed to be attributed to identifiable sources. This may include both indirect quotes and those where quotation marks are used to indicate the "exact words" of the source.[77] More than half of the stories on network TV newscasts contain anonymous attribution, in contrast to a third of newspaper stories and 70-85% of newsmagazine stories (Wulfemeyer and McFadden, 1986). Burriss (1988) found that 42% of radio network news stories carried no attribution at all. St. Dizier (1985) found a decline in the use of unnamed sources from 1974 to 1984. Wulfemeyer (1985) found international stories in weekly newsmagazines contained more anonymous attribution than did national stories. Regardless of attribution, the reporter still has to decide what's included or excluded, and objectivity has had rather little to say about the problem except for "balancing" reporting with representative spokespeople from differing positions.

One way to balance is to represent a situation as a dichotomy of pros and cons. About a fifth of controversial stories containing defamation are one-sided, while more than 70% of such stories reported both sides.[78] Prestige newspapers such as the *New York Times* are more likely to cover both sides of a community controversy, with better balanced news, than less prestigious newspapers (Lacy, Fico, and Simon, 1991). Tuchman (1972) argues that objectivity has become a ritual that stands between journalists and the public—including their critics. Objectivity is used similarly by doctors and lawyers vis-á-vis their clients. A ritual is a routine procedure with little relevance to the end sought in that particular situation. The ritual becomes more important when the goals are more vague.

What other evidence do we have that bears on reporters' objectivity? Looking at how a reporter's attitude toward the role of the press in society affects the kind of story produced, Starck and Soloski (1977) found that journalists with a participant bias tended to write stories of an analytic or interpretive nature and de-emphasized simple factual presentations; however, another study found that editors' personal beliefs about campus demonstrations were not related to whether they gave them favorable or unfavorable coverage (Martin, O'Keefe, and Nayman, 1972).

Others have looked at media bias towards groups like the Ku Klux Klan and similar extremist groups, finding that the media gave considerable attention to politically deviant groups (Monti, 1979), but used more negative terms to characterize them (Shoemaker, 1984). News coverage over time is more difficult to judge. Individual stories may be highly accurate, but a variety of factors affect what many observers may consider biased reporting. Bias also has been found in the European press, where opinion and factual coverage have traditionally been interwoven rather than separated.[79]

Views and Evidence on Message Construction

There are a variety of ways to describe the activity represented in news-gathering and message construction processes. Richard Carter (1967) looked at journalists as communicators and viewed communication as a process by which situations are conveyed across time and space. Situations here are occurrences.[80] The basic purpose is to give the audience the opportunity to attend to a situation. There are two basic reportorial functions here: observation and description of situations. The standard of performance is "accuracy"— the fidelity of the reported situation, and the criterion used by the reporter is "relevance." If a report is to be accurate, the relevant must be included and the irrelevant excluded. "Completeness" is a problem because what's omitted can contribute to inaccuracy.[81]

As we learned earlier, news value refers to the relationship of readers to the situation and it implies the use of two criteria—interest and significance. Interest is the reader's likelihood of seeking out the situation, and significance is the likelihood the situation will affect the audience. Park (1940) a half century ago distinguished between "acquaintance with" a topic and "knowledge about" the topic. Whatever is known through acquaintance with is likely to be concrete and descriptive, while that known through knowledge about tends to be abstract and analytic. The former emphasizes facts while the latter deals in concepts. Though the two categories can be located along a continuum, they are distinct forms of knowledge, each having different functions in the lives of individuals.[82]

Daily news gathering is a combination of personal judgments and role performance. The latter consists of conventions and processes adopted consciously or unconsciously to reach professional goals. Eliasoph (1988) argues that news content would not change dramatically if the government tomorrow started offering unconditional funding to all news outlets, largely because of the importance of news-gathering routines. Journalists also recognize the procedures followed in reporting. Despite folk notions that journalists operate intuitively, Parsigian (1987) found support for a model in which journalists follow pre-writing procedures much like social scientists, starting with a statement of the assignment or problem, then researching (gathering background), devising information-collecting strategies, collecting information, organizing the material, analyzing the material, drawing conclusions, and writing the story. Journalists usually have hypotheses in mind when working on a story, some implicit and some explicit, such as the belief that businesses are not complying with a new ordinance (Stocking and LaMarca, 1990). Thus, journalists have expectations and harbor assumptions about their story subjects that direct subsequent information gathering.

Tools for Gathering News

Journalists rely on a series of tools for collecting information—interviewing people, consulting published references and other materials, and examining public records. The patterns represented by each also have changed through time. For example, broadcast interviews during the 1940s and earlier were prearranged and deferential but shifted in the mid-1950s to include challenging questions, probes, and efforts by journalists to retain control (Greatbatch, 1986). While some journalists are infrequent or nonusers of the Freedom of Information Act (FOI), others are "paper chasers," who pour through hundreds of pages of documents in search of information (Fagans, 1984). International differences have been noted on use of documents and sources.[83]

Routine Channels and Initiative.   Journalists seek out news but the reverse also occurs.[84] Most front-page stories in major daily newspapers come from "routine channels" of news gathering such as press conferences, press releases, and official proceedings, in contrast to stories driven by reporter initiative (Brown, Bybee, Wearden, and Straughan, 1987; Sigal, 1973). Even smaller dailies show heavy use of routine channels (Soloski, 1989).[85] Local and national broadcast journalists also rely on routine channels.[86] Looking at news of a local TV station, Seo (1989) found 40% of news originating from routine news channels; 52% of 232 sources were identified with government organizations, 33% with nonprofit and nongovernment organizations, 14.5% with business organizations, and only 16% as unattached individuals. A fourth of news releases survived the "first cut" by producers and assignment editors at one TV station studied (Berkowitz and Adams, 1990); information from nonprofit organizations and interest groups was kept most frequently, while releases from government and business were kept least frequently.[87] Harmon (1989) observed newscasts at three Cincinnati commercial TV stations, finding that two-thirds of the sources were "active" rather than "passive," and enterprise stories—those initiated by a reporter, editor, producer, or videographer— accounted for 19% of primary sources.

The Beat System

Perhaps the most important structural feature of newspaper information gathering is the "beat system" (Lacy and Matustik, 1983). Imagine that your group was asked to organize itself for reporting all the news in tomorrow's daily paper. If you scattered in all directions without any pattern to your efforts, you'd likely find duplication and many significant events ignored. Newspapers cope with the uncertainty of news gathering by organizing reporters to cover geographic areas or topics. Local newspaper editors rate the top four beats as education, sports, local government-politics, and business-economy (McGill, 1991).[88] Tuchman (1978) calls this method of deployment the "news net." Beats produce daily features for the news organization written by reporters located in such locales as city halls, police stations, or school offices. Freelancers are used but infrequently. The "net imposes order on the social world" by assuming news will occur at certain places and not at others, thus creating a news net rather than a "news blanket." The net today is intended for "big fish," with reporters placed at institutions where stories are expected. The news net assumes: 1) readers are interested in occurrences at specific localities; 2) they are concerned with activities of specific organizations; and 3) they are interested in specific topics.

Nationally, the news net concentrates on government offices in Washington, D.C., but here too there are gaps. Editors blame reporters and reporters blame editors for various holes in the net of Washington correspondents, including not just neglected areas such as the Agriculture Department or regulatory agencies but also the Pentagon and Congress (Thomas and Boyd, 1984).[89] At the international level, a relatively small number of correspondents can be supported by any individual newspaper, but one survey found that the number of American foreign correspondents had actually grown from 309 in 1975 to 539 in 1990. The greatest numbers are stationed in Great Britain, Japan, Russia, France, Germany, Hong Kong, Israel, Mexico, the People's Republic of China, and Italy, in that order (Kliesch, 1991).

Major beats of a daily newspaper are listed in Figure 4-1, though the specific beats would match the area and audiences served. One of the oldest beats is the police or crime beat. In the early 19th century, London newspapers provided steady diets of crime news, as reporters wrote about the roasting to death of a 7-year-old by her mother, the strangulation of another child by a mother who had tied her to a bedpost as punishment, and the murder of an elderly mother by a daughter tired of waiting for her modest inheritance. Day after day, space was allotted to coverage of particularly interesting or sensational trials (Knelman, 1990). In covering crime and law enforcement today, reporters have tended to report the side of a crime story presented by police and prosecution and not to contact the person arrested or charged, although that position does emerge in subsequent trial stories (Simon, Fico, and Lacy, 1989).[90] In an analysis of homicides and coverage in Milwaukee, Pritchard (1985) found that homicides allegedly committed by blacks or Hispanics tended to be covered less extensively than those allegedly committed by whites; the race of the victim had no impact on reporting. Police complain about high turnover on the police beat and the need to "train" young reporters.

New beats emerge when the context changes and audience interests have grown. Environmental beats began from the late 1960s onward as papers focused on environmental quality and pollution. The environmental beat of the 1990s is "not very different from what it was in the 1970s," although the quantity is up and topics vary and change (Friedman, 1990).[91] However, some studies have found a decline in the number of environmental beats (De Mott and Tom, 1990) and a shift toward development and economic issues (Howenstine, 1987). Newspaper business news staffs increased markedly in the past decade or so, particularly at larger newspapers (Hubbard, 1987). In terms of actual space, sports remains one of the most popular beats at small newspapers. Many popular dailies devote almost 50% of news space to sports (Bailey and Sage, 1988),[92] and the broadcast media provide a similar emphasis.[93] Papers with science sections also have increased (Bader, 1990).[94] Religious beat reporters have shifted from event coverage to longer, indepth stories that are more issue-oriented and cover trends and ideas within religions and society as a whole (Buddenbaum, 1986, 1988).[95]

Editorial Views

Editorial pages reflect the opinions of management, but op ed pages increasingly include a diversity of opinions and views designed to stimulate debate. Considerable political diversity is found among opinion-page editors, who also tend to differ from the publishers who hire them more than would be expected (Kapoor, Cragan, and Cooper, 1990).[96] Editorial writers make wide use of newsmakers and local leaders and attend meetings for ideas and background material (Endres, 1987). Once the topic has been selected at larger papers, editorial writers begin formal research, while smaller papers' editorial writers have other duties and often set aside one day a week to do research for the upcoming week. Most editorial writers try to present several sides of an issue as well as state the paper's opinion (52%), while 38% try to build a case for their position (Hynds, 1990).

Sources—Selection and Relationships

Sources are selected just as events are. People stand out through group affiliation, location, status, and ability, all of which may promote the likelihood of being chosen as a media source. Journalists tend to rely upon authoritative sources in gathering news for obvious reasons. Authorities possess needed expertise and information. Most are highly educated and may be more articulate and prepared. Such sources also tend to be more visible[97] because they are in prominent positions (mayors), in prominent locations (making them more observable), and in the public arena (where much of the "hard" news occurs).

A variety of studies have looked at the prominence of authoritative sources in the media. A content analysis of some 5,190 news stories appearing on network TV newscasts found a strong preference for use of established institutional sources, particularly those in the government, military, politics, business, or professions (Whitney et al., 1989). In their analysis of network TV news, 28% of all identifiable domestic sources were federal officials, while state and local officials accounted for an additional 7%, other government sources about 1%, political sources 4.6%, business sources 9.2%, private individuals 26.5%, political and social interest groups, 5.2%, and others (academic, religious, sports, professional) 19.3%.[98] Other studies have found a reliance on government sources in the *New York Times* and *Washington*

Post,[99] Canadian TV news,[100] American TV news, and a small daily newspaper (Soloski, 1989).[101] Hansen (1990, 1991) found that newspaper stories which win or are nominated for Pulitzer prizes or other awards reflect more source diversity, are less likely to use official or government sources, and include more ordinary people and those representing special interests. Political figures and government officials are not the only authoritative sources appearing regularly in the media (Seo, 1989). Soloski's (1989) study of a small daily paper found that community leaders were primary sources in 15% of the stories and educators 8%. Stempel and Culbertson (1984) found physicians the most prominent sources of health-care news. In recent years "news shapers" have appeared more frequently in media reports to provide background or insights about news events. Soley (1990) found in a study of TV network newscasts that the same news shapers—former government officials, experts, journalists, think tank scholars, and university professors—were used repeatedly. Experts who are sought out tend to have particularly desirable characteristics—a popular area of expertise, providing good quotes, responding to queries quickly, and permitting one's name to be used with quotes (Belkin, 1988). Business executives and medical sources also are popular sources (Brown, Bybee, Wearden, and Straughan, 1987; Hertog et al., 1992). Computer data bases are increasingly important sources for journalists.[102]

Even among those with status and authority, there is controversy over media access. Noting that both business and labor complain about their image on TV, Pasadeos (1990) did a content analysis of network TV news and found that more than two-thirds of all automotive strike stories used a labor source, while fewer than a third used a management source. Pasadeos speculates that TV journalists view a strike as a labor rather than a management event but also notes that management representatives may fail to respond to queries by journalists. Dunwoody and Ryan (1987) found that journalists do not always take into account scientists' areas of expertise in selecting sources. Women are poorly represented as news sources (Bybee, 1990; Silver, 1986). Tuchman's (1972, 1978, 1979) concept of "symbolic annihilation" refers to the ways in which women are trivialized by news or are simply invisible.

Sources themselves have motives for cooperating with reporters, so reliance on particular sources has consequences for the news that emerges. In general, stories that rely on public documents and official proceedings are much more likely to contain defamation (Fico, Simon, and Lacy, 1991; Picard and Adams, 1987). Scientists who agree to be interviewed by the media do so for three reasons—to educate the public, to create public interest, and to represent an organization (DiBella, 1988). Judges who are elected interact more with journalists than do those who are appointed (Dreschel, 1985).

Relations with Sources.   The relationship between journalists and sources has special significance for our understanding of media operations. Some people act as news sources only once in their lives, but many have enduring links with journalists, particularly sources such as press secretaries, legislators, and professional spokespeople. These links also connect organizations and benefit both reporters and their sources.[103] Viewed as an exchange, the reporter gets publishable information while sources get to highlight things that are beneficial to them.[104] News executives frequently rotate beat assignments so journalists can't easily be coopted in their relationships with sources (Culbertson, 1975-76). Relationships with confidential sources are crucial for particularly sensitive information.[105] Journalists acknowledge the importance of public relations practitioners but tend to be antagonistic towards them.[106] Public relations practitioners themselves attribute journalists' negative attitudes to bad experiences in role relationships as well as a belief that journalists feel their own work is more important. PR representatives accept some of the blame for negative relationships but do not feel that journalists' negative attitudes are justified by the facts (Ryan and Martinson, 1988). Several studies have found that PR practitioners are more successful in assessing views of their journalistic counterparts than the reverse (Stegall and Sanders, 1986).

Relations among Reporters.   Reporters also rely on each other for news leads. A study of how crime is reported in New York City showed that a crime theme spread throughout the news organizations and even into the law community, where authorities used the theme to make news (Fishman, 1984). Working in the field, political reporters from different media organizations organize themselves in a social network (Shields and Dunwoody, 1986). Reporters share routine story information to promote accuracy and consistency. Rather than duplicating wire service reports, reporters depend on them to supplement their own enterprise reporting. Within Washington, D.C., more than other locations, the press corps has been accused of being susceptible to pack journalism. Some observers have charged that the Washington-based TV talk shows are destructive to independent thinking (Shaw, 1989). Traditionally TV has followed newspapers, which set the agenda for unfolding stories (Mayer, 1987). Foreign correspondents with limited budgets and staff rely on American media as sources of news (Ghorpade, 1984).

Gatekeeping

The term gatekeeper seems to have originated with Kurt Lewin, making its way to journalism in the 1950s (Gieber, 1964; White, 1950).[107] The concept of gatekeeping links the structure of media organizations to encoding activity. More than three-fourths of potential TV stories, for example, are discarded by the assignment editor before the news day begins, with a majority of the remaining stories ending up on the morning news budget or assignment list (Berkowitz, 1989). Furthermore, once stories are written, taped, or filmed by the troops in the field, the gatekeeping process continues before the final content emerges.[108] Research shows that editors choose news in patterned ways but select stories proportionately from what's available. Thus, if 20% of the wire news available is about politics, the final news published or aired will represent a similar percentage (Whitney and Becker, 1982). Dunwoody and Shields (1986) extended this further, finding that raw content made available to reporters by sources was similar to the content found in published stories.[109] Stempel (1985) found that nine major media—including network TV news and both regional and national daily papers—agreed on the relative emphasis on various types of news but not in the selection of individual items.[110]

Writing Routines and Conventions

Encoding messages ultimately takes the form of writing articles in print media or scripts in broadcast media, though there also is considerable unscripted encoding of messages not put down on paper first. A command of writing mechanics is an integral part of what is considered professional writing (Ward and Seifert, 1990). With experience, professionals learn how to cram more information into fewer words (Pitts, 1987).[111] One writing technique used often by journalists is the use of metaphors. So (1987) found coverage of a U.S.-Soviet summit depicted by metaphors from business, sports, and war. Writing also is a mental activity. A study of cognitive processes in news and editorial writing by journalism students found that those writing news stories paused more often, suggesting greater monitoring activity (Schumacher et al., 1989). They also were more concerned with accuracy and appeared to use a preorganized structure to guide writing and a priorities list to determine order of mention. Editorial writers paused less often but for longer periods.[112]

An analysis of the journalistic writing process shows that journalists spend one-fourth to one-third of their time writing the lead, which helps them plan the direction of the entire story (Pitts, 1982, 1989). Journalists do not set global plans for the story but concentrate on planning, writing, and editing one section of the article at a time. Steinke (1992) looked at science writers and found similarities in composing processes. Planning and writing were the most time-consuming tasks, followed by editing and considering constraints.

The journalistic story form itself is a constraint on writing (Berner, 1986; Bonk, 1990).[113] Ettema and Glasser (1988) interviewed investigative journalists, finding that they plotted events and skillfully arrayed them as identifiable moralistic stories, but the story form narrowed the types of "truths" that could be told. Major newspapers have tended to avoid including "mobilizing information" (details and specifics such as phone numbers, addresses, dates, and times) which would allow readers to take action to influence public issues.[114] The most basic element of writing-language can be subject to controversy. For example, media are split over how to avoid sexism in the use of pronouns (Kingsolver and Cordry, 1988; Ward, 1975).

Producing Broadcast News

Technology is a major difference between newspapers and TV broadcasting. Although both increasingly are involved with sophisticated technology, the technical component itself intrudes more visibly and significantly in gathering news for television. When a TV reporter collects news, he or she is accompanied by a camera crew with its technical and logistical requirements. A more significant difference is their organization for collecting news. While newspapers use a beat system that encourages topic or area specialization, TV reporters tend to be generalists. For the most part, TV news reporters are dispatched to cover whatever events or situations need attention. There are specialists in sports, weather, and soft features, but the news organization itself does not reflect specialization by topic or area generally. TV reporters on one story may interview the mayor, leaving immediately afterwards to cover a house fire or school board meeting.[115] (See Figure 4-2 on page 111.)

Duties are assigned to specialists. A TV newscast is divided into shooting, film editing, copy writing, graphics creation, etc. This work is supervised and coordinated at higher levels. In this process individuals are organized into interest groups that may be called subcoalitions. These groups have different goals and make conflicting demands. This coalition model seems to apply equally well to nonprofit systems as to commercial concerns (Dimmick, 1979). Although there are assorted ways of looking at what is a complex process, one of the most interesting analogies is provided by Bantz and his associates (1980). They argue that the local TV news organization is best described as a "factory" in which the 6 P.M. newscast is churned out through a five-step process that begins with story ideation and moves through task assignment, gathering and structuring materials, assembly, and presentation (see Figure 4-4). The sequence reflects an assembly-line approach which limits individual involvement in the organization and its product. Such specialization, routinization, and mechanization of TV newswork has four observable consequences: inflexibility, lack of personal investment in the product, evaluation of newswork in terms of productivity, and a mismatch between newsworkers' expectations and the reality of the news factory. "While the popular conceptions of television news usually encompass some image of the glamorous on-the-air news personality, television has an underlying structure little different from any other organization that markets a product," Bantz and his colleagues note.

Five factors encourage routinization of newswork at media organizations: 1) the nature of news staffs—high mobility and specialization following growth in size; 2) technological developments—portable video equipment and microwave transmission, the latter bringing live reporting into reality; 3) the impact of news consultants; 4) considerations of profit—news often makes considerable profit at larger stations and thus rates strong management interest;

Figure 4-3

The News Factory Model

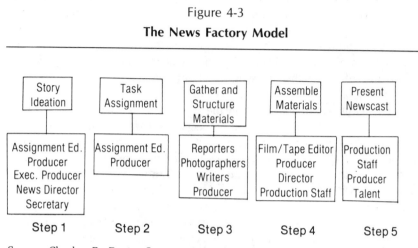

Source: Charles R. Bantz, Suzanne McCorkle and Roberta C. Baade, "The News Factory," *Communication Research* (January, 1980) 7(1): 53.

and 5) demand for a product where technical uniformity, visual sophistication, ease of understanding, a fast pace, and a people orientation are produced in a minimum of time and using the fewest resources.[116]

The factory model divides tasks into chunks or pieces for different reasons than a typical assembly line. The size of the piece is related to the skill of the worker rather than to the amount of time required to perform the task. Thus, an educated, experienced reporter has a larger chunk of the process than does a film editor.

The first step in the assembly line is producing story ideas. Two related activities are involved: 1) individual newsworkers and especially the assignment editor assess information flowing into the newsroom from various sources such as PR releases, other media, phone calls, etc.; and 2) story ideas are examined during the daily story meeting of the assignment person, news director, early evening producer, and executive producer. The story meeting functions as a meeting of management and supervisors to approve the day's work schedule.

Step two is task assignment by the assignment editor, followed by gathering and structuring materials. At its simplest this involves rewriting a wire story but more often involves five related tasks: 1) obtaining any information the assigner had; 2) talking to someone on the phone or in person; 3) going somewhere to gather material; 4) shooting film or tape; and 5) writing copy.[117] In step three, materials are gathered and structured by reporters, photographers, writers, and producers.

Step four is the assembly of materials by constructing individual segments and assembling the segments into a newscast. Assembly of a segment is done by a film/tape editor who edits according to instructions. The producer and director oversee the assembly of the newscast, going over the script, adjusting times, and planning. Step five is presentation of the newscast, the producer remaining involved with the news product throughout the telecast and overseeing the progress of the program—watching time, dropping stories if necessary, informing the newscasters of any new information, etc.

Using the factory model, Snyder (1990) examined three local TV stations' practices in trying to understand how the process affects the visual-verbal match or mismatch, a factor which has an impact on audience comprehension. He found that how to illustrate stories visually was not a concern at the ideation and selection stage, though mention was made that a story was "good" visually. In the second stage, visual treatment received more attention, but reporters were more often left on their own to determine visual treatment. In the next stage, reporters have primary responsibility for visual treatment as actual footage is shot, with both the reporter and camera person involved in selecting visuals. The next stage—actual editing of videotape and scripted narration plus file footage into one package—also is primarily reporter-driven, though the senior tape editor often provides a different perspective on the use of video and often makes his or her own decisions on which shots to use. In the final stage, changes may be made in the visual-verbal match because the newscast is done live and there are technical glitches or other problems. However, in general, reporters have the primary visual input into a story no matter who edits the final piece.[118]

News Management.   Like their colleagues in print media, TV journalists also want more influence over their own work. Local TV news staffs are more satisfied when managers emphasize good relationships as well as accomplishing job tasks (Powers, 1991). A majority of TV news directors see their management style as consultative, with some tending toward participative and a few towards authoritarian (Adams and Fish, 1987).[119] One analysis of a TV station found above average cooperation and moderate role specialization; conflict between departments was the second most common source of problems, following poor communication.[120]

As one moves up the chain of command, TV newsworkers become less critical of their craft (Smith, 1988). A national survey of TV reporters, producers, and news directors found that reporters were more inclined than producers to agree with TV news critics about a variety of items on TV news coverage—that visual hoopla is stressed in campaign stories, that ratings pressures and advice from TV consultants reduce TV news quality, and TV tends to overdramatize news. Some 40% of TV and radio stations have a code of ethics (Wulfemeyer, 1990), which provides standards for employees on such things as accepting free tickets, going undercover for stories, and paying sources for news.

On-Air Broadcast Conventions. TV news innovations were developed in the 1940s and early 1950s by NBC and later picked up by other networks (Karnick, 1988). NBC personnel tried to deal with questions of format, news gathering, and presentation policy. Ratings for the "Camel News Caravan" showed that the public liked the early news format, although critics disagreed. This and other shows were attempts to find a suitable format to present news on TV. They relied heavily on newsreel footage and tended to emphasize news for which such footage was available. NBC expanded the news with bureaus in New York, Chicago, Washington, Cleveland, Los Angeles, Dallas, and San Francisco in the 1940s and 1950s, and efforts were made to establish exchange agreements with newsreel companies in other countries, including the British Broadcasting Corp., Italian radio, and the Soviet government. By 1952, NBC had recruited stringers in thirty-six countries. By the mid-1950s, emphasis shifted more toward pre-planned coverage as the network's own resources grew, and in 1956 Chet Huntley and David Brinkley became the first TV news anchors to become superstars. Media practices continue to change in response to new technologies.

Today, the TV newscast in many Western countries is remarkably similar, but a comparison of TV news interviews in the U.S., Britain, and South Africa also found differences (Cohen, 1989). U.S. newscasts carried the most interviews, the fewest questions on screen, and the most challenging questions, while South African TV had the fewest interviews, the most questions used on air, and the fewest challenging questions. The British TV newscast fell in between on those items. American interviews also were shortest. In TV news interview shows, interviewers interact with advocates and protagonists on various issues. In a study of American TV news programs, three procedures were identified for displaying neutrality in interactions with guests: embedding statements within questions, attributing statements to third parties (the equivalent of attribution in print), and mitigating statements (Clayman, 1988). In British news interviews, a "turn-taking system" operates (Greatbatch, 1988). The public seems to value what they "see" on TV, but those working in broadcast recognize the value of people in roles less visible.[121]

New technologies have affected news-gathering patterns at TV stations. About three-fourths of all U.S. TV stations subscribe to satellite news networks and a significant portion (17% in one survey) have access to SNG (satellite news gathering) vehicles locally (Lacy, Atwater, and Powers, 1988). News directors tend to feel that both satellite news networks and SNG vehicles improve the quality of local and state news coverage and coverage outside of the state. SNG vehicles made new demands on reporters, making them think quickly and do stories which are concise and accurate under more severe time constraints (Cleland and Ostroff, 1988). TV reporters and producers tend to agree on the use of electronic news-gathering technology to go "live" in covering events (Smith and Becker, 1989).

The importance of structure and technology is underlined when different broadcast organizations exhibit similar patterns of news making. One study found the average length of TV network news stories differed only once in nine years analyzed (Riffe et al., 1986). Radio and TV station managers and editors generally agree on such factors as pacing and use of remote reports.[122] The importance of visuals for television news has been found many times (Greenberg et al., 1989; Carroll, 1988). Newscasts in large and small markets are similar in their emphasis on visual stories (Harmon, 1989). A recent study of network TV news found that 78% of the stories used some kind of visual (Foote and Saunders, 1990). Graphics were used to introduce a story 41% of the time or to explain an element of a story 32% of the time; only 14% of the graphics were used as background. Evidence on the importance of visuals and technological imperatives vs. news values is mixed. Harmon (1989) found that the technical abilities of TV as a medium were second in importance in deciding how a story was treated. Traditional news values (for example, prominence, timeliness, proximity) were the major reasons used for selecting or rejecting local TV news stories, while perceived audience interests and competition with other stories also were cited frequently.

Judging Accuracy

Accuracy may be defined to include not only correct or incorrect facts but also what sources consider problems of omission and the accuracy of quotes.[123] In a study of how accurate sources thought local TV news was, Singletary and Lipsky (1977) found that 65% thought the story was "entirely correct" and 31% "generally correct."[124] Comparing tape recordings of interviews and public events with news accounts, Lehrer (1989) found only 2 of 138 sentences with differences in meaning which were "incompatible." Contacts with sources showed that claims to being misquoted were generally reliable. Most of the discrepancies could be explained by short-term memory problems. Reporters who used tape recorders did not produce stories of greater accuracy than those who used notes. Burriss (1985) interviewed sources of articles in national news magazines to check the accuracy of quotes, finding that the only inaccuracy reported was that the quote had been taken out of context; 90% of stories were considered accurate. A study of sources in TV news reports found that the most frequent complaint was that inadequate air time was devoted to the story (38%), followed by the assertion that essential detail was omitted (35%) and the treatment was too sensational (29%) (Moore and Singletary, 1985). Science news has been the focus of numerous studies because of its complexity and the ability to compare specifics reported with original reports of research.[125] Studies of media science coverage show media do a better job of reporting events than of describing context.

Accuracy of specific articles may not be the most appropriate criterion for assessing news accounts (Graber, 1992; Smith, 1989). It's unfair to expect media audiences to be fully informed by single news stories. News accounts over time should be examined. Smith (1989) looked at newspaper and news magazine articles about the 1988 Yellowstone fires and contacted both reporters and sources that represented a wider range of people than just political figures or authoritative figures such as scientists. The error rate was 1.8 per article, more than the .5 typically found in accuracy studies but far less than high rates found by other researchers.[126] Reporters attributed errors to flaws in reporting skills, poor selection of news sources, and complex logistics of covering the story.[127]

Constraints on News-Gathering and News-Making Processes

Many different attempts to "explain" behaviors of media professionals focus on constraints from one source or another. (Shoemaker and Mayfield, 1987).[128] McManus (1988, 1990, 1991) proposes an economic theory of news making in which the probability of an event becoming news is negatively related to the expense of discovering its existence and "assembling it into a news narrative" and positively related to the anticipated intensity of interest among audiences that advertisers will pay to reach. If the news is only a commodity, the production of news at TV stations and news making in general should follow economic logic, with more emphasis on news that costs less to gather. If news follows a public service or professional model as well as being sold for a profit, then journalistic norms and values should influence the selection process. In a study of three local TV stations' discovery efforts, the economic model had more impact than the professional model—inexpensive and passive discovery methods were used much more than more expensive active methods.

More evidence of economic and professional influences is found in a survey of reasons public TV and radio stations do not editorialize (Kleiman, 1987). Some 14% said it would alienate audiences, while 17% said it would hurt the station's funding base; both reasons are examples of constraints from either the general public or others with resources. However, more important reasons were: a lack of resources to prepare editorials (cited by 61%), the belief that it would be ethically wrong (30%) a concern that only limited viewpoints would be aired (23%), and the judgement that editorials make no contribution to understanding issues (23%).

Altschull (1984) argues that media content reflects the views of society's elites, particularly advertisers and business. Evidence of advertisers' influence on media has varied through the years. Pressures have been reported most frequently in the magazine industry,[129] but TV networks also have been criticized for blurring the line between programming and ads. Although newspapers appear to have had a better track record at resisting advertising pressures than magazines. As barriers between newsrooms and advertising departments and other sections of the newspaper fall, journalists also are finding greater pressure (Soley and Craig, 1992).[130] Relying on almost a hundred interviews with news sources in Toronto, Ericson, Baranek, and Chan (1989) conclude that the image of society reflected in the press is shaped not by direct ties between media owners and the local political and economic establishment but by the understanding between reporters and sources on the working level.

Social elites themselves do not form a cohesive body, and other pressures on the media may originate in special interests or ethnic, social, political, or cultural groups. This sometimes leads journalists to self-censor their work (Kurtz, 1991). The threat of legal action by such groups or individuals also is a threat (Bowles, 1990; Hansen and Moore, 1990).[131] Local and national government restrictions take many forms in constraining news gathering. For example, newspapers often have to struggle to distribute the paper, battling with municipalities over placement of vending boxes (Eberhard, 1989).

Although most newspapers and radio and TV stations are "local" media, few observers have looked at the close relationships between community characteristics and media organizations.[132] An exception is the long stream of work by the Minnesota team of Tichenor, Donohue, and Olien (1980). They view the press as a subsystem within a total community system. Local media reflect the larger community. Thus, larger communities are more diverse (pluralistic) and conflict laden, while smaller ones are more homogeneous. Small-town media tend to report less conflict than media in large towns, where editors see themselves in the watchdog tradition (Donohue, Olien, and Tichenor, 1985). The Minnesota team found that changes in community pluralism[133] over two decades were related to conflict reporting. Newspapers in more pluralistic communities devote more space to crime, education, and politics (Donohue, Olien, and Tichenor, 1985; Donohue, Olien, Tichenor, and Demers, 1990). Smith (1987) looked at a single community across time to see whether a growth in population, diversity, and pluralism would lead to more conflict in the media, as Tichenor and his colleagues predicted. He found a steady increase in conflict reporting from 2% of all articles in 1945 to 20% in 1985. Furthermore, the percentage of articles reporting conflict increased for 15 of 17 different topics—from human relations and zoning to agriculture, street maintenance, and education. However, professional norms often are more important than community factors.[134]

In their surveys of more than 150 editors in the upper Midwest, Olien, Tichenor, Donohue, Sandstrom, and McLeod (1990) found that editors, as community elites, favored community planning, but those from more complex, pluralistic communities were more likely to see planning as part of maintaining social order and control more than editors from smaller communities. A comparison of editors from the United States and five European nations found they shared the same general priorities on news and information and priorities in reporting the issues in government, education, and business. However, editors in the United States showed less support for a government watchdog role than did the European editors. European weekly editors were more likely than United States weekly editors to say the local paper is one of the best outlets for getting views of citizen groups to the public, but United States daily editors were more likely than European daily editors to agree to the same statement. United States editors also were more likely than European editors to see their paper helping citizen groups learn what local government is doing (Olien, Tichenor, and Donohue, 1989).

Journalists seek autonomy and control over the news-making process, regardless of the culture or organizational environment in which they operate. A survey of journalists from 22 nations found that those from commercial systems wanted less commercialism while those in paternalistic countries wanted less government involvement (Sparks and Splichal, 1989).

Characteristics, Roles, and Perceptions of Journalists

Journalists and other media professionals are a diverse lot, with differences by organization and role. There also is a hierarchy within mass media. National networks and wire services, large city newspapers, and major film producers all fall into the elite category, while free-lancers and media in smaller towns carry less prestige. What do we know about "media people"?[135]

Distribution by Geography and Medium.   National surveys show that American news journalists are concentrated in two major news centers— Washington, D.C. and New York City, but the distribution of journalists has generally come closer to approximating the distribution of the United States population. While the Northeast had 36% of all journalists in 1971, the figure dropped to 20.9% in 1982, slightly below the percentage of the national population living in that area (Johnstone, Slawski, and Bowman, 1976; Weaver and Wilhoit, 1986). The largest concentration of journalists is in daily newspapers, but the greatest growth has been in weekly papers and the broadcast media.[136] In 1986, a fifth of journalism graduates went into daily newspapers, while 19% went to advertising agencies, 17% public relations, 10% weekly newspapers, 9% television stations, 7% radio stations, 5% commercial magazines, and 12% other media-related jobs (McCombs, 1988).

Age and Gender.   Journalists are generally younger than the U.S. civilian labor force, and the addition of more young people in the past couple of decades has made this feature even more pronounced. In the earlier part of this century, women were welcome in U.S. newsrooms only to work on women's pages, and they were barred from the National Press Club and the Gridiron Club (Beasley, 1988; Eberhard and Meyer, 1988). Discrepancies between women and men in the media also have been found in other countries

(Gallagher, 1990; Lent, 1985; Pollard, 1989; Muramatsu, 1990). The status of women has changed dramatically, and women have increasingly occupied important positions in the media (Lavrakas and Holley, 1989; Ogan, 1983), particularly at weekly papers and in broadcasting.[137] Women also have made some gains in formerly male-dominated assignments in the media, such as war correspondents (Rosenberg, 1991). As women have made advances, some have asked whether gender would redefine news values or change media content (Creedon, 1989). Some case studies suggest that women working in TV often present the story of underdogs in society, identify with the oppressed, have a more practical view of daily life, and are less likely to judge other women by appearances (Muramatsu, 1990). Wide differences between men and women's salaries have been noted in a variety of media areas (Ferguson, 1990; Gallagher, 1990; Kelly, 1989; Lafky, 1989; McMane, 1992), although the relationship between one's gender and earnings is quite complicated (Smith, Fredin, and Ferguson, 1988). Sexual harassment has been noted in both newspapers and TV stations (Duhe and Stone, 1992; Mills, 1988). Bias also has been noted toward gays and lesbians on daily newspapers, although papers were largely hospitable (Aarons, 1990).[138]

Ethnicity and Religion.   In 1991 minority employment in newsrooms had risen to 4,900, comprising 8.7% of the newsroom work force.[139] Colleges and universities also are graduating increasing numbers of minorities (McCombs, 1988; Pease, 1989). Minorities still tend to be poorly represented in upper management (Lavrakas and Holley, 1989)[140] or among owners (Gerard, 1990). Though most minority journalists are satisfied with their jobs, perceived discrimination in promotion and assignment opportunities persists (Pease, 1992; Pease and Stempel, 1990; Regan and Shin, 1988). How does ethnicity affect job performance? In a study of Hispanic journalists, Liebler (1988) concluded that the impact of ethnicity on news gathering was less in more integrated communities. Journalists tend to match the general U.S. population in their religious preferences (Weaver and Wilhoit, 1986; Stinnett, 1989).[141]

Educational Background.   The education level of journalists has grown as younger journalists have joined the profession.[142] Education is highest among those working for wire services (96% college graduates) and news magazines (95.7%). Media elites also have more graduate training (Lichter, Rothman, and Lichter, 1986). Journalism and communication are the major areas of study in college (Fisher, 1978; Stinnett, 1989; Weaver and Wilhoit, 1986). Education for journalists has been subjected to cross pressures between those advocating more training in writing and practical skills and those arguing for a more diverse or theoretical program.[143] Journalism majors fare well above average on national test scores. The United States has tended to rely on colleges for education of journalists, while France and Britain have emphasized on-the-job training, but that is changing as schools of journalism play an increasingly important role in Europe as well (Gaunt, 1988). Self (1988) found that those holding journalism degrees had greater confidence in their profession. Career paths in the media vary (Smith and Becker, 1988; Tharp, 1991).

Political Backgrounds.   There is more political diversity inside newsrooms and across the media than is portrayed by many critics (Kapoor, Cragan, and Groves, 1992). National surveys of the general public and newspaper journalists in 1985 found that a majority of journalists but less than a fourth of the public called themselves liberals (Schneider and Lewis, 1985). Those at the most prestigious media organizations also tend to be more liberal.[144] A national survey of TV journalists found that half described their political philosophy as moderate, while the rest were evenly split between liberal and conservative (Coulson and Macdonald, 1991). General managers and news directors at TV and radio stations are more likely to be middle-of-the-road (58%) than conservative (27%) or liberal (15%) (Lipschultz and Hilt, 1992).[145] Since editorials represent newspapers' opinions, the political backgrounds of editorial writers are particularly noteworthy. Opinion-page editors and publishers at newspapers across the country show a political diversity that is surprising since publishers are expected to appoint opinion-page editors with similar views (Kapoor and Cragan, 1989; Kapoor, Cragan and Cooper, 1990). One survey of newspaper editorial writers found that 50% were liberals, 34% conservatives, and 17% middle-of-the-road (Wilhoit and Drew, 1991).

Looking at trends in party affiliation, we find that 35.5% of journalists were Democrats in 1971, 38.5% in 1982-83, and 44% in 1992. Republicans went from 25.7% in 1971 to 18.8% in 1982-83 and 16% in 1992, and the percentage of independents went from 32.5% in 1971 to 39.1% in the early 1980s.[146] Among editorial writers at daily newspapers, 42.4% were Democrats or leaned toward Democrats in 1979, compared to 53% in 1988, while Republicans went from 34.8% to 29.4% and Independents from 22.8% to 17.6% (Wilhoit and Drew, 1991). Some 17% of general managers and news directors at radio and TV stations were Democrats, 40% Republicans, and 43% Independents or others in one national survey (Lipschultz and Hilt, 1992). Interestingly, journalism also is a route to politics for some people.[147]

Salaries and Compensation.   Journalists' salaries in the 1970s and 1980s failed to keep pace with inflation and lagged behind that for other professionals. Salary level is tied to the size of news organizations, regions of the country, and media sector (Weaver and Wilhoit, 1986).[148] With the growth of "big" media, we see further stratification of journalists, with some making large salaries and others barely surviving at the other end (Hill, 1988; Lichter, Rothman, and Lichter, 1986). In 1990, one poll showed that half of newspaper journalists earn more than $40,000 a year, while only 18% of the public did that year. The president of the American Society of Newspaper Editors said journalists often are too comfortable and part of the establishment, losing touch with their readers. Unionization of journalists has declined, providing reporters with less economic clout in bargaining for higher salaries (Scardino, 1988). In other countries the compensation and general status of journalism varies, often suffering in Third World nations (Masterton, 1989). Salary remains at the bottom of most journalists' list of important job factors in the United States (Weaver and Wilhoit, 1986).

Job Satisfaction. A variety of factors affect job satisfaction—market factors, individual factors, organizational factors, and leadership or management factors (Powers and Lacy, 1992).[149] Five dimensions of satisfaction with work are: prestige, creativity, autonomy, power, and income (DeFleur, 1992). The most important predictors of job satisfaction for younger journalists are esteem for their media organization and positive feedback from supervisors (Weaver and Wilhoit, 1986). A survey of TV journalists in several states found that job satisfaction was linked to beliefs that they were successfully producing a quality news show, that their newsrooms had achieved success in creating a less autocratic and more democratic environment, and a positive relationship with the news director (Powers and Lacy, 1991, 1992). Journalistic prize winners also are generally more satisfied with their jobs than other journalists.[150] Job satisfaction also has been linked to the degree of autonomy for both journalists and public relations practitioners (DeFleur, 1992; Olson, 1989; Rentner and Bissland, 1989). The percentage of black journalists not satisfied with their work is twice the rate of white journalists, although more than 70% indicate satisfaction.[151]

Media People's Media Use and Communication Patterns. Journalists tend to be heavy consumers of print and news media in general. Each week they read an average of 3.5 different newspapers and watch an average of 3.3 TV network news shows and 4.2 local TV news shows (Weaver and Wilhoit, 1986). The number of different papers read is significantly higher for those with some college education and those who majored in journalism in graduate school. The most frequently read newspapers by U.S. journalists are the *New York Times*, the *Wall Street Journal*, and the *Washington Post*. Local and network TV news viewing by journalists was about the same frequency as the general public's.

Most journalists have a fair amount of contact with the public, but a substantial number are isolates. There is concern that a gulf may exist between journalists and their public (Burgoon, Burgoon, Buller, and Atkin, 1987), and journalists are split on whether they should be involved with outside groups and activities, 46% favoring it, 27% being opposed and 27% neutral. However, 62% of journalists report a lot of contact with people of diverse backgrounds, and 75%

have frequent conversations about news with nonjournalists. The younger journalists are more likely to be isolated (Burgoon, Burgoon, Buller, and Atkin, 1987; Gaziano and McGrath (1987). Newspaper journalists strongly endorse knowing many people in the community, but most avoid involvement in community organizations.

Professionalism and Role Perception

The novice reporter for the county weekly newspapers and the network TV anchor may seem to have little in common. One arrives on foot, the other in a limousine. They certainly have different audiences, but both may share the same role perceptions when they confront a public official with probing questions, and both are members of the journalistic profession. Critics from left and right, business and politics, academia and the general public question what roles journalists should attempt to play.

Defining "Professionalism."[152]   News gathering occurs for the most part within organizations. Thus, obligations and control operate at more than one level, and we can look at the professionalism of individuals and organizations.[153] Beam (1990) found professional organizational practices were related to the staff size of newspapers, which underlines the strong effect of financial resources. Merrill (1986) fears that individualism within journalism will slowly disappear with professionalization as reporters abdicate much of their real autonomy to the "collective will of the profession." Defining professionalism as an "ideology," Soloski (1989) argues that it is an efficient and economical method for news organizations to control the behavior of editors and reporters. However, while some note strong links between the organization and its members (Chan and Lee, 1988), another found the organizational structure had little impact on news-making activities (Pollard, 1988).[154]

The Role of Journalist.   Journalists have described their roles and rated the importance of various functions in a variety of studies.[155] Generally at the top of the list is the investigation of claims and statements made by the government (Bridges, 1991), followed by providing analysis and interpretation of complex problems, getting information to the public quickly, discussing national policy as it develops, and staying away from stories whose factual content cannot be verified. The first underlines the significance American journalists attribute to what is usually called their "watchdog function."[156]

The watchdog function itself is often elaborated into subroles. Sigal (1973) identifies several roles that journalists play which are essentially definitions of the relationship between journalists and the government. One is that of "neutral observer" trying to avoid involvement and not taking sides. Second is "participant"—either as an insider connected with government sources and influencing policy by reporting news, or as an outsider by active involvement, making news as well as reporting it. Third is the "good citizen," who tries to weigh interests of the paper, readers, the nation, and various sources in deciding how to write and whether to publish a story. Fourth is the "adversary of the government," a long-established role that includes "gadflies" who persist for years as well as temporary adversaries who confine themselves to specific topics or time periods (Zhu, 1990).[157] Journalists and management often differ on the extent to which their organization actually exercises the option to offend business interests and the powerful.[158] This watchdog function is not limited to Great Britain or the United States, although it is practically restricted to the democracies.[159]

Some journalists are generalists and others specialist, but both are needed for the media to be an independent watchdog of society (Culbertson, 1978).[160] Specialized journalists are harder to control in some cases because they may know more about stories than do their bosses. The journalistic role also is not "singular" and various roles are assumed by journalists—news commentators, on-air personalities, columnists and editorial writers, straight-news reporters and editors, etc.[161]

The role of journalists is constrained by the immediate organization, although this varies.[162] This means journalists must cope with role conflict when presented with incompatible expectations and conflict between demands of art, professional goals, and what is needed for the organization to survive (Biddle, 1986; Curran, 1990; Elliott, 1977). These role conflicts often surface as dilemmas involving distinctions between: high and low culture (sometimes characterized as art vs. popular culture), professional or craft standards and commercial judgment, self-regulation and close bureaucratic control of the work situation, self-motivation and financial inducement, and self-monitoring and serving an audience.[163] The journalist's role in the United States has changed through the years and will continue to evolve.[164]

Newman (1990) invokes Plato's parable of the cave to discuss illusion, public opinion and journalism, and we can extend the parable to include all media. In Plato's cave, the masses spent their lives chained to fixed positions from where they could see only shadows on a wall in front of them. The shadows were created by puppeteers operating behind them. Power inside the cave rests with the Sophists, relativists with no absolute values who used their power to manipulate public opinion. Journalists are the puppeteers in this scenario, creating the illusions that affect the public's perceptions of the world. Newman (1990) expects a lot of journalism and the press, which is "truly free" when it is dominated by free men and women who "draw on moral insight, intellectual skills, and their special gift of communicating clearly and impressively so as to educate their readers about important matters of the day and the relevance of those matters to the higher aims and ideals of a civilized society."[165]

Summary

In this chapter we examined several different media organizations, including film studios, newspaper newsrooms, and television stations. News gathering was separated out from our analysis of individual media. The concepts of "news" and "news values" were discussed, along with evidence of their use and importance. A discussion of news frames followed. Evidence on the news-making process then was presented and tools for gathering news were discussed, including routine channels and initiative reporting. The beat system was analyzed along with prominent sources used by the media, gatekeeping, writing routines, and conventions and constraints from the community and other sources. The final section focused on characteristics and roles of journalists, concluding with a discussion of professionalism.

Chapter Four Footnotes

1. Turner (1990: 87) says a "social role is a comprehensive pattern of behavior and attitudes, constituting a strategy for coping with a recurrent set of situations, which is socially identified— more or less clearly—as an entity." There are four types of social roles: basic roles—age and gender roles; structural status roles—occupation, family, and recreational roles attached to position or organizational settings; functional group roles—such as "mediator," which are not attached to a particular group position or office but which are recognized in the culture; and value roles—traitor, criminal, saint, which implement some value. Also see Biddle (1986).
2. Shoemaker and Reese (1991) describe organizational analysis as an effort to explain variations in output not due to differences in routines and individuals. They ask four questions: What are the organizational roles? How is the organization structured? What are the policies and how are they implemented? How are policies enforced?
3. Many film scripts are adaptations of books rather than original screen plays, but, as Maslin (1992) notes, adaptations vary greatly in their faithfulness to the book.
4. Recently, court decisions allowed the major film producers-distributors to merge and re-enter the exhibition business.
5. In 1988 the majors averaged 143 screens per release while independents averaged 24.5 (Cronin and Litman, 1990).
6. A study reviewing film production from 1984 to 1991 by Paul Kagan Associates, Inc. found that 41% of PG films, grossed more than $20 million in the U.S. while only 36.2% of PG-13 films, 30% of G films and 27.4% of R films achieved that figure. The release of PG films declined steadily over the period studied, going from 43 in 1984 to 25 in 1991, while the release of PG-13 and R films increased, the former from 8 to 37 and the latter from 42 to 78. No more than 10 G films were released in any year. G films are open to all audiences, PG films suggest parental guidance, PG-13 strongly cautions parents regarding possibly objectionable material, and R requires minors under age 17 to have an accompanying adult.
7. They estimated the effects of nominations and awards on movie distribution and revenues using 500 movies from 1975 to 1984. Smith and Smith (1986) looked at successful films across three time periods, finding that the characteristics making films successful have changed over the 40 years studied, but with a continuing impact from receiving an Oscar.
8. An example of advertising pressure on editorial content is found in magazines, where *Healthline* magazine promised potential advertisers editorial content featuring their products. Examples

of alleged advertiser interference were reported to be growing (Lipman, 1991).

9. Women are underrepresented as news executives and photographers. Minorities are more likely to be photographers and news executives than women (Stinnett, 1989). At the national *USA Today*, only 25% of the 338-person news staff covered general news, while 21% were in sports, 16% the "life" section, 15% business, 13% graphics and photography, 6% page one stories, and 4% editorial page.

10. Research by Blankenburg (1989) found support for the view that expenditures for news-editorial departments are sound investments because they are positively related to circulation.

11. As with other industries, unions have lost ground at newspapers and other media. An example is found in the struggle between unions and the management of the *New York Post* in New York City. The newspaper guild accepted a 20% pay cut and lost up to 43 union jobs to keep the paper operating (Goltz, 1990).

12. A study of AP managing editors found that managing editors on larger papers were more involved as managers while those on small papers spent more time on editorial tasks. Most managing editors appeared to have "blank checks" as far as their newsroom role was concerned. About two-thirds of the editors' time was spent on activities not dealing directly with production of the paper (Trayes, 1978).

13. Likert (1961, 1967, 1973) classifies organizations into four increasingly participative systems: 1) exploitive authoritarian; 2) benevolent authoritarian; 3) consultative; and 4) participative.

14. Gaziano and Coulson (1988) found that a plurality of journalists at two papers wanted a moderate amount of guidance from supervisors, while another third wanted little or none. Poor communication, leadership, and planning were cited as the greatest weaknesses of management. Nearly all journalists said their participation in decision making was important in improving the work environment. Joseph (1985) noted that reporter alienation still exists in some newsrooms structured in a hierarchy where management controls most reporter decision making. A survey of journalists at Ohio daily newspapers found 90% affected by stress (Endres, 1988).

15. The highest of nine content standards was strong local coverage, followed by accuracy, good writing, visual appeal, a strong editorial page, community press standards, news interpretation, lack of sensationalism, and comprehensive coverage. Larger papers place higher value on staff enterprise, staff professionalism, comprehensive news coverage, and news interpretation. Editors of smaller papers placed greater value on community leadership and strong local news coverage.

16. The study tried to identify what contributes to excellence at smaller daily papers. High quality papers were the *Jackson* (Tenn.) *Sun*, *Lewiston* (Idaho) *Morning Tribune*, *Worthington* (Minn.) *Globe*, and *Columbia* (Mo.) *Daily Tribune*.

17. Litman and Bridges (1986) found that staff size, subscription to news services, and the amount of space devoted to news were not related to quality performance indicators, though publication of a Sunday edition was significant.

18. A Communication Audit was conducted in newsrooms of 11 daily newspapers (Incitti, 1992). The audit measured participant satisfaction and uncertainty within the communication system (on receiving information, sending information, sources of information, channels of communication, and following up messages). The greatest uncertainty on receiving information from others was for problems faced by management, chances for advancement and organizational policies; the lowest uncertainty concerned job duties. There was relatively little uncertainty about sending messages, though "evaluating the performance of my immediate supervisor" produced a fairly high level of uncertainty. Sources of information producing uncertainty were top management, department meetings, presentations, mid-management, and supervisors.

19. Fowler and Shipman (1984) found that 29 of 34 daily newspaper newsroom managers prefer to use interpersonal communication to communicate in the newsroom. They also regularly

evaluate their personnel and the news product. The newsroom atmosphere—the degree to which people feel free to say what they want—was related to participation in the paper.

20. This is based on a survey of 662 newspaper editors ("Newsroom Ethics: How Tough Is Enforcement?" *Journal of Mass Media Ethics* (Fall/Winter, 1986/1987) 2(1): 7-16). Also see Anderson (1987), who reports that a fourth of managing editors surveyed had codes of ethics posted in their buildings and Anderson and Leigh (1992), who found that 37% of newspapers use the code of the Society of Professional Journalists. Singletary, Caudill, Caudill and White (1990) found most professional journalists and students were concerned with credibility, their personal sense of morality, standards of the field and their employer, and the public's need to know.

21. Some 59% of 200 newspaper and broadcast organizations have formal written statements of policy, many devised in recent years (also see Fridriksson, 1985). McAdams (1986) found that four types of non-monetary conflicts of interest are handled on a case-by-case basis: conflicts involving political ties; conflicts involving family ties; a history of antagonism toward sources; and a history of affinity toward sources. A review of written standards says benefits outweigh possible negative effects ("Standards Governing the News: Their Use, Their Character, and Their Legal Implications," *Iowa Law Review* (March, 1987) 72(3): 637-700).

22. Ettema and Glasser (1987) note that people in this role struggle between conceptions as press critics or public relations practitioners.

23. The ads rejected most often are those for bingo, abortion services, escort services, lotteries, massage parlors, work-at-home opportunities, and X-rated movies. What's rejected varies with the region and local cultures.

24. Hale and Vincent (1986) found in a sample of 21 markets that 2.5% of the programming was locally produced, an average of 3.6 hours per week; the range was from 5.1% in top-ten markets to 1% in the smaller markets.

25. Atwater (1986) found that five factors explained decisions by public TV stations selecting programs for broadcast: audience measures, personal feedback, program strategy, station resources, and intuition. Audience measures were the most important, and the same factors are important for commercial stations. Atkin and Litman (1986) note that the broadcast industry is unique in that consumers express their preference through ratings rather than explicit patronage of market products.

26. Independent producers were pleased with Congress' policy declaration that the Corporation for Public Broadcasting should "encourage the development of programming that involves creative risks and addresses the needs of unserved and under served audiences, particularly children and minorities" (Michaelson, 1988). However, when controversial programs focused on a gay population a couple years later, members of Congress were among the first to object.

27. Cantor (1988) notes that the production process for TV programs and the role of the producer have changed little over the past couple decades, though the influence of women has grown dramatically. Furthermore, current producers are drawn to TV itself rather than seeing themselves as refugees from film, a characteristic of earlier TV producers.

28. Observers often look at particular roles as "creative," but some studies suggest that creativity is more the result of collaboration within limits than a collision between particular roles and restraints (Ettema, 1982; Peters and Cantor, 1982). Shields (1990) looked at music radio announcers (disc jockeys), who often place a premium on creative aspects of their work, finding age and the amount of time one has worked negatively related to creativity measured on a scale.

29. Long shots were emphasized in Japan and medium shots in Germany. Both employed more left-to-right movement in directing the cameras. The Japanese version was cut more rapidly, so the German version had fewer changes of images and a slower tempo. The German producer said their aim was to allow viewers once a day to interrupt the overwhelming flow of information around them and to show different types of gardens, while the Japanese

producer said he hoped to introduce historic gardens and show how the creators "yearned for a lost paradise and searched for a paradise in the future."

30. Tramer and Jeffres (1983) found that 24% of callers to three talk radio shows used the program as a forum; 27% called to chat. The most frequent callers sought companionship.

31. Turow (1984) says the three American TV networks have four major goals in protecting their own creative centers: 1) limiting the influence of various publics, or interest groups; 2) keeping issues out of the public regulatory arena; 3) minimizing the disruptive influence of programming changes made; and 4) deterring other publics from exerting new pressures. An example of the influence by a particular interest group—the medical community—shows that involvement comes at a price. Turow (1989) found that the American Medical Association and other medical organizations attained considerable power over scripts of the TV medical drama, "Medic."

32. The news-reality link is underlined in a study by Erfle and McMillan (1989), who found network news coverage of the oil industry affected by market conditions within the oil industry; thus, media attention varied with changes in the industry.

33. Berkowitz (1990) notes that broadcast journalists say they rely on instincts in deciding what makes a good newscast. Beasley (1989) suggests that current values used to identify news are male-oriented and female journalists may use different values.

34. Adams (1986) shows how the interaction of several news values affects the reporting of natural disasters. TV news coverage was affected by the number of U.S. tourists (social interest and cultural proximity), the severity of the news event, and distance from New York (geographical proximity).

35. See Abbott and Brassfield (1989), Berkowitz (1990), Bridges (1989), Chang and Lee (1990), Chang, Shoemaker, and Brendlinger (1987), Harmon (1989), Logan and Garrison (1983), Luttbeg (1983), Martin (1988), Shapiro and Shofield (1986), Shapiro and Williams (1984), Singer, Endreny, and Glassman (1991). One might expect neighborhood coverage to represent the most proximate news, but Smith (1988) found newspaper coverage was more strongly related to perceived community issues than to neighborhood issues.

36. Also see Berkowitz (1990), Carley (1988), and Sloat (1990).

37. Buddenbaum (1986) found larger churches received more coverage than smaller denominations; Randall, Lee-Sammons, and Hagner (1988) found elite crimes getting more national attention than common ones.

38. Simon, Fico, and Lacy (1989) found that 41% of stories about controversy involved conflict and 45% law enforcement. Also see Ajuonuma (1987) for conflict coverage in Africa, Carragee (1990) for conflict reporting on the Solidarity movement, and McCartney (1987), whose analysis of content in newsmagazines, newspapers, and TV programs found that 58% of conflict stories dealt with conflict between people, 21% conflict with laws and social customs, 4% conflicts with unknown sources, and 4% conflicts with nature.

39. See Driel and Richardson (1988) on media treatment of new religious movements in the 1970s and 1980s as not integral to U.S. society and connected to conflict and Chang, Shoemaker and Brendlinger (1987) on deviance as a factor increasing media coverage of an international event.

40. Shoemaker (1984, 1987) and her colleagues argue that an assessment of deviance underlies many of the indicators of newsworthiness. They find evidence that deviance of world events is a useful predictor of U.S. media coverage of international events. Ericson, Baranek, and Chan (1987) argue that deviance and control are not marginal to society but of central significance and journalism is a process by which journalists provide a "common sense" version of deviance and control processes. Also see Shoemaker, Chang, and Brendlinger (1987) and Shoemaker, Danielian, and Brendlinger (1991).

41. Hayes and Mitchell (1989) found TV news directors emphasizing "stories that affect the viewer." Singer and Endreny (1987) found that media emphasized rare but serious hazards, almost always mentioning actual or potential harm. Greenberg, Sachsman, Sandman, and Salomone

(1988) found that risk calculated by scientists had little to do with the amount of coverage provided by the 3 networks' evening news broadcasts for environmental risk (12 categories, including acid rain, oil releases, water pollution, etc.).

42. The worst performance was on predicting the order of interest in unexpected events.
43. The Gannett chain, for example, relies on extensive polling and focus groups to find out what readers want in their newspapers. Recently, one paper created a roving van of editors, reporters, and photographers that drove to a different neighborhood each week, featuring stories of those residents prominently in the Sunday paper. Stories emphasized neighborhood heroes and haunts. That chain and other papers have reduced emphasis on institutions— city councils, boards, commissions (Reilly, 1991).
44. Also see Stocking and LaMarca (1990).
45. Chang and Lee (1990) found American editors used U.S. involvement and perceived threats to the U.S. as factors elevating the newsworthiness of international events. Trade relations with the U.S. was not as important.
46. Whitney et al. (1989) examined TV network news stories and found the Midwest, Southwest, Middle Atlantic and Mountain regions were under-represented while the Pacific region was most over-represented. More specifically, the top four states in total news time (New York, California, Illinois, and Texas) were all over-covered, largely because they contained major cities that are centers of political, cultural, and economic power.
47. Zelizer (1990) shows how reporters personalized stories on the John F. Kennedy assassination. Coverage of Darwin's evolution theory was personalized and the event orientation of the press was apparent in the *New York Times* coverage from 1860 to 1925 (Caudill, 1987).
48. Chang, Shoemaker and Brendlinger (1987) found potential for social change increased the likelihood an international event would be reported in U.S. media. Harrington (1989) found TV networks giving greater coverage to bad economic news during nonelection years but not during election years.
49. Pasadeos (1984) used two measures of sensationalism to identify an increase in sensational appearance and semantic content of a paper purchased by Rupert Murdoch. Kochersberger (1988) found papers exercising constraint in using photos of a public suicide. Gorney (1992) developed a list of indicators of sensationalism, suggesting it is a continuum. Glynn (1985) notes that both editors and science reporters view sensationalism negatively.
50. Only 12% of the stories on local TV news were shared by local newspaper news in six cities in six different states.
51. Riffe et al. (1986) compared the TV network's newscasts in terms of news mix, finding little difference. Though there are qualitative differences in news treatment, the annual topic mix is comparable, with similar percentages of domestic, First World, Second World, and Third World news.
52. A comparison of newscasts of nine network affiliates in three Texas cities found that the percentage of stories which were unique varied by topic; the highest was for sports (70%), economics/business (61%), human interest (58%), and weather stories (58%); and lowest for fires/accidents (28%), education/schools (31%), crime/courts (38%), and government/politics (38%) (Davie, 1992).
53. Though not on our lists, significance as used here refers to a combination of size, magnitude, and importance.
54. The most frequent pairing Corrigan (1990) found was prominence with vitality-conflict (32.7%), followed by timeliness-prominence (30.2%), timeliness-vitality-conflict (26.2%), significance-prominence (13.6%), and significance-timeliness (15.7%). A national survey of newspaper editors identified these factors as most important for selecting foreign news to run—threats to the U.S. and world peace, timeliness, U.S. involvement, anticipated reader interest, and significant consequences such as loss of lives and property (Chang and Lee, 1992).
55. A comparison of two wire editors/gatekeepers, one in 1949 and another in 1989, found

that the top seven categories of news (those with the most stories) accounted for 85-90% of the news received over the wire services during the two periods; furthermore, the top news categories selected for the newspaper in 1949 (human interest, international politics, and national politics) were the same ones selected four decades later (Bleske, 1991).

56. In Europe, Kepplinger and Kocher (1990) note the changing social values of parliamentary democracies and changing values in journalism as well. Westerstahl and Johanson (1986) found the proportion of negative news stories—accidents, crime, etc.—in the Stockholm press remained fairly constant at 5% from 1912 to 1960, then rose to almost 25% in the period up to 1980, with similar changes in broadcast news. Weibbecker (1989, cited in Kepplinger and Kocher, 1990) found a similar pattern for radio news in West Germany, where negative reports went from 19% in 1955-1959 to 32% in the 1979-1985 period.

57. However, Indian papers focused more on public disorder and less on personal crime than is found in American papers.

58. Canino and Huston (1986) found radio and TV newscasts in Puerto Rico featuring politics most frequently, followed by economics, then violence, health, and sex. Ahmed (1986) found Indian newspapers featuring political news most often, followed by crime, human interest, sports, and religion.

59. We also would expect some differences by papers or medium. One newspaper chain has a program which examines news definition as a central feature ("News 2000," Gannett Newspapers presentation at the annual conference of the Association for Education in Journalism and Mass Communication, Boston, Mass., August, 1991).

60. Norton, Windhauser and Boone (1985) found 240 Mississippi journalists disagreed most strongly in cases that probed philosophical issues, e.g., deciding whether to publish an article about a right-to-life march on an inside news page.

61. Ahmed (1986) found three-fourths of the news hole in an Indian newspaper to be hard news, followed by features, letters, and editorials. Atwater (1984) found that soft news stories are used by broadcast editors to differentiate their local news from those of competing TV stations. Thus, there is an obligation to follow other media in reporting hard news but flexibility in selecting soft news.

62. Michael Zantovsky, press secretary to Czechoslovak president Vaclav Havel, bemoaned the story or event mentality of American journalists. "Stories have a beginning, middle and an end and when the end comes everybody picks up and goes home" ("Refashioning Media's Definitions of News," *Communique* (February, 1991), p. 1; Gannett Foundation Media Center).

63. In the political era, news was presented as the discussion of ideas, in the information era as events, and in the entrepreneurial or business era as dramatic stories, she suggests.

64. Also see: Solomon (1992), Servaes (1991), and Dickson (1992).

65. See: Altheide (1984) and Carragee (1990). Soderlund and Schmitt (1986) analyzed news coverage of the El Salvador civil war in papers from different countries, finding American and Argentine articles used a "cold war orientation" more often than Chilean papers, which depended more on European sources for news. The South American papers portrayed the Salvadorean *junta* and the U.S. positively and were critical of Cuba and Nicaragua, while North American papers were more international in their portrayal and more critical of all parties involved in the war. Comparing 10 Italian and 15 American news broadcasts, Hallin and Mancini (1984) found American TV news placing a premium on individual political leadership, while the process of ideological debate dominated the news on Italian TV.

66. However, he found coverage often used framing devices that denigrated and depoliticized the Greens, labeling them as lost children, idealists, romantics, and quasi-religious zealots who upset political stability. The party's opposition to American foreign policy also was consistently portrayed, leading Carragee (1990: 25) to conclude that, while "sweeping assessments concerning the ideological consistency of American news media coverage of

alternative parties or movements are likely to be misguided, [the] hegemonic framing of foreign alternative political parties or movements becomes most evident when these parties or movements directly challenge American foreign policy interests."

67. Schiff (1991: 16) concludes that decisions about news content seem "to reflect and reproduce a dominant corporate capitalist ideology in determining the makeup of paper as a whole but not in their choices of news play." Meyers (1990) looked at a Midwest daily paper's coverage of a farm crisis, finding that 59% of the articles reflected free trade ideology and 29% supply management ideology. Also see: Kapoor, Cragan, and Cooper (1990) and Kanso and Nelson (1992).

68. All professional encoders use parts to stand for the whole, whether they be journalists or scriptwriters for TV sitcoms. Zelizer (1990) refers to the "synecdoche," a narrative strategy in which the part stands in for the whole. The technique is similar to use of symbols and metaphors to make the abstract concrete or the situation more understandable.

69. Salwen and Bernstein (1986) found that Detroit papers covering civil disturbances in that city contained more favorable assertions than did nonlocal prestige papers covering the same events.

70. A survey of journalism students in 22 nations found diversity in the significance of the concept; objectivity was rated as an important journalistic quality by 56% of U.S. and Canadian students, 27% of those in Japan and only 9% of those in Peru and Brazil (Walker, 1991).

71. Though some suggest the debate over objectivity has ended (Hage et al., 1983), such an announcement may be a bit premature. McQuail (1986) suggests abolishing the rigid dichotomy between "objectivity" and "bias" as being counterproductive, and Hackett (1984) suggests that researchers make objectivity and bias the objects of investigation rather than dismiss them.

72. Pritchard and Morgan (1989) found no support in a survey of reporters at two Indianapolis papers for the view that ethics codes would directly influence the decisions journalists make.

73. McManus (1991) found that 20 of 34 stories broadcast by three TV stations failed to meet one or more norms of journalistic objectivity.

74. Reese (1990) examines the reactions of journalists to A. Kent MacDougall's disclosure that he had consciously sought to advance radical views while a reporter for the *Wall Street Journal* and the *Los Angeles Times*. Reese notes that MacDougall's disclosure violated journalistic views about what was appropriate behavior and resulted in reassertions of journalistic routines (editing, citations, etc.) as well as efforts to minimize MacDougall and his message. Another distinction centers around whether objectivity refers to any particular "relationship." Do we determine intentions by comparing performance with others, with one's past record, or with some external measure? How do we do this?

75. The whole of Canon 5 is: "Impartiality—Sound practice makes clear distinction between news reports and expressions of opinion. News reports should be free from opinion or bias of any kind. This rule does not apply to so-called special articles unmistakably devoted to advocacy or characterized by a signature authorizing the writer's own conclusions and interpretations."

76. In 1943, AP general manager Kent Cooper proclaimed that objective news was the "highest original moral concept ever developed in America and given to the world." In 1969 critic Andrew Kopkind argued that "objectivity is the rationalization for moral disengagement, the classic cop-out from choice making."

77. Culbertson and Somerick (1976) found that almost 85% of those surveyed knew what quotation marks were designed to tell. Almost 40% said they notice bylines, which essentially attribute the article to a particular reporter.

78. The remainder reported unsuccessful attempts to contact both sides (Fico, Simon, and Lacy, 1991)

79. Hagen (1992) looked at bias of leading German newspapers in coverage of a controversial issue, finding that arguments which agreed with the newspaper's editorial position were favored for publication.

80. Staab (1990) notes the theoretical difficulty in defining the boundaries of an "event."
81. In Carter's view the observation function is achieved when the five Ws + H (Who, What, When, Where, Why, and How) questions have been answered. The description function is achieved when the most important value is placed first, the second most important second, etc. This is the "inverted pyramid" style of writing.
82. "Because news concentrates on describing signals rather than analyzing their significance, a reporter and a scholar examining the same events are usually concerned with different data," Roshco (l975) notes.
83. British journalists approve of using personal documents without permission and making payments for confidential information; in contrast, American and German journalists disagree with such actions (Kepplinger and Kocher, 1990; Kocher, 1986).
84. In general, the more integrated one is into the journalism profession, the more one is aware and concerned about the impact of source-initiated news (Berkowitz, 1991).
85. His study of a small daily paper's local news found that the seven most common channels used in by-line stories were official proceedings (31%), non-spontaneous events (21%), interviews (21%), background briefings (18%), reporters' analysis (5%), news conferences (2%), and spontaneous events (2%). Using Sigal's categorization of news channels, 53% of the stories in the paper came from routine channels, 19% from informal channels, and 28% from enterprise channels.
86. See Berkowitz (1987), Fico, Atwater and Wicks (1985), Ramaprasad (1991), and Hackett (1985).
87. Local city releases were discarded less often (64%) than state (86%) or national (93%) releases. And only 57% of releases about planned events were discarded, while 87% of informative material was discarded. Thus, journalists use releases as starting points to consider stories but not as background material.
88. Others, in order of importance, were: general assignment, police-crime, state government-politics, courts, social issues, science-medical-technology, arts-entertainment, national government-politics, and religion.
89. UPI correspondent Helen Thomas notes that there are fewer than a dozen reporters at the White House all day, though there are large numbers at daily briefings (Kiesel et al., 1978).
90. Studies of daily newspaper editors show them using fewer names and addresses in identifying crime victims, with most favoring increased attention to privacy rights over the public's right to know (Wolf, Thomason, and LaRocque, 1987; Thomason and LaRocque (1990, 1991). While 70% of victim advocates' representatives think broadcasters should contact victims and seek their opinions in crime story coverage, only 36% of news directors feel that way. Some 62% of victim advocates and 31% of news directors think TV is less sensitive than other media to victim privacy.
91. Burnham (1990) notes changes in the environmental beat and science over three decades, from Rachel Carson's classic book *Silent Spring*, to the 1970 media event, Earth Day, to anti-environmental policies in the Reagan administration, to a sense of globalism today. Burnham notes that "environmentalism, it turns out, works into the media world particularly well. Once the basic idea developed that every event is related to every other event by ecological links in 'the chain of life,' all other science became facts" (p. 33).
92. Sportswriters regard their work as creative and tend to like their jobs but feel they are tested ethically more often than other reporters (McCleneghan, 1990).
93. Radio stations broadcast more than 300,000 hours of sports annually and more than 1,500 hours of sports are televised by the three major networks each year, with an additional 5,000 hours provided by cable TV (Bailey and Sage, 1988).
94. Only the *New York Times* had a science section in 1978 but 66 had weekly science sections by 1986 and 80 more had started shorter science pages.
95. A survey of the religion beat at daily papers found that only 25% worked full-time covering

religion. Coverage at three major dailies focuses primarily on Christian religious topics, while the *New York Times* religious coverage stresses conflict and change rather than routine coverage of churches and events.

96. Wilhoit and Drew (1989) found that 47% of editorial writers felt they were similar to their publishers on most issues while 32.8% said they agreed half the time, 11% felt they were similar on only a few issues and 4.4% said they were unlike the publisher on most issues.

97. Source selection often depends on the channel used to communicate information. Because of TV's greater focus on visual activity, broadcast journalists place greater emphasis on visibility and activity (Fico, 1984). Atwater and Fico (1986) found that state house broadcast reporters relied on activity sources—those associated with floor action, etc.—while print reporters relied on personal or print sources—agency experts, legislative leaders, and the paper's morgue.

98. Hornig, Walters, and Templin (1991) found that government sources dominated over scientific and technical experts in reporting on natural disasters.

99. See Sigal (1973) and Hess (1986). Squire (1988) found that national news media focus on senators who seem to wield institutional power.

100. Hackett (1985) found 52% of news stories in a sample of Canadian TV news originated from government politicians or representatives.

101. See Kuklinski and Sigelman (1992), Seo (1989) and Soley (1990). Soloski (1989) studied a small daily paper's news sources, finding that 56% of the stories relied on elected or appointed governmental officials as the primary source. Kuklinski and Sigelman found that Republicans and Senate leaders received more coverage on TV network news. They found no evidence that network news programs favored presidential critics over supporters during the period examined.

102. See Endres (1985), Hansen, Ward, and McLeod (1987), Jacobson (1989), Jacobson and Ullman (1989), Kerr and Niebauer (1987), and Ward and Hansen (1986, 1991).

103. See Dunwoody and Ryan (1985), Fico (1984, 1985), and Shields and Dunwoody (1986).

104. See Davison (1975), Feldman (1985), Lipschultz (1991), Miller (1978).

105. A recent case has underlined the sensitive nature of this relationship (Bunker and Splichal, 1992). In *Cohen v. Cowles Media Co.* (1991), the Supreme Court said the First Amendment does not preclude states from treating reporters the same as any other person who makes a promise that can be enforced as a contract. The case involved an oral agreement by a reporter for a Minnesota newspaper not to identify the source of information about old misdemeanor charges against a state political candidate. The editor forced the reporter to disclose the name in print, causing the source to lose his job.

106. For more on the growing importance of public relations and relationships with journalists see: Aronoff (1975), Habermann, Kopenbauer, and Martinson (1988), Kleinfield (1989), Kopenhaver, Martinson, and Ryan (1984), Neuwirth, Liebler, Dunwoody, and Riddle (1988), Turk (1985). Public relations efforts may fit naturally with other factors determining media attention rather than distorting what would occur otherwise; Dionisopoulos and Crable (1988), Stocking (1985).

107. Schudson (1989) proposes other perspectives from sociology.

108. The earliest work here examined values of editors who selected and edited stories submitted by reporters or wire services. See Buckalew (1968-69), McCombs and Shaw (1976), Snider (1967), and White (1950).

109. Two earlier studies found considerable difference between newspapers in the proportion of space devoted to 11 categories of news (Deutschmann, 1959; Stempel, 1962).

110. Abbott and Brassfield (1989) found both TV and print gatekeepers emphasizing localness as the major selection criterion for using news releases; however, initial newspaper gatekeepers frequently re-routed releases to a second gatekeeper for the final decision, whereas the initial gatekeeper made the final decision for television.

111. Three dimensions explain editors' ratings of reporters' specific writing skills in one study of

reporters and editors—writing mechanics (spelling, grammar, punctuation, knowledge of journalistic style), expressive abilities (liveliness, writing style, ease with language, word usage), and journalistic abilities (preparing good copy under time and other journalistic constraints, conciseness, speed, clarity, organization, and self-editing).

112. Reporter motivation and editor-reporter rapport are major contributors to good writing, while newsroom procedures and deadline pressures are major obstacles (Coulson and Gaziano, 1989).

113. Berner (1986) argues that traditional inverted pyramid and objective story forms are no more truthful than literary journalism, which may more accurately represent reality. Literary form employs techniques of narration and scene, summary and process, point of view, drama, chronological organization, rhythm, imagery, foreshadowing, and metaphor. Roch (1989) argues that news stories are narratives, more like than unlike other narratives.

114. See Lemert (1984) and Stanfield and Lemert (1987). Rossow and Dunwoody (1991) found that only a fourth of the opportunities in covering a nuclear waste site controversy provided sufficiently complete information for readers to act immediately. More of such information was included in less pluralistic communities. Leftist magazines include more of such information than conservative or mainstream news magazines (Lemert and Ashman, 1983).

115. The difference in structure may account for a greater reliance on "assigned stories" than enterprise reporting among broadcast journalists. Wickham (1989) found that the bulk of story ideas at one station were generated by middle management employees such as the assignment editor rather than reporters.

116. Newscasts vary based on station size and the amount of resources available. Bernstein, Lacy, Cassara, and Lau (1990) found larger TV stations devote less news space to local news and more to national and world events than did smaller stations, while Carroll (1985) found that small TV stations depend more on anticipated news and preplanned events. Both of these may be tied to the amount of resources available.

117. Hayes and Mitchell (1989) found TV news directors rated effective writing and anchors who were journalists as the most important criteria for quality in local newscasts.

118. Interviews with newsworkers found that most felt viewers could "get the point" of a story even if the narration and video did not match, which contradicts message-processing findings (Snyder, 1990). Berkowitz's (1990) analysis of local TV newscasts found that decision making was a group process shaped by group dynamics and not controlled by a single person.

119. Patterns of interpersonal communication are important in managing creative people in any organization. Owens and Infante (1988) looked at TV directors and how production crew members regarded their communication in routine situations. Time pressures can be extreme, there often is inadequate rehearsal time, and the expected pace is harried (Blumenthal, 1987; Hilliard, 1978; Kindem, 1987; Owens and Infante, 1988).

120. Allen et al. (1988) used multiple methods to analyze the activities of a TV network affiliate. More than half of employees said there was little participation in making decisions, and all employees wanted more influence over their own work.

121. TV news anchors surveyed identified the news director as most important, followed by anchor, reporter, writer, sportscaster, and weathercaster. They predicted that the public would name the anchor first, followed by the weathercaster, sportscaster, news reporter, director and, lastly, the writer (Ferri, 1989).

122. They disagree on how to get audience information. Radio editors surveyed had a negative reaction to audience feedback (Hewitt and Houlberg, 1986). Regardless of market size, TV stations get about the same volume of audience complaints, which focus on program scheduling, not on the quality of TV programs (Smith and Kapoor, 1985).

123. In an international survey of journalism students, accuracy was deemed an important journalistic quality by 51% of U.S. and Canadian journalism students, 28.6% of Peruvian and Brazilian students, 15.3% of Japanese students and 14% of those in Bulgaria, Poland

and Yugoslavia (Walker, 1991). Edwards and White (1992) conducted a small study of journalism students' language skills and right v. left brain dominance. When brain dominance and media were better "matched" (right-dominant and nonprint news media users or left-dominant and print users), there was more accuracy on such editing skills as identifying misspelled words.

124. Some 78% who noticed an error found only one, and 63% of the errors were what the researchers called "objective," e.g., wrong time, identification, description, etc., while 37% were "subjective," e.g., misleading statements.

125. See: Dunwoody (1980, 1983), McCall (1988), Long (1992), Long et al. (1991), Molitor (1991), Moore and Singletary (1985), Singer (1990), and Weiss (1985).

126. Some 69 of the 146 news sources described one or more kinds of errors they had seen in general media coverage of the fires and 45% of the errors referred to types of hype, sensationalism, or exaggeration of the effects of the fires. Some 46 of 68 reporters also described errors they had seen in news coverage of the fires, and half were basic factual errors.

127. Looking at sources and journalists' assessments of stories on environmental risk, Salomone, Greenberg, Sandman, and Sachsman (1990) found scientists and representatives of industry and government to be more interested in supporting the status quo than journalists and advocates are in undermining it.

128. They cite five theoretical explanations for what becomes news—the view that content reflects social reality with little or no distortion, the notion that content is a function of news-gathering routines, the view that personal biases and backgrounds of journalists are factors, and the view that content results from social and institutional pressures both in and outside media organizations.

129. A survey of 50 popular American consumer magazine editors found that 78% claimed that giving favorable coverage to advertisers in exchange for purchasing advertising was not allowed. Pressure from the business office was noted by 49%, while another 49% said they had complete autonomy (Hesterman, 1987). Another survey of journalists in the business press found more than a third said advertising intruded on editorial content (Endres, 1988). Weis and Burke (1986) suggest that the importance of advertising by the tobacco industry in magazines has affected their willingness to convey the health hazards of smoking.

130. They found 90% of daily newspaper editors in a national survey said they had been pressured by advertisers because of the type and content of stories carried by the paper.

131. Journalists have lived with the threat of libel for generations (Miraldi, 1988). Unfavorable lawsuits may have a "chilling effect" on news reporting in some situations (Labunski and Pavlik, 1985, 1986) but not others (Bow and Silver, 1984).

132. Much of the work analyzing political and cultural constraints on the media operate at the national level (See, for example, Herman and Chomsky, 1988).

133. Structural pluralism was measured by an index of the proportion of labor force outside agriculture, per capita income, community population, and the county population. They surveyed editors and content-analyzed the newspapers of 78 Minnesota communities in 1965 and 1985.

134. They found several news-making decisions unaffected by community pluralism, including editors' perceptions of their papers' most important news sources (Donohue, Olien, Tichenor, and Demers, 1990), perceptions of community constraints on publication of negative information or problems of news selection and display (Donohue, Olien, and Tichenor, 1989). Pritchard and Berkowitz (1991) found that letters to the editor influence editors to write about particular issues.

135. Our earliest evidence is found in a profile of Chicago journalists at the turn of the century. Journalists were overwhelmingly male (93.6%) and a fifth were born outside the U.S. Incomes varied widely, and only 7.8% owned their own home, but 9.2% had servants in their homes. They were a fairly mobile group. They also tended to live in neighborhoods populated

by people working in service-oriented occupations rather than by industrial workers (Green, Lacy, and Fokerts, 1988).

136. Considerable research describes the backgrounds of specific media roles, including film critics (Wyatt and Badget, 1988), journalists covering the religion beat (Buddenbaum, 1988), editorial cartoonists (Riffe, Sneed, and Ommeren, 1985), editorial writers (Wilhoit and Drew, 1989, 1991), graphics editors (Kelly, 1990), music critics (Wyatt and Hull, 1990), investigative journalists (Dillon and Newton, 1992), and public relations practitioners (Nayman, McKee, and Lattimore, 1977).

137. See: Beasley and Theus (1988), Cramer (1989), Ferguson (1990), Ferri and Keller (1986), Gallagher (1990), Harwood (1984), Hastings (1990), McCombs (1988), McMane (1992), Puig (1991), and Stone (1988).

138. Almost two-thirds were male and 76% were 40 or younger. Their job categories included reporter (41%), supervisor (26%), and editor (23%). Three-fourths rated their papers' coverage of AIDS as good to excellent, but coverage of gay or lesbian lifestyles, civil rights issues, community events, and violence against gays received poor or fair ratings from 75% to 80%. Bernt and Greenwald (1991) compared responses of these gay journalists with those of senior editors in a national study, finding editors generally believing that their papers' coverage of gay issues was more favorable than that seen by gay journalists.

139. "Editors' Survey Shows Increase in Number of Minority Journalists," *AAJA Newsletter* (Summer, 1991), p. 12. Asian American Journalists Association. Data represent annual survey of the American Society of Newspaper Editors. Figures vary, depending on what jobs are included. Also see Weaver and Wilhoit (1986), Stinnett (1989), and Haws (1991). For more on minorities in broadcasting see Downing (1990), Schultz (1988), Stone (1987, 1988), and Weaver, Drew and Wilhoit (1987).

140. "Surveys Show Employment Gains," *Minorities in the Newspaper Business* (May/June, 1987) 3(3): 6.

141. Among daily newspaper journalists in 1988, 42% were Protestant Christians, 27% Catholic Christians, 4% Jewish, 9% other religious beliefs, and 18% agnostics/nonbelievers (Stinnett, 1989). A study of 238 media elites at TV networks or national news organizations found them distinctly nonreligious, with 86% seldom or never attending religious services (Lichter, Rothman, and Lichter, 1986).

142. Some 85% of all entry-level newspaper journalists came directly from journalism schools or departments of communication (Dennis, 1988).

143. See Abel and Jacobs (1975), Becker, Fruit, and Caudill (1987), Dennis (1988), and Weaver and Wilhoit (1989).

144. A survey of 238 elite, high-level working journalists at the TV networks of New York/Washington news organizations, found 54% describing themselves as liberal and 17% conservative (Lichter, Rothman, and Lichter, 1986).

145. The managers and news directors thought that 63% of the community would be conservative, 22% middle-of-the-road, and 15% liberal.

146. A breakdown of partisanship by medium shows that 36% of TV journalists said they were Democrats, 22% Republicans, 41% Independents, and 1% others. For radio journalists, 30% were Democrats, 30% Republicans, 38% Independents, and 2% others; for daily newspaper journalists, 41% were Democrats, 17% Republicans, 40% Independents, and 2% other. Several sources report these data (Weaver and Wilhoit, 1986; Weaver, Drew, and Wilhoit, 1987; Weaver and Wilhoit replicated the earlier surveys in a telephone survey of U.S. journalists conducted June 12-Sept. 12, 1992 ("Survey Finds Journalists Tend To Be Democrats," *Plain Dealer*, Nov. 26, 1992, p. 1E). Also see Stinnett (1989), who found that nearly two-thirds of daily newspaper journalists surveyed in 1988 defined themselves as Democrats or liberals or leaning in that direction, while 22% were conservatives or Republicans or leaned that direction, and 17% were independents.

147. People go from journalism to politics and vice-versa. In the 101st Congress, 248 of the senators and representatives were lawyers, while 166 came from business or banking, and 114 from public service or politics, but 25 came from journalism ("101st Congress," data from the *Congressional Quarterly* and Senate Library). Kessler (1989) found that most dissident, leftist journalists examined from the 1960s felt loyalty to the politics and the movement but not to the profession of journalism. Most retained the leftist tilt to their politics, and most managed to integrate the countercultural values into their current jobs and lives.
148. Salary discrepancies also are noted on the basis of gender and race (Bielby and Bielby, 1987).
149. In 1972 49% of journalists said they were very satisfied with their job and 39% fairly satisfied, but in 1982-83 40% were very satisfied and 44% fairly satisfied (Weaver and Wilhoit, 1986).
150. See: Beam, Dunwoody, and Kosicki (1986), Coulson (1989), and Ha (1992).
151. Bramlett-Solomon's (1992) national survey of black journalists found they were more satisfied if they felt their organizations were doing a good job of informing the public and if they received positive feedback from superiors.
152. See Parsons (1957: 381) for the purpose of professionalism. In 1988, a judge ruled that 13 editors and reporters working for the *Washington Post* could not earn overtime because they were professionals who "produce original and creative writing," have "far more than the general intelligence," are "thoroughly trained before employment," and write in an "individual, interpretive and analytical" way (Crossen, 1988).
153. Beam (1990) summarizes the various traditions for examining professionalism. The phenomenological approach looks at how journalists themselves invoke the term in daily usage. Second is the trait approach, which looks for a professional orientation among journalists and develops scales for measuring them; Henningham (1984) notes three different scales for identifying people high and low in professionalism. A third approach is power-relations, which emphasizes the exercise of power by the professional, the client or consumer, colleagues, and third parties such as regulators.
154. An instrument developed by McLeod and Hawley (1964) has been used to show that professional journalists generally are more concerned with ethical standards, are more educated, are more critical of their own employer, are more independent on the job, are less likely to take a nonjournalism job, and are less concerned with money and prestige (Idsvoog and Hoyt, 1977). Merrill's (1974) social responsibility philosophy argues for an autonomous, individualistic inner-directed model of the professional journalist. Culbertson (1983) found newspaper journalists could be characterized as falling into three distinct clusters consistent with the classic Johnstone et al. (1976) study and other research: traditionalists (who emphasize local and spot news and downgrade interpretative and national-international material), interpreters (who are somewhat inclined to downgrade local news and to upgrade national material), and activists (who are more cause-oriented). Journalists' values may be common to modern Western democracies (Henningham, 1984), but differences also have been found. See Henningham (1984), Kang (1987), Pollard (1985), Ruofolo (1987), Self (1988), (Shamir, 1988).
155. See Dicken-Garcia (1989) for an assessment of journalistic standards in 19th century America.
156. A survey of Minnesota reporters found the majority divided between "interpretive" and "traditional" reporter roles, with a small minority choosing an "advocacy" role (Ismach and Dennis, 1978). Weaver and Wilhoit (1986) found that about half of journalists saw themselves in an information-dissemination role similar to a "neutral" role. In 1982-83, 62% fit into the "interpretive" role and 17% in an "adversary" role (Weaver and Wilhoit, 1986). Dillon (1990) found that communication college majors also could be divided into adversary, interpreter, and disseminator types. In Great Britain, 57% of British journalists feel their role in society is that of an informant, while about a quarter feel their job is to entertain, and a fifth to mediate between individuals and social institutions (Osiel, 1986). One survey found that more educated people in the U.S. were less likely to support either a "watchdog"

role or "consensus" role for the media (Griswold, 1988).

157. In 1983, 26% thought it was extremely important and 21.6% quite important that journalists reflect an adversarial relationship with public officials; those percentages were 19.5% and 30.7%, respectively, in 1988. And 39% thought it was quite or extremely important to be adversaries of business in 1983, while 40.7% felt that way in 1988.

158. While 68% of non-management (TV journalists) felt their stations covered stories that offend advertisers and other business interests in the community, 77% of management agreed in one survey of news directors of network TV affiliates (Coulson and Macdonald, 1992).

159. Tichenor, Donohue, and Olien (1988) found the watchdog role stronger among editors of both weekly and daily papers in Europe than in the U.S. In Holland, a critic argues that the main thrust of the muckraking journalist should be in awakening a pervasive distrust among the populace, one which sharpens people's perception of social reality.

160. "The specialist's knowledge of rules of evidence and the implications of data can aid sensitivity. The generalist's insistence on clarity can help understandability." Generalists apparently are preferred because they can write in lay language, express themselves briefly, and avoid cooptation by the technical specialities which they must cover.

161. Breiner (1988) examined how TV news commentators fulfill controversial roles during periods of instability in government. Interviews with David Brinkley, Harry Reasoner, Eric Severeid, and Howard K. Smith found differences in role perceptions. Possibilities discussed were: explaining the cause, making predictions, exploring repercussions, reflecting on the press, taking the pulse, explicitly advocating courses of action, and criticizing government without explicitly advocating directions. Garrison and Salwen (1989) found that sports journalists increasingly exhibit the same traits and assume the same values as other journalists.

162. The British Broadcasting Company, for example, rejected the informality and personality in American broadcasting, emphasizing a "collective personality" instead (Kumar, 1975).

163. Laliberte (1976) notes the journalist is a specialized professional with neither more nor less freedom than other professionals. He also argues that the more internal pluralism and professional autonomy there appears to be in the press, the more likely journalists will conform to prevailing social views. Rothenbuhler (1985) found that personnel in the popular music industry were more sensitive to national industry-wide criteria than they were to local contingencies.

164. The rise of the popular press and the distribution of information to everyone challenged the right of the mercantile elite to continue its political control. Thus, journalists perceived the public as a group to be protected as opposed to a group of peers. Professional journalists tended to accept the idea that professionals are more qualified than their audience to determine the audiences' own interests and needs. After World War I, professionals argued that their impartial methods guaranteed a fair assessment of occurrences, and, thus, guaranteed free speech (Turner, 1990).

165. In another view, May (1986) says that journalism has no body of knowledge serving as a basis of authority and no ancient traditions and does not serve individual clients like other professions.

5

The Audience
Who's Paying Attention?

I. How big a slice do media take?
   A. Introduction—relative constancy theory
   B. Leisure-time activities
   C. Time use—"time budgets"
   D. Television
   E. Use of new media technologies—cable, VCRs
      1. Cable television
      2. Video Cassette Recorders
      3. Other technologies
   F. Newspapers
   G. Radio—drive time
   H. Films
   I. Books and magazines
   J. Daily media diets and news diets—dependence
II. Media use over the life span—life cycle and life span concepts
   A. Childhood media behaviors
   B. Adolescent media behaviors
   C. Adulthood—a sequence of eras
III. Media orientations: What do people think about the media?
   A. Content preferences
      1. News
      2. Newspapers
      3. Television
      4. Cable and public access
      5. Radio and music
      6. Films
   B. Perceptions about TV and film
   C. Perceptions about media technologies
   D. Perceptions about print media
   E. Perceptions of commercials and advertising
   F. Perceptions of media influence
   G. Perceptions of media as a whole
      1. Confidence in the media as an institution
      2. Media as sources of information
      3. Perceptions of media practices
      4. Public support for the First Amendment
      5. Media credibility
      6. Summarizing the audience's media orientations
   H. International Comparisons
      1. Media use
      2. Media orientations
IV. Summary

T
he mass media take a big slice of our daily lives—in many cases, more than any other activity except sleeping. Today, the media account for half of our free time, and their importance has grown as people's leisure time has expanded. Most Americans spend the bulk of their leisure hours inside their homes and almost half of this time is spent either watching TV, listening to the radio, or reading a newspaper or magazine. TV viewing itself is the favorite leisure activity of more than 40% of U.S. adults. Most Americans spend at least two to three hours a day in front of a TV set, though their attention certainly varies.

Most media consumption is viewed as a leisure activity, but entertainment is only one reason for media's prominence in people's lives. Mass communication behaviors are both expressive (reflecting personal leisure needs) and instrumental (means to productive ends). It is this multifaceted nature of mass media that probably accounts for their large, diverse audiences.

How Big a Slice Do Media Take?

Despite a rapidly changing media environment and constant changes in people's media behaviors, media may attract a fixed share of our economic resources. We introduced McComb's (1972) **relative constancy theory** in chapter 2. According to the theory, spending for media tends to be a constant proportion of economic activity, and new media attract spending from existing media.[1] If people spend only a fixed percentage of their income for media, then the introduction of new technology, such as interactive computer programs, would divert expenditures from existing sources such as cable or network television. Attempts to test the theory have had mixed results. Fullerton's work (mentioned in chapter 2) found that the introduction of TV in the United States did divert resources from other media during that period.[2] However, a European study found no such exchange of dollars when VCRs were introduced in the 1980s (Roe and Johnsson-Smaragdi, 1987). Tradeoffs are undoubtedly more complicated than initially thought. We might find that the amount of money people devote to media fluctuates relatively little over time, but the amount of time individuals devote to a specific medium varies because of factors associated with aging, lifestyle, and the environment.

Leisure-Time Activities

Virtually everyone today has at least some "free time," but this was not always the case. Leisure time resulted from political and social struggles to reduce working time (Pronovost, 1989). People's attitudes toward leisure also have changed, moving from an image of leisure as a waste or hindrance to a view of leisure as positive and central to the economy and culture.[3] We are now at the end of what one observer called the "Golden Age of Leisure." Since the Industrial Revolution in the 18th and 19th centuries, there had been a steady increase in leisure hours until the past two or three decades, when it began to stabilize.

While the amount of time devoted to one's job has declined from 47% of the day in 1850 to 30% in the 1990s, the amount of "committed time" devoted to household tasks and child care went up from 10% in 1850 to 23% in 1960 and 25% in the 1990s. "Necessary time" for sleeping, personal care, etc. remained at about 38%, as discretionary time—time spent in leisure pursuits—went from 5% in 1850 to 15% in 1960 and 7% in the 1990s.[4]

How much free time do we have?[5] Estimates depend on how people define "free" or "leisure" time (Foxall, 1984).[6] One definition is an "attitude or state of mind in which the individual" believes that he or she is pursuing an activity for personal reasons rather than as a result of external coercion (Howe and Rancourt, 1990; Tinsley and Tinsley, 1982). People's leisure behaviors can be distinguished from other behaviors on the basis of several criteria, with almost universal agreement that a perception of freedom and choice is the critical regulator of what becomes leisure and what does not.[7] Leisure offers rich opportunities for developing personal satisfaction; thus leisure activities are important for the quality of people's lives (Kelly, 1983).[8] Frey and Dickens (1990) argue that leisure has become a primary institution in contemporary advanced societies because of its organized nature and significance for those searching for social bonds or a sense of community.[9]

Time Use

Survey researchers use time budgets to see how people distribute their activities throughout the day (Andorka, 1987). The diary method, in which people describe all of their activities from midnight to midnight for a particular 24-hour day, is one means of measuring the distribution. Using this information to estimate a week's activities, Robinson (1977, 1989, 1990) found that people had 39–40 hours "free" each week, which represents about 23% of the week's 168 hours. The rest of the week breaks down like this: 31.6% sleeping; 19.2% working for pay; 7.4% family care; 7.8% housework; and 9.2% personal care other than sleeping. Looking at it this way, the average person has 41.6 hours "free" once personal and family obligations are taken care of, work is done, and sleeping is subtracted.

An impressive array of activities compete to fill the hours of free time we have each week. Media take about half (20.8 hours) while organizational activities and education fill 10%, our social life another 18%, sports and various leisure pursuits about 8%, and walking, resting, and attending "spectacles" the rest (Robinson, Andreyenkov, and Patrushev, 1989).

How we spend our time varies by age, as Table 5-1 suggests. The greatest amount of free time is available at the youngest and oldest ends of the age scale. While men age 18-29 have about 44 hours free and those age 60-65 49.3 hours free weekly, those age 50-59 have only 34.9 hours free and those age 30-39 36.9 hours free (Robinson, Andreyenkov and Patrushev, 1989). We also see that media behaviors take a larger share of leisure time at the top of the age ladder.[10] Now let's look at how people distribute their media time.

Television

More leisure time is devoted to TV than to the other media combined. The average number of sets per household went from about 1 in 1950 to almost 2 in 1988, and Americans average more than 1,500 hours with TV each year.[11] According to diary data, the average adult (age 18-64) spends more than 15 hours each week giving his or her "undivided attention" to TV, with 2.1 hours spent Mondays, Tuesdays and Wednesdays, 2 hours Thursdays and Fridays, 2.2 hours Saturdays and 2.6 hours Sundays. Heaviest viewing is among the oldest age group and the lightest among middle age groups (Cutler, 1989, 1990; Robinson, 1990; Robinson et al., 1989). Nielsen data show that the average amount of time spent viewing TV each day reached a peak of 7 hours, 10 minutes in 1985 and fluctuated a few minutes below that over the next half dozen years, dropping to 6 hours and 53 minutes in 1990.[12]

New technologies have altered how TV viewing data are collected. **People meters**, hand-held computerized audience measurement devices, replaced the viewer diary system for A.C. Nielsen in the fall of 1986.[13] Viewers push buttons on a device to indicate which programs are being watched. More accurate demographic information is provided because family members must punch in personal code numbers when they start viewing and also when they stop. The switch from diaries to meters suggested that audiences for many TV programs were smaller than had previously been estimated. The new data created controversy. The new methods were criticized by the networks for undercounting viewers and by others who objected to the obtrusive nature of the meters (Milavsky, 1992). Soong (1988) compared people meter and diary sample data on reliability of repeat-viewing, finding results favorable for the people meter technology. Viewing away from home is not counted by the people meters, and one estimate said 1 million viewers age 12 and older watch TV in prime time or on weekend afternoons away from home.[14] A people meter snapshot of prime time TV found that 55% of women and 41% of men

Table 5–1

Time Devoted to Media Behaviors and Other Activities

Activities:	Total Number Hours	Men	Women		18-24	25-29	30-39	40-49	50-59	60-65
Work-related (jobs,				(M)	39.9	39.0	46.3	40.8	48.6	22.6
trips to work)	32.2	41.2	24.0	(W)	21.8	24.5	29.4	26.6	24.7	13.5
Housework (preparing food, laundry,				(M)	5.4	11.3	8.4	6.6	9.0	15.0
cleaning, pets, etc.)	13.1	8.5	17.1	(W)	9.8	15.9	17.1	18.5	21.6	24.6
Family tasks (child care, shopping,				(M)	9.9	9.4	9.3	10.8	9.7	7.2
non-work trips)	12.4	9.6	14.9	(W)	15.3	19.2	16.1	16.3	9.9	12.1
Personal needs (sleeping, eating,				(M)	62.6	64.4	67.3	65.9	65.8	73.6
personal care)	68.6	67.3	69.8	(W)	72.8	70.8	66.6	68.4	77.2	70.2
Total free time	41.6	41.3	42.0	(M)	43.0	43.7	36.9	43.6	34.9	49.3
				(W)	48.4	37.6	38.8	38.1	40.9	47.7
Television	17.4	18.3	16.4	(M)	19.6	19.5	16.4	18.9	14.2	23.8
				(W)	18.5	15.4	13.4	11.9	21.0	20.1
Reading	3.1	3.0	3.3	(M)	1.7	2.7	2.7	3.4	3.6	6.4
				(W)	2.3	1.5	3.3	4.4	4.3	3.8
Radio	.3	.7	.1	(M)	.3	.3	.6	.6	1.6	1.0
				(W)	.3	.2	.1	.1	.1	.0
Social life	7.6	7.2	8.0	(M)	9.6	5.5	7.2	9.0	4.1	6.2
				(W)	9.4	9.7	8.6	5.6	4.4	10.4
Conversation	2.4	1.9	2.9	(M)	1.5	2.3	1.6	2.6	1.9	1.4
				(W)	2.1	2.8	3.4	3.5	2.4	3.6
Education	2.2	1.9	2.6	(M)	5.2	2.4	1.3	.0	.2	.3
				(W)	8.2	.7	.6	3.1	.9	.0
Resting	2.1	2.2	2.1	(M)	.9	2.3	1.6	2.8	3.8	2.0
				(W)	2.0	3.8	2.1	2.3	1.9	1.3
Organizations	2.0	1.7	2.2	(M)	.9	1.3	1.2	2.7	2.8	2.4
				(W)	.9	.6	2.0	3.6	3.3	3.5
Sports	1.7	2.1	1.4	(M)	2.4	4.7	2.0	1.4	.0	2.1
				(W)	.8	2.1	2.1	.0	.7	1.9
Walking	.5	.8	.1	(M)	.7	1.4	.5	.7	.5	1.4
				(W)	.1	.3	.2	.1	.2	.0
Spectacles	.5	.3	.7	(M)	.3	.2	.6	.6	.0	.2
				(W)	2.0	.3	.8	.1	.0	.0
Various other				(M)	.5	.8	1.0	1.0	2.1	2.0
leisure activities	1.6	1.2	2.0	(W)	1.7	.6	2.3	2.3	1.7	3.0
Total Time Per Week:	168.0									

Note: The figures are based on time-use diary data (Robinson, Andreyenkov and Patrushev, 1989:78, 79, 84). M = men, W = women for age groups.

age 18-49 were watching the three major TV networks, while 15% of women and 20% of men were watching independent stations. Cable networks accounted for 9% of women and 11% of men in the audience, while the Public Broadcasting System (PBS) took 3% of both groups and pay cable 10-12%. Superstations accounted for 13% of the men and 8% of the women in the audience.[15] The three networks' share of viewers has fallen to 63% (1990-1991),[16] while independent stations and ad-supported cable increased theirs.

Yet TV use is **elastic**—TV viewing tends to be the choice when people have nothing better to do.[17] Although TV is readily abandoned to pursue more satisfying activities such as visiting friends, TV use still provides considerable satisfaction on a regular basis. Roper (Miller, 1989) reports that 75% of Americans say they watch TV every day and another 15% several times a week, leaving 7% only once a week and 3% less often than that. As Table 5-2 shows, TV viewing tends to rise with age and viewing of TV news is a favorite of older viewers. Some 68% of adults watch TV news sometime during the day, 27% before the midday meal, 26% after the midday meal but before the evening meal, and 49% after the evening meal.[18] In 1992, 25.4% of U.S. homes used TV in the morning (10 A.M.-1 P.M.), 29.4% in the afternoon, and 52.7% during prime time (8-11 P.M. EST).[19] The types of network TV shows drawing the largest audiences were: situation comedy (48% share of programming), general drama (14%), feature films (12%), and suspense and mystery programs (8%).

Pervasive TV use is a worldwide phenomenon and Americans are no more addicted to TV than are other people.[20] The percentage of Japanese who say they watch TV almost every day has reached 94%, with an average of 3 hours per person and sets in use an average of 8 hours a day in each household (Tamura, 1987). The daily reach of TV in Western Europe averaged 76%, from a low of 70% in Portugal to 87% in Spain (McCain, 1985). In Belize, high school juniors and seniors watched an average of 7 hours of Mexican TV and 12 hours of United States TV each week (Johnson and Oliveira, 1988). In Nigeria, half of the respondents in a survey who had no TV set at home said they visited neighbors or relatives to watch TV. The daily network news was the program 92% of respondents watched most regularly (Talabi, 1989).

The constraints of other activities on people's TV viewing decisions is recognized in the repeat-viewing data. The main reason people don't watch the programs they enjoy regularly is lack of availability—they are elsewhere or busy with other activities—rather than disloyalty (Kamerer, 1990). Data of U.S. TV viewing gathered by people-meter panels shows little variation by program type, whether programs are on the network affiliates, cable or independents, or whether the programs have high or low ratings. From one week to another, about a fourth of programs watched one week are viewed

Table 5–2
Television Viewing

By Age:	Watched any TV Yesterday	Saw TV News	Watched TV but No News
18–24	82%	64%	18%
25–29	85%	74%	11%
30–34	86%	68%	18%
35–44	87%	78%	9%
45–54	85%	79%	6%
55–64	87%	84%	3%
65 +	93%	91%	2%
All Adults	87%	78%	9%

Source: *News and Newspaper Reading Habits: Results from a National Survey.* New York: Newspaper Advertising Bureau, 1988.

the following week (Ehrenberg and Wakshalag, 1987).[21] However, weekly drama serials with a continuing story line had repeat viewing 10 points higher than that for series with the same rating levels; Kamerer, Mundorf, Wakshalag and Bhatia (1986) found repeat levels of 67% for daytime viewing.

TV also is popular among college students, and TV sets, once found only in dormitory and fraternity lounges, increasingly appear in students' rooms (Gitlin, 1983). Kubey and Larson's (1990) study based on sampling people's experiences found that TV accounted for almost three-fourths of all media time of adolescents and children, while reading took 9.1% of media time, and music 8.4%; new video media took a total of 6.8% of media time, with radio, movies, and other media accounting for the rest.

Media audiences have grown because of increased access to videocassette recorders, cable TV systems, and other media technologies. Almost half of all U.S. households had access to more than 28 TV channels (the number of cable networks grew from 25 in 1980 to 97 in 1989). More than 60% of U.S. households now get cable TV, representing some 56 million homes in 1991. VCRs allow people to regulate their viewing time (Levy, 1983; Levy and Fink, 1984) or to watch videos when nothing they like is available on cable or network TV. VCRs are selling so quickly that some 50 to 60 million households may have them by the end of this decade.[22] Even college students (69%) are likely to have TV sets and VCRs (29%) with them at school (Shapiro, 1992).

These technologies are altering TV viewing patterns and may increase total viewing time or affect attention to news.[23] The longer people have VCRs, the more likely they are to record TV shows, particularly sports, news magazines, and public TV shows (Klopfenstein et al., 1991). They also are more likely to seek particular tapes at video stores and to wait for movies to come out on video.

Cable Television.   Time devoted to cable rather than over-the-air stations went from 8% of all TV viewing in 1982 to 12% in 1984 and 16% in 1987, while the three major networks' share dropped.[24] Furthermore, there appears to be a steady decline of network news viewers, especially among those with pay-TV, because of increased viewing of CNN and the related "Headline News" (Baldwin, Barrett, and Bates, 1992). Cable faces a fairly high churn rate, which refers to the need to replace cable subscribers who disconnect after fairly short periods of time. While 27% of cable subscribers eventually disconnect their service, those who subscribe for a full year are likely to continue.[25] Pfetsch and Kutteroff (1988) found cable subscribers watched more TV than comparable nonsubscribers in former West Germany.

Video Cassette Recorders.   An estimated 34.3 million households with VCRs took home 111.9 million cassettes a month, an average of 3.26 movies per household, in late 1986. By the end of 1989, the average rental figure had dropped to 2.07 as the novelty wore off and videos became part of the TV entertainment mix (Nichols, 1990).[26] VCR use in other countries, including developing nations, is extensive.[27]

More than three-fourths of the homes with TVs also have VCRs. Households with VCRs report more hours of TV usage. They record an average of 154 minutes per week and play an average of 257 minutes per week, the largest percentage during the 8–11 P.M. hours. The most popular day for recording is Sundays (19%), while the most popular day for playing is Saturdays (22%). More than two-thirds of the material recorded is from the major TV networks, with independents accounting for an additional 16% and cable another 14%. On an average day, 6% of all VCR persons reported zapping or zipping through commercials.[28] Adolescents often have their own VCRs and access to cable TV. Greenberg and Heeter (1987) found that 32% of 9th graders and 34% of 10th graders had VCRs and 85% or more of these had access to cable TV.

A survey of VCR usage in homes with people meters found that the average number of hours spent recording and playing tapes was 7.1 per week in January and 6.4 in April (Sims, 1989). Playing prerecorded tapes accounted for about 50% of this time; playback home recording accounted for 16–17%. Unaccompanied recording (no one watching) accounted for 23%, and accompanied recording 11%. In homes with pay cable, VCR usage was 16%

less than in homes without cable. VCR usage was greatest among adolescents, followed by children (age 2-11), and then women age 18 and older, followed by men age 18 and older. The most popular day for recording was Sunday (26%), followed by Monday (15%), Thursday (14%) and Tuesday (13%). About 16% of VCR time is devoted to **time shifting**, and 44% of recordings made in the daytime (10 A.M.-4 P.M.) are replayed in the early fringe (4-8 P.M.). VCR owners are heavy movie viewers but it is not clear whether VCR ownership causes increased movie viewing or the reverse. Purchase of a VCR does not seem to affect the types of programs viewed on TV (Greenberg and Lin, 1989).[29]

Other Technologies. TV satellites, remote control devices, and computer-linked data bases are enriching the media environment and altering media patterns. More than 1.7 million U.S. households have TV satellite systems that provide a menu of 100 channels to choose from, even with scrambling of many signals. Despite the large variety, Lochte and Warren (1989) found in a survey of 227 viewers with satellite dishes that half of respondents watched local TV during the week. TV satellite viewing was divided between cable networks (61.5%), super stations (23.6%), and broadcast networks (13.7%), with minimal viewing of other satellite transmissions such as feeds of syndicated programming that are not intended for use by TV viewers. **Channel repertoire**[30] refers to the number of different stations, or channels, used by viewers. Among viewers with satellite dishes, the number ranges from 1 to 22, with about 69% of respondents choosing 2-6 channels.

More than three-fourths of U.S. households with TV sets have remote control devices (RCDs), and viewers often use them to **graze**—flipping through channels, largely because of boredom or a concern for missing a better program on another channel (Ainslie, 1988). Ferguson (1991, 1992) looked at the impact of remote controls on channel repertoire and found that the number of channels used ranged from 0 to 15, with an average of 5.3. Channel repertoire was related to "grazing" using remote controls and cable subscription.

Audiences in some cities also have access to **videotex**, which offers pages of information on a TV screen accessed by entering commands on a keypad. In one experimental study of videotex, shopping (21%) was the most frequently used content, followed by news (17%), sports (14%), and games (12%); those with prior computer experience found it a more positive experience (Atwater, Heeter, and Brown, 1985).

Ownership of personal computers has grown, providing access to information data bases and services that could compete with newspapers and other media. However, Schweitzer (1991) found no radical changes in use of traditional news media among owners of personal computers. PC owners did read a newspaper more often and watch less TV, but those differences could be attributed to occupation and education.

Newspapers

Daily newspaper circulation (note that circulation does not necessarily imply readers; subscribers do not always find time to read and some do not subscribe but read others' papers) has been shrinking relative to households. In 1970, total U.S. daily newspaper circulation of 62.1 million was equal to about 98% of households counted in the census that year. By 1980 daily circulation edged up to 62.2 million but comprised only 77% of U.S. households, a figure that has dropped to less than 70% in the 1990s.[31] The readership slide may have ended in 1992.[32] One study showed a jump from 62.1% of adults who were daily newspaper readers in 1991 to 62.6% in 1992,[33] representing an increase from 113.3 to 115.3 million readers. Sunday readership grew more sharply (Glaberson, 1993).

Newspapers have been fighting back to increase readership by targeting their best customers: older readers. Those age 45-64 are 13% more likely than the average person to read a newspaper. A little over 40% of those under 25 buy newspapers, compared to more than 60% for age groups between 25 and 75. The highest readership is among those age 55-64 (Cutler, 1989).

The decline in newspaper readership appears to reflect some differences in generations (Miller, 1987), as well as current life styles. New readers have not followed the traditional reading and buying patterns of previous generations. Readership habits have been eroded by a variety of factors: life-style changes (less time to read, particularly afternoon papers, and more women working outside the home), competition from TV and other media, and physical delivery problems (in high rise apartment houses), etc. People have become more occasional readers[34] rather than everyday readers (Gollin, 1991), and papers have shifted from emphasizing total readership to satisfying market niches (Miller, 1987). Readers also are more likely to read only some sections rather than look at every page of the paper. Stone (1988) found little difference between subscribers to one rather than two newspapers.

Treating newspaper reading and subscription as a single behavior can be misleading. As Table 5-3 shows, 49% of adults get a newspaper delivered to their home and another 25% sometimes buy single copies. While older adults get home delivery, younger adults rely more on buying a newspaper from a vendor box or newsstand. Motivations for starting and dropping subscriptions are different—(length of time living in a community affects restarting a subscription but not dropping, while the length of time living at an address has an impact on dropping but not restarting) (Zhu, 1988). Two contrary

Table 5–3

Newspaper Readership

By Age	Read Paper Yesterday	Has Home Delivery	Buys Single Copies	Reads Paid Weekly	Reads Free Weekly	Read at 1 Sitting	Pick It Up Several Times
18–24*	53%	34%	28%	30%	51%	64%	32%
25–29		27%	33%	40%	60%	53%	36%
30–34		42%	28%	43%	48%	59%	31%
35–44		46%	29%	34%	60%	49%	41%
45–54*	69%	58%	26%	47%	54%	58%	37%
55–64*		63%	19%	47%	65%	52%	39%
65+		66%	14%	38 %	47%	50%	41%
All Adults		49%	25%	39%	55%	55%	37%

Note: The first column includes two percentages; 53% refers to those age 18–24 who read the newspaper "yesterday" and 69% refers to those in the 45–64 age groups combined (Gollin, 1991:5). The third column refers to "sometimes buys single copies" at a newsstand, store, or vending machine. Source: *News and Newspaper Reading Habits: Results from a National Survey.* New York: Newspaper Advertising Bureau, 1988.

principles are offered: the inertia principle—the longer a household stays with a subscription, the less likely it will be dropped; accelerative principle—the longer a dropped household stays outside subscription, the more likely it will restart.

Americans spend some 180 hours with newspapers in a given year (Cutler, 1989). However, the amount of time spent reading overall dropped from 3.7 hours per week in 1965 to 3.1 hours in 1975 and 2.8 hours in 1985 in studies utilizing time-use diaries (Cutler, 1990). Daily newspaper readers spend an estimated 45 minutes with their paper over the course of the average day, with that time rising sharply among those who read two or more dailies. The amount of time spent reading newspapers has changed little from the early 1980s.

Clearly, the daily newspaper serves as an information source at various times of the day rather than being picked up and read at one sitting. Reading takes place almost around the clock, so at any hour between 6 A.M. and midnight, some small percentage of the adult population can be found reading a newspaper. Both morning and evening newspapers are read soon after they arrive but also at other times throughout the day. Some 59% of daily newspaper reading takes place in the morning before lunch, about a third in the afternoon after lunch, and another third after the evening meal.[35] Some

85% of adult readers do their reading at home, while 15% read at work, 2% while commuting and 3% at other locations. Those age 45-64 are the heaviest readers of paid weeklies. Some 55% of adults read free weeklies now available in 82% of their areas. While 55% of adults read the paper in one sitting, more than a third pick it up several times during the day. One adult in eight lives in a home where some other language is used, generally Spanish, and a fifth of those homes get a foreign-language newspaper.[36] Sunday and weekday subscribers are mostly the same people and reading habits carry over strongly, so that 80% of the frequent readers of daily papers also are frequent Sunday readers (Gollin, 1985). The Sunday paper is particularly popular among those with higher incomes and more education.

Radio

Almost all U.S. households have at least one radio and most have several sets. Some 66% of American adults listen to the radio on an average day. Except for **drive-time** hours (6-10 A.M.), younger people are more likely than older adults to listen to the radio, with 93% listening to the radio at least some time on an average weekday.[37] In the U.S., almost 40% of those under age 25 listen to the radio between 7 P.M. and midnight, double the figure for those age 65 and older (Cutler, 1989). A third of teenagers manage to listen to the radio during school hours (10 A.M.-3 P.M.), while 31% have their radios on between midnight and 6 A.M. As Table 5-4 notes, the youngest adults (age 18-24) are most likely to listen to the radio (81%), with declining percentages as one moves up to older age groups. While younger adults are about as likely to hear radio news as older groups, some 31% of those age 18-24 listen to the radio but hear no news, compared with only 9% of those age 65 and older. Clearly, music is the attraction for younger adults.

Radios are highly portable and readily integrated into diverse locations by our highly mobile population, with radios in more than 95% of all cars as well as large percentages of our living rooms, kitchens, and bathrooms. Some 24% of the adult population listens to the radio while in an automobile, and the figure varies little. Listening at home is higher for the oldest groups, while listening at work is higher among younger and middle-aged adults—those in the workforce.[38]

Despite the enormous impact of television in the 1950s, radio has continued to grow and prosper. Since its development in 1920, it has achieved growth rivaling that of all other media. Radio is an especially strong medium among both the general population and specialized audiences. The overall radio listening audience is larger than the TV audience for a sizeable segment of the day. The largest audience is at approximately 8-9 A.M., then tapers off before climbing back up to a plateau between 3-7 P.M. These "highs" are commonly called drive-time, when many people listen while commuting to

Table 5–4

Radio Listening

By Age	Listened to Radio	Heard News	Listened but Heard No News	Where Heard Radio News:		
				Listened in Car	Listened at Home	Listened at Work
18–24	81%	46%	31%	28%	21%	8%
25–29	73%	50%	21%	31%	22%	10%
30–34	76%	54%	20%	34%	17%	10%
35–44	69%	47%	18%	32%	19%	9%
45–54	62%	47%	11%	26%	20%	8%
55–64	54%	41%	11%	15%	28%	2%
65 +	46%	35%	9%	7%	28%	1%
All Adults	66%	45%	17%	24%	22%	7%

Note: The responses refer to radio listening "yesterday" in a national survey.
Source: *News and Newspaper Reading Habits*. New York: Newspaper Advertising Bureau, 1988.

and from work. TV begins to take over the audience after 8 P.M. Radio also is immensely popular in other countries.[39]

Films

Film attendance in the United States has ridden a bumpy path since the 1930s when movie attendance was at its peak. Average weekly movie attendance was 85 million in 1939, dropping to 60 million in 1950, 40 million in 1960, and 17.7 million in 1970, then recovering somewhat in the 1980s and 1990s (about 20-21 million).[40] For four in ten Americans, going out to see movies is a popular leisure-time activity (Austin, 1989). In 1987 the United States average annual attendance per person was about 5.2, compared to 1.3 in Japan, 3.8 in France, 3.4 in Italy, and 1.1 in Great Britain (Tamura, 1987). In a recent survey, 46% of Americans said they go out to see a movie in a theater less than once a month, while 24% go once a month and 30% twice a month or more often. In contrast, three-fourths watch movies at home twice a month or more often.[41] With recent films available on cable TV and videocassettes, theater exhibition must compete with the newer technologies to convince people to leave home to see movies. The most frequent moviegoers do not subscribe to cable TV, suggesting they prefer the cinema (Williams and Shapiro, 1985). While only half of infrequent moviegoers prefer to see movies in a theater, three-fourths of frequent moviegoers do (Austin, 1989).

Movie-going audiences tend to be quite young in the United States as well as other countries.[42] Some 47% of Americans claim they never go out to see films and 48% say they never watch films on prerecorded video cassettes. Among those age 15-24, only 18% say they never go to films.[43] What types of films do people go to see? Although family films have been maligned as "box office poison," 24% have been successful according to a study of 5,000 films rated during the first 11 years of the Motion Picture Association of America (1968-1979). While 27% of parental guidance films were successful, only 14% of movies rated R, and 5% of X-rated films were financially successful. Persons under age 17 are not admitted to R-rated films without adult permission, and no one under age 18 is admitted to X-rated movies. Some 70% prefer American films to foreign films (Gertner, 1985). Numerous studies of art film audiences have found them to be different from the general movie-going population.[44]

Books and Magazines

Only two out of five United States households bought a book during 1991, and professional and white-collar workers buy half of all books sold. Two-thirds of all books purchased are fiction.[45] Only 10-25% of American adults read "works of literary merit" and only 7-12% read worthwhile contemporary literature.[46] One national survey in the United States conducted in 1992 asked people if they had a collection of books at home or would have to go out to a library or store to find a book to read for pleasure right now. A third said they would have to go to a library or store.[47] About a third of regular newspaper readers said they were currently reading a book in 1987, about half of them reading a nonfiction book.[48] In Japan, 13% of the population claims to read books almost every day, while 8% read books three or four times a week, a relatively high level of reading compared with other countries (Tamura, 1987).

Magazines are found in most American homes. A national survey conducted in 1990 found that 81% of U.S. households buy magazines in the course of a year, with the average household purchasing six different magazine titles. Some 83% subscribe to at least one magazine and more than three-fourths buy single copies of one or more magazines at newsstands or retail outlets. Heavy magazine buyers—those purchasing seven or more different magazines—account for 58% of all magazines sold.[49]

The highest readership of magazines occurs on Saturdays, with slight seasonal variations. Some 42% of the reading occurs after dinner but before going to bed. Another 5% actually occurs in bed before sleeping, while 35% occurs from lunch through dinner. The average copy of a magazine is passed on and eventually read by 4.8 adults, who generally read each magazine purchased on three different days for a total reading time of 51 minutes.[50]

Reading as a leisure activity starts early. Greaney (1980) found that reading ranked seventh of nine leisure activities among fifth graders, and other studies have reported most children rarely read for pleasure, with an increase in the number of non-book-readers rising from 9% at age 10 to 40% at age 14.[51] Neuman (1986) looked at the home environment of fifth graders, finding that leisure reading was associated with parental encouragement of reading, involvement in diverse leisure activities outside the home, and the degree of independence given to the child to develop responsibility in work and social tasks. Leisure reading was associated with socioeconomic status but not with television viewing. The availability of daily newspapers and magazines was associated with reading. Parental reading habits did not appear to affect leisure reading once gender and socioeconomic status were controlled.

Daily Media and News Diets

Do the media complement each other or compete for a share of people's free time? If the former occurs, then TV viewing, for example, might stimulate newspaper reading. If the latter occurs, TV viewing might displace newspaper reading. We can envision various combinations of media substitutions or complementary use among radio listening, TV viewing, and newspaper reading. We also might find a pattern of complementary media use within one generation but substitution in another.

In general, heavy users of one medium are likely to be heavy users of another (Robinson and Jeffres, 1979; Scherer, 1989).[52] While subscribers to one newspaper are virtually identical to those subscribing to two newspapers, the latter are more likely to be subscribers to weekly newsmagazines, to subscribe to cable TV, and to watch TV-magazine shows more often (Stone, 1988). PBS news viewers, who use more TV news sources than do regular network news viewers, also view more news analysis programs (such as "Nightline" or "This Week with David Brinkley") and read more newspapers (Chew, 1990). Those who watch little TV also do not read newspapers regularly or listen to the radio as much.[53] Thus, the media complement each other at a single point in time.

Dependence is a relationship between people and information sources which can satisfy a variety of needs. Gaziano (1990) analyzed a national U.S. sample and identified six dependence groups: 1) those highly dependent on both TV news and daily newspapers for their news (9%), 2) those with low dependence on either medium (59%), 3) those highly dependent on TV news but with low dependence on daily newspapers (17%), 4) those highly dependent on daily newspapers but with low dependence on TV news (14%), 5) those dependent on radio news (3-12%), and 6) those dependent on news magazines (1-12%).[54] The largest group, non-dependents, had few characteristics distinguishing them from the other groups, although they were more likely to include men, people under age 35, single people, and those employed full-time. Those dependent on both TV and daily newspapers tended to include more women, older people, less-educated people, lower incomes, retired people, and residents of smaller communities. Those dependent on TV news were lower on education and income, more likely to be black, separated-divorced, and urban. Newspaper dependent people tended to be older, have higher education and income, be married, retired, and live in larger communities. Radio dependents included more people age 35-44, household incomes between $15,000-$30,000 (in 1985-86), and those in professional-technical occupations. People dependent on news magazines were much higher on education, income, and occupational status than the other groups and included more urban residents, separated-divorced or single people, males, renters, and newcomers to their communities.

Tradeoffs within people's media diets are likely to occur among media that directly compete for particular audiences, as Robinson (1981) suggests. In one study, cable TV subscribers and nonsubscribers in two cities were similar in news consumption (Reagan, 1989), suggesting that new technologies may not "siphon people away from news use." However, Baldwin, Bates, and Barrett's (1990) analysis of national data found that the network news audience for both basic and pay cable households dropped considerably from 1982 to 1989, a decline that "must stem from the increasing availability of attractive alternative programming and the added channels." Local broadcast news held its own against cable attractions except for small losses in audiences for early evening news in small markets and late evening news in large markets. In another competition among technologies, Henke and Donohue (1986) studied audiences for a teletex system, which offered 100 pages of updated news and other services, finding a decline in viewing after the novelty wore off but increased viewing of the local TV news program among teletex enthusiasts.[55]

News media are quite competitive in attracting audiences. As the amount of TV news has expanded in the past two decades and newspaper circulations have failed to grow as rapidly as the population, a host of researchers and observers have focused on relationships between different media use, particularly newspapers and TV.[56]

In the 1970s, the National Opinion Research Center (NORC) at the University of Chicago documented a 9% decline in the public's reported daily use of newspapers (between 1975 and 1978). Moreover, the NORC survey shows a pronounced generation effect—the tendency of the youngest adults to read newspapers at a lower rate than previous generations of adults at that stage in their lives.[57] In 1982-1983 a study conducted for Scripps-Howard found that 72% of a national sample of adults watch TV every day, compared with 70% who read a newspaper. Summarizing trends across two decades, Gollin (1991) notes that newspaper readership declined from 1970 to 1991 for four age groups, but the spread between them widened over the years, reaching 16 percentage points in 1991; 53% of 18-24-year-olds read a newspaper "yesterday" vs. 69% of those age 45-64.

There has been a running debate over the importance of newspapers and television as news sources. The debate has been fueled by results of Roper polls conducted since 1959 documenting an apparent rise of television as America's preferred news source. People were asked: "Where do you usually get most of your news about what's going on in the world today?" Since 1959, TV has been the key source for a growing number of adults, rising from 51% to proportions that have stabilized at about 65% since the early 1970s (see Table 5-5). Newspapers, in contrast, have declined from 57% in 1959 to 42% in 1988 (Miller, 1989). Basil (1990) analyzed the Roper public opinion data for the period 1937-1987, finding that question wording, media availability (the more available a medium is, the more likely it's cited as the major source of news), and generational effects are all-important. He concludes that TV has displaced radio more than newspapers as a source of news.

Moore, Howard, and Johnson (1988) compared newspaper readership and TV news viewing across the top 50 markets in the United States, finding no relationship between highly rated TV newscasts and the presence of an evening newspaper. In Britain, 44% cited newspapers as the source of most local news, followed by 26% who cited TV and 14% radio (Golding, 1992). Henke (1985) found heavier use of news media among students who were viewers of Cable Network News (CNN); CNN supplemented already healthy "news appetites"— supporting the tendency of heavy users of one medium to be heavy users of another. Melton and Galician (1987) found that TV was viewed as a major news source by 47% of a sample of college students, while 25% read papers daily, 11% viewed radio as the major news source, and 18% cited other sources.

One national study probed people's use of the media for specific news stories.[58] Two-thirds of all adults surveyed recalled something in the news "yesterday or today" that was of particular interest to them, with a wide range of topics covered by the stories mentioned. U.S. news stories were mentioned

Table 5–5

News Sources

	1959	1968	1978	1988
Television only	19%	29%	34%	44%
Newspapers only	21%	19%	19%	22%
TV and newspapers	26%	25%	27%	18%
All media except TV	10%	6%	3%	2%
All media except papers	6%	5%	6%	3%
All media except TV, newspapers	17%	13%	11%	10%

Note: The question was: "Where you usually get most of your news about what's going on in the world today" (Roper data, Miller, 1989).

frequently (by 14%). Topics mentioned by at least 5% were: world news items, professional sports news, natural disasters, business and financial news, and crime news. Those who recalled a news story were asked what their "main sources" were and what the "one main source" was for that story. Television was named most frequently not only as a news source (by 75%) but also as the one main source across topics (by 57%). Newspapers were named as a source by 48% and as the main source by 25%. Radio was named as a source by 26% and as the main source by 12%; only a few named any other source. Newspapers were identified by 44% as the main source for state/local and community news, compared with 37% who cited TV and 11% citing radio. TV was cited as the main source for national and international stories, sports, disasters, business/financial news, weather, and health/science/environment news. For crime stories, TV was cited by 48% and newspapers by 37% as the main source.

The same study sought to contrast the strengths of the media—TV's role as a medium of first exposure for big news stories and newspapers' varied role both as a back-up source and in providing desired additional details.[59] TV news programs were preferred in general by 44%, while 24% named newspapers as their preferred source on big news stories. About a fourth (26%) volunteered that both TV and newspapers are valuable. However, newspaper readership is not always based on an interest in the news printed in the daily paper, any more than watching TV news necessarily signifies interest in what is being presented. News is but one element in a mix of offerings by both media.

Media Use Over the Life Span

Patterns of media behaviors change and evolve over the life span as individuals experience physical, psychological, social, and environmental changes. Thus, we see changes in the amount of time devoted to media as a whole and to specific media. Content preferences also change, as do orientations to the media, the uses and gratifications fulfilled by media behaviors, and how media fit into people's life styles.

No single all-encompassing theory has been developed to account for development of media behavior patterns over the life span. However, several theories focus on pieces of the puzzle. For example, physical developments in children and the growth of message-processing capacities have led researchers to investigate cognitive development and media behaviors developmentally. Furthermore, the influence of parents and others on children's media use has been studied in the socialization literature. At the other end of the age spectrum, researchers have looked at how the media fit into lives of the elderly as they disengage from a more active life style. Some of these theories are discussed briefly here and some in the following chapter.

Childhood

Mass media consumption begins very early in a child's life. TV is the first medium to occupy much prominence in most contemporary children's lives in the Western world.[60] However, children's short attention spans mean early viewing is usually for brief periods. Preschool children are exposed to about 25 hours of TV each week. Children typically begin their TV viewing three to four years before entering first grade. Most children watch at least some TV every day, the majority for two hours or more. Nielsen data show that children age 2-11 watch about 4 hours per day during the colder months, a figure which drops to 3-3.5 hours the rest of the year.[61] The amount of viewing increases during the elementary school years, but there is no agreement on when peak viewing occurs.[62]

When children watch TV depends on their daily schedule. For pre-schoolers the largest amount of viewing occurs on weekday and Saturday mornings, decreases in early afternoon and rises in mid-afternoon until about 5:30 P.M., when it drops until increasing during the early evening. After 8 o'clock it drops drastically as bedtime arrives. Children of elementary school age (6-11 years) spend most of their TV viewing time during prime time, followed by late afternoon and early evening hours.

Children's early preferences for TV content are animals, puppets, etc., but that begins to change by school age when situation comedies rank first. Sitcoms remain popular into adolescence, but interest also grows in adult dramas, mysteries, variety shows, and crime shows. Rubin (1986) compared three age groups (5-7, 8-9, 10-12), finding decreased viewing of children's programs and cartoons and increased viewing of comedies and adventure-drama programs. For older children, TV is less important and less realistic. Although gender differences are not important for the amount of TV children watch, content preferences begin to appear in elementary school. Boys seem to like adventure programs and girls prefer popular music.

Children are not highly adventurous TV viewers and tend to like the familiar rather than new shows (Wakshalag and Greenberg, 1979). Children age 5 or younger watch more TV when cable TV is available in the home, but cable apparently makes little difference among older children age 6-12 (Wartella, Heintz, Aidman and Mazzarella, 1990). There is some evidence of a tradeoff between watching TV and playing video games among children age 2-11; ironically, many of the video games are based on TV programs deserted for game playing.[63]

What about other media use? Selnow and Reynolds (1984) found that sixth-eighth grade children who watch a lot of TV also listen to more records and tapes, listen to the radio more often, and have more hobbies. Radio grows in importance among older children. Christenson and DeBenedittis (1986) found that a third of a sample of elementary school children (grades one through five) listened to the radio the previous night, with 27% listening every day after school; 69% reported having a favorite radio station and most of the reasons for listening to radio involved music.

Low print use has been found among children, but by the sixth grade, a fifth of students read at least some part of the newspaper daily and a third read some portion several times a week.[64] Comic book reading decreases between first and sixth grades, while use of other print media—newspapers, magazines, and books—increases. Use of newspapers and print media is strongly linked to education. The Newspaper in Education program has provided newspapers to students in school for many years.[65] Those who use papers in school also have less difficulty reading papers and are more likely to be regular newspaper readers. In general, heavy TV viewing is associated with less book reading, but time spent reading comics is positively associated with viewing time (Van der Voort and Van Lil, 1989).

Sometime during the early school years gender differences in reading begin to emerge. Whereas boys and girls have an even start at the beginning of school, by the end of the third grade boys are significantly lower than girls on reading tests (Landsberger, 1981). There is some evidence that boys striving to develop a masculine sex role resist involvement in feminine situations. Reading is often considered a feminine activity, although the content of the book or magazine affects this assessment (Kelly, 1986). In one study boys saw reading in general, reading poetry, and consulting dictionaries as more feminine activities, while reading TV Guide, mysteries, comics, science books, animal books, and running books was more masculine. Female students tended to agree with the boys, except for an assessment that reading running books was more feminine. Looking across the grades, the researchers found an increasing perception of reading in general as feminine from kindergarten to high school (Kelly, 1986).

Scholars also have looked at how children use the media. What a child gets out of early media use is limited by the level of cognitive development. For example, younger children see TV as more real than do older kids.[66] Children's motivations for using media and the uses to which they put their viewing and the gratifications derived are similar in many respects to those of adults—using TV for topics to talk with friends, to alleviate boredom or control moods, to stimulate thinking, to learn about others, and so forth. In general, informational uses become more important with advancing age. In the early years, many children say they watch TV so they can join in conversations with friends about TV. This decreases as the children get older, with a rise in the selection of other media for social conversations. Similar switches are seen in media use to forget unpleasantness and when one feels sad.

Adolescence

Adolescence, generally referred to as age 12 to 18, is a time of searching and introspection in which the adolescent confronts the need to find a suitable place in an adult-dominated society. Early and mid-adolescence are periods of attempted escape from parental influence and often disassociation from others in the family.[67]

Social relations with other teenagers grow dramatically as a preferred activity during adolescence,[68] and media use as a leisure preference drops (Smith, 1987). Nonetheless, most media capture the attention of adolescents for significant portions of time in the United States and around the world.[69] Watching TV followed visiting friends as a favorite way to spend an evening in a major survey of American adolescents. Some 24% said visiting friends was their favorite way to spend an evening, 15% cited watching TV, 12% going on a date, 9% going to movies, 8% playing or watching sports, 7% reading, 7% staying home with the family, and 7% going to a party. TV viewing was higher among boys than girls, younger teens (age 13-15), and those with blue-collar backgrounds; similar findings have been found in Sweden (Rosengren and Windahl, 1989).

TV viewing in the United States and elsewhere reaches its peak at the beginning of adolescence. By the end of adolescence, it has declined by 10% or more.[70] Nielsen data show that teens age 12-17 watch three to four hours per day during the colder months, a figure which drops to about three hours the rest of the year.[71] The major decrease comes in prime time and late afternoon viewing. Looking at younger teens (age 12-14) in another sample, Brown et al. (1990) found an average of 45.1 hours of TV viewing during a typical school week (46.3 for 12-year-olds; 45.9, 13-year-olds; 43.4, 14-year-olds). Boys watched more than did girls and blacks more than whites at each age.

Adolescents are fans of music videos and new technologies around the world.[72] Teenagers are heavy users of VCRs, particular younger teens (age 12-14), perhaps because they are less mobile but can still easily rent a movie. Watching videos is a peer group activity among older adolescents, while younger ones are more likely to watch with other family members.[73]

The size and nature of the family affect adolescent media use; Tangney and Feshbach (1988) found that children who live with one natural parent and one stepparent watch more TV than children from households with either two natural parents or only one natural parent. Late adolescence sees the development of self-awareness shaped by environmental realities and a redefinition of personal values. As the adolescent's interests and activities extend beyond the home arena, TV viewing declines (Selnow and Reynolds, 1984). This process starts earlier in higher socioeconomic status homes, although the differences are small. Viewing patterns and program preferences are linked to emerging adult sex roles (Avery, 1979).

Potter (1992) looked at changes in adolescents' perceptions of TV reality across a five-year period, examining three dimensions: identity (the possibility of interaction with TV characters); utility (that some of the lessons on TV are useful in their own lives); and magic window (that TV provides a window to reality and depicts what could happen in real life). Declines in the perceived reality of TV occurred on all three dimensions with advancing age.

While TV viewing declines, other media use increases during adolescence. Radio listening grows dramatically during adolescence because listening to music is a favorite way to relax, be entertained, or fill a lonely void. In one large survey of early teens, the average radio listening per week rose from 33.7 hours at age 12 to 34.7 at age 13 and 39.3 at age 14. Girls spent more time listening to the radio than did boys at each age, and blacks spent more time listening than did whites (Brown et al., 1990). Moviegoing during adolescence fluctuates, depending on availability of theaters and other recreation facilities in the community. However, moviegoing is a popular dating activity and provides topics for discussions among teenagers.

Reading newspapers and magazines grows as children move into adolescence. A national survey of more than 2,000 teenagers in 1988 looked at how newspapers and other media fit into their lives. The percentages who said they read the newspaper "yesterday" rose through the adolescent years: 33% of those age 12-13; 43%, age 14-15; 47%, age 16-17; 53%, age 18-19.[74] Some 91% said they look at a newspaper at least sometimes, and 81% read at least one issue each week. During the five weekdays, 68% read at least one issue but only 16% read the paper each of the five days. Cobb (1986) found in a Texas study that teenagers average less than 15 minutes per day reading newspapers and magazines, although 80% have access to newspapers in their home. Newspaper reading levels were highest among the 38% of teenagers who said their parents read to them almost every day when they were little. More than two-thirds of teenagers said they had had school assignments requiring use of a newspaper. While 37% of the teenagers felt they were reading more newspapers in the past year, 27% reported reading less.[75] Some 74% of teenagers had seen a film within the past 90 days and those who went most often also were the most regular newspaper readers.[76] A 1989 study by Simmons Market Research found that 81% of teenagers read the newspaper at least once a week, with nearly half of those age 12-17 looking at the general news in daily papers and 27% opening to the business pages regularly.[77]

While younger children are attracted to papers by comics, in adolescence there is increased readership and interest in local news, sports, personal advice columns, and entertainment sections. Adolescents read newspapers for general information and to keep up with what's going on in their environment.[78] Magazine reading also grows during adolescence, as does use of books. Gender-related content preferences also appear, as boys, for example, show a greater preference for sports magazines than do girls.

Adulthood—A Sequence of Eras

Although little has been done to conceptualize the nature of adult development, researchers are beginning to look beyond adolescence in studying development of the individual over the "life course." The idea of a life cycle is metaphorical, suggesting that there is an underlying order in the course of human life and a definable sequence of forms corresponding to "seasons." The developmental perspective of the first 20 years or so is: prenatal, infancy, early childhood, middle childhood, pubescence, and adolescence. The adult life cycle also can be viewed as a sequence of **eras**, each with its own character and connected by transitions (Levinson, 1986). Each era is defined by our relationships with others in the external world; family, marriage, and occupation are the chief components for laying out the structure to one's life. Mass and interpersonal communication are major links to that external world as well as expressive, leisure-time activities. Biological, psychological, and social factors mark changes from one era to another. Thus, we might expect changes in communication patterns which link individuals to other people and the larger environment. The fit between media and people's lives continues to evolve. Riddick (1986) found there was no difference in leisure satisfaction among different age groups.[79] Others have found stable patterns of leisure behaviors over time.[80]

Efforts to track media use of people across long time spans are rare, largely because of costs, but several studies are available. Scott and Willits (1989) looked at leisure activities during high school years and again when almost 1,300 respondents were in their early fifties 37 years later. In general, people involved in three types of activity during adolescence also were more likely to participate in the same types at midlife—socializing (including going to movies), intellectual activities (including reading stories), and formal organizations. A panel study by Scott and Willits (1989) also found a positive relationship between people's adolescent and adult leisure choices. A British study tracked media use of a group when they were teenagers (13-14 in 1951), age 24-25 (in 1962) and age 32-33 (1970). Ability, skills, role models, and opportunities provided by the home and school counted for a good deal in the crucial adolescent period when the basis for future taste was laid (Himmelweit and Swift, 1976). Age culture also affected people's tastes, so that different types of content appealed at different times of people's lives. However, adolescent media tastes predicted later media usage and taste almost as well as information about one's educational attainment, job level, outlook, and personality predisposition as an adult. Predictions of media preferences at age 32-33 showed significant influence from media habits, tastes, and content preferences from earlier age periods.[81]

TV viewing was the most popular leisure activity (90% viewed TV) among a sample of adults age 50-92, followed by reading newspapers or magazines (82%), reading books, plays, or poetry (75%), visiting friends (71%), and listening to the radio (69%) (Thornton and Collins, 1986). Kelly and Ross (1989) found that home-based leisure activities (including media use) were negatively related to life satisfaction among those in their twenties but were the most significant positive contributor to life satisfaction among those age 75 and older. There were no relationships for the 30-74 age groups.

Although general leisure patterns may be relatively stable, the importance attached to leisure activities varies with the life cycle. For those age 40-54, cultural activities and travel are most important for life satisfaction, with social and exercise/sport activities of moderate importance. Family activities, home-based and community organizational activities contributed relatively little in one study. For those age 55-64, no activity stood out for its significance in deter- mining people's satisfaction. For those age 65-74, life satisfaction was tied to activities that increased interaction with other people, while those age 75 and older found more satisfaction in reading at home and community organizational activities such as going to church (Kelly, Steinkamp, and Kelly, 1987).

Media exposure patterns across adult age groups differ for specific media. Cutler (1989) reports that those age 55-64 are most likely to buy newspapers, followed by adjacent age categories (45-54 and 65-74) and then those age 35-44. The lowest rate is found for those age 75 and older (slightly less than 60% buy newspapers) and those under age 25 (slightly over 40%). One set of national surveys found that 37% of those age 18-30 read a daily newspaper, compared to 49% of those 30-49 and 65% of those age 50 and older.[82] Those age 35-44 are most likely to buy magazines (more than 40%), followed by those age 24-34 and then those age 45-54. Those age 75 and older are least likely (Cutler, 1989). The *Times Mirror* nationwide studies found a slightly higher magazine use among younger adults.[83]

There is a steady decline in radio listening (to any content—news, music, or talk) across three major time periods[84] for each age group, with a high among those under age 25 and lows for those age 65 and older. For the morning drive-time (6-10 A.M.), those in the middle age categories (particularly 35-44 but also adjacent age groups) are more likely to listen because they commute to work (Cutler, 1989). In one set of nationwide surveys, 43% of young adults (age 18-30) listened to radio news regularly, compared to 50% of those age 30-49 and 44% of those age 50 and older.[85]

Watching TV is the prime leisure activity for the elderly (Fouts, 1989; Singleton, Mitic, and Farquharson, 1986). Roberts' (1987) study of the TV nonviewer found nonwatching was significantly associated with age, TV avoidance increasing during early adulthood, remaining fairly high into the late 40s, dropping off between 50-80, and increasing again for those older than 80. Rahtz (1989) found only weak support for a positive relationship between age and TV orientation. Lamude and Scudder (1988) found differences in TV program preferences across young, middle-aged and senior adults. As numerous researchers have noted, the elderly are a diverse audience (Glass and Smith, 1985), with other factors affecting media use more than age itself. The elderly are less likely to rent videocassettes and are subscribers to basic cable if they subscribe at all (Reagan, Ducey, and Bernstein, 1985).

TV news viewing increases with age, from 62% reporting regular viewing among those age 18-30, to 69% of those age 30-49 and 83% of those 50 and older.[86] Other TV news and magazine shows are popular among older adults.

A study of reading behavior of older adults (average age of 78) found that 36% read two or more hours per day, 28% one to two hours and 19% less than an hour. Newspapers were read most often, followed by magazines and then books (Fisher, 1988). People older than 65 were the largest single group of book buyers in 1990-1991, accounting for 16% of sales.[87]

What Do People Think about the Media?

People's attitudes toward the mass media are often quite ambivalent. Americans generally like their media systems but fear the potential control over their lives and feel guilty about how much time they spend with the media. They have what many would call a healthy skepticism about what they see, hear, or read, but it is combined with a large measure of confidence in the performance of media people. People's perceptions, images, and attitudes are particularly important because they can have an impact on the subsequent processing of media messages and media effects (Fulk, Steinfield, Schmitz, and Power, 1987).

Content Preferences

Each person has a unique set of content preferences, perhaps liking sitcoms and talk shows on TV, adventure and mystery film genres, and how-to books. However, some preferences tend to be associated with a specific medium and some stretch across media. Hirschman (1985, 1987) looked at people's preferences for different types of film genres, book content categories, and TV program formats. In her sample of adults, three TV program dimensions emerged: a) game-quiz shows, situation comedies, soap operas, and variety specials; b) police-crime-detective shows, westerns, and sports events; and c) movies and docudramas. That is, people who like police shows also tend to like westerns and sports events on TV. Film genre preferences grouped as follows: a) liking adventure movies, science fiction films, westerns, and mysteries, and disliking love-romance movies; b) liking movie classics and mysteries and not liking erotic-pornographic films; c) liking horror films and science fiction; d) liking musicals, comedies and love-romance movies. Four book content factors were obtained: a) liking historical, adventure, biographical, and finance books; b) liking the classics, art books, and historical books and disliking erotic-pornographic books; c) liking science, science fiction, self-help and horror books; and d) liking humor, love-romance, and biographical books and disliking science books. When content preferences across the three media were analyzed, Hirschman (1985) turned to a theory described in the next chapter to explain the groupings—uses and gratifications.

News.   News is the major attraction for newspapers and TV around the world. A national survey done for the Newspaper Advertising Bureau found that 84% of readers usually read the local community news, 75% international news, 74% news briefs, summaries, 72% news about the president and Congress, 69% local politics and government news, 68% economic news, 65% news about celebrities and famous people, 60% TV listings, 59% advice columns, 58% comics, 57% local events calendars, and 51% sports news (Bogart, 1988). In a Chinese survey, 77% of an urban audience said the news was the first reason they turned on their sets (Hollstein, 1989).

Audiences have considerable interest in specialized areas of news, such as medicine (Aida, 1987). One survey found 84% were interested in consumer economic news, 65% in science news, and 56% in business news (Blick et al., 1986). Four out of 10 Europeans claim to take at least an occasional interest in business news such as stock prices and currency exchange rates.[88] People also are interested in environmental news, particularly disposal of wastes, water quality, and hazardous substances (Atwater, 1988).

Media in recent years have been criticized for being the bearers of bad news. However, Galician (1986) found that more than half of the respondents of one survey did not feel that "bad news" was more interesting than "good news." A majority agreed that TV newscasts report too much bad news and not enough good news.[89]

Newspapers.   Other newspaper features capture audience interest. When the *Washington Post* tried to drop several venerable comic strips, they received 15,000 phone calls and 2,000 letters, many passionate declarations of love for the comic strips (Jones, 1991). A national survey of American teenagers found that the top three contents read in daily newspapers were: comics (68%), sports (66%), and entertainment (52%).[90] In Japan, topics about TV and radio programs attract the most readers (64%), while 58% read social topics and half read sports. Politics attracted 44%, local news 43%, and economic news 32% (Aida, 1987).

The percentage of people who read something regularly in a newspaper does not indicate how important they consider the content. Thus, while local community news is read by most people and is also a favorite newspaper content, sports news is read by less than half but also rates high as a favorite. Similarly, economic news is read by two-thirds of the readers but is enjoyed by relatively few, and book reviews get low readership and a low preference rating (see Table 5-6).

Table 5–6

Newspaper Content Preferences

Type of Content:	% Readership	% Like Most	Intensity Score
High Readership/High Intensity:			
Local community news	84%	30%	33
International news	75%	25%	30
Comic strips, funnies	58%	17%	26
Advice columns	59%	16%	24
Supermarket ads	58%	12%	19
News briefs/summaries	74%	15%	18
Local politics, government	69%	14%	18
High Readership/Low Intensity:			
Economic news	68%	9%	13
Editorials/opinion	55%	8%	13
President/Congress	72%	9%	12
Letters to the editor	55%	7%	12
TV program listings	60%	8%	11
Celebrity news	65%	7%	10
Store ads (clothing)	57%	6%	09
Calendar of local events	57%	5%	08
Low Readership/High Intensity:			
Sports news (professional sports)	51%	23%	42
Sports news (local schools)	53%	15%	26
Business/financial news	46%	10%	20
Crossword puzzle	26%	5%	18
Obituaries	50%	9%	17
Help wanted/classifieds	43%	8%	17
Low Readership/Low Intensity:			
Food pages	54%	9%	15
Fashion and lifestyle	47%	7%	13
Investigative reports	53%	6%	10
Movie ads	50%	6%	10
Real estate classifieds	31%	3%	10
Movie reviews	48%	4%	07
Book reviews	27%	1%	05
Public opinion polls	52%	2%	04
Political opinion columns	45%	2%	04

Note: The percentages refer to the percentages of total newspaper readers surveyed who said they "usually read" each item and who identified the category as one of their three favorites. To measure the relative intensity of appeal or interest, the number who picked each one as one of the three they liked most was divided by the number who usually read it. The four categories were then divided into four groups based on high (at least 55% usually read) or low readership and high (at least 16% intensity of appeal) or low intensity of appeal. News and Newspaper Reading Habits: Results from a National Survey. New York: Newspaper Advertising Bureau, 1988, pp. 32, 34.

Television. Viewers generally like what they watch and watch what they like (Barwise and Ehrenberg, 1987). Furthermore, how much an individual likes a particular TV series is related to how often he or she sees it.[91] Menneer (1987) found that women, older adults, and people in lower socioeconomic groups tend to think more highly of what they watch. Preferences for particular TV formats vary across time, and particular shows often capture the attention of "everyone." Johnny Carson's final appearance on "The Tonight Show" in 1992 drew 55 million viewers, 62% of those watching TV at that time.[92] A study in Britain found that TV viewers are loyal to particular formats, with the greatest loyalty found for news and current events programs and dramas. Within dramas, loyalty is strongest for specific soap operas. Loyalty is lower for action/adventure programs (Brosius, Wober, and Weimann, 1992).

Based on the average Nielsen ratings for prime-time programming, the most popular TV format in 1989 was situation comedies, watched by an average of 23.75 million viewers. Second was feature films, followed by drama, suspense, and adventure programs.[93] Sports is a popular form of TV programming. The number of Americans watching sports on TV is greatest for professional football, followed by baseball, college football, boxing, and college basketball.[94] Preferences for particular TV formats may vary around the world, but large audiences are universal for several types. For example, Lull and Sun (1988) found in a small sample of households in four cities in China that drama, particularly series and specials, was the favorite type of TV programming, followed by sports, information, and light entertainment.[95]

How are preferences for different TV formats related? A British study constructed a typology based on such patterns, identifying four types of TV use: 1) Light Mixers—people who do not watch a lot of TV and mix different types and formats; 2) Heavy Mixers—viewers who watch many TV programs, combining different types into their TV diet; 3) Light Devoted—those who watch little TV but devote their time to a few types of programs; and 4) Heavy Devoted—viewers who watch a lot of TV and devote their time to a few types of programs. The two largest groups were Light Devoted (about 36%) and Heavy Mixers (about 30%).[96]

The Public Broadcasting Service scored highly with audiences in 1990 when it offered the 11-hour series, "The Civil War," the most-watched public TV program in history.[97] In an earlier national survey using viewer diaries, 9 of the top 10 shows rated most highly were from PBS, including: "Great Performances," "Nova," "Nature," "American Playhouse," and "Masterpiece Theatre."[98] However, while one study found public TV appealing to a broader audience, another found that an increasing percentage of public TV viewers saw cable channels as equal or better substitutes for public TV (from 40% in 1986 to 65% in 1989), with a growing importance of the Discovery Channel, Cable News Network (CNN) and Arts & Entertainment (A&E).[99] Waterman (1986) found that the audience for cultural fare on public TV or on cable represented a fragmented group among whom major increases in viewing were unlikely. While some types of programming are rated as socially desirable for most Americans, they are viewed infrequently. Hoover (1987) found that religious TV programming falls into this category.[100] Religious programs are preferred by those who are more religious, less advantaged and feel unhappy with the moral direction in which the culture appears to be heading (Wuthnow, 1987).

Music TV is popular fare for adolescents and young adults. The rating for MTV in 1990 among adolescents age 12-17 was .6, compared to .2 among adults age 18 and older.[101] Hall, Miller, and Hanson (1986) found that youth watch more than they listen and prefer the storyline to match the lyrics. One experiment which manipulated sex and violence in music videos found that sex and violence separately enhanced appreciation of the music, but together they had no impact (Zillmann and Mundorf, 1987).

Cable and Public Access. Public access channels suffer from poor advertising, less professional production standards, and nontraditional content. However, Hardenberg (1986) found that content, not production values, was what viewers liked about public access channels on cable TV. Being aware of public access is no guarantee of viewership; Porter and Banks (1988) found that 65% of those aware of public access never viewed, although they recognized it provided alternative viewpoints and represented decentralization of control. Sharp (1984) found a more favorable reception to public access cable among the less educated, lower income, and minority population in one community. Atkin and LaRose (1988) analyzed data from a national survey that 16% of the overall audience watched a community channel and 70-80% of viewers were satisfied with access fare.

Radio and Music.   As many people age, they turn to "soft rock" and "new age music." New age radio station listeners tend to be urban and upscale.[102] Children listen to radio primarily for music, with an overwhelming preference for FM rock music stations (Christenson, DeBenedittis, and Lindlof, 1985). In Sweden, Roe (1985) found boys preferring rock and jazz and girls preferring mainstream pop, classical, and folk music. Though musical tastes vary by culture, popular music has fans around the world.[103]

Those who like beautiful music or religious stations also like all-news formats (Wright and Hosman, 1986). Radio listeners who are most interested in news prefer a broad range of news topics, with particular interest in local news, political news, and soft news. Crime, traffic, and weather information received high overall ratings but were not preferred by news-oriented listeners.

Films.   How do people pick films to go see or rent for viewing on their VCRs? The types of movies that VCR households rent do not differ much from those they previously viewed in the theater (Lindstrom, 1989). The most important factor is the film genre, followed by the description of the film on the video box, the recommendations of friends and family, and actors in the film (Cohen, 1987).[104] People who rent films to watch on VCRs at home can be divided into those who think what they do is like watching TV vs. those who think it is more like theater film viewing. Silva (1992) found that more than half of a student sample said they had seen a foreign movie in a theater; enjoyment of foreign movies was the lowest of 13 film categories rated. Highest were comedies, followed by adventure films, drama, romance, mystery, science fiction, family, horror, war, musical films, cartoons, and westerns.

Perceptions about TV and Film

TV.   Asked to describe TV, the most frequently cited adjectives are entertaining, interesting, and informative, all picked by more than half of a national Roper sample in 1988. However, 14-20% called TV dull, too simple minded, or annoying.[105] An analysis of data by the National Opinion Research Center from 1975 to 1982 found that African-Americans had significantly more positive feelings about television than did whites (Bales, 1986). However, while there was a positive relationship between the amount of time spent viewing TV and feelings of confidence in the institution among whites, the pattern was unclear among blacks.[106]

People often feel guilty about the amount of time they spend watching TV. In Canada, a group which believes "TV addiction" is North America's top mental health problem has worked to get a series of 15-second anti-TV spots aired ("Tubehead—The Campaign Against TV addiction") in Canada and the United States. However, Gantz (1985) studied 416 married adults on how TV fit into their lives. His findings indicated that most saw viewing as a shared and valued activity that generally did not disrupt activities with spouse or friends. Some 14% thought TV interfered with the amount of time they spend with their friends.

Films.   One national poll of 1,084 adults found that 27% rated most new movies as poor and 34% as only fair, while 31% rated them good and 3% excellent. Overall, 56% said the quality of movies has been getting worse over the years, a perception shared more by older respondents and women.[107] Attitudes vary depending on the types of films. A study of college students found that they saw colorized films as more contemporary, more positive, and more potent than their black-and-white counterparts (Sherman and Dominick, 1988). Americans also have long-held negative attitudes towards sexually explicit films, with significant numbers wishing to ban such movies.[108]

Perceptions about Media Technologies

The best thing about cable TV is the number of channels. Audiences also like being able to watch programs without commercial interruptions, better reception, less censorship, and 24-hour programming (Everett, 1990). *Consumer Reports* (September, 1991) found that its readers like cable TV but not the way it's run. A third thought that too many channels were similar, a third wanted particular cable channels that weren't available and a sixth said their cable systems offered too few channels. Using 0–100 point scales, most cable channels were rated higher in program quality than the commercial networks, with the Discovery Channel receiving the highest rating (77); followed by CNN and PBS (76 each); the Disney Channel and CNN Headline News (74 each); ESPN (70); Arts & Entertainment (69); The Weather Channel and American Movie Classics (66 each); TNT (65); The Learning Channel (64); The Family Channel, TBS, and Nickelodeon (62 each); WGN, Lifetime, HBO, and Showtime (61 each); and Cinemax, The Movie Channel, and the USA Network (60 each). Of the three national broadcast networks, NBC rated highest at 57, followed by ABC at 56, and CBS at 53. The lowest consumer ratings went to MTV (40) and Black Entertainment Television (39).[109]

Media technologies have moved into increasing numbers of households, and Americans tend to share a positive image of VCRs, home computers, etc. More than half of one large sample rejected the idea that new computer technologies will benefit only the few, a view held by such critics as Schiller (1980). Some 58% thought new technologies would give them greater control over their information consumption and 69% agreed that everyone should know about computers. On the negative side, a majority also thought the new technologies would allow the government to invade people's privacy. Differences in expectations were found by age and social status. The more well-off individuals were less concerned that high cost might limit access to the new technologies among poorer people. They were more likely to believe that the technologies would provide "the electronic equivalent of Head Start" (Reese et al., 1984). Age was related to pessimistic views about the distribution and personal control of new technologies. Older people may feel they won't be around long enough to realize the potential benefits of new technologies and they are more likely to be apprehensive about the technical operation of computers, VCRs, etc., a fear which may be at the base of such negative attitudes.

Media technologies are viewed as "modern." Three quarters of VCR households in Germany thought a video recorder "simply belongs to a modern lifestyle," while only 35% of those from homes without VCRs agreed with this assessment (Schoenbach and Hackforth, 1987). VCR households hold more positive images of technology. A study which compared pay-per-view cable TV and VCRs found that VCRs were seen as more difficult to operate but providing more selection and control (Childers and Krugman, 1987).

Attitudes toward new technologies are modified by experience. People who owned VCRs for longer periods were more likely to express positive attitudes about watching and recording network TV (Klopfenstein, Spears, and Ferguson, 1991). Attitudes toward cable evolve from initial enthusiasm to disappointment and finally a modified appreciation by subscribers (Sparkes and Kang, 1986). Evaluations of cable news services grow more positive over time.

Perceptions about Print Media

What are audience images of newspapers? Burgoon, Burgoon, and Butler (1986) looked at image ratings for more than 150 newspapers, finding that image had at least three components: community involvement/personalism (includes concern for community's well-being, care for reader's feelings, courage, and professionalism); bias/sensationalism (reflecting paper's impartiality and restraint); and surveillance (watching over environment). In a national survey, 78% felt that reporters don't worry much about hurting people, while 46% thought papers look out mainly for powerful people, 29% thought the local paper usually tries to cover up its mistakes, 51% thought the paper was sometimes inaccurate, and 70% felt the local paper was sometimes sensationalist (MORI Research, 1985; Lavrakas and Holley, 1989).

Several studies have looked at how audience perceptions were influenced by appearances of newspapers. Newspapers with a modern design format are seen as more pleasant, important, interesting, informative, responsible, and professional. Modular designs—where stories are arranged in blocks or rectangles—are seen as bolder, more readable, and more modern but less professional (Pasternack and Utt, 1986). Traditional papers are considered more old-fashioned and boring, less informative, and less pleasant than modular and modern papers (Smith, 1989). Covert (1987) found that visual compositions which may please makers—designers, graphic artists, page editors, and photographers—may not be as acceptable to readers. Readers prefer an active style of writing, which they judge to be more interesting and one they can read faster (Bostian, 1983).

How newspapers treat their readers also affects audience perceptions. Hartung, Jacoby, and Dozier (1988) found that people who complained to a newspaper ombudsman were satisfied with the newspaper's response to their call, particularly those complaining about errors of facts. Those complaining about news policies or news judgments were less satisfied. Readers differ on whether they prefer the use of courtesy titles (Mr., Mrs.) in newspapers, but a survey in a southern state found some support for a return to courtesy titles (Cloud, 1989).

Perceptions of Commercials and Advertising

Advertising creates intense feelings and disagreements. Zanot (1984) chronicles 38 public opinion surveys concerning advertising since the depression. Roper's annual survey of public perceptions of TV asked "is having commercials on TV a fair price to pay for being able to watch it?" In 1963, 77% agreed, 80% in 1968, 84% in 1974, 78% in 1978, and 74% in 1984.[110] In 1989, a survey by Opinion Research Corp. found only 17% of consumers viewed advertising as a source of information,[111] while 80% saw it as a "deceptive persuader" and 44% thought advertising had become more deceptive in recent years. The percentage of consumers who considered advertising to be fair or very believable was 35% in 1989, up from 26% in 1988.[112]

Attitudes toward advertising may be media-specific. One study found that 88% of adults surveyed thought magazine advertising was "usually appealing," compared to 66% for TV advertising. While 80% thought magazine ads were usually informative about products, only 62% thought TV ads were usually informative. A similar difference was found for believability.[113] Using different dimensions for making comparisons, another survey showed people rating TV advertising as more authoritative, exciting, and influential than the other media.[114] The 1989 Opinion Research Corp. survey found 47% considered TV ads the most annoying, but 79% also thought they were the most entertaining and 32% the most believable. Newspaper ads were cited as most believable by 30%.

In general, American and Canadian studies have found a concensus that commercials are a fair price to pay for TV but that they are too numerous and too long.[115] The American Association of Advertising Agencies has found that opinions of advertising are primarily influenced by TV advertising, although newspaper, radio, and magazine advertisements also have impact. Credibility, entertainment value, role as a social force, and consumer benefits of advertising are the most important issues. People are concerned about how advertising manipulates and motivates us, its clutter and intrusiveness, its content, and media support of advertising as an institution. Negative opinions center on credibility, content, intrusiveness, and ability to manipulate and motivate us.[116] Advertising presented as TV programs and often employing celebrities ("infomercials") became successful in the 1990s, blurring the lines between programming and advertising and adding to the clutter, generally on cable TV.

Attitudes toward advertising develop early. In a study comparing attitudes of American and Chinese children and adolescents, American youth were more critical and generally inclined to believe "little" they see in media advertising (Ku, Yoon, and Greenberg, 1991). For Chinese youth, TV commercials were the most believable, followed by radio, newspaper, and magazine ads. For United States children and adolescents, newspaper ads were the most

believable, followed by TV, radio, and magazines. While
believability was tied to attention (the greater the attention t
greater the credibility attached to its advertising), that was
American youth, who paid the greatest attention to TV ads but
ads highest. Both groups were more likely to feel that ads give good information
than that they told the truth or were likeable.

Attitudes toward advertising and marketing vary from one country to another.
One critic noted that commercialism is almost revered in Hong Kong but
everyone is presumed to be a critic of ads in the United States. A study by
Ogilvy and Mather found that people in Hong Kong, Colombia, Brazil, and
Britain are much more positive about advertising than are Americans. However,
West Germans disliked ads more than did Americans in that study.[117] When
the Berlin Wall fell, Eastern Europeans were introduced to a heavier diet of
advertising. After being told for 40 years about advertising as one of the evils
of capitalism, East Germans were distrustful of advertising. Those feelings
persist, according to one study. Easterners surveyed were more likely than
Westerners to feel advertising takes advantage of people (59% vs. 52%). They
also believe that advertising makes them buy things they don't need (87% vs.
82% of Westerners). And 64% said advertising gives people a misleading
impression of products, compared to 60% in the West.[118]

Perceptions of Media Influence

When given a choice about who should have the most to say about what
appears on TV, Americans overwhelmingly (78%) opt for "individual viewers
by deciding what they will/will not watch." A fifth cite the TV networks and
stations themselves, while 11% cite advertisers, 9% the federal government,
and 6% social action and religious groups.[119]

A five-country survey found that Americans were most concerned that the
media had too much power (49%), followed by people in Spain (46%), Britain
(43%), Germany (32%), and France (29%). Americans also were more likely
than people surveyed in other countries to believe that media influence was
larger on the judiciary, legislative, executive branches of the federal government
and on public opinion. Furthermore, larger percentages of Americans felt these
branches of government and the public opinion exerted reciprocal influence
on the media (Parisot, 1988).

Local media are important actors in American communities. Janowitz (1952)
found, for example, that people in smaller homogeneous communities thought
local newspapers should promote social consensus. Tichenor, Donohue, and
Olien (1980) have demonstrated that residents of larger diverse communities
are more likely to support media content which is controversial and conflict-
oriented. Smith (1984) found that newspapers and TV were considered the
most influential of 12 community groups in one city. Broadcast media got

almost 30% of the nominations as institutions exercising the "greatest influence," followed by daily newspapers with 21%. Most residents were satisfied with the media's role in supporting the community, and two-thirds felt that the media projected at least a positive image of the community, with strong consensus among racial and income groups. Those rating the quality of life highly were more likely to feel the media conveyed a positive image of the community than those less satisfied with the area.

Perceptions of Media as a Whole

Audience perceptions of the media are multi-dimensional. In a series of studies, Kosicki and McLeod (1990) found five dimensions to audience perceptions: 1) news information quality, a positive summary evaluation of media as accurate, complete, thoughtful, and responsible; 2) patterning of news, an expression of faith in the ability of the news to make sense and provide a comprehensive picture of the world over time; 3) negative aspects of content, a summary of four frequent criticisms of the news as dull, sensationalistic, dominated by bad news, and biased; 4) dependency and control, a tendency to see media institutions as too powerful; and 5) a view of the media as representing special interests in their reports or the media themselves being special interests in society. Each of these dimensions has been subjected to scrutiny by mass communication scholars.

Confidence in the Media as an Institution.   Americans' confidence in the media has declined through the years. According to Gallup polls (1986), 39% said they had a high level of confidence (great deal or quite a lot) in newspapers in 1973, a figure that went to 51% in 1979, 38% in 1983, and 37% in 1986. Some 37% said they had a high level of confidence in TV in 1973, compared to 38% in 1979, 25% in 1983 and 27% in 1986. In a ranking of 10 major institutions in 1986, the military received the highest level of confidence, followed by churches/organized religion, the U.S. Supreme Court, banks and public schools (tied), Congress, newspapers, organized labor, big business, and, lastly, television. In a comparative study of four European countries and the United States, public confidence in the media was highest in the United States (69% saying they had a great deal or some), followed by France (48%), Spain (46%), Germany (41%), and Britain (38%) (Parisot, 1988).[120]

Media as Sources of Information.   Media are generally cited as preferred sources of information about what's going on in the world today. Roper (Miller, 1989) found that television and newspapers top the list of preferences, followed by radio, magazines, and then people.[121] Travis and Violato (1985) found that veteran teachers cited newspapers first, television second, and magazines third as important sources of ideas and information about social, political, and economic matters.

Perceptions of Media Practices.   Audiences have been critical of media news-gathering techniques and presentation styles.[122] Braman (1988) sifted through complaints to the National News Council. While media present techniques as neutral and procedures as objective, public complaints suggest they believe that techniques are biased and can be used to serve particular purposes, such as private interests. The public also assumes intentionality in errors or distortions, in contrast to media codes that suggest media practices are designed to serve broader goals. Complaints about reporting standards suggested a need for presenting all sides in a conflict, including context and not being sensationalist. Complaints about style included not using loaded adjectives. Complaints about news-gathering procedures included objections to interrupting people during interviews, using more than one source, using the same type of source for both sides of a story, and watching for conflicts of interest. Izard (1985) found in a national survey that a majority said they believe the major news media often cover up stories that ought to be reported,[123] and 70% said journalists violate the privacy of individual citizens. Whitney (1985) found that key complaints about the media by residents of Baltimore and Toledo were sensationalism, invasion of personal privacy, and reporters' lack of concern about whether their stories hurt people.[124]

Specific events often affect people's perceptions of media practices. For example, in the 1991 Persian Gulf war, 42% of those surveyed in one state said they had more respect for network TV, and 49% said they had more respect for the Cable News Network (CNN) for its coverage of the "first live war."[125]

Journalists and the public differ widely in their judgments about what news-gathering practices are acceptable. While three-fourths of the public think a photographer should never take a picture of a women held hostage who escaped and ran half-naked into the street, 53% of journalists said they "sometimes" would take such a picture (Gaziano, 1987). While 68% of the public said secret government documents dealing with an important national security issue never should be reported, 72% of journalists said they should "sometimes." Similar discrepancies are found in other situations. Weaver and Daniels (1992) found that public support for investigative reporting techniques—such as using hidden cameras and microphones—may depend on a city's tradition.[126] Criticism of media practices also is found in other countries and is not limited to the United States.[127]

Public Support for the First Amendment.   Freedom of the press in the United States depends on the First Amendment to the Constitution. Although crucial for the expression of unpopular ideas, the First Amendment often seems to be held with little esteem by Americans. Queried in public opinion polls, most Americans voice their support for civil liberties such as free speech, but given specific situations in which these same principles should be applied, they withhold their support. One survey of young Americans age 15-25 learned that they would fight to preserve freedom of speech, religion, and career but not the press. However, this is not a recent phenomenon. The first Gallup Poll question in 1936 asked people if they thought "the press should have the right to say anything it pleases about public officials," and only 52% said yes. Also, the Agenda Foundation study found that a majority of respondents agreed with 10 of 15 statements about freedom of expression which were contrary to established law (Stempel, 1991; Wyatt, 1991).

A national survey on free expression and the American public in 1991 found that political speech fared better than other forms of communication in both ordinary and extraordinary times, with more than two-thirds willing to protect the right to disagree with the president. Actions and speech viewed as seditious received minimal protection. Media rights rated lower than individual rights, with more than a fourth offering no protection to newspapers that editorialize during political campaigns. In only a few circumstances (for example, journalists criticizing politicians or retaining books in a library despite protests over the content) did even a majority endorse what the Constitution demands (Wyatt, 1991). In another analysis of this survey, Voakes (1992) found that people dissatisfied with the media also tended to support press rights. Education and knowledge of civil liberties were positively related to support for media rights. Men were more supportive than women; those who were younger, more liberal, and more educated also showed greater support for media rights (Miller, Andsager, and Wyatt, 1992; Andsager, 1992).

Do media users differ in their tolerance for others and respect for civil liberties? Earlier work by Gerbner et al. (1982) showed that heavy TV viewers were more distrustful of the world in general. Elten and Rimmer (1992) analyzed a national survey conducted in 1987 by the Gallup Organization on attitudes toward political issues. They found that people who were more newspaper reliant (who said they relied on that medium for most of their information on national affairs) showed more tolerance than did those who relied on TV for such information. The difference persisted even when other variables such as age, education, religiosity, and church attendance were taken into account. Newspaper reliant individuals showed higher support for three civil liberties— free speech, free press, and privacy.

Media Credibility.   Considerable resentment of the press is found in the general public, and it affects their assessment of media credibility. In the past decade or so, journalists and others in the news media have been concerned about what many see as a significant decline in media credibility among the general public. Credibility has been the subject of considerable controversy in the literature. Sometimes it is left undefined, and audiences are merely asked which source of information they would believe first or how much credibility they place in the media. The following have been identified in different studies as components of credibility: dynamism, competence, trustworthiness, safety, authoritativeness, character, and honesty (Singletary, 1976). Trustworthiness and expertise of source, objectivity, and clarity are related to credibility (Salwen, 1987).

Surveys conducted for the American Society of Newspaper Editors in 1985 showed that three-fourths of the American public had serious reservations about the credibility of the press, but that included a broad assessment of not only image but also practices such as rudeness and insensitivity. Gaziano (1988) concluded that the 1985 credibility studies do not portray a crisis in public confidence in the media but that the public has a largely favorable impression. However, the data do indicate the public has major reservations about such issues as bias, the amount of bad news, coverage of groups, invasion of privacy, and media treatment of the average citizen. In general, the public was most critical of the media in their coverage of ordinary people and issues of accuracy and bias (McGrath and Gaziano, 1986). Many felt the media often hurt people while trying to get a good story, don't give enough favorable coverage to the average person, or take advantage of victims of circumstances. At the same time, about 60% rated media coverage of stories with which they were familiar very fair or very accurate and 78% said their daily newspapers were doing an excellent or good job covering controversial news topics (66% said TV news was doing an excellent or good job).

Robinson and Kohut (1988) analyzed another national survey conducted by Gallup for Times Mirror Co. in 1985, focusing specifically on credibility as believability. Results showed that nearly all serious news sources scored highly, with the highest ratings going to newscasters Walter Cronkite, Dan Rather, Peter Jennings, and Ted Koppel. The *Wall Street Journal* was the most highly ranked media organization, followed by CBS News, the local TV news, CNN, ABC News, *Time* magazine, NBC News, *Reader's Digest*, *Newsweek*, radio news, and daily newspapers. Only the *National Enquirer* and *Rolling Stone* had more doubters than believers. Top newscasters, daily newspapers and network news were judged more believable than the president at the time, Ronald Reagan.[128] The news media rate better on accuracy when the questions are more specific and less general (Whitney, 1985).

Credibility seems to be linked to authority and visibility.[129] Many people base their views of credibility or confidence in a newspaper on its performance as an institution, while they base their perception of credibility of TV news on the performance of on-camera personalities (Newhagen and Nass, 1989).[130]

Perceptions of political bias are at the center of many perceptions. The 1985 ASNE study found that a majority of people believe the media have political leanings, although they disagree on the direction. Almost half feel that papers which endorse a political candidate would not be fair to all candidates. A large portion of the public misunderstand media practices about separating out management opinion in editorials from the news columns; 4 in 10 said the editorial page contained about the same amount of opinion as the rest of the paper. A substantial minority (40%) showed a desire for curbs on freedom of the press and 71% said a person's right to a fair trial outweighed the public's right to be informed. Gunther (1988) looked at trust in the media and people's attitudes towards abortion, welfare, and Latin American policy. Media trust ratings went up as the extremity of the attitude increased from low to moderate but then turned down again as attitude extremity increased from moderate to high. Thus, at both extremes, there was less trust in the media. Becker, Kosicki, and Jones' (1992) analysis of 1985 Gallup data showed that more than half of white Americans thought the media were influenced by advertisers, business corporations, Democrats, the federal government, liberals, the military, and Republicans. Some 47.7% of whites thought blacks influenced the media, compared to 26% of blacks surveyed. People's perceptions of the media are important for their potential impact on how people evaluate what appears in the media. For example, Fredin and Kosicki (1989) found that people compensate for distortions they think occur in the news because of how the news media operate; thus, images that the media are boosters, speak for powerful interest groups, convey too much bad news, and are of high quality affect people's personal evaluations of various topics appearing in the media.

Perceptions of media credibility by government officials show newspapers and news magazines with a slight edge over network TV news, though we need to update this information (Yankelovich, Skelly, and White, 1979). A survey of black elected officials across the country found them generally dissatisfied with the predominantly white-controlled press coverage of blacks on a variety of dimensions (Riffe, Sneed, and Van Ommeren, 1990). Metropolitan media were seen as more credible and accurate than the community media in a New England suburban survey (Nwankwo, 1982). Perceptions of bias and low credibility are not static.[131]

Newspapers and TV news have battled for credibility at least since 1961 when, for the first time, the Roper polling organization reported that the public found TV news more believable than newspapers. Since then, TV news has steadily drawn audience away from newspapers so that the margin is now about 53-24% (Roper, 1985). Roper's finding have been criticized from several angles. For example, the definition of credibility as believability has been questioned. That is, when people consider newspaper believability, are they thinking about coverage of a local news event while in the case of TV they associate credibility with national newscasts rather than local news? TV seems to win in direct comparisons. Rimmer and Weaver (1987) analyzed data from the 1985 study, finding that credibility ratings of individual media were not related to media use but were related to people's choices of media for news (local, state, national/international, and all). However, TV and newspaper credibility are moderately correlated, suggesting that attitudes toward these media are similar (Gaziano and McGrath, 1986). Some research has suggested the geographic scope of news was related to credibility. Meyer (1988) found evidence that newspaper credibility has two dimensions—believability and community affiliation; thus, the public may believe but disapprove of how a paper covers a sensitive local story. The 1985 ASNE study showed that newspapers did better than TV in only one context—"a situation in your local area that is hard to understand or is controversial." TV was the choice as most trusted to help understand national and international news. For coverage of particular topics, both TV and newspapers received similar marks, except that newspapers did better on local news and TV did slightly better on coverage of natural disasters (Gaziano and McGrath, 1986). Salmon and Lee (1983) found limited support for the idea that residents of a community would see the local paper as fairer in general than newspapers in general.

Channel dimensionalities are probably strongly related to credibility. TV's ability to show events happening may give people the feeling that they have almost direct contact with the news and newsmakers. Even if they are informed enough to recognize that pictures are edited, the visual element is a powerful factor that grey print cannot match.[132] Perhaps the most important factor is audience expectations concerning the media. Greenberg and Roloff (1975) say that audience orientation skews results of the credibility polls. People turn on the TV expecting entertainment; they go to newspapers for information rather than entertainment. TV news is a mass appeal medium—it does not cater to role interests as much as newspapers. TV builds a familiarity and is more easily digested than the complex world offered by newspapers. People who seek news find newspapers to be the most credible medium, while those who passively consume news thought TV news was more credible. Thus, credibility was linked to patterns of uses and gratifications. Even within media, context affects credibility. Cohen, Mutz, and Nass (1988, 1989) found that page location affected perceptions of fact or opinion in newspapers. Articles on the front page were viewed as more factual than articles on the editorial page.

Media skepticism may occur when people find discrepancies between what they see in the mass media and what they personally experience or learn from interpersonal communication with other people. An experiment found that introducing conflicting information from other sources increased media skepticism (Cozzens and Contractor, 1987).

A long-range view of media perceptions is found in a study which repeated the celebrated Middletown studies of Robert and Helen Lynd from the 1920s and 1930s (Caplow and Bahr, 1979). The entire high school population was surveyed in 1924 and again in 1977, more than 50 years later. There was a considerable increase in people's confidence in sources of information on public issues, one dealing with the major morning newspaper, one dealing with national magazines, and one concerning the campaign speeches of candidates. Students showed significantly more confidence in the newspaper in 1977 than they did in 1924. Fifty years earlier, 60% said the Middletown newspaper presented a fair and complete picture of the issues in the recent election; 71% thought so in 1977. While only 5% of the students in 1924 said voters can rely on statements of fact made by political candidates in campaign speeches, 21% of the 1977 students expressed such confidence a half-century later. However, there was a 9% drop in 1977 from the 50% who thought in 1924 that it was safe to assume that a statement appearing in an article in a reputable magazine was correct.

A variety of audience factors also can affect one's media credibility—people's membership in social groups, demographic characteristics, and personal skepticism. Gunther (1992) argues that trust in the media is best understood as a relational variable—an audience response to media content. Thus, one's distrust of media is linked to an individual's personal involvement with issues or groups. Analyzing data that looked at people's political, religious, and ethnic affiliations, he found group involvement strongly related to judgments of news coverage. If one identified with a particular group, he or she was more likely to say the media gave unfavorable coverage to that group. General skepticism was linked to distrust of media in coverage of Democrats and Republicans and born-again Christians. Media characteristics and audience perceptions of the media (ownership or structure) were not related to perceptions of media credibility. Other studies have linked audience characteristics to media assessments.

Social categories of members of the audience (for example, education, income, ethnicity) influence assessments of the media. Robinson and Kohut (1988) found that social categories were only weakly related to audience assessments of media credibility. This is consistent with Whitney (1985) and Lipset and Schneider's (1983) findings. However, Robinson and Kohut (1988) did find that the youngest adults (age 18-24) thought the three TV networks were more believable. The strongest factor, however, was gender; women consistently were more willing to believe the news media. Lowry (1986) found that education was related to the ability to recognize news bias. Race also has been related to credibility.[133]

Who is most critical of the media? Whitney (1985) found that the best read people were more critical of the news media. Gaziano and McGrath (1987) identified two groups of people as highly critical of newspapers. One segment was called "sophisticated skeptics" and was composed of more highly educated and wealthier people with more knowledge of news coverage and a tendency to act when angered by media content.[134] A second group was less well informed and suspicious, had lower education and incomes, less knowledge of the media, and a lower tendency to act when provoked.[135] Izard (1985) found that men and those over age 60 were more critical of the media. Lund and Rolland (1987) found older respondents more skeptical of TV news than younger ones in Norway. Gunther and Lasorsa (1986) found that audience trust in newspapers as sources of news about four issues increased as the importance of the issues increased.

Summarizing the Audience's Media Orientations. People's attitudes towards the mass media are quite ambivalent. They fear potential media control and feel guilty about how much time they spend with the media, although they have positive perceptions about its content and find it useful, interesting and entertaining. People also are quite critical of particular media practices and feel reporters don't worry much about hurting people. Americans also have a healthy skepticism about what they find in the media and are more concerned with the power of the media than are people in other countries. Confidence in newspapers has remained fairly stable in the past couple decades, while confidence in TV dropped from the 1970s to the 1980s. Public support for the First Amendment often seems quite limited, with more support offered for free speech and civil liberties in general but withdrawn when applied in specific situations. Public resentment of the press affects their assessment of media credibility but serious news sources such as the TV networks and major newspapers are rated as highly credible. Media evaluations also are affected by audience characteristics.

International Comparisons

There are many similarities and differences in media use and orientations around the world, though international comparisons are difficult because of differences in data.

Media Use.   While media (TV, reading, radio) capture about half of the free time available for United States men, they capture about a third of leisure time among Japanese men. TV use is pervasive worldwide and reaches substantial percentages of audiences in not just the United States (87% watched "yesterday") but also in Japan (94% watch daily), Western Europe (76%), Belize (student sample watched 19 hours of United States, Mexican TV each week), and Nigeria (where those without TVs go to others' homes to watch). The spread of cable TV or VCRs has been higher in many countries than it has in the U.S., e.g., VCRs in Germany, cable TV in Canada. Radio also is a ubiquitous medium around the world. While two-thirds of United States adults listen to the radio on an average day, about 40% of Japanese listen to the radio daily, and Japanese households have about a third as many radio sets as do American households. While only 20% of United States households bought a book in 1991 and 10-25% of United States adults read "works of literary merit," 13% of Japanese claim to read books almost every day. Americans appear to be slightly more avid fans of magazines, the average household purchasing 6 different titles each year and 83% subscribing to one or more. In Japan 8% read magazines three or four times a week. TV viewing patterns and motivations for media use among United States teenagers and their cohorts in other countries (Sweden, Australia, Scotland, Japan) tend to be similar, with much peer-group video viewing.

Media Orientations.   News attracts people to the media around the world. While 78% of United States adults watched TV news "yesterday," some 77% of an urban audience in China said news was the first reason they turned on their TV sets. Specialized areas also attract attention in both the United States (e.g., 84% interested in consumer, economic news and 56% in business news) and in Europe (4 of 10 claim at least occasional interest in business news). Preferences for particular TV formats vary across time within countries as well as around the world, but some major formats—situation comedies, drama, news—attract major audiences almost everywhere. A preference for Western music (rock, pop, jazz, and classical) has been found in youth audiences of the United States, Europe, and Japan. Public perceptions of new media such as cable TV and VCRs are similar in the United States, Britain, and Germany. Both Americans and Canadians think commercials are a fair price to pay for TV but agree there are too many and they are too long. Attitudes toward advertising show American youth more critical than youth in China, and the former thought newspaper ads were most believable while TV ads were most believable for the latter. Americans in general are more critical of advertising than people in Brazil, Britain, Colombia, and Hong Kong. Eastern Europeans remain distrustful of advertising and are more likely to feel it takes advantage of people than Westerners do. Americans also are more concerned that the media have too much power (49%), compared to people in Spain (46%), Britain (43%), Germany (32%), and France (29%). While Americans are highly critical of common media practices, criticism and skepticism also have grown in Britain, Japan, and Norway. However, Americans show more overall confidence in their media (69% had a great deal or some) than do the public in France (48%), Spain (46%), Germany (41%), and Britain (38%).

Summary

In this chapter we examined audiences of the mass media. First, we looked at how big a slice of our lives is taken by the mass media. We also outlined audience exposure patterns for TV use, newspaper reading, radio listening, attending the cinema, and reading books and magazines. A review of media diets showed a competitive situation in which TV increasingly is pitted against the print media. Then we analyzed media behavior patterns across the life span, inspecting media exposure for children, adolescents, and adults. In the last section, we reviewed people's orientations toward the media, including content preferences, media images, and evaluations. In the next chapter we will take a systematic look at origins of media behavior patterns.

Chapter Five Footnotes

1. Wood (1986) suggests modifying the principle to conclude that the public's demand for mass media grows only at the same pace as overall income.
2. Werner (1986) also found support for the relative constancy hypothesis in an analysis of media expenditures in Norway from 1958 to 1982, when media expenditures increased less rapidly than expenditures on leisure and other educational activities. Media expenditures went from 3.5% to 5.6% of total consumer expenditures.
3. See Horna (1988), Hunnicutt (1980), and Sylvester (1987).
4. These data come from several sources, the Federation of German Employers Association and the Naisbitt Group study of leisure life styles in Western Europe and the United States, reported in John Elkins, "Out of Time," *American Way*, Dec. 15, 1987, p. 16, 18, 19.
5. Some reports suggest Western European countries maintain a traditional view of work and leisure as separate; one study showed Germans with 30 vacation days, Italians 25, French 21 and Americans 12. Juliet Schor and Laura Leete-Guy found that Americans had an average of 16.1 days (paid time-off)in 1989, down from 19.8 in 1981. The average United States worker put in about 140 more hours on the job in 1992 compared to two decades earlier ("Work Rises, Leisure Drops," *New York Times*, Feb. 17, 1992, p. 7A.) See Roper (1980).
6. See Hamilton (1991) and Juster and Stafford (1991) for a discussion of the amount of time spent working or in leisure pursuits.
7. Some leisure situations also are seen as having some element of obligation (Shaw, 1985). For more on leisure, see Ellis and Witt (1984), Iso-Ahola (1979), Mannell and Bradley (1986), Ragheb and Beard (1982), and Riddick (1986).
8. See Andrews and Withey (1976), Campbell, Converse and Rodgers (1976), and Sneegas (1986).
9. Opportunities for leisure activities exist in the homes, neighborhoods, and cities where daily activities occur. Research has matched increased public interest as scholars have focused on leisure programs, social needs, leisure businesses, and life styles (Barnett, 1988; Kelly, 1983; Olszewska and Roberts, 1989).
10. In a time budget study in Japan, media captured about a third of the time devoted to leisure—2 of 6 hours for men (Aida, 1987).
11. "Trends in Television," report prepared by the Research Department, Television Bureau of Advertising, New York, March, 1988, p. 6. The number of people per TV set reported by the *Book of Vital World Statistics* (Random House, 1990) was: China, 1 TV for every 101 people; India, 155; U.S.S.R, 9; U.S., 1; Indonesia, 25; Brazil, 5; Japan, 2; and Nigeria, 170.
12. A. C. Nielsen Co. data, "Trends in Television," TVB Research Department, Television Bureau of Advertising, New York, November, 1991, p. 7.
13. A similar meter was introduced earlier and used by AGB, a British ratings company. The company eventually left the American market because Nielsen introduced its own meter (Rothenberg, 1990) but made plans to re-enter (Kneale, 1990).
14. Bill Carter, "Study Finds 'Uncounted' TV Viewers," *New York Times* Aug. 29, 1990, p. 2C;

Joanne Lipman, "Networks Find 'Missing' Daytime Viewers," *The Wall Street Journal*, July 6, 1989, p. 4B.

15. "'The Soul of a New Machine': Industry Views on the People Meter," *Gannett Center Journal* (Summer, 1988), p. 52. A.C. Nielsen Co. data.

16. Dennis Kneale, "NBC Draws Top TV-Viewer Ratings, As Networks' Prime-Time Audience Falls," *The Wall Street Journal*, April 19, 1989, p. 10B; Nielsen data for February of each year showed that the average number of households watching network TV during the nighttime (Mondays–Saturdays) dropped from a peak of 15,240,000 in 1980 to 14,510,000 in 1985 to 12,540,000 in 1990 and 11,810,000 in 1991. "Trends in Media," a TVB research trend report, TVB Research Department, Television Bureau of Advertising, 477 Madison Ave., New York, N.Y. July, 1991.

17. One-third of the audience deserts the average hour-long program before it's over (Brown, 1983).

18. *News and Newspaper Reading Habits: Results from a National Survey*. New York: Newspaper Advertising Bureau, Inc., 1988.

19. "U.S. Television Audiences," *Broadcasting & Cable Market Place 1992*, p. 111E. Nielsen Media Research National Audience Demographics Report, August, 1991.

20. In Great Britain, people watch an average of 25 hours and 21 minutes of TV each week, and the amount viewed and channels watched are quite consistent from one week to the next. Examining almost 2,400 British viewers, Brosius, Wober, and Weimann (1992) found strong correlations between the amount of TV viewed during each of two weeks in June, 1989. Correlations were high (r = .82 to .90) for people from different social classes, for light, medium and heavy viewers, and for other subgroups ("Decline of British TV," *Wall Street Journal*, April 12, 1990, p. 10A).

21. Soong (1988) found 28% repeat viewing (day and night) and Barwise (1986) found that repeat viewing of weekly prime-time series on the U.S. networks was typically about 40% or so for adults and lower for children and teenagers.

22. Some 77% of homes in the U.S. had VCRs in January, 1992, while 98% had a TV set, 98% a home radio, 97% color TV and 17% a camcorder, according to the Electronic Industries Association, *New York Times* dispatch. According to Nielsen data in a report prepared by the Television Bureau of Advertising, New York, in 1992, 65% of households had several TV sets, with an average of 2.08 sets per household, and 72.5% had VCRs ("Trends in Television," TVB Research Department, November, 1991).

23. See: Becker, Dunwoody and Rafaeli (1983), Henke et al. (1984), Reagan (1984), and Webster (1984).

24. "Trends in Cable TV," report prepared by the Research Department of the Television Bureau of Advertising, New York, April, 1988, pp. 13-14. Sources: A.C. Nielsen.

25. Those who disconnected cable in one study gave as major reasons inadequate religious programming and low variety of movies (Burkum and Niebauer, 1988).

26. This continues to change. The first week of January, 1992 saw the largest one-week total of video rentals (106.6 million) ever recorded by Alexander & Associates, an industry consultant. A national survey reported that 40% rented or bought movies more often than they did two years previously and 67% said they preferred to watch movies at home rather than go out to a theater. However, rentals increasingly are concentrated among the top 20 hits (Peter M. Nichols, "Home Video: Rentals Set a Record in January, but Some People Are Hoping for a Broader Base than Just the Top 10 or 20 Films," *The New York Times*, Feb. 6, 1992, p. 2B).

27. See: Boyd (1987), LeDuc (1987), Lin (1987), Roe (1987), Noble (1987/1988), Boyd (1989), Gunter and Wober (1989), Levy (1989), and Ogan (1989). LeDuc (1987) notes that the rate of acquisition of VCRs in what was then West Germany was one of the highest in the world, going from 3% of households in 1981 to 10% in 1983 and 28% in mid-1986.

28. "Trends in VCR Usage," report prepared by the Research Department of the Television Bureau of Advertising, New York, March, 1988, p. 5. Source: Paul Kagan Associates; Nielsen Media Research data reported in 1989 said 62% of all shows recorded on VCRs were network shows, 13% independents, 10% pay cable, 9% basic cable, and 6% PBS ("Market Watch/VCR Favorites," *Wall Street Journal*, May 8, 1989, p. 4B).

29. See White (1987). Harvey and Rothe (1985-1986) found that VCR owners increased their TV viewing time as a result of owning a VCR, and Murray and White (1987) found a similar relationship with viewing pay cable movies and VCRs. Henke and Donohue (1989) found that people who use VCRs to tape programs increased their overall TV viewing after purchasing a VCR, while those who purchased the VCR largely for playing back rented or purchased tapes decreased their regular network viewing after the VCR purchase and increased their viewing of X-rated programming.

30. The term apparently originates with Heeter (1985), Ferguson (1991) notes.

31. "Black and White and Not Read All Over," *Wall Street Journal*, April 27, 1988, p. 25. Sources: American Demographics; Editor & Publisher; Gollin (1991).

32. In the early 1980s, from 68% to 80% of American adults read a newspaper on an average day (Bogart, 1981). A 1978 survey (NORC) found that only 57% of the sample said they read a newspaper everyday, down from 62% in 1977, 69% in 1972, and 73% in 1967. Robinson's 1975-76 diary study found that 90% of those age 66 or older had read a daily newspaper the previous day, compared with 51% of those age 18-24. The percentage of people reading a newspaper rose consistently with advancing age groups: 66% of those in the 30-39 group, 79% in the 50-65 group, for example. Newspaper use also does not appear to depend on how much free time people have available (Robinson and Jeffres, 1979, 1981).

33. The annual surveys by the Simmons Market Research Bureau reported 77.6% of U.S. adults reading daily newspapers in 1970, 66.9% in 1980, 62.4% in 1990, 62.1% in 1991 and 62.6% in 1992 (William Glaberson, "Press Notes," *New York Times*, Jan. 4, 1993, p. 12C).

34. In major metropolitan areas, there is a growing preference to buy copies of papers rather than subscribe for home delivery (*Home Delivery and Single Copy Buying: Results from a National Survey*. New York: Newspaper Advertising Bureau, 1988; "The Marketing Value of Single Copy Buyers," Research Department, Research Note, No. 21. New York: Newspaper Advertising Bureau, October, 1988).

35. Fowler (1985) looked at changes in people's readership patterns when a paper switched from evening to morning publication. The amount of time spent reading the paper changed little but when the reading occurred did shift. Reading around breakfast and in the evenings remained stable, but reading at home or the office in the afternoons and around dinner time shifted to mornings at home or the office. Miller, Chen, and Everett (1988) looked at audience changes when two newspapers in Knoxville traded publication times. About 2% of respondents surveyed canceled their subscriptions because of the switch, but the largest percentage loss of readers came in the paper which moved to the afternoon slot.

36. *News and Newspaper Reading Habits: Results from a National Survey*. New York: Newspaper Advertising Bureau, Inc., 1988.

37. *Today's Teenagers: Tomorrow's Readers*. Report of study conducted for the Newsprint Information Committee by the Simmons Market Research Bureau. New York: Newspaper Advertising Bureau, April, 1989.

38. *News and Newspaper Reading Habits: Results from a National Survey*. New York: Newspaper Advertising Bureau, Inc., 1988, pp. 61-65. A study of radio use in urban Hong Kong found that 77% listen to radio at home and 20% at work, with 25% spending less than 30 minutes a day listening to the radio (Leung, 1986).

39. For example, in Japan radio receivers can be found in almost every household, and 39% of Japanese listen to the radio almost every day (Tamura, 1987).

40. In 1990, 10% fewer Americans went to movies than the previous year, according to the

Motion Picture Association of America, and the downturn continued. Initial estimates for 1992 suggested that the number of people going to the movies in theaters had fallen below 1 billion tickets sold, making that the third consecutive year of a drop in the number of tickets sold and perhaps the worst since 1976 (see Austin (1989:36); David J. Fox, "Movies had 3rd Best Year Despite Flat Attendance," *Plain Dealer*, Jan. 5, 1993, Los Angeles Times dispatch).

41. Some 12% said they watch movies at home once a month and 13% less than once a month (Keith Carter, "How Often People Watch Movies," *USA Today*, Feb. 10, 1992, p. 1D). Source: American Communications Group poll of 1,000 households for the Electronic Industries Association.

42. A comparison of 1949 and 1984 film-going behaviors in Britain shows younger people have always gone out to films more often than older people (Docherty, Morrison, and Tracey, 1986). Currently, the most regular attendees are age 16-24, 30% of whom go to films at least once a month.

43. "Film Audience Bias to Young," *Marketing* (March 12, 1987) 28(10):76. In 1985, some 71% of those age 18-24 went to a film at least once a month, compared to 43% of those age 25-29, 37% age 30-49, 15% age 50-64, and 6% age 65 or older ("Flick Figures," *Wall Street Journal*, Jan. 16, 1987, Sec. 2, p. 21).

44. Foreign film audiences are: better educated in a university community (Smythe, Lusk, and Lewis, 1953), older in Rochester, N.Y. (Austin, 1984), single in Austin, Texas (Faber, O'Guinn, and Hardy, 1988), more educated with a higher foreign orientation among renters of foreign film videos (Ogan, 1990).

45. "Only 40% of Households Bought Books in '91," *Plain Dealer*, Jan. 13, 1992, p. 5D. Associated Press dispatch. Survey of 16,000 U.S. households from April, 1990 to March, 1991, sponsored by American Book Sellers Association, Association of American Publishers, and the Book Industry Study Group, Inc.

46. The figures draw on several large-scale surveys done for the National Endowment for the Arts ("U.S. Literary Tastes Lean to the Lightweight," *Wall Street Journal*, July 14, 1989, p. 1B).

47. Howard Goldberg, "Yawning Apathy in Home Entertainment Center," *Plain Dealer*, Feb. 26, 1992, p. 10G. Associated Press dispatch. AP poll of 1,001 adults taken Jan. 22-26 by ICR Survey Research Group of Media, Pa.

48. *News and Newspaper Reading Habits*. New York: Newspaper Advertising Bureau, 1988, p. 66.

49. The chief source for subscriptions is publisher mailings (43%), followed by cards inserted in magazines (22%) and stamp sheets (12%) (*The Study of Magazine Buying Patterns*, conducted by Audits & Surveys and sponsored by Publishers Clearing House in collaboration with the Magazine Publishers of America. New York: Publishers Clearing House, 1991).

50. *The Magazine Handbook*. No. 59. New York: Magazine Publishers of America, 1991. Although various lists exist, an analysis of audience surveys found that 10 categories best describe consumer magazine preferences: home operations/literary (e.g., *McCall's*), home operations/nonliterary (e.g., *Family Circle*), glamour (e.g., *Cosmopolitan*), sensationalistic (e.g., *True Story*), intellectual/cultural (e.g., Psychology Today), general interest/mass audience (e.g., *Reader's Digest*), business (e.g., *Forbes*), sexually-oriented (e.g., *Playboy*), home decorating (e.g., *American Home*), home operations/young mothers (e.g., *Parents*) (Cannon and Williams, 1988).

51. See: California Department of Education (1980) and Whitehead, Capey, Maddren, and Wellings (1977), cited in Neuman (1986).

52. This has been found in several countries. Nordberg and Nordstrom (1986) note that three-fourths of the Swedish population watch TV, listen to radio, and read morning newspapers each day, while 20-40% use other media. Even in Bali, Indonesia, use of TV was associated with greater use of traditional media (puppet shows, music, dances) and more interpersonal

communication (Anshary, 1988). An Australian survey found that four out of five people reported watching TV news regularly and reading the newspaper each day (Schibeci, 1989).

53. Analysis of six National Opinion Research Center (NORC) surveys (1975 through 1983) found a total of 477 respondents who reported watching less than 30 minutes of TV per day (Roberts, 1987). They also were less likely to read newspapers than others.

54. Dependence was determined by six questions ascertaining how people felt about the media, which they preferred for news, which they would miss the most if they had to do without, which they believed most reliable, and which they thought would help them best understand a situation. Different questions were used for identifying radio- and magazine-dependent groups, so those percentages were not "constructed" in the same manner and the percentages vary.

55. These included: stockmarket quotations, sports, consumer news, features, local entertainment news, local merchant price comparisons and advertising, instant headline news updates, and puzzles for children and adults.

56. Also see Robinson and Jeffres (1979), who found time devoted to newspapers declined while that spent watching TV rose from 1965 to 1975, particularly among older people.

57. Between 1975 and 1977, the percent of 18-30-year-olds claiming to read the newspaper daily dropped from 51% to 42% and those aged 31-43 from 68% to 60%. A greater decline was found among the younger age groups, particularly those aged 30-39.

58. *News and Newspaper Reading Habits: Results from a National Survey.* New York: Newspaper Advertising Bureau, Inc., 1988.

59. The specific question was: "Some people feel that, generally, you can find out all you want to know about big news stories from 'TV news programs.' Others generally want the additional details that 'newspapers' give you on a big story. Which best describes the way you feel?" Another version switched the position of "newspapers" and "TV news programs" to avoid biasing responses.

60. Even when TV is unavailable in the home, as is often the case in developing countries, children get access to TV. Erdogan (1985) found that 55% of children in a Turkish town didn't have TV but still viewed it elsewhere. Exposure to radio and TV generally was low until children reach the seventh or eighth grade.

61. "Trends in Viewing," Research Department, TV Bureau of Advertising, July, 1988. Viewing data from A.C. Nielsen's people meter sample.

62. In the 1970s, Comstock and his colleagues (1978) reported that children age 2-5 watch TV 29 hours a week and children age 6-7 some 26.7 hours a week. Older studies show less viewing, suggesting there has been a general increase over the past couple decades.

63. Kevin Goldman, "Ratings at Kids' Viewing Times Are Off," *Wall Street Journal*, Oct. 30, 1992, p. 5B.

64. Barnhurst and Wartella's (1991) analysis of student recollections about how newspapers fit into their lives shows that newspapers were almost invisible in childhood, gaining some attention during the school years and finally being tied to adulthood.

65. After reviewing research on this program, Stone (1988) concluded that it provides papers for many youth not having papers at home and that those who read a newspaper in the classroom reported enjoying reading papers more than those who did not.

66. See Wartella (1979) and Ward, Wackman, and Wartella (1977). Greenberg and Reeves (1976) found the perceptions of reality of TV among children increasing as the specificity of content increases.

67. Current research has shifted to process-oriented approaches which look at the individual's interactions with other people and contexts (Peterson, 1988). Also see Dornbusch (1989).

68. For more on the adolescence period see: Hall (1904) and Peterson (1988).

69. In German-speaking portions of Switzerland, more than 50% of a sample of students reported using TV, radio, and phonograph records daily; while 40% read books, 25% newspapers,

and 14% comics (Bonfadelii, 1986). Kam and Valbuena (1988) found in a survey of teenagers in Singapore that 98% read newspapers, 77% read a daily paper, 73% read world news, 70% checked TV/cinema listings, 50% read news of Asia, 79% read magazines, with music magazines read most frequently, followed by comics and local entertainment magazines, Western fashion magazines, and sports magazines. Some 85% listen to the radio, with 48% tuning in daily and a majority listening to music programs, 65% to Western pop programs, 40% to rock music, and 71% to English-language programs. More than 97% watch TV, 79% daily, with most shows watched of Western origin.

70. See: Comstock (1975), Cowie (1981/1982), von Feilitzen (1976), and Robinson (1977).

71. "Trends in Viewing," Research Department, TV Bureau of Advertising, July, 1988. Viewing data from A. C. Nielsen's people meter sample. Smith, Sachs, Chant, and Carss (1988) found that young people in Australia and Sweden watch TV two hours or more each school day, with 50% watching 2-3 hours each day on the weekends.

72. Stipp (1985) found that more adolescents (95%) watch music videos than do children (85%). Music videos are more attractive than other types of TV programming among Japanese youth (Kojima, 1986).

73. Smith, Sachs, Chant, and Carss (1988) examined Australian and Swedish adolescents.

74. The increase in use of news-oriented print media in senior high school is greater among boys than girls (Weber and Fleming, 1983).

75. Comparable figures for other media were: watching TV, 18% more, 48% less; radio listening, 60% more, 14% less; reading magazines, 46% more, 23% less.

76. *Today's Teenagers: Tomorrow's Readers.* Report of study conducted for the Newsprint Information Committee by the Simmons Market Research Bureau. New York: Newspaper Advertising Bureau, April, 1989.

77. "Odds and Ends," *Wall Street Journal*, Sept. Results from a National Survey. New York: Newspaper Advertising Bureau, Inc., 1988.

78. Elliott and Quattlebaum (1979) found support for earlier findings that newspapers are found to be most useful by adolescents for learning about civic leaders, keeping an eye on government, keeping involved in important events, and finding information about daily life. Adoni (1979) found that teenagers who read newspapers also attach importance to political and voluntary activities; use of other media was not related to such values.

79. Crowther and Kahn (1983) also found different age groups had the same patterns of interest, participation, and enjoyment in leisure activities.

80. Crawford, Godbey, and Crouter (1986) also found modest correlations between media leisure preferences over a two-year period. Reading books, magazines, and newspapers and watching daytime TV were more stable than watching evening TV and going to movies. Listening to the radio, tapes, or records was least stable among media behavior preferences. Highest stability was found for active sports and skilled hobbies such as playing musical instruments. Lounsbury and Hoopes (1988) also found considerable stability of leisure participation over a five-year period.

81. As adolescents, the students were oriented to active leisure pursuits: only 14% mentioned reading as their favorite interest and only 5% cited radio, TV, or the cinema. At age 24-25, media use was considerable and two-thirds watched TV two or three evenings a week, 46% had been to the cinema in the past two weeks, 38% read two or more newspapers daily, 55% subscribed to periodicals, and half read at least two books per month, yet the majority thought they spent little time on the various media; 54% thought so about reading, 62% about radio, and 62% about TV. At any given time, an individual's tastes in one medium were consistent with preferences in others; those who liked TV adventures also liked reading adventure stories in books. In adolescence, the boys liked action pursuits and adventure content, but by early adult life tastes were more varied, and interest grew for the informative, nonfiction, and the useful. Taste, in part, also reflects what the medium offers; thus, researchers

believe the media "create as well as reflect taste." Tastes were found to be related to socializing experiences as well as personality predispositions and outlook on society, although the strengths of these influences vary across periods. Background and ability were the most important factors predicting "highbrow" preferences, but personality also contributed. In the adult stage (age 24-25) tastes again were related to background factors such as education and occupation, and to personality predispositions and outlook on adult life. The researchers conclude from other analyses that a positive outlook orients the individual toward the varied, the demanding, and the factual. Conversely, poor adjustment, a sense of powerlessness, and an authoritarian outlook on society are associated with interest in strong stimulation within a safe, predictable, and stereotyped format.

82. Times Mirror Center for the People & the Press, "The Age of Indifference: A Study of Young Americans and How They View the News," June, 1990.
83. Times Mirror Center for the People & the Press, "The Age of Indifference: A Study of Young Americans and How They View the News," June, 1990. The percentages reporting regular readers were: news magazines such as *Time*, 18% of those age 18-30, 16% of 30-49, 17% of 50 + ; personality magazines such as *People*, 12% of 18-30, 8% of 30-49, 5% of 50 + ; supermarket newspapers such as *The National Enquirer*, 8% of 18-30, 5% of 30-49, 8% of 50 + ; business magazines such as *Fortune*, 5% of 18-30, 5% of 30-49, 3% of 50 + ; magazines such as *Atlantic*, *Harpers*, or the *New Yorker*, 2% of 18-30 and of 30-49, 3% of 50 + . Another study found that more than 40% of those age 35-44 purchase magazines, while more than 30% of young adults (under age 25) buy magazines and less than a fifth of those age 75 and older buy magazines (Cutler, 1989).
84. The three time periods are 10 A.M.-3 P.M.; 3-7 P.M.; 7-12 P.M.
85. Times Mirror Center for the People & the Press, "The Age of Indifference: A Study of Young Americans and How They View the News," June, 1990.
86. Times 20, 1989, p. 1B. Simmons Market Research Bureau data for the Newspaper Advertising Bureau.
87. Survey of 16,000 households sponsored by three book sellers, publishers, industry groups.
88. *European Omnibus Survey: Europeans and the ECU.* International study conducted in Belgium, Germany, France, Italy, Luxembourg, the Netherlands, and Great Britain (International Coordination, *Faits et Opinions*, Paris, November, 1985, p. 1).
89. Galician and Pasternack (1987) found that 82% of a sample of commercial TV news directors also thought network TV news presented more bad than good news and half said local TV news and radio news exhibit a similar pattern.
90. *Today's Teenagers: Tomorrow's Readers.* New York: Newspaper Advertising Bureau, April, 1989, p. 13.
91. Litman and Kohl (1992) found that the minority of people who frequently watch reruns on TV are close to TV addicts satisfied with current programming.
92. This represented almost 32% of all TV households and surpassed his previous record of 45 million witnessing the marriage of Tiny Tim and Miss Vicki on Dec. 17, 1969 ("Carson 'Tonight' Farewell Sets Record for the Show," *Wall Street Journal*, May 26, 1992, p. 2.).
93. Aaron Hightower, "Most Popular Programming," *USA Today*, July 3, 1989, p. 1D. Source: Nielsen Television Report, 1989.
94. "Television Sports," *Wall Street Journal*, March 25, 1987, p. 31. Simmons Market Research Bureau, Inc. data. Contrast this with the percentage of Americans age 7 or older who have attended sporting events in person, major-league baseball game, 15%; high school football game, 15%; high school basketball game, 9%; college football game, 7%; minor-league baseball game, 6%; professional football game, 5% ("Sports Fans," *Wall Street Journal*, April 4, 1988, p. 15. National Sporting Goods Association data.).
95. In addition to drama series, Chinese opera was very popular. Men were more likely to cite sports, and women preferred drama and light entertainment, such as variety shows.

96. Light Mixers had higher shares of viewing drama, films, and music/arts and lower shares of news/current affairs, sports, and children's programming, but they also showed no pattern of combining formats and had low consistency across time. Heavy Mixers watched many programs from different formats and tended to favor news/current affairs, while Light Devoted had higher shares of viewing drama, films, light entertainment, music/arts, and hobbies/ leisure/documentaries. The Heavy Devotees were heavy consumers of sports, children's programming and, to a lesser extent, films and music/arts (Weimann, Brosius, and Wober, 1992).

97. "'Civil War' Series Attracts Most Viewers Ever for PBS," *Wall Street Journal*, Oct. 1, 1990, p. 3B.

98. However, when asked which programs they planned to watch in advance, only "Wall Street Week" from PBS was in the top category, which was dominated by prime-time serial dramas (Steve Sonsky, "Viewers Like What They See on PBS," *Dayton Daily News and Journal Herald*, Aug. 28, 1987, p. 48. Knight-Ridder News Service dispatch).

99. See Sparkes (1989) and Norton, Windhauser, and Norton (1992).

100. Hoover (1988) notes that estimates of the size of the electronic church audience has ranged from 10 to 130 million. A 1984 survey found viewers of religious TV went to church more often and were more conservative. Scandals among some religious broadcasters saw ratings plummet, e.g., Jimmy Swaggart's weekly program lost 1.5 million households from February, 1988, when he held the No. 1 spot before his sex scandal surfaced, to late 1989 (Michael Hirsley, religion writer, "TV Religion Lives Despite Scandals," *Chicago Tribune*, Nov. 17, 1989, sec. 2, p. 10).

101. "Demographic Delivery of Cable Networks: 4th Quarter 1990," TVB Research Report, Television Bureau of Advertising, New York, February, 1991, p. 29. The Nielsen Homevideo Index Cable Network Audience Demographic Report for the fourth quarter, 1990, applied to 8-11 P.M. Monday-Sunday.

102. Meg Cox, "'New Age' Music Wins Wider Following as Many People Grow Too Old for Rock," *Wall Street Journal*, April 1, 1987, p. 29.

103. Darrow, Haack, and Kuribayashi (1987) found an overall preference for Western music by both Japanese and American college students.

104. Stokes (1992) found that a small sample categorized films based on five dimensions, but genre was used only in clear situations. Mood or feeling appeared to be used more often.

105. Steven Miller (Ed.) *America's Watching: 30th Anniversary, 1959-1989*. The 1989 Television Information Office/Roper Report. New York, N.Y., p. 24.

106. Bower (1973) found a U-shaped relationship between attitudes toward TV and one's position in the life span. Those younger and older were more positive in their ratings of TV than those in the middle.

107. Gary Langer, "Majority of Filmgoers Give Movies Low Marks," *Plain Dealer*, July 6, 1989, p. 9C. Associated Press dispatch; in the same poll 80% said there was too much profanity and violence in current films, "It Came from Hollywood," *USA Today*, July 3, 1989, p. 1D.

108. Some 43% feel theater showings of X-rated movies should be totally banned, while 38% favor no public displays and 16% no restrictions (*The Gallup Report*. Report No. 251, August, 1986, pp. 5, 8).

109. Similarly, a British survey of public perceptions of new media found that variety and availability of specialty channels were the two most frequent descriptions (Negrine and Goodfriend, 1988). Some 59% of subscribers said they were satisfied with cable programs but only 51% said cable was "good value" for the money. Cable audiences were more satisfied with lighter, entertainment-oriented channels, such as Sky Channel, which features music and general entertainment, and Music Box, a music video channel later absorbed into Super Channel; both had satisfaction rates over 70%. Channels specializing in children's entertainment, sports, and films also were well received. Channels such as public access, teletex information channels

and foreign language channels were seldom watched.
110. Steven Miller (Ed.) *America's Watching: 30th Anniversary, 1959-1989.* The 1989 Television Information Office/Roper Report. New York, N.Y., p. 25. A poll for the Ogilvy and Mather advertising agency found that 59% of the public thought advertising did not "present an honest picture" in 1974 and the figure had grown to 70% more than a decade later (Garfield, 1985).
111. Other surveys have found the public questioning the informational value of advertising (Norris, 1983; Soley and Reid, 1983).
112. John Freeh, "Advertising Is Losing Credibility with Consumers," *Plain Dealer*, Feb. 27, 1990, p. 2D.
113. *A Study of Media Involvement.* New York: Magazine Publishers of America, April, 1991; *The Study of Magazine Buying Patterns.* New York: Magazine Publishers of America, conducted by Audits & Surveys, 1991.
114. "Media Comparisons," TVB Research Department, New York: Television Bureau of Advertising. Bruskin Associates, 1990. The question asked was: "Which of these kinds of advertising 1) is the most authoritative, 2) is the most exciting, 3) has the most influence on people?"
115. Rich, Owens, and Ellenbogen (1978) found that 58% of their Montreal sample thought commercials were a fair price to pay for TV, but 86% thought there were too many commercials on TV. In the U.S., Sandage, Barban, and Haefner (1976) found that farmers maintained a positive view of advertising as an institution since a study 16 years earlier, though there was a less positive view than earlier.
116. When people are interested in a topic or object, they do not distinguish between advertising and news content (Grotta, Larkin, and Carrell, 1976).
117. Ronald Alsop, "Advertisers Find the Climate Less Hostile Outside the U.S.," *Wall Street Journal*, Dec. 10, 1987, p. 25.
118. Joanne Lipman, "Eastern Germans Distrust Deluge of Ads," *Wall Street Journal*, Oct. 4, 1991, p. 7B.
119. Steven Miller (Ed.) *America's Watching: 30th Anniversary, 1959-1989.* The 1989 Television Information Office/Roper Report. New York, N.Y., p. 25.
120. A ranking of the ethical standards for various fields in 1991 gave the highest rating to physicians (ranked high by 54%), engineers and college teachers (each 45%), then journalists (26%), lawyers (22%), business executives (21%), Senators and Congressmen (19%), labor leaders (13%), and advertising executives (12%) ("Congress Trails Almost Everybody," poll conducted by Gallup Organization, *USA Today*, April 1, 1992, p. 11A).
121. Steven Miller (Ed.). *America's Watching: 30th Anniversary 1959-1989.* The 1989 Television Office/Roper Report, 1989, p. 27.
122. A survey of business executives listed sensationalism, lack of knowledge about business, and overemphasis on the negative as criticisms of business reporting ("Criticizing the Press," *Wall Street Journal*, May 1, 1987, p. 19. Source: Egon Zehnder International).
123. A comparison of the public and journalists in Kentucky found the public much more likely to believe that newspapers sometimes withhold accurate, important stories because of fear they will be sued for libel if the story is published; 60% of the public agree this happens but only a fifth of editors do (Hansen and Moore, 1992).
124. Polls show Americans believe the press goes too far in examining the private lives of public officials (David Shribman, "Public Backs Inquiries of Official Acts by Politicians, Not Their Private Lives," *Wall Street Journal*, May 17, 1991, p. 16A).
125. "Press Won Respect in War, Pollster Says," *Plain Dealer*, June 2, 1991, p. 5B. Associated Press dispatch on Ohio Poll.
126. In a 1984-85 national poll, 42% approved of using hidden cameras, 29% of hidden microphones, and 32% of reporters not identifying themselves as reporters.

127. In Japan, public criticism of the media grew in the 1980s when journalists took photos but did nothing to prevent the murder of the head of a company, and when reporters exposed the private lives and activities of fire victims and high school athletes (Nakasa, 1987). In Norway, two-thirds of respondents in one survey said they could not always rely on the news in the newspapers, largely because of skepticism regarding editorials and opinions rather than news coverage itself (Lund and Rolland, 1987).

128. In Gallup's 1980 national survey of teenagers age 13-18, 31% said journalists have either "very high" or "high" ethical standards. Higher ratings of journalists were given by older teenagers (age 16-18), nonwhites (39%), teenagers from white-collar backgrounds, and those living in the South.

129. A 1985 survey by Media Opinion Research found that 40% of respondents gave high credibility to TV news anchors, 28% to TV reporters, 27% to newspaper editors and 18% to newspaper reporters.

130. In an experiment, Harp, Harp, and Stretch (1985) found that newscasters wearing "conservative" styles of clothing were rated more credible and effective than those wearing other styles.

131. Tillinghast (1983) found increased credibility among news sources (and journalists) following two newspapers' mergers and changes in management.

132. A TV newscaster's credibility may be affected by the camera angle and similar technical factors. McCain, Chilberg, and Wakshalag (1977) examined the effect of high vs. low camera angle on the credibility of televised speakers, finding that higher camera angles enhanced the speaker's perceived competence, composure, and sociability.

133. Looking at two national data sets, Becker, Kosicki, and Jones (1992) found that African-Americans were less critical of the media than whites and saw fewer outside influences on the media from a variety of sources. In a study of perceptions of media by white ethnic groups, Jeffres and Hur (1979) found that people who saw a positive image of their ethnic group in a particular medium also tended to evaluate that medium's performance in covering the ethnic community positively. International students are critical of U.S. media for their international news coverage (Viswanath, 1988).

134. Three surveys in Columbus sought to understand public knowledge of how the news media operate (Becker, Whitney, and Collins, 1980). Results found significant gaps in public understanding. Audience members were more knowledgeable about TV stations than about newspapers, and knowledge was related to exposure. Knowledge also seemed to lead to a decrease in confidence concerning people who produce the news.

135. They were analyzing the 1985 ASNE (American Society of Newspaper Editors) study data.

6

Origins of Media Behaviors
The Why Question

  I. Ways of viewing media audiences
     A. Media use and the environment/social system
     B. The individual level
     C. Structuring the media use situation
 II. Defining "media use"—active or passive
     A. Social categories—ascriptive and achievement factors
III. Impact of environment on media use
     A. Home environment
     B. Community context
     C. Natural environment—seasons, weather
 IV. Uses and gratifications
     A. Uses-and-gratifications theory
     B. Mapping influences on media behaviors
     C. Linking uses and gratifications to media/media content
     D. Influences from traits, social context, and the environment
     E. Criticism and summary
  V. Media socialization—the longer view
 VI. Communication and life styles
     A. Where do life styles come from?
     B. Why do new life styles arise?
     C. Relating life styles and media-use patterns
VII. Summary

or many years, communication researchers focused almost exclusively on media effects, although marketers have long constructed profiles of media audiences relevant to advertisers. In the 1970s, "uses and gratifications" theory emerged in investigations of how audiences develop and people's media behavior patterns emerge and evolve. At the same time, ideological debates focused on how "active" people were as media users, an issue important for "media effects" research but also a stimulus for efforts focusing on media behavior patterns themselves. Theories "explaining" the development of individual media patterns are ultimately linked to changes in media organizations and media industries that survive because of those audiences. Today, the picture describing the origins of media behaviors is more complex as work has coalesced under various traditions, and scholars have put forward several limited theories and clarified some of the concepts.

"Why do people engage in mass media behaviors?"—This sounds like an easy question but it isn't. The question is posed at different levels, some targeting specific media use situations (why you curl up with a book rather than TV on a cold winter night), some asking questions about individual patterns of media use (comparing, for example, a TV fan with a newspaper fan), and others seeking answers to the "why" question at even higher levels where they examine the impact of the media system or social system on people's media behaviors (seeking, for example, the impact of government regulation on content diversity and audience choices). Answers to the different questions are not necessarily incompatible; one "why" question often leads to another.

Ways of Viewing Media Audiences

One set of "why" questions locates the origins of media-use patterns outside the individual, although it doesn't claim that everything is determined by the social system. This structural/cultural explanation either stresses the importance of such national/cultural factors as social stratification and economic equality, or it emphasizes the way that the national media system and availability of content affect people's media-use patterns.[1] The size and nature of the local community also have been cited as factors (Webster and Newton, 1988). This structural perspective suggests that much media consumption is low involvement behavior that is essentially unplanned. Thus, people are more or less acquiescing to nationally laid plans beyond our individual control: we watch TV sitcoms because that's what the networks give us, or we enjoy some media because that's what we can afford, based on our place in the social structure. Much of the literature that focuses on the why question at this level is descriptive or anecdotal, although comparisons across time and comparisons of different countries will eventually provide more grounded explanations.

Media Use and the Environment/Social System

Certainly availability is a prerequisite for people to use media, and the more time a medium is available, the more time one can devote to its use. In Japan, Yoshida (1986) tracked an increase in the time people spent watching TV as programming expanded from a limited number of hours to morning broadcasts and eventually all-day broadcasts. Choices available at the time people decide to use the media are not endless for any particular medium,[2] and this limits people's ability to be selective. This simple fact has been used by media programmers to devise strategies for capturing audiences. For example, audience size of local TV news is related to lead-in shows and competing programs (Webster and Newton, 1988), and repeat viewing of TV programs is affected by scheduling and a continuing story line, both structural factors (Webster and Wang, 1992). Tiedge and Ksobiech (1986, 1988) found support for the sandwich strategy as a means of building audiences for half-hour prime-time TV shows, placing them between strong leading and following programs. Programming itself is not static as networks jockey for advantage. Davis and Walker (1990) found that inheritance effects (audience for one TV program continuing to watch the next program) were affected by program type compatibility and the number of options.[3] Some data also support the effectiveness of **counter programming** (scheduling an appealing but different program at the same time to compete for audience share) over **blunting** (offering a similar program that appeals to the same target audience as those on other networks; Tiedge and Ksobiech, 1987). Other media face similar situations—radio's dependence on commuter audiences and formats targeting specific groups.[4]

In its early days, TV offered one program during a brief time period. The choice for people who happened to have TV sets was simple—to watch TV meant to watch that program or nothing at all. With the spread of TV around the world, we have systems with structural differences that allow us to see how programming affects audience viewing. The American system—structured so programs generally start and end on the hour or half hour—encourages audiences to consider alternatives at those points rather than planning for the entire evening and then continuing with the flow.[5] The Swedish TV system's policy of not ending programs simultaneously discourages changes. A comparison of viewing styles in both countries found more viewing, more channel changes, more genre changes, and more choice behaviors in general in the U.S. (Pingree, Hawkins, Johnsson-Smaragdl, Rosengren, and Reynolds, 1990).

Bower's (1985) study of public TV viewing found that the environment was more important than age, sex, race, and education, which explained only 1% of the variance in the amount of TV viewing done on weekends and after 6 P.M. weekdays. Geographical location proved more relevant, with those in large cities viewing more. Since large cities represent a richer menu, location may reflect the access and opportunity that come with urbanization.[6] However, a national comparison of newspaper reading and TV viewing among seniors living in central cities, urban fringe areas, smaller towns, and open country found no significant differences (O'Keefe, Burull, and Reid, 1990).

The Individual Level

Since the nature of the media system or social system fails to explain all audience behaviors, diversity in individual media patterns or behaviors is linked to individual differences. Why do people use media differently and how do individual media use patterns develop? This question locates the origins of TV viewing and newspaper reading within individuals, who are viewed as having some responsibility for their own media use.

The tradition of looking at demographic characteristics of media audiences continues to be profitable. Also called social categories, these can be divided into ascriptive factors that we inherit or carry around with us—such as sex, race, ethnicity, and achievement-oriented factors—such as education, income, and occupational status. More recently, media behaviors have been linked to personality traits. For example, compulsively curious people may be hyperactive information seekers. Research into personality and social categories such as education and income is quite extensive.

One "why" question seeks to identify the uses and gratifications that attract people to the media and hold their attention. This perspective tries to link basic human needs with the gratifications people derive from media and the uses to which they put media. For example, if entertainment is important, we may use the entertainment guides of newspapers to help plan our weekends. If we want to ease loneliness, we may use constant background music from a radio for relief.

However, our own patterns of media consumption are not created in a vacuum with no influence from our families. Customs, beliefs, values, roles, and behavioral patterns are passed along from one generation to the next. The family is a major socialization agent involved in teaching us how to think about and use the media. More recent investigations ask how media use fits into life styles.

Structuring the Media Use Situation

Although the impact and origins of media use are more difficult to pin down, there are vague boundaries to media behavior units themselves. Rubin and Windahl (1986) define "media use" to include "the selecting, consuming, processing, and interpreting of media and their content," thus combining initial exposure, decoding activities conceptualized as message or information processing, interpretation, and reflection.[7] We can separate out aspects for particular attention. Thus, one decides to watch TV, sits down, makes choices, processes messages, and eventually concludes that behavior to begin another symbolic or nonsymbolic experience. The media behavior unit occurs in time and space and is the subject of the next two chapters on message processing. One "why" question focuses on why people actually engage in media behaviors in specific situations. What leads one to read a newspaper, watch TV or listen to the radio at a point in time? What are the intentions that lead people to seek media or other activities, and are such intentions triggered by different situations—dinner, commuting, companionship with family, etc.? Within the "uses and-gratifications"-tradition researchers have looked at how intentions are related to gratifications sought from the media. Others have linked specific emotional states to subsequent media behaviors. If the newspaper doesn't arrive in the morning, many of us are at a loss during breakfast. Our "media situations" themselves form patterns that are more or less peculiar to individuals, which is the focus of other "why" questions.

People's processing of media messages tends to fall into patterns that can be characterized in terms of decision making, starting and stopping points, and paths pursued. These are generally broken down by medium.

Reading Situations.   The context in which we read newspapers, glance through magazines, or study books affects our attention, comprehension, and retention. Some of the environmental distractions are deliberate, some aren't. Klein (1989) looked at three modes of reading—reading while listening, listening, and silent reading, finding that sixth grade children made more correct inferences following reading in the combined modality, followed by the listening situation and then the silent reading situation. Background TV has a deleterious impact on recall of difficult reading material, with stronger effects from background commercials than from TV drama (Armstrong, Boiarsky, and Mares, 1991). Activities with similar information processing demands are more likely to interfere with one another. Also, background TV might interrupt concentration, disrupt short-term memory, create physiological (physical, biological) changes advantageous to message processing at the expense of internally directed thinking, or affect capacity interference. However, Armstrong and Greenberg (1990) found that background TV had only a weak effect on reading comprehension among college students.

Although reading for pleasure and reading to learn material for coursework are different tasks, the literature on instructional reading is relevant. Kiger (1989) notes that music has been used in various educational settings to enhance learning. College students showed improved recall on reading tasks when they listened to music but adverse effects were noted on eighth graders, perhaps because the former have more experience and a greater ability to adapt to repetitive auditory stimulation (Fogelson, 1973; Wolfe, 1982).[8] If audio demands grow excessive, attention can be affected.

How do people read the newspaper? Bogart (1988) looked at adults' reading style for weekday newspapers. Some 45% start with the front page and go through the paper, while 18% turn first to some other section and then go through the rest. A fifth read only certain parts and skip the rest of the paper and 14% read some sections, skimming the rest.[9] With the larger Sunday edition, only 32% begin with the front page and march through the paper, almost a fourth turn first to other sections and then go through the rest of the paper, and a quarter of readers read only certain sections and skip the rest.

TV Viewing Situations.   When people decide to watch TV, they start with specific or indefinite goals. The latter refer to decisions where one adopts a goal that can be satisfied by any of several alternatives and the selection is based on information generated within the process (Heeter, 1985, 1988). An orienting search pattern follows, with viewers examining channels (in a purposive, numerical, or other regular order), consulting a particular number (called search repertoire) and evaluating alternatives—searching until one is found or searching all channels and returning to the best choice.

Heeter (1985, 1988) identified three stages of TV viewing decisions: preveiwing planning; switching channels (once the set is on) for an orienting search, and reevaluating the current choices by switching around to find a better one. These decisions are affected by media technologies, particularly the availability of cable TV and remote controls.

Viewers with a more diverse menu—such as cable TV—are more likely to switch channels. Before starting to watch TV, cable subscribers and nonsubscribers behave the same but differences are quite marked once they get in front of the TV set (Greenberg, 1988). Cable subscribers do much more channel checking, checking more than twice as many channels as nonsubscribers and generally more likely to do it in some sequential order. They also sample lots of channels before returning to the program selected as the best option, and they continue to check alternatives even when viewing commences. Cable viewers do more channel changing at all points, during shows, during breaks between programs, and during commercials.[10] A study which gathered data on minute-by-minute changes in TV viewing found that the number of channel changes was positively related to adventurous viewing (e.g., watching two shows concurrently) and the extent to which people in the household were upset or disagreed over the viewing choices made (Greenberg, Heeter, and Sipes, 1988).

The remote control device, which reaches more than three-fourths of TV households in the U.S., has had a significant impact on how people watch

TV (Ferguson, 1991; Shagrin, 1990). Zapping—the deliberate avoidance of commercials using a variety of electronic means—is common. Viewers use remotes to switch channels when a commercial appears, largely to scan other channels (Stutts, Eure, and Hunnicutt, 1985). Although people flip through channels to avoid boredom or commercials, or because they're curious what's on other channels, they also often watch two or more shows. In watching two shows at the same time, clearly the viewer misses substantial chunks of programs and must fill in those spaces with inferences. This must be accomplished while trying to maintain a similar continuity on the competing program. This clearly will have an impact on how people process TV in comparison with the viewer who sits down, regardless of the initiating motivation, and then watches a TV program from beginning to end.

Hawkins, Reynolds, and Pingree (1990) used a variety of measures to tap the ways people move through an evening of TV viewing, with particular focus on transitions between programs and channels. They identified five different styles of viewing in a sample of adolescents, four of them representing ways of being active viewers and one corresponding to the stereotype of inactivity. Viewing styles were based on level of activity (number of times decisions made to watch TV vs. other alternatives, etc.), content loyalty, and program stability (frequency of channel changes during a program). In their sample, 46% were moderate runners (watched TV more times, changed channel less frequently, made moderate format changes), 17% heavy changers (changed channel most frequently), 14% light channel users (few channel or format changes and light viewing), 17% moderate zappers (highest in format changes and second highest in channel changes), and 7% light genre users (lowest in format changes and second lowest in channel changes).

Media compete with other people in the processing environment for viewer's attention. In an ethnographic study which watched seniors as they viewed soap operas in a community center, Irwin (1989) found the viewing was treated as an interactive social event. Soap operas were involving to the point of blurring the distinction between real life and the fictional soap opera world, though viewers were aware of the soap opera as an industry.

Viewing styles change with the season. Channel changing is greater early in the TV season, with viewing blocks lengthening later on (Heeter, 1988). The type of content available also affects the viewing style. Movies are slightly more important to watch in their entirety than other types of TV formats, but there is much more viewing of parts of movies than watching them from start to finish (Heeter and Baldwin, 1988).

In general, data show that TV viewing is a more active pastime than radio listening, with viewers doing more planning, checking more channels, zapping more often and watching more channels (Heeter and Cohen, 1988). Eventually, we need to integrate the message processing literature with that focusing on media-specific motivations and various aspects of the media use situation. The work by Armstrong and his colleagues is a move in that direction. The complexity of symbolic activity in mass communication will require moving beyond current lab experiments to consider more natural decoding environments that take into account patterns of audience activity/inactivity, different motivations, and influences such as distractions and interpersonal communication.

Defining "Media Use"

People often speak of "media use" or "TV consumption" as if they were self-explanatory. Sometimes the terms refer to the amount of time people spend engaging in particular media behaviors, but this captures only one dimension of these complex behaviors. "Television viewing," for example, may refer to the amount of time spent watching TV during particular periods, frequency of viewing, addiction to TV, attentiveness during exposure, the amount of content absorbed, activeness, decision-making behavior one performs in the service of personal gratification, and others (Hill, 1983; Salomon and Cohen, 1978).

For years there has been controversy over how **active or passive** people are in their media use. As Schramm (1973) noted long ago, the audience is no longer viewed as simply a passive mass of individuals but rather as active entities who interact with the sender of the messages. From World War I to the 1950s, the audience was considered passive and took the label of "target" audience, but research showed that the audience was not always responding as predicted. This led to the view that audiences may be divided into social categories—education, income, beliefs, etc. These categories served as reference groups for comparing media content processed; there was thus a dramatic shift in perspectives. The audience no longer was a passive, defenseless target. Bauer (1973) wrote that "people actively seek out information for such diverse purposes as reinforcing or consolidating their existing opinions, preserving or strengthening their self-image, ingratiating themselves with other persons, or even for the solving of cognitive problems."

In the 1970s and 1980s, critics debated whether particular theories were more "conservative" or "liberal" in their assumptions about the audience. Some critics preferred to think of the audience as either active or passive because it justified their view of what the media system should look like. Blumler (1979) noted that the concept of an active audience is an empirical question and subject to testing. He suggested that the viewer is active prior to exposure if he or she consults information about what is available, plans what will be consumed, has a prior expectation, or sets criteria as to what is preferable to consume. We might expect people to be active in some situations and inactive in others (Levy and Windahl, 1984). In general, the debate over whether people are "active" has moved from treating it as a dichotomy (yes or no) to one of deciding how active and when.

Social Categories

Demographic variables represent links between the individual and the social-structural environment. Some have suggested that demographic groups constitute distinctive cultural formations or interpretive communities that share basic interests in the media (Jensen, 1990). Demographic factors include both ascriptive factors and achievement factors.[11] **Ascriptive status** refers to those factors over which the individual has no control, including those based on one's position in the social structure at birth. **Achievement** refers to characteristics the individual is able to control and change, such as education and income. Life cycle factors—generally represented by age and marital status—reflect one's location in the life span.

Three achievement-oriented factors have received the bulk of attention because they seem to be the most significant: income, education, and occupation. Sometimes the three are combined into "socioeconomic status" (SES) or used to figure "social class."[12] Americans seem to apply the labels "working class" and "middle class" to such things as a college degree or a managerial position rather than to relative ranking in a status hierarchy (Vanneman and Cannon, 1987). Values, social status, and personality influence each other.[13]

Social class and social structure can have an impact on the individual's total media use, greater use of one medium than another, or content preferences. Self (1988) found education and income more powerful predictors of media choice than age or sex. The activities on which people spend the most time as leisure activities—watching TV and relaxing at home—are the same for low, middle, and high SES levels, although those in the highest SES group spend significantly less time viewing TV than those from the lowest SES group (Francken and van Raaij, 1981).

Education.   Education is related to use of several media, particularly print media. In general, the higher one's education, the more likely one is to listen to the radio, read a newspaper (Gollin, 1991; Lain, 1986), go to a film (Peterson and Davis, 1978; Waldrop, 1990), own a VCR (Scherer, 1989), and watch less TV (Robinson, 1990). The largest percentage of those watching the least amount of TV is among the most highly educated (Roberts, 1987).[14] People with more education are heavier readers of both morning and evening papers (Einsiedel, 1983), but the largest differences are for morning papers. College graduates turn to a newspaper more often during the day. They say they are less satisfied with what they get from TV news and want added details from newspapers. Robinson found that the better educated spend slightly more time reading the newspaper, but they spent considerably more time reading magazines and books. Some 48% of those with some college education or higher degrees buy magazines, compared to only 32% of high school graduates and 20% of those with less education.[15] Shoemaker (1989) found that more-educated individuals tend to use print information sources compared to less-educated counterparts, who prefer electronic media or none at all.[16] More education results in greater credibility for the print media than for electronic media (Ostman and Parker, 1986-1987).[17]

Education affects not only the amount of time we spend with different media but also content and format preferences (Mobley, 1984). The better educated are more likely to listen to classical or easy-listening radio stations, the lesser educated to top-40 or country-western stations. The more highly educated also tend to prefer public broadcasting on TV more than less educated people (Peterson and Davis, 1978). Henke (1985) found an increase in the importance and use of national and international news media. In general, people with more education also are more critical of the media (Schneider and Lewis, 1985).

Income.   Relationships between income and media use are similar to those for education, but there also are differences. Those with higher incomes are less likely to have watched TV yesterday, but they are more likely to have turned on the radio or to have read a paper (Gollin, 1991). In Roberts' (1987) analysis of surveys to locate non-TV-viewers (those who watch less than 30 minutes per day), he found the highest percentage of non-TV-viewers was among the lowest income group (10.58%, compared to the 4.32%-6.28% found for higher income groups).[18] Higher income families also are more likely to have videocassette recorders (Scherer, 1989) and cable TV.[19]

Income also interacts with age in affecting media use. Older people, especially those retired, are heavier daily viewers of TV and watch news more often. Magazine buying also is associated with household incomes, where 44% of those with annual incomes of $35,000 or more buy magazines but only 17% of those making less than $15,000 yearly.[20] Households earning $50,000 or more buy a fifth of all books in the U.S. and account for 40% of sales; households with incomes under $30,000 account for nearly half of all books sold and about 25% of dollar sales.[21] The percentage of income spent on media is quite similar for different educational groups but educated householders are 20% more likely to buy a newspaper and 50% more likely to buy a magazine because of unequal incomes;[22] thus, income acts as a constraint on some education groups. A study of poor working women who were the sole support for their families found magazines rated higher than newspapers as a preferred medium (Chatman, 1985). Household income is linked to expenditures for entertainment, including going to films, etc. (Talbot, 1989).

Occupation.   If we look at occupations in terms of a ladder of status, we find increasing print media use with advancing status (Einsiedel, 1983). Almost a fourth of managers and officials read both morning and evening papers— twice the figure for most occupational groups (Gollin, 1978). Blue collar workers read a daily paper less than those in white collar occupations or those who are not employed. Professional and white-collar workers also buy half of all the books sold in the United States. A study of chief executive officers at major corporations found that 43% watch 1-4 hours of TV per week, while a third watch 5-7 hours and 12% 8-10 hours. Only 7% watched more than 10 hours and 5% reported watching none at all.[23] Occupation and class also have been related to media use in other countries.[24]

The importance of occupation is found in a comparison of the media use among the oldest Americans (age 65-74, and 75 and older). The older of the two categories spends more time watching TV, listening to the radio, and reading newspapers than does the other group, but differences in time use between the new old and old old are not as great as those between pre- and post-retirement populations. Thus, employment is the major influence on an older person's time use—those age 18-64 spent 2.8 hours a week reading, compared to 6-7 hours among the elderly (Robinson, 1991).

Gender.   Changes in gender roles in the United States today are likely to show up in changed leisure behavior in the future. Robinson's earlier diary data showed the total time spent with mass media was greatest among single housewives.[25] Recent data show that women watch more TV than men do (Cutler, 1989; Robinson, 1990).[26] While 54% of women buy magazines, only 46% of men do.[27] Males age 18-40 are heavier filmgoers than females of the same age (Knapp and Sherman, 1986). Above age 35, men and women differ very slightly in average weekday newspaper readership but below that age the gap widens to 7-9 percentage points, men reading more than women. This suggests that newspapers may be losing ground faster among younger women than younger men (Gollin, 1991: 6). More gender differences emerge when we look at media content and format preferences.[28]

Race and Ethnicity.   Ethnic and racial differences also have been found in media use and preferences for leisure time activities.[29] Earlier diary data showed that blacks and whites spent about the same percentage of their free time with the media (44%).

Whites are more likely than blacks to read a daily newspaper on an average day (59% of adult blacks read a daily paper compared to 67% of adult whites).[30] Lavrakas' (1990) study of readership of Chicago dailies found whites reading dailies more frequently. However, Gollin (1991) points out that much of the difference in newspaper readership among racial and ethnic groups largely is a matter of education and income. Cobb and Kenny (1986) found black youth in a Texas survey had less access to newspapers but were generally receptive and had favorable attitudes toward them.

Although the earlier diary data showed no racial difference between the percentage of whites and non-whites who watch TV or TV news on an average day, more recent data are mixed. A 1981 national survey of black Americans found lower TV viewing among blacks in the South; rural residents also reported lower viewing compared to urban residents (Fairchild, Stockard, and Bowman, 1986). Bales (1986) found more TV viewing among blacks, who also had more positive feelings about TV than whites. Nielsen data show that black audiences watch an average 44% more TV than white audiences, 74.1 hours per week compared to 51.4 hours per week (Lipman, 1989). Black youth show heavier TV usage than white youth, even when differences in family structure and social status are taken into account.[31] Black adolescents also watch more music videos than whites (39.1% vs. 32.5%) and watch videos to learn how to dance and see the latest fashions.[32]

Surveys show blacks favor programs featuring black performers; the most popular shows among blacks are those with black casts.[33] Hispanic, black, and white residents of a southwestern city differed in their preferences for various TV formats in one study (Albarran and Umphrey (1992). Blacks were the most frequent viewers of sports, situation comedies, game shows, police/detective shows, and dramatic shows. Hispanics joined blacks in preferring soap operas, movies, music programs, talk/interview shows, reality programming, and westerns. Strong black viewership increasingly is important for the success of individual shows (Wynter, 1989).[34] Blacks also prefer black newscasters to white newscasters and rate them more highly (Johnson, 1984). The cable network, Black Entertainment Television (BET), launched in 1980, tends to do better among younger, more racially-oriented blacks than does black-oriented programming on major network channels (Jones, 1990).

Ethnicity affects media use patterns. Dobrow (1989) found that different cultural groups use the VCR to view foreign language videos, most from their country of origin. First-generation immigrants preferred to watch programs on the VCR to the exclusion of American TV shows, although their children were less attracted to viewing foreign language videos. Foreign students in the U.S. and elsewhere also use media from their home countries.[35]

Surveys of Hispanics show that those who are more traditional are oriented toward Spanish-language radio (O'Guinn and Meyer, 1984) and TV programs, while nontraditionals—younger and more educated—prefer radio and TV programs in English (Dunn, 1975; Greenberg et al., 1983).[36]

White ethnic groups also are not homogenous media audiences. By providing news of the ethnic community and the mother country, ethnic media seem to meet needs not fulfilled by the metropolitan media. Czechs, Hungarians, Irish, Slovenes, and other ethnics in one study spent a considerable amount of time with both ethnic and metropolitan mass media. Those who identify more strongly with their ethnic groups and who have lower levels of English proficiency use the ethnic media more often (Bednall, 1988; Jeffres and Barnard, 1982; Jeffres and Hur, 1980; Korzenny et al., 1983). A survey of ethnic school children age 5-15 found differences among whites, blacks, and Hispanics.[37]

Race and social class are often intertwined. Stamps and Stamps (1985) found both racial and social class differences in a study of leisure activities in a northern U.S. community. Within the middle class, reading was first and TV/radio fourth among both blacks and whites; among lower class respondents, TV was first and reading second among whites, but socializing/partying was first, TV/radio second and reading fifth among blacks. Similarly, social class differences were found within racial groups—among blacks, reading was first, socializing/partying second, and TV/radio fourth among middle-class respondents, compared to socializing/partying first, TV/radio second, participation in sports third, and reading fifth among lower class blacks. Woodard (1988) also found social class differences among black Americans.

Other Ascriptive and Life Cycle Factors.   Exposure to some TV programs is affected by **religious affiliation**.[38] Religious people are more faithful viewers of religious TV fare such as the "PTL Club."[39] According to some studies, Catholics and members of conservative protestant churches are more likely to watch Sunday morning televangelists, and Catholics and Protestants are least likely to be nonviewers of TV compared to Jews and other non-Christians.[40] Since religion reflects personal values, it also has been linked to motivations for media use.[41]

Marital status is another important factor. Married people tend to be heavier newspaper subscribers and cable TV subscribers (LaRose and Atkin, 1988). Compared to single people, they are more likely to have watched TV on a given day, to see TV news, and to spend more time watching TV. However, single people listen to the radio more often.[42] Bush and Burnett (1987) found in an annual life style survey of single women that divorced and those that never married both made heavy use of pay cable services, and all-talk radio programs were the favorite of widowed females. Robinson (1990) found that widows watch more TV than other groups.

The importance of marital status for media use was found in a study of five leisure pursuits (Stover and Garbin, 1982). Over a five-year period, changes in marital status were found to interrupt reading and media-use patterns. Those who continued as students with no change in marital status showed more stable reading and overall media behaviors; however, status changes did little to interrupt participation in sports or hobbies.

Impact of Environment on Media Use

All media use occurs in a physical environment, and that environment can have an impact on people's media behaviors. The physical context may trigger or inhibit media use or affect message processing. Since most media use occurs in the home, the family is the most important context. Here we examine that context and the community.[43]

Home Environment

TV viewing isn't the only media use that occurs in the family or at home. A sample of people's experiences found that 55% of childhood and adolescent TV use was done with the family and only 36% alone; 36% of reading occurred in the family context, 54% of VCR use, and 36% of music video viewing (Kubey and Larson, 1990). Several aspects of the home environment are important, but researchers have focused primarily on competing activities, family size and structure, joint decision making to use media, family communication patterns, coviewing, and parents' rules for media use.

Not surprisingly, TV has received more attention than other media in studies of the home environment. What does it mean to "watch TV" in a context? If viewing occurs alone, we have individual processing of messages and other behaviors engaged in at the same time. If viewing occurs with others, then issues of rules, styles, etc. arise. Here the research is meager but growing. Lull (1988: 17) points out that TV viewing is a "family activity that involves an intermeshing of the constantly changing personal agendas, moods, and emotional priorities of each family member with the fluctuating agenda of programs that emanates from TV sets." Furthermore, TV viewing doesn't just happen but is constructed by family members. Lull (1988) concludes that life with TV is best understood by examining the rituals—repeated, regular activities elevated to nearly a ceremonial level because of TV's cultural power—that families and their members create at home. Thus, TV viewing reflects the culture, household, and the individual at the same time.[44] Family viewing involves a set of rules, meanings, and practices.[45]

Media's physical location in the home also is a factor (Barrios, 1988; Moores, 1988). The practice of prominently displaying the TV set reflects the status a TV confers on its owners in urban India (Yadava and Reddi, 1988) and China (Lull and Sun, 1988), but wealthy homes in the U.S. often hide the TV.

Competing Activities at Home. The context and conditions of TV viewing are important for the subsequent experience: "Viewers watch TV while reading, writing, cleaning, cooking, eating, drinking, talking on the telephone, interacting verbally and physically with friends, family, and lovers" (Giles, 1985: 12). This makes it "messy, impure, contaminated with non-television activities."

Hopkins and Mullis (1985) interviewed parents and children on their viewing habits twice each week for two weeks, finding that fathers gave their "complete" attention to TV viewing 55% of the time and mothers 36% of the time, with the rest of the viewing done during domestic chores, child care or playing with children, and other personal activities that included reading, studying, and writing letters.

Family Size and Structure and Media Use.   Adolescents in homes where there is no father generally spend more time with radio and television.[46] Two-parent families and those with more children are more likely to have rules about TV viewing and use of VCRs which discourage children from viewing particular shows and encourage them to watch others; parents also are more likely to discuss the content of shows and videos (Lin and Atkin, 1989). Access to cable TV increases children's viewing of R-rated movies but doesn't prompt more parental rules on viewing (Atkin, Heeter, and Baldwin, 1989). Parents were more likely to set VCR-use rules for males than females.

Decisions to Use Media.   Decisions to engage in media behaviors and subsequent decisions on content often emerge after discussions and negotiation or are joint decisions. In a 1980 poll of adult women, 21% cited TV viewing decisions as a source of marital disagreement, more than twice the figure for politics and three times the number citing sex as centers for discord (Roper, 1980). In an observational study, Lull (1990) found that fathers controlled more program decisions than any other single family member or combination of family viewers (30% vs. 16% for mothers, 18% one child, 12% a consensus, 8% both parents, 8% several children, 3% parent-child combination, and 5% unclear). About 21% of those decisions occurred following discussions with others in the family. Half of the respondents in one survey said their video rental decisions and VCR recording decisions often followed discussions with spouses or children (Lin, 1989). Other evidence suggests that children have some influence in selecting VCR tapes for viewing, although parents feel they have more control than children over the children's viewing (Kim, Baran and Massey, 1988). Both agree that they watch TV together often. VCR use may be both a cause and a symptom of family conflicts.[47] Gantz (1985) found in one survey that many adults often watch TV because their spouses are watching. Most adults feel TV is a positive force in their marriages, with few expressing dissatisfaction with the amount of TV their spouses watch.

Communication and Other Activities while Viewing TV.
Increasingly, researchers are observing media use in natural contexts. Although these have limited generalizeability, they do move us closer to the actual behaviors.[48] They also shift our attention to the context of viewing from the object of viewing (Morley, 1988). A British study of what people do during

program breaks or between programs on commercial TV showed that conversation with other people was the most frequent behavior. For breaks within programs, watching commercials was second, followed by preparing refreshments, flicking through channels, and reading the newspaper or other print media. People showed more mobility during breaks between programs than during commercials within programs (Kitchen and Yorke, 1986).

While the TV is on, interpersonal communication is less frequent. Kubey (1990) found that talking coincided with 21% of all TV viewing in the family. The figure for conversation during other, non-TV activities, was 36%. Data in Germany show that the media have a definite place in family communication patterns, structuring the daily and weekly scheme of activity (Rogge and Jensen, 1988). Lull and Sun (1988) found that families in China have adjusted their routines around TV viewing.

Men and women may have different styles of viewing, men preferring a situation where viewing is done in silence, without interruption, and with fuller attention, while women prefer viewing as a social activity conducted with conversation and at least one other domestic activity (Morley, 1988).

Family Communication Patterns and Media Use.   Parents' attitudes about their children's viewing are related to family interaction.[49] Negative attitudes towards TV are associated with fewer TV sets per family member and more regulation of children's TV use. The frequency with which family members discuss what they watch on TV with each other is positively related to a measure of expressiveness—the extent to which family members can act openly and express their feelings directly.

Two dimensions have been used to describe family communication patterns.[50] In socio-oriented families, parents stress maintaining good relations with other people (encouraging their children to get along with other family members and friends) repress anger, give in on arguments, and avoid controversy. In concept-oriented families, parents emphasize ideas and challenge their kids to express ideas, question beliefs, and engage in debates or discussions over controversies. Lull (1990) found that socio-oriented individuals were more likely than concept-oriented people to use TV for social purposes (as background noise, for companionship and entertainment). Socio-oriented people also were more likely to use TV for a variety of other purposes, including regulative uses (to plan activities, for something to talk about), to facilitate communication (for common illustrations, topics to talk about), for affiliation and avoidance (to avoid verbal contact, to relax and be with family members, to reduce conflict), and for social learning (problem solving, behavior modeling, consumer decision making). Mothers in families that emphasize familial harmony (high socio-oriented communication patterns) report greater use of TV as a babysitter.[51] Family communication patterns also are related to other media use, including print and radio[52] and VCRs.[53] How families communicate also is related to the manner in which conflicts over viewing decisions are solved. Families that stress concept orientation solve TV viewing disputes via voting or compromise to a much greater degree than the other types.[54]

Watching TV Together.   Some studies suggest that children model their parents' behaviors, while others argue that children's viewing patterns influence their parents or that both patterns grow out of the same set of internal and external conditions (McDonald, 1986).[55] One study found that most TV viewing is not done alone and most of that occurs with peers (McDonald, 1986). Male and female heads of households were least likely to watch TV alone, and their coviewing was generally done with peers, while others in the household, generally children, spent almost a third of their viewing alone, a fourth viewing with peers, another third with nonpeers and the rest with mixed groups. When parents and children do watch TV together, it is largely the result of similar viewing habits and preferences.[56]

Parent-child interaction during coviewing begins early. Lemish and Rice (1986) found consistent "language-related behavior" among parents and children age 6-8 months. Gantz and Masland (1986) found that TV was low on preferred activity lists for busy mothers (below playing with friends or mothers) but that TV was often used as a babysitter. Mothers reported using TV as a babysitter about 1.2 hours daily, with mothers of younger children reporting more frequent use this way.[57]

Sibling coviewing is a dominant TV viewing pattern among American children. Almost two-thirds of the viewing time spent by adolescents is done with another family member (Lawrence et al., 1986), and children actively interact during TV viewing, with an impact on subsequent interpretations (Alexander, Ryan, and Munoz, 1984). The evidence on whether VCRs are used alone or with others is conflicting.[58]

Coviewing by siblings is an opportunity for influence and conflict. Haefner and Wartella (1987) found that younger children (first and second graders) were influenced in their evaluations of TV programs by older siblings when they watched TV programs together. Younger siblings spent more than a third of their talk asking TV questions while older siblings devoted more time to reacting and describing actions or characters or directing the other child's attention to program content.

Conflict over what to watch on TV occurs in about two-thirds of situations where siblings watch TV together (Haefner, Metts, and Wartella, 1989). A third of the time, there is no conflict over program choice because siblings like the same things, agree amiably or watch different TV sets when conflict occurs. When conflict occurs, most children use "low power strategies"—taking turns, bribery, or promises—rather than "high power strategies" such as using physical force or taking control of the set. Males use more high power strategies than females. Older siblings are more likely to win program choice younger ones (Zahn and Baran, 1984).

Parental Rules on Children's Media Use. Many parents try to set rules for TV viewing by their children. Such rules may apply to the amount of TV viewed, the time when TV is viewed, program content, the program selection process, activity accompanying viewing, and rewards or sanctions used to achieve parental goals. A Gallup Poll found that 60% of parents who watch TV with their children at least occasionally feel uncomfortable about the content of the programs they see, and sex, violence, and bad language are the principal causes of distress. The most common response is to switch channels (cited by 46%), followed by turning the TV off (24%), and explaining the situation to their children.[59] Lull (1990) identifies three **types of rules within families**: habitual rules (firmly established rules which are not negotiated or modified and generally apply to younger children), parametric rules (which allow media behaviors under particular conditions, such as TV viewing when homework is done), and tactical rules (pragmatic means-to-end strategies, such as not arguing over which radio station to listen to in the car to maintain harmony). Many parents try to limit the amount of TV viewing (44%) or to require tasks be done before TV watching is permitted (31%), according to one study.[60] Evidence is contradictory on whether children spend less time with TV and radio when their parents have rules about what can be watched.[61] Parents also rely somewhat on warning statements about TV programming for judging the suitability of a program for children's viewing (Slater and Thompson, 1984).

Community Context

The local community is the broader context within which media use occurs.[62] The strength of **people's links to the local community** is positively related to local media use. Lundy (1988) found that identification with the local community was strongly related to community TV use. Neuwirth, Salmon, and Neff (1989) found that listening to local radio was related to identifying with the local community and having a local orientation. Lain (1986) found that newspaper subscribers were more integrated into the community where the newspaper was published.

Merton (1950) identified **two types of community ties**—local and cosmopolitan, the former referring to membership in local community organizations, which was associated with an interest in the content of local newspapers. Janowitz (1952) proposed that community integration—participation in and identification with local facilities and institutions—would be linked to greater use of local newspapers. A host of studies since then have suggested community ties are multi-dimensional and many are strongly related to media use (Jeffres, Dobos, and Lee, 1988; Stamm, 1985; Viswanath, Finnegan, and Potter, 1989).

Community links are **associated with information needs** (Stamm, 1985). Community integration can be viewed as a process in which people construct new ties or disengage from existing ones.[63] Stamm, Guest, and Fiedler (1990) looked at people's thought processes when they move to a new community, identifying three dimensions corresponding to the amount of effort put into social integration (finding schools, child care, church-community groups, a doctor-dentist), neighborhood integration (finding a house and neighborhood), and institutional integration (finding jobs, spare-time interests, local stores). People used more sources, particularly newspapers, when they put greater effort into each type of integration.[64] Four different ties to a community were related to media use by Viswanath, Finnegan, Rooney, and Potter (1990): primary (family) ties, secondary (friends) ties, the number of community groups residents were involved in, and political involvement and frequency of voting.[65] Collins-Jarvis (1992) found that community identification predicted community newspaper use.

The **size of a community** and **people's commitment to living there** are also predictors of daily newspaper circulation. People living in larger cities are more likely to read morning papers while radio news captures a larger percentage of people in smaller towns and cities. TV viewing does not seem to differ much by size of population. Other research shows that people living in rural areas are less likely to read daily papers regularly, primarily because of availability. Commitment is expressed as homeownership and local involvement.[66]

Individual links to community (community integration) should depend upon the **structure of the community** (Viswanath, Finnegan, and Potter, 1989). In large, diverse communities with many more subgroups, people are more likely to depend upon the mass media for communication. Finnegan and Viswanath (1988) found that use of community weekly papers, metropolitan dailies, and community cable systems were associated with different patterns of community ties. Knowing and contacting neighbors in the suburbs was associated with regular reading and time spent with the community weekly papers but not to metro newspaper or cable TV use. Finnegan, Viswanath, Strickland, and Hannan (1990) compared exposure to sources of health information in small cities, regional cities, and metropolitan suburbs. Residents in larger, more pluralistic communities reported greater exposure to mass media, interpersonal, and group sources for heart disease prevention information.[67]

Natural Environment

The amount of TV viewing also is affected by the seasons—weather or the amount of daylight, temperature, and precipitation.[68] People watch less

TV when longer days allow them to be outside more. In 1987, the average number of hours of TV usage per day ranged from highs of 7 hours, 50 minutes in January and 7 hours, 35 minutes in February to lows of 6 hours, 31 minutes in August and a minute more in July.[69]

Uses and Gratifications

One of the most important theories explaining people's patterns of media behavior is called **uses and gratifications** (U&G). This perspective examines media behaviors from the view of the audience member; it seeks to examine the uses to which people put their media behaviors and the gratifications that people derive from media use. Without such uses and gratifications, the media behavior pattern would change or be extinguished in its existing form; thus, uses and gratifications is a theory explaining not only audience behavior but, in the long run, the form and structure of media themselves. Uses-and-gratifications research has grown dramatically in the past couple decades.[70]

Uses-and-Gratifications Theory

The uses-and-gratifications tradition takes the audience member as the focus. According to this view, audience members can articulate their needs and the uses to which they put the media. The media also are seen to compete with other sources of need satisfaction. The research goes back to the 1940s.[71] The audience member's relationship to the media is affected by a large number of factors—including those derived from one's personality, social background, symbolic and nonsymbolic experiences, immediate social contact, and from the content itself (McQuail, Blumler, and Brown, 1972). The individual has certain expectations and responds according to them—deriving certain affective (feelings), cognitive (thoughts), and instrumental satisfactions (reaching goals) as a consequence.

Where do uses and gratifications come from? Dimmick, McCain, and Bolton (1979) identify two sources. One is an individual's need structure, which itself may be affected by changes in one's physical tastes or socio-psychological states, personality factors, and the larger social and physical environment. As one grows older, for example, some needs increase while others fade in importance, and one's media use pattern will change to fit the new constellation of uses and gratifications that matches the underlying needs. A second factor which may alter one's uses-and-gratifications pattern is changes in the available media (Sparkes, 1983) and nonmedia sources of need satisfaction. New media or leisure-time innovations such as cable TV, and video discs offer new avenues that compete with existing ones for fulfilling different uses and gratifications.

People do not develop their uses of the media in a vacuum. **Orientations toward the media**—including attitudes, expectations about content, and more specific expectations about gratifications offered—also direct our behavior. The newer technologies offer us a clear example of how people develop pictures of the media and their potential uses as manufacturers try to figure out how to market videotex or interactive cable services. The public needs to learn how the new services can be used and what gratifications can be derived from that use before they diffuse widely throughout the population. This is a social process as individuals consult with friends and neighbors, experts, and advertising messages. Later, individuals use what they've learned in matching potential uses and gratifications with personal needs. The decision to use mass communication channels has two parts (Lichtenstein and Rosenfeld, 1984): first, acquiring normative expectations about gratifications from different media; second, making individual decisions about how to seek gratifications within the defined environment. Thus, an individual makes decisions from among socially and culturally defined possibilities. Stanford (1984) found some support for this view. She concluded that general orientations to TV (e.g., TV's most important function is entertainment) give a better explanation of actual gratifications received from a particular TV program than do efforts to link them to needs.

Though intentions to engage in a behavior are strong predictors of what people will actually do, they are less than perfect and "best intentions" may be altered in a complex environment affected by family, friends, and other factors. The closer intentions are to the anticipated behavior, the less likely they will be altered or not acted upon. Rust (1987) looked at children's attentions to TV programs at one location, their expressed intention to watch the program in the future, and their actual program selections at home a week later. Intention was strongly associated with subsequent program choices among those with high attention but not among those with low attention.

Mapping Influences on Media Behaviors

The number of concepts involved in uses and gratifications has grown as various traditions have been invoked to look at origins of media behaviors. We can array these concepts in mapping out media behavior sequences, demonstrating various influences linked to TV viewing, newspaper reading, and other audience behaviors.

Locating Activity. "Activity" is the concept around which many of the relationships in Figure 6-1 evolve. Audience members are not uniformly active in their media use nor consistent in the level of activity across all situations. Audience activity is an important mass communication variable for investigation, and several researchers have confirmed some of the relationships in Figure 6-1,

Table 6–1

Mapping Influences on Media Behaviors

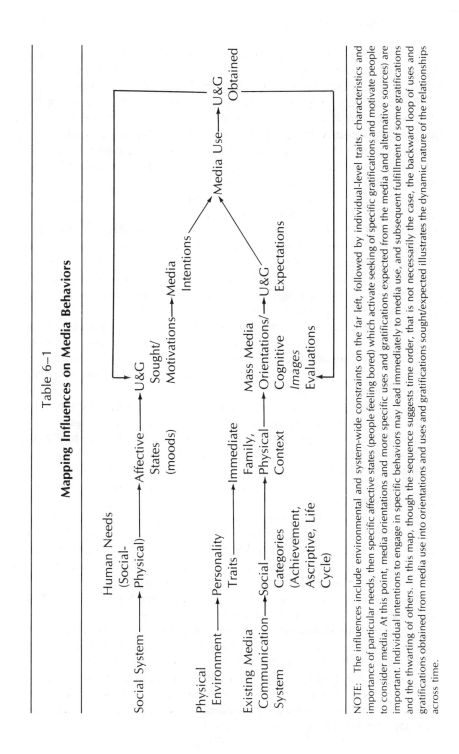

NOTE: The influences include environmental and system-wide constraints on the far left, followed by individual-level traits, characteristics and importance of particular needs, then specific affective states (people feeling bored) which activate seeking of specific gratifications and motivate people to consider media. At this point, media orientations and more specific uses and gratifications expected from the media (and alternative sources) are important. Individual intentions to engage in specific behaviors may lead immediately to media use, and subsequent fulfillment of some gratifications and the thwarting of others. In this map, though the sequence suggests time order, that is not necessarily the case, the backward loop of uses and gratifications obtained from media use into orientations and uses and gratifications sought/expected illustrates the dynamic nature of the relationships across time.

though some of the elements in the model are difficult to separate. Rubin and Windahl (1986) note that motives are difficult to separate from needs since the latter are manifested in motives. Rubin and Perse (1987) found links among motives or gratifications sought, attitudes, and three types of audience activity: 1) **intentionality**, the extent to which news viewing is planned, purposive behavior; 2) **selectivity**, the degree to which the viewing is a nonrandom selection of content from available alternatives; and 3) **involvement**, the extent to which audience members attend to and reflect on the content.[72] Perse and Rubin (1988) also found audience activity was the major predictor of viewing satisfaction for soap opera viewers; thus, those who were more active also were more satisfied with the program.[73]

A link also has been noted between particular motives and types of audience activity before, during, and after exposure. Perse (1990) looked at motivations and four indications of audience involvement: 1) intentionality—anticipating TV viewing,[74] 2) attention-focused cognitive effort, 3) elaboration—thinking about program content, and 4) engaging in distractions while viewing. She found that ritualistic TV viewing (to pass the time, out of habit) was associated with greater selectivity before and during exposure but less involvement during exposure (e.g., program selection, channel changing). Salient viewing motives were linked to more pre-exposure activity, and instrumental viewing (to learn or be excited) was associated with greater activity before exposure and more involvement during exposure.

Hoijer (1989) found from in-depth interviews that viewers of TV programs can be engaged in deep cognitive activities, supporting an active theory of TV viewing. A national sample of prime-time TV viewers reported that two-thirds of the viewing was decided on in advance, while a third of the viewing decisions were made at the time people sat down to watch. Only 9% of program decisions were passive, where viewers merely watched what came on next (Lometti and Addington, 1992).[75]

Do people actively seek out news information rather than passively accept information or become aware of events during exposure to media?[76] Looking at the 1986 summit between the U.S. president and U.S.S.R. premier and other topics, Gantz, Fitzmaurice, and Fink (1991) found that most people engaged in information seeking about a variety of topics at least several times a week. The topic sought most often was local weather information, for which respondents said they turned to the media four days a week for more information. No other topic was sought more than every other day. Catastrophes such as plane crashes were the subject of information searches an average of three days a week. A fifth of the people said they had not sought information during the week about any topic. Adults who sought information more frequently also tended to be heavier users of the media. Interest in topics was linked to information seeking, and most of the efforts involved use of media normally used rather than additional news outlets.

Links from the immediate media use context and earlier influences in the sequence have been studied. Levy (1987) found that different kinds of communication technologies (e.g., VCRs) are linked to differing levels of audience activity, suggesting that VCR use is associated with content or process gratifications.[77] Ferguson (1991) notes that remote control devices have changed the way people watch TV, making them much more active. Interventions through family or other socialization agents can have an impact on media orientations (images, attitudes, knowledge) and subsequent activity; several projects have demonstrated that children can be taught to become more critical, active viewers of TV.[78]

Individual orientations toward the media do affect media use patterns. McDonald and Reese (1987) found newspaper-reliant and TV-reliant individuals choose different types of news programs. Stanford (1984) found general TV orientations (entertainment, information, personal guidance) related to gratifications from specific programs but the former were generally unrelated to such social categories as sex, age, and education. Babrow (1988) contends that motives are "rooted" in the content and operation of audience members' "interpretive frameworks"—the patterns of meaning that people bring to the media and which are used in processing messages. He notes the limited evidence for the claim that perceived outcomes of exposure comprise much of the content of interpretive frames. More research is suggested for audience perceptions of media content structures, such as TV formats and film genre.[79]

Expectancy-Value Theory. An application of "expectancy-value theory" says that media exposure is under an individual's control and one's behavior is guided by perceptions of the probability and value of the potential consequences (Fishbein and Ajzen, 1975). Palmgreen and Rayburn (1985) draw upon expectancy value theory for gratifications research. Thus, people have beliefs that affect their expectations and evaluations, which in turn influence the seeking of media gratifications. Actual media use results in the fulfillment of particular gratifications, which subsequently affect perceptions of what media can and do offer members of the audience. Evaluations are not affected by perceptions of the gratifications obtained because they are seen as relatively stable elements that are tied to one's needs and value system. Rayburn and Palmgreen (1984) found support for their hypothesis that gratifications are strongly related to beliefs about media attributes but not to evaluations of those attributes.

Looking at student viewing of TV soap operas, Babrow (1989) applied expectancy-value theory and found that student attitudes toward soap operas were strongly related to what they expected to get out of such viewing and the strength of those evaluations. Attitudes toward soap operas strongly predicted intentions to watch them. Babrow and Swanson (1988) found that gratifications sought and expectancy-value orientations were highly related but distinctly different judgments. Expectancy-value judgments affected intentions to watch TV news and the frequency through their impact on attitudes, while gratifications sought had direct impact on both intention and exposure levels. Some support for the link between expected values and media use decisions is found in a study by LaRose and Atkin (1988, 1991). They found that the strongest predictors of intentions to disconnect cable TV were perceived value (of pay-per-view, pay-TV, and commercial TV) and whether expectations had been met, along with related factors—complaints and customer service.

Linking U&G Sought with U&G Obtained. Motives for viewing TV, particularly watching for exciting entertainment or escapist relaxation, are major predictors of audience satisfaction (Perse and Rubin, 1988). Watching to pass the time is negatively related to satisfaction. Some studies have found similarity between gratifications sought and those obtained (Dobos and Dimmick, 1988; Levy and Windahl, 1984), although others have found differences in dimensions (McLeod et al., 1982; Palmgreen et al., 1980).

Linking U&G/Motives to Affective States. Media are sought out in response to emotions, and media behaviors are events provoking emotions. **Arousal theories** are based on the premise that one's physiological arousal or level of wakefulness can explain media behaviors. Thus, people use calming, arousing, distracting, and comforting media content to facilitate, maximize, and reduce their levels of affective arousal (Zillmann, 1988). Symbolic information generally has weaker impact, compared to the actual events or impact of pictures of events—the vividness effect (Fisk and Taylor, 1984). Frijda (1988) notes that emotions arise in response to events that are important to the individual. Events that satisfy the individual's goals or promise to do so yield positive emotions. Furthermore, the emergence of emotions is dictated by how one perceives a situation—the "law of apparent reality" (Frijda, 1988: 352).[80]

Media use is linked to mood management.[81] TV viewers report lower moods before a heavy night of TV viewing than before a light night, suggesting that depressing/negative mood states lead people to seek out TV for escape or gratifications (Kubey and Csikszentmihalyi, 1990). The less educated, less affluent, and divorced or separated are more inclined than others to use TV to avoid negative moods that often coincide with solitude and unstructured time (Kubey, 1986). Bryant and Zillman (1984) conducted an experiment in which subjects who faced stress were more likely to turn to "tranquil programming" than bored subjects, who were more likely to turn to more exciting fare. Media also are used for mood management by pregnant women.[82] TV viewing has been associated with those who perceive their lives as "lousy" (Morgan, 1984). Heavy viewers are more likely to say their lives are "intense" rather than calm, secure, and peaceful.

Several TV viewing motives have been linked to measures of affect and other psychological variables: authoritarianism (liking to get one's way, relying on authority), attributional complexity (extent to which people enjoy analyzing reasons, causes of people's behavior), sensation-seeking (enjoying adventure, not being inhibited), locus of control (feelings one has control over one's life), anxiety (feeling overwhelmed by life), creativity (feeling one is original, inventive), assertiveness (feeling one expresses opinions freely, confidently), and parasocial interaction (feeling one is interpersonally involved with a media personality). Conway and Rubin (1991)[83] found that anxiety and parasocial interaction were positively related to watching TV to "pass time." Entertainment TV viewing motives were related to parasocial interaction, while information and relaxation viewing motives were linked to creativity and parasocial interaction. Escape gratifications/motives were predicted by sensation and anxiety. Viewing TV for status enhancement was predicted by anxiety and assertiveness.

Linking Needs to Media Uses and Gratifications.   Five groups of needs were identified by Katz, Gurevitch, and Haas (1973) in their classic study, which was conducted in Israel: 1) cognitive needs, such as the need to understand; 2) affective needs strengthening aesthetic or emotional experience; 3) integrative needs strengthening one's confidence, credibility, stability; 4) needs relating to strengthening contact with family, friends, and the world; and 5) needs related to escape or tension release. Results of the Israeli survey showed that books cultivated the inner self while films and TV gave pleasure. They also found TV the most diffuse medium, and users applied it to a wide range of functions. Movies and newspapers were the most specific media. Cohen, Levy, and Golden (1988) found that children ranked TV highest or second highest among media in its perceived utility to gratify three-fourths of the needs measured. VCRs were ranked second best in satisfying half of the needs, while cinema received only one first-place rank, and both newspapers and books rated first or second best in meeting only a third of the needs. Choi, Wright, and Ferguson (1991) found that gratifications for surveillance and social utility were associated with the need for cognition.[84] People who regularly watch TV, go to films, and read fiction rate these leisure activities higher on intellectual stimulation and providing solitude and low on companionship, Tinsley and Johnson (1984) found.[85]

Uses-and-Gratifications Dimensions.   McQuail, Blumler, and Brown (1972) developed a typology of gratifications: diversion, including emotional release and escape from problems and the daily routine, personal relationships, which include vicarious (parasocial) companionship and social utility such as conversations, family viewing, and viewing to meet the standards of a group; personal identity, which includes personal reference (self-evaluation), reality

248   Chapter Six

exploration (ideas about personal concerns), and value reinforcement; and the surveillance function (McDonald and Glynn, 1984).

Dobos and Dimmick (1988) provide an excellent summary of the dimensions of gratifications which have emerged from studies over the past couple decades: surveillance—to keep in touch with area, state, national, and international events[86]; knowledge—to get information about issues and events, the government, things affecting family, to help make decisions;[87] escape/diversion—to fill time, put mind at ease, divert attention from personal problems, for relief from boredom;[88] excitement—news stories are dramatic, often entertaining, often exciting;[89] interpersonal utility—for things to talk about, for facts to back up opinions, for facts and opinions that will interest others, for facts and opinions to help influence others.[90] Noting methodological differences, they asked respondents to evaluate the extent to which they sought 20 different gratifications from news in general. They found support for a distinction between cognitive (grouping surveillance and knowledge dimensions) and affective gratifications (grouping escape, excitement, and interpersonal utility dimensions).[91] Similar dimensions have been found when uses and gratifications have been studied in different countries and cultures, including Japan,[92] Venezuela,[93] and Poland.[94]

We also learn what people get out of the media by examining unavailability. Windahl, Hojerback, and Hedinsson (1986) looked at media deprivation by adolescents during a Swedish TV strike, finding 62% felt at least partially deprived and 11% very or fairly deprived.[95] During a TV-radio strike in Iceland, Broddason and Hedinsson (1986) found that adults missed radio the most, followed by TV. Respondents missed the surveillance/awareness function of radio and the entertainment function of TV. In a Korean experiment which removed TV from people's homes for a month, Auh (1991) found that the bulk of the newly obtained free time went to such activities as listening to the radio, hobbies, socializing, and resting, with a small increase in use of books and magazines. Newspapers became the major source of information, and radio tended to fulfill uses and gratifications previously linked to TV—for news, for fun, to kill time, to relax. Interpersonal communication with family members increased about 7 minutes a day when TV was removed, but the figure dropped back to the earlier level when the TV was reintroduced. Winick (1988) studied a New York City sample of people whose TV sets were not operating and found six basic functions served by TV: surveillance and information (missed by 83%), relaxation and entertainment (82%), conversation (72%), social cement (71%), punctuating the day and week (63%), and companionship (60%).

Leisure Motives/Satisfactions.[96] Watching TV, reading newspapers and books, going to films and listening to the radio have frequently been investigated in studies of leisure motivations.[97] Dimensions which have been identified as underlying such motivations are similar to those found for use and gratifications: self-expression/achievement, education/ information, interpersonal companionship, relaxation/diversion, physiological/health, sophistication/intellectual, and beauty/ aesthetic.[98] Hirschman (1985) found several of these dimensions—expressive values, instrumental values—related to people's TV content preferences.

What directs you to turn on the TV set rather than go visit a friend? And what leads you to read a book rather than go for a walk? At a given moment in time, the individual has various alternatives (constrained by past choices and the larger system) that can be selected to move him or her toward goals and maximize one's personal growth (Grunig, 1979). Rather than classifying all media use as "pleasure seeking," some observers have found it useful to distinguish between situations in which people seek media content and situations in which the process of reading, viewing, or listening is central. Jeffres (1975) distinguished between media seeking and content seeking. The first refers to situations in which you turn to the media because the act of consumption— reading, watching, listening—is more important than the content. You might, for example, turn on the TV because you're bored and the content is a secondary consideration; you may pick the "lesser of several evils" available at that moment. In content-seeking situations, you decide to use a medium because of the content. Here you rush home to find out the latest developments in a soap opera, or you anxiously wait for your favorite film director's latest work to arrive in town and plan accordingly. Some of our content seeking aims at larger parcels than others—TV programs vs. the weather. The actual seeking of particular items may be called information seeking. How often do you pick up the newspaper to find out the outcome of a sports event, what's on TV (Gantz and Eastman, 1983), or what's for sale at the grocery store? Another type of media use might be called non-seeking (Jeffres, 1975), where the individual does not actively seek either content or media but is virtually sought out by other people or the media. Here, you're sitting in the back of someone else's automobile and are "forced" to listen to the radio whether you want to or not.

The content/process distinction, also noted by others (Csikszentmihalyi, 1975; Cutler and Danowski, 1980; Kelly, 1978), is important for pragmatic reasons too. We might hypothesize that media seeking, or a concern for process, is related to habitual use and patterns that are likely to continue over time. Thus, people who media-seek newspapers may be more likely to continue their reading for a longer period than those whose newspaper use is characterized as information-seeking. An emphasis on "process" does not mean that people are not selective once reading or viewing has begun. Jeffres (1975) has elaborated this in terms of TV viewing and newspaper reading.[99] His findings indicate that people who media-seek newspapers are more likely to start reading on page one while content-seekers are more likely to begin with other sections of the paper.

Boredom has been tied to leisure dissatisfaction. Research suggests that media use and other leisure activities should be arousing in order to be psychologically rewarding. Boredom results if leisure skills are greater than the challenge of leisure opportunities or if there isn't a balance between novelty and familiarity.[100] Boredom also has both cognitive and affective components (Hill and Perkins, 1985; Perkins and Hill, 1985).[101] Those unaware that leisure can be psychologically rewarding also are more likely to see leisure as boredom; thus, boredom may be powerful enough to make the person feel more depressed, hopeless, worthless (Iso-Ahola and Weissinger, 1990); we might expect this to occur more often with TV, particularly in situations of limited choice and challenge.

Similarly, Csikszentmihalyi and LeFevre (1989) look at the extent to which people engage in challenging vs. more passive activities. They note the paradox of teenagers finding involvement in sports more challenging and positive than watching TV, to which they devote much more of their time. They found that TV viewing by adults was less likely to be "flow time"—challenging, requiring people to use skills, concentrate, etc. They note that people may need to recuperate from the intensity of work in low-intensity activities, which would explain why people prefer to watch TV, sleep, or relax, recuperating from stimulation at work. Yet in some traditional societies, people in more demanding work situations spend more of their free time in challenging pursuits.[102]

Linking Uses and Gratifications to Media/Media Content

TV and other media have been linked with such a broad range of uses and gratifications that many critics have feared TV would lead to the "colonization" of virtually all leisure time (Robinson and Sahin, 1981). Uses and gratifications may be associated with the behavior itself—enjoying reading, with the medium itself—reading magazines, or with particular content—reading articles about people in entertainment.

Media Technologies.   Audiences look at new media technologies as mere extensions of existing media, although they increase alternatives and promote interaction with messages (Williams, Phillips, and Lum, 1985). A sample of elementary children found that TV gratified the largest number of needs, while VCRs satisfied one need most of all and lagged in satisfying others, suggesting that VCRs had not established a separate "identity" among respondents but were blended with cinema, tapes, and TV (Cohen, Levy, and Golden, 1988).[103] Uses associated with technologies shift as novelty wears off. Morgan, Alexander, Shanahan, and Harris (1990) found that the dominant use of the

VCR by adolescents in 1985 was to watch rented tapes (87.5%), compared to 77.6% using VCRs for off-air taping and about a fifth using VCRs to watch tapes they owned; in 1988, almost 60% were using the VCR to watch tapes they owned, while slightly lower percentages cited the two other purposes (84.5% to watch rented tapes and 69.3% for time shifting). Walker and Bellamy (1991, 1992) looked at gratifications derived from using remote control devices (RCD), which have been responsible for an increase in the "zapping" (avoiding commercials by switching channels), "zipping" (fast-forwarding VCR tape) and "grazing" (using RCD to sample viewing environment) phenomena. Use of RCDs was associated with getting more from TV (watching bits and pieces of several shows), annoying others, selective avoidance (changing channels to avoid something), controlling family viewing, accessing TV news, accessing music videos, avoiding commercials, and finding out what's on TV.

Rubin and Bantz (1987) identified eight dimensions to motivations for VCR use, ranging from socializing at home video parties to time shifting.[104] Lin (1991, 1992) found that more satisfied VCR users reported more home entertainment and video party activity than those less satisfied; since these heavier "video partiers" were more likely to be single, less affluent and with fewer children, VCRs were a means for expanding social options. Umphrey (1988) notes that motivations for subscribing to cable TV differ, with basic cable subscribers citing improved reception and pay cable subscribers citing greater program variety.[105] Dobos (1992) found that gratifications obtained explained some of people's satisfaction and choice of media channels in organizations—electronic media and interpersonal communication.[106]

Television Viewing. Rubin (1983) found two TV viewer types. The first uses TV out of habit, to pass the time, and for entertainment; this model of audience use emphasizes the communication medium itself. A second type of TV viewer—the escapist viewer—uses TV to forget about personal problems and to get away from other people or tasks. Escapist viewing occurs at reduced levels. In a Roper survey in 1989, the third most popular activity people engaged in to feel better when they felt sad or depressed was TV viewing (29%).[107] Satisfaction with TV viewing in general as a source of gratifications is suggested in a study by Litman, Kohl, and Pizante (1989), who studied network rerun viewing; those who watched more TV were more likely to be satisfied with reruns rather than seeking out alternatives. Furno-Lamude and Anderson (1992) found that those who watched reruns said it reminded them of their past, their parents used to watch the program, and it reminded them of their younger years.[108]

Uses and gratifications associated with watching TV news include personalities and content sections as well as overall characteristics. Wicks (1989) found that five dimensions of uses and gratifications explained viewing of TV news: sports-related uses and gratifications (to keep up on sports, to find out if my favorite teams have won, sports is entertaining), credibility (like professionalism in local newscasts, should just stick to the news), reinforcing news (enjoy human interest stories, people-oriented stories, family-oriented stories with happy endings), production considerations (the station is on top of the story, can catch up quickly without too much effort, enjoy causal manner of presentation), and weather information (weather forecast helps me to plan ahead). Lin (1992) found both personalities and content major criteria in selecting which news program to watch; the weather person was more important than news anchors, reporters, or sports anchors. Gratifications associated with TV news viewing also are related to different types of news stories. Thus, Henningham (1985) found that information seeking was associated primarily with political or conflict news, scientific and cultural news, while interpersonal utility gratification was related to human interest items, sports news events, and news depicting tragedy.[109]

Other TV formats also have been linked to specific uses and gratifications. Livingstone (1988) found escapism the major reason for watching soap operas, followed by realism, relationship with characters, critical responses, problem solving, their role in the viewer's life, emotional experience, and entertainment.[110] Abelman (1988) found six factors of viewing motivations for religious TV: dissatisfaction with commercial TV, information, entertainment, faith, habit, and escape.[111] Teenagers watch music videos primarily for diversion, because they are seen as exciting and because they help get adolescents into desirable moods (Brown, Campbell, and Fischer, 1986).[112] Sports provide a substantial chunk of content in all mass media. Duncan and Brummett (1989) argue there are three types of pleasure provided by viewing sports on TV: voyeurism (pleasure of watching without being invited), fetishism (pleasure of watching a spectacle), and narcissism (pleasure from identification with the athletes performing).[113]

Movie-going.   Entertainment isn't the only gratification attracting people to theaters. Analyzing student reasons for moviegoing, Palmgreen et al. (1988) found a variety of factors, from mood control to a desire to avoid communicating with others.[114] Another college student sample revealed three types of moviegoers based on reasons for going to films: self-escape, purely for entertainment value of films, and for self-development (Tesser, Millar, and Wu, 1988). Tamborini and Stiff (1987) found three important appeals specifically for horror films: a desire to experience the satisfying resolutions usually provided in such films, a desire to see the destruction characteristics of such films, and sensation seeking per se (thrill and adventure seeking, experience seeking, disinhibition).

Radio Listening.   Radio listening attracts larger young audiences because of the gratifications provided. Radio listening also is associated with other activities. In Japan 86% of all radio listening occurred with other activities, particularly among people age 30-40 (Aida, 1987). Listening to music on the radio is important to college students, who use radio music as a background for studying, exercising, driving, and lovemaking (Edwards and Singletary, 1989). Listeners to call-in programs seek useful information about daily life, want to know what's going on in the country, and wonder why others have various ideas (Surlin, 1986). Other gratifications are reinforcement and companionship.

Reading and Print Media.   Reading itself is a gratifying experience for many people, yet 45% of U.S. adults do not read books at all. However, at least a third of adults say they draw "creative satisfaction" from reading books. The print media that manage to attract and to hold larger audiences are newspapers and magazines, which attract people with not only news but also advertising, comics, bridge columns, etc. (Larkin and Grotta, 1979). Three sets of uses and gratifications—diversion, surveillance, interaction—draw readers to consumer and trade magazines (Payne, Severn, and Dozier, 1988). Diversion (to be happy, relax, pass the time, for companionship, improve life style) is greater for consumer magazine readership, while trade magazine reading is higher for surveillance gratifications (do job better, get immediate news, stay up on events, teach common issues) and interaction gratifications (to pass info on to others, understand what's happening).[115]

Newspaper Reading.   Newspaper readers belong to one of five types (Ruofolo, 1988): **instrumental readers**, who use the paper as an information tool for daily living; **opinion makers**, who use information to form and compare opinions and who read papers for guidance and analysis of news events; **pleasure readers**, who read papers primarily as an enjoyable habitual activity; **ego-boosters**, who read to enhance their self-image and who are strongly information-oriented; and **scanners**, who skim the paper for a variety of purposes.[116] Of 15 uses and gratifications examined in the Ruofolo study, learning about the environment (surveillance) was the strongest, followed by guidance, social comparisons, social interactions, and opinion confirmation. Enjoyment and habit also were strong motives, while participation in and control of the environment, companionship, excitement, relaxation, passing time and escape were less important.[117] Among teenagers, three newspaper image factors help explain whether they are likely to be newspaper readers (Cobb-Walgren, 1990): perceptions of time—"I generally don't have time to read the paper," perceptions of content—"There aren't many newspaper articles relevant to my hobbies," and competition from TV—"I would rather watch the news on television than read about it in the newspaper."[118] *USA Today* has been more successful in attracting younger readers.[119] In general, the relevance of all gratifications declines from the 60s to the 80-plus segment, particularly for information gain and arousal. An exception is companionship, a gratification which increases slightly with age. Involvement and information are the most sought-after gratifications from newspapers among the elderly (O'Keefe, Burull, and Reid, 1990).

News Media In General.   News is the major ingredient of newspapers and a major content in TV, radio, and other media. Wenner (1985) identified four areas of media news gratifications with common boundaries—across all media. Orientation gratifications refer to messages used for information that puts things in context and reassures people about their place in the world. Social gratifications link media information about society to one's interpersonal network. News process gratifications include parasocial uses.[120] We also can distinguish between news providing gratifications which are immediate vs. delayed (Singletary, 1985).[121]

Media use as sources for particular topics has been studied by a variety of scholars. Mass media are the major source of information about the environment in the U.S. and other countries (Blum, 1987; Pierce, Lee-Sammons, and Lovrich, 1988), with more educated segments preferring print media (Ostman and Parker 1986-1987). Local TV has been identified as a major choice for specialized news,[122] newspapers follow interpersonal sources for hospital information,[123] magazines are a major source for information about sexually-transmitted diseases,[124] and advertising is a major source of consumer information.[125]

News media gratifications have been linked to particular social categories and the life cycle (age). Kebbel (1985) found that older, more educated, politically active people tend to use multiple media as news sources about politics compared to younger, less educated, less politically active respondents. Andreyenkov, Robinson, and Popov (1989) found that a majority of samples of adolescents in both the U.S. and Soviet Union said that TV was their main source of information about nuclear issues, particularly among Soviet teens. Newspapers were second in importance. News from home is important when one is out of the country.[126]

Functional Equivalence of Media.   Earlier we noted that many uses and gratifications may be fulfilled by any of the media. Are the media complementary in their uses—TV specializing in particular gratifications while newspapers serve other uses—or are the mass media functionally equivalent and interchangeable in their satisfaction of people's needs? After reviewing more than 100 studies, Weaver and Budeenbaum (1979) concluded that people value both newspapers and TV in complementary manners for knowledge and diversion as well as an adjunct to interpersonal communication. While TV is seen as fulfilling a general surveillance function, papers are associated with information seeking, in-depth subject knowledge, and election guidance. Only for escape is there a clear difference between newspapers and TV.[127]

Media compete with each other in fulfilling gratifications, particularly the entertainment function commonly provided by a host of media technologies, including TV, VCRs, Cable TV, and films shown in theaters. Yoshida (1986) shows the tradeoff of radio prime-time listening for TV viewing in the 1950s and 1960s in Japan. There also appears to be functional equivalence of TV viewing and going to the cinema among older people.[128]

Uses and gratifications associated with TV viewing, VCR use, and other communication behaviors are interrelated (Rubin and Rubin, 1989).[129] In Germany, Schoenbach, and Hackforth (1987) found that TV viewing was greater in households with VCRs, suggesting an extension rather than a substitution of uses. LaRose and Atkin (1988) also found that cable subscribership was positively related to VCR ownership, total TV viewing, and weekly newspaper readership. However, differences in offerings of the media technologies made them less functionally equivalent. Burkum and Niebauer (1988) found that families who replaced cable TV with other electronic entertainment and information sources, such as VCRs, tended to be families with adolescents who were seeking better youth-oriented programming and were not satisfied by cable and wanted more movies than were available on TV or cable.

Advertisers also need to find out the conditions under which new media technologies are sought as functional alternatives to traditional media. Henke and Donohue (1989) sought to determine how VCRs displaced other media by distinguishing between those who used VCRs for "time shifting" vs. those who used them to play back purchased or rented tapes; the former use the new technology to complement and provide flexibility in the use of other media (over-the-air TV and cable TV) while the latter use VCRs to functionally displace existing TV behaviors, such as playing X-rated tapes. Zohoori (1988) found that children's exposure to modern media technologies—VCRs, video games, and PCs—supplemented traditional media exposure.[130]

When there are changes in the media system, people's media behavior patterns and associated uses and gratifications are disrupted, demonstrating how the media complement and displace each other. People read more suburban and out of town newspapers during a Philadelphia newspaper strike (Elliott and Rosenberg, 1987). When a newspaper switched from afternoon to morning publication, Rarick and Lemert (1988) found a temporary change in TV news viewing patterns but a year later viewing returned to pre-existing patterns. Adolescents listened to records, went out with friends, and listened to the radio when they couldn't watch TV during a strike in Sweden (Windahl, Hojerback, and Hedinsson, 1986),[131] and viewers increased their use of VCRs and engaged in more interpersonal communication during a TV-radio strike in Iceland (Broddason and Hedinsson, 1986). In an experiment which removed TV from the home, families with children reported much higher use of radio and music, but reading was unaffected (Knowles et al., 1989).

Media also compete with other sources of gratification—including both symbolic behaviors (interpersonal communication) and other activities—such as jogging. Looking at the introduction of TV among Turkish squatters from 1962 to 1985, Ogan (1987) found that visiting, once the only source of entertainment in the evenings, was partly replaced by TV viewing. Selnow and Reynolds (1984) found that an increase in TV viewing time produced a decline in playing home video games, sleeping, and playing musical instruments. Buller and Pease (1990) found that TV programming was selected over interpersonal sources for a variety of uses and gratifications.[132]

Influences from Traits, Social Context, and the Environment

Particular needs and uses and gratifications will be more important for some people than others. Some of these individual differences are personality factors, while others are social categories or location in the life cycle. The larger physical environment or the more immediate family/social context also are important.

Blumler (1979) sought to link people's social situations and their media-related needs, grouping them into factors which act as influences on what people get out of the media,[133] compensators which are sources of a need to compensate for the lack of opportunities and capacities,[134] facilitating factors which enable one to have a richer involvement with media content,[135] and subjective reaction or adjustment to one's situation (indicated by satisfaction with work, leisure).[136]

Earlier critics of uses and gratifications argued that the theory treated mass communication in isolation from other social factors that can be generalized to categories of people but not to social structures. Rubin and Windahl (1986) respond to this criticism, noting the social-structural conditions that affect media uses and suggesting how a host of variables could be integrated into a media dependency model of mass communication.

Although little work has linked personality types or traits to particular uses and gratifications, some researchers have looked at individual levels of loneliness, shyness, self-esteem, assertiveness, need for activation, need for stimulation, etc. Some of these have been studied as individual traits, others as levels experienced in specific affective states. An overall dissatisfaction with life was linked to TV viewing by Espe and Seiwert (1987), who found that the amount of time spent viewing TV increased with life dissatisfaction among all viewing types (entertainment viewers, information viewers, sports viewers, infrequent viewers, etc.), while controlling for age, education, and size of household. Assertiveness is a predictor of particular readership patterns (Andreasen and Steeves, 1984). Assertive, employed women are more interested in national news than unassertive women, who are more interested in information relating to the home and family. Extroversion and locus of control have been related to heavier TV viewing (Wober and Gunter, 1986). Sneegas (1986) found that reading for pleasure was positively related to perceptions that one was socially competent. Watching TV was not related.

Based on arousal and activation theory, individuals differ in their need for and tolerance for arousal (Littlejohn and Jabusch, 1987), and this has been linked to media uses and gratifications. In an experiment, Lawrence and Palmgreen (1991) found that arousal needs affected movie motives. Among young adults, three arousal needs influenced five of the nine motives for going to films. Need for internal cognitive novelty was linked to four uses and gratifications (entertainment/diversion, mood control/enhancement, personal identity, and general learning). The need for physical excitement was linked to two uses and gratifications (mood control/enhancement and general learning. The need for internal sensation was related to social facilitation or audience involvement. For older adult moviegoers, the need for internal sensation was positively linked to five motives/gratifications sought (entertainment/diversion, medium characteristics/involvement, mood control/enhancement, personal identity, and general learning) while the need for disinhibition was negatively associated with seeking movies for social facilitation or involvement.

Activation also has been linked to news and information-seeking motivations. Sparks and Spirek (1988) found that an individual's tendency toward activation or arousal was related to information seeking of highly negative emotional information in the media when the space shuttle, the *Challenger*, exploded. Lain (1985) found that need for stimulation was a strong predictor for viewing TV news but not newspaper readership. Collins and Abel (1985) found that need for activation was not a good predictor of information-seeking behavior and exposure to news sources.[137]

Use of media behaviors for companionship or to escape loneliness is a major dimension of uses and gratifications. Finn and Gorr (1988) found loneliness positively related to viewing TV for social-compensation motivations (companionship, pass time, habit, escape), but, for the extremely lonely, there was less desire to watch TV at all. Shyness was positively related to viewing TV for social-compensation and mood management (relaxation, arousal, entertainment). People's self-esteem was positively related to viewing TV for mood management and negatively associated to viewing for social-compensation. Chronically lonely people use interpersonal channels less, have increased use of TV and movies, and watch TV soap operas to pass the time rather than for exciting entertainment or social utility viewing motives (Perse and Rubin, 1990).[138]

When lonely, people may seek media for parasocial interaction,[139] the illusion by audience members that they are engaged in a face-to-face relationship with a broadcast media performer (Houlberg, 1984). A study of adult TV viewers found that they placed favorite TV personalities in an intermediate position between friend and acquaintance in "semantic space" (Koenig and Lessan, 1985).[140] Characters in a long-running TV program and the situations in which they become involved take on a significance for the regular viewer that they do not have for the casual viewer, Berger (1989) suggests. However, relationships with a media person do not follow from loneliness and exposure alone (Perse and Rubin, 1989).[141]

Linking Social Categories and Life Cycle Position to U&G.   Social categories, such as occupation, have been related to media uses and gratifications in the U.S. and other countries.[142] Decision-making women—such as professionals—use media more for work-related information than do hourly workers and homemakers (Johnson and Gross, 1985). They also spend less time with the media, particularly TV, and they spend more time reading newsmagazines and trade magazines and newspapers. Uses and gratifications are better predictors of public TV viewing and print media use than such traditional social categories as education and income (Atkin, 1973; Palmgren and Rayburn, 1979; Wang, 1977). Kirsch and Guthrie (1984) found different uses for reading in work and in leisure settings. At work, reading for specific information (48 minutes per day) dominated all other uses, followed by reading for regulation, evaluation (21 minutes per day), and construction of messages (21 minutes per day). In leisure, three uses of reading prevailed—relaxation (23 minutes per day), keeping informed about current events (19 minutes per day), and knowledge (14 minutes per day). In leisure, reading for relaxation was slightly higher for managers and professionals than the average and the most frequently named content was novels and stories in magazines.[143]

Ethnicity and cultural differences also are factors. Zohoori (1988) found that American and foreign children both used TV for escape but that foreign children used TV more to learn about others and themselves. Slight differences on use of TV for companionship and social interaction were noted but were not significant. Disentangling the various social categories and individual differences is difficult and their joint impact complex. Kubey (1986) found that lower SES (socioeconomic status) and divorced or separated demographic groups felt depressed in unstructured or solitary situations and turned to TV when it was available, compared to higher SES and married respondents. The former also were more likely to continue to watch TV to avoid being left alone with their feelings and thoughts; thus, TV provided an alternative during unstructured time. Kubey suggests that heavy TV viewers have fewer inner resources to maintain emotional control and balance and turn to TV for help.

One's age, or position in the life span, can affect the uses and gratifications that link people to media behavior patterns.[144] Age also is related to five motives for using TV—to learn things, to forget, to overcome loneliness, to pass time when bored, and to find something to talk about (Ostman and Jeffers, 1983).

Using TV to escape boredom and to forget were both negatively correlated with age but the others were all positively correlated with age in a sample of residents age 18-87. Rubin (1985) notes the importance of fantasy motives for media use in younger children, the emergence of informational use in adolescence, and the relative continuity of gratifications sought through the early and middle adult years. Uses and gratifications associated with broadcast media have been the focus of those examining children and adolescents.[145]

The elderly provide an example of a social group whose media use is linked to particular needs, although the evidence is still unclear. Goodman (1990) found older people preferring TV for national and world news but newspapers for local news. Information seeking and entertainment are the primary motives for TV viewing by the elderly, followed by use of TV for companionship, to help schedule daily activities and as a source of common experiences (Fouts, 1989).[146] Less than 9% of a sample of older adults reported they never use TV for companionship, while 16% did sometimes, 58% fairly often and 17% frequently (Davis and Westbrook, 1985). Activity theory (Lemon, Bengston, and Peterson, 1972) suggests that the elderly are forced to disengage from society. Rahtz, Sirgy and Meadow (1989) found that the elderly use TV for entertainment and information-gathering purposes to cope with the alienating effects of social disengagement and more limited activity. Interactive cable TV and other communication technologies also are being used to help the elderly cope with loneliness and isolation.[147]

Environment.   The environment in which the audience finds itself affects people's "need structure" and the list of behavioral alternatives. The environment includes the broader physical environment as well as the immediate viewing context.[148] The larger community or environment also can affect the pattern of people's uses and gratifications. Changes in geographic location may mean different facilities are available to meet people's needs. Kelly (1978) looked at leisure styles in three cities to examine factors that shape leisure choices. Importance of leisure activities was similar in all cities; marriage intimacy, reading, and family activity led all rankings while TV ranked no higher than sixth out of more than a dozen. Differences were explainable by the environment—climates, natural resources available, and community opportunities. Though rural-urban differences in the U.S. may be disappearing, they remain in other areas. Rota and Tremmel (1991) found rural Mexican youth lower on all TV gratifications compared to urban children. However, rural children seek several types of TV programs more often, suggesting their behavior is more purposive. In a national sample of elderly residents in the U.S., surprisingly little variation was found in media exposure patterns across different sized communities, but several differences were found in gratification-seeking patterns (O'Keefe, Burull, and Reid, 1990). Reading newspapers for entertainment was higher in rural communities, while urban fringe residents used papers less for companionship and escapism than did other elderly persons. A similar pattern was found in TV uses for companionship and escapism, suggesting that suburbanites have less need for media for those purposes. They also found a tendency to use TV to keep involved in the world among central city and small town elderly, both isolated but perhaps for different reasons. Pearson (1990) found no difference between urban and rural Alaskans' perceptions of the functions of newspapers, magazines, or friends across a wide range of uses and gratifications.[149]

Criticism and Summary

A decade ago uses-and-gratifications research was criticized for producing little more than conflicting lists of "uses and grats." Others pointed to conceptual confusion or asked where the uses themselves come from (Swanson, 1979). Work since then has responded to much of that criticism but more research is necessary and the nature of the questions has shifted from ideological battles to a more theoretical domain. For example, where earlier critics argued that the uses-and-gratifications perspective seemed to emphasize stability and maintenance of the status quo, more current questions would seek answers to the following. How "flexible" are people in learning to satisfy particular needs with media behaviors, e.g., to what extent can children be taught to seek "intellectual" gratifications from print media? What "precise" uses and gratifications must be fulfilled for a particular media pattern to persist, e.g., can U&G scales be developed for use in studies across time that test the crucial relationship of the theory? The relationship between general media orientations and uses and gratifications would seem to be one of the most important areas for future study. Studies should include not only attitudes, images, and perceptions but also "knowledge" measures. What media orientations are related to uses and gratifications—are positive perceptions of media technologies related to more diverse media behavior patterns? Ultimately, we need to move to higher levels, linking changes in patterns of uses and gratifications sought with changes in media content patterns and shifts in media organizations.

In summary, the uses-and-gratifications perspective has been used to understand how people view their media behaviors. Attributing a measure of activity to the audience, researchers have developed typologies that tap various dimensions of meaning including: diversion/escape, coping with relationships (with family, friends, or via parasocial communication with strangers), establishing and reinforcing personal identity (as a personality and role enactment), and surveying the environment (understanding the political, social, economic systems). Some have linked use of particular media to categories of needs (cognitive, affective, integrative, and escape) or particular uses and gratifications (e.g., watching TV to pass time is the dominant use for all age groups). Social situations have been linked to media-related needs. Individual differences have been found in people's U&G patterns—college students use media for behavioral guidance more than many other groups. We also discussed the functional equivalence of media with some evidence that TV viewing and newspaper use both provide the same range of uses and gratifications, but each medium specializes in particular functions (TV viewing for escape, newspaper reading for indepth knowledge).

Media Socialization—The Longer View

"Socialization" refers to the process by which behaviors, values, and customs are learned by each new generation. We learn many of our behaviors in the family and school; our parents serve as models, and teachers encourage us to read. Thus, we find some continuity from one generation to the next. We expect, for example, that children in homes with reading material are more likely to become heavier readers than those from homes without such material. Gades (1988) studied lifetime newspaper reading patterns of 30- to 45-year-olds through indepth interviews, finding that people establish their newspaper reading habits as children and that readers find the process pleasurable in contrast to nonreaders and change their newspaper reading habit only in extreme circumstances. Attitudes toward children's socialization have changed through the years.[150]

Socialization prepares one to take on the way of life of his or her family and the larger social groups one needs in order to perform adequately as an adult. How does this process occur?[151] Modeling and reinforcement are two specific processes that have been studied in mass media socialization. Evidence of actual reinforcement is scanty, however, since relatively few parents bother to reward or punish their children for exhibiting media behaviors (Mohr, 1979).[152] In modeling, a child uses the parents' media pattern as an example for his or her own behavior. Families exert influence by making media available.[153] In a study of 1,300 11th and 12th graders in Dallas, Cobb (1986) found that the best predictors of adolescent newspaper readership were availability of the newspaper in the home, perception of time spent by parents in newspaper reading, and usage of other media.[154] Hopkins and Mullis (1985) found the TV viewing patterns of children age 3-6.6 years more similar with their fathers than with their mothers, with no differences by age. Heeter (1988) found parent and child viewing styles related in a study of fifth and sixth grade children.[155] Most of the attempts to use reward and punishment to influence children's media behavior come before adolescence (Lyle and Hoffman, 1971).[156]

Evidence for learning through social interaction is more abundant. Studies on family communication patterns (McLeod and O'Keefe, 1972) show that the amount of time adolescents spend watching TV and the type of content viewed are affected by parent-child interaction. In families that stress social relations, adolescents spend the most time watching TV; they also prefer entertainment to news and public affairs programs. In homes with strong and varied conceptual development but low insistence on obedience, adolescents spend relatively little time watching TV and show relatively great interest in news and public affairs programs. The third type of home, "laissez-faire," is characterized by both low socio-orientation and low concept-orientation. In such homes, adolescents' TV viewing is moderately high but they seem disinterested in newspapers or public affairs programs on TV.

While parents are a major force in the socialization process, they are not the only force. There are many different agents of socialization. Peer groups and siblings also are important. Teachers, spouses, one's own children, work associates, friends, and neighbors all may influence one's media pattern. The potential importance of agents changes as the individual influenced matures and grows old. From early childhood to adolescence, the parents' influence wanes and the influence of peers and teachers increases.[157] Recognizing the importance of schools as a socialization agent, newspapers have sought to encourage use of their medium through a program that provides newspapers in the classroom.[158] In adulthood, occupational peer groups, friends, spouses, and the various reference groups we adopt as bellwethers for our opinions should increase their power to influence media usage.

Communication and Life Styles

How does TV viewing relate to housework, child care, household obligations, study, travel, or personal care? In general, our attempts to explain people's media behaviors have failed to show how they fit into individual patterns of daily activities. Perspectives which look at alternatives considered in specific media-use situations or contexts often do not look at such relationships across time or fail to integrate media use with other domains of people's lives. Social categories locate people in the physical environment, and uses and gratifications tie media to individual needs. Yet each media behavior is an activity that must compete with a host of other symbolic and nonsymbolic behaviors.

As culture becomes more homogeneous with respect to language and custom, it may become more heterogeneous, or diverse, with respect to life styles, especially material life styles (Felson, 1976). The question is how to relate media consumption to other behavioral domains. Newspaper use is linked to social categories, reading is a leisure-time activity, and leisure pursuits may be connected with such obligatory behaviors as work. The perspective which seems to come closest in recognizing the need for looking at "interconnections" is the life style perspective. Closely related is the research on the quality of life, which slices people's lives into various domains and examines how each contributes to an overall assessment of satisfaction and well-being.[159]

Even the life styles of people on the same block have become varied as the once tightly knit middle class becomes divided and fragmented (Koten, 1987; Kotlowitz, 1987). Society imposes much less of a common mold on people and there is greater tolerance for different patterns of behavior. Although media fit into this pattern, they also are seen as a contributor to the splintering which has occurred. Modern industrial nations have seen a proliferation of alternative life styles in the past few decades, although people use the term in quite different ways.[160] Zablocki and Kanter (1976) define life style in terms of shared preferences or tastes, where the people sharing a life style are a "collectivity that otherwise lacks social and cultural identity." Thus, people sharing a life style may not communicate with each other and may not share characteristics such as ethnic background. Although it originally referred to young, urban, professionals, the term "yuppies" now refers to a life style rather than a group based on social characteristics. People from different age groups have identified with the complex of product purchases (computers, sport cars), style preferences (nontraditional, modern), and personal goals (high achievement-oriented, self-development) that have generally represented "the good life" in advertising campaigns. People also differ considerably in their ability to match personal resources with the price tag accompanying this life style, but that doesn't stop them from trying. Contrast the "yuppies" life style with one which might fit well under the heading "back-to-nature." The media use patterns that fit each would differ considerably.

Consumption behaviors alone are insufficient for identifying life styles; we also have to examine the meanings that people attribute to their media use and other consumption behaviors (Zablocki and Kanter, 1976). Levine (1968) defines life style as what "emerges from the mutual adaptation of parts of experience felt so intensely that their contacts and organization produce an emotionally gratifying whole." Mass communication scholars interested in how media use "inter-connects" with other behaviors are concerned with how media content, the media use process itself, and the "meanings" attributed to media behaviors fit into different life styles. Sobel (1983) analyzed spending patterns on leisure activities to identify four patterns, including one which was entertainment-based (TV expenditures, camping, etc.).[161]

Where Do Life Styles Come From?

Mitchell (1983) conceptualizes nine American life styles based on Maslow's hierarchy of needs.[162] The nine fit into three categories: need-driven, outer-oriented and inner-oriented life styles. Need-driven groups include "survivors" and "sustainers," groups which are poverty-stricken and struggling to make ends meet. Outer-oriented life styles, which make up two-thirds of the U.S. population, include: "belongers" (middle-class, traditional, conforming), "emulators" (ambitious, striving to be like those richer, more successful than themselves), and "achievers" (diverse, gifted, hardworking, self-reliant, status-seeking). Inner-oriented life styles ("integrateds") include people combining outer-oriented and inner-oriented personality characteristics (maturity, sense of belonging).[163]

Social class and socioeconomic status are the factors cited most often for influencing life styles. Three basic types of economically determined life styles are: 1) property-dominated; 2) occupation-dominated; and 3) income or poverty dominated. These roughly correspond with conventional designations of the traditional upper class, upper middle through working classes, and the lower class or the poor.[164] While life style has been related to social class and status, tastes and preferences are neither completely determined by economic status, as Marx implied, nor completely individualized. "Tastes are determined in part by relative position in the markets for wealth and prestige, in part by individual choice informed by education and experience, and in part by voluntarily chosen, collectively-held standards that determine life styles" (Zablocki and Kanter, 1976).[165]

Although economic position no longer dominates the definition of a life style for a growing segment of the U.S. population, the very rich and the very poor may still find their life styles more or less automatically given by their location in the economic system. One sign of the arrival of the post-industrial society was the relative independence of production, consumption, and distribution, leaving people "relatively free to make a range of independent, even hedonistic, consumption decisions little constrained by their productive roles" (Bell, 1976).

Why Do New Life Styles Arise?

New life styles emerge when members of a society cease to agree on the value of the markets in commodities and prestige or come to recognize other sources of value (Zablocki and Kanter, 1976). With consensus absent, people use several strategies to cope with the loss of "value coherence." Two alternative hypotheses explain the proliferation of life styles in the U.S. since World War II. The transitional society hypothesis argues that the growth of different life styles is associated with the breakdown of one cultural tradition and occurs prior to the emergence of a new one (Etzioni, 1968). The consumer society hypothesis (Bell, 1976; Lewis, 1973) says that society has accumulated sufficient capital to generate enough leisure time for many people so "alternative standards of value and alternative life styles become a permanent feature" of society. In either case, mass media use is a major factor in at least two ways. First, media themselves are a primary vehicle for "creating" or aiding in the formation of many life style collectivities by providing symbols and objects for sharing values and by legitimizing the "sharing" itself. Secondly, media use itself is a significant portion of people's lives, making media use a major ingredient of current life styles (Bryand, Currier, and Morrison, 1976). The question is how and what patterns of media and other leisure behaviors fit into life styles.

Efforts to explain leisure activities often center on socioeconomic factors, but so far studies have detected few clear patterns. Income level is associated with the absolute amount of money spent on leisure but otherwise only shapes leisure activities by placing limits on those that are affordable. Education is positively related to strenuousness of leisure pursuits and engaging in a diversity of leisure activities (Cheek and Burch, 1976). Occupation is correlated with leisure choices, but socioeconomic differences in type of leisure activity are "not marked" and predicting one's leisure behaviors on the basis of SES is "all but impossible" (Wilson, 1980).

What is the relationship between work and leisure? Spreitzer and Snyder (1987) identify four perspectives: spillover—continuity of interests, attitudes, activities flowing from the job to the leisure context; compensation—participation in leisure activities that are the opposite of the job context to obtain satisfactions not realized at work; segmentation—leisure and work as autonomous spheres of experience, independent and unrelated; joint determination—leisure and work are reciprocally related, with two-way influence between them.[166] In a summary of research, Wilson (1980) finds evidence for a spill over into leisure pursuits of the "kinds of activities required by work." Examples would be work-acquired skills, mental vs. physical activities, job autonomy and leisure planning, etc. Kabanoff and O'Brien (1986) found evidence supporting a compensatory pattern among professionals.[167]

Besides work, the immediate environment affects one's choice of leisure activities, including the media. This includes facilities available, the type of home one lives in, whether one has children or not, etc. (Kelly, 1978). A report on life styles and demographics by area shows that particular media behaviors rank higher in some areas than others; reading books is popular in Charlottesville, Virginia, while VCR viewing is popular in Las Vegas, as is watching TV sports in Indianapolis.[168] An adult's leisure-time pursuits are affected by early family influences, Kelly notes, but not all adult leisure activities have origins in childhood.

Our definition of life style refers to a sharing of both behavior patterns and the meaning, or values attributed to them. As major components of various life styles, leisure activities themselves may be engaged in for a variety of meanings. Different activities favored by different social groups may have the same meaning, while a jointly popular activity may conceal a variety of satisfactions. Csikszentmihalyi (1975) found that leisure does have intrinsic meaning, and Kelly (1978) found that people chose more than half of their most important leisure activities for intrinsic reasons (where the behaviors are ends in themselves) such as "it's exciting," while the rest of their activities "acquired meaning as a result of their relation to work, family or community" (extrinsic, where behaviors are means to other ends). The intrinsic vs. extrinsic meaning of leisure pursuits is a useful way to identify whether media use and other leisure activities are related to work, family, etc. The "meaning" of leisure activities is another way of identifying the uses and gratifications which attract and sustain people in their media behavior patterns—"watching TV makes me relax, feel good" and "I read the stock market tables because it's useful at work." Uses and gratifications may link media not only to needs but to other behaviors that form a coherent life style (Villani, 1975).

Relating Life Styles and Media Use Patterns

People can be grouped on the basis of their leisure interests and activities and underlying psychological needs (Greenberg and Frank, 1983). One taxonomy identified 18 patterns of interests, including: comprehensive news and information and popular entertainment (radio, films, popular music, etc.). Analyzing clusters of interests and needs, they identified 14 groups, 3 for adult males, 4 for adult females, 3 for youth, and 4 mixed. News and information emerged as a "mixed" life style interest cluster. Popular entertainment formed part of an adult-female and home/community pattern. Leisure life style interest segments were closely related to TV viewing patterns; for example, children's programs were watched more frequently by those in the family-integrated activities cluster, and those in the arts and cultural activities cluster watched musical programs more often.

An effort to link life styles with individual needs, uses and gratifications, and media behavior patterns is found in a study by Donohew, Palmgreen, and Rayburn (1987). They analyzed a sample of cable TV subscribers, finding four life styles: disengaged homemakers, outgoing activists, restrained activist, and working class climber.[169] These were compared in terms of individual need for arousal and gratifications sought from cable TV. Need for external and internal sensation was highest for outgoing activists, while external and internal cognitive needs were highest for restrained activists. Corresponding to these needs were higher rates of consumption of newspapers and newsmagazines, while TV exposure was higher among working class climbers and disengaged homemakers. Surveillance and local orientation gratifications were highest for restrained activists, as were gratifications related to reception and religious programs. Disengaged homemakers sought all-day programming, companionship, and family viewing gratifications from cable TV more than those with other life styles. Working class climbers were highest on parasocial/entertainment gratifications, passing the time and variety gratifications. Valette-Florence and Jolibert (1990) also found that the life style concept—defined in terms of activities, interests, and opinions—explained differences in consumption patterns beyond social categories. Particular interests and media gratifications[170] were significant predictors for particular consumer patterns.[171]

While life styles characterize patterns of behaviors, quality-of-life assessments represent people's assessments of well-being. Concern with the pursuit of happiness is not novel to modern consumer societies, but it has grown as a topic on personal, public, and political agendas (Andrews and Withey, 1976; Andrews, 1986). Which domains of life contribute most to global measures of the quality of life? Satisfaction with self has the strongest correlation, followed by satisfaction with the following: standard of living, family life, marriage, family income, friendships, savings, work, housework, life in the U.S., housing, neighborhood, health, community, and the amount of education (Campbell, 1981). People's lives can be sliced up in many ways. Although mass communication researchers have examined relationships between media behaviors and uses and gratifications, explicit measures of the quality of life are rare. Recently, however, Kubey and Csikszentmihalyi (1990) examined people's TV viewing, relating it to personal feelings (passive, relaxing, sometimes negative feelings) and to the quality of family life (viewing may lead to more positive experiences with family members but greater passivity within that interaction; Kubey, 1990).

Summary

In this chapter we examined the diverse origins of media behaviors—the "why" question. At the highest level, people's media behaviors are seen as low involvement activity, with people picking choices from a menu determined largely by the larger social system or environment. At the individual level, we examined personality traits associated with media use, as well as social categories (achievement-oriented factors such as education and ascriptive-oriented factors such as gender). The home and physical environment also affect media use, which often is a joint activity rather than individual behavior. The community represents the broader environment affecting people's media behaviors; several community linkages are related to media use. The theory and research on uses and gratifications (U&G) represents the most extensive investigation into why people watch TV, read newspapers, and turn to various media. We discussed a host of concepts and mapped influences on media behaviors according to this theory. Finally, we reviewed the literature on media socialization and life styles that integrate media behaviors with competing alternatives in our daily lives.

Chapter Six Footnotes

1. See Tiedge and Ksobiech (1988) and Webster and Wakshalag (1983).
2. Signorielli (1986) found that action-adventure programs predominated (45%) on network TV, followed by situation comedies and serious dramas (about 28% each).
3. Audience inheritance (the percentage of the audience watching a program who also watch the next program on the same network) was stronger when programs and their lead-ins were of the same type and when programs were in the one-option rather than two- or three-option situation (Walker, 1988).
4. National Public Radio audiences are more diverse than those of commercial stations which offer a specific format because they attract audiences of subgroups whose allegiance to the station is partial and linked to particular types of programming available only some of the time (Woal, 1986).
5. In a comparison of Swedish and American TV viewing behaviors, Pingree, Hawkins, Johnsson-Smaragdl, Rosengren, and Reynolds (1990) note that the policy of not ending programs simultaneously makes exercising choice difficult in the Swedish context. The same structure may require Swedish viewers to make choices early on (consulting listings and planning ahead) rather than drift through an evening of viewing as is more feasible with the structure of American TV programming. Thus, decisions by media organizations about how media content is organized impact on the viewing process. Rust and Eechambadi (1989) suggest that audience size may be more sensitive to scheduling (what's shown on TV when and against what competition) than many have thought. Webster (1985) also finds evidence of audience flow—inheritance effects, repeat viewing, and channel loyalty.
6. Overbeck (1987) found in a study of 54 new housing developments in Los Angeles suburbs that rules frequently prohibited outdoor antennas, leaving residents with no choice but to subscribe to cable TV. Thus, desired "appearance" of the neighborhood leads to a choice of either poor reception or wide choices with cable TV.
7. Since the boundaries of a specific "media-use" unit are unclear, questions about why people use the media also are intertwined with questions about how—audience processing of media messages.
8. When people hear a variety of sounds simultaneously, the resulting barrage of noise so overwhelms attentive processes and arousal that music interferes with concentration. Music can have different information-load characteristics (loudness, variety, complexity, and tonal range) which produces overarousal (Kiger, 1989; Mehrabian, 1976). Effects of music on learning from reading books and other print media also may be the result of one's prior and current study/listening habits (Etaugh and Ptasnik, 1982; Rice, Meyer and Miller, 1988). In Kiger's (1989) study, two types of music were played to represent low- and high-information conditions as well as one without music. Reading comprehension was significantly higher in the low information-load condition than in either the silent or high information-load condition for these students, almost all reporting that they occasionally studied with background music. Kiger suggests that high information-load music may produce tension and anxiety that hurt performance of complex tasks requiring concentration, while slow, soft, repetitive (low information-load) music lowers arousal for better performance, with silence producing a subthreshold arousal that impairs performance.
9. Of younger readers (age 18–24), almost 39% read only certain parts of the daily paper and skip the rest, while 19% start with page one and go right through the paper.
10. Lin (1988) found that viewers with access to more options tended to be more selective. Program choice was positively but weakly correlated with viewing planning, program-guide use and channel switching. A comparison of cable and noncable viewing styles found that cable viewers consulted guides more often, had larger channel repertoires and engaged in more orienting

searches than did those restricted to over-the-air broadcast channels (Greenberg, Heeter, D'Alessio, and Sipes (1988).

11. These are traditional sociological descriptors that Talcott Parsons saw as central to sociological theory (Tomovic, 1979; Mann, 1984). Ascriptive, achievement, and life cycle categories help distinguish between influences on media use into those which an individual can control and those which are out of one's control or which are tied to the life cycle.

12. Wright (1989) looks at three types of class differences: those based on unequal control over means of production, those based on unequal control over organization assets—bureaucratic or organizational differences—and those based on unequal control over scarce skills. He attributes differences in people's identification with social class ("class consciousness") to a combination of actual social position and politics.

13. A study of the psychological effect of social class in the U.S., Japan, and Poland found that men with higher class status were more self-directed, valued self-direction for their children, and were more intellectually flexible than men less advantageously located in the class structure. Data showed effects of personality on class position and of class position on personality (Kohn, Naoi, Schoenbach, Schooler, and Slomczynski, 1990).

14. Roberts (1987: 107) combed several national surveys for those who claimed to watch less than 30 minutes of TV per day, finding 10.86% of post-graduates falling into this category, compared to 7.43% of college graduates, 6.91% of those with some college, and 3.76% of those with high school diplomas.

15. *The Study of Magazine Buying Patterns*, conducted by Audits & Surveys and sponsored by Publishers Clearing House in collaboration with the Magazine Publishers of America. Port Washington, NY, 1991.

16. A national survey shows that 35% of college graduates favor newspapers as their main source of information, while 46% favor TV news and 13% radio; in contrast, of those with less than a high school education, only 15% prefer newspapers and 74% prefer TV news (*News and Newspaper Reading Habits: Results from a National Survey*. New York: Newspaper Advertising Bureau, 1988.).

17. Education also has been positively linked to newspaper readership in other countries (e.g., Kenya, Ugboajah, 1985).

18. Earlier, Jackson-Beeck (1977) found that non-TV viewers are rare in the U.S., "not a meaningful population subgroup" and socially insignificant.

19. "Cable TV, VCRs, and Newspapers: Results from a National Survey," New York: Newspaper Advertising Bureau, July, 1988. Those in the top income category ($40,000 +) were more likely to have cable TV (64% vs. 38% of the lowest income category) and to have recorded TV programs in the past month (60% vs. 41% of lowest income category).

20. *The Study of Magazine Buying Patterns*, conducted by Audits & Surveys and sponsored by Publishers Clearing House in collaboration with the Magazine Publishers of America. Port Washington, NY, 1991.

21. Survey of 16,000 households from April, 1990 to March, 1991, sponsored by the American Book Sellers Association, the Association of American Publishers and the Book Industry Study Group, Inc.

22. They spend similar portions of their income on reading material (.7% vs. .6%). The total includes money spent on reading and TV, radio, and sound equipment (Waldrop, 1990).

23. "Executive Style Survey," *Wall Street Journal*, March 20, 1987, p. 21D.

24. Such as Yugoslavia, Australia, and Great Britain (Dzinic, 1974; Palmer, 1985). In Britain, interviews with working- and middle-class adults found differences in how some news is interpreted, but papers were the most important source of information on industrial relations for both groups, then TV, radio, and finally other media (Hartman, 1979). Two other British researchers studying a group of boys over two decades found that TV was a major home-based activity in the working class where it occupied a more central place in the home-based

leisure compared with middle-class counterparts (Himmelweit and Swift, 1976).

25. This refers to the 1975 diary data. As women have entered professional and managerial occupations, their readership patterns have shifted (Sparks, 1987).

26. However, Roberts (1987) found no significant gender differences in not watching TV.

27. *The Study of Magazine Buying Patterns*, 1990 survey conducted by Audits & Surveys and sponsored by Publishers Clearing House in collaboration with the Magazine Publishers of America. Port Washington, NY, 1991.

28. See: newspaper content (Weaver and Mauro, 1978); magazine preferences (Sosanie and Szybillo, 1978); types of magazine advertising (Griswold and Moore, 1989); graphic design in advertising (Surlin and Kosak, 1975); radio formats (Lull, Johnson, and Sweeny, 1978); TV programs (Frank and Greenberg, 1979; Gerbner et al., 1984; Paugh, 1989), music videos (Brown, Campbell, and Fischer, 1986), music preferences (Christenson and Peterson, 1988), going to X-rated films, watching TV sports, reading sex-oriented magazines, watching TV soaps, reading newspaper society pages, and reading home-oriented magazines (Gentry and Doering, 1979).

29. See Stamps and Stamps (1985) and Woodard (1988).

30. Simmons Market Research Bureau, *The 1984 Study of Media and Markets*. New York: SMRB, 1984. Cited in Cobb and Kenny (1986), who also found that 69% of blacks reported having a newspaper available in the home, compared to 86% of whites in their study.

31. See Brown, Childers, Bauman, and Koch (1990).

32. See Brown, Campbell, and Fischer (1986).

33. See Allen and Bielby (1979), Jones (1988), and Lipman (1989).

34. For example, in the late 1980s, "In the Heat of the Night" was 26th among white households but a sixth place ranking among blacks pulled it up to a 16th place overall.

35. See Okigbo (1985) and Young (1986).

36. Viewers of one Spanish-language station spend almost 38% of their total viewing time with that station, and greater attention to Spanish-language programs also was found in Texas. See Webster (1986) and Chang et al. (1988). Shoemaker et al. (1987) found the concentration of Hispanics in the community positively related to Spanish-language media use, particularly print media and radio listening.

37. Whites exceeded blacks in frequency of going to the school library, while blacks got a newspaper and went to the movies more frequently than whites. Blacks watched more TV and got a newspaper more frequently than Mexican children. Mexican children exceeded their black peers on frequency with which they went to the school and public libraries, but Puerto Rican children were not more frequent users than blacks of any media. In general, white children were more frequent media users than their Hispanic peers. Access and social class differences were noted (Blosser, 1988). Tangney and Feshbach (1988) found black children viewed nearly twice as much TV as white children, independent of parents' level of education.

38. See Gaddy (1984) and Tanney and Johnson (1984).

39. See: Abelman (1987, 1988, 1989), Gerbner, Gross, Hoover, Morgan, and Signorielli (1984), and Hoover (1987).

40. See Litman and Bain (1989) and Roberts (1987).

41. Religious conservatives are less motivated to watch TV because characters are sexually appealing. They also watch fewer programs with sexual content and feel TV is less important in their lives (Hamilton and Rubin, 1992).

42. *News and Newspaper Reading Habits: Results from a National Survey*. New York: Newspaper Advertising Bureau, 1988.

43. Media use occurs in a variety of physical contexts outside the home. TV viewing is common in college lounges, newspaper and magazine reading are common in hospital waiting rooms, and radio listening often occurs in the automobile. Lindlof (1986) looked at one constraining environment—media use by prisoners in a state institution, finding that those who had greater

community contacts (phone calls, visits, letters) and who were more involved in inmate organizations or educational programs also were higher on magazine reading and ownership; the former also was related to higher radio listening and the latter to higher movie attendance. Those alone in cells valued TV more for its help in passing the time or passing lonely hours away from family, while those in double-occupancy cells liked TV for privacy and control of program selection.

44. Lull (1988: 245-246) describes the complexity of TV viewing at home: "Family viewing takes place within the household, a complex mixture of people, social roles, power relations, routine activities, processes of interpersonal communication, ecological factors that characterize the home environment, and technological devices and appliances that exist there. The home surrounds viewers, and viewing, with all the intricacies and complications of family life."

45. See Bryce (1987), Lindlof (1987), Traudt and Lont (1987).

46. This is based on a survey of more than 2,000 12-14 year olds in 10 southeastern U.S. cities (Brown, Childers, Bauman, and Koch, 1990).

47. See Morgan, Alexander, Shanahan, and Harris (1990).

48. See Lewis (1990), Lull (1988), and Morley (1986).

49. Christopher, Fabes, and Wilson (1989) interviewed 55 parents to study the relationship of family TV viewing and family interaction.

50. See Chaffee et al. (1971, 1973) and McLeod et al. (1972).

51. Mothers who encouraged their children to express their own ideas reported less use of TV this way (Gantz and Masland, 1986). Jordan (1992) links many of the differences within families to social class differences.

52. Studying juveniles in Thailand, Cheyjunya and Lerklang (1988) found that families with a concept-oriented communication pattern also tended to have higher levels of newspaper and magazine reading, radio listening, and movie going.

53. Morgan, Alexander, Shanahan, and Harris (1990) found that adolescents in families with socio-oriented communication patterns used the VCR more for all specific types of uses— viewing owned or rented tapes, time shifting, etc.; those in more concept-oriented families also rented more tapes. The socio-orientation was related to arguing with siblings about TV and the concept-orientation was related to fewer arguments with parents, about TV or in general. The greater the usage of the VCR, the more frequent adolescents argued with each other and their parents, about the VCR, TV, or in general.

54. Some voting and compromise are evident in consensual families for children of all ages and in protective and laissez-faire families with older adolescents age 15-17 (Dimmick, 1976).

55. Fabes, Wilson, and Christopher (1989) argue that family professionals need to help parents and families cope with television; they provide a checklist focusing on building awareness of family TV viewing patterns, processing what is watched and questioning the role of TV in family life.

56. Parents who believe TV can influence children have kids who watch TV more for learning and escape. The study involved second, sixth, and tenth graders and their parents (Dorr, Kovaric, and Doubleday, 1989).

57. Some 17% of mothers said they send their child to the TV when they need to cook, 11% when they have housework to do, and 16% when they want to relax.

58. One study found that VCR use is more individualistic than off-the-air TV, with less coviewing even among family members (Gunter and Levy, 1987). Another study found the opposite—a tendency for adolescents to use the VCR with others; while 44% of one sample reported often watching TV alone, only 23% said they frequently use the VCR by themselves (Morgan, Alexander, Shanahan and Harris, 1990).

59. Gallup Poll conducted nationwide in late 1988.

60. Chicago elementary school children were surveyed (Sarlo, Jason, and Lonak, 1988).

61. See Atkin, Greenberg, and Baldwin (1991) and Brown, Childers, Bauman, and Koch (1990).

62. Community linkages have been related to media use since Robert E. Park's (1929) work in Chicago more than half a century ago.
63. Also see Stamm and Guest (1991).
64. Newspaper subscription and frequency of reading were related to the social effort dimension.
65. Primary ties had no relationship to media use, and secondary ties were only related to subscription of the local newspaper. People who participated in more local volunteer associations were more likely to subscribe to both local and regional newspapers. Political involvement and voting in local elections also were linked to newspaper subscriptions. Cable TV was not associated with any of these ties.
66. See: Jackson (1981), Rarick (1973), Stone (1977), Stamm and Fortini-Campbell (1983), and Weaver and Fielder (1983).
67. The three types of communities also have widely different media systems, with suburban communities having a much richer media environment—2 weekly papers compared to none in the small cities and 1 in the regional cities.
68. See Barnett and Chang (1989) and Barnett, Chang, Fink, and Richards (1991).
69. "Trends in Viewing," report prepared by the Research Department of the Television Bureau of Advertising, New York, July, 1988, p. 3. Source: A.C. Nielsen. Seasons also affect TV viewing in Australia (Correll and Biggins, 1984).
70. Numerous scholars have sought to place "uses and gratifications" into broader frameworks or to organize the literature for a clearer picture. Altheide (1985) locates the uses-and-gratifications approach within the broad theory of symbolic interaction, noting that research shows audience members are involved interactively with media content, their own feelings and social situation and that the impact of specific messages is not uniform and cannot be solely attributed to such social variables as education. Palmgreen (1984) and Palmgreen, Wenner, and Rosengren (1985) summarize research findings into major categories that reflect not only gratifications sought and obtained but also theories that focus on media behavior situations—expectancy value approaches and audience activity.
71. Early studies looked at the functions of radio soap operas (Herzog, 1942), the use of the media to orient oneself to other people (Lasswell, 1948), and use of films for escape.
72. They found that intentionality to view local TV news was predicted by affinity, selectivity and involvement. Lack of selectivity was predicted by pastime motives, perceived realism, and reduced intentionality. Involvement was predicted by information and nonentertainment motives, perceived realism, and intentionality.
73. Viewing attention, parasocial interaction, and two motives for viewing (for exciting entertainment and escapist relaxation) also were major predictors.
74. Mele (1989: 25) notes that there is widespread agreement among philosophers of action that intention is a motivating cause of actions, with both initiating and sustaining functions; however, intentions are not "raw motivation" but have cognitive or representational content.
75. Looking at Nielsen data, Lometti, Hyams, and Zhang (1992) find added support for the view of an active audience in the relatively quick review and rejection of new programs by viewers. Early rejection was higher among children, teens, and young adults than among older adults.
76. A national survey found that only 15% of people who watched TV news "yesterday" said the news came on while they were watching TV, in contrast to 51% who said they tuned in specifically to watch the news at that time of day. The most frequent readers were even less likely to watch TV passively (12% vs. 20% of infrequent readers and 19% of nonreaders) (*News and Newspaper Reading Habits: Results from a National Survey*. New York: Newspaper Advertising Bureau, 1988, p. 60.).
77. Dobrow (1990) also found that TV viewers who owned VCRs sought to select and control their viewing, and heavier viewers used their VCRs to watch more of the same type of programming they preferred. Jeffres (1978) referred to this as "interest maximization." Scherer

(1989) found that those who were heavy print users and whose information gathering was more focused and purposive were more likely to use VCRs to increase control over their TV/video environment.

78. See Baron (1985) and Kelley, Gunter, and Buckle (1987). Frazer (1987) found that girls reading an adolescent magazine were not the passive readers depicted but were critical consumers.

79. Finn (1992) looks at models of TV addiction with different assumptions for individual responsibility: the disease model where one is free from personal responsibility for the development of addiction, and change is impossible without some treatment program; the moral model where one is blamed for becoming addicted; the enlightenment model which assigns some personal responsibility for the addiction; and the compensatory model which says one learns to compensate for a problem by assuming active responsibility and self-mastery in the change process but is not personally responsible for the problem. Each model assumes a different origin for the "activity" of the individual in TV viewing. Looking at TV "addiction" and drug use, Finn (1992) found alcohol and marijuana use negatively correlated with motives for watching TV, but sensation seeking was positively correlated with drug use and negatively correlated with TV viewing. The disease model of TV addiction lacked support, and the other models appeared more appropriate for developing strategies to correct compulsive TV viewing.

80. "Input some event with its particular kind of meaning; out comes an emotion of a particular kind"—the law of situational meaning (Frijda, 1988: 349). This is a framework used to organize findings on cognitive variables that account for various emotions.

81. People's leisure preferences are less stable than commonly assumed, and individuals' psychological states of anxiety, stress, fatigue, and depression may affect their leisure preferences (Crawford and Godbey, 1987).

82. Helregel and Weaver (1989) looked at pregnant and non-pregnant women and new mothers to see how they used TV as a mood-management device, finding that affective states during pregnancy strongly influenced TV program choices. Also see Meadowcroft and Zillman (1987).

83. They controlled for social categories.

84. They also found that surveillance gratifications mediated the relationship between need for cognition and media reliance.

85. They looked at psychological benefits of participation in 34 leisure activities for 1,375 respondents who described themselves as knowledgeable participants of at least a year. Analysis showed the activities were grouped into nine categories based on benefits.

86. See Lain (1986), Katz et al. (1973), Weaver et al. (1980), and Kippax and Murray (1980).

87. See Katz et al. (1973), Kippax and Murray (1980), Levy and Windahl (1984), Palmgreen et al. (1980), Wenner (1982, 1986), McLeod and Becker (1974), McLeod and McDonald (1985), and Levy (1977).

88. See Frank and Greenberg (1980), Katz et al. (1973), Lain (1986), Rubin (1981, 1983, 1984), Rubin et al. (1985), Rubin and Perse (1987), Weaver et al. (1980), Levy (1977), and Wenner (1982, 1986). Looking at nostalgia as a media gratification, Lamude (1990) and Davis (1979) suggest that people who wish to avoid current anxieties and discontinuities often seek media in a flight to the past.

89. See Lain (1986), Levy and Windahl (1984), Palmgreen et al. (1980), Wenner (1982, 1986), Frank and Greenberg (1980), Katz et al. (1973), Kippax and Murray (1980), Levy and Windahl (1984), Palmgreen et al. (1980), Rubin (1981, 1983, 1984), Rubin et al. (1985), Rubin and Perse (1987), Weaver et al. (1980), Wenner (1982, 1986), Greenberg (1974), Lain (1986), Levy (1977), McLeod and Becker (1974), McLeod et al. (1982), McLeod and McDonald (1985).

90. See Katz et al. (1973), Kippax and Murray (1980), Levy (1977), Levy and Windahl (1984), McLeod et al. (1982), McLeod and McDonald (1985), Palmgreen et al. (1980), Wenner (1982, 1986), McLeod and Becker (1974), and Frank and Greenberg (1980).

91. McDonald and Glynn (1984) found surveillance gratifications more stable over a one-year period than communicatory utility gratifications.
92. See Arai and Fujiwara (1987) for the pattern of information needs identified in Japan.
93. Izcaray and McNelly (1987) found audience interests and tastes accounting for most of the differences in individual media use patterns in Venezuela, despite geographic, educational, and economic constraints.
94. In Poland, Dohnalik (1989) found six clusters of gratifications associated with viewing a popular TV series, "Return to Eden," which portrayed a world of the Australian "high life": 1) escape (daydreams, to forget reality, find out things, get better knowledge of people and problems, to feel one knows heroes of the series, to look in others' lives, to satisfy oneself that capitalism offers greatest possibilities to become rich and enjoy a comfortable life); 2) ritualistic viewing (to pass time, kill time, do the usual thing); 3) confirmation of one's proper place in society (to find out nature of struggle for money in capitalist societies, to satisfy oneself that struggle for money is always and everywhere accompanied by cheating, to have a closer look at lives of people likely never to be encountered, to satisfy oneself that one would be out of depth in a capitalist state); 4) suppression of comparisons (to participate in conversations about the series, to derive pleasure from watching the series with others and comment on it, to present opinions of series to others, to become agitated and get suspense from what happens next); 5) entertainment without involvement (to get to know life style of heroes, to get away from daily worries and problems, to pass time pleasantly, to amuse self by guessing further course of events); and 6) limited identifications (to feel like a participant in the series events, to compare one's own behavior and others with those in series). Dohnalik (1989) suggests that differences in the dimensions of gratifications gained from this series and those in some American studies reflect differences in samples and cultures. We would expect some of the differences to be related directly to the particular program and the dramatic changes occurring in Poland at the time.
95. Respondents missed serials, movies, and crime shows the most, but three activities (listening to records, going out with friends, and listening to the radio) supplanted TV viewing during the strike.
96. Audience motivations affect mental effort, attention, and memory of message processing (Rothschild, Thorson, Reeves, Hirsch, and Goldstein, 1986; Reeves and Thorson, 1986).
97. See Hirschman (1985) and Holbrook and Lehmann (1981).
98. See: Beard and Ragheb (1980), Bishop (1970), McKechnie (1974), Pierce (1980), and Witt (1971).
99. This is a complex area. It should be mentioned that some media behavior is done for negative reasons—for example, other people turn on the TV. Jeffres (1975, 1976) reports that 74% say they are content-seeking when they turn on the TV as opposed to media-seeking. Newspapers (66%) and radio (45%), on the other hand, are more associated with media-seeking. People just wanted to "listen to the radio" or "read the newspaper." A significant portion of radio use (19%) is non-seeking.
100. See: Csikszentmihalyi (1975), Iso-Ahola and Weissinger (1990), Kelly (1974), McCall (1974).
101. The cognitive component is related to perceptions of behavior as instrumentally unsatisfying, not satisfying salient needs, monotonous, homogeneous. The affective component is related to frustration, a result of perceptions of constraints that limit the satisfaction that can be derived from the experience. Thus, boredom consists of displeasure and low arousal (Iso-Ahola and Weissinger, 1990).
102. Alternative explanations are personality traits (a dislike for challenging situations that require skilled performance), cultural factors (lack of socialization in flow activities), or overreliance on TV and other media that makes people less able to engage in active leisure.
103. However, a study of graduate students' perceptions of new interactive media and their uses for personal financial planning found that print media grouped together (newspapers,

magazines, direct mail), as did media typically used for entertainment purposes (cable/broadcast TV, videocassette programming); however, videotex and teletext grouped with interpersonal communication, suggesting different uses and gratifications for those new technologies (Cowes, 1989).

104. Others were: library storage (creating copies for later use); music or music videos (motives attached to music); exercise tapes (for exercising at home); movie rentals (convenience, choice, ease, selection attached to film videos); child viewing (movies available for kids); critical viewing (to review, study program content).

105. Umphrey (1989) also found no differences in attitudes toward cable services of those who disconnected and those who continued to subscribe.

106. O'Keefe and Sulanowski (1992) found gratifications linked to telephone use.

107. "Feeling Depressed?" *Public Opinion*, May/June, 1989, p. 40.

108. Swartz and Meyer (1986) found five variables discriminating between individuals who use TV primarily for news and information, entertainment, or both: viewing educational programs, viewing informational programs, the number of hours spent watching TV daily, personal views of TV on the info-entertainment dimension, and the importance of TV in one's life.

109. Perse (1992) found that utilitarian motivations for viewing news were related to watching local government reports, while passing-the-time motives were linked to avoiding government reports and watching sports reports instead. Jensen (1990) used qualitative analysis of interviews with TV news viewers to identify social uses of TV news (information, legitimation—get sense of control over events in the world, and diversion.

110. Also see: Alexander (1985); Rubin (1985); Babrow (1987), who found that 16 types of gratifications accounted for differences in why college students watched soap operas; Babrow (1988, 1990) and Lemish (1985), who found that college students derive significant gratifications from viewing soap operas in social settings; Schrag and Rosenfeld (1987), who found that college students generally do see such values as loving, cheerful, true friendship, and equality in daytime TV dramas; Johnstone and Allen (1984), who found a "glamour" factor for urban soap viewers.

111. People who devote 50% or more of their TV viewing to religious programs are purposeful, selective information seekers who do not watch much (Abelman, 1987). Gaddy and Pritchard (1985) found that people who watch religious TV go to church less often, suggesting a functional similarity.

112. Walker (1987) found that seventh graders who watched MTV also were more likely to watch romance and comedy motion pictures and teen films and to listen to the radio more often. Eleventh graders who watched MTV also were more likely to watch daytime soap operas and go to films more often. Also see: Zillmann and Mundorf (1987) and Wells and Hakanen (1991).

113. Becker and Creedon (1989) identified three motives for viewing male vs. female sports: familiarity (people prefer the known), perceptions of female sports as inferior, and views that competitive sports are not consistent with how females should behave. They found modeling and spectating motivations. Groves (1986, 1987) found that people active in sports watch TV daily, read books or magazines daily, and liked sports programming best in comparison to those not active in sports. The Olympic games are a focus of celebrations and communal gratifications for many (Lee, 1992; Rothenbuhler, 1988).

114. Ten factors were found: general learning, mood control/enhancement, characteristics of the medium, social utility, personal identity, entertainment, social facilitation, communication avoidance, communication utility, and great expectations.

115. Towers (1986) found the same three dimensions predicting magazine and other media use. Newsmagazine subscribers tended to read them for surveillance and interaction, while those who bought single copies emphasized surveillance of particular and exciting events. Consumer magazine subscription was related to dimensions of passing time and life-style quality.

Malaysian youth were found to read magazines to acquire knowledge (20%), stay abreast of current events (12%), as a hobby (11%), and for relaxation (6%). Others used magazines as substitutes for friendship (Idid, 1988).

116.   Nonreaders of newspapers cite usefulness, interest, trust, use of radio-TV, and the amount of detail in newspapers as reasons for not reading a newspaper (Lipschultz, 1987). Analysis of motivations for starting and stopping subscriptions of daily newspapers shows that households are less likely to drop if their members mainly look for information rather than ads from the newspaper (Zhu and Weaver, 1989).

117.   Surveillance is more important for regular subscribers and readers while occasional weekday readers use papers more for interaction (Lain, 1986; Towers, 1985, 1986). Hu and Wu (1991) found that readers and nonreaders of newspapers could be distinguished by their responses to the following: "There is not much in newspapers that is useful to me in my daily life; newspapers do not print much of interest to me; Newspapers cost more than they are worth to me; it takes too much time to read a newspaper regularly; By the time I see a story in a newspaper, I have already heard about it from television or radio."

118.   Also significant were: daily usage of magazines, mother's usage of the newspaper, the newspaper as most valuable medium, and availability of newspaper in the home. The image factors reflect uses and gratifications teenagers associated with newspapers.

119.   Some 36% of its readers are between age 18 and 29, compared to 26% of those who read the *Los Angeles Times* ("Where Have All the Readers Gone? Publishers Struggle to Win Over Younger Generation—Quickly," *Media/Impact/Update* (Fall, 1989) 2(2):1, 3.). Hartman's (1987) study of 18-35 year old readers found about a fourth reading *USA Today*, about half spending 5-15 minutes with the paper, most with either the main news or sports sections. Half of this group said they would like other papers to be more like *USA Today*. A third of the respondents said they read the paper half for information and half for entertainment, while an additional third placed more emphasis on information (75%) and 22% said entirely for information.

120.   McDonald (1990) found that two uses explained people's news information-seeking behavior from newspapers and TV: surveillance—to know about the community and world events; and communicatory utility—information to use in social interaction with others.

121.   This distinction was first suggested by Wilbur Schramm in 1949. Mazharul Haque (1986) found that Indian elite papers devoted 72% of their newshole to delayed-reward news stories and 28% for immediate reward stories (for example, most sports and popular amusements stories).

122.   Howard, Blick, and Quarles (1987) found that local TV stations were the preferred choice for specialized news (about medicine, science, business, consumer economics), followed by local newspapers, magazines, radio, cable networks, national newspapers, and other sources.

123.   One survey found that the physician was the chief source of people's hospital information, followed by friends and neighbors, newspapers, and then other sources; electronic media were mentioned by fewer than 1% of respondents (Reagan and Collins, 1987). In another study, half of middle-class women approaching menopause age got most of their ideas about menopause from friends, with 45% citing magazines, 40% books, 32% their mothers and 21% doctors (Brazaitis, 1991). A study of male athletes found that media were cited as sources of information about nutrition by less than 10% (Shoaf, McClellan, and Birskovich, 1986).

124.   Magazines were cited by single men and women as the major source of information on sexually transmitted diseases, followed by TV, newspapers, and physicians ("The Best Source?" *Wall Street Journal*, July 30, 1987, p. 21. Survey of single men and women. Source: Abbott Laboratories.).

125.   Giese and Weisenberger (1985) found that advertising was a source of information used

by consumers for purchasing a variety of products: by 38% purchasing small appliances, 14% purchasing home repair services, 32% buying lawn and garden equipment, 9% purchasing insurance policies, and 20% buying eyeglasses/contact lenses.

126. Barber and Smith (1989/1990) found that Chinese students in the U.S. relied more heavily on interpersonal sources rather than media sources for local news. Temporary Canadian residents in the U.S. express a greater need for home news than do permanent residents (Sherman, 1985). Similarly, a study of media use by Americans in Britain and Britons in the U.S. found both groups relying on newspapers and TV to keep up with the home country (McKenzie, 1988). Americans relied most on British TV and British newspapers, followed by U.S. magazines, while Britons relied on U.S. TV, British newspapers, U.S. newspapers, and then U.S. magazines.

127. Other studies find: paper subscribers using TV as a complementary medium (Grotta et al., 1975); TV and papers evenly split in satisfying the need to keep tabs on things, while TV was favored for relaxing, killing time, and being entertained (Weaver, Wilhoit, and Riede, 1979); people paid not to use TV turned to radio, magazines, newspapers, friends, and associates for entertainment (Tan, 1977).

128. In a British study, Docherty, Morrison, and Tracey (1986) note that 70% of those age 50 or older say the best way to watch a feature film is by TV, while 6% favor the VCR and 21% favor going to the cinema. Among those age 16-29, 26% said they prefer to watch a film on TV, 31% on VCR and 39% by going out to a theater. In Santa Monica, a survey found that respondents went to see movies at a theater 2.6 times a month before they acquired VCRs, pay-TV subscriptions, and videodisc players; afterwards the figure dropped to an average of 1.8 movies a month, suggesting a functional equivalence of the different media (Mazingo, 1987).

129. Atkin (1991) found a positive relationship between cable subscription and VCRs, video games, camcorders, and audio technology use, which represents functional similarities in meeting entertainment needs.

130. The new technologies were preferred over TV, and TV was favored over radio and print media. In a panel study of adolescents, Morgan, Alexander, Shanahan, and Harris (1990) found that the amount of TV viewing predicted VCR ownership three years later, but early VCR ownership did not predict later TV viewing.

131. Some 62% of Swedish adolescents reported feeling at least partially deprived by the TV strike, and these feelings were related to habitual motives for TV viewing.

132. These included: instrumental uses (to learn things, get information, keep up with events) and ritualized gratifications (to escape problems, pass the time, be entertained) when interpersonal opportunities were restricted by psychological and socio-demographic conditions (e.g., loneliness, unemployment). Increasing media opportunities increased use of TV programming but not interpersonal communication.

133. Here he included one's life cycle position and place in the social structure.

134. Examples are lack of a phone, car, or satisfying job.

135. Examples are organizational affiliation and frequent social interaction.

136. Results showed that newspaper gratifications tend to be linked to facilitating influences while TV uses and gratifications are connected to compensatory ones.

137. From this perspective, viewer responses to specific segments of TV content are a function of three things: viewers are activated or aroused by the content, they adapt to the material, and their interest in the material rises (Behnke and Miller, 1992).

138. Austin (1985) found no relations or weak ones between loneliness and media use among a sample of college students, suggesting this group turned to other methods for help.

139. The concept is linked to Horton and Wohl (1956).

140. Rubin, Perse, and Powell (1985) found a relationship between people's loneliness, infrequent interpersonal communication and use of TV for parasocial interaction. Armstrong and Rubin

(1989) found that listening to talk radio also was an alternative to interpersonal communication for those who were less mobile.

141. Parasocial interaction follows a path of development similar to social relationships with others—moving from exposure to attraction to parasocial interaction to greater importance of the relationship (Rubin and McHugh, 1987). Perse (1990) found that parasocial interaction from watching local TV news was associated with feeling happy while watching the news and with higher levels of perceived news realism.

142. Greenberg and Dominick (1969) found uses of TV viewing different for lower class and middle income children, with the former more dependent upon TV for "school of life" gratifications. Also see Moore, Moschis, and Stephens (1978) and Greenberg and Dervin (1970).

143. Clerical workers reported reading for excitement in leisure reading more than other groups. Semi-skilled and service employees spent more time reading to keep abreast of things during their leisure reading than the average did.

144. See Rubin (1986) and Wigand and Craft (1985).

145. Rubin (1977) investigated differences among children, young teenagers, and adolescents in their TV viewing behaviors and motivations to use TV. Six sets of reasons for viewing emerged: to learn, as a habit or to pass time, for companionship, to forget or for escape, for arousal, and for relaxation. Viewing to pass time was the prominent reason for viewing TV across all age groups. American grade schoolers listen to radio to create a private, self-defined domain within their households; music also seems to provide children with vocabulary and behavioral scripts needed in adolescence, as part of "anticipatory socialization" (Christensen, DeBenedittis, and Lindlof, 1985). Though adolescents use TV for information and entertainment, media play a relatively small part in teenage lives; the most frequently-cited use of radio by youths is to pass the time, as filler or background (Gantz et al., 1978). Also see Boyd and Najai (1984), Bryant and Zillman (1984), Lometti, Reeves, and Bybee (1977), Roe (1985), and Wade (1973).

146. Davis and French (1989) found 25% of a sample of elderly females were more socially active and engaged in life; they were more innovative and felt that information from advertising helped them make better buying decisions but often insulted their intelligence. Kaiser and Chandler (1985) found that people over age 70 with more education use TV more for fashion information.

147. See Monk (1988) and Elton (1988). Davis (1971) did not find support for the view that older adults use TV as a substitute for social involvement, but Hess (1974) found that TV viewing can substitute for face-to-face communication no longer available to the elderly. Three nonmedia sources of gratification—job, social activity, and solitary activity—were more important than the media in a study of the elderly by Swank (1979); print media and radio use may facilitate interpersonal contact rather than function as substitutes for missing activities.

148. An example of the latter was studied by Lindlof (1986), who looked at prisons, finding that inmates who displayed a "time-doer adaptation" used TV to displace relationships with inmates and staff members.

149. However, rural Alaskans were less likely to use radio ritualistically or for escape. Newspapers were preferred by urban residents for information about state government but, rural residents preferred TV as a source.

150. Early Americans thought children were capable of learning to read at very young ages and should be taught as soon as they could talk. During the 1830s and 1840s a shift occurred as educators and physicians thought childhood education could be harmful to the child. Thus, infancy schools disappeared until reinvented through the Headstart Program (Juster and Vinovskis, 1987).

151. Corsaro and Eder (1990) note various theories relevant for childhood socialization: behaviorist, constructivist, and interpretive. The behaviorist approach places little emphasis on social

interaction and peer cultures, while the constructivist stresses the child's active role in interpreting, organizing, and using information from the environment as he or she acquires adult skills and knowledge. The interpretive approach sees children's development as a process of interacting and negotiating with others, including not only parents and the family but also others in peer cultures and the adult world. Some activities are more dominant in some subcultures of youth than are others, and the functions certain speech activities serve may change over time.

152. In a study of high school sophomores, Thorn (1978) found only 28% said their parents ever suggest or require that they not watch certain programs.

153. The TV set is always on in more than a third of inner city families whether anyone is watching or not. In these families, parents are less likely to control, regulate, or monitor their children's viewing. The majority of children in such TV households were heavy viewers and could watch as much as they wished. The larger the household, the more likely the family will subscribe to cable TV for greater variety (Metzger, 1983).

154. Also see Einsiedel (1983) and Jeffres (1968), who found that modeling is more likely to occur among teenage boys when they strongly identify with their fathers.

155. However, children's channel repertoires were higher than those of adults by one or two channels, and children watched more different channels and spent more time viewing.

156. Parental messages need to be clear to be effective. Dornbusch et al. (1987) found a tendency for inconsistent messages from parents to adolescents to be associated with a lower correlation between hours of homework and grades, suggesting that inconsistency in the home environment creates anxiety that affects children's work.

157. The influence of peers on media use appears to have grown (Adoni, 1979). Looking at seventh, eleventh, and twelfth graders in the U.S., Chaffee and Tims (1976) found that adolescents from socio-oriented families tended to vary their viewing patterns more in the direction of their parents than did those in families where this orientation was weak. Strong peer orientations were found to be associated with conformity to peer viewing norms when viewing with friends.

158. Reviewing research on the Newspaper in Education program, Stone (1988) concluded that the program provides papers for many youth not having papers at home and that those who read a newspaper in the classroom reported enjoying reading papers more than those who did not. Those who use papers in school also say they have less difficulty reading papers and are more likely to be regular newspaper readers.

159. See: Campbell (1981), Campbell, Converse, and Rodgers (1976), and Meadow and Sirgy (1990), and Sirgy et al. (1992).

160. The concept of "way of life" or "style of life" dates back at least to Max Weber, but it became more popular beginning in the 1960s and 1970s (Andorka, 1987; Sobel, 1983).

161. Though income, education, and occupational status accounted for differences in life style forms, the relationships were complex rather than straight forward.

162. Heylighen (1992) reconstructed Maslow's theory of self-actualization, concluding the definition was confusing and gratification of all needs was an insufficient explanation. His hierarchy comprises the needs for homeostasis, safety, protection, feedback, and exploration. Self-actualization is defined as perceived competence to satisfy basic needs in due time (with material, cognitive, and subjective components).

163. Loov and Miegel (1990) argue that Mitchell's theory is individual-oriented and ahistorical. They note Bourdieu's (1984) theory that life styles are products of the struggle for power between social classes. Life styles are cultural phenomena, existing at both the individual and societal level. This theory accounts for outer-oriented life style values but neglects inner-oriented life style values.

164. Life styles dominated by property ownership are characterized by extended family and strong kinship ties and occupation of their own insulated, territorially distinct social world, such

as that found in private clubs and schools. In occupation-dominated life styles, life is shaped largely by selling one's labor for wages; one's feeling of self-worth tends to stem from measures provided by the work situation. The first indicator of identity is likely to be occupation or current job. Poverty-dominated life styles are also characterized by strong kinship and a reliance on family for a host of activities and support.

165. The inadequacy of class as the sole economic factor identifying life style is underlined by the fact that it is often difficult to determine whether emerging patterns of consumption are attributed to the blurring of class boundaries or to the upward mobility of whole classes themselves as a society becomes more affluent. Another view is presented by Dawson (1986), who proposes that leisure plays a role in the formation of class structure itself.

166. Parker and Smith (1976) identify ways that work and leisure are related: 1) leisure can be an extension of work so that the demarcation between the two is weak and work is the individual's primary interest; 2) leisure can be set in opposition to work, where leisure activities are deliberately counterposed to work and clearly set apart from it; and 3) the relation can be one of neutrality, where the boundary between them is not strong and the person is slightly more interested in leisure than work. Also see Shaffer (1987).

167. Stress was associated with a leisure pattern that provided escape from routine but also sociability, variety, and stimulation. Poole and Cooney (1986) found adolescents in Asia viewing leisure preferences and occupational aspirations as independent spheres, supporting a segmentation hypothesis that people split their lives into different areas of activity and interest existing independently of each other. The boundary between work and leisure and their relationship may not be fixed over a lifetime. Near and Sorcinelli (1986) found a high degree of spillover between work and life away from work among academics, compared to the general population.

168. *The Lifestyle Market Analyst*, report by National Demographics & Lifestyles, Inc., reported in *USA Today*, June 1-3, 1990, p. 1.

169. These were based on social, political, economic, cultural, and communication related attitudes, behaviors, self-perceptions, and needs.

170. These included: entertainment appeal of mass media, informative appeal of mass media, and entertainment in general.

171. People identified as "do-it-yourselfers" in a life style survey were more likely to own video cassette recorders (VCRs), to read newspapers, to read news and business sections of the paper, and to listen more often to classical music radio stations (Bush, Menon, and Smart, 1987). Yanclay and Metcalf (1985) surveyed readers of seven alternative life style magazines, finding a wide range of occupations and few unconventional ways of earning an income.

7

Processing Print and Broadcast Messages
What Do We Do?

A single mass media message, whether a TV commercial or a newspaper article, is decoded with relative ease by diverse members of the audience. In decoding, people perceive, interpret, categorize, and make sense of what they find on MTV or in radio bulletins, but the complexity of a solitary media unit—a magazine article or a TV commercial—is beyond the scope of a single theory in communication or related social or behavioral science disciplines. How audiences process media content clearly is a complex issue, one which also is significant for concerns over media effects.[1] For example, are there long-term effects on people's "thinking" from watching TV rather than reading print media? What formats and techniques best enable audiences to learn from watching TV or listening to the radio?

This chapter examines how audiences process print and broadcast messages. The media and larger environment represent an almost infinite potential for constructing different meanings. Two concepts of processing emphasize the importance of the environment (or message) vs. the importance of cognition and memory (images) one brings to the TV viewing or newspaper reading situation. When features of the message or environment are paramount, it's called **bottom-up processing**.[2] When memory and cognition become influential, it's called **top-down processing**. This chapter emphasizes the former by examining how characteristics of media messages affect audience processing.

Although we can examine how people learn from all media, the unique aspects of print versus audio/visual (broadcast) media argue for separate treatment. Researchers have focused on how audiences recognize, recall, and comprehend media forms and content. These have been linked to specific forms (for example, typefaces, movie genre) and content of media messages (such as negative news), generally those in newspapers and television.

Processing Print Media

What aspects of print media affect people's processing activities? At this stage, no exhaustive list is available, but several areas have been laid out for investigation. First, we need to identify relevant media units for study because they affect how people process print media. Units include global forms such as articles and advertisements, as well as further subdivisions such as typefaces, paragraphs, and illustrations. Once the units themselves have been identified as potential influences on how people process messages, we need to examine the size and shape of various message units, relationships among different components within messages, and relationships among messages within print media themselves. All of this occurs in a larger processing context (maybe a favorite easy chair) in which the media forms compete with nonmedia influences—noises heard while trying to read the paper and visual distractions. We also need to understand how audiences recognize, segment, and "chunk," these units individually and in combination with each other. Since print media are "read" as well as "viewed," we need to pay close attention to reading itself.

Reading Processes

Reading is an interactive process and does not proceed in strict sequence from basic perceptual units to overall interpretation of a text. Instead, the skillful reader gets information from many levels simultaneously and integrates them.[3] In comprehending print media, readers construct meaning by integrating information from successive sentences (Just and Carpenter, 1980). Each sentence is processed in a cycle during which the reader (a) buffers[4] information from the current sentence, (b) integrates the new information at clause and sentence boundaries, and (c) purges information from working memory to clear space for the next sentence (Chang, 1980; Miller and Kintsch, 1980; Haberlandt and Graesser, 1989).

Newspaper articles and magazine stories are composed of both **content words** and **function words**. The former include nouns, verbs, adjectives and adverbs, with the remaining words—prepositions, conjunctions, etc.— function words (Clark and Clark, 1977). Content and function words also differ in a variety of linguistic characteristics, such as the frequency with which they occur in the language, word length, and position within clauses (Haberlandt and Graesser, 1989). Newspaper word puzzles and the TV show "Wheel of Fortune" rely on these and similar factors; thus, contestants and audiences select the most common letters and identify function words first in solving the puzzle. Readers process these words differently, largely because of these linguistic characteristics.[5] Function words require more processing resources to recall than do content words; in comprehension tasks the opposite occurs (Haberlandt and Graesser, 1989).[6] Thus, content words provide the backbone for constructing the reader's text representation and add to the buffering load, while function words play an important processing role but require fewer buffering resources.

Our ability to process newspaper articles and other print information is restricted by our information processing ability.[7] People are limited in the amount they can perceive in a single fixation, how quickly the eyes can move, the number of chunks of information that can be held in short-term memory, and the rapidity with which information can be recalled from long-term memory.

Reading is strategic. Reading depends as much on the person reading as on the text read (Bransford and Johnson, 1972). The reader brings to a text his or her expectations, prior knowledge of language structure and content, and cultural background, all of which influence the comprehension and interpretation of the written word constructed during reading.[8] A skilled reader continuously monitors his or her comprehension, is alert to breakdowns in understanding, is selective in allocating attention to various aspects of print material, and progressively refines the interpretation during reading (Brown, Armbruster and Baker, 1986; Hall, 1989).

Human cognitive processes are geared to achieve the greatest possible cognitive effect for the smallest possible processing effort; to achieve this, people focus attention on what appears to be the most relevant information (Sperber and Wilson, 1986). Britton, Muth and Glynn (1986) found in an experiment that readers spent more time reading important information than unimportant information in twelve stories. Important information also was recalled more accurately.

Assumptions of readability are embedded in assumptions of reader motivation (Finn, 1985). If the reader engages in newspaper reading as a civic-minded information-seeking activity, then easy-to-read copy is likely to facilitate the reader's quest for information. If the reader is motivated by a need for emotional activation, sensation and arousal, then novelty may facilitate readability up to a point and then have a negative impact. Finn (1985) found in one study that reader enjoyment of news articles was enhanced on one level by the use of predictable syntactic forms and on another level by the use of unpredictable semantic content. Thus, content and function operate in different directions.

Model for Analyzing Comprehension of Print Media. Jacoby and Hoyer (1987) present a model for analyzing comprehension of print media.[9] Once the reader has given some attention to the media message, he or she begins processing this information at various levels simultaneously to extract meaning. Top-down processing emphasizes the pre-existing mental contents that the receiver brings to the situation. Bottom-up processing emphasizes the physical characteristics of the newspaper or magazine articles themselves (Tourangeau, 1984). Both involve the use of prior knowledge by the reader and recognize the influence of inferential processes during comprehension, but the top-down approach emphasizes large pre-existing structures that can organize an entire text while the bottom-up approach emphasizes lower-level structures that can be used piecemeal. The two perspectives are complementary rather than contradictory (Jacoby and Hoyer, 1987).

Bottom-up processing involves two types of analysis: sensory and semantic analysis. In **sensory analysis**, selected sensory features of incoming information are identified and these features integrated into larger structures. Acoustic information is first considered in terms of basic phonetic sounds (e.g.,'e'), which are then fused into larger units (namely syllables, e.g., 'ed'), and eventually into words (e.g., 'educate'). Visual information in alphanumeric form first is considered in terms of its discrete features.[10] Visual images other than numbers or letters are expected to go through a similar process, the person looking at a photograph first recognizing a shape then seen as part of a person and later fleshed out with specific details (Jacoby and Hoyer, 1987).

In **semantic analysis**, meaning is assigned to the sensory input via two overlapping stages: morphemic and thematic representation. Just as a phoneme is viewed as the smallest unit of human speech and the basis for distinguishing one linguistic sound from another, a morpheme (the smallest meaningful linguistic unit) is the most basic unit of meaning. Morphemes may be either single letters (such as I) or clusters of letters (separate words, such as "news," or part of larger clusters of letters that together form a word, such as "news" and "paper" in the word "newspaper"). In morphemic representation, the reader, for example, assigns relatively isolated meanings to the incoming sensory data, relying on past experience and knowledge of syntax and context to give each the most likely meaning. Especially with print communication, the assignment of meanings may not occur in the same sequential order as the words appear in the newspaper or magazine article. At this stage, the meanings exist in relative isolation, with no understanding of how the information can be used. Only when these rather preliminary meanings become integrated to form larger semantic units has the reader arrived at some useful level of understanding of all or some of the article being read. Jacob and Hoyer (1987) call these larger units "thematic representations,"[11] which are constructed in each situation to comprehend the specific article or material. They include both asserted meanings (those explicitly expressed in the media message)[12] and implied meanings (non-explicit inferences the reader draws from the media message).[13]

Four additional layers of complexity are identified as readers process media content (Jacob and Hoyer, 1987), and these represent opportunities for **top-down influences**: 1) fleeting meanings (those evoked for an instant and present only in short-term memory) vs. retained meanings (those given further cognitive attention and, thus, stored as beliefs for further use); 2) communication beliefs (those relating directly to aspects of the medium or message, focusing on what the reader believes the message contained—Does the editorial say an issue such as abortion should be opposed?) and referent beliefs (those pertaining to the content of the message itself—Does the reader oppose an issue such as abortion?); 3) asserted and implied communication beliefs in evaluative and affective terms—the process of evaluating the issue; and 4) other communication beliefs not tied to the message content, for example, Why did they print this editorial now?

Outcomes of this comprehension process include: 1) non-comprehension (no meanings extracted—nothing made sense); 2) comprehension of one or more asserted or logically implied meanings; and 3) complete or partial miscomprehension—extracting thematic meanings which are incorrect or making faulty inferences.

Jacoby and Hoyer (1987) sampled advertising and editorial content from eighteen consumer magazines—including *Reader's Digest, Time, Life, Redbook, Outdoor Life, Bon Appetit*—and asked more than 1,300 respondents what the main points of individual items were after reading each of two ads and two editorial items. A modified true-false quiz also was developed for each item to assess asserted and implied meanings. Graphic (type sizes, number of words, line length, etc.) and linguistic (number of sentences, passive verbs, noun strings, adjectives, etc.) features for ads and editorial items were analyzed.

A single reading of a magazine communication resulted in an average of 63% correct answers to questions about content, with correct answers ranging from a high of 83% to a low of 37%. Comprehension was higher for advertising content (65%) than editorial content (61%) and higher for facts (64%) than for inferences (62%). Some 37% of the meanings associated with the information content were miscomprehended. While all of the 108 test messages showed some miscomprehension, the percentage of incorrect answers ranged from a low of 6% to a high of 32%. None of the eighteen magazines were immune from miscomprehension. Tested across four messages, only 3 of 1,347 respondents were able to answer all 24 quiz items correctly and another 18 (1.4%) made no incorrect answers but had at least one "don't know" response. Thus, 98% of the readers misunderstood at least some portion of the four ads or articles on which they were tested. A fourth of the messages (articles and ads) had less than a 16% miscomprehension rate and another fourth had more than 25%.

Comprehension was related to individual differences[14] and content[15] but there were few differences attributed to message structure (graphic features) or specific magazine. Using comparable measures, results for this study of print media and an earlier study of TV (Jacoby, Hoyer and Sheluga, 1980) were similar, with 29.4% incorrect answers in the TV study and 25-29% incorrect answers in the magazine study.

Size and Shape of Typefaces and Words within Articles. The **size** and **shape** of **typefaces** have an impact on reading of print media. This book, for example, is typeset in 10 point Souvenir, a serif font (typestyle). Everett and Everett (1988) found that readers have increasing difficulty identifying type size differences when the size decreased from 6 points to 4 points to 2 points, all of which are very small type sizes. Difficulty in detecting size differences was not related to differences in text. **Serifs** (the short lines stemming from the ends of strokes of letters) increase character recognition by making letters more perceptible, particularly for small print (Robinson, Abbamonte and Evans, 1971). Changing script—for example, from handwritten to typewritten affects reading, as does changing letter case—from lower case to capitals.

Print media vary in **word selection**. Moriarty (1986) sampled newspaper stories, newsmagazine articles and magazine advertising copy, finding that newspapers used the longest words (5.9 characters per word), with newsmagazines second (5.4) and advertising copy third (4.6). For some time there has been a debate on how words are recognized and the processes involved. According to **word-shape theory**, the meaning of the word is cued in top-down processing by the actual shape of the composite word, not from individual letter characteristics or features. The word is abstracted as a semantic unit (Healy, Oliver and McNamara, 1987). The contrasting bottom-up view sees recognition of a word based not on overall word-shape but on specific letter shape features and combinations of letters assembled which cue semantic retention (Paap, Newsome and Noel, 1984). Recent research in which a scanner allowed researchers to see a word being remembered in the brain supports the word-shape, top-down view, because word recall was processed as though it were visual stimuli (Hilts, 1991).

Color vs. Black-and-White.   Color affects people psychologically and physiologically. Click and Stempel (1976) found that the use of color on pages resulted in higher ratings of the newspaper on several dimensions—style, potency, activity, evaluation. "Color conveys meaning, aside from the content of whatever it is in color" (Bohle and Garcia, 1987: 733). Color has the power to attract and pulls the readers' eyes.

The addition of color to black-and-white newspaper pages affects how readers process content. Bohle and Garcia (1987) used twenty-four different versions of a front page, sports page, and life-style page that differed in the use of color. They found that the main photo on all pages drew the most attention, whether it was in color or whether spot color was used on the page, but color on the page diminished the photo's power of attraction. On the front pages, after viewing the main photo, readers usually were attracted to the color, which also drew eyes below the fold. Color sometimes was more powerful than black-and-white photos in moving the eye after initial entry to the page.

Color is an important perceptual feature that combines with size, shape, location, brightness, line, angle, and contour to highlight the physical aspects of visual images found in photographs and illustrations in print media. Research examining color as a visual feature shows that it is analyzed immediately by a specialized set of receptors that map the color information in a specific area of the brain (Zeki, 1976). This information then is integrated with other basic features so that the image is perceived.[16] Objects in any visual field are fixated more quickly on the basis of color than on the basis of size or shape (Williams, 1966). Arnheim (1974) suggests that color is fundamental to seeing the information presented in mediated messages correctly.

Color photographs are expected to require less **mental effort** than black-and-white photos. Since color helps people discriminate between objects, audiences looking at black-and-white pictures have difficulty identifying specific background items in the photograph. However, research is mixed on whether color or black-and-white photographs are better remembered. Color photos were better remembered in several studies[17] while black-and-white photos were better remembered or no differences were found in others.[18] Gilbert and Schleuder (1988, 1990) found that responses to color photographs were faster than responses to black-and-white photographs, another indication that color photographs require less mental effort to process to a level at which meaning can be extracted.[19]

Much of the earlier color research focused on advertising, where color generally pulled more reader attention and was more effective than illustrations. While color is better for quick appeal, black-and-white is better for recall,[20] as was the case with photographs.

Graphic Elements—Charts, Maps, Tables.   In addition to words, sentences, and paragraphs, print media use photographs and graphic elements such as charts, maps, and tables to convey information. According to design principles, photographs and artwork can attract attention, aid in retention, entertain, show a relationship, inform, and help pull a reader into a design. Smith (1989) found that newspaper design (traditional, modular, modern) was the best predictor of differences in the perception of neatness and organization. Design and the use of color also were the best predictors of perceptions of how modern, colorful, stale, and bold the papers were. Color alone was the best predictor of differences in how interesting and exciting the newspapers appeared.

The use of bar charts, maps and tables increases reader retention (Peterson, 1983), recall (Amlund, Gaffney and Kulhavy, 1985), and accuracy (Sundar, Perkins and Zillmann, 1991).[21] Pasternack and Utt (1990) found that 15-25% of readers read the graphic before the text or headline accompanying it and 45% of these did so for appearance-related reasons (location, color, size of graphic) rather than content-related reasons (graphic would help one understand story). Stark and Hollander (1990) found that readers were more accurate in answering questions about an airline crash when the story they read had an accompanying informative graphic than those who read the text only or the text with a photograph. Those reading the text, graphic, and photograph about the crash were the most accurate. In an experiment, Griffin and Stevenson (1991, 1992) found that understanding of an event was greatest when the background information was in both the text of the story and an accompanying graphic.[22] Ward (1992) found similar results when a bar chart accompanied a news story.[23] Bar graphs provide for more efficient and more accurate recall (Multer and Mayson, 1986). Waller and Whalley (1984) found that readers of graphic-organized text were better able to write a summary of the material than those who read text only. Graphics also can divert and entertain those in the audience who find the text too difficult (McGregor and Slovic, 1986), although more complex graphs require a more sophisticated audience (Peel, 1978).[24]

Not all graphics are equally efficient in helping people understand or comprehend ideas. David (1992) looked at eight quantitative graphics in a test of the Stevens' (1975) law, which says that the perceived magnitude of a stimulus is a function of its physical magnitude. Using this theory, a graphic showing increasingly larger stacks of coins to indicate the cost of postage in different countries would convey the message that postage costs more/less in the countries cited. The figures had been published by USA Today. Some readers saw those graphics while others saw pie charts or typical bar charts. Five of the eight graphics tests supported the idea.[25] Tufte (1983) said that graphics need to do more than merely decorate a page or describe some phenomenon. A large share of the ink on a graphic should present data-information (Pasternack and Utt, 1990) rather than distract by presenting other visuals designed to attract.[26] Tankard (1989) found that chartoons (charts with cartoons incorporated into a chart or graph) were more appealing to readers than straightforward charts but did not significantly increase retention of information. McCombs and Smith (1971) found that simply adding more white space to stories of otherwise equal readability increased readers' liking, interest, and understanding of the news stories.

Print media images vary greatly in terms of **complexity**, particularly in modern newspaper or magazine designs that employ many different graphic elements. Studies looking at visual complexity show a variety of results. Loftus and Bell (1975) found that photographs were better recognized than either sparsely detailed or highly detailed line drawings of the same subject;[27] other studies have found that outline drawings are better recalled than highly detailed line drawings (Coulter, Coulter and Glover, 1984; Ritchey, 1982).[28] Gilbert and Schleuder (1988, 1990) predicted that simple photographs would require less mental effort at the perceptual stage and, thus, they would move more quickly to the meaning level for processing and be more memorable than complex photographs. However, they found no difference in reaction times between simple and complex photographs.

Photographs. People are quite good at recalling photographs and other visual materials. Standing (1973) found that people scored an average of 73% correct on identifying photographs even after seeing 10,000 different pictures. Weldon and Roediger (1987) studied the "picture superiority effect," which refers to the finding that pictures are typically better remembered than words. In a series of experiments, free recall of pictures was better than that of words.

Pictures may facilitate the recall of information presented in accompanying prose passages.[29] Swann and Miller (1982) have suggested that visual information may increase people's memory in three ways: by serving as highly memorable cues to retrieval, by strengthening people's organization of social information, and by motivating more elaborate processing of the material.[30] Levin (1981) identifies functions[31] that may be served by pictures accompanying text, two of which are relevant for how the picture affects audience learning of the textual content—representation and transformation. A **representational picture** would make the information in the prose passage more concrete, and a **transformation picture** makes information in the prose passages more memorable. Levin (1981) argues that representational pictures make the information in the prose passages more specific and provide a second mode for the information to be represented in the brain. Anglin (1987) found that people remembered more information from stories with accompanying pictures than did those who read only the prose. Lynn, Shavitt and Ostrom (1985) found that photographs enhance people's memory by fostering elaboration on incoming information at the point of encoding. Photographs accompanying news stories also affect how readers evaluate people in the stories. Lain and Harwood (1992) found that readers saw people in different mug shots as more or less congenial and as having more or less integrity and credibility based on their facial expressions in the mug shot accompanying the story featuring them as a source.

Structure of Headlines. Newspaper headlines are syntactically impoverished and often can be ambiguous to readers because definite articles and auxiliary verbs are omitted, the present tense is used to indicate past actions—"Madonna Visits Cannes"—and infinitives indicate the future—"President To Visit City." Given these syntactic obstacles, the question is how readers achieve comprehension of headlines. Two theories have been offered—the traditional reliance on syntax and problem solving. In a syntactic explanation, readers arrive at a meaning of a headline through the application of normal parsing processes (dividing a sentence into its component parts). These processes are assumed to be partly autonomous in that they operate according to structural principles first and then allow pragmatic influences. In the other explanation, comprehending newspaper headlines is more a matter of problem solving than of reading. By this account, the normal processes of parsing are inadequate and, therefore, generally abandoned in favor of conceptually guided problem-solving procedures. Words are encoded and combined, and then quickly checked for plausibility. Perfetti et al. (1987) found support for the syntactic explanation, which said that ambiguous headlines would take more processing time. Readers carry forward only one meaning after reading an ambiguous headline.

Length of Sentences, Paragraphs within Articles. In the 1940s researchers began developing formulas to measure readability, emphasizing two major factors: sentence length and word difficulty. Early research indicated that writing using simple sentences was more readable than that with more compound sentences (Westley, 1980). It was included in readability formulas of Rudolf Flesch and others (Stapler, 1985) who argued that sentence length affected memory span and mental energy required for reading. One study showed that Ernest Hemingway averaged only 13.5 words to a sentence, although the range was from 3 words to 49 words (Mencher, 1981). Studies in the 1950s showed a trend to shorter sentences, but more recent studies suggest more difficult readability levels (Porter and Stephens, 1989; Stapler, 1985). Danielson, Lasorsa and Im (1992) traced the readership level of the *New York Times* and *Los Angeles Times* from 1885 through 1989, finding a steady decrease in reading ease of the two newspapers; in contrast, there was a steady increase in reading ease among a sample of 98 novels published over that period. Editors underestimate the reading difficulty of news stories (Porter and Stephens, 1989). McAdams (1991) found that readability of news stories had no impact on reader interest.

Most leads (the first paragraph) of newspaper stories contain only one sentence. Stapler (1985) examined leads of 360 stories in 12 newspapers, finding that the lead paragraph clearly exceeded lengths of the three subsequent paragraphs. The mean length of sentences in leads was 26.1 words, with an average of 21.7 words in paragraphs 2 through 4. The longest lead sentences were found in the *Washington Post* (35.8 words) and the *Los Angeles Times* (31.1 words). One wire service chart lists average sentence length of 21 words as "fairly difficult to read," with 25 words "difficult to read," and 29 or more words "very difficult to read" (Stapler, 1985). The ease of reading is related to overall image of print media. Burgoon, Burgoon and Wilkinson (1981) found that ease of reading and image of the newspaper as competent and trustworthy were positively correlated.

Structure of Print Messages.   Print messages come in many traditional forms. Newspaper news articles are written in an inverted pyramid style, while magazine articles and books follow essay and narrative styles. Furthermore, within each format, there are differences in writing styles—use of more active verbs, more personal pronouns, more metaphors. We also can look at how the sequencing of "content" (types of information about a topic such as AIDS) within messages affects audience processing.

General Message Structure.   Relatively little work has been done on the cognitive effects of message structure. People remember connected discourse better because prior information and expectations allow them to form a highly interconnected representation (Nolan, 1990). Research also shows that people tend to remember elements of a text that are central to the theme.[32] In theory, all text is assumed to be structured according to some specific pattern of underlying organization that depends on the goal of the text.[33] These forms have been characterized as **narratives** or stories for simple fiction[34] and a variety of other structures for nonfiction.[35] Chief among the latter for mass media are the **inverted pyramid** news structure for print messages, although **chronology** and other structures also are used.

Numerous studies indicate that a reader's familiarity with the way in which information is organized in a message has a significant impact on how well he or she remembers or comprehends it.[36] This suggests that people develop message-relevant schemas over time, using those schemas for subsequent processing. **Schemas** are "generic knowledge structures that guide the reader's interpretations, inferences, expectations, and attention.[37] A schema is generic in that it is a summary of the components, attributes, and relationships that typically occur in specific instances" (Graesser and Nakamura, 1982: 60-61). What is the evidence that people develop and use message-relevant schemas that guide their processing of newspaper articles and stories in magazines and books?

The basic story usually is the first text structure acquired by readers, through early exposure to stories in childhood (Hoover, 1981). Nonfiction structures are learned later, generally beginning in the third grade (Gillet and Temple, 1986).[38] Mandler and Johnson (1977) refer to a story schema as an idealized representation of the parts of a typical story and the relationships among those parts. The basic organizational pattern of story narratives includes the following elements: the setting of the story, an event—an action or idea that precipitates further story developments; an internal reaction—the character's simple or complex reaction, which is followed by an effort to reach that goal; an outcome resulting from the protagonist's attempt to arrive at the set goal; and an ending (Mandler and Johnson, 1977). For students, the textbook represents a significant structure they must master. The **enumerative** or **attributional structure** is the most common type of textbook organization, including the book you're now reading.[39]

Developing Message-Relevant Schema.   Evidence suggests that the inverted pyramid schema and other message-relevant schema develop over time with growing experience (Nolan, 1990: 39).[40] In one study, college students and newspaper professionals familiar with the inverted pyramid form tended to retell stories in inverted pyramid form regardless of whether the story had been written in chronological or inverted pyramid style (Nolan, 1990). Nonjournalism students with no background in inverted pyramid writing showed no preference for either form when retelling the story. However, children who read a chronological story retold it with a strong tendency toward chronological form, while children who read an inverted pyramid story retold it with about equal tendencies toward the two story structures.

Effects of Story Structure on Comprehension. More than a half century ago, Bartlett (1932) suggested that recall of written material depends on a reader's schema for the structure of a written passage. Various studies have demonstrated that a knowledge of story grammars facilitates both reading comprehension and recall of stories.[41] Knowledge of nonfiction text structures helps readers better recall and comprehend nonfiction materials (Durham, 1990).[42]

Nolan's (1990) results give no indication that readers in any of the four groups (children, professionals, journalism students, nonjournalism students) had any more difficulty with stories in the inverted pyramid form than with chronologically ordered stories. Reading times for both chronological and inverted pyramid stories were similar. However, school children who read inverted pyramid stories put more of the gist, or essential elements, into their free recall of the story, suggesting that the inverted pyramid form has a focusing strength.

Recent research indicates that recall and comprehension are interactive processes in which a reader brings his or her prior knowledge into play while encoding new information and later activates that knowledge for retrieval of the information.[43] Much of the existing research on the processing of mass media news messages focuses on comprehension or memory for news content rather than story structure itself.[44] Woodall, Davis and Sahin (1983) incorporated a variety of experimental findings to propose a theoretical framework for memory and understanding of news based on principles of episodic memory and the trace theory of memory and understanding. Other studies which have explored cognitive aspects of news processing have shown that prior knowledge is vital to the comprehension and recall of news (Findahl and Hoijer, 1981, 1985) and that schema-based strategies are employed in processing information gained from news (Graber, 1988).[45]

Inverted Pyramid News Form. Most newspaper articles are written in inverted pyramid news form.[46] Nolan (1990) studied the impact of familiarity with this writing style and ease of reading and retelling the content. Determination of the importance of news items is made by reporters. "These encoding decisions are made under the assumption that the stories thus encoded can be easily decoded by an audience of readers comprised of members who need share only basic literacy in English" (Nolan, 1990: 2-3). Little regard is given to temporal links in inverted pyramid stories because the story is not ordered according to what happened when.

Researchers have examined the impact of the structure of news articles on the cognitive processing of news messages.[47] Durham (1990) compared comprehension and recall of news stories written in either an inverted pyramid news style, a narrative style, or expository text style, seeking to test Green's (1979) hypothesis that the organization of news stories hinders comprehension and recall of messages.[48] Recall and comprehension were expected to be best for the narrative story, then for the expository textbook style, and then the modified inverted pyramid. Results showed that both the narrative and expository text stories were recalled better in the short-term than were the news stories, but there was no difference between the short-term recall of narrative and expository stories. The same pattern was found for long-term recall a week after reading. These results indicate that readers' structural schemas for narrative text are stronger than their schemas for news text (Durham, 1990), the former developing earlier in life and the latter not encountered until adolescence (Nolan, 1989). In addition, we would expect individual differences, with regular newspaper readers having better news structure schemas than those who read newspapers less often.

However, altering the structure of stories in another study (expository vs. news structure) had no significant effect on comprehension of the stories' content, suggesting that comprehension is likely due to readers' prior knowledge of the topic and differences in inferential and evaluative abilities.[49] Content schemas might be more important than structure schemas, which would be consistent with results obtained by Olhausen and Roller (1988), who found that content schemas played a more important role than text structures when texts were well structured, following a familiar pattern of organization. Comparing readers' interest in the article topics, Durham (1990) found that comprehension was higher for the high-interest group, which may be an indicator of high prior knowledge, or of more careful text processing and subsequent higher comprehension.

There is some suggestion that the impact of news structure depends on the topic or content. In experiments on reading of news stories, Thorndyke (1977) found that readers followed information relevant to the main topic, whatever the story organization, but narratives produced better comprehension and recall for historically based news stories, and the inverted pyramid stories produced better comprehension and recall for current news.

Writing Styles. Writing styles can be characterized in a variety of ways, but we have research tapping only a few. Journalists operate under the assumption that an active, verbal style is the more understandable and preferred style of writing. That was confirmed in a study showing that active styles were significantly easier to comprehend than passive or nominal styles (Bostian and Byrne, 1984).[50] **Intensity** refers to the use of language and passages which indicate the author's attitude toward the concept or content. Deviations from neutrality—for example, emotionalism and extreme adjectives—are characterized as high intensity. While print journalists typically try to keep themselves out of their writing, media professionals using other formats often do the reverse. Badzinski (1989) found that likelihood of inferential processing was greater for high-intensity texts than for texts low in intensity for both adults and children. Intensity was believed to affect inferential processing by affecting one's perception of the importance of information communicated (Walker and Meyer, 1980).[51]

Journalistic style also can be an impediment to comprehension. Smith and Voelz (1983) looked at style rules governing abbreviations, identification of the location and source of stories, and similar conventions used by journalists following Associated Press style. They found that many adults age 18-34 experienced difficulty in comprehending information based on the traditional style. Differences were noted for frequency of readership, with greater comprehension among those who read newspapers more often.

Sequencing of "Content".   The order of content within messages affects audience processing. Yarborough and Gagne (1987) found greater recall when information appeared earlier in a text.[52] Content schematic theorists believe that understanding of a text involves top-down processing in interaction with bottom-up processing. For example, encountering information at the beginning of an article about MTV may activate schemata that the reader has about MTV, with these in turn affecting comprehension of what follows in the article. Content schemata function flexibly in that they affect diverse goals, including comprehension, memory, learning, and summarization of text.[53]

Print Media Design.   Print media themselves have a structure that affects audience processing. Segmentation of content into sections, the arrangement on individual pages, and the relationships among the various elements of design all can affect processing.

The study of typography (overall page design)[54] has been concerned largely with the aesthetics of the printed page alone. Page location and amount of space are the key variables in predicting reader attention to specific newspaper articles. Location also affects readers' assessments of content. For example, placing the same article on the op-ed page led readers to see the article as opinion more than when the leads appeared on the front page. Thus, "page environment" is important in drawing fact/opinion distinctions. McCombs, Mauro and Son (1988) found that placement on the front page of a section was the most important predictor of readership, followed by the amount of space devoted to an item ("the bigger, the better") and placement on the upper half of the page. Readership also declined as items were located further back in the paper. McCombs and Mauro (1977) found that the page on which an item was placed was the biggest predictor of readership, followed by the amount of space devoted to it. Headlines may activate particular attitudes and act as "agenda setters" for subsequent reading of attached newspaper articles (Shapiro, 1991).[55]

Fico, Heeter, Soffin and Stanley (1987) conducted a study to test the extent to which the ordering of information within a newspaper affected how readers process content. They prepared **indexed** and nonindexed versions of an 18-page newspaper with 38 stories; in the former, news was indexed topically. There was no difference in the number of stories read in the two different versions (about 6 stories each), but readers of the indexed paper were less likely to read the major stories than those in the traditional nonindexed version.

Technological innovations may make the idea of the mass audience obsolete by eliminating the structure of print media through **videotex** and other electronic delivery systems (Rogers and Chaffee, 1983). As new technologies offer audiences more choice, the composition of those audiences may change considerably, with fewer people sharing the same media content (Fico, Heeter, Soffin and Stanley, 1987).

Processing TV and Film Media

TV and film images change through time and include both audio and visual modes of representation. This adds a dynamic dimension and increases message complexity in our efforts to understand audience message processing.

What do people understand or recall from processing TV content? A national study conducted for the American Association of Advertising Agencies (AAAA) found that a large proportion of the U.S. TV-viewing audience tends to miscomprehend TV messages (Jacoby, Hoyer and Sheluga, 1980). The average amount of miscomprehension was about 30%, with higher levels of miscomprehension for non-advertising messages than for TV commercials. Research by Robinson, Levy, Davis, Woodall, Gurevitch and Sahin (1986) found an average accurate retention rate of less than 15% for TV news items. When respondents were tested only four hours after viewing the news, aided recall (where viewers were asked whether they recalled seeing specific stories/topics) averaged about 28%. Lipstein (1980) found an average miscomprehension of 30% on quizzes assessing comprehension of the advertising and program content of the CBS show, "60 Minutes." A median miscomprehension of 23% was found among viewers of the 1980 pre-election debate between then President Jimmy Carter and candidate Ronald Reagan (Jacoby, Troutman and Whittler, 1986).

The task of decoding filmed or televised messages consists of two critical **processes** (Hobbs, Frost, Davis and Stauffer, 1988). First, the visual and auditory information presented must be recognized as representational, e.g., an image of a horse is seen as representing that object.[56] However, when rapid pacing or unusual lighting and camera angles are used, even decoding the representational aspects requires complex perceptual skills.[57] Second, the viewer must decode two kinds of symbolic codes, including familiar symbolic codes such as gestures, speech, facial expressions, and graphic-pictorial messages (Salomon, 1979) as well as the structures and conventions specific to film, television, and broadcast media.[58]

Again, we face the message unit problem, since TV messages can be divided into units that range from a single video frame to an entire program (McLeod and Reeves, 1980). A single frame may be defined in terms of a picture's structural properties (such as color, brightness, spatial frequency) or meaningful characteristics such as picture content (the story in a picture, its personal relevance, aesthetic appeal). Furthermore, since information is presented both aurally and visually, we also can segment the audio track into chunks of content with structural properties (pitch, loudness) or meaningful characteristics. Ultimately, we have to integrate the two modes for conveying information. Similar descriptions could be given for increasingly larger units—5 seconds, 30-second commercials, 5 minutes, entire programs, entire viewing sessions. Clearly, processing explanations differ by unit. In addition to the size of the message unit, Reeves and Thorson (1986) identify several other issues for understanding how audiences process TV content: complexity of TV stimuli, interdependence of time units in TV presentations (time units may vary from scenes and visual shots to story segments, commercials, etc.), differences and similarities among units in similar and different contexts, content vs. form and active vs. passive processing.

Structure of Film and TV Messages

The structure of film and TV messages has been linked to different processing consequences as observers have sought to identify the principles which must be followed for film and TV narratives to conform to audience expectations and produce comprehensible visual sequences (Kraft, 1987).[59] Audiences judge from clues in TV guides and newspaper ads that a film or TV program belongs to a particular genre or format. Characteristics associated with a genre or format then are used to judge or reason about the program or film itself. **Montage**—the connection of different film shots or segments— historically has been recognized as crucial for understanding films (Cowen, 1988). Analogies frequently have been made between media literacy and print literacy, with the notion that learning to decode the symbols of film or television is something like learning to read (Greenfield, 1984).

Narrative/Story Structure. Work on comprehension has focused on narrative structure of TV and film and the minimum number of components necessary for a story, the nature of these components, the order in which they occur and links between them. Clearly, recognition of typical instances is crucial for following the story lines of films, and professional writers and directors rely on particular symbols or combinations of symbols—visual and audio—to direct people's attention and comprehension. In one experiment, Cowen (1988) found that the relationship between **montage linearity** (chronological ordering of images), comprehension and recall strongly resemble what is typically found in story comprehension for print texts. Cowen constructed four versions of a film representing decreasing linearity of montage: a chronological version with a beginning, middle, and end and no deletions; a quasi-linear version which moved the beginning to the end; another linear version which created a more serious break from the order by putting part of the beginning in the middle; and a nonlinear version which reversed the order of episodes so the film went from the end to the middle to the beginning. The linear version was highest on recall and comprehension and the nonlinear version lowest. Recall of action and linearity of comprehension were strongly correlated.[60]

Rules governing message structure serve a syntactic function and prescribe how visual events should be restructured so they meet audience expectations and allow them to comprehend the messages. Some of these rules are expressed in terms of message structure, while others are identified through production or encoding techniques such as camera angles. Perceptually based rules prevent unintended apparent movement and brief misidentification of depicted objects (Hochberg and Brooks, 1978), while continuity-based rules tell the producer how to conform to viewers' narrative expectations. The latter involve focus, space, sequencing, causality, identity, and viewpoint. Reverse angle shots can disrupt both perceptual operations and narrative expectations (Kraft, 1987), with the perceptual disruption being brief (Hochberg and Brooks, 1978) and the disruption of spatial expectations more enduring (Frith and Robson, 1975).

Kraft's (1987) study sought to determine the influence of pictorial form on the evaluation and retention of pictorial events. One grammatical rule— **directional continuity**—and one technique—alteration of camera angle— were manipulated independently of the simple visual narrative. Violation of directional continuity was expected to inhibit the viewers' ability to see a coherent flow of action within the scene. Rotating the camera angle was expected to affect connotative meaning of the depicted characters (low angles connoting strength, action, and superiority and high angles connoting weakness, passivity, and insignificance). Results showed that violating the rule of directional continuity significantly impaired subjects' ability to remember the underlying flow of action in the visual stories, but changing the camera angle had no effect.[61]

Processing Consequences of Earlier/Later Material. Since processing of TV programs and films occurs over substantial blocks of time, reactions to content and structure at one point can affect processing at a later point. Sequence is clearly very important. Reeves and Thorson (1986) found that relationships between memory for messages and liking of material that either preceded or followed the target message were quite apparent. Memory was positively related to highly involving prior material and negatively predicted by subsequent messages that were highly involving. Thus, to get attention, one would position a message segment following highly interesting material but follow that with something dull.

Talking Heads vs. Dramatic Presentations.   Studies on the effectiveness of production techniques used in instructional TV have been surprisingly few (Morris, 1988). However, overall learning from three videotaped versions of an economics tape found that TV production techniques can affect recall of information presented in a telecourse. Recall was higher for students watching a version with music and drama than for a version with a "talking head" presenting the same information (Morris, 1988).

Color vs. Black-and-White Film.   No difference was found in one study where people rated black-and-white and colorized film on 14 dimensions, including dramatic value, emotional value, special effects, pace, visual imagery, etc. However, the colorized film was seen as easier to watch and more interesting (Cutler, Dalseide, Plummer and Bacon, 1988).

Impact of Encoding Techniques

Techniques used to create film and TV message structure include camera angle, lighting, perspective, framing, cutting, pacing, sequencing, zooming, tracking, and panning. These can be manipulated separately from narrative content (Huston and Wright, 1983), and the choices made by directors and other professional encoders can affect the audience's understanding and recall.[62] These techniques are frequently compared to syntax in language,[63] because of the way editing conventions such as cuts, fades, and dissolves are used to structure the content, make shifts in time, place, or action and separate programs from commercial messages (Hobbs, Frost, Davis and Stauffer, 1988; Rice, Huston and Wright, 1982).

Moving vs. Fixed Camera.   Filmmakers and critics have long noted the spatial qualities of camera movement. Zettl (1973) noted that a camera that moves into a scene on a dollie produces a continually changing visual perspective that allows the viewer to better experience spatial relationships between objects. The outcome, in contrast to the zoom shot, which does not create such changes, is a sense by the viewer that he or she is actually entering the scene. Similarly, Lewis (1968) observed that a camera which moves into a scene gives the viewer the sense of being within the locality rather than watching as a detached observer. Kipper (1986) found that the physical properties of scenes presented with a moving camera were better understood and recalled than when scenes were shown from fixed-camera versions.[64] The moving camera provides viewers with more information about the physical form of objects and about the three-dimensional layout of a TV scene. People who saw the moving-camera version of a film remembered more objects from the scene and were better able to reconstruct it.[65]

There is little disagreement that **motion** itself provides key information about the environment, although researchers differ in their explanation of how the eye-brain system receives and processes visual information. People's perceptual systems are tuned to abstracting information from images changing over time (Johansson et al., 1980; Kipper, 1986).[66] In the case of TV and film, most movement occurs on the screen rather than by movement of the audience through the environment.

Camera Angle. Several studies have found that camera angle affects audience perceptions of TV newscasters. McCain, Chilberg and Wakshlag (1977) found that a newscaster's perceived sociability, character, competence, task attractiveness, and composure were increased when he or she was viewed from a higher camera angle. Kraft (1987) found that camera angle influenced subjects' evaluation and retention of stories in a slide presentation.[67] In an experiment, vertical camera angle was varied to see how it affected viewers' recall of the characters and the story. Results supported hypotheses that changes in vertical camera angle would alter the viewer's evaluation, with low angles connoting strength, action, and superiority, eye-level connoting parity, and high angles connoting weakness, passivity, and insignificance. In general, as one changes from a high-angle shot to an eye-level shot to a low-angle shot, the characters in these shots appear stronger, taller, less afraid, bolder, and more aggressive. Camera angle also affected recall of the gist of the story but was not equally effective across all stories.

Special Effects. Elaborate special effects can inhibit learning of content in accompanying dialogue. Ginsburg, Bartels, Kleingunther and Droege (1988) found that highly stimulating visual materials interfered with the viewer's ability to process aural information effectively. Viewers were given brief episodes from an educational TV series that used an extensive amount of abstract visual effects. Recall was diminished because viewer attention was focused on the visual effects.

Editing Conventions. Carroll (1984) provides evidence that the structural boundaries in film (frames/major cuts involving changes in camera distance or angle) also are perceptual boundaries for audiences. Reeves and Thorson (1986) found a relationship between brain activity (alpha, EEG data) and the exact points at which scenes changed in a TV presentation.

Editing techniques can be organized along a continuum, from those representing changes or mobility in specific scenes to those which move the viewer substantially across time and between locations, to those implying more complex ideas such as causality (Messaris, 1982, 1987).[68] Shifts in camera position or magnification often achieve the visual effect of bringing the viewer into the scene instead of relying on a fixed camera position. These point-of-view editing conventions are comprehensible to most viewers because they represent an aspect of ordinary visual experience. When the camera shifts position within a scene (close-up shot), the visual effect is similar to moving to get a different view. When the camera shifts to enlarge or magnify something within a scene, the visual effect resembles the process of paying attention (Hobbs, Frost, Davis and Stauffer, 1988).

Editing conventions such as transitional editing alter the viewer's time and space, moving the viewer forward or backward in time or shifting the viewer from one location to another (Messaris, 1982). "Because they integrate actions across time and space, a complex cognitive activity not grounded in pure perceptual experience, transitional editing conventions may be more difficult for viewers to comprehend than point-of-view techniques" (Hobbs, Frost, Davis and Stauffer, 1988: 52). Lang et al. (1991) look at related and unrelated cuts and their impact on viewer understanding. Related cuts occur when the scenes on either side of the cut are tied together by either visual information (a cut from one camera to another in the same visual scene or setting) or by audio information (a cut from one scene to another in which the new scene was expected because it was introduced in the audio channel). In related cuts, there is no change in content. Unrelated cuts occur when scenes on either side of the cut are completely detached from each other in both visual setting and message content. In the experiment, viewers remembered more of the information around related cuts.[69] Viewers have limited resources for processing and must allocate more of those resources to coping with the structural feature of TV than to understanding the content of the story or message.

Much research supports the idea that cuts and other visual and audio conventions increase short-term attention to TV (Lang, Strickwerda, Sumner, Winters and Reeves, 1991).[70] The mechanism that causes this increase is the orienting response, an involuntary, automatic response elicited by changes in the environment (for example, someone walking into a room) or by learned signals (someone calling your name).

The extent to which an understanding of particular editing techniques requires a set of skills depends on how much the editing departs from everyday visual experience (Messaris, 1982). In Africa, a study found that adult viewers with little prior experience with photos, film, or TV[71] were able to recall the critical features of a narrative that used point-of-view editing. There were no significant differences in recall between villagers who saw an unedited tape and those who viewed the version using point-of-view editing (Hobbs, Frost, Davis and Stauffer, 1988). The researchers manipulated the point of view with editing conventions, producing two film versions, one using a stationary camera and fixed focal length and the other version using editing to make shifts in perspective and to enlarge details within the scene.[72]

However, we also know that altering the point of view can affect audience evaluations of media content. Lassiter and Irvine (1986) found that subjects' interpretations of police coercion from a videotape of a mock police interrogation were affected by the point-of-view, whether the camera was focused primarily on the suspect, on the detective, or on the two equally. Greater coercion by police was found for those who saw the version with the camera focused on the detective, followed by the equal condition and lastly the suspect-focus condition.[73]

Cutting Rate.   Filmmakers often make assumptions about the way in which certain editing procedures affect the emotional experience of the viewer. One technique for intensifying the viewer's affective experience of a scene is to increase the rate of cutting, which means viewers see rapid changes from one visual shot to another. Heft and Blondal (1987) found that cutting rate enhanced viewers feelings while watching films. As cutting rate increased in the version with happy content, the individual portrayed was evaluated as being more pleasant and controlling, while in the film with angry content, increased cutting rate had the opposite effect, where the individual was seen as being less pleasant and less controlling.

Relationship between Visual, Audio Content.   The relationship between the audio and video portions of TV programs and films affects audience processing. Much of the concern focuses on "congruence" of audio and visual messages—seeing exactly what the words describe. However, the nature of the match is more complex than merely trying to see how the "meanings" or "representations" fit together. For example, Neuendorf and Fennel (1988) found that canned laughter produced greater mirth behavior (smiling, laughing) for a TV show compared to a version without the laugh track.

Although results are mixed,[74] most research relating the visual and audio modes shows that audience processing of TV messages is hampered when the meaning of the pictures does not match the meaning of the audio text.[75] Heuvelman (1989) notes that the relationship between the audio and video—"congruency of picture and sound"—represents the degree of match between the meanings of two simultaneously presented sign systems—visual and verbal. Edwardson, Grooms and Proudlove (1981) found that recall of news was greater when viewers were shown an interesting visualization which was highly consonant with the audio news information than when subjects only saw a talking anchorman. Thus, higher recall is obtained when information is both visually and aurally encoded. Drew and Grimes (1987) found that people exposed to conflicting information attended to the video at the expense of the audio. The nature of the visuals themselves also may affect memory—shocking visuals may interfere with comprehension of the audio channel (Newhagen and Reeves, 1991).

As the content becomes more abstract and less realistic, a good match is increasingly difficult. Using visualized analogies is a way to explain something unknown using something known to the viewer. Heuvelman (1989) conducted an experiment to see if there were differences in processing of visual analogies, using videotapes of topics (such as filtering of blood in the kidneys) presented to adults in one of several ways: realistic pictures, schematic pictures (a diagram or roadmap), and using a visual analogy to explain something else—a water purification plant representing a kidney. There were no differences between the verbal or visual recognition of content for the three different videotapes, but open-ended responses were best for those watching the schematic tape, compared to the other two.

The audio sometimes can compensate for video discontinuity. Drew and Cadwell (1985) studied the effects of an editing convention—the jumpcut (when the camera stops and restarts, producing a discontinuity. A common compensation when using a jumpcut is to change the camera distance, angle, or both each time the camera stops, which is believed to help viewers overcome the disruption and discontinuity. In the experiment, people focused their attention on the audio when watching a TV news story. Video discontinuity failed to produce negative evaluations. Viewers apparently were unable to attend to both channels simultaneously so they concentrated on the audio, which traditionally contains the factual information. Attention to the audio seemed to be constant, while attention to the video depended upon its utility. When the story was shown without audio, moving in for a closeup—either with or without an angle change—was effective in masking jumpcuts. Changing only the camera angle was not very useful. Stories with the most severe jumpcuts received less favorable evaluations.

People appear to detect information in both the audio and video channels simultaneously, regardless of their selective attention. Furthermore, processing visual information in TV scenes is not equivalent to processing auditory information. Basil (1992) conducted an experiment in which viewers showed better memory for both types of information in scenes described as visually-based rather than audio-based. However, memory for audio content did improve when attention was focused on the audio.[76]

Processing Complex Forms of Visual Media

Complexity at one level may complicate sensory processing, while complexity on a global message level may affect processing of meaning, requiring more effort to make sense out of the message. We will need more research examining the various combinations of structure and content to understand the complexity of TV messages. For example, the presence of printed copy in a TV ad was associated with more miscomprehension (Hoyer, Srivastava and Jacoby, 1984), and the presence of music lowered the rate of miscomprehension slightly (Hoyer, Srivastava and Jacoby, 1984).

Several popular TV formats have been examined to see how audiences process these particular structures or the content conveyed using these structures. Most of the attention has focused on news broadcasts, although others have examined music videos (Rubin, Rubin, Perse, Armstrong, McHugh and Faix, 1986), soap operas, and commercials (Thorson and Reeves, 1986). Many of the structural elements discussed above have significance for the news format.

TV News Broadcasts.   The combination of verbal information, visual images, structure and pace of presentation, and the skills and cognitive abilities that viewers bring to the situation make TV news viewing complex (Woodall, Davis and Sahin, 1983).TV news broadcasts compete for audiences. Content is presented in an entertaining manner, using the various conventions and structures which have been associated with positive audience reactions. Critics have suggested that a reliance on brief items and emphasis on entertainment foster low levels of attention and poor memory for the content presented (Miller and Reese, 1982; Miyo, 1983). Audiences seeking entertainment engage in lower-level processing, paying less attention to the content and, thus, recalling less information.[77] Information thoroughly analyzed at both a structural and semantic level represents higher order processing and is more likely to be retained than information that only receives preliminary (lower-order) processing (Lang, 1989). This occurs when audiences are seeking information and are motivated to "learn" or understand, not relax. Support for this is found in a study where subjects who were asked to pay attention to news items recalled 58% more items than subjects who were not similarly cued (Stauffer, Frost and Rybolt, 1983).

The viewers' inability to control the time frame of presentation also has been held responsible for audiences' poor recall of news broadcasts (Garramone, 1983; Miyo, 1983). Since viewers cannot back up and review material incompletely perceived or poorly understood, they fail to process and store the information in the newscasts, producing low levels of recall for TV news (Lang, 1989). To improve learning for information in newscasts, viewers must either increase the level of effort expended or the newscast must be changed so less effort is required.

Structure/Chronology of Stories in TV Newscasts.   The structure of content presented in TV news stories may affect audience processing. Findahl and Hoijer (1981) have suggested the typical TV news story is produced mainly for the initiated: what is new or different is presented first, followed by what caused the change, followed by the consequences of that change. This requires the viewer to have previous knowledge of the situation. Stephens (1986) says that broadcast news style is not designed to ease processing but to maintain attention.[78] This style may demand much more cognitive processing effort than TV viewing audiences are generally prepared to expend. To adequately process a news story written in this manner, the viewer must immediately access what is already known while simultaneously processing the incoming information (Lang, 1989).

Theories of human memory suggest that the current broadcast news style may require viewers to do more processing and exert greater effort by requiring them to activate both **semantic** and **episodic memories** for comprehending and storing information contained in news stories. Episodic memory generally is defined as memory for the day-to-day activities of life, while semantic memory stores general world knowledge.[79] Some have argued that information doesn't get into semantic memory without first being a part of episodic memory (Friestad and Thorson, 1985; Ortony, 1978). As a consequence, when we learn something, initially, it is remembered as what we did today and only later stored as simply a fact that we know (Lang, 1989).

If all information originally enters memory as **episodes**, the mental operations performed on episodic memory create semantic memory (Friestad and Thorson, 1985).[80] It has been suggested that the strength of the episodic memory trace helps determine whether it becomes a part of semantic memory.[81] This view of message processing suggests that information gain will occur if a person first perceives the information, then processes and stores it episodically, and then stores the information in semantic memory. Ultimately, whether the information becomes a part of one's general knowledge or semantic memory depends on its relevance or importance, its comprehensibility, its temporal order, and the amount of effort the individual expends on the creation of the episodic trace (Lang, 1989).

Applying this theory to processing of TV news broadcasts, we would expect the level of effort required to be much higher than the effort audiences typically expend (Findahl and Hoijer, 1981; Miller and Reese, 1982; Miyo, 1983).[82] Without increased effort, viewers incompletely process the news and are left with weak episodic memory and low levels of information transferred from episodic to semantic memory. This leads to poor recall for broadcast news and low levels of information among those who rely primarily on the broadcast media for information (Lang, 1989).

Newscasts designed to reduce the need for semantic processing would decrease the cognitive work required of viewers. TV news stories written in an episodic manner—the story presented in chronological order with the causes first, the change next, and the consequences last—would require only on-line episodic processing and maximize the strength of the episodic traces being laid down. This should increase viewers' recall of the news by allowing them to process the entire story without accessing semantic memory. In an experiment,

Lang (1989) found that people who viewed a chronological story in a newscast were more accurate in recollections than those who viewed a traditional broadcast style.

Images which generate **emotional responses** can affect processing of subsequent aspects of TV news stories, and this can occur whether the content is presented in a chronological order or some other writing style. Newhagen and Reeves (1991) investigated the relationship between compelling negative images in TV news and memory for information appearing before, during, or after the negative images. They found that negative images produced interference for preceding material; that is, memory was worse for material that preceded the negative scenes. However, memory for visual material after compelling images was better than for material not preceded by negative images. During the presence of negative images, memory was worse for semantically intact audio information (such as speech) than for audio material with no semantic meaning (crashing noises, screams).

The order of stories and their grouping within newscasts also affects processing. Grouping related news stories together negatively affects their recall (Gunter, 1981). Also, items at the beginning or end of a newscast are recalled better (Gunter, 1981; Gunter, Clifford and Berry, 1980). Memory for news items involves a complex interaction of cognitive factors, environmental factors and individual differences.[83] For example, some evidence shows that people recall more from seeing the news at 9:30 A.M. than at 5:30 P.M. (Gunter, Furnham and Jarrett, 1984; Gunter, Jarrett and Furnham, 1983).

Formats affect processing of the news. Brosius (1991) developed four different formats for a TV news program, one composed of eight stories presented by a "talking head," one composed completely of stories pictured in film, and two mixed format versions. The format of items and the format of the newscast as a whole influenced comprehension. Within each format, pictured items were somewhat better understood than were talking head items. For both types of items, their presentation in a mixed newscast enhanced learning, suggesting a clear additive effect to using both filmed material and mixed formats. Both talking head and film items were comprehended better in mixed formats.

Images Recalled in TV Newscasts.   What aspects of TV news stories are best recalled? There are two trends in research on recall: the study of microprocessing—processing of media messages in extremely short periods (Thorson and Lang, 1989); and the study of understanding the totality of news stories rather than the recall of isolated facts.[84]

What specifics are best recalled? Graber (1990) found that the type of video most remembered by news viewers is close-ups of people, with familiar faces remembered best. Also, visuals were remembered more readily than were verbal themes. Edwardson, Kent, Engstrom and Hofmann (1991) found that stories with video generated higher recall. Results also showed that free recall of news topics in stories with video elements would be better remembered than topics of stories presented by the visible newscaster, perhaps because stories presented by the newscaster without video were seen as less interesting.

We also have evidence that a graphic (a bar chart or screenful of information) can distract viewers from what a newscaster is saying. To avoid this, the audio presented with such a graphic should be maximally redundant. Information presented with the audio alone may be lost (Edwardson, Kent, Engstrom and Hoffman, 1991). Burriss (1987) found that viewers prefer and remember more from a story with few production elements than from a story that is more elaborately produced. Story complexity—in terms of variety of audio and video production elements—decreased recall of news items.

Recalling Audio vs. Video.   Based on the notion that attention is limited, Broadbent (1958) asserts that only one image at a time can be admitted to consciousness.[85] Applying the limited capacity model, we would not expect viewers of TV news broadcasts to perform equally well on auditory and visual recognition.[86] Watching and listening to TV news stories requires capacity; the less the two information channels relate to each other, the more processing capacity they require (Grimes, 1989: 4).

Even mild **audio-visual channel conflict**, which characterizes many TV news stories, weakens the visual channel as an effective conveyor of information (Drew and Grimes, 1987; Grimes, 1989).[87] Viewers sacrifice the visual channel and attend to the story-telling auditory channel—where more of the who, what, when, where, why, and how information is located. Since news events are often presented "live," channel conflict cannot be eliminated. The most likely conflict between channels occurs when the audio and visual information are thematically related but the specific messages conflict: for example, showing pictures of a snowstorm in progress but talking about how it ended and the weather has changed (Grimes, 1989).

Three types of changes in video momentarily disorient viewers so that they pay less attention to the audio while they try to draw meaning from newly-appearing video; this occurs only when video and audio are non-redundant (Edwardson, Kent, Engstrom and Hoffman, 1991). This momentary disorientation could be caused by the sudden appearance of three types of video: exciting video such as portrayal of a disaster, a statement by a newsmaker identified only by a caption under the face, and a table, chart, or screenful of words used to explain statistical information, or to provide added information in words (Edwardson, Kent and McConnell, 1985).

Expandable capacity models suggest that the number of tasks that can be engaged in simultaneously is not fixed but can grow, within limits.[88] Research also shows that performance on multiple tasks improves with practice (Schneider and Shiffrin, 1977), which would suggest that effects of auditory-visual channel conflict in TV newscasts might lessen with practice.

Grimes (1990) examined the translation phenomenon, where people recall pictures as words and words as pictures. His experiment sought to examine how facts conveyed in narration would be remembered as having been conveyed in video, and vice versa. Visual and auditory messages that were exclusive to each channel—not duplicated by the other channel—were created and exposed to different groups, with the expectation that people's surface memories would contain the tags necessary for later distinguishing between visual and audio messages. Comparing recall immediately after viewing the news with recall after a 48-hour delay, more people incorrectly remembered messages as having been conveyed visually or auditorily two days later. Thus, both audio and video message channels were encoded into surface memory but decay occurred so only the semantic content of both messages remained in long-term memory, making them vulnerable to being recalled incorrectly. Thus, video and audio have the potential for altering memory of one another.

Processing Radio/Audio Content

Unfortunately, we have little information on audience processing of radio content.[89] However, we do know that changes in voice have been found to have minor negative effects on memory tasks in word-identification tests (Richardson-Klavehn and Bjork, 1988). Grady (1987) found no difference in the perceived appeal of different radio news formats (voice reports with no sound, voice reports with background sound, and a straight newscast) or the recall of facts in the news stories.

Auditory research shows that people listening to rapid sequences of sounds may perceive them as a single perceptual stream or split the music, sound track, or other auditory stimuli into a number of perceptual streams, a process known as primary auditory stream segregation, or fission. Usually, we attend primarily to one perceptual stream at a time, and that stream stands out from the background formed by other streams. Stream formation places constraints upon attention, but attention also may influence the formation of streams (Moore, 1982). Given the popularity of various music formats in radio and the importance of audio in MTV and TV, it is surprising that so little effort has centered on understanding how audiences segregate auditory streams.

In an experiment which exposed students to either a music-audio group or a music-video group, Rubin, Rubin, Perse, Armstrong, McHugh and Faix (1986) found that music videos were seen as more active and potent than were music audios.

Modality Differences among the Media

McLuhan (1989) contended that media are defined by their extension of the human senses, with radio extending the ear and TV the eyes. Neuendorf, Brentar and Porco (1990) summarize the literature which notes that individual media tend to rely primarily on one sense modality but others are still important (e.g., Welch and Watt, 1982). A number of studies have shown modality effects on memory, and people generally recall pictures more readily than text.[90] Wartella and Reeves (1987: 635) note that different symbol systems may require different amounts of mental energy to process and represent internally: "The types of symbols present in a particular medium . . . cultivate a style of information processing dependent primarily on the effort required to produce internal representations of content. The most obvious example is that pictures (from television or film) are easier to represent than written words because words require translation into a visual code before the information is stored for later use."[91]

Although the media can be differentiated in many ways, it is the print vs. broadcast comparison which has captured the most attention. At the base of this attention is a concern that reading is declining as a leisure-time activity, particularly among youth. Negative consequences for education may be linked with this fact. In a 1926 study, reading occupied 15% of the hours awake (Duker, 1969) but that has declined dramatically.[92] The superiority of print vs. audio or visual media for recall has been noted in several studies (Browne, 1978; Jacoby and Hoyer, 1987). Gunter, Furnham and Gietson (1984) found that the recall of story content by teenagers was best for print and worst for stories presented audio-visually; results indicated that reading the news can produce more effective retention than listening to or watching the news. Furnham and Gunter (1989) found that subjects who received news stories in print remembered the material better than those who received them aurally—by tape recorder. Research has shown for some time now that television viewing leads to poorer recall and retention of information than newspaper reading (Robinson and Levy, 1986, and Gunter, 1987). Robinson and Levy (1986: 17) note that TV news stories "are transitory; they cannot be reread. Learning of content must occur quickly. Complex combinations of powerful visual and auditory stimuli must be rapidly decoded . . . Accurate comprehension of such fast-changing, diverse information requires cognitive processing skills of a high order—higher than some audience members may possess." Melwani (1989) points out that, "Reading, on the other hand, because it is self-paced, allows us to replay information as we encode it. The process of reading itself, seems to engage the brain in a more complex way than does the more passive act of watching" (Melwani, 1989: 10).

People also tend to do a better job of **understanding** print media. A study using six audio/video messages, six converted to audio only, and six typewritten print versions revealed lower miscomprehension rates for the print versions than for the radio or TV versions (Jacoby, Hoyer and Zimmer, 1983). The rate was 17% miscomprehension when respondents were given unlimited time to read the messages and 21% when given only 30 seconds (the time corresponding to the broadcast conditions. Rates were 25% for TV and 26% for radio.[93] Singer (1980) asserts that the human brain constantly plays and replays the material that it stores as it processes information. Singer feels that the basic problem with TV lies in its strength—TV holds people's attention with a constant sensory bombardment, a rapid fire pace that catches and holds attention but which gets in the way of processing information.

Salmon (1981) uses the concept of "amount of invested mental effort" to study children's comprehension of media information, finding that comprehension increases when children expect TV messages will be difficult to process (Salomon and Leigh, 1984), when viewing departs from expectations and when children are instructed to learn (Salomon, 1983).[94] Furthermore, TV may "signal that little effort is required whereas reading suggests from the outset that processing will be difficult" (Wartella and Reeves, 1987: 635). Salomon (1981, 1983, 1984) and others have found that students learn more from a book than from watching a televised presentation of the same content, largely because the perceived demand characteristics of reading are higher and students invest more mental effort in processing the content (Salomon and Leigh, 1984). Others report similar results for adult assessments of investments of mental effort for viewing TV and reading books (Csikszentmihalyi and Kubey, 1982).

The new technologies provide an opportunity to separate out reading as a process from the print media themselves. Videotex may be thought of as a video newspaper, with words rather than video images dominating the screen. One reads videotext just as one reads a newspaper, eliminating a major difference between TV and newspapers. Melwani (1989) conducted a videotext experiment to examine the effect of medium on the information processed as people formed impressions of political candidates. There were three conditions—print, TV news broadcast, and videotext. Recall was highest for videotext, then the newspaper, and then TV. The difference in recall between subjects in the TV and those in the other two media was statistically significant. In another experiment, Zerbinos (1990) also found that people remembered more from videotext than from a newspaper.[95]

Linking Audiences and Messages

Although focusing only on television content, Biocca (1991) demonstrates broadly how links may be drawn between media messages and images that audiences bring with them to media use situations. Mass media tend to be "user friendly," assisting viewers, readers, and listeners by providing conventions that help audiences arrive at understandings. In the case of TV, for example, structure is built into programming as demonstrated by our use of the following terms—genre, plot, characters, shot sequence, camera flow, argument, etc. (Bordwell and Thompson, 1986).[96] These features of the media "frame" audience processing by guiding and limiting the kinds of inferences people make. These media frames help the viewer activate content-relevant schema in an on-going, continuous process of semantic activation (Biocca, 1991).[97] In the actual media use "situation," content is seen as being processed in cycles[98] strongly influenced by the structure of the message (Carroll, 1980; Jarvella, 1975).

Thus, media structure—called syntactic cues and **semantic frames** by Biocca (1991)—is seen as promoting the use of schema frames—which include both propositions and images[100]—for processing media messages. These images and propositions eventually become linked in some way.[101] One schema audiences use to understand TV programs in particular is called a **script**, a term which refers to a predetermined, stereotyped sequence of actions that defines a well-known situation. Scripts are structures that describe appropriate sequences of events in a particular context and are made up of slots and requirements about what can fill those slots (Schank and Abelson, 1977). The structure is an interconnected whole, and what is in one slot affects what can be in another. Scripts help people to cope with familiar situations and, in the case of mass media, familiar content. They provide no help for totally novel situations. Frames differ in patterns of dominance or priority for processing media messages, and the use of a particular frame leads to other frames closely associated in people's minds (Biocca, Neuwirth, Oshagan, Zhongdang and Richards, 1987).

Biocca (1991) identifies seven frames which may be active in generating "mental models" of TV messages: 1) Possible World Frame, social-psychological constructs with scripted values for spatial, temporal, and actantial variables that locate the message and help in decoding linguistic propositions and images[102]; 2) Discursive Schematic Frames—the problem space for cognitive procedures that automatically are used to organize the thematic structure of incoming messages; 3) Actantial Frames—TV scenes and other media messages are filled with actors or agents of propositions, which may be organized by a set of referent nodes in an associative network representing the television scene;[103] 4) Point-of-View frames—which allow audiences to see the possible world of the TV program, magazine article or other media message 'through the eyes' of some agent;[104] 5) Narrative Frames—which help audiences understand stories and guide how messages are split into components, inferences are made, etc. Research supports existence of such schemata (Bower, 1976; Mandler and Johnson, 1977; Rumelhart, 1977; Schank and Abelson, 1977; van Dijk, 1988) across cultures (Labov, 1972; Propp, 1968), specifically to process media messages (Thorndyke, 1977); 6) Ideological

Schematic Frames—used to refer to underlying assumptions and the logic of ideas that underlie any statement about a state of a possible world (Livingstone, 1987); 7) Self-Schematic Frames—which refer to self schemata, prototypical concepts of the self constructed from self observation, etc. Processing schemas about oneself have been characterized as more complex, elaborated, and requiring greater cognitive effort.[105]

Summary

In this chapter we looked at the expanding literature dealing with audience processing of specific media messages. Beginning with print media, we looked at reading processes in general before discussing the research on how audiences process typefaces and words in articles, color vs. black-and-white, graphic elements such as charts and tables, photographs, headlines, sentences and paragraphs within articles, structures of print messages and specifically the inverted pyramid news form, writing styles, sequences of content within messages, and print media design.

Audience processing of TV and film was then outlined, beginning with the narrative/story structure. We also looked at the impact of encoding techniques such as moving vs. fixed camera, camera angle, special effects, editing conventions, and cutting rate, as well as the relationship between the visual and audio content processed. Finally, we looked at processing of complex forms of visual media, in particular TV news broadcasts and the structure of particular stories within that format. Modality differences in processing were addressed.

Chapter Seven Footnotes

1. Researchers have looked at cognitive processing as mediating variables for social effects on children (Wartella and Reeves, 1987), advertising effects on consumers (Ward, 1987), media effects during political campaigns (Graber, 1984), and cognitive effects from exposure to news.

2. Recent support for the idea of bottom-up processing from machine vision (Cutting, 1987) suggests that new information is initially encoded in memory in a fraction of a second, leaving little opportunity for interference from storage processes. Thus, when interference does occur later it appears to come after the information is acquired from disruption of processing necessary for subsequent retrieval (Miller, Kasprow and Schachtman, 1986).

3. We can examine reading at various levels, looking at our small perceptual spans (Meyer and Schvaneveldt, 1971; Rayner, 1975) and how our eyes pause, or fixate, most of the time rather than move through newspaper articles or magazine stories without disruption (Carpenter and Just, 1986; McConkie, Underwood, Zola and Wolverton, 1985).

4. **Buffering** is a process of intersentence integration that involves three operations: accessing the meaning structures that correspond to the new textual information in semantic memory; transferring the meaning structures to working memory; and maintaining the information in working memory. In addition to buffering of new information, integration involves two other

subprocesses: linking the new information with earlier information from the text (Jarvella, 1979) [Continuity with earlier information is provided by repeated argument nouns (Haviland and Clark, 1974), by the global text topic (Kieras, 1981), and by conceptual structures associated with the predicates of sentences, particularly the verbs (Carpenter and Just, 1977; Graesser and Clark, 1985; Haberlandt and Bingham, 1978; Haberlandt and Graesser, 1989; Keenan, Baillett, and Brown, 1984).] and purging the buffered information from working memory (Chang, 1980; Kintsch and van Dijk, 1978; Miller and Kintsch, 1980).

5. Carpenter and Just (1983) found that readers tend to fixate more on content than function words even when obvious differences such as word length and occurrence frequency were controlled.

6. In comprehension, we identify intended meanings, make associations with context, etc. In recall, we consciously remember symbols, images, messages previously perceived. It is possible to recall what is not understood.

7. Miller (1956, 1965, 1973) presented seven ideas that had implications for research into reading: 1) Not all physical features of speech are significant for vocal communication, and not all significant features of speech have a physical representation; 2) The meaning of a symbol or an utterance should not be confused with its reference; 3) The meaning of an utterance is not the simple sum of the meanings of the words that comprise it; 4) The syntactic structure of a sentence imposes groupings that govern the interactions between the meanings of the words in that sentence; 5) There is no limit to the number of sentences or the number of meanings that can be expressed; 6) Descriptions of language and of the language user are distinct; 7) There is a large biological component to the human capacity for articulate speech (Hall, 1989: 157).

8. In an experiment with seventh- and eighth-grade students, both prior knowledge and topic interest were related to higher comprehension of materials read (Baldwin, Peleg-Bruckner, and McClintock, 1985).

9. Their model has four stages prior to comprehension: exposure (which may be unplanned or the result of a deliberate act), peripheral sensory reception (print may be too faint or the screen too snowy, reception by the peripheral nervous system is a prerequisite for comprehension), central cortical representation (given activation of the peripheral sensory system, not all neuronal transmissions reach the audience member's cortex), and attention (since people cannot attend to all incoming sensory information, the reader is selective, so much of the cortical stimulation does not register on consciousness and fails to be translated into psychological form).

10. Just as the more than 600,000 words in the English language are constructed using 26 letters, the letters themselves are made up of a smaller number of characteristics (called critical features) that include lines, segments, curves, juxtapositions, and angles and allow readers and viewers to distinguish one letter or number from another. In English, the features are integrated to form separate letters (or numbers) which then are combined to form letter clusters (e.g., 'un') and eventually entire words and word strings (Jacob and Hoyer, 1987). For descriptions of this process, see Estes (1977) and Rumelhart (1977).

11. Thematic representations are not schemata, which refer to pre-existing knowledge structures with extensive meaning that are built up over time and brought to the reading or media use session by the audience member (Norman and Bobrow, 1975).

12. Technically, an assertion is a linguistic construction in which a referent is associated with or dissociated from a complement via a verbal connector (Osgood, 1959).

13. Implied meanings may be either logical (necessarily implied) or pragmatic (inferred but not logically necessary). Meanings exist only in the minds of individuals, as communication encoders or decoders, but here they refer to those intended by the professional encoder who constructed the message.

14. Of the demographic characteristics assessed, only age, education, and income were related to miscomprehension. Readers over age 54 tended to miscomprehend slightly more than those in other age groups. More significantly, level of formal education was negatively related to the degree of miscomprehension. A small inverse relationship also was found between income and miscomprehension.

15. Miscomprehension was highest for national affairs editorial content (28.5%), followed by building (26.8%), sports/hobbies (26.8%), beauty and grooming (26.4%), food and nutrition (25.4%) and then business and industry (25.3%). Miscomprehension was lowest for wearing apparel (19.5% incorrect), fiction (19.9%) and general interest content (20.8%). Miscomprehension was highest for toiletries (26.7%), automotive (23.9%), jewelry, and sporting goods (each 22%) advertising, and lowest for office equipment (14.5%), home entertainment (14.6%) and entertainment (14.8%) advertising.

16. See Triesman (1977), Triesman and Gelade (1980), Triesman, Sykes and Gelade (1977).

17. See Bousfield, Esterson and Whitmarshk (1957), Denis (1976), and Franken (1977).

18. See Paivio, Rogers and Smythe (1968) and Wicker (1970).

19. Most media researchers examining the effects of color on memory and comprehension have used television messages (Scanlon, 1967, 1970; VanderMeer, 1954). These studies suggest that color adds information to a pictorial message, facilitates the identification of objects, and may increase image memorability. Early studies of color vs. black-and-white TV messages suggest that color hinders learning of central information and attracts viewers to irrelevant details such as color of hair or style of clothing (Scanlon, 1967, 1970). These studies were conducted when color television was a new phenomenon. More recent studies have found that colored visual messages elicit greater learning and are better remembered than black-and-white messages (Franken, 1977; Gilbert and Schleuder, 1988, 1990; Power, 1978; Reid, Beveridge, and Wakefield, 1986).

20. Bohle and Garcia (1987) summarize the research on advertising reported in dissertations and elsewhere.

21. Sundar et al. (1991) found that infographics in a news story increased perceptual accuracy compared with stories missing infographics. They concluded that vivid, graphically presented information was readily accessible in memory.

22. Ramaprasad (1991) found no difference in overall recall by two groups of students, one reading a story with an accompanying graph and one without the graph, but the former did score higher on statements which had received high visual support.

23. Readers of the story and bar chart were more accurate in their comprehension than those who read stories alone, stories with tables, or stories with sidebars. Kelly (1992) also confirmed earlier studies that graphs are more accurately read than tables but density of information and format also are factors. Tables are read more quickly when there are only 8 data points but graphs are read more quickly when there are 16.

24. Expecting a graphic to lead to a more systematic processing of the accompanying message, Hollander (1992) found no attitude change when a graphic accompanied an article. The experiment included graphic public opinion data, a newspaper article about results which were either high or low in relevance to the audience, and other details about the poll. Though the graphic had no impact on attitude change, results suggested a graphic can increase cognitive effort.

25. The data are much more complex than presented here. The four findings were: 1) angle may be the dominant cue used during magnitude estimation of components of a whole; 2) if the central angles serve as the dominant cue, the center of the whole may be important as a cognitive anchor; 3) volumetric shapes can be used to represent data as accurately as length representations.

26. Tufte (1983) proposed the data-ink ratio, which says that a large share of the ink on a graphic should present data-information to avoid distraction and aid understanding. Ironically, increasingly newspapers are using considerable non-data ink in graphs to attract reader attention

(Kelly, 1989). In his study with students, there was no difference between the perceived accuracy of graphs differing in the portion of ink devoted to information. Kelly (1989) found no support for the data-ink ratio theory of Tufte (1983), finding no difference in errors between those who received more data-ink in a graphic than those who received less.

27. Similar results are found in Daw and Parkin (1981) and Loftus and Kallman (1979).

28. Also, studies of visual recognition in TV commercials show that people recalled visually simple commercials better than visually complex commercials (Schleuder et al., 1987, 1988; Thorson et al., 1985, 1986).

29. See: Alesandrini (1984), Levie and Lentz (1982), Levin (1981), Levin and Lesgold (1978); for simple stimuli, Madigan (1983); Paivio (1979); for more complex social stimuli, Swann and Miller (1982).

30. Lynn, Shavitt and Ostrom (1985) formulate each of these three explanations in terms of associative network theory (Anderson, 1977; Anderson and Bower, 1973) to identify cognitive processes through which visual information improves social memory.

31. The seven functions are decoration, remuneration, motivation, reiteration, representation, organization, interpretation and transformation (Anglin, 1987).

32. See Mandler and Johnson (1977), Rumelhart (1977), and Thorndyke (1977).

33. See, for example, Mandler and Johnson (1977), Marshall and Glock (1979), Meyer (1977), Rumelhart (1975, 1977), Stein and Glenn (1979), Taylor (1980), and Taylor and Samuels (1983).

34. See Mandler and Johnson (1977), Rumelhart (1975), and Stein and Glenn (1979).

35. Meyer (1975) has identified the following organizational structures and relationships as characteristic of nonfiction texts: taxonomical, chronological, cause and effect, directive, comparison and contrast, and enumerative or attributional. Also see Gillet and Temple (1986).

36. See Anderson (1977), Bower, Black and Turner (1979), Gourley (1984), Marshall and Glock (1979), McGee (1982), Pearson and Camperell (1985), Ruddell and Speaker (1985), Rumelhart (1985), Taylor (1980), and Whaley (1981).

37. Fiske and Linville (1980: 543) say schemas are "cognitive structures of organized prior knowledge, abstracted from experience with specific instances; schemas guide the processing of new information and the retrieval of stored information."

38. Richards (1978) has observed that many students who are reading fluently in the beginning grades start to experience reading problems in the fourth and fifth grades, when a greater amount of nonfictional material is introduced into the curriculum. This may be due to the children's lack of familiarity with text structures other than the fictional narrative.

39. A major feature of the attributional expository text structure is the theme paragraph which begins with a topic sentence followed by elaborative sentences (Durham, 1990).

40. Van Dijk and Kintsch (1983; van Dijk, 1988) proposed that readers develop a "superstructure" schema for the form of stories.

41. See Fitzgerald (1984), Fitzgerald and Spiegel (1983), Mandler (1978), Spiegel and Fitzgerald (1985), Stein and Nezworski 1978), and van Dijk and Kintsch (1983).

42. See Meyer (1975), Meyer (1977), Meyer, Brandt and Bluth (1980), Meyer and Freedle (1979), Mulcahny and Samuels (1987), and Olhausen and Roller (1988).

43. See, for example, Bobrow and Norman, 1975; Freebody and Anderson (1983), Graesser and Nakamura (1982), Pearson, Hansen and Gordon (1979) Schank and Abelson (1977), and Stahl and Jacobson (1986).

44. For research which quantifies news recall see Booth (1970), Edwardson, Grooms and Pringle (1976), Edwardson, Grooms and Proudlove (1981), Edwardson, Kent and McConnell (1985), Findahl and Hoijer (1975, 1981, 1985), Gunter (1980, 1981), and Neuman (1976).

45. Donohew, Finn, and Christ (1988) examined the complementary roles of cognition, schemas, and affect in processing news (Durham, 1990).

46. Newsom and Wollert (1988) see most news stories as containing the following elements: a lead giving the main point, secondary points in a transition, elaboration on the major point,

support for the lead, background, development of the main idea, and details.

47. See Green (1979), Housel (1984), Nolan (1989), and Thorndyke (1977).

48. Durham (1990) used the Newsom and Wollert modified inverted pyramid structure (excluding elements such as comments on or analyses of events) in an experiment exploring the connection between the schematic organization of news stories and readers' cognitions regarding news messages. Past research has supported the view that narrative writing is better received by readers than news stories (Donohew, 1982; Smith and Voelz, 1983).

49. Farnan (1992) compared a traditional inverted pyramid news structure with a "mapping" structure in which the inverted pyramid lead was followed by a body broken into sections under subheads. The mapping structure was rated as more appealing by readers but there was no difference on material learned.

50. Active style uses verbs in the active voice, with the cause of the action before the verb and object. Passive styles put the actor at the end of the sentence or delete the actor. Nominal style substitutes nouns for verbs, with most remaining verbs in passive or "to be" forms. The study used Cloze procedure to discriminate among writing styles, e.g., active vs. passive. Cloze procedure is based on gestalt theory, with readers following a sequence to first understand the whole, or broader issue, and then grasping individual details. It also has been used to measure reader comprehension (Bostian and Byrne, 1984).

51. In a general associative memory model, a concept's importance is determined by the number of connections that the concept has to all the other concepts and propositions in the system (Walker and Yekovich, 1984). The intensity of a passage could influence a reader's perception of the concept's importance and likelihood that its associative network would be activated.

52. Walker and Meyer (1980) found that the ordering of facts affects inferential processing of material.

53. The content schematic approach focuses more on describing text in structural terms, with meaning presumed to be more text driven (bottom-up) than top-down. Structural-schematic approaches describe abstract text structures, beginning, middle, end of a TV commercial or magazine article, rather than particular content or symbols within them (see Galambos, Abelson and Black, 1986).

54. This includes page size, proportion, use of color, use of illustrations and art, typeface and size, placement, fitting.

55. In an experiment, exposure to a headline speeded up subjects' responses to attitude questions about the topic.

56. According to Gibson's (1979) ecological theory of pictorial representation, a picture is not something made to be similar to a scene but is a specially contrived means of providing information to enable observers to see a scene not present to them (Reed, 1988). Gibson's theory explains that there can be some degree of "illusion of reality" in pictures but it is incomplete because the information displayed by a picture surface is not of the same kind as that displayed by a real scene. People scrutinizing a picture eventually reach the limits of the displayed information and begin to detect information about the picture surface or screen, the texture of the pigment, or the graininess of the photographic reproduction (Reed, 1988: 249). If pictures are displays of information rather than surrogates of scenes, then their display allows perception not only for remembering something in the past but also for conceiving something in the future, for considering in visual terms what might be as well as what might have been.

57. These are not well developed in young children (Greenfield, 1984; National Conference on Visual Information Processing, 1974; cited in Hobbs, Frost, Davis and Stauffer, 1988).

58. See Huston, Wright, Wartella, Rice, Watkins, Campbell and Potts (1981), Rice, Huston and Wright (1982), and Salomon (1979).

59. Kraft (1987) distinguishes between two sets of principles governing structure of film and TV narratives, rules for a coherent presentation and strategies for an effective presentation.

60. Deviations from linearity were associated with negative evaluations of the editing and the

film as a whole, suggesting people prefer chronological narratives (Cowen, 1988). However, not all effects of film structure are due to chronological ordering of events since the differences in comprehension and recall are so small.

61. However, changing the vertical camera angle predictably influenced subjects' evaluations of the relative dominance of the two characters in each story.

62. See Arnheim (1974), Chandler (1934), Kraft (1987), Shoemaker (1964), and Tannenbaum and Fosdick (1960).

63. Gershon and Gantz (1992) analyzed changes in the production style of TV by looking at how features of music videos were integrated into TV commercials. They found that music video style was used in TV advertising during the 1980s, with a peak in 1985. Elements of music video style were: movement across frames/editing (including pacing, jump cuts, cuts made during a camera movement, and music-video montages); movement within frames (including electronically matted visuals, new wave graphics and altered motion); static visualization (including shots with non-standard camera framing and lens distortion, shots with chroma distortion, polarized images and extreme close-ups); audio (including use of popular music and music in the foreground); narrative (including visual inclusion of other cameras in the shot, self reflexive references to TV, intertextual references to other mass media, and amateur appearance).

64. In this study, camera movement was defined as fluid motion achieved by a camera that arcs, trucks, or dollies smoothly through a scene. Viewers of the moving-camera scene were expected to have more information available to them and thus remember objects better and better comprehend the scene's three-dimensional reality. Free recall, recognition and spatial comprehension, and memory tests were developed and subjects watched either a moving-camera or fixed-camera version (Kipper, 1986).

65. The moving camera apparently has an influence on the viewer's comprehension and understanding that is quite different from the symbolic or conventional meanings that are sometimes the result of visual techniques (Kipper, 1986).

66. Considerable experimental evidence supports this view, e.g., motion affects one's ability to separate foreground and background (Braunstein, 1966; Kaplan, 1969; Mace and Shaw, 1974) and motion can enhance depth perception (Hay, 1966; Wallach and O'Connell, 1953).

67. In the experiment, camera angle in a series of slides was varied, e.g., low angle-high angle, eye-eye, or high-low (low, meaning shooting up to the subject; high, meaning shooting from a higher point down to the subject).

68. Lang (1992) discusses a limited capacity theory of TV viewing, suggesting that attention and mental effort are two distinct parts of the TV-viewing process. Both attention and mental effort are required for viewers to remember what they watch but they are not sufficient. When cognitive capacity is exceeded, attention and mental effort will not result in memory.

69. They also found that audio information was recalled better than video information, and information before the cuts was recalled better than information after the cuts. Both audio and visual memory were damaged by unrelated cuts and improved by related cuts.

70. Other features are edits, loud noises, funny voices, movement, flashes of light, and music.

71. Among the more isolated and rural of African tribes, 90% of the villagers had heard audiotape or radio before but only 40% had seen a film before, 60% had seen photographic images and 35% had seen newspapers, magazines, or other printed matter. Experience with media was limited. In the U.S., Worth (1972, 1981) found that groups of Navajo Indians taught to make films discovered the editing process within a few days, recognizing that close-ups of a horse could be combined with images of a whole horse. They also used many editing techniques that are unfamiliar or "wrong" to viewers used to Western models of film production and editing, including unusual camera movements.

72. The use of point-of-view editing to fragment the visual scene and reconstruct it by changing the distance between the viewer and the camera did not affect the ability to comprehend the story, supporting a belief that some media-specific conventions and specifically those

manipulating point of view operate much like perceptual processes which arrange the viewer's experience in a manner which facilitates its encoding and storage.

73. A closely-related technique, one which affects point of view, involves talking directly to the audience. Auter (1992) found that viewers ranked higher on a parasocial interaction scale when the "fourth wall was broken" and actors in the sitcom spoke directly to the audience.

74. Basil (1992) summarizes the research on understanding of video-audio information, noting that half of the studies demonstrate that visuals interfere with understanding of audio content, e.g., Burriss (1987), Edwardson et al. (1991), Hoffner et al. (1988), while the other half suggest visuals do not interfere with memory for audio information, e.g., Gunter (1980) and Kisielius and Sternthal (1984). Katz, Adoni and Parness (1977) had hypothesized that lack of consonance between sound and picture would produce a distraction effect and reduced recall of content but they failed to confirm this hypothesis.

75. See Hsia (1977), Miller (1982), Nugent (1982),and Wember (1976).

76. Basil (1992) notes that the experiment suggests only one channel of information gets into the processing system for semantic processing. Visual information appears to be detected and processed equally well, regardless of viewers' focus, while viewers show improved memory for auditory information when they are focused on the audio channel.

77. This is consistent with Craik and Lockhart's (1972) level of processing theory, which suggests that memory is directly related to how deeply information is processed.

78. Stephens (1986) describes broadcast news style as follows: having a lead that points the viewer toward the heart of the story, followed by information supporting the claims made by the lead and ending with the 'snapper' (which may be a final fact, the other side of an issue, or the main point of the story).

79. See: Friestad and Thorson (1985), Ortony (1978), Shoben, Wescourt, and Smith (1978), and Tulving and Donaldson (1972).

80. Ortony (1978) theorizes that "we create an episodic 'subgraph' of our experiences which contains three types of information: the surface structure, corresponding to what actually happened; the semantic structure, made up of semantic information that was required to understand the experience; and input associates, which are concepts related to the subject of the experience." In Ortony's theory, episodic processing requires creation of a complete subgraph. Later the information contained in the episodic subgraph is stripped of source and circumstances and stored in semantic memory. According to this perspective, all semantic memory (or world knowledge) begins as episodic knowledge, and the completeness of the episodic processing largely determines whether episodically stored and processed information makes the transition from episodic to semantic memory (Lang, 1989).

81. Theories suggest that episodic trace strength (intensity) is influenced by such factors as the intensity of the experience, the importance or relevance of the experience, the person's ability to understand the experience, the emotional content of the experience, the completeness of the episodic trace, and the temporal ordering of the experience (Friestad and Thorson, 1985; Lang, 1989; Ortony, 1978; Tulving, 1972).

82. Viewers "must first identify, from the lead, the subject of the story. In order to understand that lead, the viewer must access semantic memory to retrieve what information is stored on that subject . . . while simultaneously processing the incoming story episodically. Later the viewer must shift that information from episodic to semantic memory for later recall." (Lang, 1989: 444).

83. Miscomprehension of TV messages was related to age and education but differences were minor across age, income, and education groups in a national study (Jacoby, Hoyer and Sheluga, 1980). There was no relationship between accurate retention of TV news four hours after viewing and education or occupational status, but age was related in a curvilinear fashion. Those in the age 25-54 bracket showed better retention than those above or below it (Robinson, Levy, Davis, Woodall, Gurevitch and Sahin, 1986). Introverts remember more than extroverts (Gunter, Furnham and Jarrett, 1984).

84. See Edwardson, Kent, Engstrom and Hofmann (1991), Berry, Gunter and Clifford (1981), and Woodall, Davis and Sahin (1983).

85. Much research has demonstrated human difficulty in processing two items of information simultaneously. Broadbent (1971) proposed that audiences process fully only one information channel at a time although they can change the focus of attention rapidly. Treisman (1968) demonstrated limits on the division of attention in analyzing multiple input.

86. Grimes (1989) suggests that narration may "drive" the processing of visuals when there is channel redundancy. "If viewers actually do rely on the narration for the principal story message, perhaps the narration promotes semantic comparisons between what is heard and seen. Thus, one would expect to see more attention expended on the visual channel in this condition" (Grimes, 1989: 24). More research is needed to resolve the question.

87. In general, people orient toward visual stimuli. Posner, Nissen and Klein (1976) report that this orientation is depressed when visual stimuli do not provide adequate information in comparison to auditory stimuli. With extreme channel conflict, people shift their attention toward the channel that is easier to process, the audio (Grimes, 1989).

88. See Hirst, Spelke, Reaves, Caharack and Neisser (1980), and Schneider and Shiffrin (1977).

89. See Harris, Dubitsky and Bruno (1983) for research on comprehension of simulated radio commercials.

90. A large literature examines modality effects on memory; see, for example, Biggs and Marmurek (1990), Huttenlocher and Kubicek (1983), Richardson-Klavehn and Bjork (1988), and Smith and Magee (1980).

91. See Reeves and Thorson (1986).

92. A 1965-1966 study indicates that reading of newspapers, books, and magazines occupied only 3% of an adult's day, while TV dominated with 7%. A 1957 study reported that 53% of the school day involved listening, most of it to the teacher. Downing and Leong (1982) concluded that listening serves information needs better than reading does until grade 7 (Klein, 1989).

93. It should be pointed out that the messages in this study were only typescripts of the radio and TV communication and not like those generally found in broadcast or print media. A large-scale study conducted for the U.S. Food and Drug Administration utilized quizzes to test miscomprehension of fictitious drug products embedded in either a magazine or a TV show. Somewhat greater miscomprehension rates were found for the magazine ads (20%) than for the TV commercials (17%) (see Jacoby and Hoyer, 1987).

94. Salomon's model draws on schema theory and the relationships between: the perceived demand characteristics of the situation, the individual's perceived self-efficacy for using a particular medium, and the amount of mental effort the individual invests in processing the message. Demand characteristics are linked to motivations.

95. Zerbinos (1990) also found that subjects in an experiment assigned to videotext engaged in more information-seeking behavior and recalled proportionally more factual information than did those assigned to read a newspaper with similar material.

96. These conventions are not unique to television and also help in processing other media and everyday experiences (Biocca, 1991), for example, knowing how to follow the plot of a mystery or drama must make use of skills that share features with deducing plots from mystery novels or following a sequence of causally related events.

97. Biocca (1991: 6) describes the on-going process: "Starting in the very first milliseconds of the programming, the viewer constructs an early mental model of the overall message. The viewer does this automatically by calculating values in some of the schematic frames. This in turn primes and instantiates selected schema, leading the viewer to infer default schema consistent values (Minsky, 1975) to the other schematic frames. For example, the viewer makes inferences about the setting of the programming and the topic of the program. This may activate inferences about the type of people and behavior typical of the world of the program, and some projection about how the story of the program or commercial 'will turn out.'"

98. The concept of cycle is an effort to resolve the unit problem of how to slice up the message in units, perceptually and conceptually. Biocca (1991) suggests that television is processed in cycles just as language is (Kintsch and van Dijk, 1978), and, as in language processing, the cycling is strongly influenced by the structure of the message. A cycle could be a scene or other unit of video equivalent to a phase or sentence of language.

99. These schematic frames are seen as analogous to problem spaces in artificial intelligence (e.g., Newell, 1981). Problem spaces are areas, or subroutines, where specific semantic or problem-solving tasks are carried out.

100. Some have proposed that visual images are stored and used as a set of key frames (Reeves, Chaffee and Tims, 1982; Wyer and Gordon, 1984). Wyer and Gordon (1984) suggest that subjects use key frames to code continuous event sequences. These key frames capture non-propositional relationships in visual or acoustic images that store such things as prototypical features of a scene, object, or person (Wyer and Gordon, 1984) and may be used to derive further conclusions about events, plot, characters, etc.

101. Wyer and Gordon (1984) suggest that key frames may be referred to by pointers (networked links) in propositions about messages. Pointers, located in a proposition about the message, would refer to key frames and integrate frames into propositions about event sequences, causal attributions, and trait inferences. Some support for this is found in research showing that viewers are better able to remember static images that occur close to break points in filmed sequences of events (Newtson and Enquist, 1976).

102. Violations can affect subsequent processing of messages, e.g., if one is not familiar with science fiction, the injection of something not "possible" in the physical-temporal world would raise questions and confusion for the audience.

103. Biocca (1991) says audiences appear to better understand and remember the behaviors or agents by organizing them around traits and motivations, and media techniques and conventions support this by judiciously using single traits to prompt audiences to "see" an entire trait from a single behavior and to continue on to visualize a role or character based on a set of actions or traits.

104. In TV, point of view has two interacting dimensions: mode-of-address and positions of sight. Because of these dimensions, point of view in television and film is significantly different than it is in literature (Biocca, 1991: 27). Mode-of-address is part of the semantic framing of the television sequence, where a number of cues are used to guide the viewer to hold a particular point of view, e.g., actors/agents directly addressing the camera, active or passive camera movement, camera angles suggesting the position-of-sight of various actants within the scene (Biocca, 1991). Position-of-sight refers to the position of the viewer in space as cued by the camera's position in space. Points of view found in TV are: first person viewer identity, often cued by actors speaking directly to the audience; second person borrowed identification, where the viewer is encouraged to role play or model action from the character's viewpoint; third person nomadic identification, where the audience sees the possible world from a variety of perspectives and the point-of-sight continuously changes; third person voyeur, where the point of view is always that of outsider to the narrative. Point of view may affect the images and inferences of the audience (Strange and Black, 1989; Taylor and Fiske, 1978).

105. Messages that stimulate audiences to think about themselves receive qualitatively and quantitatively different levels-of-processing (Borgida and Howard-Pitney, 1983; Petty and Cacioppo, 1986). Thompson (1992) found that viewers of a music video who invoked referential frames of involvement connected the program to their own lives more than those who invoked a metalinguistic frame—discussing roles in the script from a distance.

8

Patterns of Media Content

I. Introduction
II. Major content structures of the media
   A. Radio—news and music, major formats
   B. Film structures
   C. TV content structures
   D. Media advertising
   E. Print media content structures
   F. News in print and broadcast media
III. Media images, stereotypes and portrayals
   A. Ethnicity—increasing diversity
   B. Age and images of the elderly
   C. Families and children—portraying the rest of the life cycle—childhood, families, family life
   D. Gender—images of men and women in TV, music videos, film, TV commercials, print media
   E. Occupations and professions—general social class, medical professionals, science, advertising, journalists, others
   F. Organizations and institutions—government agencies, religion, health institution and diseases
   G. Problems and issues—crime, interest groups, cities and nations
   H. Other behaviors in media content—slice of daily activities, conflict and prosocial events, values
IV. Summary

T V newscasters often label their programs "eyewitness news," implying that they provide the same direct experience people in the audience would have if they were present at news sites. Journalists, however, must be selective in choosing from the huge volume of potential facts. They have access to information that the average person would not have in the same situation. The "news content" of media is an effort to represent some aspect of reality. "Non-news content" is equally important in its representation of the human experience, although the purposes are quite different—to excite, to stimulate, to express sentiments, to persuade or to sell products.

Media content of all types can affect political perceptions, cultural tastes, and consumer preferences. Traditionally, media content "reflects" reality, but creative, "fictionalized" aspects of the media—television entertainment programs, radio formats, films, and interactive computer programs—also create new perceptions of reality. Commercial-advertising content of the media surrounds us daily. Media content is an important area of study, because it has tremendous impact.[1]

We can slice up media content in a variety of ways. We do this every day when we recognize the **content structures** that media practitioners themselves use to identify and analyze their work—the "urban sound" of radio, "horror" films, newspaper "op-ed" pages, and TV formats like "Roseanne."[2]

Communication is the encoding and decoding of messages; media content represents symbolic "messages," a unit which can be abstracted from the rest of the process (see Fisher, 1978). These messages can be subjected to content analysis, which is conducted for several purposes: to infer something about the encoders themselves (for example, whether journalists are biased); to find out something about the channel (such as, which medium presents images of minorities most similar to the general population?); to find out what decoders/audiences have been exposed to (for example, how much stereotyped gender material are children exposed to?); and to see if media content reflects the larger "culture."[3]

The relationship between media content and social reality is a major concern of various groups critical of their media images. Often fearful of the impact media may have on society over time, these groups analyze media content to see whether it reflects those aspects of society that are important to them. Thus, women and ethnic groups criticize media images and stereotypes. Criticism also comes from others who want to control how they're portrayed—including business, professions, agencies, cities, and others.

This chapter will focus on two types of media content. First, we will look at content forms which have been used by media professionals and observers to describe the major recurring patterns or structures. These include radio formats, film genre, TV formats, newspaper features, and forms of print and broadcast news. These are the structures that emerge from the message construction conventions described earlier. These also have been linked to information processing and audience choices. Secondly, we will look at media images, stereotypes, and portrayals of different types of people and their institutions.

Major Content Structures of the Media

Radio

Today, radio content falls into two large categories: **news** and **music**. This represents a major change from the days when flipping the dial would provide you with sounds of variety programs, comedies, cops-and-robbers serials, westerns, soap operas and big band musical programs.[4] When homogenization occurs on one dimension, efforts to create variety (differentiation) occur on other dimensions. News itself is diversifying into various specialties that include business news and talk formats that focus on sports or emphasize banter among personalities, interviews with guests, or public call-in programs. Since most stations offer music-and-news, more distinctions are made in terms of the type of music played.

Radio content is structured as **formats**, patterns of programming that represent increasingly specialized musical tastes. Radio station formats are infinite in variety and subject to constant reappraisal and change (Routt et al., 1978). A formula that stresses progressive rock music today may be changed to feature rhythm and blues music tomorrow. Once a decision to adopt a format is made, it is subjected to a dozen subtle shifts and adjustments because the "execution of conceptualities is the essence of any format." Today formats are shaped by extensive audience research that extends to testing of individual songs played on the air (Hall and Hall, 1977). In the extreme, the final configuration of musical content is based on the collective reactions of audience targets identified by age, sex, income, ethnic status, etc. According to a recent listing of radio formats, country music is the most popular (See Table 8-1), followed by adult contemporary. Rock music is part of many formats, including top-40 rock, which emphasizes hit singles.

The figures in Table 8-1 change rapidly. From 1985 to 1990, the number of radio stations following the Oldies format increased 166%,[5] with other large increases noted for new age/jazz formats, gospel-oriented formats and all-talk stations. There are also new formats created to fit market segments or to rejuvenate old ones. Free-form programming, where disk jockeys are put on

Table 8-1

Major Programming Formats of U.S. Radio Stations

Format	AM	FM	Total No. Stations	% of Total
Country	1,391	1,213	2,603	18.1%
Adult contemporary	831	1,516	2,347	16.2%
Rock formats:			3,247	22.5%
Oldies	599	421	1,020	7.1%
Top 40	119	726	845	5.9%
Middle-of-Road	450	100	550	3.8%
Album-oriented rock	65	474	539	3.7%
Classic rock	48	245	293	2.0%
News and Talk formats:				
News	276	254	530	3.7%
News/Talk	471	59	530	3.7%
Talk	288	61	349	2.4%
Religious formats:			1,392	9.7%
Religious	590	514	1,104	7.7%
Gospel	228	60	288	2.0%
Variety	122	405	527	3.7%
Ethnic formats:	574	4.0%		
Spanish	242	89	331	2.3%
Black	112	59	171	1.2%
Foreign/ethnic	31	18	49	
Portuguese	7	1	8	
American Indian	3	1	4	
Greek	3		3	
Italian	2		2	
Japanese	2		2	
Polish	2		2	
Filipino	1		1	
French	1		1	
Classical	22	407	429	3.0%
Jazz	30	338	368	2.6%
Beautiful music	98	191	289	2.0%
Urban contemporary	107	146	253	1.8%
Progressive	10	234	244	1.7%
Big band	145	41	186	1.3%

Note: Other radio formats and the number of stations listed with each are: agriculture, 96; bluegrass, 18; blues, 30; children, 3; comedy, 3; disco, 1; drama/literature, 1; folk, 8; new age, 45; nostalgia, 99; polka, 7; public affairs, 50; reggae, 1; other, 187.

Source: *Broadcasting & Cable Market Place 1992*, p. 486A.

the air because of their musical knowledge and are allowed great freedom to talk over music and to play a variety of music is fairly common (Goldman, 1990).

Musical formats have changed through the decades. The 1920s abounded with the work of George Gershwin and Duke Ellington. With the 1930s came Benny Goodman and "swing" music. Programming music in the 30s and 40s was simple because popular music was not splintered; country music was played in rural areas and progressive music rarely made the airwaves (Routt et al., 1978). Music went from pop to rock in the 1950s as the spread of TV forced radio to rely increasingly on formats that were exclusively music and news. The late 1950s and early 1960s also saw the high-water mark of folk music. As rock music grew in popularity and became more established, it diversified so that by the 1970s, 1980s, and 1990s audiences were harder to identify, capture, and retain. The music has become "almost everything."

Film Structures

People go to films for a variety of gratifications. The choice of film often is not based on the actors alone but also on the "type" of film. Some people like adventure films; others prefer comedies or science fiction. For decades, film scholars have employed the concept of **genre** in their analyses of film structure (Cawelti, 1985; Landrum, 1985). Borrowed from art-history terminology, genre referred to paintings with unidealized scenes and subjects of everyday life. Because of its commonplace subject matter, genre art was not deemed worthy of critical attention. The concept has had similar origins in film, speaking of popular forms and structures that appealed to the masses; this contrasts with the cinema produced by artists who experiment with structure and violate audience expectations. In recent years, the concept has migrated from film to other media—particularly television—but also radio and print media.[6]

The film *J.F.K.* by director Oliver Stone created a controversy in 1992 by challenging the conclusion of the Warren Commission that a lone assassin was responsible for the death of President John F. Kennedy. The controversy also indirectly focused on the concept of genre because the discussion blurred lines between art, biography, and docudrama[7]. Novelist Normal Mailer said that "the surplus of theories about the Kennedy assassination makes a factual movie on the subject impossible," while an editor for *Nation* magazine said filmmakers cross the line when they bend the facts to suit their thesis (Grimes, 1992). Toplin (1988) notes that people have come to expect "conventional history" from film rather than innovative approaches for looking at the past. Although many work hard to achieve verisimilitude, filmmakers also strive to excite feelings and emotions in storytelling, using personal chronologies and perspectives. If the concept of genre depends on both the form of a film and audience expectations, then violation of those expectations may represent art but may also represent efforts to change the structure of a given genre. Cohen (1987) notes that postmodern critics blur genres, cross boundaries, and generally question whether such things as genres can exist in uncertain times. Technology contributes to the innovations, allowing for the manipulation of forms and altering content of "real" photographs or documentary footage (Miller, 1987).

The commercial cinema in general is identifiable by recurring formal and narrative elements (Schatz, 1981). These include a story of a certain length focusing upon a protagonist (such as a hero, a central character), certain standards of production, a style of editing, the use of a musical score, and so forth. However, the "genre film" contains not only these general film devices but also a predetermined structure in which the characters, setting, plot techniques, etc. have prior significance to the audience. Tudor (1977) notes that to call a film an example of a genre means that it draws on a tradition, on a set of conventions. This is significant because it means people have prior expectations that guide their media seeking and message processing. Genre films are often criticized because they appeal to a pre-existing audience. Critics used to ignore genre films because of their prejudice for the unique (Braudy, 1976), but film studios rely on such forms.[8]

There are many lists of contemporary and historically important genre. Defining genre as a "category, kind, or form of film distinguished by subject matter, theme, or techniques," Geduld and Gottesman (1973) list 75 genres of film, including fiction and nonfiction. The western is a typically American genre. Traditionally, the setting—the American West—defines the genre, but the issues raised and the character traits of the personalities are equally well defined. There are noble or ruthless Indians, strong, silent gunmen, single women, powerful cattle barons, and tireless soldiers. The western genre has been so generative its elements have been translated to Japanese, Italian, and German settings and have retained sufficient unity to be recognizable as the same genre by audiences. Table 8-2 provides a sample of genres cited by film scholars and critics.

Jeffres, Neuendorf, and Giles (1990) found that a broad range of college students varied in their agreement about what constituted popular genres. Students were presented with 20 different film genres and TV formats and asked to match them with 38 items representing themes, characters, settings, or film techniques cited in the literature as being associated with particular genres. Analyses showed that audiences can articulate their genre expectations, but these do not conform to some uniform critical standard. For only eight genres did a 50% majority agree on even one component. For many others consensus emerged on only one or two components. The popular horror genre was the most precisely defined genre in the study, while the musical and epic genres were less clear for this young audience. Austin and Gordon (1987) found a student audience agreeing on attributes for documentary/biography/

Table 8-2

A Sample of Film Genres

---

adventure film: a pattern of social unrest and revolution to solve social ills; more recently characterized by fast action and quests for treasures or other goals (Bourget, 1977:69).

art movies: "deliberately and obviously intellectual," bleak compositions, minimal dialogue, grey photography, self-indulgent surrealistic imagery, these characterized European films in the 1960s (Tudor, 1977:21).

black new wave: considers African-American experience on its own terms, from a black perspective and often focusing on taboo subjects by prominent directors such as Spike Lee (Ebert, 1991; for other ethnic and regional films, see Goldman, 1983; French, 1981).

crime or **detective film**: there may be anti-social, violent acts but somewhere there is a moral order of community and group benefit, with the police/detective or someone vindicating the ideal, and restoring the community; (Sobchack, 1977:49; Clarens, 1980; Douglass, 1981; Wakshalag, Vial and Tamborini, 1983; **film noir**, a body of about 25 black-and-white U.S. films with a distinctive vision of despair, loneliness, and dread, often focused on crime (Miller, 1989).

disaster: a situation of normalcy erupts into a persuasive image of death; basic types include: natural attack of nature or other worlds, the ship of fools—dangers of an isolated journey, the city falls—advances of civilization are fragile, the monster, survival—after journey, etc., war, the comic disaster film; conventions include: tendency to be in current time, cross section of society represented, class conflict often dramatized, is based on idea of isolation, which exacerbates conflicts between characters, men have savage side, reoccurring characters include religious figures, scientists, all systems fail in the disaster, the hero is a layman, there is a romantic subplot, people's problems are partially deserved (Yacowar, 1977; Quarantelli, 1985).

documentaries: now largely restricted to television rather than first-run theaters, documentaries are historical, nonfiction approaches tracing events, ideas, people (Corner, 1986).

epic: always connected with action, extroversion, often extravagant, expensive, historical, large size, grandeur (Durgnat, 1977).

erotic/pornography: characterized by sexual images and romances; Limbacher, 1983; Rollin, 1982).

gangster: recurrent patterns of imagery, the physical presence-attributes-dress of actors, the milieu, and the technology; includes racketeers, gangsters, cops, private eyes; firearms, autos, phones; speeding cars, screaming tires, images of aggression (McArthur, 1977).

horror: fear and pity aroused by spectacular means, often supernatural, violent death, bizarre love, manipulation of fear, fear of the unknown, fear of rejection/isolation, abnormal mental processes, suspension of normal frames of reference (Blonsky, 1989; Frank, 1982; Grant, 1985; White, 1977).

musical: ends with a wedding or the promise of one as boy and girl come together after overcoming all obstacles (Sobchack, 1977); music and dance help tell a story, feelings, emotions, instincts are given expression through music, dance (Scheurer, 1977); libretto essential—fusion of music, dance, book (Feuer, 1982; Green, 1981; Altman, 1981; Shout, 1982).

samurai: this genre is Japanese but has traveled abroad so that it now includes western actors and scenes (Desser, 1983).

sports: themes include transitory nature of success, sports settings-locker room (Sayre, 1977).

science fiction: there is no survival outside the group (Sobchack, 1977:49); science will save us if anything, not the individual (Tarratt, 1977); deeply involved with concepts of Freudian psychoanalysis, anxieties about repressed sexual desires (Frank, 1982; Slusser and Rabkin, 1985).

screwball and **slapstick comedy:**   man out-of-keeping with his culture or man vs. woman (Leach, 1977); slapstick comedy depends on collision between man and things or rules; little man as victim (Cavell, 1984; Gehring, 1983; Seidman, 1981).

teenage movies: seen as "beach blanket" films that were popular in the 1950s and early 1960s but in the 1980s teenpics shifted to sex, horror, and other forms for exploitation of teenage concerns, themes, and values; Cruz (1988) found Filipino youth films featuring youth as victim, as villain, as heroes who strike back at perpetrators of injustice or anti-heroes (Doherty, 1988).

war: most popular plot involves a group of men, individuals thrown together from disparate backgrounds, who must be welded together to become a well-oiled fighting machine; Comber and O'Brien, 1988; Dick, 1985; Kane, 1982; Rubin, 1981; Rowe, 1988; Sobchack, 1977:48).

western: "The 'western'. . . has certain crucial established conventions—ritualistic gunfights, black/white clothing corresponding to good/bad distinctions, revenge themes, certain patterns of clothing, types villains, and many, many more" (Garfield, 1982; Hardy, 1983; Jarvie, 1970; Sarf, 1983; Tudor, 1977:18).

women's films: characterized by strong roles for actresses and, more recently, feminist themes (Kuhn, 1984; Waldman, 1984).

---

drama as well as crime/war /action/adventure genres; action and adventure genres were similar on a dimension representing potency or strength. Glass and Waterman (1988) found that students judge new films by reference to past films with similar characteristics—in other words, students naturally used genre to classify films.[9]

TV Content Structures

Some TV stations specialize in particular types of content such as religious programming, classic movies, reruns of past network programs, and so forth.

Within daily schedules we also find patterns or concentrations of TV content designed to appeal to audience segments. We could characterize TV content as "entertainment" or "actuality" programming (news, documentaries); this distinction is similar to the fiction/nonfiction division in literature. However, it is the **TV program** itself which is the most important **content unit** and the one which has some sense of coherence and unity for both the creators and the audience.

The **television format** represents a concept similar to genre in film. Again, the notion is that the public has prior conceptions about what constitutes a particular TV format, such as a situation comedy. This form has a limited, generally indoor setting, a small cast of characters whose interaction is the focus, and "substantive" content which, although it may be of major import in some cases, is generally mundane. Goedkoop (1983) notes that an important ingredient is the development of strong characters. Sitcoms, thus, offer predictable settings and situations that allow the audience to roleplay and vicariously enjoy somewhat exaggerated characterizations.

The number and diversity of formats is limited only by human creativity. Most of us do not seek constant stimulation, particularly the kind that requires attention to structure in order to understand the content or to enjoy the process. Were that the case, all film would be experimental and TV content would represent public acceptance of the artist's desire to be "expressive." A format or genre reduces the need to pay close attention for understanding. It also allows the audience to plan one's behaviors, to watch a sitcom in order to laugh, to enjoy predictable characters acting out roles that make us feel good about our own lives, or to watch a news program that makes us feel we're current on world affairs. In such low-involvement situations like TV viewing, the public has certain expectations about the redundancy of content. Although such expectations exist to some extent in all creative situations, it is much more evident in the case of mass media.

TV formats, like film genre, represent successful compromises between creative ideas and **public expectations**. In the case of TV, new formats generally represent combinations of older formats or subtle changes in the elements generally associated with an existing one. "New" also often means a return to the "old," as formats from the past appear new when recast with today's popular culture, language, and problems (White, 1985). Although TV is a relatively new medium, its history is long enough to suggest that formats or genre may go through cycles of popularity and acceptance. We see some evidence of these ideas in a tabulation of the top-rated programs through the years (Brooks and Marsh, 1981). The format which has enjoyed the most consistent presence among the top programs is the situation comedy. Beginning with "Mama" in 1950, sitcoms have remained among the most popular programming on TV. They were particularly dominant during the early 1970s when they included 15 of the top 25 programs. Examples of sitcoms through the years are: "I Love Lucy," "Gilligan's Island," "The Mary Tyler Moore Show," "Happy Days," "The Cosby Show," and "Murphy Brown" (all in syndication).

Shifts in Popularity of TV Formats.   Shifts in the popularity of TV formats are documented in two overlapping studies covering the period from 1950 to the mid 1980s. In an analysis of 15 years of prime-time TV programming, situation comedies went from 45% in 1970, to 34% in 1975, 39% in 1980, and 28% in 1985 (Signorielli, 1986). The percentages for action-adventure programming were: 40%, 1970; 54%, 1975; 34%, 1980; 45%, 1985. Percentages for serious drama were: 15%, 1970; 12%, 1975; 27%, 1980; 27%, 1985. Looking at a longer time-span, Wakshalag and Adams (1985) used 37 categories to classify all regularly scheduled prime-time TV programs from 1950 through 1982, finding no decline in the variety of network programming.[10] In general, each season was dominated by two to four categories, each accounting for 12-25% of available time. Twenty of the 33 years studied were dominated by three program categories, 7 years were dominated by two categories and 2 years were dominated by four categories. However, the dominant categories shifted through the years. From 1950 to 1969, the top three formats each year tended to change each season following various fads, with westerns popular for a year or two and then replaced by medical shows.[11] The program format categories were: action/adventure, animal shows, animation, children's shows, comic book, crime drama, dance, documentary, dramatic anthology, education, family drama, game shows, general drama, interviews/talk shows/debates, lawyers, light family, magazine series, medical, miscellaneous, films, music, news, occult/horror/suspense, religion, romance, science fiction/fantasy, situation comedy, soap opera, sports, spy, talent, travelogue, variety-comedy, variety-general, variety-music, war, and western. Since 1971, films, crime dramas, and situation comedies have occupied an average of 60% of all regularly scheduled prime time programs and constituted 53% of all new series, with no other format entering the top three since 1971.[12]

A complete listing of TV formats would have to extend beyond the major formats found on daytime or prime-time TV to include the occasional fare that appears on one of the major networks or the programs presented on cable channels—dance contests, Sunday public affairs panel shows, how-to-do-it/fishing/bridge/hobby/cooking shows, educational instruction, weather programs, C-SPAN, music TV and other videos, nature programs, travelogues, musical concerts and opera, videotex, and community access programs.[13]

Nonfiction television is becoming increasingly ambiguous, particularly with TV formats which blend aspects of documentaries and dramas. Barker (1988) notes that the notion of "realism" is encrusted with ideas from centuries of debate and suggests substituting the term "verisimilitude" because it implies the notion of work ("real seeming") and varies by degree. Bower (1985) found that the amount of time devoted to news and information on TV grew from 13% in 1960 to 24% in 1970 and 27% in 1980; that growth in news programming continued into the 1980s and 1990s. In the 1970s actuality programming provided new formats with such popular programs as "60 Minutes." In the 1980s and 1990s, reality programming reappeared in programming featuring real-life violent crime, lurid sex, bizarre behavior, and disasters in such programs as "Rescue: 911" (Cox, 1989).

Some formats enjoy immense popularity for a decade or more and then fade. Examples are the western which peaked with "Bonanza," "Gunsmoke," and "Wagon Train." The variety program in any form virtually disappeared from TV after enjoying top ratings for two-and-a-half decades. "The Ed Sullivan Show," the longest-running example of this format, was first telecast in 1948 and ended in 1971. We also see the **blending of formats**—from pure comedy and dramatic adventure to comedy adventure programs. The format which has grown increasingly differentiated is "drama," which has been represented by medical shows, mini-series, romantic drama, and adventure drama.[14]

TV formats may evolve slowly rather than emerge full-grown. Networks, producers, and creative people often extend a TV format by spinning-off programs from those which have been successful. The spin off has a greater chance of success because the audience is already familiar with the characters or situational aspects of the program. Spin-offs fall into several categories: character spin-offs, such as "Gomer Pyle"; situational spin-offs, where the same locale is used with different or supporting characters—"Mayberry R.F.D."; guest-star spin-offs, in which the lead characters are introduced as guest stars in another series—"Mork and Mindy" from "Happy Days" (Bellamy, McDonald, and Walker, 1990).[15]

Programmers try to follow audience tastes by airing programs similar in type to those currently enjoying success (Beville, 1985). McDonald and Schechter (1988) found support for this proposition, finding higher audience ratings for programs in a particular format were related to the prevalence of programs in three of five program types—physical conflict, comedy, and drama (Auter, 1990).

Ultimately it should be possible to identify TV formats by researching audience perceptions and expectations.[16] Although TV formats may have their origins in the creative minds and interactions of small groups of people, their survival depends on audience acceptance and subsequent use in seeking out and processing content. Thus, the TV show "Law and Order" combined elements of the police detective format with the lawyer/ prosecutor format but it will not emerge as a full-blown format until: a) the public recognizes unique elements or a pattern (perhaps not articulated in the same manner as observers would expect), b) additional creative organizations "produce" other TV programs which would elicit the same public response, and c) the public comes to identify those elements as a particular format.

Public TV emphasizes different program formats from those found on commercial prime-time network television. The two major categories of programs are "informational" (24%) and "cultural" (23%). Children's programming[17] accounts for another 22%, instructional programs for 13% and news/public affairs for 12% (Eastman, Head, and Klein, 1985). Waterman (1986) found that four cable networks provided the same range of cultural programming as public TV, much of it from the same British sources.

Independent TV stations, with fewer resources than network affiliates, produce relatively little original programming. Hale and Vincent (1986) found U.S. independent TV stations producing an average of 3.6 hours weekly (2.5% of total programming). About 30% of the programs were discussion/information programs, followed by 20% religious programming, 17% news, 13% sporting events,[18] and 9% news/feature magazines.

Soap Operas.   The soap opera as a form was developed first on radio, but "The Guiding Light" was transferred to TV in 1952 (Matelski, 1988; Allen, 1985). Analyses of soap operas show that most characters suffer because they are unable to cope with their specific life situations. The soap opera resembles the romance novel (Allen, 1985). An analysis of 33.5 hours of 13 daytime network TV soap operas found that there were 66 acts or references to acts of sexual intercourse (14 visual and 52 verbal), 17 of petting, 8 of prostitution, 3 of rape, and 8 other acts, with the age of most characters involved ranging from 20 to 40.

Game Shows/Contests.   The game show has weathered the quiz show scandals and survived changes in network programming strategies to prosper as a format in syndication (Shaw, 1987). Competition and rewards are essential ingredients of this format, and almost all are contestant-oriented to some degree.[19] The "Wheel of Fortune" is one of the highest-rated syndicated series in TV history, reaching more than 43 million viewers each day.

Late-Night Talk Shows.   The late-night talk show host operates as both a reinforcer of mainstream social values and moderator of potential chaos (Timberg, 1987). Examining "The Tonight Show" starring (at that time) Johnny Carson and "Late Night with David Letterman," Timberg notes that both shows were organized as ritual quests for social knowledge and experience, proceeding through a series of tensions between the host's control and lack of control while touching upon current topics, enduring social values, and championing common sense.

MTV/Music Videos.   Music videos, which now dominate not only MTV but also other cable networks featuring country music and black-oriented music, share characteristics of both commercials and drama. Fry and Fry (1987) did a content analysis of commercials and three types of music videos: concert, conceptual and combination videos.[20] Concert videos focus on the concert performance of a singer or group, while conceptual videos focus on images unrelated to the actual performance of the music, and others combine concerts and conceptual images. Concert videos had an average of 17.91 shots-per-minute, while conceptual videos averaged 20.38 and combination videos 22.90. The shots-per-minute variations made the visual pacing of concert videos more like that of drama, while conceptual and combination videos were more like commercials. Analysis of other features of videos shows them more similar to drama in relying on scenes (continuous flow of action without temporal or spatial breaks). Music videos rely on special effects (Baxter et al. (1985), portrayal of sexual feelings or impulses, dancing, and themes of violence,[21] wealth, friendship, and isolation.[22]

Media Advertising

The diversity of advertising has increased through the years. In the 1970s, the top five categories (over-the-counter medicine,[23] food and beverages, household goods, personal care and automotive) accounted for more than 75% of all commercials aired during evening newscasts, but the figure dropped to about 60% in the mid-1980s as the product mix diversified to include more financial services, office/school supplies, TV shows, transportation, utilities, and department stores.

The **level of information** in advertising also has increased, according to a sample of 2,000 magazine advertisements from the twentieth century to the present (Pollay, 1984, 1985). About one-third of the advertisements focused on product characteristics and two-thirds focused on benefits from use or consumption. A focus on simple description of product characteristics was popular at the turn of the century but declined steadily afterwards. Materialistic themes and appeals to luxury and pleasure also increased in frequency (Belk and Pollay, 1985, 1987). Another study of magazine ads showed an increase from 1967 to 1984 in ads reflecting social-responsibility issues. Receiving the most attention were health and safety, consumerism, ecology, and the physical environment (Lill, Gross, and Peterson, 1986). One study of magazine ads from the 1930s to the 1980s indicated a movement toward simplification, with fewer illustrations, fewer words in headlines, fewer people in visual parts of ads, and a less cluttered look overall (Feasley and Stuart, 1987). Although radio ads generally are not seen as containing much information, a study of more than a thousand such ads found 99% contained at least one information cue, with a third containing three or more cues.[24]

Advertising appeals vary across countries. For example, a sample of Japanese and American magazine advertising showed that Japanese ads were more emotionally oriented than U.S. advertising and contained fewer comparative ads. Both U.S. and Japanese TV commercials used cues emphasizing similar kinds of information, but they differed in the number employed for various products and strategies. The most commonly used cues referred to package, performance, content, price/value, taste, quality, and availability.[25]

Print Media Content Structures

The print media themselves vary as content structures. Books represent the most indepth treatment of concepts, themes, or stories. Magazines are more timely, but still present a somewhat lengthy treatment of materials. Newspapers generally represent the briefest and most current treatment. Certainly, there are lengthy newspaper articles, short magazine pieces, and book collections of little more than isolated anecdotes. Furthermore, like the visual media, we have some content structures which are found across the media forms themselves. Examples would be news articles, news magazines, and instant news books relying heavily on pictures.

The two major content areas in newspapers are **news** and **advertising**. News must occupy at least a third of the available space for a paper to obtain second-class mailing rates. Advertising is the most important content in shoppers and freely distributed papers (Hunt and Cheney, 1982). Advertising generally accounts for more than half of newspaper space.[26] Newspapers have become increasingly segmented as content is aimed at target audiences. Some content has the intent of informing readers, but it must also attract attention and maintain interest. This marriage of factors is partly responsible for the changing content structures found in newspapers and other print media.

Content varies by newspaper size, with smaller newspapers devoting greater percentages of their total space to news and editorial material as a whole but smaller percentages to foreign news, editorial/op-ed content, letters to the editor, guest columns, and copy generated by local staffs (Lacy and Bernstein, 1988). In a survey of more than 1,310 U.S. daily newspapers, Bogart (1985) notes shifts in U.S. newspaper content. A typical weekday paper now has an average of 18 news and editorial pages with a growing use of zoned editions aimed at particular geographic regions within the circulation area. He notes that one striking change has been sectionalization. For example, 25% of the daily papers added "lifestyle" sections between 1981 and 1983. Increases in news coverage of sports and business also were reported. A wide variety of features is now regularly found in American newspapers.[27] Bogart concludes that the mix of newspaper subject matter has not changed much in recent surveys, with no dramatic shifts in newspaper content devoted to crime, public health, taxes, or Hollywood. Three trends which were identified are: an increase in the ratio of features to hard news content, a reduction in the number of regular standing columns and features dealing with specialized interests, and a reduction in the ratio of national and world news to local news.

Newspaper **editorial pages** continue to play vital roles, with 97% of daily papers devoting at least one page a day to editorials and such related features as cartoons, columns and letters to the editor (Hynds, 1984, 1990). The amount of space devoted to editorials also seems to be growing. Most of the larger papers include op-ed pages. More than a quarter of dailies employ local cartoonists for these pages and most use syndicated cartoons such as Pat Oliphant and Herbert Block. Nine in 10 include syndicated columnists such as James Kilpatrick, and more than 60% have local columnists as well; the former are selected more for their ability to draw readers regardless of philosophy.[28]

Today editorial pages include features that make them a forum for the exchange of information and opinion across diverse readership groups. Editors themselves see not only a community leadership function in the editorial page content but also a variety of other goals. These include: attracting readers to the papers, educating people on issues, sorting out important issues and stimulating the public's thoughts about them, helping people understand trends and developments, stirring the community to get a public opinion response, reflecting wants and needs of the community, allowing public access to the medium, encouraging a local exchange of ideas, making people think, criticizing official malfeasance, evaluating candidates for public office, being the community's conscience, and establishing the character of the paper. Clearly, the content of the editorial pages has changed to meet what editors see as an expanding range of functions, often including interpretations, guest essays, cartoonists, columnists, letters, editorials, and analyses by journalists and contributors.

Print Media Graphics. The appearance of newspaper content—the **typography**—is increasingly important today, a fact which is illustrated by the success of Gannett's national daily, *USA Today*, with its use of color and charts. The "graphics" of newspapers parallel the "visual style" of TV and film. Gottschall (1989) describes the remarkable power of graphics to make information more noticed, more attractive, more understandable. Major design changes are not new to newspapers. Barnhurst and Nerone (1991) looked at changes in front pages of three newspapers over a century, finding that changes were gradual rather than revolutionary, with a steady increase in the width of columns and headlines and a steady decline in the average number of headline decks[29] and the percentage of stories with bylines. In the 1960s a revolution of sorts occurred as papers moved to more readable type, eliminated rules between columns and emphasized horizontal makeup (Sissors, 1965). Today more papers than ever are paying attention to their appearance and many are hiring graphics designers. In a survey of front pages of American newspapers, Utt and Pasternack (1989) found that 57% are printed offset— which allows for sharper photographs, 82% use a 6-column front page, and

70% begin six to nine stories on the front page.[30] A third of papers run an index and a digest on their front page.[31] In one study, newspapers averaged 4.5 graphics per edition (Smith and Hajash, 1988), with more used in Sunday editions. Maps were used the most frequently, half of the time associated with weather (Monmonier, 1989).

The latter half of the 1980s and the 1990s have produced even more far-reaching design shifts.[32] Movement toward modular design is affecting the way news is emphasized on the front page. Utt and Pasternack (1989) found that papers still tend to follow the traditional practice of placing the day's main headline in the upper right corner (40%) or spanning the top of the page, but 32% follow no pattern for placement of the lead story headline. A majority of the papers run an average of two photos on page one and 95% use a dominant, large photograph. Some 56% use four-color photographs and 65% use spot color every day on page one.[33]

The significance of graphic design is not limited to newspapers. Moriarty (1982) looked at elements of magazine ads, concluding that those in special-interest magazines seemed to be striving for a distinctive fashionable statement in a manner which led them to risk functional problems such as legibility or readability. Those appearing in magazines aimed at general audiences tended to follow design strategies which avoided such problems.

Other Features in Newspapers.   In addition to news, papers include a variety of special features, some produced by local staffs and others purchased from national syndicates. Bogart (1990) notes that **columns** and **features** carried by newspapers have been cut back in the past two decades because of emphasis on staff-written stories and reduced use of syndicated material. In 1987, 63% of newspapers carried an **entertainment section** at least once a week, while 58% did on Sunday and 34% every weekday. **Reviews** of TV programs and movies were carried by 47–49% of newspapers at least once a week, and weekly book reviews were available in 26% of daily papers. Almost three-fourths of articles in a sample of nationally distributed **gossip columns** were positive in tone, with 61% focusing on celebrities from show business or politics (Levin, Mody-Desbareau, and Arluke, 1988). A national sample of daily newspapers found that 82% devote a fourth of a page or less to **weather news**, temperatures and weather graphics on an average day, while 18% devote a half page to weather; 38% had increased the space devoted to weather in recent years, with a fourth citing the influence of USA Today, which devotes a full page to weather (Anderson and Anderson, 1986). In the 1980s, newspaper space devoted to **letters from readers** increased, (Kapoor and Botan, 1989). One-half of newspapers publish more than 80% of letters received, a figure that drops to less than 5% for large papers. Editors agree that letters help to personalize the newspaper, "reflect a multitude of views and moods" and "provide a safety valve for readers."[34]

News in Print and Broadcast Media

News content has been analyzed on various dimensions: soft vs. hard news (Scott and Gobetz, 1992; Turow, 1983),[35] events vs. situations or issues,[36] straight news vs. features vs. opinions (Hohenberg, 1978; Wyatt and Badger, 1990), news reports (succinct reporting of facts about events), articles (more analytic form), and stories (more literary form) (McCombs, Son, and Bang, 1988),[37] and news focusing on the established and powerful vs. the powerless and unknown.

At the **local TV news** level, Wulfemeyer (1982) divided TV newscast content into seven categories: non-news, issues, unexpected events, entertainment, banter, sports, and weather. At the station analyzed, coverage of unexpected events took up about 6 minutes of each newscast, while sports took 5 minutes and weather 4.5 minutes. Discussion between on-air personalities was less than 3 minutes per newscast and non-news items took up the largest amount of newscast time, reaching a third of one station's content. The newscasts were fast paced and averaged 28 separate stories.

Patterns are found in the style of presentation,[38] which has been affected by **technology**. Use of film or video, particularly in news originating abroad, has been linked to the spread of satellite technology (Larson, 1984).[39] A breakdown of U.S. network themes by story format shows that 37% were anchor reports, while 34% were foreign video reports and 29% domestic video reports (Larson, 1984). Butters (1990) looked at the impact of electronic news gathering (ENG) on news presentation of a network affiliate, concluding that satellite news gathering expanded the geographical area from which stories were generated (for greater state and regional coverage) and increased use of live shots. Smith (1989) found that the length of sound bites in evening network TV newscasts shrank from 31.5 seconds in 1968 to 10.3 seconds in 1988, while the number of sound bites per newscast story grew. This was attributed in part to a shift to video tape.

Topical Emphasis.   What are the topics of news stories? Analysis of front pages of five newspapers[40] found that politics accounted for 24% of news topics, followed by human interest, 18%; sports, 17%; economics, 12%; crime, 7%; entertainment, 6%; violence, 5%; accidents, 4%; science, 2%; health, 2%; and recreation, social news, social problems, and education, 1% each (Lester, 1988).[41]

In addition to politics and social accounts, economics is a major topic in the news. Reese, Daly, and Hardy (1987) found in a ten-year study of network TV broadcasts that economic news occupied significant portions of the news. Government economic reports accounted for 37% of economic news and the private sector 38%, while economic indicators, e.g., unemployment rate, cost of living, stock market, accounted for 9% and foreign economic reports for

16%. Looking at the two Chicago dailies and both network and local news broadcasts of network affiliates for a year ending in August, 1991, Graber (1992) grouped news stories into five topics, finding governmental affairs accounting for 20-22% of the newspaper topics, 47-57% of network TV topics, and 32-35% of local TV news topics. Her sample showed that sports and entertainment accounted for 42-51% of newspaper topics and about a fourth of those on local TV newscasts. Economic issues were more important in newspapers and national TV newscasts, while social issues were more important in all TV newscasts compared to the two newspapers.

Looking only at TV broadcasts, Whitney, Fritzler, Jones, Mazzarella, and Rakow (1989) found the most frequent topics in a sample of national network TV newscasts were: economic matters (25.8%), domestic politics (19.3%), military and defense (18.4%), international politics (17.8%), and crime, judicial, legal topics (16.5%). While three-fourths of network TV news focused on the U.S., the Mideast was the next most frequent focus, followed by Western Europe, Central America, the former Soviet Union, and then Central Europe. Within the U.S., 22.8% of stories focused on the Northeast region, followed by the Pacific (19.5%) and Midwest (18.7%); weighting regions by population, the Pacific region was the most over-represented region in the news and the Midwest the most under-represented.[42] McGill (1991) content analyzed the evening news programs of the three broadcast networks from 1988-1990, finding that wars and the economy led in 1990.[43] The five major U.S. TV networks examined in one study are similar in topics covered; however, the Cable News Network (CNN) emphasizes more popular amusement and has a stronger international orientation, while the Public Broadcasting Service (PBS) emphasizes classic arts and education more (Stempel, 1988).[44]

Cable News Network's "World Report" has received growing attention because it includes reports produced by many countries. The program carries stories collected by broadcast news organizations around the world and run unedited and uncensored. The most common story topics in one study were: national politics (18%), economics (8.1%), diplomacy (7.5%), culture (6.9%), and military (5.6%). The topic mix varied over time, with coverage of only three topics remaining relatively stable (arts, economics, animals).[45] Ganzert and Flournoy (1992) found significant differences between that program and news broadcasts of the three largest U.S. TV networks. For example, the arts category ranked first on the World Report but only thirteenth in network reporting.[46]

Foreign vs. Domestic News. The foreign vs. domestic news distinction has been analyzed most frequently. American newspapers devoted 30% of the newshole to foreign news in 1809, 17% in 1810 and about 7% in 1812 (Avery, 1986). In recent decades, international news decreased from more than 10% in 1971 to only 2.6% in 1988 (Emery, 1989). A content analysis of three national newspapers in Japan put the figure at 5.2% in 1984 (Tamura, 1987). Studies show a consistent picture of foreign news on the major TV networks from the 1970s through the 1980s. About 40% of network news deals either with other countries or with activities of the U.S. that involve other countries.[47] Topical content was diverse but concentrated in the following four areas: military-defense, foreign relations, domestic political activities, and crime-justice-terrorism. Similar emphases have been found on national TV newscasts and in newspapers of other countries and on international wire services.[48]

Good vs. Bad News.   Some people avoid the news because they find so much of it depressing, and critics have often chastised the media for emphasizing negative stories. How much of the news is "good" vs. "bad"? Stone, Hartung, and Jensen (1987) sampled local evening TV news in three cities, finding 43% of the items covered represented "bad news," compared to 47% in a national network TV news study. In all three local markets, there were more bad news stories than good news stories. In an earlier study, Stone and Grusin (1984) found almost twice as many bad news stories as good news stories on national TV evening newscasts.

Media Images, Stereotypes, and Portrayals

Media images are central to discussions about the impact of communication on relationships between people, the sexes, age groups, ethnic groups, cities, and countries. Representatives from these groups decry what they see as unfair media images. For example, the cultural indicators project compares its findings with the demographic profile provided by U.S. census figures (Signorielli, 1983). The world of TV drama has a very different demographic structure than the U.S. and is dominated by white men in traditionally powerful, important, and adventurous occupations. Such critiques represent an effort to change the images. However, concern with media images extends beyond the traditional categories to include those concerned with institutions, professions, diseases, social interaction, problems like drugs and alcoholism, etc. In most cases, the issue is whether media portrayals are negative or "fair" in the eyes of their proponents, and whether an adequate amount of attention is being paid.

Debates over whether media images are fair often assume that media content should represent some definition of "real life," often described in terms of demographics. However, the purpose of much media content is to portray the dramatic rather than the mundane, the unusual (a defining aspect of news) rather than the average, the deviant rather than the typical or the norm. Whether one chooses a particular side in these debates is a matter of personal values.

Ethnicity—Increasing Diversity

Concern with media stereotypes has long been an issue among different ethnic groups. The concern has spread across all media—from stereotypes of Chinese and American Indians in Hollywood movies of the 1930s to charges that Arabs are stereotyped in U.S. TV programs and film today. A national survey of 1,700 adults showed that both Anglos and Hispanics believe there were more media portrayals of Mexican-Americans doing bad things than good things. Many of these groups note that some of their individual identity is tied to these "corporate entities." If the larger entity suffers, the individual suffers in some smaller way (Van Dyke, 1977).

What are the images of ethnics in various mass media?

African Americans.   The media portrayal or news coverage of African-Americans has received increasing attention (Harris, 1992). Berry (1980) notes that there have been three major periods in the **portrayal of blacks on TV**: 1) the stereotypic age, 1948-1965, when the medium reflected and reinforced the attitudes of the dominant culture; 2) the new awareness, 1965-1972, when TV was sensitized by the Civil Rights movement and urban unrest; blacks were consciously represented as competent, positive members of society; and 3) stabilization, 1972 to the present, when there is less pressure to include a black in every situation but more effort to be realistic and focus on universal personal concerns of specific characters.[49] Lichter, Lichter, Rothman, and Amundson (1987) found that blacks have gradually progressed from invisibility to integration on TV, moving from a low of 1% of characters in the 1950s to one in ten since 1975. Atkin (1992) found a steady increase in series with minority lead characters from 1948 to 1991. Gerbner reported in 1993 that African-Americans comprise about 11% of the network primetime dramatic population but only 3% of the casts of children's programs after analyzing more than 19,000 speaking parts on news and programs of the major networks and cable.[50]

MacDonald (1983) notes that TV in the 1950s offered better roles for blacks than any other medium, but the bright promise was unfulfilled for many years. Early TV often spotlighted black talent on variety series; thus, Pearl Bailey, Louis Armstrong, and Cab Calloway appeared on "Your Show of Shows" and the "Garry Moore Show," etc. This was a breakthrough for black entertainers who had not been used consistently in network radio in the preceding two decades. However, blacks found few opportunities in video drama; a program with both a black and a white detective, "Harlem Detective," lasted only three months in 1953. There were roles in such stereotyped situation comedies as "Amos 'n Andy." The break-through for black drama stars came when Bill Cosby joined Robert Culp in "I Spy" in the mid-1960s. Nat King Cole in the late 1950s was the first black performer to host a TV show of his own.

Three consecutive seasons of U.S. network TV in the 1970s were sampled by Greenberg and Neuendorf (1980), beginning with the fall of 1975. They looked at black families' role interactions and how they compared with white TV families. The findings showed that black TV families were almost exclusively nuclear and had more children than their white counter-parts. Black mothers and sons were overrepresented and the male role in black families was generally more energetic than white male TV roles. Black family members also were more often portrayed in interpersonal conflict.[51] This scenario was updated in the 1980s by Stroman, Merritt, and Matabane (1989).[52] Unlike earlier years when men vastly outnumbered women, the gender ratio was about equal. Also, a sizeable 44% of the characters were 35 years or older and 16% age 50 or older, a reduction in the emphasis on youth from earlier studies. Most African-Americans were portrayed as belonging to the middle and upper social classes, with 31% cast as professionals or managers; however, law enforcement-related roles still constituted the single largest category (38%). Characters tended to be portrayed as competent, and some 19% were cast in major roles, 59% in supporting roles. Sixty percent of the characters were members of families.[53] Half of the characters lived in racially-mixed neighborhoods and 38% lived in all-black neighborhoods. A majority of the males (60%) and females (82%) appeared in situation comedies. Thus, like other groups, blacks tend to do better on TV than they do in real life (Gates, 1990). A comparison of Brazilian and U.S. commercial TV showed that black and brown Brazilians of African origin also were underrepresented on TV there (Leslie and Barlow, 1991).[54] Others have looked at blacks in TV news[55] and TV commercials. Black representation in TV commercials approximates their numbers in the U.S. population[56] and has grown considerably over the past three decades in all advertising.[57]

Films with urban themes have increased, as have influences by black directors in recent years. Berry (1992) analyzed 15 popular films by black directors featuring black stars and plots, all distributed in 1989-1991. The recent renewal period is reminiscent of the black exploitation era of the 1970s when black directors and independent films were afforded unprecedented popularity. While some positive changes in the roles of black women were noted, the black woman as sex object was still prominent.[58] Black women were relegated to minor roles or bit parts in most films. Of the 105 roles, 38% showed black women as sex objects, 36% as the lady/good woman, 18% as mammy/mother, 5% as tragic mulatto/addict, and 3% as super woman.

Turning to **print media**, we see blacks again underrepresented but their numbers increasing over the decades. Several studies have documented an increasing attention to African Americans in **magazines** (Zinkhan, Cox, and Hong, 1986).[59] A breakdown by subject categories shows that advertisements accounted for 44% of African-American images in 1937-1952, compared to only 25% by 1978-1988. In general, African-American images were distributed more evenly across categories in the more recent period (1978-1988), with 10.6% representing prominent persons, 9.4% people engaging in everyday life activity, 10.1% crime, 14% social commentary, 18.3% sports figures, 12.6% entertainment figures, and 2.1% magazine covers. Ortizano (1989) looked at photographs in advertisements and editorial content to see if they were segregated by race. He found photographs in editorial content of six magazines[60] were more racially mixed than were those in advertising content. A sample of *New Yorker* magazine cartoons showed that all cartoons from the earliest period presented blacks in stereotypic occupational roles, but by the 1960s and early 1970s, racial themes dominated (Thibodeau, 1989).[61]

Coverage of blacks in **newspapers** also has increased. Martindale (1985, 1986, 1990) found that the percentage of the newshole devoted to covering blacks went up from the 1950s to the 1960s but then dropped in the 1970s for three of five papers analyzed, rising again in the 1980s.[62] However, while space in the 1950s tended to reflect stereotypic images, in the 1960s coverage was related to civil rights activities and in the 1970s shifted toward blacks' activities in everyday life, a trend that intensified in the 1980s.[63]

Crime news is important because it has the potential for casting minorities in an unfavorable light. Pritchard (1985) found racial differences in coverage of homicides in two Wisconsin newspapers. However, it was the race of the suspect, not the victim, that best predicted how a homicide would be covered. Stories about homicides with minority suspects tended to be shorter than others. Entman (1990, 1992) looked at 55 days of local TV news of three network affiliates and one independent station in Chicago, finding that politics comprised the largest single category of stories involving blacks, followed by crime. Together they accounted for almost half of all stories in which blacks appeared.[64]

Hispanic Americans.   As the population of Hispanic Americans has grown, attention to the images portrayed in the media have also increased. In recent years, a gradual change in images of Hispanics in U.S. films has occurred, particularly in films where Hispanics helped create the product—*La Bamba* (1987) and *Stand and Deliver* (1988). However, when such inputs are not involved, shifts in attitudes represent only variations in prevailing stereotypes of Mexican characters. Berg (1989) identifies six Hollywood stereotypes of the Hispanic: "El Bandido," the Mexican bandit, an older image in films; the "half-breed harlot," the corresponding female image common in early westerns; the "male buffoon," second banana comic relief as in the roles of Pancho in "The Cisco Kid"; the "female clown," a way of neutralizing the overt sexual threat posed by the half-breed harlot; the "Latin lover," stemming from Rudolph Valentino; and the "dark lady," mysterious, virginal, inscrutable. One study of prime-time TV reported Hispanics were disproportionately portrayed as criminals.[65]

Hispanic **news coverage** is changing, with some evidence Hispanics are favorably covered. Underrepresentation of Hispanics in news stories was noted in an analysis of six southwestern newspapers (Greenberg et al., 1983), but a cross-media study found Hispanic news presented as prominently across the media as non-Hispanic news (Heeter et al., 1983). Turk, Richstad, Bryson, and Johnson (1988, 1989) studied two daily papers in New Mexico and Texas, finding Hispanic stories and photos were larger, had bigger headlines and were more prominently placed than were those focusing on Anglos. Hispanic news also was less likely to focus on bad news or problem people, compared with coverage of Anglos.[66]

American Indians. Coverage of Indians in North America has been examined in both the U.S. and Canada. Murphy and Avery (1982, 1983) looked at eight Alaskan newspapers and found coverage in native-owned papers was more pro-native than that in the non-native press, although attitudes toward native peoples were positive in both. The establishment press paid relatively little attention to native Alaskan news, but the types of stories were similar to those in the native press. In Ontario, Canada, a study found that the image of the Indian or Eskimo was based on land claims and dependence on government help (Singer, 1982).

Other Ethnics. Media images of Asians, white ethnic groups,[67] and immigrant groups also have been examined. Simon (1985) notes that media coverage of new immigrant groups in the late 1800s also tended to be hostile, with many of the same biases found today even though the groups have changed. Asian groups, though growing in numbers, have been fairly small and have also been portrayed stereotypically when represented in the media (Jen, 1991). That too is changing as Asians become more involved in the creation of media images. Dodd, Foerch, and Anderson (1988) found no Asian-Americans or American-Indians on the cover of *Time* or *Newsweek* magazines from the 1950s through the 1980s. Shaheen (1988) found stereotypical images of Arabs in TV programs from 1975-1985, with Arab villains appearing frequently in children's programming. General themes identified were: Arabs are wealthy; Islam is radical; Arabs are sex maniacs and white slavers; Arabs are nomads; Arabs are buying up America; Iranians are Arabs; and Arab is synonymous with OPEC—the Oil Producing and Exporting Countries group.

Age and Images of the Elderly

Although there is interest in other stages in the life cycle, most of the attention on age has focused on media images of the elderly. How are **seniors** portrayed in the media? Historically, most people did not believe they would live a long life; thus, little attention was likely to be paid to old age. In the various scenarios on the stages of life, old age was a time for contemplation, wisdom, spiritual restoration, and repentance, as well as decay, lust, foolishness, poor health, and dementia (Covey, 1989). Age-appropriate behaviors were tied to the stages of life. As the proportion reaching old age has grown, old age and other stages of the life cycle have become less defined by the appropriateness of behaviors.

As the American population ages, we would expect older people to receive greater attention in the media. Numerous studies in past decades have shown age biases in media portrayals of old age (Powell and Williamson, 1985). The Greenberg et al. (1980) sample of three TV seasons found that persons in the 65 and older age group were increasingly less visible on TV, comprising about 3% of all TV characters by the 1977-78 season. A disproportionate percentage of older characters was found in situation comedies, and there was a clear male bias in portrayal of the elderly.[68] More recently, Dail (1988) analyzed 193 characters playing elderly adults on 12 family-oriented prime-time **TV programs**, finding that 22% were in family roles and 78% in other contexts, such as jobs. Males accounted for 46% and females 30.5% on the programs. A comparison of the top ten programs in the U.S. and Japan found younger age categories portraying 58% of characters in the U.S. and 75% in Japan (Holtzman and Akiyama, 1985). U.S. programs were more heavily weighted toward roles of people age 40 and older (42% of U.S. characters, 25% of Japanese characters).

The elderly also are infrequently found in **TV commercials**. Swayne and Greco (1987) found that 6.7 to 7.2% of a sample of commercials on network TV used elderly people, compared to the 12% they represent in the U.S. population. In this case, the number of elderly females was higher than that for males.[69] A similar portrait has been found in magazines. Bramlett-Solomon and Wilson (1989) found 1.8% of advertisements in *Life* magazine from 1978 to 1987 featured the elderly, while 1.7% of those in *Ebony* featured seniors.[70]

Newspaper coverage of the elderly was examined in a comparison of 10 **newspapers** that included the *St. Petersburg Times* (a city which has a concentration of elderly people). The Florida paper had the most coverage of the aged and devoted almost 5% of its space to them, almost double the average of 2.5% for all ten papers. Second highest was the *New York Times*, which devoted 3.5% of its space to the aged. The tone of newspaper stories was positive or neutral and did not support criticism that newspapers are creating negative images of the aged (Broussard et al., 1980). In another study of two newspapers, Flocke (1990) found 12.2% of all stories mentioned older persons, although only 1.4% were about an elderly topic.[71]

Families and Children—Portraying the Rest of the Life Cycle

Those at the other end of the age spectrum, children, also receive proportionately little media coverage (Dennis and Sadoff, 1976). The coverage received often is more institutionally oriented rather than people-oriented, emphasizing administrative issues such as school boards and taxes. Jackson (1986) notes that the American conception of childhood has undergone several variations which have been mirrored in the media, particularly film. At the turn of the century, the image of the "good child" predominated in films dealing with children. This view of innocence continued into the 1920s—Charlie Chaplin's "The Kid" and "America's Sweetheart," Mary Pickford. Films of the early 1920s espoused the glories of childhood innocence and adult corruption. In the following decade, the era of the child star continued as children solved problems adults could not during the depression. In the 1940s, nostalgia of childhood became a major theme; after the war, children often were portrayed as alone or troubled. In the 1950s the child-as-monster emerged along with the rebellion of youth and a focus on parent-child problems.

Starting with the 1960s, images of the child have included precocious children (such as *The Bad News Bears*), mature geniuses, emotionally starved and confused children (*Taxi Driver*), and both passive tykes and monsters (*Rosemary's Baby, The Omen*). In the 1970s and 1980s, the precocious child image in films suggests social disintegration of the family, although Steven Spielberg's films tried to recapture child-as-innocent images in *Close Encounters of the Third Kind* and *ET*. A comparison of American and Dutch programming found that children were underrepresented in relation to their numbers in the population (Bouwman and Signorelli, 1985). Children also have been used as sex objects in advertising in recent years (Kilbourne, 1991). Falchikov (1986) found that victimization and criminal activity of adolescents were overemphasized by British newspapers, while sports was underemphasized. Hendrickson (1992) found that press coverage of child maltreatment has shifted from an emphasis on crime earlier in the century to a psychological frame in the 1960s and 1970s, to an emphasis on social problems more recently.

One report (Kaplan, 1984) found that 36% of families on new series in the fall of 1984 were traditional, two-parent families while 10% of all the women portrayed on TV were divorced and 9% widowed. Skill, Robinson, and Wallace (1987) found that 21 of 58 series per year used the family as the primary story vehicle, with more than half of situation comedies using the family as the program focus, while 24% of dramatic series emphasized the family unit. Some two-thirds of prime-time network series from 1979 to 1985 focused on the conventional family, while 34% emphasized the nonconventional family configuration.

The Greenberg et al. (1980) study included an analysis of 73 family units depicted during one TV season. Four basic types of families were presented: the nuclear family, one parent with one child, couples without children, and the "conglomerate" of many relatives. The vast majority of TV characters portrayed had no relatives and divorce was infrequent. An analysis of family interaction showed that nuclear family males were the initiators of 50% of all family acts, with nuclear females accounting for 36%.[72]

How is **family life** portrayed on TV? Three popular prime-time TV shows were analyzed to determine the interaction between siblings. Most encounters were positive (almost two-thirds of interactions were positive on "The Cosby Show"), but the behaviors emphasized conflict, particularly between older brothers and younger sisters (Larson, 1989). During the 1950s, interaction between siblings was more positive (Larson, 1991). Another study of 23 prime-time network entertainment programs with family relationships in 1987–1988 found an average of almost 9 conflict situations per hour of programming (Comstock and Strzyzewski, 1990). Most instances of conflict occurred in situation comedies (55%), rather than evening serials (26%) or dramas (19%).[73]

Three major strategies are used to resolve conflict on TV: integrative strategies, which include emphasizing commonalities, accepting responsibility, initiating problem solving, and showing empathy or support; distributive strategies, which are destructive and entail competition and primacy of personal goals, involve blaming, hostile questioning or joking, and personal rejection; and conflict avoidance strategies, such as pretending to be hurt, postponing the issue, shifting the topic, denying the conflict exists, etc. Mothers initiating conflict with children used integrative strategies (45%), while dads tended to use distributive strategies (50%) (Comstock and Strzyzewski, 1990).[74]

Interaction and decision making within families reflects power relationships and efforts to solve problems while mediating relationships. With a growing concern that children are learning how to act by modeling communication patterns on TV, researchers have begun looking at what models are presented on TV programs. In the 1992 election campaign, the vice president attacked the TV sitcom "Murphy Brown" for "glorifying" unwed motherhood and not representing "family values." Skill and Wallace (1990) looked at all prime-time series where the family unit was the major story vehicle in 1987 and analyzed family communication and interaction patterns. Intact family units (married couples alone or with children or other family members) accounted for 40% of the roles portrayed, while non-intact families (those lacking one or both parents but with children) represented another 30% and mixed family units (two or more families representing both intact and non-intact units) about 30%. Intact families were the most harmonious and their family members least likely to engage in power acts or rejection acts and less likely to exhibit conformity behaviors. Mixed family units were least harmonious and exhibited rejection and conformity behaviors. Non-intact families were between the other two in terms of harmony. Results also showed that brothers tended to contribute little to family harmony in any family configuration.[75]

The role of mothers and fathers within families has shifted in **print media** through the years. Day and Mackey (1986) note that the American father portrayed in the *Saturday Evening Post* before the 1970s was shown as one of bumbling irrelevance and ineffectiveness, an image which has changed to "mother substitute" since. Henry (1984) looked at seven women's magazines, concluding that charges they perpetuated the "superwoman myth" were only partially warranted. Many of the problems of combining job and family were consistently recognized.

Depiction of sexual behavior on prime-time TV has not diminished over a 10-year period from 1979 to 1989, according to a study by Sapolsky and Tabarlet (1991). Explicit intercourse, not found in 1979, was "shown" in 1989. Portrayal of touching, hugging, kissing, implied intercourse, and various combinations increased per hour of viewing. Sex in prime-time occurs primarily among the unmarried, and sexual acts and words are generally initiated by males. Larson (1991) analyzed a year of the sexual activity on the soap opera "All My Children," finding that 31% of the kissing occurred among married people, while another 24% was among those committed and planning to marry and 28% was among committed partners not intending to marry. Only 11% was between people in uncommitted relationships.

Gender—Images of Men and Women

The feminist movement in the 1960s focused attention on media portrayals of women. Researchers around the world have looked at how media treat men and women differently.[76] Numerous studies now document an **improving picture of women** in the media,[77] although a recent study found that women still are underrepresented and portrayed as less successful and aging faster on TV.[78]

There has been some increase in the representation of women and the diversity of their **occupational portrayals** on TV. Vande Berg and Streckfuss'(1992) analysis of 116 prime-time TV programs on the three major networks in a 1986-1987 sample found that male characters outnumbered female characters two to one. Both men and women were featured in service roles most often—51% of the women and 44% of the men. Men also were featured frequently in public administration roles, such as law enforcement, courts, national security (29%); 15% of women's roles were in this area, while 18% of women's roles and 12% of men's roles were in no industry at all. Signorielli (1989) analyzed sex roles presented on prime-time network dramatic programs from 1969 to 1985, finding more than 14,000 male characters and almost 5,700 female characters. Men tended to be older while women were younger.[79] While 68% of men were in working roles, only 48% of women were in working roles;[80] women were more likely to be in student roles or in roles where the occupation was unknown (37%, compared to 18% for men).[81] Men were more likely to commit violence in their roles (22.5% vs. 9.5% for women) and to be hurt (21% vs. 13% for women) or killed (4.7% vs. 2.2% for women). Atkin (1991) found that the number of TV series with single working women grew from 1966 to 1990, with the greatest growth in the late 1970s and early 1980s when networks experimented and cable competition began. The trend stabilized in the early 1980s and the average remained above pre-1975 levels. More women are featured in situation comedies than action-adventure or serious dramatic programs (Atkin, 1991; Signorielli, 1986).

The **role of men as fathers** has evolved as that of women has changed. Cantor (1990) looked at domestic TV comedies from the 1950s through the 1980s, noting that the women in more recent TV families are more independent and fathers more caring and domesticated. However, certain basic attitudes about male-female relationships have remained constant in two general themes persisting over the decades in sitcoms: the myth of female dominance and the breakdown of male authority, and the theme that men also can be good, kind and understanding.

An analysis of prime-time TV humor showed that men were the object of humor or disparagement more than females—perhaps because of their greater numbers on TV. Males were more likely to disparage females than the reverse. Nonsexual humor was more frequent than sexual humor (Suls and Gastoff, 1981). An analysis of male-female interaction on daytime serials showed that male dominance of females occurred most often in business dyads.[82] Spangler (1989) notes that realistic female friendships are the trend in 1980s TV portrayals, with women friends discussing not only emotional concerns but current issues in general. A preference for viewing men's faces and women's bodies in pictorial media has been termed **face-ism**. Copeland's (1989) study of prime-time network TV programs confirmed the gender difference, with women seen via longer shots from a distance.[83]

Women are less likely than men to appear in **TV news programs**, though their numbers have grown considerably. Foote (1992) looked at the gender of correspondents on TV newscasts of the major networks from 1983 to 1989, finding that 84% of the correspondents were men and 16% women. The figures for women were static over the seven years. Women also registered no gains in the frequency of exposure during this period.[84] Men also tend to be the newsmakers in TV news reports in numerous countries, including the U.S., India, and Japan.[85] Rakow and Kranich (1991) found that 50% of on-camera appearances by women as network TV news sources in a 1986 sample were as private individuals, while 16% were as experts and authorities, 13% as spokespersons, 8% candidates and politicians, 8% celebrities, 4% political activists, and 2% others.

Gender in Music Videos.   Music videos tend to be male-dominated and contain heavy sex-related themes consistent with the interests of youthful audiences. Vincent, Davis, and Boruszkowski (1987) looked at a 1985 sample of music videos aired on Music TV (MTV), finding the depiction of gender roles to be fairly traditional and sexism high. Women were portrayed in "condescending" roles that emphasized them as one-dimensional sex objects in more than half of the videos, while only a fifth presented women in fully equal roles. Almost two-thirds of the characters were male. For the most part, occupational roles were stereotypically male (for example, manual laborer, mechanic, firefighter) or stereotypically female (for example, secretary, librarian). More evenly distributed roles were artists, singer, actor, lab assistant. Male characters were more adventuresome, domineering, aggressive, violent, and victimized than female characters, who were more affectionate, dependent, nurturing, and fearful.[86]

Women in Film.   The portrayal of women in American cinema over the past 60 years confirms the differential treatment found in TV and other media (Levy, 1990).[87] For example, while men are more likely to receive Oscars for performances in drama (60%) and adventure (19%) films, women are recognized for drama (51%) and romance (18%). While male Oscar-winners include 30% identified as old, 51% middle aged and 18% adolescent or young, only 15% of women winning Oscars were old and 21% middle aged, with more than 62% young and 4% adolescent. The distribution of roles by gender also shows sex-role stereotyping.[88] Among men the occupations of Oscar-winning roles include: soldier, 14%; sheriff, 8%; criminal 8%; politician, actor, writer, and laborer, about 6% each. Among women, occupations were: actress, 15%; prostitute, 12%; heiress, teacher, artist, hotel proprietress, farmer's wife, and secretary, about 4% each. Thus, while women are presented in personal-domestic roles more than 60% of the time, men are presented in public-career roles with about the same frequency.[89] Looking at how women are portrayed in advertisements for a single genre, horror films, over a 50-year period, Spirek (1992) found female victims more prominent than males, who were more frequently portrayed as the evil protagonist. A sample of 121 adult movie titles available in videocassette rental stores showed half contained explicitly sexual scenes with themes of domination and exploitation (Cowan et al., 1988).

Males and Females in TV Commercials.   Differences also have been found in the portrayal of men and women in TV commercials (Craig, 1992), although the gaps seem to be narrowing in some studies. Bretl and Cantor (1988) summarized 15 years of research from 1971-1985. In 1971 as little as 39% of primary characters in prime-time TV commercials were female, but the two sexes have generally appeared equally often since then. Also, females seem to have become more equal to men in the arguments used to promote a product. When TV is aimed at the general audience, men tend to dominate in commercials, but those appearing during programs aimed at primarily male or female audiences show some differences. Osborn (1989) sampled commercials during prime-time network programs, male-oriented sports programs, and female-oriented daytime soaps and morning game shows in

1988, finding that males accounted for 90% of the voice-overs in prime-time commercials, 88% in those airing during sports programs and 77% of those slotted between soaps and game shows.[90] Also, while 57% of central characters in ads in the 1970s were male, the figure rose to 62% in the 1988 sample. However, differences again were noted by programming. While only 39% of characters in prime-time commercials were females in 1988, 59% of those in commercials during daytime soaps or morning game shows were females. Only 31% of those in commercials shown during sports-programming were women. The female presence in radio commercials is similar to that in TV; females, typically placed in consumer work roles, represented only 7% of the commercial slots on two AM and FM stations (Melton and Fowler, 1987). Male dominance and sex-role stereotyping in TV commercials also have been noted in Canada,[91] Europe,[92] Asia,[93] and elsewhere.[94]

Gender in Print Media.   In 1992, *Newsweek* printed two different covers, one featuring a man, the other a woman, both saying "Oh God . . . I'm really turning 50!" The split editions were run to avoid appearing sexist. Portrayal of gender has been analyzed in different print media. Potter (1986) looked at samples of five elite newspapers in the U.S. from 1913, 1933, 1963, and 1983, finding that females were the main character in only 7.3% of the stories, while males were prominent in 62% and both genders were featured in 3.2% (neither were featured in 28%). Contrary to expectations, the number of stories with females as the main character decreased over time, a downward trend also found for stories featuring men as the main character. A study of news in the *New York Times* in 1885 and 1985 found that men were given more prominence in the 1985 sample, but women were presented in a much wider range of roles in the recent sample. While no women were found in politics, government, war and defense, or foreign relations stories in 1885, they accounted for figures approximating those for men in 1985. Women also were found in professional roles and those of sports figure, entertainer, and public official, from which they were absent in the nineteenth century sample (Jolliffe, 1989). Gender differences also have been found in the wire services which serve the media.[95]

Different features of print media have been noted for gender differences. Luebke (1989) found that photographs of men outnumber those of women on all pages except life style. A study of Sunday comics found that females appeared in 59% of the strips examined and men in 74%.[96] Women also are underrepresented as both sources and subjects of stories in newspaper business sections, even when the writers or editors are women (Greenwald, 1990).[97]

Although some **magazines** are aimed at general audiences, most tend to be targeted at more narrow audiences. Thus, we have an opportunity to see the link between audience gender and images of women. Hynes (1981) looked at fiction and nonfiction short stories in the *Saturday Evening Post*,

Cosmopolitan, Ladies Home Journal and *Atlantic Monthly* between 1911 and 1930. Only 300 of the nearly 8,500 stories had at least one female character. Twenty-four of the 29 stories which mentioned women's involvement in politics portrayed them as basically uninterested in political affairs or inept.[98] Johnson and Christ (1988) found that women were pictured on only 14% of the covers of *Time* magazine from 1923 to the 1980s, but there was a marked increase in covers featuring women in the 1970s. LaFollette (1988) found that men also dominated in articles on science in 11 mass circulation magazines published between 1910 and 1955. More recently, Clark (1981) looked at how five magazines treated women living alone. Some 11% of the nonfiction articles made some reference to women living alone and few of the references presented a positive view. A similar study (Loughlin, 1983) focusing on magazine fiction in 1979-81 found that the fiction mirrored some of the changes occurring in America, such as increased female education and employment, with somewhat less emphasis on romance and personal appearance than in the past. Gender differences also have been examined in new vs. established magazines,[99] magazine cartoons,[100] picture books,[101] magazine photos,[102] and computer magazines.[103]

Sex-role portrayals in advertising are seen as important because of their potential impact on uninvolved members of the audience. Magazine advertising is significant for the range of roles in which women are portrayed and the models of appearance and behavior presented as desirable. Marked increases in the employment status of women have been found in several studies from the 1950s to the present.[104] One study looked at changes in advertising in 22 different magazines and found small shifts between 1974-1975 and 1979-1980. Women appeared less frequently as dependent upon men, and men were less likely to be depicted in themes of sex appeal, dominance over women, and as authority figures. Women were portrayed more frequently as career oriented and in non-traditional activities. However, the physical attractiveness stereotype remained prevalent and sex object themes continued to be used to sell certain types of goods (Lysonski, 1983). Gagnard (1986) found that the ideal body type presented in magazine advertising from 1950 to 1984 became thinner with each decade, with 46% of models being thin in 1980. There has been an increase in sexually explicit content and nudity in magazines, with more emphasis on sexy dress or nudity for females than males in three magazine segments: men's, women's, and general interest news magazines (Soley and Reid, 1988).[105] Another study found changes in male sex-role portrayals in ads paralleling the change in women's roles; men are increasingly portrayed in decorative roles and less often in traditional "manly" roles in magazine ads (Skelly and Lundstrom, 1981). Textbooks also have been examined and one analysis of 11 books used as introductory texts in college found that females were underrepresented in examples in every type of textbook (Bertilson et al., 1982).

Occupations and Professions

As people have invested greater personal identity into their jobs, they have become concerned about the images of their occupation or profession. Consistent with earlier studies, daytime[106] and prime-time TV continue to be dominated by characters with higher-status professions. A study of prime-time programs on the three major TV networks identified a broad range of occupations (Smith and Ferguson, 1990), the most frequent being police officers or private investigators (17%), lawyers (7%), and business executives (6%). Grouped into three major categories, a third of the characters were executives, proprietors of major businesses, or professionals such as physicians, lawyers, nurses, accountants, engineers, or military officers. Another 29% were administrators (including executives of small businesses) and minor professionals (as termed by the authors): actors, journalists, detectives, and school teachers. Some 18% were clerical or sales workers, technicians, skilled manual laborers, machine operators, or unskilled workers. A tenth of the characters were unemployed outside the home. Another sample of prime-time TV in 1987 ranked professions by the number of hours of portrayal: police, journalists, doctors, lawyers, religion, private eyes, entertainers, politicians, and teachers (Stone and Lee, 1990). Vande Berg and Trujillo (1989) report that the major characters in organizations on prime-time network TV tend to be professional (20%), managerial (14%), or in service occupations (19%).[107] Studies of sitcoms show a similar bias toward higher status occupations.[108]

One of the high-status professions consistently portrayed in TV series is **medicine**.[109] Although TV focuses on higher-status occupations requiring lengthy education, actual TV series centering on education are rare and transient.[110] On the news side, media pay more attention to education, and larger newspapers have been increasing their education coverage, with attention to school board meetings and general curriculum as well as problems such as drugs in schools, race relations, sex education, discipline in schools, etc. (Hynds, 1989).[111] **Science** is a frequent theme of TV drama, but the scientist is a relatively rare dramatic character. Positive portrayals outnumber negative ones. While scientists are "smart," they tend to be less attractive, sociable, warm, or as young as other characters.[112] The image of **advertising** as a profession in the media shifted from negative when it began at the turn of the century to positive and then back to negative.[113] **Journalists** appear often in prime-time TV.[114] Newspaper and television journalists appeared with about equal frequency, but the former received more negative treatment and were portrayed as unethical more often (Stone and Lee, 1990). Journalists also have been negatively portrayed in films (Talbott, 1990; Vaughn and Evensen, 1991).[115] A variety of other occupations and professions have received scrutiny for their media coverage or portrayal: **police officers**,[116] **attorneys**,[117] and **artists**.[118]

Business and Labor.   Business and labor are concerned about their media coverage, but studies suggest the picture is a mixture of good and bad. Thomas and LeShay (1992) monitored prime-time fiction programs on the three major TV networks in 1988-1989. They found that a fourth of the business characters were upper class, 31% upper middle class, 38% middle class, and only 6% working class. They found that it is wealth, not business, that is stigmatized in the popular media.[119] A content analysis of organizational life on prime-time TV series showed that 60% of the actions of workers were depicted as positive, 16% negative, and 24% neutral, compared with 43% of management depicted as positive, 20% negative and 37% neutral (Vande Berg and Trujillo, 1989). Broken down by industry, finance received a more negative depiction, while retail trade received the most positive image. Some industries get more attention than others.[120] Vande Berg and Trujillo (1989) report on the analysis of 116 episodes of prime-time TV series in 1986-1987, finding that the largest portion of characters worked in the service and public administration industries. A media monitoring project by the Machinists Union concluded that unions were almost invisible on TV (Rollings, 1983). TV depicted unions as violent and obstructive; workers in unionized occupations were clumsy, uneducated fools with little leadership ability.

News coverage of business and industry has grown from 1970 to the present (Nelson, 1992), with greater recognition that audiences are interested in stories about jobs, the economy and consumer issues. Economic news extends beyond businesses themselves to reporting on trends and statistics.[121] Hackett (1983) analyzed Canadian TV and CBS network TV newscasts for two months in 1980, finding business mentioned in 17% of the items and labor mentioned in 11% of the items. Overall, business people and corporations were shown in a broad range of social activities and roles. Business performance was cited as an indicator of the general economic climate (also see Gale and Wexler, 1983). Threats to business health were seen as threats to the health of the country. Unions, on the other hand, were portrayed primarily as engaged in strikes or other socially disruptive activities. Workers were sometimes shown as the victims of economic conditions but also were portrayed as causing trouble for the economy. Douglas, Pecora, and Guback (1985) found that the majority of labor-related news items in three newspapers concerned issues initiated by union members (strikes or contract negotiations), while a fifth focused on social issues and 31% on institutional issues (government actions, union policies, business employment policies).[122] Randall (1987; Randall and DeFillipi, 1987) found that the 40% of network TV newscasts over a 10-year period contained at least one story on corporate crime.[123]

What **values representing business** are found in the media? Nord (1984) looked at three Chicago newspapers' coverage of three great business-labor crises, finding they had sharply opposing views on the crises but shared several fundamental values including commitment to public interest, commercial order, social harmony, and the ability to resolve conflicts through organized modes. Dionisopoulos (1988) found print media used several themes in covering Chrysler's financial problems from 1977-1985, focusing on saving Chrysler as a heroic task and Lee Iaccoca's role in achieving the success. At the turn of the century, the *Saturday Evening Post* sought to provide an early business education for young men (Cohn, 1987). More recently, attitudes about business expressed in popular music show that a tenth of songs in one sample made some reference to business; a third were allusions to companies, industries, or professions, while 27% mentioned the rich, 18% specific trade names, and 18% technologies (Grady and Baxter, 1985). Looking at comic books as a mass medium, Belk (1987) analyzes four popular comics which have produced potential models for acquiring and using wealth.

Organizations and Institutions

Government agencies tend to get media coverage when social regulatory issues are involved, and most reports are neutral.[124] The government institutions receiving the bulk of media attention in the U.S. are the presidency and Congress, with coverage of the former increasing.[125] Stories about the U.S. Supreme Court are infrequent in any media (Davis, 1987).

Religion has received considerable attention in the media, although less than many other institutions. Network TV news focuses on issues and conflicts in stories involving religion (for example, North Ireland's political-religious conflict), with infrequent mentions of religious practices or beliefs.[126] Religious media attention tends to be focused on established religions, and new religious movements get little coverage until a surge of interest emerges (Van Driel and Richardson, 1988).[127] Analyses of religious TV programming have shown that offering or seeking information accounted for 25% of all communication observed in a sample of the 27 most widely available religious programs. The type of interaction on religious programming tends to be affiliative, or one of people moving toward each other (Neuendorf and Abelman, 1987). More religious and social topics are discussed (58% and 23%) than political topics (19%).[128]

The **health institution** includes hospitals, illnesses, and issues as well as physicians. Hospitals get generally favorable attention on TV (Turow, 1985). Messages about health and illness are scattered across all types of TV shows and commercials,[129] comic books,[130] cable TV,[131] and news media.[132] Media tend to support medical research and emphasize medicine and technology over interpersonal and psychological attempts to cope with illness (Fisher, Gandy, and Janus, 1981). Indirect messages about health also are portrayed in the life styles of TV programs. One study found that almost two-thirds of the food servings on three popular sitcoms were nutritious, but the most frequently eaten meal was "the snack."[133]

When President Ronald Reagan's colon **cancer** dominated the news in the summer of 1985, many observers noted that the coverage might save many lives by alerting others in "at risk" categories to have checkups. Public fears of diseases or other health problems have concerned many professionals. They have examined the media to see how such problems are portrayed. Stories on cancer tend to stress dying rather than coping.[134] Coverage of **infectious diseases** has been examined with greater interest since AIDS (Acquired Immune Deficiency Syndrome) emerged as a major health issue in the media.[135] Media tend to focus more on the life style of victims than on medical aspects of the disease (Albert, 1986). Since AIDS and venereal diseases are associated with sexual behavior, Lowry and Towles (1989) expected that TV would increasingly emphasize possible consequences of sexual behavior; however, although some verbal references were found (31.5 instances out of a total of 722 sexual behaviors), not one example of someone acquiring a sexually transmitted disease was found in prime-time programs. **Mental illness** is often misunderstood in real life as well as the reality presented in the media (Wahl, 1992). While small in numbers, mentally ill are the group most likely to commit violence and to be victimized in the world of TV.[136] **Disabilities** also tend to be negatively portrayed in the media.[137] **Drug and alcohol abuse** have grown as social issues and prompted investigations of their treatment in the media.[138] One study suggests that someone watching TV at night would witness about 11 drinking acts per hour.[139] Drinking is portrayed as social,[140] but youth are seldom seen actually drinking on TV.[141] Films also have commonly included drinking activities, with changes in how they have been portrayed over the decades.[142] Print media focus on alcohol and smoking as social problems.[143]

Problems and Issues

Crime is probably the major problem portrayed on TV and in other entertainment content because of its dramatic value and themes of conflict. Several analyses of TV programming show murder and robbery to be the most frequently depicted crimes, far more than they occur in real life. Furthermore, more women than men are murder victims, which is inconsistent with crime data.[144] **Interest groups** of all types are concerned with media images, and research has focused on media treatment of a wide variety of behaviors and issues as a result.[145] **Cities** and **nations** also worry about their images, and some even advertise.[146]

Other Behaviors in Media Content

Although much of the concern about media images has focused on people and institutions, media present a much more complex picture of human behavior. According to the notion of mainstreaming, media pull audiences toward the middle by ignoring the extremes and telling people what is normal or typical. What is the pattern of "normal activity" presented in the media?

The range of activities on TV representing a normal person's day are reported by Henderson and Greenberg (1980). Restricting their analysis to two TV seasons of network programs, coders identified more than 4,500 acts grouped into 16 major categories. Two types of behavior occurred more than 5 times per program hour—driving and media use. Three other behaviors were seen at a rate of 3-4 incidents per hour: personal grooming, eating, and riding. Appearing almost as frequently were making business phone calls and entertaining. Drinking and smoking occurred about twice per hour.[147]

Entertainment media content, particularly the TV drama, focuses on problems and conflicts. What are the typical issues presented? Cassata, Skill, and Boadu (1983) content analyzed life and death for 341 characters on 13 soaps during a one-year period. There was a total of 191 occurrences of health-related conditions and 43 deaths; some 13% of the characters died of some disease,[148] accident, or crime. They found 79 accidents or violent incidents (homicide, suicide, etc.); of these, 28 ended in death. Selnow (1986) found that prime-time network programming in the U.S. focuses most frequently on affect-sentiment, or romantic problems, which provide the basis for nearly one in three subplots. Physical problems accounted for about a fourth of the subplots.[149]

Although conflict is the norm for dramatic media content, what are typically seen as **prosocial events** also receive considerable attention. Lee (1988) found that 97% of 235 prime-time entertainment programming on TV analyzed during one season contained at least one prosocial event. Major themes were: overcoming one's fears, the priority of people over material gain, lying and deceit are destructive, and lessons of tolerance and accepting individual differences.

What **values** are **presented in the media**? Selnow (1990) applied a values inventory in a content analysis of 54 regularly scheduled TV shows. Some 1,148 values incidents were identified, with personal values (96.5%) greatly outnumbering citizenship values (3.5%). There were 471 instances of "compassion for others" (41.1%). The major values explored were "courage to express conviction" (20.1%), "sense of duty" (9.6%), and "pride and respect" (9.5%). Only minor differences in values were found among demographic categories (age, gender, occupation). Frith and Wesson (1991) compared the values in British and American magazine advertising, finding the U.S. ads portraying characters in more "individualistic" stances while British ads emphasized social class differences.

Summary

In this chapter we analyzed media content structures and images presented in the media. First, content structures were examined for different media including: radio formats, film genre, TV program formats, print media editorial forms and graphic design, and news distinctions. Then we looked at media images, stereotypes, and portrayals that are central to discussions about whether the media affect or reflect society. We reviewed the literature on media images of ethnic groups, age and the elderly, children and families, gender and sex roles, occupations and professions, organizations and institutions, problems and issues, and other behaviors represented in media content.

Chapter Eight Footnotes

1. Historical trends in the media often represent changes in media content such as evolving definitions of news or a new medium offering different images. Activity inside media organizations includes conventions established to cope with the demands of encoding specific types of content—newscasts, feature films, newspaper stories. Audience attention to the media is often defined in terms of the specific contents attended to—such as radio format preferences or favorite movie genres. Content structures differ in how they are processed by media audiences and media effects are linked to particular types of content.

2. Some scholars look at media content as just more symbolic representation of culture. Those employing this view may group TV sitcoms with clothing styles and eating patterns as representations of particular cultural forms (See Berger, 1984; Peterson, 1979).

3. The last purpose focuses on sign-systems and "meaning." Semiology explores the nature of sign-systems, and its use in communication focuses attention on connotative meaning as well as denotative meaning. For example, one might analyze an episode of a particular TV show as a text to demonstrate how that TV format treats women using techniques from semiotics or structuralism (Jaddou and Williams, 1981). See Eco (1976), Fiske and Hartley (1978), and Crowley (1982). Examples of such structural content analyses include both broadcast (Fiske and Hartley, 1978) and print media (Corrigan, 1983) and communication in general (Crowley, 1982; Davis and Walton, 1983). This contrasts with social science methods which must follow established procedures and be reproducible by other researchers. Although structuralists often appear at odds with those using such social science methods as surveys and content analyses, that need not be the case. We now see a merging of **semiology** as a conceptual area from which social scientists pursue questions which can be addressed by **scientific methodologies**. The significance of structural concepts may be achieved only when they are included in audience analyses that employ various quantitative strategies. For example, "genre" is a concept used to describe a particular kind of film. Its significance is found in the fact that people have prior expectations about what a "western" is, and this can affect subsequent media seeking, information processing, and understanding. These are issues for scientific research and that line of research, though growing, is still in its early stages.

4. In earlier decades, music and talk also formed the bulk of radio schedules. Major network radio programs on the air in January, 1927 included: 1 general variety hour, 9 programs of concert music, 12 programs of musical variety, 4 light music programs, 4 religious talk programs, 1 news commentary, 2 other talk programs (travel and bridge), and 1 daytime homemakers talk show (see Summers, 1958). Shifts occurred through the decades, with

growth in the number of thriller dramas, news and commentary, and religious talk programs from 1935 to 1945 and 1955. Musical variety also retained its popularity. Some formats popular in the 1930s had disappeared two decades later—Broadway and Hollywood gossip programs, for example. Appearing somewhat later on the chart were formats like sports interviewing and magazine-type variety programs.

5. The number of stations programming "oldies" increased 20% from 1989-1990 alone. Included here are stations that play Elvis Presley, The Supremes, and other favorites of people age 35-45. Goldman (1990) notes that oldies formats are the favorite for baby boomers just as the big band format is favored by their parents.

6. In its travels, the concept has taken on meanings different from its artistic anchor. Genre has become a fashionable metaphor for media content structures, sometimes replacing the concept of "TV format" or journalistic "story forms." Implicit in almost all definitions is a presumed relationship between the audience and media content. However, it has not provoked empirical research which would test the validity of assumptions or reliability of critics' assessments.

7. In a similar fashion, some argue that TV docudramas that appear before a case goes through the legal process represent a pervasive form of pretrial publicity (Cooperstein, 1989).

8. Dominick (1987) finds that film studios took more chances during periods when production costs were low (1969-1973). Films released were fairly diverse, with more pronounced differences in the types of films released among studios. Those differences began to decline as costs escalated.

9. Silva (1992) found that college students' enjoyment of foreign films was predicted by the star, settings, language, and director.

10. See Kaminsky with Mahan (1985) for more on American TV formats.

11. In 1969, films and situation comedies moved into the top positions. In 1971, crime dramas joined them to form the top three positions.

12. Dominick and Pearce (1976) looked at fall schedules of TV networks from 1953 to 1974 and found mutual interdependence among program formats—as adventure rose, other types decreased. Network programming was marked by relatively regular periods of change and permanence. All three networks seldom undertook major content shifts in the same year. Peaks in diversity occurred in 1961-63 and 1969-70 but otherwise generally declined over the two decades. The three network schedules also became increasingly similar.

13. Public access on cable represents great freedom to generate novel formats, although the lack of resources is a major constraint. Janes (1987) looked at two years of programming (4,000 programs) for one cable system, finding half were informational programs, with instructional or religious programs accounting for a third—"Side-by-Side Obesity" and "Social Security and You." Manhattan's cable TV system for 14 years has had explicit sex advertising and pornographic programming. "Hate TV" featuring white supremacists groups also has appeared on public access cable outlets in the U.S.

14. See Hawes (1986) for the history of the development of the TV drama format.

15. Their analysis showed that ratings for spin-off programs was higher than for non-spin-off programs. Also, the average yearly rating for spin-off programs was lower than for parent programs.

16. An example is provided by Schrag and Rosenfeld (1987), who looked at student ratings of values associated with prime-time and daytime serials, finding differences between the two. Prime-time serials were associated with self-oriented values such as ambition, logic, a comfortable life, and family security, while daytime soap operas were more relationship-oriented and demonstrated values of loving, cheerfulness, true friendship, and equality. They conclude that their findings support Cantor and Pingree's (1983) contention that prime-time serial dramas are not soap operas but a different format.

17. An analysis of children's programming available on national cable services, public TV, and commercial TV networks in 1983-1984 found basic cable networks offered 46% of the total, pay cable networks 39%, and commercial and public broadcast services the remaining 14% (Siemicki, Atkin, Greenberg and Baldwin, 1986). The amount of time devoted to program material (80%) and nonprogram content (20%, mostly commercials) remained steady in samples of children's TV broadcast Saturday mornings and weekday afternoons in 1983, 1985, and 1987 (Condry, Bence and Scheibe, 1988). After an absence of many years, a

variety of high-quality cartoon shows were offered for afternoon viewing, beginning in 1990.

18. Sports makes up almost 7% of TV programs in the U.S., compared to 15.6% in Switzerland, 12.1% in Belgium, 10.8% in Ireland, 10.7% in Finland, and 8.3% in Canada (Little, 1992).

19. The diverse programs in this format fall into the following categories: games of logic and chance, where those who master the rules of the game are rewarded (for example, "Wheel of Fortune"); talent showcase, where the basis of competition is not knowledge or logic but performance ("Star Search"); host-centered game shows, where the contestants and game function as a pretext for the host to perform ("You Bet Your Life" with Groucho Marx in the 1950s and "Family Feud" with Richard Dawson in the 1980s); celebrity-oriented shows, which focus on celebrity performance ("What's My Line" in the 1950s and 1960s and "Hollywood Squares" in the 1960s and 1970s)(Shaw, 1987).

20. Kaplan (1988) provides another set of categories, including romantic, socially conscious, nihilistic, classical and postmodern videos.

21. Caplan (1985) found an average of 10.2 acts of violence per hour in a 1983 sample of MTV videos.

22. A content analysis of popular music also is relevant here. Bridges and Denisoff (1986) updated earlier studies in the 1950s and 1960, finding that a 1977 sample also showed love songs the predominant theme, with 68% of the sample consisting of love songs. More than half were in a conversational mode and 15% in a narrative mode, while 7% were novelty or comic songs and 6% dance songs.

23. Verer and Knupka (1986) looked at over-the-counter drug advertisements in 111 different mens and women's magazines published in the spring and summer of 1985, finding that seven times as many such ads were found in women's magazines as in men's magazines. Some 79% of women's magazines had one OTC drug ad, compared to 27% of men's magazines.

24. See Pasadeos, Shoemake and Campbell (1992).

25. See Hong, Muderrisogiu and Zinkhan (1987) and Ramaprasad and Hasegawa (1992).

26. This also is the case in Japan, where the figure has hovered around 50% for many years (Tamura, 1987).

27. Walker (1983) found in a content analysis of the *Washington Post* that the editorial mix included the following proportions (newspaper columns per issue); style, 17; sports, 14; national news, 14; comics/features, 12.5; financial news, 12; metro news, 10; foreign news, 8.

28. Looking at three major dailies (*New York Times, Chicago Tribune, Los Angeles Times*), Hynds found politics and government accounting for 40-52% of all editorials. Other major topics were war and defense (second at the *Los Angeles Times* and *Chicago Tribune*), economic activity, human interest, popular amusements, and public health and welfare.

29. Each deck refers to a separate "sentence" or idea; often each deck is in a different—larger or smaller—type size.

30. For 88% of the papers, the flag—containing the name of the newspaper—spanned the entire page and for a third, the flag remained at the top of the paper all the time. Half of the papers used a 9-point type for body text, with almost universal use of a serif face; headlines were split between serif typefaces (48.9%) and sanserif faces (47.8%). Three-fourths of papers use graphics wires and Macintosh systems, while 56% use electronic scanning systems and satellite transmission systems (Utt and Pasternack, 1989).

31. Utt and Pasternack (1984) also conducted an earlier study of the front pages of American newspapers with daily circulations of 25,000 or more. They found that 85% of the dailies used a 6-column front page and the others 5 or 7, with varying column widths and a flexibility in their use. Most papers also included a boxed index on the front page. The "flag," or newspaper name, spanned the width of the page but was not always at the top and periodically was in color. Some two-thirds of the papers also used a modular format, while 30% used a horizontal layout and only 4% a vertical format. The number of stories on the front page ranged from 3 to 10, with an average of 5-6. Many of those stories concluded inside the paper, a factor readers dislike (Bain and Weaver, 1979).

32. Utt and Pasternack (1989) identify three stages describing the changes in design among daily U.S. newspapers: 1960s to about 1981, when early innovators adopted wider columns, spot color, large black-and-white photos, and four-color photos; 1981-1986, the homogenization period, when almost all papers were changing graphically and the Standard Advertising Unit

was introduced, forcing papers to change their standard 11 pica line, and *USA Today* introduced widespread use of modern design in all markets; 1986-present, the refinement period, as papers continue to readjust their overall look and even larger papers invest in the new changes.

33. The impact of design elements cannot be assumed, however; Berner (1983), for example, found structural content changes such as the style of the headline and first paragraph had less impact on readers' decision making than the story's actual relevance. Brown (1989) looked at one newspaper's switch to color and its impact on photographs used, finding that fewer news photos and more feature photos appeared on front pages after the switch. Fewer of the photos also were attached to specific stories and stood alone instead. The paper also relied less on wire services and generated their own photos for use.

34. A combined survey and content analysis of a mid-sized daily's letters to the editor found that 30.5% of letters were written to share expertise in a subject, while 25% wrote because they were aware of an event or situation, 19% blew off steam, 22% wrote to correct an error, 17% opposed an editorial, 49% reacted to a news story, and 32% wrote to fulfill a civic obligation. Some 22% of letters submitted were rejected because the topic was already exhausted (22%), while 17% were rejected because they were not from the audience area, 12% because better letters were available and 9% because no address was included (Pasternack, 1988).

35. Soft news in a study by Scott and Gobetz (1992) referred to stories that focused on features, human interest topics, and nonpolicy issues. The average annual soft news time for all networks varied for the years 1972-1987, going from 70 seconds per broadcast in 1972 to 63.44 seconds in 1975, 77.5 seconds in 1980, 140.79 seconds in 1985 and 89.21 seconds in 1987. The years from 1981 through 1986 showed a jump in soft news to more than 100 seconds for each year.

36. Brown and Atwater (1986) found that the news on three videotex services tended to be event-oriented and focus on breaking stories rather than issue-oriented, with international relations and violent crime among the most frequent topics presented.

37. A sample of adult readers showed higher readership of reports than stories, particularly among women, older readers, and those with lower income or education.

38. Foote and Saunders (1990) looked at the use of graphics in network TV evening newscasts, finding 78% of all stories contained some type of graphic coverage. Some 41% were used to introduce a story, 32% to explain an element of a story, and 14% as background.

39. The percentage of nations with earth stations for sending and receiving satellite signals grew from almost 30% in 1972 to 76% a decade later; those with such international links are more likely to originate video reports for TV newscasts.

40. *USA Today, New Orleans Times-Picayune, Chicago Tribune, New York Times, Los Angeles Times.*

41. Topical emphases and structure have changed through the decades. Shaw (1981, 1984) focused on the 1820-1860 period when new printing press technology allowed newspapers to expand their audiences and reduce prices. He found that the content did not become less political and more social; rather, the papers carried a substantial amount of social/cultural news continually.

42. The most underrepresented states were North Carolina, Ohio and Indiana, and the most overrepresented were New York, California, and Illinois.

43. In a 1990-1991 sample of network coverage, Graber (1992) also found the Middle East topping the list, followed by the former Soviet Union and Western Europe.

44. Politics and government were ranked first for four of the five networks. An international project found considerable convergence on the top news stories among 18 different TV news organizations around the world (Roeh and Dahlgren, 1991). Politics also dominates TV news in Puerto Rico (Canino and Huston, 1986).

45. Fryman and Bates (1992) conducted a census of stories on CNN's "World Report" from Oct. 25, 1987-Sept. 8, 1991.

46. Agriculture/fisheries/ecology ranked fifth in the CNN newscast but sixteenth in network coverage. While natural disasters were ninth on U.S. networks, they were only seventeenth on CNN's "World Report." Topics appearing equally frequent on both were foreign relations (second on both) and domestic relations (third). Crime/justice/ terrorism was fourth and

economics fifth on U.S. networks and tied for seventh on CNN's broadcast. Differences between the networks' international coverage of events were fewer than expected.

47. See Gonzenbach, Arant, and Stevenson (1992), and Weaver, Porter, and Evans (1984).
48. See Golding and Elliott (1979), Larson (1984), and Stevenson and Shaw (1984).
49. Seggar et al. (1981) examined TV portrayals of minorities in comedy and drama from 1971 to 1980 to see whether gains made in the 1960s were retained over time. They found that blacks generally were slightly less frequently shown in the late 1970s than at the beginning and the black female had become almost invisible. Both black men and women decreased in major roles while other minority men gained in role significance. Mexican-Americans, Asians, Native Americans and foreign-born ethnics dropped considerably in terms of their representation over that period.
50. The study was done by the Cultural Indicators research team, which studied 1,371 programs, including major network prime-time and Saturday morning programs, daytime serials, game shows, cable-originated programs, and network news on ABC, CBS, NBC, Fox, and 11 major cable networks. A typical prime-time network viewer may see an average of 355 characters in speaking parts during a given week. At a press conference, George Gerbner is reported as saying that it has become a "new civil right" for people "to be represented fairly and equally in the cultural environment in which we grow" (John Carmody, "Women, Minorities Still Shut Out, Survey Reports," the *Washington Post*, June 16, 1993, p. 1B).
51. A 1977 sample showed that blacks were concentrated in situation comedies (Baptista-Fernandez and Greenberg, 1980); also, half of the blacks were in virtually all-black shows and the other half spread out one to a show in a "token fashion."
52. They looked at African-Americans appearing during prime-time programming on the three major TV networks in the fall 1987–1988 season. Some 26 shows featuring 58 recurring African-American characters were identified.
53. A study of families portrayed on the top 30 programs on commercial TV in a 1984 sample found that the majority of white families were nuclear, while the dominant black family type consisted of a single parent plus children, the result of a broken marriage (Abelman, 1989). In the Stroman et al. (1989) study, 58% of those in families belonged to a two-parent family.
54. Brown and Campbell (1986) found nonwhites accounted for only 5% of the leaders of groups shown in a sample of music videos airing on MTV in 1984.
55. Ziegler and White (1990) looked at minorities appearing on the evening network news, finding 6.9% of correspondents appearing were nonwhite for a 1987 and 1989 sample. In 1987, 85.4% of newsmakers appearing in the news were white, with 12.2% nonwhite males and 2% nonwhite females. In 1989, 73% of newsmakers were white, with 23% nonwhite males and 3.7% nonwhite females. Most nonwhites were black.
56. Wilkes and Valencia's (1989) sample of prime-time commercials on network TV in the fall of 1984 showed that blacks appeared in 26% of commercials using live models, a figure that drops to about 17% without duplication. Commercials with blacks were overwhelmingly racially integrated, and the proportion of commercials in which only blacks appeared (11%) closely approximates their representation in the U.S. population. Riffe, Goldson, Saxton and Yu (1989) found that a third of commercials featuring humans during Saturday morning children's programs contained one nonwhite character. Looking at commercials broadcast during college basketball tournament games in 1988, Wonsek (1992) found that almost 10% had minor black images and 9.5% major black spokespersons or images, while 68% had white spokespersons/images and 13% were neutral (no black or white images).
57. Zinkhan, Qualls, and Biswas (1990) look at the results of 40 years of studies on blacks in both print and TV advertising, summarizing data representing 13,000 TV commercials and 205,000 magazine ads. They note that the black presence reached 16% of TV commercials in 1986. Humphrey and Schuman (1984) looked at the occupational levels of blacks in *Time* and *Ladies' Home Journal* advertisements during 1950 and 1980. The percentage rose considerably in that period, with a disappearance of blacks in roles as maids or servants (also see Sentman, 1983).
58. Five negative recurring messages for black women were noted: black women are submissive and controlled by men; black women sleep their way to the top or use their bodies to get what they want; black women are defined by their bodies as evidenced by close up camera shots of behinds, legs, and breasts; educated and successful black women are snobbish, fake,

and money-hungry bitches; and black women have no self-respect or self-love when it comes to men.

59. Zinkhan, Cox, and Hong (1986) looked at *Ladies Home Journal, Life, New Yorker, Time,* and the *Saturday Evening Post,* finding the percentage of black ads going from .57 in 1949-1950 to 2.17 in 1967-1968 and 3.95 in 1983-1984. Increases were noted in blacks as professionals and entertainers, with decreases for consumer roles. Lester and Smith (1989, 1990) looked at African-American photo coverage in three major magazines, finding the percentage of images which were African-American making significant and generally steady increases from 1937 to 1988.

60. The magazines were *Ebony, Essence, Players, Ladies' Home Journal, Life,* and *Playboy.*

61. Wiggins (1988) found that images of black boxers in newspaper cartoons moved from crude, ape-like drawings in the pre-1920 period to more humane sketches of Joe Louis in the 1930s. Only 6.6% of Americans on the cover of *Time* and *Newsweek* magazines in the 1950s through the 1980s were racial minorities, and, except for one Hispanic, all were black (Dodd, Foerch and Anderson, 1988).

62. The newspapers were: the *New York Times, Atlanta Constitution, Boston Globe, Chicago Tribune,* and *Youngstown* (Ohio) *Vindicator.*

63. Pease (1989) looked at minority news coverage in a Columbus newspaper, finding little change from 1965 to 1987, although the emphasis shifted from bad news to a more upbeat tone. Analysis of coverage of congressional representatives showed greater visibility for African-American than for white representatives in nine major U.S. dailies (Barber and Gandy, 1990).

64. Although there were no racial differences on many dimensions, the researcher concludes that blacks accused did appear to be treated in a less favorable manner than whites accused.

65. The Center for Media and Public Affairs in Washington, D.C., reported that Hispanic TV characters commit twice as many crimes as whites and three times as many as blacks. The 40% of Hispanic characters who were negative was higher than the rate for whites or blacks (Gregory Katz, "Mixed TV Reviews on Minorities," *USA Today,* July 1, 1987, p. 1).

66. However, both Mexican-American and Puerto Rican leaders in one survey complained of negative portrayals of Hispanics and an overemphasis on crime-related news about Hispanics in Anglo and Spanish-language media (Nicolini, 1986, 1987).

67. Raub (1988) found that the magazine *National Geographic* portrayed urban ethnics in two ways, focusing on "exotic traits" or their contribution to the American "melting pot." Before the emergence of middle-class ethnic pride in the 1970s, the magazine tended to equate ethnic with working class. Coverage of blacks and Hispanics has increased significantly; 6.5% of people depicted were black in 1950-1969, compared to 27% in 1970-1984.

68. Elderly people were increasingly cast in regular roles rather than guest roles, and they were increasingly represented as lower-class. They also were presented as victims rather than perpetrators of aggressive acts. Also see: Cassata et al. (1983) and Elliott (1984).

69. A 1981 study of 136 TV commercials found that only 11 included one or more people age sixty or older (Hiemstra et al., 1983), and two-thirds were males.

70. Another study focused on advertisements in five magazines (*Vogue, Ms., Playboy, Time, Ladies' Home Journal*) from 1960 to 1979, finding that 62% of the adults appeared to be under 30, compared with about 28% of the U.S. population. Women depicted in ads were usually younger than the men they were pictured with; only 4% of all the women were judged to be 40 or older compared to 57% in the general population. There was no major change in the portrayal of ages during the period studied (England et al., 1981).

71. Most of the stories in which older persons appeared were reports of some event (67%), while another fifth were related to an event and the remainder enterprise stories. Polivka (1988) identified four components of 84 magazine cartoons seen as indicators of successful aging in the U.S.: sexuality, power, authority, and self-sufficiency, all delivering an overwhelmingly negative message about growing old in America. A fifth, age-relatedness, was the only one indicating some positive social recognition.

72. An analysis of family life in magazine advertisements from 1920 to 1978 found a significant increase in the portrayal of intimacy between spouses and between brothers and sisters, with greater emphasis on companionship in household tasks among younger couples (Brown, 1981).

73. The average number of conflicts per hour was 11.8 for situation comedies, 8.1 for evening

serials, and 5.4 for family dramas. Females were involved in more conflict situations than males, and 30% of the conflicts involved parents and children, while 19% involved husbands and wives, and 13% involved siblings (50% brother-sister, 40% brother-brother, 10% sister-sister).

74. Sons responded to both parents with integrative strategies (50% with dads and 46% with moms), while daughters responded to mothers with avoidance strategies (56%) and to fathers with distributive strategies (67%). Brothers and sisters initiating conflict used distributive strategies about 85% of the time.

75. In Japan, changes in themes of contemporary dramas from 1974 to 1984 showed a decreased emphasis on male-female relations (from 43% in 1974 to 25% in 1984), while social problems and crime grew from 11% to 33% (Makita and Muramatsu, 1987). Portrayal of relationships within families and among friends showed a drop in emphasis on warm family ties (from 43% to 22%) and an increase on family troubles (from 40% to 53%).

76. For examples of research on portrayal of gender in media, see Malaysia (Adnan, 1987), Mexico (Hinds and Tatum, 1984), Philippines (Fernandez, 1987; Lent, 1985), Japan (Ledden and Fejes, 1987), Australia (Bell and Pandey, 1989), and Czechoslovakia (Salzmann, 1990).

77. For earlier studies see Greenberg, Richards, and Henderson (1980), Henderson, Greenberg, and Atkin (1980), Kaplan (1984), Matelski (1985), and Weigel and Loomis (1981).

78. In a study of more than 19,000 speaking parts, women accounted for 29% of major roles. In news, women accounted for 35% of news broadcasters, 20% of authorities cited, and 17% of other newsmakers (John Carmody, "Women, Minorities Still Shut Out, Survey Reports," the *Washington Post*, June 16, 1993, p. 1B).

79. Men were 72% middle aged, 2.8% old, 16% young adult. Women were 10% child/adolescent, 27% young adult, 57% middle aged, 3.7% old. The same phenomenon was found for women in contemporary TV dramas in Japan (Yasuko, 1986).

80. Men included: 19% professional, 12% white collar, 32% blue collar. Women included: 18% professional, 13% white collar, 13% blue collar.

81. Portrayal of women as single professionals working successfully with men was found in analysis of six 1985-1986 prime-time TV shows. The women were financially successful but were less than perfect mothers and lacked romance (Reep and Dambrot, 1987). Makita and Muramatsu (1987) note that women in Japanese TV dramas also tend to be employed less than they are in society. A major change in the status of Japanese women from 1974 to 1984, the period studied, was a sharp rise in the number of married women employed outside the home, a trend not fully reflected in TV dramas.

82. A pattern characterized as competitive symmetry (where both spouses try to talk) was the most common pattern in families; submissive symmetry (where neither person seeks control) was more common in exchanges between socially linked men and women (Arliss, Cassata and Skill, 1983).

83. Clothing also has been studied for sex-role presentations. Lennon (1990) found that the attire of female leads in three 1988 TV sitcoms contained fewer elements of "bondage" as sex roles changed from traditional to nontraditional, suggesting that sex roles and clothing were closely related. Bondage refers to restrictiveness of clothing (short skirts, tight pants, buttoned bodice, fitted waistline, high heels, uplift bra, etc.).

84. In Canada, 57% of TV news anchors are male and 43% female, while 79% of reporters are male (Soderlund, Surlin and Romanow, 1989). A larger discrepancy has been noted in Japanese news programs (Muramatsu, 1990).

85. In India, 71% of total time was devoted to male newsmakers in one study (Behera, 1989). In Japan, in a 1978 study, one national TV news program had an average of 1 woman and 9.4 men in the news; in 1984, an average of 3.1 women appeared in a half-hour news program (Muramatsu, 1990).

86. Endres (1984) found that the percentage of male vocalists among the top songs declined from 75% in 1960 and 1970 to 50% in 1980, but Wells (1986) found males still dominating in another study of singles and album charts in 1979-1984. Since music is the major content of radio and MTV, the portrayal of men and women in contemporary music takes on greater significance. Hyden and McCandless (1983) analyzed the lyrics of 110 songs popular from 1972-1982, finding 68% were sung by males and 26% by females; while men were pictured as possessing both masculine and feminine characteristics, women largely conformed to

traditional stereotypic feminine attributes. Women were most frequently described as being young, childlike, passive, and powerful.

87. Levy analyzed 218 screen roles which won the Academy Award as best actor/actress or best supporting actor/actress from 1927 through 1986.

88. Cooper and Descutner (1992) compared the treatment of gender in two autobiographies and a film version, finding the film shifted the focus toward romantic relationships and changed the role of the woman from a strong independent individual to a more traditionally weak and dependent woman. The film was *Out of Africa*, based on autobiographies of Isak Dinesen.

89. Fishbein (1989) notes changes in the image of New York City in films about fallen women from the turn of the century through the 1930s, suggesting, for example, that the image of the fallen woman served as a metaphor for public anxieties about urban life.

90. Ferrante, Haynes and Kingsley (1988) found that the use of male voice-overs on TV commercials declined only 4% from the early 1970s to 1986.

91. Rak and McMullen (1987) found a sex-stereotyped pattern of male-female differences in daytime commercials more than in prime-time commercials in Canada. Morre and Cadeau (1985) found that 88% of voice-overs were male and 85% of experts were male in a sample of Canadian TV commercials.

92. Furnham and Voli (1989) found gender stereotyping in Italian commercials constant across time-of-day and more apparent than in the U.S. but as frequent as in England. Livingstone and Green (1986) found men dominating voice-overs in British TV commercials. Women also were placed in more familiar roles and for promoting personal and domestic products. Harris and Stobart (1986) found women more frequent in daytime commercials and men in evening commercials on British TV. Furnham and Schofield (1986) found men accounting for 83% of the central figures in a sample of British radio commercials.

93. In Japan, commonplace sexist ads have provoked relatively few complaints. A comparison of news magazine ads in the U.S. and Asia found similar percentages of females to be in working roles but Asian women in working roles occupied positions of less prestige (Sengupta, 1992). Adnan (1987) reports on a study analyzing about 1,800 TV commercials in Malaysia, finding that more women were featured than men (56% women) but nearly all were in stereotyped images of women, as mothers, housewives, or sexual objects. Men also accounted for 84% of the voice-overs.

94. Gilly (1988) analyzed samples of TV commercials in Mexico, Australia, and the U.S. in 1984-1985, finding TV commercials of all three countries reflecting stereotypic gender roles, women in more dependent roles and males dominating in voice-overs.

95. See: Luebke (1985) and Wanta and Leggett (1989). Moslem (1989) found women portrayed as passive objects of news 17% of the time, active newsmakers 17% of the time, and as victims of events 66% of the time in a study of women's images in Bangladesh newspapers.

96. Females were seen in the home context in 71% of the comics, compared to 33% for males but female characters were less likely to be seen engaged in home or child care compared to a similar study a decade earlier (Brabant and Mooney, 1986; Thaber, 1987).

97. A study of two dailies' business sections found that men were the subject of 44% of stories and briefs and were quoted as experts 61% of the time. Women were the subject of only 3% of the business news and were quoted as experts 7% of the time.

98. List (1986) found that three magazines published in the late 1700s did not portray women as politically active in any meaningful way; a woman's place was in the home. Magazines analyzed were: *The Ladies Magazine* (1792-1793), *The American Magazine* (1787-1788) and *The Weekly Magazine* (1798-1799).

99. Ruggerio and Weston (1985) looked at how established and newer women's magazines differed in their presentation of women's work options. Results showed that established magazines were more likely to profile women in traditional occupations.

100. Lisenby (1985) found five stereotypes of women in magazine cartoons from 1930-1960: the incompetent woman driver; the reckless spender, the talkative, gossipy woman; the unpredictable, indecisive, hyperemotional female; and the woman of limited understanding of public affairs or culture. These cartoon put-downs of women were decreasing by the late 1950s.

101. A study of picture books aimed at preschool-age children found females no longer were invisible in award-winning books and were about as frequent as males. All males were

portrayed as independent, persistent, and active but females did not share specific characteristics (Williams et al., 1987). Also see Reinstein (1984).

102. An emphasis on women's bodies rather than their faces, noted earlier with newspapers, also has been found in magazines (Dodd et al., 1989), but a study of photos of male and female candidates did not find such differences (Sparks and Fehlner, 1986).

103. Ware and Stuck (1985) found females in 31% of illustrations in a sample of computer magazines, while males were portrayed in 69%.

104. See Sullivan and O'Connor (1988) and Saunders and Stead (1986).

105. Even Ms. magazine has increasingly portrayed women as alluring sex objects, according to a study by Ferguson, Kreshel and Tinkham (1990).

106. Rondina et al. (1983) found that 49% of the soap opera work force was made up of professionals, with managers shown at twice the rate they occur in the general population.

107. Others were unidentifiable (11%), customers (10%), students (8%), lawbreakers (5%), or in other categories. Of the major characters, 58% were depicted in a positive light, 24% negative and 18% neutral. In terms of depictions of total actions, 51% of managers were seen as positive and 36% negative, while 60% of professionals were positive and 20% negative and 65% of service workers positive and 15% negative.

108. A study of TV situation comedies over several decades (1946 to 1978) found that 64% were middle-class families; professionals accounted for 43% of heads of households on TV compared to 14.5% in the general population. The self-employed also were overrepresented but the largest discrepancy was in the representation of the working class, which accounted for only 8% of the heads of TV households but 65% of the actual population (Butsch and Glennon, 1983). One analysis of TV sitcoms found that characters' aspirations for upward mobility typically required personal sacrifice and self-reliance for success (Freeman, 1992).

109. A sample of TV series from 1950 to 1980 found 240 nurses and 287 physicians portrayed; 99% of the former were female and 95% of the latter male (Kalisch and Kalisch, 1984). Four major treatments of nurse characters were identified: the nurse as nonentity (nurses in "Medical Center" or "Ben Casey"), the good nurse ("Marcus Welby"), the nurturing nurse (Julia Baker of "Julia"), and the professional nurse (Margaret Houlihan of "M'A'S'H"). Kalisch et al. (1983) conclude that the image of nursing depends exclusively upon the image of the good doctor.

110. Mayerle and Rarick (1989) looked at prime-time network TV series from 1948 to 1988, finding a total of 40 education series, 4 in the 1950s, 7 in the 1960s, 10 in the 1970s, and 19 in the 1980s. Male teachers outnumbered female teachers almost two to one, with a similar gender ratio among students. Series themes included 30% which were personal/family comedies, 28% education dramas, 22.5% non-traditional educators, 15% education comedies, and 5% teacher as bumbler.

111. Others looking at coverage of education in specific newspapers have found most articles either positive or neutral in tone (Criscuolo, 1985), paying more attention to post-secondary rather than elementary or preschool education and placing greater emphasis on events rather than people (Ross, 1983). Also see: Reber (1990), Johns, Brownlie and Ramirez (1986), and DeRiemer (1988).

112. Gerbner et al. (1981) analyzed TV programming and found that science was the main focus of 4% of primetime and 9% of weekend-daytime programs. Scientists complain that they are too often portrayed as odd and peculiar on TV (Gerbner, 1987). The old movie image of the mad scientist and nineteenth century newspaper exaggerations of scientific findings made the scientific community leery of media coverage and concerned about media contributions to the understandings of what scientists do. Media coverage of social science often is chosen for its dramatic value or obvious reader relevance (Weiss and Singer, 1988). Science and medicine get considerable attention in the supermarket tabloids, which devote more of their space to medicine than science. In contrast, the mainstream press focuses more on technology and hard science (Hinkle and Elliott, 1989). Caudill (1987) content analyzed the New York Times index from 1860 to 1926, showing how coverage of Darwin's theory shifted from portraying evolution as a radical idea in 1860 to presenting it as valid scientific theory by 1925. Conflict between religion and science remained a theme throughout.

113. Initially negative, the image became more positive in the prosperous 1920s and then declined with renewed criticism during the depression. In the 1940s, there was a slight improvement

but the image of the "huckster" advertising man became firmly fixed in the mid 1940s and has continued to the present (Maddox and Zanot, 1985).

114. A content analysis of 1987 programs from three TV networks found that journalists were second to police in the number of hours of portrayals. Some 19 of 20 journalists were white and most between age 30 and 50. A third of the time journalists were found in crime-drama programs and a little more than a fifth in situation comedies.

115. Vaughn and Evensen (1991) found that reporters in films of the early 1930s often were portrayed as drunks or other less than glamorous roles. However, World War II films often portrayed reporters as searchers for truth in a free democratic system. Journalists became one of Hollywood's moral compasses in a disoriented world.

116. Police officers are dismayed that their TV counterparts are often portrayed as ignoring civil rights of suspects and are too violent (Daly, 1972).

117. Attorneys worry that glamorous TV portrayals will create unrealistic expectations for their courtroom performance (Dershowitz, 1987; Lewis, 1974; Winick and Winick, 1974). Sharf (1986) found that much of the media commentary aimed at expert witnesses during the trial of John Hinckley (convicted for trying to assassinate President Ronald Reagan in 1981) ascribed ulterior motives to the psychiatric testimony.

118. Ryan and Sim (1990) looked at portrayals of art and artists on network TV news from 1976 to 1985, finding 310 stories related to art during this period. Some 14% of the stories related in part to financial or marketing aspects of the art world, while another 14% focused on controversy and 16% on the artwork itself. Ten percent were political stories and another 10% reports about thefts, fraud or recovery of stolen art.

119. Wealth often intersects with business, but they found no evidence that the media emphasize the wealth/evil connection in business portrayals any more than in other contexts.

120. Trujillo and Ekdom (1987) found that mining, construction, manufacturing, and finance industries appeared least on prime-time TV between 1946 and 1984, while trade, agriculture, and transportation/communication industries appeared more often. Retail trade, generally as background context, appeared most often.

121. Reese, Daly and Hardy (1987) found that economic news represents a significant portion of evening newscasts in a study of 10 years of network news broadcasts. Harrington (1989) found that TV news coverage of the unemployment rate, the Consumer Price Index and the growth rate of real Gross National Product (GNP) was twice as likely to lead the evening newscast when these indicators were deteriorating. Also see: McGee and Weaver (1988) and Thompson, Olsen, and Dietrich (1987).

122. A study of British media coverage of a coal miner's strike found that media concentrated on violence and explained events in terms of two polarized sides, while ignoring industrial, social and historical context (Wade, 1985).

123. Each week between 1974 and 1984 network news covered an average of 9.34 stories per week on business crime, while news magazines examined carried about 2 stories per week. Both media tended to focus more on the investigative and sentencing stages rather than the trial stage.

124. An analysis of network news stories about six federal regulatory agencies during 1980 found that news centered on social regulatory matters rather than conflicts between agencies or with Congress (Thomas and Boyd, 1984). Most of the stories were judged to be neutral (87%), while 11% depicted agencies in a negative manner and 2% in a positive light. The agencies were EPA, FDA, CAB, ICC, FTC, and OSHA.

125. Coverage of the American president has increased over the years (1900-1980s) in the periodical press (Orman, 1984), although coverage varies during election campaigns (Stempel and Windhauser, 1984).

126. A sample of network TV newscasts from 1976, 1981, and 1986 found that the time devoted to religion stories remained fairly constant over this period, with religion mentioned in an average of 7-8% of all stories (representing 9-12% of the total news time). Roman Catholics received the most coverage, followed by mainline Protestant churches and Jewish groups. The type of information predominating in religion news stories was issues, including conflicts in the Middle East and Northern Ireland. Religious beliefs and practices were the least frequently mentioned topic (Buddenbaum, 1988, 1990). Also see Buddenbaum (1987).

127. Analysis of four major metro dailies and three news weekly magazines shows that legal conflicts

and controversies surrounding criminal allegations were the most frequent topics for coverage of such religious movements as the Unification Church, with little attention to their historical development or social conditions underlying their existence.

128. Of the political topics discussed, terrorism, communism, Reaganomics, the Supreme Court, and federal spending were most frequent (Abelman and Pettey, 1988).

129. A review of more than 90 hours of network TV revealed 723 interactions in which ill persons appeared, a third in commercials, a third in prime-time fiction programming, 18% in afternoon serials, 12% in news magazines, and 3% in the news (Turow and Cole, 1985).

130. An analysis of all comic strips in two newspapers during 1956, 1968, 1972, and 1980 found that health-related topics were found in 8% of the strips, with 14% focusing on illness and 11% on safety. Three-fourths of the health-related comic strips used humorous themes to deal with the topics (Sofalvi and Drolet, 1986).

131. An appraisal of three years of Lifetime cable TV programming found health-related programming dropping from 54% in 1984 to 27% in 1987, with the decline found largely in consumer health education programming. An increase was found in programming for health-care professions (Banks and Banks, 1988).

132. Health news is event-oriented much like the rest of the news (Kristiansen, 1988).

133. Another analysis of food and beverage commercials shown during daytime serials found that 43% promoted nutrition, 85% alluded to the palatability of the product, and a fourth used social and emotional appeals. See Larson (1991) and Lank, Vickery, Cotugna and Shade (1992).

134. The National Cancer Institute conducted studies of news media coverage of cancer in 1977 and 1980 (Freimuth et al., 1984). Fewer than 5% of the stories dealt with the support services available to cancer patients and their families. Headlines of cancer news stories were generally accurate and neutral in tone. Clarke's (1986) review of coverage of cancer in periodicals from 1961 to 1984 found fewer than half of the articles described cancer in a neutral or informative manner, with 54% portraying cancer or its treatment in emotional or moral language.

135. Ziporyn (1988) looked at magazine coverage of three infectious diseases—diphtheria, typhoid fever, and syphilis—in popular magazines in the U.S. from 1810 to 1920. Each disease was portrayed in a manner which characterized the need for optimism, relevance, and certainty, with particular attention to nonscientific aspects of the disease. Content analyses of coverage of infectious diseases on the three major TV network evening news broadcasts from 1978 to 1987 found that the diseases mentioned most often were Legionnaires' disease, AIDS, and influenza (Greenberg and Wartenberg, 1990).

136. Signorielli (1989) analyzed prime-time programming from 1969 to 1985, finding that a fifth of dramatic programs depicted mental illness, although less than a tenth presented mental illness as a major focus of the story line. Of all prime-time dramatic adult major characters, 42% were violent, but 72% of those characterized as mentally ill hurt or killed others. And 45% of all characters but more than three-fourths of the mentally ill became victims of violence. Daytime soap operas also present a negative image of mental illness (Fruth and Padderud, 1985). Looking at the print media, Bonnstetter (1986) found a sample of magazines from the 1950s and 1970s tended to be neutral in reporting about mental illness, with the 1970s articles expressing a more positive viewpoint from those from the earlier decade.

137. They were depicted in 11% of a sample of films between 1976 and 1983, with most negatively portrayed (Byrd and Elliott, 1985). Emotional-behavioral disorders appeared more frequently and males outnumbered females two to one. Zola (1985) looked at coverage of persons with disabilities, finding that TV focused more on adjustment problems and deviant behaviors while newspapers focused more on successful adjustments and the availability of special services. Yoshida, Wasilewski and Friedman (1990) looked at five U.S. metropolitan newspapers' coverage of people with disabilities, with the mentally retarded mentioned most frequently (28%), followed by the emotionally disturbed (24%), the orthopedically impaired (21%), general handicapped (17%), and the deaf (11%). Coverage in the *New York Times* has shown a decline in the portrayal of disabilities in a traditional economic sense (dependent on charity) and a rise in coverage from a civil rights perspective. Medical views remained constant over the 50-year period studied (Clogston, 1992).

138. Breed and De Foe (1982) report on an effort to influence the portrayal of drinking on TV

by working with production personnel and within the dramatic framework of the medium. Contacts were made with studio personnel who were assisted in using more accurate and authentic material about alcohol use. They concluded that the process was most effective in increasing the authenticity of alcohol use portrayal. Other evidence suggests that the campaign to reduce TV presentations of alcohol has been successful in some instances (Chan, 1985). Between 1982 and 1985, the TV show "Dallas" trimmed 70% of its drinking.

139. About 80% of episodes from a sample of 122 hours of prime-time TV programs in the fall of 1984 contained one or more appearances of alcohol, with a particularly high 9 of 10 episodes in dramatic series containing such references (Wallack, Breed and Cruz, 1987). This confirms the 80% alcohol use found in a 1979 sample of the 15 most popular prime-time TV programs (Futch, Lisman and Geller, 1984).

140. An Australian TV study found that the most common format for drinking on TV was in groups. When men and women were presented in couples (28%), wine was the favored drink, but men-only groups mainly drank beer (Shoebridge, 1988).

141. Focusing on youth and alcohol, DeFoe and Breed (1988) sampled eight seasons of prime-time TV in 1976, 1980, 1982, 1983 and 1986 to locate some 900 episodes with drinking. They found that young people were seldom seen drinking on prime-time TV, with less than 2% of all drinking done by those under the drinking age. Furthermore, many of the youth seen drinking were associated with negative role models—gangs or criminal activity.

142. Room (1989) found that between 1945 and 1962 at least 34 Hollywood films were made in which at least one major character was marked by drunkenness as a character trait. Herd (1986) looked at 100 films produced during the 1920s and 1960s that dealt with alcoholism. During both decades, the chief cause of alcohol problems of film characters was loss of love or romantic problems (47% in 1920s and 37% in 1960s), but there was a tripling of instances in which psychological problems were the basis (from 11% of 1920s film characters to 33% of 1960s characters). A significant drop was found in citing victimization by others (dropping from 17% to 4%). Effects of alcohol problems also showed changes, with drops in family or romantic problems and general antisocial behavior but increases in sexual deviance and job failure. Resolution of alcohol problems in the 1920s generally was more positive (69% vs. 38% in 1960s), often achieved through marriage or reconciliation with lover or spouse. By the 1960s, death had grown from 25% to 41% of the solutions.

143. See Craig (1981), Finn and Strickland (1982), Jones (1984), Kessler (1989), Litman (1980), and Strickland et al. (1982).

144. See: Estep and MacDonald (1983, 1984), who looked at three different seasons of TV—1976-77, 1978-79, and 1980-81; Lichter and Lichter (1983), who content-analyzed a six-week sample of prime-time TV programs from 1980-81, finding 250 criminals who committed 417 crimes; Greenberg et al. (1980), who studied antisocial behavior on TV during three fall seasons in the 1970s, finding verbal aggression the most frequent; and Graber (1980).

145. These include: consumer behaviors (Way, 1984), driving (Greenberg and Atkin, 1983), insects (Moore et al., 1982), gambling (Abt and McDowell, 1987), forensic hypnosis (McConkey, Roche and Sheehan, 1989), the coming of the Holocaust (Lipstadt, 1986; Seaton, 1987), destruction of the rainforest and other environmental issues (Bendix and Liebler, 1990; Friedman, Gorney and Egolf, 1987; Howenstine, 1987; and Sullivan, 1985), natural history (Fortner and Wiggington, 1989), technology (Goldman, 1989), government regulation and energy issues (Erfle, McMillan and Grotman, 1989).

146. U.S. media have been examined for their treatment of Greece (Zaharopoulos, 1984, 1989), Italy (Pittatore, 1983), Iran (Altheide, 1982; Meeske and Jayaheri, 1982; Tadayon, 1980), Israel and the Middle East (Barranco and Shyles, 1988), Australia (McCracken, 1987), and Canada (Flournoy, Mason, Nanney and Stempel, 1992). The U.S. image has been examined in media of Greece (Zaharopoulos, 1984, 1989) and China (Blackwood, 1990; Lee, 1981), and Ata (1984) found Moslems portrayed as aggressive, violent, and homogeneous in the Australian press.

147. Other activities and rates per hour were: food preparation, 1.4; playing games, 1.36; writing, 1.1 1; using firearms, 1.02; social courtesies, .86; personal phone calls, .73; athletics, .71; and indoor housework, .51. Five other categories of behavior occurring infrequently (less than .02 incidents per hour were: yard work, shopping, child care, office work, and sewing.

148. There also were some 51 diseases identified by organ system—from neurological to congenital—with 9 resulting deaths. Some 61 other diseases and health-related conditions were found (psychiatric disorders, pregnancy-related problems, and undefined), with 3 deaths resulting.
149. Of the 222 subplots identified in the two-week sample, some 89% had clear, unambiguous resolutions, while about 5% of the problems were not resolved definitively and 6% reached no resolution at all. A variety of analysts have looked at the problem-resolution and other themes of specific programs: music videos (Bennett and Ferrell, 1987), "The A-Team" (Schwichtenberg, 1987), mini-series (Liebman, 1987), the late-night talk show (Buxton, 1987; Timberg, 1987), "Dallas" and "Dynasty" (Cassidy, 1989; Hirschman, 1988), courtroom dramas (Dumble, 1989), and soap operas (Norton, 1985).

Concluding Note

For centuries, mass media have persisted by changing their form and function rather than going out of existence. That's not likely to change, and the 21st century will be populated by books, magazines, and newspapers which originated in earlier centuries, as well as radio, television, and film—which emerged as full-blown media in the current century. The 21st century also will witness other technologies developed in recent decades and some currently "on the drawing boards." These innovations are sure to affect the existing mass media. These new technologies—500 channel cable systems, media content accessible as data banks, high definition TV, magazines and newspapers available through computers, virtual reality TV/video/film, satellite distribution, hand-held electronic books, and other technologies—will continue to blur the lines between media forms and increase links among media institutions themselves. At some point, we could see an existing medium transformed and emerging as a new medium, for example, hologram films replacing flat screen cinema. However, such grand forecasts in the past seldom have been vindicated by events.

Media content and the patterns used to create those messages also will evolve. Content forms available in one medium are crossing boundaries, as fiction and non-fiction forms become increasingly indistinct—dramas presented as documentaries, for example. Furthermore, professional communicators are likely to need skills and knowledge that prepare them to handle many more forms than have been necessary in the past. Journalists, for example, will likely prepare alternative stories of the same news item with different emphases desired by audiences. With interactive media, audiences will become more involved in structuring their media agenda rather than having it constructed for them. Media more and more will resemble point-to-point communication, sharing more characteristics with interpersonal communication. Links between media organizations and competition to attract audiences by fulfilling uses and gratifications also will challenge existing professional standards and conventions—as when entertainment goals and news values clash on TV.

Although economic links have integrated media around the world, we are likely to see a more profound internationalization of media forms. Struggling to fill insatiable channels, media organizations will audition formats from Japan, sports from Europe, and news ideas from anywhere. American forms will continue to dominate as they increasingly become vehicles for reaching international audiences. This probably will continue, but any national culture or subculture—from the U.S. or other nations—can obtain access by

373

demonstrating a minimum of audience acceptance, measured by commercial viability most of the time, although acceptance by substantial elites also may be sufficient.

While some traditions argue for the cultural reflection hypothesis, the trends suggested here argue that mass communication evolves toward an international unity despite cultural constraints and political realities. The ultimate arbitrator of media messages—their content and form—is audience acceptance. In the long run, the uses and gratifications of American and international audiences will continue to second guess the best attempts at commercial exploitation, political manipulation, and cultural myopia in message construction. Public preference for easily-accessible fare in any medium is seen by some as the triumph of commercialism, but the increasing diversity of the media menu for all audiences also is a triumph of intellectual diversity.

With an increasingly complex environment, we will need to conduct research on existing relationships and re-examine what we know about mass media processes. We also need to develop and test more theories focusing on symbolic activity as the legitimate focus, not an appendage to economic, political or cultural processes. Some of those theories will focus on limited domains, perhaps those cited in specific chapters of this book. Thus, for example, we might expect to see theories that explain how new technologies alter audience processing of media messages or reconcile influences of "bottom-up" (message characteristics) and "top-down" (schemas, knowledge brought to the media by audiences) factors in message processing. Some theories may focus entirely on competition among groups of encoders, not just in economic terms but encoding goals and traditions. Theories focusing on audiences may identify the "minimum set of uses and gratifications" needed for maintenance of a media behavior pattern.

Other theories will attempt to link the various chapters in this book by examining patterns of encoding and decoding in dynamic models that cross time. Thus, for example, we might theorize along the following lines in "fleshing out" the "internationalization theory of media forms and content" cited earlier. We begin with two premises. First, audiences struggle between needs for familiarity and diversity in form and content of media messages. Second, encoding organizations and individuals strive for a combination of personal-professional satisfaction and commercial-resource viability. Pressures to achieve a balance between encoding-organizational goals while facing the constraints of audience needs for familiarity and diversity will lead to increasing expansion of the "domains" linking encoding and decoding activity. This expansion occurs in three ways. First, encoding organizations from one country seek message forms or encoders from other domains (cartoons or cartoonists from Tokyo) in a search to be creative, different, and competitive. Second encoders seek new audiences in other countries and cultures for existing messages (American football in England). Third, audiences from one culture or country seek novelty and gratification by seeking out media content and forms from other cultures and countries; with increased travel to other countries, diversification of populations through immigration, and greater interpersonal communication among people from different cultures, the opportunity and inclination for this third option increases. Thus, over time, media forms and content may become increasingly "internationalized." There are many consequences that could accompany this process, the "dilution" of national cultures and, perhaps, the disappearance, of smaller, weaker forms in this international exchange. However, the majority of any population tends to be more satisfied with media presentations that are familiar. Will they eventually reject innovations or be attracted to a form which incorporates a few novel concepts into an accustomed genre? The international "marketplace" or exchange of messages offers intriguing possibilities—and no predictable, "safe" ground. This fact is precisely what makes the study of media processes so fascinating: limitless possibilities grounded in a rich and fascinating history.

References and Author Index

The bold numbers in brackets at the end of each citation
are the pages on which authors are cited in the text.

Aarons, Leroy F. "Alternatives: Gays & Lesbians in the Newsroom," *Newspaper Research Bureau* (Summer, 1990) 11(3): 38-49. **[148]**

Abbott, Eric A. "The Volunteer Newspaper: A Communication Solution for Small Rural Communities? A Case Study," paper presented to the Newspaper Division at the annual conference of the Association for Education in Journalism and Mass Communication, Portland, July, 1988. **[71]**

Abbott, Eric A. and Lynn T. Brassfield. "Comparing Decisions on Releases by Television and Newspaper Gatekeepers," *Journalism Quarterly* (Winter, 1989) 66(4): 853-856. **[156, 161]**

Abel, John D. and Frederick N. Jacobs, "Radio Station Manager Attitudes Toward Broadcasting Graduates," *Journal of Broadcasting* (Fall, 1975) 19(4): 439-451. **[164]**

Abelman, Robert. "A Comparison of Black and White Families as Portrayed on Religious and Secular Television Programs," *Journal of Black Studies* (September, 1989) 20(1): 60-79. **[270, 364]**

Abelman, Robert. "'PTL Club' Viewer Uses and Gratifications," *Communication Quarterly* (Winter, 1989) 37(1): 54-66. **[270]**

Abelman, Robert. "Motivations for Viewing 'The 700 Club.'" *Journalism Quarterly* (Spring, 1988) 65(1): 112-118. **[252, 270]**

Abelman, Robert. "Why Do People Watch Religious Television? A Uses and Gratifications Approach," *Review of Religious Research* (December, 1987) 29(2): 199-210. **[270, 275]**

Abelman, Robert. "Religious Television Uses and Gratifications," *Journal of Broadcasting & Electronic Media* (Summer, 1987) 31(3): 293-307. **[270, 275]**

Abelman, Robert and Gary Pettey. "How Political Is Religious Television?" *Journalism Quarterly* (Summer, 1988) 65(2): 313-319, 359. **[370]**

Abrahamson, David. "A Quantitative Analysis of U.S. Consumer Magazines: Baseline Study and Gender Determinants," paper presented at the annual conference of the Association for Education in Journalism and Mass Communication, August, 1992. **[73]**

Abt, V. and D.J. McDowell. "Does the Press Cover Gambling Issues Poorly? Evidence from a Newspaper Content Analysis," *Sociology and Social Research* (April, 1987) 71(3): 193-198. **[371]**

Adams, Edward E. "Market Subordination and Secret Combinations: Scripps Howard Newspapers and the Origin of Joint Operating Agreements," paper presented to the History Division at the annual conference of the Association for Education in Journalism and Mass Communication, Montreal, August, 1992. **[88, 90]**

Adams, Edward E. "A Comparison of Local Editorial Issues in Competitive, Joint Monopoly and Joint Operating Agreement Newspapers," paper presented to the Media Management and Economics Division at the annual conference of the Association for Education in Journalism and Mass Communication, Montreal, August, 1992. **[88, 90]**

Adams, R.C. and M.J. Fish. "Television News Directors' Perceptions of Station Management Style," *Journalism Quarterly* (Spring, 1987) 64(1): 154-162. **[140]**

Adams, W.C. "Whose Lives Count? TV Coverage of Natural Disasters," *Journal of Communication* (Spring, 1986) 36(2): 113-122. **[156]**

Adnan, Mohd. Hamdan. "Women and the Media in Malaysia," *Media Asia* (1987) 14(4): 194-203. **[47, 366, 367]**

Adoni, Hanna. "The Function of Mass Media in the Political Socialization of Adolescents," *Communication Research* (January 1979) 6: 84-106. **[216, 279]**

Agbese, Pita Ogaba and Chris W. Ogbondah. "The Press and Authoritarian Regimes: A Critical Analysis of Public Reactions to Press Control Laws in Nigeria," paper presented at the annual conference of the Association for Education in Journalism and Mass Communication, Minneapolis, August, 1990. **[59]**

Ahmed, S.A. "The Language Press in India: A Case Study of Malayalam Newspapers," *Gazette* (1986) 38: 71-82. **[158]**

Aida, Toshihiko. "Mass Communication Behavior of Japanese Audience--Changes from the 1950's to the 1980's," *Studies of Broadcasting* (1987) 23: 73-104. **[193, 211, 253]**

Ainslie, P. "Confronting a Nation of Grazers," *Channels* (September, 1988), pp. 54-62. **[176]**

Aitken, Hugh G.J. *The Continuous Wave: Technology and American Radio, 1900-1932.* Princeton: Princeton University Press, 1985. **[26]**

Ajuonuma, Livi. "U.S. Television Coverage of Crisis in the Third World: The Case of the Sub-Saharan Hunger Crisis," Ph.D. dissertation, University of Minnesota, 1987. **[156]**

Akhavan-Majid, Roya. "The Effect of Chain Ownership on Editorial Independence: A Case Study," paper presented in the Newspaper Division at the annual conference of the Association for Education in Journalism and Mass Communication, Minneapolis, August, 1990. **[90]**

Akhavan-Majid, Roya, Anita Rife and Sheila Gopinath. "Chain Ownership and Editorial Independence: A Case Study of Gannett Newspapers," *Journalism Quarterly* (Spring/Summer, 1991) 68(1/2): 59-66. **[90]**

Akhavan-Majid, Roya and Gary Wolf. "American Mass Media and the Myth of Libertarianism: Toward an 'Elite Power Group' Theory," *Critical Studies in Mass Communication* (1991) 8(2): 139-151. **[54]**

Akst, Daniel. "New Magazine Tries to Carve Out a Niche by Reporting on the Business of Sports," *Wall Street Journal*, Dec. 15, 1987, p. 29. **[73]**

Albarran, Alan B. and Don Umphrey. "Ethnic Diversity: The Uses of Television and Cable Television Services by Hispanics, Blacks and Whites," paper presented to the Mass Communication Division at the annual conference of the International Communication Association, Miami, May, 1992. **[233]**

Albert, E. "Acquired Immune Deficiency Syndrome: The Victim and the Press," *Studies in Communication*, ed. T. McCormack. Vol. 3, Greenwich, CT: JAI Press, 1986, pp. 135-158. **[358]**

Alesandrini, Katheryn L. "Pictures and Adult Learning," *Instructional Science* (1984) 13(1): 63-77. **[316]**

Alexander, A., M.S. Ryan and P. Munoz. "Creating a Learning Context: Investigations on the Interaction of Siblings during Television Viewing," *Critical Studies in Mass Communication* (December, 1984) 1(4): 345-364. **[238]**

Alexander, Alison. "Adolescents' Soap Opera Viewing and Relational Perceptions," *Journal of Broadcasting and Electronic Media* (Summer, 1985) 29(3): 295-308. **[275]**

Alexander, Suzanne. "'Interactive TV' Test Is Watched to See Who's More than Remotely Interested," *Wall Street Journal*, May 10, 1990, p. 1B. **[74]**

Allen, Myria Watkins, Joe Hart Seibert, John W. Haas and Stephanie Zimmermann, "Broadcasting Departmental Impact on Employee Perceptions and Conflict," *Journalism Quarterly* (Fall, 1988) 65(3): 668-677. **[162]**

Allen, R.C. "Reader-Oriented Criticism and Television," *Channels of Discourse: Television and Contemporary Criticism*, ed. R.C. Allen. Chapel Hill: University of North Carolina Press, 1987, pp. 74-112. **[16]**

Allen, Richard L. and William T. Bielby. "Blacks' Attitudes and Behaviors Toward Television," *Communication Research* (October, 1979) 6: 437-462. **[270]**

Allen, Robert C. *Speaking of Soap Operas*. Chapel Hill: University of North Carolina Press, 1985. **[20, 335]**

Altheide, David L. "Three-in-one News: Network Coverage of Iran," *Journalism Quarterly* (Fall, 1982) 59(3):482-486. **[371]**

Altheide, David L. "Media Hegemony: A Failure of Perspective," *Public Opinion Quarterly* (1984) 48: 476-490. **[158]**

Altheide, David L. "Symbolic Interaction and 'Uses and Gratification'" Towards A Theoretical Integration," *Communications: The European Journal of Communication* (1985) 11(3): 73-82. **[272]**

Altman, Rich (Ed.). *Genre: The Musical*. Boston: Routledge and Kegan Paul/British Film Institute, 1981. **[331]**

Altschull, J. Herbert. *Agents of Power*. New York: Longman, 1984. **[52, 145]**

Altschull, J. Herbert. "What Is News?" *Mass Comm Review* (December, 1974) 2(1):17-23. **[129]**

Amlund, Jeane, Janet Gaffney and Raymond Kulhavy. "Map Feature Content and Text Recall in Good and Poor Readers," *Journal of Reading Behavior* (1985) 17(4): 317-330. **[289]**

Andersen, R. "Visions of Instability: US Television's Law and Order News of El Salvador," *Media, Culture and Society* (April, 1988) 10(2): 239-264. **[126]**

Anderson, D., E.P. Lorch, D.E. Field and J. Sanders. "The Effects of TV Program Comprehensibility on Preschool Children's Visual Attention to Television," *Child Development* (1981) 52: 151-157.

Anderson, D. "How Managing Editors View and Deal with Newspaper Ethical Issues," *Journalism Quarterly* (Summer/Autumn, 1987) 64(2/3): 341-345. **[155]**

Anderson, Daniel R. "Television Literacy and the Critical Viewer," *Children's Understanding of Television*, ed. Jennings Bryant and Daniel Anderson. New York: Academic Press, 1983.

Anderson, Douglas A. and Claudia J. "Weather Coverage in Dailies," *Journalism Quarterly* (Summer, 1986) 63(2): 382-385. **[339]**

Anderson, Douglas A. and Frederic A. Leigh. "How Newspaper Editors and Broadcast News Directors View Media Ethics," *Newspaper Research Journal* (Winter/Spring, 1992) 13(1/2): 112-22. **[155]**

Anderson, J.M. and S. Harris. "Communications and Future Employment Trends," *Telematics and Informatics* (1989) 6(2): 71-80. **[65, 316]**

Anderson, J.R. "Memory for Information about Individuals," *Memory and Cognition* (1977) 5: 430-442. **[316]**

Anderson, James A. and Robert K. Avery. "The Concept of Effects: Recognizing Our Personal Judgments," *Journal of Broadcasting & Electronic Media* (Summer, 1988) 32(3): 359-372. **[20]**

Anderson, John R. and Gordon H. Bower. *Human Associative Memory*. Washington, D.C.: Winston, 1973. **[316]**

Anderson, Mary A. "Two-Newspaper Towns: Competition Endures in 12 Smaller Places," *Presstime*, July, 1990, pp. 44-46. **[85, 97]**

Andorka, Rudolf. "Time Budgets and Their Uses," *Annual Review of Sociology* (1987) 13: 149-164. **[170, 279]**

Andreasen, M. and H.L. Steeves. "Assertive Response to the On-the-Job Sex Discrimination as a Possible Predictor of Newspaper Reading Behavior," *Newspaper Research Bureau* (Summer, 1984) 5(4): 27-40. **[256]**

Andrews, Frank M. (Ed.). *Research on the Quality of Life*. Ann Arbor: Institute for Social Research, University of Michigan, 1986. **[267]**

Andrews, Frank and Stephen Withey. *Social Indicators of Well Being: Americans' Perceptions of Life Quality*. New York: Plenum Press, 1976. **[211, 267]**

Andreyenkov, V., J.P. Robinson and N. Popov. "News Media Use and Adolescents' Information about Nuclear Issues: A Soviet-American Comparison," *Journal of Communication* (Spring, 1989) 39(2): 95-113. **[254]**

Andsager, Julie L. "Differentiating Media Practices: How Demographic Variables Relate to Support for Freedom of the Press," paper presented to the Communication Theory & Methodology Division at the annual conference of the Association for Education in Journalism and Mass Communication, Montreal, August, 1992. **[204]**

Anglin, Gary J. "Effect of Pictures on Recall of Written Prose: How Durable Are Picture Effects?" *Educational Communication and Technology Journal* (Spring, 1987) 35(1): 25-30. **[291, 316]**

Anshary, Isa. "A Comparison of Media Use of Acehnese and Balinese Natives, Indonesia," master's thesis, Iowa State University, 1988.

Arai, Hirosuke and Norimichi Fujiwara. "The Information Consciousness of the Japanese in the Present Age," *Studies of Broadcasting* (March, 1987) 23: 105-140. Tokyo: NHK Theoretical Research Center. **[274]**

Arliss, L., Mary Cassata and Thomas Skill, "Dyadic Interaction on the Daytime Serials: How Men and Women Vie for Power," *Life on Daytime Television*, ed. M. Cassata and T. Skill. Norwood, NJ: Ablex Publishers, 1983, pp. 147-156. **[366]**

Armstrong, C.B. and A.M. Rubin. "Talk Radio as Interpersonal Communication," *Journal of Communication* (Spring, 1989) 39(2): 84. **[277]**

Armstrong, G. Blake. "Background Television and Reading Performance," paper presented to the Communication Theory & Methodology Division at the annual conference of the Association for Education in Journalism and Mass Communication, Minneapolis, August, 1990. **[226]**

Armstrong, G. Blake, Greg A. Boiarsky and Marie-Louise Mares. "Background Television and Reading Performance," *Communication Monographs* (September, 1991) 58: 235-253. **[226]**

Armstrong, G. Blake and Bradley S. Greenberg. "Background Television as an Inhibitor of Cognitive Processing," *Human Communication Research* (1990) 16(3): 355-386. **[226]**

Arnheim, R. *Art and Visual Perception: A Psychology of the Creative Eye*, Berkeley, CA: University of California Press, 1974. **[288, 318]**

Arnold, Jay. "Copycat Money Pitches Dismay Public TV Outlets," *Plain Dealer*, Nov. 7, 1989, p. 6E. **[77]**

Aronoff, Craig. "Credibility of Public Relations for Journalists," *Public Relations Review* (Fall, 1975) 1: 45-56. **[161]**

Arundel, John. "Time Warner and Soviets to Build Theaters in U.S.S.R.," *Plain Dealer*, March 8, 1990, p. 15E. New York Times dispatch. **[67]**

Ash, Rene' L. *The Motion Picture Film Editor*. Metuchen, NJ: Scarecrow Press, 1974. **[105]**

Ata, A.W. "Moslem Arab Portrayal in the Australian Press and in School Textbooks," *Australian Journal of Social Issues* (August, 1984) 19(3): 207-217. **[371]**

Atkin, Charles. "Instrumental Utilities and Information Seeking," *New Models for Communication Research*, ed. Peter Clarke, Vol, 2, Sage Annual Reviews of Communication Research, Beverly Hills: Sage Publications, 1973, pp. 205-242. **[258]**

Atkin, David. "An Analysis of Television Series with Minority Lead Characters," *Critical Studies in Mass Communication* (December, 1992) 9: 337-349. **[343]**

Atkin, David. "Uses of Cable Television amidst a Multimedia Environment," paper presented at the annual conference of the Midwest Association for Public Opinion Research, Chicago, November, 1991. **[277]**

Atkin, David. "The Evolution of Television Series Addressing Single Women, 1966-1990," *Journal of Broadcasting & Electronic Media* (Fall, 1991) 35(4): 517-523. **[277, 350, 351]**

Atkin, David. "The (Low) Power Elite: Deregulated Licensing Criteria for Low-Power Television in the USA," *Telecommunications Policy* (December, 1987) 11(4): 357-368. **[68, 69]**

Atkin, David, Bradley S. Greenberg, and Thomas F. Baldwin. "The Home Ecology of Children's Television Viewing: Parental Mediation and the New Video Environment," *Journal of Communication* (Summer, 1991) 41(3): 40-52. **[271]**

Atkin, David, Carrie Heeter and Thomas Baldwin. "How Presence of Cable Affects Parental Mediation of TV Viewing," *Journalism Quarterly* (Autumn, 1989) 66(3): 557-563, 578. **[236]**

Atkin, David and B. Litman. "Network TV Programming: Economics, Audiences, and the Ratings Game, 1971-1986," *Journal of Communication* (Summer, 1986) 36(3): 32-51. **[155]**

Atkin, David and Robert LaRose. "News and Information on Community Access Channels: Market Concerns Amidst the Marketplace of Ideas," paper presented to the Radio-Television Division at the annual conference of the Association for Education in Journalism and Mass Communication (AEJMC), Portland, OR, July, 1988. **[196]**

Atwater, Tony. "Reader Interest in Environmental News," *Newspaper Research Journal* (Fall, 1988) 10(1): 31-37. **[193]**

Atwater, Tony. "Consonance in Local Television News," *Journal of Broadcasting & Electronic Media* (Fall, 1986) 30(4): 467-472. **[123, 155]**

Atwater, Tony. "Factors of Program Choice in Public Television: A National Survey," *Journal of Educational Television* (1986) 12(2): 105-117. **[123, 155]**

Atwater, Tony. "Product Differentiation in Local TV News," *Journalism Quarterly* (Winter, 1984) 61(4): 757-762. **[158]**

Atwater, Tony and Fred Fico. "Source Reliance and Use in Reporting State Government: A Study of Print and Broadcast Practices," *Newspaper Research Journal* (Fall, 1986) 8(1): 53-61. **[161]**

Atwater, Tony, Carrie Heeter and Natalie Brown. "Foreshadowing the Electronic Publishing Age: First Exposures to Viewtron," *Journalism Quarterly* (Winter, 1985) 62(4): 807-815. **[176]**

Auh, Taik Sup. "Deprivation of Television Viewing Opportunities and Its Impact on Lifestyle, Leisure Activities, Media Use and Family Interaction," paper presented at the annual conference of the Association for Education in Journalism and Mass Communication, Boston, August, 1991. **[248]**

Austin, B.A. "Loneliness and Use of Six Mass Media among College Students," *Psychological Reports* (February, 1985) 56(2): 323-327. **[277]**

Austin, Bruce A. *Immediate Seating: A Look at Movie Audiences*. Belmont, CA: Wadsworth Pub. Co., 1989. **[180, 214]**

Austin, Bruce A. "Portrait of an Art Film Audience," *Journal of Communication* (Winter, 1984) 34(1): 74-87. **[214]**

Austin, Bruce A. and T.F. Gordon. "Movie Genres: Toward a Conceptualized Model and Standardized Definitions," *Current Research in Film: Audiences, Economics, and Law*, ed. B.A. Austin. Vol. 3. Norwood, NJ: Ablex, 1987, pp. 12-33. **[329]**

Auter, Philip J. "Analysis of the Ratings for Television Comedy Programs 1950-1959: The End of 'Berlesque,'" *Mass Comm Review* (1990) 17(3): 23-32. **[334]**

Auter, Philip J. "TV that Talks Back: An Experimental Validation of a Parasocial Interaction Scale," *Journal of Broadcasting & Electronic Media* (Spring, 1992) 36(2): 173-181. **[319]**

Avery, Donald R. "American Over European Community? Newspaper Content Changes, 1808-1812," *Journalism Quarterly* (Summer, 1986) 63(2): 311-314. **[30, 341]**

Avery, Donald R. "The Emerging American Newspaper: Discovering the Home Front," *American Journalism* (1984) 1(2): 51-66. **[30]**

Avery, Robert K. "Adolescents' Use of the Mass Media," *American Behavioral Scientist* (September/October, 1979) 23(1): 53-70. **[188]**

Babrow, Austin S. "Student Motives for Watching Soap Operas," *Journal of Broadcasting & Electronic Media* (Summer, 1987) 31(3): 309-321. **[275]**

Babrow, Austin. "Audience Motivation, Viewing Context, Media Content, and Form: The Interactional Emergence of Soap Opera Entertainment," *Communication Studies* (Winter, 1990) 41(4): 343-361. **[275]**

Babrow, Austin S. "Theory and Method in Research on Audience Motives," *Journal of Broadcasting & Electronic Media* (Fall, 1988) 32(4): 471-487. **[245, 275]**

Babrow, Austin S. "An Expectancy-Value Analysis of the Student Soap Opera Audience," *Communication Research* (April, 1989) 16(2): 155-178. **[245]**

Babrow, Austin S. "Social Creation of Media Entertainment: The Integration of Audience Motives, and the Context, Content, and Form of Soap Operas," paper presented at the annual conference of the Speech Communication Association, New Orleans, LA, Sept. 4, 1988. **[245]**

Babrow, Austin S. and David L. Swanson. "Disentangling Antecedents of Audience Exposure Levels: Extending Expectancy-Value Analysis of Gratifications Sought from Television News," *Communication Monographs* (March, 1988) 55: 1-21. **[245]**

Back, Kurt W. "Rhetoric as Communication and Performance," *Communication Research* (February, 1989) 16(1): 130-148. **[25, 27]**

Badaracco, Claire. "Alternatives to Newspaper Advertising, 1890-1920: Printers' Innovative Product and Message Designs," *Journalism Quarterly* (Winter, 1990) 67(4): 1042-1050. **[34]**

Bader, Renate G. "How Science News Sections Influence Newspaper Science Coverage: A Case Study," *Journalism Quarterly* (Spring, 1990) 67(1): 88-96. **[136]**

Badzinski, Diane M. "Message Intensity and Cognitive Representations of Discourse: Effects on Inferential Processing," *Human Communication Research* (Fall, 1989) 16(1): 3-32. **[295]**

Bagdikian, B.H. "The Media-Conglomeration Concentration," *The AFL-CIO American Federationist* (March, 1979) 86(3): 14-33. **[79]**

Bain, Chic and Dennis H. Weaver. "Readers' Reactions to Newspaper Design," *Newspaper Research Journal* (1979) 1: 48-59.**[362]**

Bailey, C. Ian and George H. Sage. "Values Communicated by a Sports Event: The Case of the Super Bowl," *Journal of Sport Behavior* (September, 1988) 11(3): 126-143. **[128, 136, 160]**

Baldasty, Gerald J. and Jeffrey B. Rutenbeck. "Money, Politics and Newspapers: The Business Environment of Press Partisanship in the Late 19th Century," *Journalism History* (Summer/Autumn, 1988) 15(2-3): 60-69. **[30, 31]**

Baldasty, Gerald J. and Myron K. Jordan. "E.W. Scripps and the Newspaper Business: The Market Niche Strategy of Competition," paper presented to the Management and Economics Division at the annual conference of the Association for Education in Journalism and Mass Communication, Minneapolis, Aug. 10, 1990. **[88]**

Baldwin, R. Scott, Ziva Peleg-Bruckner, and Ann H. McClintock. "Effects of Topic Interest and Prior Knowledge on Reading Comprehension," *Reading Research Quarterly* (Summer, 1985) 20(4): 497-504. **[314]**

Baldwin, Thomas F., Marianne Barrett and Benjamin Bates. "Influence of Cable on Television News Audiences," *Journalism Quarterly* (Fall, 1992) 69(3): 651-658. **[175]**

Baldwin, Thomas F., Benjamin Bates and Marianne Barrett. "The Impact of Cable on Television Journalism Audiences," paper presented at the annual conference of the Association for Education in Journalism and Mass Communication, Minneapolis, August, 1990. **[183]**

Bales, Fred. "Television Use and Confidence in Television by Blacks and Whites in Four Selected Years," *Journal of Black Studies* (March, 1986) 16(3): 283-291. **[197, 233]**

Balio, Tino (ed.). *The American Film Industry.* Madison: University of Wisconsin Press, 1985, rev. ed. **[102]**

Ball-Rokeach, Sandra J. and K. Reardon. "Monologue, Dialogue, and Telelog: Comparing an Emergent Form of Communication with Traditional Forms," *Advancing Communication Science: Merging Mass and Interpersonal Processes*, eds. R.P. Hawkins, J.M. Wiemann, and S. Pingree. Newbury Park, CA: Sage Publications, 1988, pp. 135-161. **[7]**

Banks, Mark J. and Sara E. Titus. "The Promise and Performance of Low Power Television," *Journal of Media Economics* (Fall, 1990) 3(2): 15-25. **[69]**

Banks, Mark J. and Mary Ellen Banks. "The Evolution of Health Programming on Cable Television," *Health Values* (November/December, 1988) 12(6): 21-27. **[370]**

Bantz, Charles R., Suzanne McCorkle and Roberta C. Baade. "The News Factory," *Communication Research* (January, 1980) 7(1): 45-68. **[140]**

Baptista-Fernandez, Pilar and Bradley S. Greenberg. "The Context, Characteristics and Communication Behaviors of Blacks on Television," *Life on Television: Content Analyses of U.S. TV Drama,* ed. Bradley S. Greenberg. Norwood, NJ: Ablex, 1980, pp. 13-21. **[364]**

Barber, Benjamin R. *Salmagundi* (Winter, 1989) 81: 159-173). **[19]**

Barber, John T. and Oscar H. Gandy Jr. "Press Portrayal of African American and White United States Representatives," *Howard Journal of Communications* (Spring, 1990) 2(2): 213-225. **[365]**

Barber, S.R. and J.H. Smith. "Domestic and Foreign Language News Reliance among Chinese and American Students," *Howard Journal of Communications* (Winter 1989/1990) 2(1): 97-115. **[277]**

Barchak, Leonard J. "Black Entertainment Television: Seeking Dr. King or Slouching toward Malcolm X?" paper presented at the annual confernece of the Association for Education in Journalism and Mass Communication, Montreal, August, 1992. **[69]**

Barker, David. "The Emergence of Television's Repertoire of Representation, 1920-1935," *Journal of Broadcasting & Electronic Media* (Summer, 1991) 35(3): 305-318. **[115]**

Barker, David. "'It's Been Real': Forms of Television Representation," *Critical Studies in Mass Communication* (March, 1988) 5(1): 42-56. **[333]**

Barkin, S.M. and Michael Gurevitch. "Out of Work and on the Air: Television News of Unemployment," *Critical Studies in Mass Communication* (March, 1987) 4(1): 1-20. **[127, 128]**

Barlow, William. "Community Radio in the U.S.: The Struggle for a Democratic Medium," *Media, Culture and Society* (1988) 10: 81-105. **[70, 74]**

Barnett, George A. and Hsiu-Jung Chang. "Seasonality in Television Viewing: A Mathematical Model of Cultural Processes," paper presented to the Information Systems Division of the International Communication Association, San Francisco, May, 1989. **[272]**

Barnett, George A., Hsiu-Jung Chang, Edward L. Fink and William D. Richards Jr. "Seasonality in Television Viewing," *Communication Research* (December, 1991) 18(6): 755-772. **[272]**

Barnett, L.A. (Ed.) *Research about Leisure: Past, Present and Future.* Champaign, IL: Sagamore Pub., 1988. **[211]**

Barnhurst, Kevin G. and Ellen Wartella. "Newspapers and Citizenship: Young Adults' Subjective Experience of Newspapers," *Critical Studies in Mass Communication* (1991) 8: 195-209. **[215]**

Barnhurst, Kevin G. and John C. Nerone. "Design Trends in U.S. Front Pages, 1885-1985," *Journalism Quarterly* (Winter, 1991) 68(4): 796-804. **[338]**

Baron, Lois J. "Television Literacy Curriculum in Action: A Long-Term Study," *Journal of Educational Television* (1985) 11(1): 49-55. **[273]**

Barranco, Deborah A. and Leonard Shyles. "Arab vs. Israeli News Coverage in the 'New York Times,' 1976 and 1984," *Journalism Quarterly* (Spring, 1988) 65(1): 178-181. **[371]**

Barrios, Leoncio. "Television, Telenovelas, and Family Life in Venezuela," *World Families Watch Television,* ed. James Lull. Newbury Park, CA: Sage Publications, 1988, pp. 49-79. **[235]**

Barron, I. and R. Curnow. *The Future with Microelectronics.* Milton Keynes: Open University Press, 1979. **[93]**

Bartlett, Frederick Charles. *Remembering: A Study in Experimental and Social Psychology.* Cambridge, England: Cambridge University Press, 1932. **[294]**

Barwise, P. "Repeat-Viewing of Prime-Time Television Series," *Journal of Advertising Research* (August/September, 1986) 26(4): 9-14. **[212]**

Barwise, T. Patrick and Andrew S.C. Ehrenberg. "The Liking and Viewing of Regular TV Series," *Journal of Consumer Research* (June, 1987) 14: 63-70. **[195]**

Barzun, Jacques. *Classic, Romantic, and Modern.* Chicago: Little, Brown, 1981. **[18]**

Basil, Michael D. "Attention to and Memory for Audio and Video Information in Television Scenes," paper presented to the Information Systems Division at the annual conference of the International Communication Association, Miami, May, 1992. **[304, 319]**

Basil, Michael D. "Primary News Source Changes: Question Wording, Availability and Cohort Effects," *Journalism Quarterly* (Winter, 1990) 67(4): 708-722. **[184]**

Bates, Benjamin J. "Breaking the Structural Logjam: The Impact of Cable on Local TV Market Concentration," *Journal of Media Economics* (Fall, 1991) 4(3): 47-57. **[84]**

Bates, Benjamin J. "Concentration in Local Television Markets," paper presented at the annual conference of the Association for Education in Journalism and Mass Communication, Minneapolis, August, 1990. **[65, 81, 84]**

Bates, Benjamin J. "Channel Diversity in Cable Television," paper presented at the annual conference of the Association for Education in Journalism and Mass Communication, Washington, D.C., August, 1989. **[65, 82]**

Bates, Benjamin. "Information Utilities and Information Societies: Considering PC-Based Information Networks as an Alternative," paper presented at the annual conference of the International Communication Association, New Orleans, June, 1988. **[75, 93, 94]**

Bates, Benjamin. "The Impact of Deregulation on Television Station Prices," *Journal of Media Economics* (Spring, 1988) 1(1): 5-22. **[75, 93]**

Bauer, Raymond A. "The Audience," *Handbook of Communication* ed. Wilbur Schramm, Nathan Maccoby and Edwin B. Parker. Chicago: Rand McNally, 1973. **[229]**

Baughman, James L. "Television in the 'Golden Age': An Entrepreneurial Experiment," *The Historian* (February, 1985) 47(2): 175-195. **[39]**

Baxter, Robert L., Cynthia De Riemer, Ann Landini, Larry Leslie and Michael W. Singletary. "A Content Analysis of Music Videos," *Journal of Broadcasting & Electronic Media* (Summer, 1985) 29(3): 333-340. **[336]**

Beam, Randal A. "Journalism Professionalism as an Organizational-Level Concept," *Journalism Monographs* (June, 1990) No. 121. **[92, 97, 151, 165]**

Beam, Randal A. "The Impact of Group Ownership on Organizational Professionalism," paper presented at the annual conference of the Association for Education in Journalism and Mass Communication, Minneapolis, August, 1990. **[92, 97, 151, 165]**

Beam, Randal A., Sharon Dunwoody, and Gerald M. Kosicki. "The Relationship of Prize-Winning to Prestige and Job Satisfaction," *Journalism Quarterly* (Winter, 1986) 63(4): 693-699. **[165]**

Beard, J. and M.G. Ragheb. "Measuring Leisure Satisfaction," *Journal of Leisure Research* (1980) 12: 20-33. **[274]**

Beasley, M. "Newspapers: Is There a New Majority Defining the News?" *Women in Mass Communication: Challenging Gender Values*, ed. P.J. Creedon. Newbury Park, CA: Sage Publications, 1989, pp. 180-194. **[156]**

Beasley, M. "The Women's National Press Club: Case Study of Professional Aspirations," *Journalism History* (Winter, 1988) 15(4): 112-121. **[147]**

Beasley, M. "The Muckrakers and Lynching: A Case Study in Racism," *Journalism History* (Autumn/Winter, 1982-1983) 9(3-4): 86-90. **[33]**

Beasley, M.H. and K.T. Theus. *The New Majority*. Lanham, MD: University Press of America, 1988. **[164]**

Becker, Carl M. "Newspapers in Battle: The Dayton Empire and the Dayton Journal during the Civil War," *Ohio History* (Winter/Spring, 1990) 99: 29-50. **[31]**

Becker, Lee B. and Pamela J. Creedon. "Coming to Grips with Sports Viewing on Television: Conceptual and Methodological Work on Motivations for Watching Sports," paper presented at the annual conference of the Midwest Association for Public Opinion Research (MAPOR), Chicago, November, 1989. **[275]**

Becker, Lee B., Sharon Dunwoody and Sheizaf Rafaeli, "Cable's Impact on Use of Other News Media," *Journal of Broadcasting* (Spring, 1983) 27(2): 127-140. **[212]**

Becker, Lee B., Jeff W. Fruit and S.L. Caudill. *The Training and Hiring of Journalists*. Norwood, NJ: Ablex, 1987. **[164]**

Becker, Lee B., Gerald M. Kosicki and Felecia Jones. "Racial Differences in Evaluations of the Mass Media," *Journalism Quarterly* (Spring, 1992) 69(1): 124-134. **[206, 220]**

Becker, Lee B., D. Charles Whitney, and Erik L. Collins, "Public Understanding of How the News Media Operate," *Journalism Quarterly* (Winter, 1980) 57(4): 571-578. **[220]**

Bednall, D.H.B. "Television Use by Melbourne's Greek Community," *Media Information Australia* (February, 1988) 47: 44-49. **[234]**

Behera, Sunil K. "Gender Role Biases on Indian Television," *Media Asia* (1989) 16(3): 119-124. **[366]**

Behnke, Ralph R. and Phyllis Miller. "Viewer Reactions to Content and Presentational Format of Television News," *Journalism Quarterly* (Fall, 1992) 69(3): 659-665. **[277]**

Bekken, Jon. "Concentration in the Retail Book Industry: The Emerging Distribution Monopoly," paper presented at the annual conference of the International Communication Association, San Francisco, May, 1989. **[88, 89]**

Bekken, Jon. "Working-Class Newspapers in the United States," paper presented at the annual conference of the Association for Education in Journalism and Mass Communication, Portland, OR, July, 1988.

Belbase, Subhadra. "Press Freedom and Political Stress in Nepal," paper presented at the annual conference of the International Communication Association, Minneapolis, May 22, 1981. **[60]**

Belk, Russell W. "Material Values in the Comics: A Content Analysis of Comic Books Featuring Themes of Wealth," *Journal of Consumer Research* (June, 1987) 14: 26-42. **[357]**

Belk, R.W. and R.W. Pollay. "The Good Life in Twentieth Century U.S. Advertising," *Media Information Australia* (November, 1987) 46: 51-57. **[336]**

Belk, R.W. and R.W. Pollay. "Images of Ourselves: The Good Life in Twentieth Century Advertising," *Journal of Consumer Research* (March, 1985) 11(4): 887-897. **[336]**

Belkin, Lisa. "For Quotable Expert on Political Messages, Phone Never Stops Ringing," *New York Times*, Nov. 5, 1988, p. 8. **[137]**

Bell, Daniel. "The Third Technological Revolution," *Dissent* (Spring, 1989) 36: 164-176. **[69, 93]**

Bell, Daniel. "Glasnost Watch: To the Other Shore," *Dissent* (Fall, 1988) pp. 407-413.

Bell, Daniel. *The Winding Passage: Essays and Sociological Journeys, 1960-1980.* Cambridge, MA: Abt Books, 1980. **[18, 64]**

Bell, Daniel. *The Cultural Contradictions of Capitalism.* New York: Basic Books, 1976. **[18, 64, 264]**

Bell, Daniel. *The Coming of Post-Industrial Society.* New York: Basic Books, 1976. **[18, 64, 264]**

Bell, J.H. and U.S. Pandey. "Gender-Role Stereotypes in Australian Farm Advertising," *Media Information Australia* (February, 1989) No. 51-45-49. **[366]**

Bellamy, Robert V., Daniel G. McDonald, and James R. Walker. "The Spin-Off as Television Program Form and Strategy," *Journal of Broadcasting & Electronic Media* (Summer, 1990) 34(3): 283-297. **[334]**

Bendix, Jacob and Carol M. Liebler. "Ideology and the Environment: U.S. Media and Deforestation in Brazilian Amazonia," paper presented to the Mass Communication and Society Division at the annual conference of the Association for Education in Journalism and Mass Communication, Minneapolis, August, 1990. **[371]**

Beniger, James R. *The Control Revolution: Technological and Economic Origins of the Information Society.* Cambridge, MA: Harvard University Press, 1986. **[64]**

Bennion, S.C. "Women Suffrage Papers of the West, 1869-1914," *American Journalism* (1986) 3(3): 125-137. **[33]**

Bennett, H. Stith and Jeff Ferrell. "Music Videos and Epistemic Socialization," *Youth and Society* (June, 1987) 18(4): 344-362. **[372]**

Berg, Charles Ramirez. "Stereotyping in Films in General and of the Hispanic in Particular," paper presented at the annual conference of the International Communication Association, San Francisco, May, 1989. **[345]**

Berger, A.A. "'He's Everything You're Not': A Semiological Analysis of 'Cheers,'" *Television Studies: Textual Analysis*, ed. G. Burns and R.J. Thompson. New York: Praeger, 1989, pp. 89-102. **[258]**

Berger, Arthur Asa. *Signs in Contemporary Culture: An Introduction to Semiotics*. New York: Longman, 1984. **[360]**

Berger, Charles R. and Steven H. Chaffee (Eds.) *Handbook of Communication Science*. Newbury Park, CA: Sage, 1987.

Berkman, Dave. "Chauvinism, Populism and Pre-War Television: Two Views as Seen by the Press, 1937-42," *Journalism Quarterly* (Summer, 1988) 62(2): 347-351. **[38]**

Berkowitz, Dan. "Routine Newswork and the What-A-Story: A Case Study of Organizational Adaptation," *Journal of Broadcasting and Electronic Media* (Winter, 1992) 36(1): 45-60. **[125]**

Berkowitz, Dan. "Non-Routine News and Newswork: Exploring a What-a-Story," *Journal of Communication* (Winter, 1992) 42(1): 82-94. **[125]**

Berkowitz, Dan. "Journalists' Perceptions of News Selection in Local Television: A Q-Methodology Study," paper presented to the Radio-TV Journalism Division at the annual conference of the Association for Education in Journalism and Mass Communication, Boston, August, 1991. **[160]**

Berkowitz, Dan. "Refining the Gatekeeping Metaphor for Local Television News," *Journal of Broadcasting & Electronic Media* (Winter, 1990) 34(1): 55-68. **[125, 156, 162]**

Berkowitz, Dan. "Routine Newswork and the What-A-Story: A Case Study of Organizational Adaptation," paper presented to the Radio-Television Journalism Division of the Association for Education in Journalism and Mass Communication at the annual conference of the Association for Education in Journalism and Mass Communication, Minneapolis, August, 1990. **[125, 156]**

Berkowitz, Dan. "Information Subsidy and Agenda-Building in Local Television News," paper presented at the annual conference of the Association for Education in Journalism and Mass Communication, Washington, D.C., 1989. **[160]**

Berkowitz, Dan. "Television News Sources and News Channels: A Study in Agenda-Building," *Journalism Quarterly* (Summer/Autumn, 1987) 64(2/3): 508-513. **[160]**

Berkowitz, Dan and Douglas B. Adams. "Information Subsidy and Agenda-Building in Local Television News," *Journalism Quarterly* (Winter, 1990) 67(4): 723-731. **[134]**

Berner, R. Thomas. "Literary Newswriting: The Death of an Oxymoron," *Journalism Monographs* (February, 1986), No. 99. **[139, 162]**

Berner, R. Thomas. "Commentary: The Narrative and the Headline," *Newspaper Research Journal* (Spring, 1983) 4(3): 33-40. **[363]**

Bernstein, James M. and Stephen Lacy. "Contextual Coverage of Government by Local Television News," *Journalism Quarterly* (Summer, 1992) 69(2): 329-340. **[96]**

Bernstein, James M., Stephen Lacy, Catherine Cassara, and Tuen-yu Lau. "Geographic Coverage by Local Television News," *Journalism Quarterly* (Winter, 1990) 64(4): 663-671. **[162]**

Bernt, Joseph and Marilyn Greenwald. "Daily Newspaper Coverage of the Gay and Lesbian Community: Perceptual Differences of Senior Editors and Their Gay and Lesbian Staffers," paper presented at the annual conference of the Association for Education in Journalism and Mass Communication, Boston, August, 1991. **[164]**

Berry, C., B. Gunter and B. Clifford. "Memory for Televised Information: A Problem for Applied and Theoretical Psychology," *Current Psychological Reviews* (1981) 1: 171-192. **[320]**

Berry, G.L. "Television and Afro-Americans: Past Legacy and Present Portrayals," *Television and Social Behavior: Beyond Violence and Children*, ed. S.B. Withey and R.P. Abeles. Hillsdale, NJ: Lawrence J. Erlbaum Associates, 1980, pp. 231-248. **[343]**

References and Author Index **387**

Berry, Venise T. "Limited Vision: Realism, The New Ghetto Aesthetic, and Black Female Representation in Today's Popular Black Films," paper presented at the annual conference of the Association for Education in Journalism and Mass Communication (AEJMC), Montreal, August, 1992. **[344]**

Bertazzoni, Donna M. "Gender-Based Differences in Attitudes Towards Stories: An Examination of Maryland Editors," paper presented to the Commission on the Status of Women at the annual conference of the Association for Education in Journalism and Mass Communication, Boston, August, 1991. **[125]**

Bertilson, H.S., D.K. Springer and K.M. Fierke. "Underrepresentation of Female Referents as Pronouns, Examples and Pictures in Introductory College Textbooks," *Psychological Reports* (December, 1982) 51(3): 923-931. **[354]**

Besen, Stanley M., Thomas G. Krattenmaker, A. Richard Metzger, Jr., and John R. Woodbury. *Misregulating Television: Network Dominance and the FCC.* Chicago: University of Chicago Press, 1984. **[83]**

Beville, H.M. Jr. *Audience Ratings: Radio, Television, and Cable.* Hillsdale, NJ: Erlbaum, 1985. **[334]**

Biddle, Bruce J. "Recent Developments in Role Theory," *Annual Review of Sociology* (1986) 12: 67-92. **[152, 153]**

Bielby, William T. and Denise D. Bielby. "Pay Equity and Employment Opportunities among Writers for Television and Feature Films," commissioned by the Writers Guild of America, Los Angeles, June 16, 1987 report. **[165]**

Biggs, Terrence C. and Harvey H.C. Marmurek. "Picture and Word Naming: Is Facilitation Due to Processing Overlap," *American Journal of Psychology* (1990) 103(1): 81-100. **[320]**

Bilby, Kenneth. *The General: David Sarnoff and the Rise of the Communications Industry.* New York: Harper & Row, 1986. **[58]**

Biocca, Frank, K. Neuwirth, H. Oshagan, P. Zhongdang and J. Richards. "Prime-and-Probe Methodology: An Experimental Technique for Studying Film and Television," paper presented to the International Communication Association, Montreal, May, 1987. **[312]**

Biocca, Frank. "Semantic Frames in Political Messages," *Television and Political LAdvertising,* ed. F. Biocca. Hillsdale, NJ: Lawrence Erlbaum, 1991. **[311,312, 320, 321]**

Biocca, Frank. "Mental Models of Television: Toward a Theory of the Semantic Processing of Television," paper presented to the Information Systems Division at the annual conference of the International Communication Association, Chicago, May, 1991. **[311, 312, 320, 321]**

Bishop, D.W. "Stability of Factor Structure of Leisure Behavior: Analysis of Four Communities," *Journal of Leisure Research* (1970) 2: 160-170. **[274]**

Bishop, Robert L., Katherine Sharma and Richard J. Brazee. "Determinants of Newspaper Circulation: A Pooled Cross-Sectional Time-Series Study in the United States, 1850-1970," *Communication Research* (January, 1980) 7(1): 3-22. **[80]**

Blackwood, Roy E. "Portrayal of the United States in the Newspapers of the People's Republic of China," paper presented at the annual conference of the Association for Education in Journalism and Mass Communication (AEJMC), Minneapolis, August, 1990. **[371]**

Blake, Reed H. and Edwin O. Haroldsen. *A Taxonomy of Concepts in Communication.* New York: Hastings House, 1975. **[14]**

Blanchard, Margaret A. *Exporting the First Amendment: The Press-Government Crusade of 1945-1952.* White Plains, NY: Longman, 1986. **[52]**

Blankenburg, William B. "Newspaper Scale and Newspaper Expenditures," *Newspaper Research Journal* (Winter, 1989) 10(2): 97-103. **[71, 154]**

Blankenburg, William B. "Consolidation in Two-Newspaper Firms," *Journalism Quarterly* (Autumn, 1985) 62(3): 474-481. **[97, 98]**

Blankenburg, William B. "A Newspaper Chain's Pricing Behavior," *Journalism Quarterly* (1983) 60: 275-280. **[97]**

Blankenburg, William B. and Ruth Walden. "Objectivity, Interpretation and Economy in Reporting," *Journalism Quarterly* (Autumn, 1977) 54: 591-595. **[130, 131]**

Bleske, Glen L. "Ms Gates Takes Over: An Updated Version of a 1949 Case Study," *Newspaper Research Journal* (Fall, 1991) 12(4): 88-97. **[158]**

Blick, T.E., H.H. Howard and J.P. Quartes. "Patterns of Consumer Interest in Specialized News," *Proceedings, Ninth Annual Communications Research Symposium,* ed. M.W. Singletary. Knoxville: College of Communication, University of Tennessee, 1986, pp. 125-133. **[193]**

Blonsky, Marshall. "Hooked on Horror," *The Plain Dealer,* Aug. 20, 1989, p. 1C. Blonsky is author of *American Mythologies* (Oxford University Press, 1990). **[330]**

Bloom, Charles P. "The Roles of Schemata in Memory for Text," *Discourse Processes* (1988) 11: 305-318.

Blosser, Betsy J. "Ethnic Differences in Children's Media Use," *Journal of Broadcasting & Electronic Media* (Fall, 1988) 32(4): 453-470. **[270]**

Blum, Abraham. "Students' Knowledge and Beliefs Concerning Environmental Issues in Four Countries," *Journal of Environmental Education* (Spring, 1987) 18(3): 7-13. **[162, 254]**

Blumenthal, Goldwyn. "Univision Fails to Pay Holders, Banks Interest," *Wall Street Journal,* Feb. 2, 1991, p. 4B. **[72]**

Blumenthal, H.J. *Television Producing & Directing.* New York: Barnes & Noble, 1987.

Blumler, Jay G. "New Roles for Public Television in Western Europe: Challenges and Prospects," *Journal of Communication* (Winter, 1992) 42(1): 20-35. **[59]**

Blumler, Jay G. "The Role of Theory in Uses and Gratifications Studies," *Communication Research* (January, 1979) 6(1): 9-36. **[229, 256]**

Blumler, Jay G. and Carolyn Martin Spicer. "Prospects for Creativity in the New Television Marketplace: Evidence from Program-Makers," *Journal of Communication* (Autumn, 1990) 40(4): 78-101. **[113]**

Bobrow, G.H. and D.A. Norman. "Some Principles of Memory Schemata," *Representation and Understanding: Studies in Cognitive Science,* ed. D.G. Bobrow and A. Collins. New York Academic Press, 1975, pp. 131-149. **[316]**

Boddy, W. "Operation Frontal Lobes versus the Living Room Toy: The Battle Over Program Control in Early Television," *Media, Culture and Society* (July, 1987) 9(3): 347-368. **[39]**

Boddy, William. "The Studios Move into Prime Time: Hollywood and the Television Industry in the 1950s," *Cinema Journal* (Summer, 1985) 24(4): 23-37. **[113]**

Bogart, Leo. "The American Media System and Its Commercial Culture," *Occasional Paper,* No. 8, Gannett Foundation Media Center, Columbia University, March, 1991. **[73]**

Bogart, Leo. "The Culture Beat," *The Gannett Center Journal* (Winter, 1990), pp. 23-35. **[339]**

Bogart, Leo. *An Update on Readership.* New York, NY: Newspaper Advertising Bureau, Inc., April, 1988. **[193, 227]**

Bogart, Leo. "How U.S. Newspaper Content Is Changing," *Journal of Communication* (Spring, 1985) 35(2): 82-90. **[337]**

Bogart, Leo. *Press and Public: Who Reads, What, When, Where, and Why in American Newspapers.* Hillsdale, NJ: Lawrence Erlbaum Associates, Publishers, 1981. **[213]**

Bohle, Robert H. and Mario R. Garcia. "Reader Response to Color Halftones and Spot Color in Newspaper Design," *Journalism Quarterly* (Winter, 1987) 64(4): 731-739. **[288, 315]**

Bohle, Robert H. "Negativism as News Selection Predictor," *Journalism Quarterly* (Winter, 1986) 63(4): 789-796. **[128]**

Bohlen, Celestine. "East Europe's Cultural Life, Once a Refuge, Now Eclipsed," *The New York Times,* Nov. 13, 1990, p. 1A, 6A. **[59]**

Bonfadelii, H. "Uses and Functions of Mass Media for Swiss Youth: An Empirical Study," *Gazette* (1986) 37(1-2): 7-18. **[216]**

Bonk, C.J. "A Synthesis of Social Cognition and Writing Research," *Written Communication* (January, 1990) 7(1): 136-163. **[139]**

Bonnstetter, Cathy Meo. "Magazine Coverage of Mentally Handicapped," *Journalism Quarterly* (Autumn, 1986) 63(3): 623-626. **[370]**

Boorstin, Daniel J. "Advertising and American Civilization," *Advertising and Society*, ed. Yale Brozen. New York: New York University Press, 1972. **[58]**

Booth, A. "The Recall of News Items," *Public Opinion Quarterly* (1970) 34: 604-610. **[316]**

Bordwell, D. and K. Thompson. *Film Art*. New York: Alfred A. Knopf, 1986. **[312]**

Borgida, Eugene and Beth Howard-Pitney. "Personal Involvement and the Robustness of Perceptual Salience Effects," *Journal of Personality and Social Psychology* (September, 1983) 45(3): 560-570. **[321]**

Borstel, Gerald H. "Ownership, Competition and Comment," *Journalism Quarterly* (Spring, 1956) 33: 220-222. **[90]**

Bostian, L.R. "How Active, Passive and Nominal Styles Affect Readability of Science Writing," *Journalism Quarterly* (Winter, 1983) 60(4): 635-640. **[199]**

Bostian, Lloyd R. and Tomas E. Byrne. "Comprehension of Styles of Science Writing," *Journalism Quarterly* (Autumn, 1984) 61(3): 676-678. **[295, 317]**

Bourdieu, P. *Distinction: A Social Critique of the Judgment of Taste*. Cambridge: Harvard University Press, 1984. **[279]**

Bourget, Jean-Loup. "Social Implications in the Hollywood Genres," in Barry K. Grant, ed. *Film Genre: Theory and Criticism* (Metuchen, NJ: The Scarecrow Press, Inc.), pp. 62-72, 1977. **[330]**

Boursfield, W.A., J. Esterson and G.A. Whitmarsh. "The Effects of Concomittant Colored and Uncolored Pictorial Representations on the Learning of Stimulus Words," *Journal of Applied Psyhchology* (1957) 4(3): 165-168. **[315]**

Bouwman, H. and N. Signorelli. "A Comparison of American and Dutch Programming," *Gazette* (1985) 35(2): 93-108. **[348]**

Bovee, Warren G. "Horace Greeley and Social Responsibility," *Journalism Quarterly* (Summer, 1986) 63(2): 251-259. **[51]**

Bovone, Laura, "Theories of Everyday Life: A Search for Meaning or a Negation of Meaning?" *Current Sociology* (1989) 37(1): 41-59. **[10]**

Bow, J. and B. Silver. "Effects of 'Herbert v. Lando' on Small Newspapers and TV Stations," *Journalism Quarterly* (Summer, 1984) 61(2): 414-418. **[163]**

Bower, G.H., J.B. Black and T.J. Turner. "Scripts in Memory for Text," *Cognitive Psychology* (1979) 11: 177-220. **[316]**

Bower, G.H. "Experiments on Story Understanding and Recall," *Quarterly Journal of Experimental Psychology* (1976) 28: 511-534. **[312]**

Bower, Robert T. *The Changing Television Audience in America*. New York: Columbia University Press, 1985. **[225, 334]**

Bower, Robert T. *Television and the Public*. New York: Holt, Rinehart & Winston, 1973. **[218]**

Bowles, Dorothy. "The Chilling Effect of Libel on Newspaper Editors," paper presented to the Newspaper Division at the annual conference of the Association for Education in Journalism and Mass Communication, Minneapolis, August, 1990. **[146]**

Bowles, Dorothy. "Newspaper Attention to (and Support of) First Amendment Cases, 1919-1969," *Journalism Quarterly* (Fall, 1989) 66(3): 579-586. **[59]**

Boyd, Douglas A. "The Videocassette Recorder in the USSR and Soviet-Bloc Countries," *The VCR Age: Home Video and Mass Communication*, ed. Mark R. Levy. Newbury Park, CA: Sage Publications, 1989, pp. 252-270. **[212]**

Boyd, Douglas A. "Home Video Diffusion and Utilization in Arabian Gulf States," *American Behavioral Scientist* (May/June, 1987) 30(5): 544-555. **[212]**

Boyd, Douglas A. and Alim M. Najai. "Adolescent TV Viewing in Saudi Arabia," *Journalism Quarterly* (Summer, 1984) 61(2): 295-301. **[278]**

Boyle, Maryellen. "The Revolt of the Communist Journalist: East Germany," *Media, Culture and Society* (January, 1992) 14(1): 133-139. **[49]**

Brabant, Sarah and Linda Mooney. "Sex Role Stereotyping in the Sunday Comics: Ten Years Later," *Sex Roles* (1986) 14(3/4): 141-148. **[367]**

Bradbury, Malcolm and James McFarlane, eds., *Modernism, 1890-1930.* New York: Penguin, 1976. **[18]**

Braman, Sandra. "Public Expectations of Media Versus Standards in Codes of Ethics," *Journalism Quarterly* (Spring, 1988) 65(1): 71-77, 240. **[203]**

Bramlett, Sharon A. "Southern vs. Northern Newspaper Coverage of a Race Crisis--The Lunch Counter Sit-in Movement, 1960-1964: An Assessment of Press Social Responsibility," Ph.D. dissertation. Indiana University, 1987. **[124]**

Bramlett-Solomon, Sharon. "Predictors of Job Satisfaction among Black Journalists," *Journalism Quarterly* (Fall, 1992) 69(3): 703-712. **[165]**

Bramlett-Solomon, Sharon and V. Wilson. "Images of the Elderly in 'Life' and 'Ebony,' 1978-1987," *Journalism Quarterly* (Spring, 1989) 66(1): 185-188. **[347]**

Brand, Stewart. *The Media Lab: Inventing the Future at MIT.* New York, Viking, 1987. **[17]**

Brannigan, Martha. "Cox to Close the Miami News at Year End," *Wall Street Journal*, Oct. 17, 1988, p. 6B. **[97]**

Bransford, J.D. and M.K. Johnson. "Contextual Prequisites for Understanding: Some Investigations of Comprehension and Recall," *Journal of Verbal Learning and Verbal Behavior* (1972) 11: 717-726. **[285]**

Braudy, Leo. *The World in a Frame: What We See in Films.* Garden City, NY: Anchor/Press/Doubleday, 1976. **[329]**

Braunstein, M.L. "Sensitivity of the Observer to Transformations of the Visual Field," *Journal of Experimental Psychology* (1966) 72: 683-689. **[318]**

Brazaitis, Thomas J. "Bridging the Menopause Knowledge Gap," *The Plain Dealer*, May 31, 1991, p. 8A. **[276]**

Breed, Warren and James R. De Foe. "Effecting Media Change: The Role of Cooperative Consultation on Alcohol Topics," *Journal of Communication* (Spring, 1982) 32(2): 88-99. **[370]**

Breiner, Rich M. "An Analysis of Controversial Role Fulfillment of TV News Commentators during Times of Crises," paper presented to the Radio-Television Journalism Division at the annual conference of the Association for Education in Journalism and Mass Communication, Portland, OR, July, 1988. **[166]**

Bremner, Brian and Gail DeGeorge. "Coming Soon to a Theater Near You: Recession," *Business Week* (Dec. 3, 1990), p. 127-128. **[87, 94]**

Bretl, Daniel J. and Joanne Cantor. "The Portrayal of Men and Women in U.S. Television Commercials: A Recent Content Analysis and Trends over 15 Years," *Sex Roles* (May, 1988) 18(9/10): 595-609. **[352]**

Bridges, J. and R.S. Denisoff. "Changing Courtship Patterns in the Popular Song: Horton and Carey Revisited," *Popular Music and Society* (1986) 10(3): 29-45. **[362]**

Bridges, Janet A. "News Use on the Front Pages of the American Daily," *Journalism Quarterly* (Summer, 1989) 66(2): 332-337. **[119, 123, 156]**

Bridges, Janet A. "Daily Newspaper Managing Editors' Perceptions of News Media Functions," *Journalism Quarterly* (Winter, 1991) 68(4): 719-728. **[151]**

Britton, B.K., K.D. Muth and S.M. Glynn. "Effects of Text Organization on Memory: Test of A Cognitive Effort Hypothesis with Limited Exposure Time," *Discourse Processes* (October-December, 1986) 9(4): 475-487. **[285]**

Broadbent, D. *Decision and Stress.* London: Academic, 1971. **[320]**

Broadbent, Daniel Eric. *Perception and Communication.* London: Pergamon Press, 1958. **[308]**

Brod, Donald F. "Classifying the World's Media: The One-Step and Two-Step Approaches," *International Communication Bulletin* (Fall, 1987) 22(3-4): 8-11. **[52]**

Broddason, T. and E.A. Hedinsson. "World without Media: Some Findings from an Exploratory Survey during the Mass Media Strike in Iceland, October, 1984," *The Nordicom Review* (1986) 2: 1-5. **[248, 255]**

Brooks, Tim and Earle Marsh. *The Complete Directory to Prime Time Network TV Shows: 1946-Present.* New York: Ballantine Books, 1981, rev. ed. **[332]**

Brosius, Hans-Bernd. "Format Effects on Comprehension of Television News," *Journalism Quarterly* (Fall, 1991) 68(3): 396-401. **[307]**

Brosius, Hans-Bernd, Mallory Wober and Gabriel Weimann. "The Loyalty of Television Viewing: How Consistent Is TV Viewing Behavior?" *Journal of Broadcasting & Electronic Media* (Summer, 1992) 36(3): 321-335. **[195, 212]**

Broussard, E. Joseph, C. Robert Blackmon, David L. Blackwell, David W. Smith and Sarah Hunt. "News of Aged and Aging in 10 Metropolitan Dailies," *Journalism Quarterly* (Summer, 1980) 57(2): 324-327. **[347]**

Brown, A.L., B.B. Armbruster and L. Baker. "The Role of Metacognition in Reading and Studying," *Reading Comprehension*, ed. J. Orasanu. Hillsdale, NJ: Erlbaum, 1986, pp. 49-75. **[285]**

Brown, Ben. "Our TVs Are on 7 Hours a Day," *USA Today* (April 29, 1985), p. 1.

Brown, Ben. "We're More Picky about Our TV Fare," *USA Today* (April 25, 1983), pp. 1-2A. **[212]**

Brown, Bruce W. *Images of Family Life in Magazine Advertising: 1920-1978.* Praeger Studies on Changing Issues in the Family. New York: Praeger, 1981. **[365]**

Brown, Cindy M. "How the Use of Color Affects the Content of Newspaper Photographs," paper presented at the annual conference of the Association for Education in Journalism and Mass Communication (AEJMC), Washington, D.C., August, 1989. **[37, 98, 365]**

Brown, J.D., K. Campbell and L. Fischer. "American Adolescents and Music Videos: Why Do They Watch?" *Gazette* (1986) 37(1/2): 19-32. **[252, 270]**

Brown, Jane Delano, Carl R. Bybee, Stanley T. Wearden and Dulcie Murdock Straughan, "Invisible Power: Newspaper News Sources and the Limits of Diversity," *Journalism Quarterly* (1987) 64: 45-54. **[134, 137]**

Brown, Jane D. and Kenneth Campbell. "Race and Gender in Music Videos: The Same Beat but a Different Drummer," *Journal of Communication* (Winter, 1986) 36(1): 94-106. **[364]**

Brown, Jane Delano, Kim Walsh Childers, Karl E. Bauman and Gary G. Koch. "The Influence of New Media and Family Structure on Young Adolescents' Television and Radio Use," *Communication Research* (February, 1990) 17(1): 65-82. **[188, 189, 270, 271]**

Brown, Karen F. "Factors of Success for Newspapers in Intracity Competition," paper presented to the Newspaper Division and Media Management and Economics Interest Group at the annual conference of the Association for Education in Journalism and Mass Communication, Washington, D.C., August, 1989. **[37]**

Brown, Natalie A. and Tony Atwater. "Videotex News: A Content Analysis of Three Videotex Services and their Companion Newspapers," *Journalism Quarterly* (Autumn, 1986) 63(3): 554-561. **[363]**

Brown, R.D. *Knowledge Is Power: The Diffusion of Information in Early America, 1700-1865.* New York: Oxford, 1989. **[37, 98]**

Browne, K. "Comparison of Factual Recall from Film and Print Stimuli," *Journalism Quarterly* (1978) 55: 350-353. **[310]**

Browning, N., D. Grierson and H.H. Howard. "Effects of a Conglomerate's Takeover and Newspaper's Coverage of the Knoxville World's Fair: A Case Study," *Newspaper Research Journal* (Fall, 1984) 6(1): 30-38. **[85, 90, 98]**

Bryant, C.G.A. *Positivism in Social Theory and Research.* New York: St. Martin's Press, 1985. **[19]**

Bryant, Barbara E., Frederick P. Currier and Andrew J. Morrison. "Relating Life Style Factors of Person to His Choice of a Newspaper," *Journalism Quarterly* (Spring, 1976) 53: 74-79. **[265]**

Bryant, Jennings and Dolf Zillman. "Using Television to Alleviate Boredom and Stress: Selective Exposure as a Function of Induced Excitation States," *Journal of Broadcasting* (Winter, 1984) 28(1): 1-20. **[246, 278]**

Bryce, J.W. "Family Time and Television Time," *Natural Audiences: Qualitative Research of Media Uses and Effects*, ed. T.R. Lindlof. Norwood, NJ: Ablex, 1987, pp. 121-138. **[270]**

Buckalew, James K. "News Elements and Selection by Television News Editors," *Journal of Broadcasting* (Winter, 1968-1969) 14: 47-53. **[161]**

Budd, Mike and Clay Steinman. "Television, Cultural Studies, and the 'Blind Spot' Debate in Critical Communications Research," *Television Studies: Textual Analysis*, ed. G. Burns and R. Thompson. New York: Praeger, 1989, p. 9-20. **[20]**

Budd, Mike, Robert M. Entman and Clay Steinman. "The Affirmative Character of U.S. Cultural Studies," *Critical Studies in Mass Communication* (June, 1990) 7: 169-184. **[13, 20, 21]**

Buddenbaum, Judith M. "'Judge...What Their Acts Will Justify': The Religion Journalism of James Gordon Bennett," *Journalism History* (Summer/Autumn, 1987) 14(2/3): 54-67. **[369]**

Buddenbaum, Judith M. "Network News Coverage of Religion," *Channels of Belief*, ed. John P. Ferre. Ames: Iowa State University Press, 1990, pp. 57-78. **[369]**

Buddenbaum, Judith M. "The Religion Beat at Daily Newspapers," *Newspaper Research Journal* (Summer, 1988) 9(4): 57-70. **[136, 166]**

Buddenbaum, Judith M. "Religion in Network Television Newscasts: 1976-1986," paper presented to the Mass Communication and Society Division at the annual conference of the Association for Education in Journalism and Mass Communication (AEJMC), Portland, OR, July, 1988. **[136, 369]**

Buddenbaum, Judith M. "An Analysis of Religion News Coverage in Three Major Newspapers," *Journalism Quarterly* (Autumn, 1986) 63(3): 600-606. **[136, 156]**

Buller, David B. and Warren Pease. "Selecting between Media and Interpersonal Sources: A Functional Alternatives Perspective," paper presented at the annual conference of the International Communication Association, Dublin, Ireland, 1990. **[256]**

Bunker, Matthew D. and Sigman L. Splichal. "Legally Enforceable Reporter-Source Agreements: Chilling Newsgathering at the Source?" paper presented at the annual conference of the International Communication Association, Miami, May, 1992. **[161]**

Burdach, K.J. "Reporting on Deaths: The Perspective Coverage of Accident News in a German Tabloid," *European Journal of Communication* (March, 1988) 3(1): 81-89. **[119]**

Burgoon, Judee K., James M. Bernstein and Michael Burgoon. "Public and Journalist Perceptions of Newspaper Functions," *Newspaper Research Journal* (Fall, 1983) 5(1): 77-85. **[122]**

Burgoon, Judee K., Michael Burgoon, David B. Buller and Charles K. Atkin. "Communication Practices of Journalists: Interaction with Public, Other Journalists," *Journalism Quarterly* (Spring, 1987) 64(1): 125-132, 275. **[110, 150, 151]**

Burgoon, Judee K., Michael Burgoon and David B. Butler. "Newspaper Image: Dimensions and Relation to Demographics, Satisfaction," *Journalism Quarterly* (Winter, 1986) 63(4): 771-781. **[199]**

Burgoon, Judee K., Michael Burgoon and Miriam Wilkinson. "Writing Style as a Predictor of Newspaper Readership, Satisfaction and Image," *Journalism Quarterly* (Summer, 1981) 58(2): 230-231. **[292]**

Burkum, Larry G. and Walter E. Niebauer Jr. "Why Subscribers Drop Cable Television: Characteristics of Three Groups," paper presented to the Mass Communication and Society Division at the annual conference of the Association for Education in Journalism and Mass Communication, Portland, OR, July, 1988. **[212, 255]**

Burnby, J. "Pharmaceutical Advertisements in the 17th and 18th Centuries," *European Journal of Marketing* (1988) 22(4): 24-40. **[39]**

Burnham, John. "Of Science and Superstition: The Media and Biopolitics," *Gannett Center Journal* (Summer, 1990) 4(3): 24-35. **[160]**

Burns, R. "A Two-Way Television System Operated by Senior Citizens," *American Behavioral Scientist* (May/June, 1988) 31(5): 576-587. **[74]**

Burriss, Larry L. "Attribution in Network Radio News," A Cross-Network Analysis," *Journalism Quarterly* (Fall, 1988) 65(3): 690-694. **[132]**

Burriss, Larry L. "How Anchors, Reporters and Newsmakers Affect Recall and Evaluation of Stories," *Journalism Quarterly* (Summer/Autumn, 1987) 64(2/3): 514-519, 532. **[308, 319]**

Burriss, Larry L. "Accuracy of News Magazines as Perceived by News Sources," *Journalism Quarterly* (Winter, 1985) 62(4): 824-827. **[144]**

Burrowes, Carl P. "Measuring Freedom of Expression Cross-Culturally: Some Methodological and Conceptual Problems," *Mass Comm Review* (1989) 16(1/2): 38051. **[60]**

Bush, A., A. Menon and D. Smart. "Media Habits of the Do-It-Yourselfers," *Journal of Advertising Research* (October/November, 1987) 27(5): 14-20. **[280]**

Bush, A.J. and J.J. Burnett. "Assessing the Homogeneity of Single Females in Respect to Advertising, Media, and Technology," *Journal of Advertising* (1987) 16(3): 31-38. **[234]**

Busterna, John C. "Price Discrimination as Evidence of Newspaper Chain Market Power," *Journalism Quarterly* (Spring/Summer, 1991) 68(1/2): 5-14. **[85]**

Busterna, John C. "How Managerial Ownership Affects Profit Maximization in Newspaper Firms," *Journalism Quarterly* (Summer, 1989) 66(2): 302-307, 358. **[79, 92]**

Busterna, John C. "Daily Newspaper Chains and the Antitrust Laws," *Journalism Monographs* (March, 1989) No. 110. **[79, 92]**

Busterna, J.C. "Concentration and the Industrial Organization Model," *Press Concentration and Monopoly: New Perspectives on Newspaper Ownership and Operation*, ed. Robert G. Picard, James P. Winter, Maxwell E. McCombs, and Stephen Lacy. Norwood, NJ: Ablex, 1988, pp. 35-53. **[85, 91, 96, 97, 98]**

Busterna, John C. "National Advertising Pricing: Chain vs. Independent Newspapers," *Journalism Quarterly* (Summer, 1988) 65(2): 307-312, 334. **[85, 91, 96, 97, 98]**

Busterna, John C. "Television Station Ownership Effects on Programming and Idea Diversity: Baseline Data," *Journal of Media Economics* (Fall, 1988) 1(2): 63-74. **[85, 91, 96, 97, 98]**

Busterna, John C. "Trends in Daily Newspaper Ownership," *Journalism Quarterly* (Winter, 1988) 65(4): 831-838. **[85, 91, 96, 97, 98]**

Busterna, John C. and Kathleen A. Hansen. "Presidential Endorsement Patterns by Chain-Owned Papers, 1976-84," *Journalism Quarterly* (Summer, 1990) 67(2): 286-294. **[90]**

Busterna, John C., Kathleen A. Hansen and Jean Ward. "Competition, Ownership, Newsroom and Library Resources in Large Newspapers," *Journalism Quarterly* (Winter, 1991) 68(4): 729-739. **[91]**

Butsch, Richard and Lynda M. Glennon. "Social Class: Frequency Trends in Domestic Situation Comedy, 1946-1978," *Journal of Broadcasting* (Winter, 1983) 27(1): 77-81. **[368]**

Butters, Barry E. "Local TV News Before and After SNG," paper presented to the Radio-Television Journalism Division at the annual conference of the Association for Education in Journalism and Mass Communication," Minneapolis, August, 1990. **[340]**

Buxton, Rodney A. "The Late-Night Talk Show: Humor in Fringe Television," *Southern Speech Communication Journal* (Summer, 1987) 52(4): 377-389. **[372]**

Bybee, Carl R. "Constructing Women as Authorities: Local Journalism and the Microphysics of Power," *Critical Studies in Mass Communication* (September, 1990) 7(3): 197-214. **[137]**

Bylinsky, Gene. "Technology in the Year 2000," *Fortune* 118(3), 1988, pp. 92-98. **[17]**

Byrd, E.K. and T.R. Elliott. "Feature Films and Disability: A Descriptive Study," *Rehabilitation Psychology* (Spring, 1985) 30(1): 47-51. **[370]**

Caine, Michael. *Acting in Film*. New York: Applause, 1990. **[104]**

California Department of Education. *Student Achievement in California Schools: 1979-1980 Annual Report*. Sacramento: California Department of Education, 1980. **[214]**

Callahan, Francix X. "Does Advertising Subsidize Information?" *Journal of Advertising Research* (August, 1978) 18(4): 19-22. **[77]**

Campbell, A., P. Converse and W. Rodgers. *The Quality of American Life: Perceptions, Evaluations and Satisfactions.* New York: Russell Sage Foundation, 1976. **[211, 279]**

Campbell, A. *The Sense of Well-Being in America: Recent Patterns and Trends.* New York: McGraw-Hill Book Co., 1981. **[267, 279]**

Campbell, Richard and Jimmie L. Reeves. "Covering the Homeless: The Joyce Brown Story," *Critical Studies in Mass Communication* (March, 1989) 6(1): 21-42. **[127, 128]**

Candussi, D.A. and J.P. Winter. "Monopoly and Content in Winnipeg," *Press Concentration and Monopoly: New Perspectives on Newspaper Ownership and Operation,* ed. R.G. Picard et al., Norwood, NJ: Ablex, 1988, pp. 139-145. **[91]**

Canino, Glorisa J. and Aletha C. Huston. "A Content Analysis of Prime-Time Television and Radio News in Puerto Rico," *Journalism Quarterly* (Spring, 1986) 63(1): 150-154. **[158, 363]**

Cannon, Hugh M. and David L. Williams. "Toward a Hierarchical Taxonomy of Magazine Readership," *Journal of Advertising* (1988) 17(1): 15-25. **[214]**

Cantor, M.G. and S. Pingree. *The Soap Opera.* Beverly Hills: Sage, 1983. **[20, 361]**

Cantor, Muriel G. "Prime-Time Fathers: A Study in Continuity and Change," *Critical Studies in Mass Communication* (1990) 7: 275-285. **[351]**

Cantor, Muriel G. *The Hollywood TV Producer.* New Brunswick, NJ: Transaction Books, 1988; original edition, Basic Books, 1971. **[114, 115, 155]**

Caplan, R.E. "Violent Program Content in Music Videos," *Journalism Quarterly* (Spring, 1985) 62(1): 144-147. **[362]**

Caplow, Theodore and Harold M. Bahr. "Half a Century of Change in Adolescent Attitudes: Replication of a Middletown Survey by the Lynds," *Public Opinion Quarterly* (Spring, 1979) 43(1): 1-17. **[207]**

Carley, William M. "In a Big Plane Crash, Cause Probably Isn't Everybody's Guess," *Wall Street Journal,* March 29, 1988, p. 1. **[156]**

Carpenter, Patricia A. and Marcel Adam Just. "Cognitive Processes in Reading," *Reading Comprehension,* ed. J. Orasanu. Hillsdale, NJ: Erlbaum, 1986. **[313]**

Carpenter, Patricia A. and Marcel Adam Just. "Reading Comprehension as Eyes See It," *Cognitive Processes in Comprehension,* ed. Marcel A. Just and Patricia A. Carpenter. Hillsdale, NJ: Erlbaum, 1977. **[314]**

Carpenter, Patricia A. and Marcel A. Just. "What Your Eyes Do While Your Mind Is Reading," *Eye Movements in Reading: Perceptual and Language Processes,* ed. K. Rayner. New York: Academic, 1983. **[314]**

Carragee, Kevin M. "Defining Solidarity: Themes and Omissions in Coverage of the Solidarity Trade Union Movement by ABC News," *Journalism Monographs* (February, 1990) No. 119. **[127, 156, 158]**

Carroll, Glenn R. and Michael T. Hannan. "Density Dependence in the Evolution of Populations of Newspaper Organizations," *American Sociological Review* (August, 1989) 54: 524-541. **[80, 81]**

Carroll, J.M. *Toward a Structural Psychology of Cinema.* The Hague: Mouton Publishers, 1980. **[312]**

Carroll, John M. "The Film Experience as Cognitive Structure," *Empirical Studies of the Arts* (1984) 2(1): 1-17. **[301]**

Carroll, Raymond L. "Changes in the News: Trends in Network News Production," *Journalism Quarterly* (Winter, 1988) 65(4): 940-945. **[126, 144]**

Carroll, Raymond L. "Content Values in TV News Programs in Small and Large Markets," *Journalism Quarterly* (Winter, 1985) 62(4): 877-882, 938. **[162]**

Carter, Richard F. "The Journalistic Function," unpublished paper. University of Washington, Seattle, 1967. **[132]**

Carveth, Rod. "The Reconstruction of the Global Media Marketplace," *Communication Research* (December, 1992) 19(6): 705-723. **[89]**

Cassara, Catherine. "The Foreign-Language Press in America: A Historiographic Analysis," paper presented at the annual conference of the Association for Education in Journalism and Mass Communication, Boston, August, 1991. **[72]**

Cassata, Mary, Thomas Skill and Samuel Osei Boadu. "Life and Death in the Daytime Television Serial: A Content Analysis," *Life On Daytime Television: Tuning-in American Serial Drama*, ed. Mary Cassata and Thomas Skill. Norwood, NJ: Ablex Publishing Co., 1983. **[359]**

Cassata, Mary, P.A. Anderson and Thomas Skill. "Images of Old Age on Day-time," *Life on Daytime Television*, ed. Mary Cassata and Thomas Skill. Norwood, NJ: Ablex Publishers, 1983, pp. 37-44. **[365]**

Cassidy, M.F. "'Dallas' Refigured," *Television Studies: Textual Analysis*, ed. G. Burns and R.J. Thompson. New York: Praeger, 1989, pp. 41-56. **[372]**

Caudill, Ed. "A Content Analysis of Press Views of Darwin's Evolution Theory, 1860-1925," *Journalism Quarterly* (Winter, 1987) 64(4): 782-786. **[157, 368]**

Cavell, Stanley. *Pursuits of Happiness: The Hollywood Comedy of Remarriage*. Cambridge, MA: Harvard University Press, 1984. **[331]**

Cawelti, John G. "The Question of Popular Genres," *Journal of Popular Film and Television* (Summer, 1985) 13(2): 55-61. **[328]**

Chabot, C. Barry. "The Problem of the Postmodern," *New Literary History* (Autumn, 1988) 20(1): 1-20. **[18]**

Chaffee, Steven and Charles Berger. "What Communication Scientists Do," *Handbook of Communication Science*, ed. Charles Berger and Steven Chaffee. Newbury Park, CA: Sage, 1987, pp. 99-122. **[11]**

Chaffee, Steven H., Jack M. McLeod and Daniel B. Wackman. "Family Communication Patterns and Adolescent Political Participation," *Socialization to Politics*, ed. J. Dennis. New York: Wiley, 1973. **[271]**

Chaffee, Steven H., Jack M. McLeod and Charles K. Atkin. "Parental Influences on Adolescent Media Use," *American Behavioral Scientist* (1971) 14(4): 323-340. **[271]**

Chaffee, Steven H. and D.C. Mutz. "Comparing Mediated and Interpersonal Communication Data," *Advancing Communication Science: Merging Mass and Interpersonal Processes*. eds. R.P. **[177]**

Chaffee, Steven H. and Albert R. Tims. "Interpersonal Factors in Adolescent Television Use," *Journal of Social Issues* (1976) 32(4): 98-115. **[279]**

Chan, Anthony B. "Gagging the Hong Kong Press: Slippery Road to 1997," *Gazette* (1988) 42: 161-175. **[43, 49]**

Chan, Joseph M. and Chin-Chuan. Lee. "Press Ideology and Organizational Control in Hong Kong," *Communication Research* (April, 1988) 15(2): 185-107. **[151]**

Chan, Joseph Man and Chin-Chuan Lee. "Shifting Journalistic Paradigms: Editorial Stance and Political Transition in Hong Kong," paper presented in the International Communication Division at the annual convention of the Association for Education in Journalism and Mass Communication, Portland, OR, 1988. **[151]**

Chan, Mei-Mei. "TV is on the Wagon to Set Good Example," *USA Today*, March 21, 1985, p.11a. **[371]**

Chan-Olmsted, Sylvia M. "Network versus Studios: An Examination of Programming Product Competitiveness and the Financial Interest and Syndication Rules," paper presented to the Media Management and Economics Division at the annual conference of the Association for Education in Journalism and Mass Communication, Montreal, August, 1992. **[84, 97]**

Chan-Olmsted, Sylvia. "A Structural Analysis of Market Competition in the U.S. TV Syndication Industry, 1981-1990," *Journal of Media Economics* (Fall, 1991) 4(3): 9-28. **[89]**

Chan-Olmsted, Sylvia M. and Barry R. Litman. "Antitrust and Horizontal Mergers in the Cable Industry," *Journal of Media Economics* (Fall, 1988) 1(2): 3-28. **[82, 84]**

Chandler, A.R. *Beauty and Human Nature.* The Hague: Mouton, 1934. **[318]**

Chang, F.R. "Active Memory Processes in Visual Sentence Comprehension: Clause Effects and Pronominal Reference," *Memory and Cognition* (1980) 8: 58-64. **[284, 314]**

Chang, Tsan-Kuo and Jae-won Lee. "Factors Affecting Gatekeepers' Selection of Foreign News: A National Survey of Newspaper Editors," paper presented to the Newspaper Division at the annual conference of the Association for Education in Journalism and Mass Communication, Minneapolis, August, 1990. **[119, 156, 157]**

Chang, Tsan-Kuo and Jae-won Lee. "Factors Affecting Gatekeepers' Selection of Foreign News: A National Survey of Newspaper Editors," *Journalism Quarterly* (Fall, 1992) 69(3): 554-561. **[157]**

Chang, Tsan-kuo, Pamela J. Shoemaker and Nancy Brendlinger. "Determinants of International News Coverage in the U.S. Media," *Communication Research* (August, 1987) 14(4): 396-414. **[120, 156, 157]**

Chang, Tsan-Kuo et al. "Sampling Ethnic Media Use: The Case of Hispanics," *Journalism Quarterly* (Spring, 1988) 65(1): 189-191. **[270]**

Chase, Donald. *Filmmaking: The Collaborative Art.* Boston: Little, Brown & Co., 1975. **[103, 104, 105]**

Chatman, E.A. "Information, Mass Media Use and the Working Poor," *Library and Information Science Research* (April-June, 1985) 7(2): 97-113. **[231]**

Cheek, Neil H. and William R. Burch Jr. *The Social Organization of Leisure in Human Society.* New York: Harper & Row, 1976. **[265]**

Cheesman, Robin and Carsten Kyhn. "The Structure of Danish Mass Media," *The Nordicom Review of Nordic Mass Communication Research* (1991) No. 2: 3-18. **[59]**

Chew, Fiona. "Television News and Communication Tactics," paper presented to the Theory and Methodology Division at the annual conference of the Association for Education in Journalism and Mass Communication (AEJMC), Minneapolis, August, 1990. **[182]**

Cheyjunya, Patchanee and Pratoom Lerklang. "Family Communication Patterns and Exposure of Bangkok Juveniles to Mass Media," *Media Asia* (1988) 15(1): 30-36. **[271]**

Childers, Terry L. and Dean M. Krugman. "The Competitive Environment of Pay Per View," *Journal of Broadcasting & Electronic Media* (Summer, 1987) 31(3): 335-342. **[198]**

Choi, Yangho, John W. Wright, and Mary Ann Ferguson. "Do Gratifications Sought Mediate the Relationship between Need for Cognition and Newspaper Exposure and Newspaper Reliance?" paper presented to the Newspaper Division at the annual conference of the Association for Education in Journalism and Mass Communication, Boston, August, 1991. **[247]**

Christenson, Peter G. and Peter DeBenedittis. "'Eavesdropping' on the FM Band: Children's Use of Radio," *Journal of Communication* (Spring, 1986) 36(2): 27-38. **[186]**

Christenson, Peter G., Peter DeBenedittis and T.R. Lindlof. "Children's Use of Audio Media," *Communication Research* (July, 1985) 12(3): 327-343. **[196, 278]**

Christenson, Peter G. and Jon Brian Peterson. "Genre and Gender in the Structure of Music Preferences," *Communication Research* (June, 1988) 15(3): 282-301. **[270]**

Christians, Clifford G. "Fifty Years of Scholarship in Media Ethics," *Journal of Communication* (1977) 27(4): 19-29. **[131]**

Christopher, F. Scott, Richard A. Fabes and Patricia M. Wilson. "Family Television Viewing: Implications for Family Life Education," *Family Relations* (1989) 38: 210-214. **[271]**

Clarens, Carlos. *Crime Movies: From Griffith to the Godfather and Beyond.* New York: W.W. Norton, 1980. **[330]**

Clark, H.H. and Eve Clark. *Psychology and Language: An Introduction to Psycholinguistics.* New York: Harcourt Brace Jovanovich, 1977. **[284]**

Clark, Rebecca L. "How Women's Magazines Cover Living Alone," *Journalism Quarterly* (Summer, 1981) 58(2): 291-294. **[354]**

Clarke, Debra. "Constraints of Television News Production: The Example of Story Geography," *Canadian Journal of Communication* (February, 1990) 15(1): 67-94. **[121]**

Clarke, J.N. "Cancer Meanings in the Media: Implications for Clinicians," *Studies in Communications*, ed. T. McCormack. Vol. 3, Greenwich, CT: JAI Pres, 1986, pp. 175-215. **[370]**

Clayman, S.E. "Displaying Neutrality in Television News Interviews," *Social Problems* (October, 1988) 35(4): 474-492. **[143]**

Cleland, Gladys L. and David H. Ostroff. "Satellite News Gathering and News Department Operations," *Journalism Quarterly* (Winter, 1988) 65(4): 946-951. **[143]**

Click, J.W. and Guido H. Stempel III. "Reader Response to Front Pages with Four-Color Halftones," *Journalism Quarterly* (1976) 53: 732-736. **[288]**

Clifford, James. "Introduction: Partial Truths," *Writing Culture: The Poetics and Politics of Ethnography* ed. James Clifford and George E. Marcus. Berkeley, CA: Unviersity of California Press, pp. 1-26, 1986. **[18]**

Clogston, John S. "Fifty Years of Disability Coverage in 'The New York Times,' 1941-1991," paper presented by the Committee on the Status of Disabled People at the annual conference of the Association for Education in Journalism and Mass Communication, Montreal, August, 1992; reprinted from the *News Computing Journal*, Vol. 8, No. 2. **[370]**

Cloud, George William. "Preference for Newspaper Courtesy Title Use in a Southeastern State," *Newspaper Research Journal* (Spring, 1989) 10(3): 11-16. **[199]**

Cobb, Cathy J. "Patterns of Newspaper Readership among Teenagers," *Communication Research* (April, 1986) 13(2): 299-326. **[189, 261]**

Cobb, Cathy J. and David Kenny. "Adolescents and the Newspaper: Images in Black and White," *Newspaper Research Journal* (Spring, 1986) 7(3): 1-8. **[232, 270]**

Cobb-Walgren, Cathy J. "Why Teenagers Do Not 'Read All About It,'" *Journalism Quarterly* (Summer, 1990) 67(2): 340-347. **[253]**

Codel, Martin. "Who Pays for Your Radio Program?" *Nation's Business* (August, 1929) 17, pp. 39. **[37]**

Cohen, Akiba A. "Answers without Questions: A Comparative Analysis of Television News Interviews," *European Journal of Communication* (1989) 4: 435-451. **[143]**

Cohen, Akiba A. "Decision Making in VCR Rental Libraries," *American Behavioral Scientist* (May/June, 1987) 30(5): 495-507. **[197]**

Cohen, Akiba A., Mark R. Levy and Karen Golden. "Children's Uses and Gratifications of Home VCRs: Evolution or Revolution?" *Communication Research* (December, 1988) 15(6): 772-780. **[247, 250]**

Cohen, Jeremy, Diana Mutz and Clifford Nass. "Testing Some Notions of the Fact/Opinion Distinction in Libel," paper presented to the Law Division at the annual conference of the Association for Education in Journalism and Mass Communication (AEJMC), Portland, OR, 1988. **[207]**

Cohen, Jeremy, Diana Mutz, Clifford Nass and Laurie Mason. "Experimental Test of Some Notions of the Fact/Opinion Distinction in Libel," *Journalism Quarterly* (Spring, 1989) 66(1): 11-17, 247. **[207]**

Cohen, Ralph. "Do Postmodern Genres Exist?" *Genre* (Fall-Winter, 1987) 20: 241-258. **[329]**

Cohen, Roger. "Paperbacks Seem to be Making a Comeback," *New York Times*, Feb. 4, 1991, p. 8C. **[73]**

Cohen, Roger. "Booksellers Cheered by Convention Crowds," *New York Times*, June 5, 1991, p. 6C. **[73]**

Cohn, J. "The Business Ethic for Boys: 'The Saturday Evening Post' and the Post Boys," *Business History Review* (Summer, 1987) 61(2): 185-215. **[357]**

Collins, Janay and John D. Abel. "Activation as News Exposure Predictor," *Journalism Quarterly* (Summer, 1985) 62(2): 316-320. **[257]**

Collins, Jim. *Uncommon Cultures: Popular Culture and Postmodernism.* London: Routledge, 1989. **[18, 19]**

Collins, Randall. "Sociology: Proscience or Antiscience?" *American Sociological Review* (February, 1989) 54: 124-139.

Collins-Jarvis, Lori. "A Causal Model of the Reciprocal Relationship between Community Attachment and Community Newspaper Use," paper presented to the Communication Theory & Methodology Division at the annual conference of the Association for Education in Journalism and Mass Communication, Montreal, August, 1992. **[240]**

Comber, Michael and Margaret O'Brien. "Evading the War: The Politics of the Hollywood Vietnam Film," *History* (June, 1988) 73(238): 248-260. **[331]**

Compaigne, Benjamin (ed.). *Who Owns the Media?* White Plains, NY: Knowledge Industry Publications, Inc., 1979. **[88, 89, 98]**

Comstock, George. *Television and Human Behavior: The Key Studies.* Santa Monica, CA: Rand Corp., 1975. **[216]**

Comstock, George, Steven Chaffee, N. Katzman, Max McCombs and Donald Roberts. *Television and Human Behavior.* New York: Columbia University Press, 1978. **[215]**

Comstock, Jamie and Krystyna Strzyzewski. "Interpersonal Interaction on Television: Family Conflict and Jealousy on Primetime," *Journal of Broadcasting & Electronic Media* (Summer, 1990) 34(3): 263-282. **[349]**

Condry, John, Patricia Bence and Cynthia Scheibe. "The Non-Program Content of Children's Television," *Journal of Broadcasting & Electronic Media* (Summer, 1988) 32(3): 255-270. **[361]**

Connery, Thomas. "Management Commitment & the Small Daily," *Newspaper Research Journal* (summer/Fall, 1989) 10(4): 59-76. **[110]**

Connor, Michael. "NBC Will Trim an Hour of Daytime Programming," *Chicago Sun-Times*, May 24, 1991, p. 35. **[68, 94]**

Connors, Tracy Daniel. *Longman Dictionary of Mass Media & Communication.* New York: Longman, 1982. **[14]**

Conway, Joseph C. and Alan M. Rubin. "Psychological Predictors of Television Viewing Motivation," *Communication Research* (August, 1991) 18(4): 443-463. **[247]**

Cook, Timothy E. "Are the American News Media Governmental? Re-examining the 'Fourth Branch' Thesis," paper presented at the annual conference of the International Communication Association, Chicago, May, 1991. **[63]**

Coon, Stephen C. and Eric Hing-Tat Tse. "Negativity and Visualization as Criteria for News Selection in Local Television Newscasts," paper presented to the Radio-Television Journalism Division at the annual conference of the Association for Education in Journalism and Mass Communication, Boston, August, 1991. **[128]**

Cooper, Brenda and David Descutner. "Through the Eyes of Gender and Hollywood: Conflicting Versions of Isak Dinesen's Africa," paper presented to the Qualitative Studies Division at the annual conference of the Association for Education in Journalism and Mass Communication, Montreal, August, 1992. **[367]**

Cooperstein, S. "Television Docudramas: Is the Titillation Worth the Risk?" *Rutgers Law Journal* (Winter, 1989) 20(2): 461-478. **[361]**

Copeland, Gary A. "Face-ism and Primetime Television," *Journal of Broadcasting & Electronic Media* (Spring, 1989) 33(2): 209-214. **[351]**

Corner, J. (Ed.) *Documentary and the Mass Media.* London: Edward Arnold, Ltd., 1986. **[330]**

Correll, R.L. and B. Biggins. "Trends in Commercial Television Ratings, 1977-1983," *Media Information Australia* (August, 1984) 33: 35-38. **[272]**

Corrigan, Dennis M. "Value Coding Consensus in Front Page News Leads," *Journalism Quarterly* (Winter, 1990) 67(4): 653-662. **[123, 156]**

Corrigan, Dennis M. "News as Symbolizing Activity," paper presented at the annual conference of the Association for Education in Journalism and Mass Communication, Corvallis, OR, August, 1983. **[360]**

Cosaro, William A. and Donna Eder. "Children's Peer Cultures," *Annual Review of Sociology* (1990) 16: 197-220. **[278]**

Coser, L.A., C. Kadushin and W.W. Powell. *Books: The Culture and Commerce of Publishing.* New York: Basic, 1982. **[20]**

Coulson, D.C. "Editors' Attitudes and Behavior Toward Journalism Awards," *Journalism Quarterly* (Spring, 1989) 66(1): 143-147. **[165]**

Coulson, David C. "Effects of Joint Operating Agreements on Newspaper Competition and Editorial Performance," paper presented to the Newspaper Division at the annual conference of the Association for Education in Journalism and Mass Communication, Montreal, August, 1992. **[88, 92]**

Coulson, David C. "Journalists' Assessment of Group Ownership and Their Newspapers' Local News and Editorial Performance," paper presented to the Newspaper Division at the annual conference of the Association for Education in Journalism and Mass Communication, Boston, August, 1991.

Coulson, David C. and Cecilie Gaziano. "How Journalists at Two Newspapers View Good Writing and Writing Coaches," *Journalism Quarterly* (Summer, 1989) 66(2): 435-440. **[162]**

Coulson, David C. and Scot Macdonald. "Television Journalists' Perceptions of Group Ownership and their Stations' Local News Coverage," *Readings in Media Management*, ed. Stephen Lacy, Ardyth B. Sohn and Robert H. Giles. Columbia, S.C.: Media Management and Economics Division, Association for Education in Journalism and Mass Communication, Montreal, August, 1992, pp. 21-33. **[88, 92, 166]**

Coulson, David C. and Scot Macdonald. "Television Journalists' Perceptions of Group Ownership and Their Stations' Local News Coverage," paper presented at the annual conference of the Association for Education in Journalism and Mass Communication, Boston, August, 1991. **[149]**

Coulter, R.G., M.L. Coulter and J.A. Glover. "Details and Picture Recall," *Bulletin of the Psychonomic Society* (1984) 22(4): 327-329. **[290]**

Covert, Douglas C. "Maker and Viewer Disagreement in Aesthetics of Visual Composition," *Journalism Quarterly* (Spring, 1987) 64(1): 133-136. **[199]**

Covey, Herbert C. "Old Age Portrayed by the Ages-of-Life Models from the Middle Ages to the 16th Century," *The Gerontologist* (1989) 29(5): 692-698. **[347]**

Cowan, Gloria, Carol Lee and Daniella Levy. "Dominance and Inequality in X-Rated Videocassettes," *Psychology of Women Quarterly* (September, 1988) 12(2): 299-311. **[298, 352]**

Cowen, Paul S. "Manipulating Montage: Effects on Film Comprehension, Recall, Person Perception, and Aesthetic Responses," *Empirical Studies of the Arts* (1988) 6(2): 97-115. **[318]**

Cowie, E. "Viewing Patterns Within the UK Population," *Annual Review of BBC Broadcasting Research Findings* (1981/1982) No. 8: 27-39. **[216]**

Cowles, Deborah. "Consumer Perceptions of Interactive Media," *Journal of Broadcasting & Electronic Media* (Winter, 1989) 33(1): 83-89. **[275]**

Cox, Meg. "'Reality' TV Shows Continue to Spread Despite Critics and Nervous Advertisers," *Wall Street Journal*, May 11, 1989, p. 1B. **[67, 334]**

Cox, Meg. "Paramount Unit to Expand Tie-In with Television to Sell Textbooks, *Wall Street Journal*, May 20, 1991, p. 5. **[77]**

Cox, Meg. "NBC Plans to Link Affiliates' Pay to Performance and Audience Size," *Wall Street Journal*, May 22, 1989, p. 5B. **[67]**

Cozzens, Michael D. and Noshir S. Contractor. "The Effect of Conflicting Information on Media Skepticism," *Communication Research* (August, 1987) 14(4): 437-451. **[207]**

Craig, Richard J. "Drug Themes in Metropolitan Newspapers: Review and Analysis," *The International Journal of the Addictions* (1981) 16(6): 1087-1093. **[371]**

Craig, R. Stephen. "The Effect of Television Day Part on Gender Portrayals in Television Commercials: A Content Analysis," *Sex Roles* (1992) 26(5/6): 197-211. **[352]**

Craik, Fergus I.M. and Robert S. Lockhart. "Levels of Processing: A Framework for Memory Research," *Journal of Verbal Learning and Verbal Behavior* (1972) 11: 671-684. **[319]**

Cramer, J.A. "Radio: A Woman's Place Is on the Air," *Women in Mass Communication: Challenging Gender Values*, ed. P.J. Creedon. Sage Focus Editions, No. 106. Newbury Park, CA: Sage Publications, 1989, pp. 214-226. **[164]**

Crawford, Duane W., Geoffrey Godbey and Ann C. Crouter. "The Stability of Leisure Preferences," *Journal of Leisure Research* (1986) 18(2): 96-115. **[216]**

Crawford, Duane W. and Geoffrey Godbey. "Reconceptualizing Barriers to Family Leisure," *Leisure Sciences* (1987) 9: 119-127. **[272]**

Creedon, P.J. (Ed.). *Women in Mass Communication: Challenging Gender Values*. Sage Focus Editions, No. 106. Newbury Park, CA: Sage Publications, 1989. **[148]**

Criscuolo, N.P. "The Public's Attitude toward Education: What Effect Do the Media Have on Formulation of Opinions," *Editor & Publisher* (March 2, 1985) 118(10): 16-18. **[368]**

Cronin, Mary M. and Barry R. Litman. "Independent Film Fortunes in the 1980s: 'The Spring of Hope, The Winter of Despair,'" paper presented in the Management and Economics Division at the annual conference of the Association for Education in Journalism and Mass Communication, Minneapolis, 1990. **[66, 105, 106, 153]**

Cronkhite, Gary. "On the Focus, Scope and Coherence of the Study of Human Symbolic Activity," *The Quarterly Journal of Speech* (August, 1986) 72(3): 231-246. **[7, 10, 19, 177]**

Crossen, Cynthia. "Washington Post Reporters Lose Overtime Ruling," *Wall Street Journal*, Jan. 15, 1988, p. 5. **[165]**

Crowley, D.J. *Understanding Communication: The Signifying Web*. New York: Gordon & Breach Science Pub., 1982. **[360]**

Crowther, B. and A. Kahn. "Arts and Leisure Activities in the St. Louis Region," *American Behavioral Scientist* (1983) 26: 509-520. **[216]**

Cruz, I.R. "Portraits of Youth in Philippine Films," *Media Asia* (1988) 15(1): 17-21. **[331]**

Csikszentmihalyi, Mihaly. *Beyond Boredom and Anxiety*. San Francisco: Jossey-Bass, 1975. **[249, 265, 274]**

Csikszentmihalyi, Mihaly and Robert Kubey. "Television and the Rest of Life: A Systematic Comparison of Subjective Experience," *Mass Communication Review Yearbook*, ed. D.C. Whitney and Ellen Wartella. Vol. 13, Beverly Hills, CA: Sage, 1982. **[311]**

Csikszentmihalyi, Mihaly and Judith LeFevre. "Optimal Experience in Work and Leisure," *Journal of Personality and Social Psychology* (1989) 56(5): 815-822. **[250]**

Culbertson, Hugh M. "Three Perspectives on American Journalism," *Journalism Monographs* (June, 1983) No. 83. **[165]**

Culbertson, Hugh M. "Specialized Journalism -- A Structural View," *Mass Com Review* (Spring, 1978) 5(2): 2-3. **[152]**

Culbertson, Hugh M. "Gatekeeper Coorientation -- A Viewpoint for Analysis of Popular Culture and Specialized Journalism," *Mass Com Review* (Winter, 1975/76) 3(1): 3-7. **[138]**

Culbertson, Hugh M. and Nancy Somerick. "Quotation Marks and Bylines--What Do They Mean to Readers?" *Journalism Quarterly* (Autumn, 1976) 53: 463-467 +. **[159]**

Curran, J. "Culturalist Perspectives of News Organizations: A Reappraisal and a Case Study," *Public Communication: The New Imperatives*, ed. M. Ferguson. Newbury Park, CA: Sage Publications, 1990, pp. 114-134. **[13, 152]**

Curran, James. "The New Revisionism in Mass Communication Research: A Reappraisal," *European Journal of Communication* (1990) 5: 135-164. **[13, 152]**

Cutler, Blayne. "Where Does the Free Time Go?" *American Demographics*, November, 1990, pp. 36-38. **[178]**

Cutler, Blayne. "Mature Audiences Only," *American Demographics*, October, 1989, pp. 20-26. **[171, 177, 178, 179, 191, 217, 231]**

Cutler, Gregory H., Angela R. Dalseide, Vincent H. Plummer and Chad R. Bacon. "Subjective Reactions to a Colorized Movie vs. Its Original Black/White Version," *Perceptual and Motor Skills* (1988) 66: 677-678. **[300]**

Cutler, Neal E. and James A. Danowski. "Process Gratification in Aging Cohorts," *Journalism Quarterly* (Summer, 1980) 57(2): 269-276. **[249]**

Cutting, James E. "Perception and Information," *Annual Review of Psychology* (1987) 38: 61-90. **[313]**

D'Agostino, Peter (ed.). *Transmission*. New York: Tanam Press, 1985. **[51]**

Dahlgren, Kathleen. "The Cognitive Structure of Social Categories," *Cognitive Science* (1985) 9: 379-398. **[20]**

Dahlgren, P. "The Modes of Reception: For a Hermeneutics of TV News," *Television in Transition*, ed. P. Drummond and R. Paterson, London: British Film Institute, 1985, pp. 235-249. **[20]**

Dail, P.W. "Prime-Time Television Portrayals of Older Adults in the Context of Family Life," *The Gerontologist* (October, 1988) 28(5): 700-706. **[347]**

Daley, Patrick and Dan O'Neill. "'Sad Is Too Mild a Word': Press Coverage of the Exxon Valdez Oil Spill," *Journal of Communication* (Autumn, 1991) 41(4): 42-57. **[128]**

Daly, R. "Police Report on the TV Cop Shows," *New York Times Magazine*, Nov. 19, 1972, pp. 39-106. **[369]**

Danielson, Wayne A., Dominic L. Lasorsa and Dae S. Im. "Journalists and Novelists: A Study of Diverging Styles," *Journalism Quarterly* (Summer, 1992) 69(2): 436-446. **[292]**

Darrow, Alice-Ann, Paul Haack and Fumio Kuribayashi. "Descriptors and Preferences for Eastern and Western Musics by Japanese and American Nonmusic Majors," *Journal of Research in Music Education* (1987) 35(4): 237-248. **[218]**

Davenport, L.D. and R.S. Izard. "News Media Restrictive Policies," *Journal of Mass Media Ethics* (1985) 1(1): 1-3. **[110]**

David, Prabu. "Accuracy of Visual Perception of Quantitative Graphics: An Exploratory Study," paper presented to the Visual Communication Division at the annual conference of the Association for Education in Journalism and Mass Communication, Montreal, August, 1992. **[290]**

David, Prabu. "Accuracy of Visual Perception of Quantitative Graphics: An Exploratory Study," *Journalism Quarterly* (Summer, 1992) 69(2): 273-292. **[290]**

Davie, William R. "Sex, Violence and Consonance/Diversity: An Analysis of Local TV News Values," paper presented to the Radio-Television Journalism Division at the annual conference of the Association for Education in Journalism and Mass Communication, Montreal, August, 1992. **[123, 156]**

Davis, Brian and Warren A. French. "Exploring Advertising Usage Segments among the Aged," *Journal of Advertising Research* (February/March, 1989) 29(1): 22-29. **[278]**

Davis, Donald M. and James R. Walker. "Countering the New Media: The Resurgence of Share Maintenance in Primetime Network Television," *Journal of Broadcasting & Electronic Media* (Fall, 1990) 34(4): 487-493. **[224]**

Davis, F. *Yearning for Yesterday: Nostalgia, Art and Society*. New York: The Free Press, 1979. **[273]**

Davis, R. "Lifting the Shroud: News Media Portrayal of the U.S. Supreme Court," *Communications and the Law* (October, 1987) 9(5): 43-60. **[357]**

Davis, Howard H. and Paul A. Walton. "Sources of Variation in News Vocabulary: A Comparative Analysis," *International Journal of the Sociology of Language* (1983) 40: 59-75. **[360]**

Davis, Richard H. "Television and the Older Adults," *Journal of Broadcasting* (Spring, 1971) 15:153-159. **[278]**

Davis, Richard H. and G. Jay Westbrook. "Television in the Lives of the Elderly: Attitudes and Opinions," *Journal of Broadcasting & Electronic Media* (Spring, 1985) 29(2): 209-214. **[259]**

Davison, W. Phillips. "Diplomatic Reporting: Rules of the Game," *Journal of Communication* (Autumn, 1975) 24(4): 138-146. **[161]**

Davison, W. Phillips. *International Political Communication*. New York: Praeger Publishers, 1965. **[56]**

Daw, P.S. and A.J. Parkin. "Observations on the Efficiency of Two Different Processing Strategies for Remembering Faces," *Canadian Journal of Psychology* (1981) 35(4): 351-355. **[316]**

Dawson, Don. "Leisure and Social Class: Some Neglected Theoretical Considerations," *Leisure Sciences* (1986) 8(1): 47-61. **[280]**

Day, R.D. and W.C. Mackey. "The Role Image of the American Father: An Examination of a Media Myth," *Journal of Comparative Family Studies* (Autumn, 1986) 17(3): 371-388. **[349]**

De Foe, James R. and Warren Breed. "Youth and Alcohol in Television Stories, with Suggestions to the Industry for Alternative Portrayals," *Adolescence* (Fall, 1988) 23: 533-550. **[371]**

DeFleur, Margaret H. "Foundations of Job Satisfaction in the Media Industries," *Journalism Educator* (Spring, 1992) 47(1): 3-15. **[150]**

DeLauretis, Teresa and Stephen Heath. *The Cinematic Apparatus*. New York: St. Martin's Press, 1980. **[105]**

Demers, David Pearce. "Effect of Corporate Structure on Autonomy of Top Editors at U.S. Dailies," paper presented at the annual conference of the Midwest Association for Public Opinion Research, Chicago, November, 1991. **[90, 92]**

Demers, David Pearce. "Corporate Structure and Emphasis on Profits and Product Quality at U.S. Daily Newspapers," *Journalism Quarterly* (Spring/Summer, 1991) 68(1/2): 15-26. **[90, 92]**

Demers, David Pearce. "Structural Pluralism and the Growth of Chain Ownership in the U.S. Newspaper Industry," paper presented to the Newspaper Division at the annual conference of the Association for Education in Journalism and Mass Communicaion, Minneapolis, August, 1990. **[81]**

Demers, D.P. "Opinion Polling Practices of Chain and Independent Papers," *Journalism Quarterly* (Summer, 1988) 65(2): 500-503. **[90]**

DeMott, John and Emmanuel Tom. "The Press Corps of Spaceship Earth: A Trend Analysis, 1968-88," *Newspaper Research Journal* (Fall, 1990) 11(4): 12-23. **[135]**

Denis, M. "Test of the Incidental Cues Hypothesis," *Perceptual and Motor Skills* (1976) 43: 175-178. **[315]**

Dennis, Everette E. "Media at the Millennium," *Media Studies Journal* (Fall, 1991) 5(4): 51-66. **[94]**

Dennis, Everette E. "Whatever Happened to Marse Robert's Dream? The Dilemma of American Journalism Education," *Gannett Center Journal* (Spring, 1988) 2(2): 2-22. **[164]**

Dennis, Everette E. and Michal Sadoff. "Media Coverage of Children and Childhood: Calculated Indifference or Neglect?" *Journalism Quarterly* (Spring, 1976) 53(1): 47-53. **[347]**

DeRiemer, Cynthia. "Education Coverage in Award-Winning and Non-Award-Winning Newspapers," *Journalism Quarterly* (Spring, 1988) 65(1): 171-177. **[368]**

Dershowitz, A. "The Verdict," *American Film*, December, 1987, pp. 15-18. **[369]**

Deutschmann, Paul J. *News-page Content of Twelve Metropolitan Dailies*. Cincinnati: Scripps-Howard Research, 1959. **[161]**

Devey, Susan M. "Umbrella Competition for Newspaper Circulation in the Boston Metro Area," *Journal of Media Economics* (Spring, 1989) 2(1): 31-40. **[87, 98]**

Dewey, J. *Reconstruction in Philosophy*, enl. ed. Boston: Beacon, 1948/1967 (Originally published in 1921). **[12]**

DiBella, Suzan, "Scientists' Reasons for Becoming Mass Media Sources: A National Survey," master's thesis, University of Nevada-Las Vegas, 1988. **[137]**

Dick, Bernard F. *The Star-Spangled Screen: The American World War II Film*. Ann Arbor: UMI Research Press, 1982/Lexington, KY: University Press of Kentucky, 1985. **[331]**

Dicken-Garcia, Hazel. *Journalistic Standards in Nineteenth Century America.* Madison: University of Wisconsin Press, 1989. **[126, 165]**

Dickson, Sandra H. "Press and U.S. Policy toward Nicaragua, 1983-1987: A Study of the New York Times and the Washington Post," *Journalism Quarterly* (Fall, 1992) 69(3): 562-571. **[158]**

Dillon, John. "Career Values as Predictor of the Perceived Role of Media," *Journalism Quarterly* (Summer, 1990) 67(2): 369-376. **[165]**

Dillon, John F. and Jenna L. Newton. "Birth Order and News Reporting Orientation," paper presented to the Mass Communication and Society Division at the annual conference of the Association for Education in Journalism and Mass Communication, Montreal, August, 1992. **[164]**

Dilts, J.P. "Testing Siebert's Proposition in Civil War Indiana," *Journalism Quarterly* (Summer, 1986) 63(2): 365-368. **[47]**

Dimmick, John. "Sociocultural Evolution in the Communication Industries," *Communication Research* (July, 1986) 13(3): 473-508. **[80, 89, 97]**

Dimmick, John W. "The Gatekeepers: Media Organizations as Political Coalitions," *Communication Research* (April, 1979) 6(2): 203-222. **[140]**

Dimmick, John. "Family Communication and TV Program Choice," *Journalism Quarterly* (Winter, 1976) 53: 720-723. **[270]**

Dimmick, John W., Thomas A. McCain and W. Theodore Bolton. "Media Use and the Life Span," *American Behavioral Scientist* (September/October, 1979) 23(1): 7-31. **[241]**

Dimmick, John W., Scott J. Patterson, and Alan B. Albarran. "Competition between the Cable and Broadcast Industries: A Niche Analysis," *Journal of Media Economics* (Spring, 1992) 5(1): 13-30. **[43]**

Dimmick, John W. and E.W. Rothenbuhler. "The Theory of the Niche: Quantifying Competition among Media Industries," *Journal of Communication* (Winter, 1984) 34(1): 103-119. **[43, 81]**

Dionisopoulos, George N. and R.E. Crable. "Definitional Hegemony as a Public Relations Strategy: The Rhetoric of the Nuclear Power Industry after Three Mile Island," *Central States Speech Journal* (Summer, 1988) 39(2): 134-145. **[161]**

Dionisopoulos, George N. "A Case Study in Print Media and Heroic Myth: Lee Iacocca 1978-1985," *Southern Speech Communication Journal* (Spring, 1988) 53(3): 227-243. **[357]**

Dizier, Bryon St. "Editorial Page Editors and Endorsements: Chain-Owned Vs. Independent Newspapers," *Newspaper Research Journal* (Fall, 1986) 8(1): 63-68. **[90, 98, 132]**

Dobos, Jean and John Dimmick. "Factor Analysis and Gratification Constructs," *Journal of Broadcasting & Electronic Media* (Summer, 1988) 32(3): 335-350. **[246, 248]**

Dobos, Jean. "Gratification Models of Satisfaction and Choice of Communication Channels in Organizations," *Communication Research* (February, 1992) 19(1): 29-51. **[251]**

Dobrow, J.R. "Patterns of Viewing and VCR Use: Implications for Cultivation Analysis," *Cultivation Analysis: New Directions in Media Effects Research*, ed. N. Signorielli and M. Morgan. Newbury Park, CA: Sage publications, 1990, pp. 71-83. **[272]**

Dobrow, J.R. "Away from the Mainstream? VCRs and Ethnic Identity," *The VCR Age: Home Video and Mass Communication*, ed. M.R. Levy. Newbury Park, CA: Sage Publications, 1989, pp. 193-208. **[233]**

Docherty, David, David E. Morrison and Michael Tracey. "The British Film Industry and the Declining Audience: Demythologizing the Technological Threat," *Journal of Communication* (Autumn, 1986) 36(4): 27-39. **[214, 277]**

Dodd, D.K., B.J. Foerch and H.T. Anderson. "Content Analysis of Women and Racial Minorities as News Magazine Cover Persons," *Journal of Social Behavior and Personality* (1988) 3(3): 231-236. **[346, 365]**

Dodd, David K. et al. "Face-ism and Facial Expressions of Women in Magazine Photos," *Psychological Record* (Summer, 1989) 39(3): 325-331. **[368]**

Dodd, J.C. and M.B. Holbrook. "What's an Oscar Worth? An Empirical Estimation of the Effects of Nominations and Awards on Movie Distribution and Revenues," *Current Research in Film: Audiences, Economics, and Law*, ed. B.A. Austin. Vol. 4. Norwood, NJ: Ablex, 1988, pp. 72-88. **[106]**

Doherty, Thomas P. *Teenagers and Teenpics: The Juvenilization of American Movies in the 1950s*. Media and Popular Culture, Vol. 3. Boston: Unwin Hyman, 1988. **[331]**

Dohnalik, Jacek. "Uses and Gratifications of 'Return to Eden' for Polish Viewers," *European Journal of Communication* (1989) 4: 307-328. **[274]**

Dominick, Joseph R. "Film Economics and Film Content: 1964-1983," *Current Research in Film: Audiences, Economics, and Law*, ed. Bruce A. Austin. Vol. 3. Norwood, NJ: Ablex, 1987. **[105, 361]**

Dominick, Joseph R. "Impact of Budget Cuts on CBS News," *Journalism Quarterly* (Summer, 1988) 65(2): 469-473. **[91]**

Dominick, Joseph R. and Millard C. Pearce. "Trends in Network Prime-Time Programming, 1953-1974," *Journal of Communication* (Winter, 1976) 26(1): 70-80. **[361]**

Donohew, L., S. Finn and W.g. Christ. "'The Nature of News' Revisited: The Roles of Affect, Schemas, and Cognition," *Communication, Social Cognition and Affect*, ed. L. Donohew, H.E. Sypher and E.T. Higgins. Hillsdale, NJ: Lawrence Erlbaum, 1988, pp. 195-218. **[316]**

Donohew, L. "Newswriting Styles: What Arouses the Reader?" *Newspaper Research Journal* (1982) 3(2): 3-6. **[317]**

Donohew, Lewis, Philip Palmgreen, and J.D. Rayburn II. "Social and Psychological Origins of Media Use: A Lifestyle Analysis," *Journal of Broadcasting & Electronic Media* (Summer, 1987) 31(3): 255-278. **[246, 266]**

Donohue, George A., Clarice N. Olien, Phillip J. Tichenor and D.P. Demers. "Community Structure, News Judgments and Newspaper Content," paper presented at the annual conference of the Association for Education in Journalism and Mass Communication, Minneapolis, August, 1990. **[146, 163]**

Donohue, George A., Clarice N. Olien and Phillip J. Tichenor. "Structure and Constraints on Community Newspaper Gatekeepers," *Journalism Quarterly* (Winter, 1989) 66(4): 807-812, 845. **[163]**

Donohue, George A., Clarice N. Olien and Phillip J. Tichenor. "Reporting Conflict by Pluralism, Newspaper Type and Ownership," *Journalism Quarterly* (Autumn, 1985) 62(3): 489-499, 507. **[146]**

Dornbusch, Sanford M., P.L. Ritter, P.H. Leiderman, D.F. Roberts, and M.J. Fraleigh. "The Relation of Parenting Style to Adolescent School Performance," *Child Development* (1987) 58: 1244-1257. **[279]**

Dornbusch, Sanford M. "The Sociology of Adolescence," *Annual Review of Sociology* (1989) 15: 233-259. **[215]**

Dorr, Aimee, Peter Kovaric and Catherine Doubleday. "Parent-Child Coviewing of Television," *Journal of Broadcasting & Electronic Media* (Winter, 1989) 33(1): 35-51. **[271]**

Douglas, Susan, Norma Pecora and Thomas Guback. "Work, Workers and the Workplace: Is Local Newspaper Coverage Adequate?" *Journalism Quarterly* (Winter, 1985) 62(4): 855-860. **[356]**

Douglas, Susan J. *Inventing American Broadcasting, 1899-1922*. Baltimore: Johns Hopkins University Press, 1987. **[58]**

Douglass, Wayne J. "The Criminal Psychopath as Hollywood Hero," *Journal of Popular Film and Television* (Winter, 1981) 8(4): 30-40. **[330]**

Downing, J. and C.K. Leong. *Psychology of Reading*. New York: Macmillan, 1982. **[320]**

Downing, John D.H. "Ethnic Minority Radio in the United States," *The Howard Journal of Communications* (Spring, 1990) 2(2): 135-148. **[164]**

Dreier, Peter and Steve Weinberg. "Interlocking Directories," *Columbia Journalism Review* (November/December, 1979), pp. 51-68. **[80]**

Drennan, Mathew P. "Information Intensive Industries in Metropolitan Areas of the United States of America," *Environment and Planning A* (December, 1989) 21: 1603-1618. **[65]**

Dreschel, R.E. "Judicial Selection and Trial Judge-Journalist Interaction in Two States," *The Justice System Journal* (Spring, 1985) 10(1): 6-18. **[137]**

Dresser, D. "Toward a Structural Analysis of the Postwar Samauri Film," *Quarterly Review of Film Studies* (1983) 8(1): 25-41. **[331]**

Drew, D.G. and T. Grimes. "Audio-Visual Redundancy and TV News Recall," *Communication Research* (1987) 14(4): 452-461. **[303, 308]**

Drew, Dan G. and Roy Cadwell. "Some Effects of Video Editing on Perceptions of Television News," *Journalism Quarterly* (Winter, 1985) 62(4): 828-831, 849. **[304]**

Dreyfus, John "The Invention of Spectacles and the Advent of Printing," *The Library* (June, 1988) 10(2): 93-106. **[26]**

Ducey, Richard V. and Mark R. Fratrik. "Broadcasting Industry Response to New Technologies," *Journal of Media Economics* (Fall, 1989) 2(2): 67-86. **[75]**

Duhe, Sonya Forte and Vernon A. Stone. "Sexual Harassment in Television Newsrooms," paper presented to the Radio-Television Journalism Divison at the annual conference of the Association for Education in Journalism and Mass Communication, Montreal, August, 1992. **[148]**

Duker, S. "Listening," *Encyclopedia of Education Research*, ed. R. Ebel. 4th ed. New York: The Macmillan Co., 1969, pp. 747-753. **[310]**

Dumble, W.V. "And Justice for All: The Messages behind 'Real' Courtroom Dramas," *Television Studies: Textual Analysis*, ed. G. Burns and R.J. Thompson. New York: Praeger, 1989, pp. 103-120. **[372]**

Dummett, Michael. *Truth and Other Enigmas*. Cambridge: Harvard University Press, 1978. **[19]**

Duncan, Margaret C. and Barry Brummett. "Types and Sources of Spectating Pleasure in Televised Sports," *Sociology of Sport Journal* (1989) 6(3): 195-211. **[252]**

Dunn, Edward W. Jr. "Mexican-American Media Behavior," *Journal of Broadcasting* (Winter, 1975) 19(1): 3-1O. **[233]**

Dunnett, Peter J.S. *The World Newspaper Industry*. London: Croom Helm, 1988. **[44, 49, 52, 59]**

Dunwoody, Sharon, "Mass Media Coverage of the Social Sciences: Some New Answers to Old Questions," paper presented at the annual conference of the Association for Education in Journalism and Mass Communication, Corvallis, OR, 1983. **[163]**

Dunwoody, Sharon. "The Science Writing Innerclub: A Communication Link between Science and the Lay Public," *Science, Technology & Human Values* (1980) 5: 14-22. **[163]**

Dunwoody, Sharon and Michael Ryan. "The Credible Scientific Source," *Journalism Quarterly* (Spring, 1987) 64(1): 21-27. **[137, 161]**

Dunwoody, Sharon and Michael Ryan. "Scientific Barriers to the Popularization of Science in the Mass Media," *Journal of Communication* (Winter, 1985) 35(1): 26-42. **[161]**

Dunwoody, Sharon and Steven Shields. "Accounting for Patterns of Selection of Topics in Statehouse Reporting," *Journalism Quarterly* (Autumn, 1986) 63(3): 488-496. **[139]**

Durgnat, Raymond. "Epic, Epic, Epic, Epic, Epic," in Barry K. Grant, ed. *Film Genre: Theory and Criticism* (Metuchen, NJ: The Scarecrow Press, Inc.), pp. 108-117, 1977. **[330]**

Durham, Meenakshi Gigi. "Is It All in the Telling? A Study of the Role of Text Schemas and Schematic Text Structures in the Recall and Comprehension of Printed News Stories," paper presented to the Communication Theory & Methodology Division at the annual conference of the Association for Education in Journalism and Mass Communication, Minneapolis, August, 1990. **[294, 295, 316, 317]**

Dutka, Elaine. "Hollywood: A Decade Driven by Dollars, Not Dreams," *Los Angeles Times*, Dec. 29, 1989, p. 6, 8F. **[66]**

Dyer, Carolyn Steward. "Political Patronage of the Wisconsin Press, 1849-1860, New Perspectives on the Economics of Patronage," *Journalism Monographs* (February, 1989) No. 109. **[30]**

Dzinic, Firdus. "Regional Differences in the Contact of Citizens with Mass media," *Sociologica* (1974): 16: 131-139. **[269]**

Eastman, Susan Tyler, Sydney W. Head and Lewis Klein. *Broadcast/Cable Programming.* Belmont, CA: Wadsworth Publishing Co., 1985, 2d ed. **[335]**

Ebeogu, Afam. "Media Comedy for Nigerian Folk: The Adventures of the 'Masquerade' Drama Group," *Nigeria Magazine* (April-June, 1987) 55(2): 1-12. **[45]**

Eberhard, Wallace B. and Margaret Lee Meyer. "Beyond the Locker Room: Women in Sports on Major Daily Newspapers," *Journalism Quarterly* (Fall, 1988) 65(3): 595-599. **[147]**

Eberhard, Wallace B. "Journalism on the Rack: Regulating Newspaper Vending Machines," *Newspaper Research Journal* (Winter, 1989) 10(2): 27-38. **[146]**

Ebert, Roger. "It's High Tide for Black New Wave," *Chicago Sun-Times*, May 26, 1991, p. 3E. **[330]**

Ebert, Teresa. "The Crisis of Representation in Cultural Studies: Reading Postmodern Texts," *American Quarterly* (Fall-Winter, 1986) 38: 894-902. **[10]**

Eco, Umberto. *A Theory of Semiotics.* Bloomington: Indiana University Press, 1976. **[360]**

Edgerton, G. and C. Pratt. "The Influence of the Paramount Decision on Network Television in America," *Quarterly Review of Film Studies* (Summer, 1983) 8(3): 9-23. **[36]**

Edwards, Clark and H. Allen White. "Right V. Left Brain Dominance and Language Skills Ability," *Journalism Educator* (Summer, 1992) 47(2): 32-38. **[163]**

Edwards, Emily D. and Michael W. Singletary. "Life's Soundtracks: Relationships between Radio Music Subcultures and Listeners' Belief Systems," *The Southern Communication Journal* (Winter, 1989) 54: 144-158. **[253]**

Edwardson, M., D. Grooms and S. Proudlove. "Television News Information Gain from Interesting Video vs. Talking Heads," *Journal of Broadcasting* (1981) 25: 15-24. **[303, 316]**

Edwardson, M., K. Kent, E. Engstrom and R. Hofmann. "Audio Recall Immediately Following Video Change in Television News," paper presented at the annual conference of the International Communication Association, Chicago, May, 1991. **[307, 308, 319, 320]**

Edwardson, Mickie, K. Kent and M. McConnell. "Television News Information Gain: Videotex Vs. a Talking Head," *Journal of Broadcasting & Electronic Media* (Fall, 1985) 29: 367-378. **[308, 316]**

Edwardson, M., D. Grooms and P. Pringle. "Visualization and TV News Information Gain," *Journal of Broadcasting* (1976) 20: 373-380. **[316]**

Ehrenberg, A.S.C. and J. Wakshalag. "Repeat-Viewing with People Meters," *Journal of Advertising Research* (February/March, 1987) 27(1): 9-13. **[173]**

Einsiedel, E.F. "Comparisons of Subscribers and Non Subscribers," *ANPA News Research Report.* No. 39. Washington, D.C.: American Newspaper Publishers Association, 1983. **[230, 279]**

Einsiedel, Edna. "Comparisons of Subscribers and Non-Subscribers," *ANPA News Research Report* (Dec. 27, 1983) No. 39. Washington, D.C.: American Newspaper Publishers Association. **[230, 232]**

Eisendrath, Charles R. "Back to the People with the Mom-and-Pop Press," *Columbia Journalism Review* (November/December, 1979), pp. 72-74. **[71]**

Ekecrantz, Jan. "The Rise and Fall of National News in Sweden," *Media, Culture and Society* (April, 1988) 10(2): 197-207. **[48, 124]**

El Nasser, Haya. "Hundreds of Magazines Come and Go," *USA Today*, July 5, 1988, p. 3B. **[95]**

Eliasoph, N. "Routines and the Making of Oppositional News," *Critical Studies in Mass Communication* (December, 1988) 5(4): 313-334. **[133]**

Elliott, J. "The Daytime Television Drama Portrayal of Older Adults," *The Gerontologist* (December, 1984) 24(6): 628-633. **[365]**

Elliott, Philip. "Media Organizations and Occupations: an Overview," *Mass Media and Society.* ed. James Curran, Michael Gurevitch and Janet Woollacott. London: Edward Arnold in association with The Open University Press, 1977, pp. 142-173. **[152]**

Elliott, William R. and Cynthia P. Quattlebaum. "Similarities in Patterns of Media Use: A Cluster Analysis of Media Gratification," *Western Journal of Speech Communication* (1979) 43: 61-72. **[216]**

Elliott, William R. and William L. Rosenberg. "The 1985 Philadelphia Newspaper Strike: A Uses and Gratifications Study," *Journalism Quarterly* (Winter, 1987) 64(4): 679-687. **[255]**

Ellis, Gary and P. Witt. "The Measurement of Perceived Freedom in Leisure," *Journal of Leisure Research* (1984) 16: 110-123. **[211]**

Ellis, Stephen. "Tuning in to Pavement Radio," *African Affairs* (July, 1989) 88(352): 321-330. **[45]**

Elton, Martin. "When Will the Information Explosion Reach Older Americans?" *American Behavioral Scientist* (May/June, 1988) 31(5): 564-575. **[278]**

Emery, Michael and Edwin Emery. *The Press and America: An Interpretive History of the Mass Media.* Englewood Cliffs, NJ: Prentice Hall, 1992. 7th edition. **[34]**

Emery, Michael. "An Endangered Species," *The Gannett Center Journal* (Fall, 1989), pp. 151-164. **[341]**

Endres, Fredric F. "Stress in the Newsroom at Ohio Dailies," *Newspaper Research Journal* (Fall, 1988) 10(1): 1-14. **[73, 154, 163]**

Endres, Fredric F. "Editorial Writers and the Research Process," *Newspaper Research Journal* (Spring, 1987) 8(3): 11-20. **[136]**

Endres, Fredric F. "Daily Newspaper Utilization of Computer Data Bases," *Newspaper Research Journal* (Winter, 1985) 7(1): 29-35. **[161]**

Endres, K.L. "Ownership and Employment in Specialized Business Press," *Journalism Quarterly* (Winter, 1988) 65(4): 996-998. **[73]**

Endres, K.L. "Sex Role Standards in Popular Music," *Journal of Popular Culture* (Summer, 1984) 18(1): 9-18. **[366]**

England, Paula, Alice Kuhn and Teresa Gardner. "The Ages of Men and Women in Magazine Advertisements," *Journalism Quarterly* (Fall, 1981) 58(3): 468-471. **[365]**

Entman, Robert M. *Democracy without Citizens: Media and the Decay of American Politics.* New York: Oxford University Press, 1989. **[20]**

Entman, Robert M. "Blacks in the News: Television, Modern Racism and Cultural Change," *Journalism Quarterly* (Summer, 1992) 69(2): 341-361. **[345]**

Entman, Robert M. "Framing U.S. Coverage of International News: Contrasts in Narratives of the KAL and Iran Air Incidents," *Journal of Communication* (Autumn, 1991) 41(4): 6-27. **[126]**

Entman, Robert M. "Modern Racism and the Images of Blacks in Local Television News," *Critical Studies in Mass Communication* (1990) 7: 332-345. **[345]**

Entman, Robert M. and Steven S. Wildman. "Reconciling Economic and Non-Economic Perspectives on Media Policy: Transcending the 'Marketplace of Ideas,'" *Journal of Communication* (Winter, 1992) 42(1): 5-19. **[79]**

Epstein, Edward J. *News from Nowhere: Television and the News.* New York: Random House, 1973. **[20]**

Erdogan, I. "Children's Media Use in a Turkish Town," *Journal of Broadcasting & Electronic Media* (Spring, 1985) 29(2): 195-199. **[215]**

Erfle, S., H. McMillan and B. Grotman. "Testing the Regulatory Threat Hypothesis: Media Coverage of the Energy Crisis and Petroleum Pricing in the Late 1970s," *American Politics Quarterly* (April, 1989) 17(2): 132-152. **[371]**

Erfle, S. and H. McMillan. "Determinants of Network News Coverage of the Oil Industry during the Late 1970s," *Journalism Quarterly* (Spring, 1989) 66(1): 121-128. **[156]**

Ericson, Richard V., Patricia M. Baranek and Janet B.L. Chan. *Negotiating Control: A Study of News Sources*. Toronto: University of Toronto Press, 1989. **[146]**

Ericson, Richard V., Patricia M. Baranek and Janet B.L. Chan. *Visualizing Deviance: A Study of News Organization*. Toronto: University of Toronto Press, 1987. **[156]**

Espe, H. and M. Seiwert. "Television Viewing Types: General Life Satisfaction, and Viewing Amount: An Empirical Study of West Germany," *Communications* (1987) 13(2): 95-110. **[256]**

Estep, Rhoda and Patrick T. Macdonald. "How Prime-Time Crime Evolved on TV, 1976 to 1981," *Justice and the Media: Issues and Research*, ed. R. Surette. Springfield, IL: Charles C. Thomas Publisher, 1984, pp. 110-123; also *Journalism Quarterly* (1983) 60(2): 293-300. **[371]**

Estes, W.K. "On the Interaction of Perception and Memory in Reading," *Basic Process in Reading: Perception and Comprehension*, ed. D. Laberge and S.J. Samuels. Hillsdale, NJ: Lawrence Erlbaum Associates, 1977, pp. 1-25. **[314]**

Etaugh, Claire and Patricia Ptasnik. "Effects of Studying to Music and Post-Study Relaxation on Reading Comprehension," *Perceptual and Motor Skills* (1982) 55: 141-142. **[268]**

Ettema, James S. "Journalism in the 'Post-Factual Age,'" *Critical Studies in Mass Communication* (March, 1987) 4(1): 82-86. **[129]**

Ettema, James S. *Individuals in Mass Media Organizations: Creativity and Constraint*. Beverly Hills: Sage, 1982. **[155]**

Ettema, James S. and Ted L. Glasser. "Narrative Form and Moral Force: The Realization of Innocence and Guilt Through Investigative Journalism," *Journal of Communication* (Summer, 1988) 39(3): 8-26. **[139]**

Ettema, James S. and Theodore L. Glasser. "Public Accountability or Public Relations? Newspaper Ombudsmen Define Their Role," *Journalism Quarterly* (Spring, 1987) 3-12. **[155]**

Etzioni, Amitai. *The Active Society*. New York: Free Press, 1968. **[264]**

Evans, William A. "The Interpretive Turn in Media Research: Innovation, Iteration, or Illusion?" *Critical Studies in Mass Communication* (1990) 7: 147-168. **[16, 20, 21]**

Evensen, B.J. "The Evangelical Origins of the Muckrakers," *American Journalism* (1989) 6(1): 5-29. **[33]**

Everett, S.E. and G.A. Everett. "The Blurring of Headline Sizes under New Editing Technology," *Journalism Quarterly* (Fall, 1988) 65(3): 627-633. **[287]**

Everett, Stephen E. "The Erosion of Network Television Audiences: Audience Opinion of Programs and Services," paper presented at the annual conference of the Midwest Association for Public Opinion Research, Chicago, November, 1990. **[198]**

Faber, R.J., T.C. L'Guinn, and A.P. Hardy. "Art Films in the Suburbs: A Comparison of Popular and Art Film Audiences," *Current Research in Film: Audiences, Economics and Law*, ed. Bruce Austin. Vol. 4. Norwood, NJ: Ablex, 1988, pp. 45-53. **[214]**

Fabes, Richard A., Patricia Wilson and F. Scott Christopher. "A Time to Reexamine the Role of Television in Family Life," *Family Relations* (July, 1989) 38: 337-341. **[271]**

Fabrikant, Geraldine. "Wooing the Wealthy Reader," *The New York Times*, Oct. 14, 1987, p. 29. **[73]**

Fabrikant, Geraldine. "Time Warner Constructing 2-Way Cable TV System," *New York Times*, March 8, 1991, p. 5C. **[67, 69]**

Fagans, A.E. "Media Use of the Freedom of Information Act," *Government Information Quarterly* (1984) 1(4): 351-364. **[134]**

Fairchild, H.H., R. Stockard and P. Bowman. "Impact of 'Roots': Evidence from the National Survey of Black Americans," *Journal of Black Studies* (March, 1986) 16(3): 307-318. **[233]**

Falchikov, N. "Images of Adolescence: An Investigation into the Accuracy of the Image of Adolescence Constructed by British Newspapers," *Journal of Adolescence* (June, 1986) 9(2): 167-180. **[348]**

Farnan, Jacqueline. "Mapping: Organizing News Stories for Improved Readability. Does It Work?" paper presented to the Newspaper Division at the annual conference of the Association for Education in Journalism and Mass Communication, Montreal, August, 1992. **[317]**

Feasley, F.G. and E.W. Stuart. "Magazine Advertising Layout and Design: 1932-1982," *Journal of Advertising* (1987) 16(2): 20-25. **[336]**

Feher, Ferenc. "The Status of Postmodernity," *Philosophy and Social Criticism* (1987) 13: 195-206. **[18]**

Feldman, Gayle. "The Organization of Publishing in China," *China Quarterly* (September, 1986) 107: 519-529. **[59]**

Feldman, Ofer. "Relations between the Diet and the Japanese Press," *Journalism Quarterly* (Winter, 1985) 62(4): 845-849. **[161]**

Felson, Marcus. "The Differentiation of Material Life Styles: 1925 to 1966," *Social Indicators Research* (1976) 3: 397-421. **[262]**

Feran, Tom. "TV-8 Follows Viewers to Cable," *Plain Dealer*, Feb. 4, 1991, p. 5C. **[74]**

Ferguson, Douglas A. "Channel Repertoire in the Presence of Remote Control Devices, VCRs and Cable Television," *Journal of Broadcasting & Electronic Media* (Winter, 1992) 36(1): 83-91. **[176]**

Ferguson, Douglas A. "Channel Repertoire in the New Media Environment," paper presented to the Mass Communication Division at the annual conference of the International Communication Association, Chicago, May, 1991. **[176, 213, 228, 245]**

Ferguson, Jill Hicks, Peggy J. Kreshel and Spencer F. Tinkham. "In the Pages of Ms.: Sex Role Portrayals of Women in Advertising," *Journal of Advertising* (1990) 19(1): 40-51. **[368]**

Ferguson, Marjorie. "Broadcasting in a Colder Climate: Canada's Cautionary Tale," *Political Quarterly* (January-March, 1987) 58(1): 40-52. **[44]**

Ferguson, Marjorie. "Images of Power and the Feminist Fallacy," *Critical Studies in Mass Communication* (September, 1990) 7: 215-230. **[148, 164]**

Fernandez, D.G. "Women in the Media in the Philippines: From Stereotype to Liberation," *Media Asia* (1987) 14(4): 183-193. **[366]**

Ferrante, C.L., A.M. Haynes and S.M. Kingsley. "Images of Women in Television Advertising," *Journal of Broadcasting and Electronic Media* (Spring, 1988) 32(2): 231-237. **[367]**

Ferri, Anthony J. "Perceptions of Broadcast News Positions by TV Anchors," *Mass Comm Review* (1989) 16(3): 39-41. **[162]**

Ferri, Anthony J. and Joe E. Keller. "Perceived Career Barriers for Female Television News Anchors," *Journalism Quarterly* (Autumn, 1986) 63(3): 463-467. **[164]**

Feuer, Jane. *The Hollywood Musical*. Bloomington: Indiana University Press, 1982. **[331]**

Fico, Frederick. "Perceived Roles and Editorial Concerns Influence Reporters in Two Statehouses," *Journalism Quarterly* (Winter, 1985) 62(4): 784-790. **[161]**

Fico, Frederick. "Statehouse Broadcast and Print Reporters: A Comparative Analysis," *Journal of Broadcasting* (Fall, 1984) 28(4): 477-483. **[161]**

Fico, Frederick, T. Atwater and R. Wicks. "The Similarity of Broadcast and Newspaper Reporters Covering Two State Capitols," *Mass Comm Review* (1985) 12(1-3): 29-32. **[160]**

Fico, Federick, Carrie Heeter, Stan Soffin and Cynthia Stanley. "New Wave Gatekeeping: Electronic Indexing Effects on Newspaper Reading," *Communication Research* (June, 1987) 14(3): 335-351. **[296, 297]**

Fico, Frederick, Todd Simon and Stephen Lacy. "Reporters' Use of Defamatory Source Materials in Qualified Privilege Contexts," *Newspaper Research Bureau* (Winter, 1991) 12(1): 34-45. **[137, 159]**

Fincham, Robin. "'From 'Post-Industrialism' to 'Information Society'" Comment on Lyon," *Sociology* (August, 1987) 21(3): 463-466. **[94]**

Findahl, O. and B. Hoijer. "Effect of Additional Verbal Information on Retention of a Radio News Program," *Journalism Quarterly* (Autumn, 1975) 52(3): 493-498. **[316]**

Findahl, O. and B. Hoijer. "Some Characteristics of News Memory and Comprehension," *Journal of Broadcasting & Electronic Media* (1985) 29(4): 379-396. **[294, 316]**

Findahl, O. and B. Hoijer. "Studies of News from the Perspective of Human Comprehension," *Mass Communication Review Yearbook 2*, ed. G. C. Wilhoit and H. deBock. Beverly Hills, CA: Sage, 1981, pp. 393-403. **[294, 305, 306, 316]**

Finn, Seth. "Television 'Addiction?' An Evaluation of Four Competing Media-Use Models," *Journalism Quarterly* (Summer, 1992) 69(2): 422-435. **[273]**

Finn, Seth. "Unpredictability as Correlate of Reader Enjoyment of News Articles," *Journalism Quarterly* (Summer, 1985) 62(2): 334-345. **[285]**

Finn, Seth and Mary Beth Gorr. "Social Isolation and Social Support as Correlates of Television Viewing Motivations," *Communication Research* (April, 1988) 15(2): 135-158. **[257]**

Finn, T. Andrew and Donald E. Strickland. "The Advertising and Alcohol Abuse Issue: A Cross-Media Comparison of Alcohol Beverage Advertising Content," *Communication Yearbook 6*, ed. Michael Burgoon. Beverly Hills, CA: Sage Publications, 1982, pp. 850-872. **[371]**

Finnegan, J.R. Jr. and K. Viswanath. "Community Ties and Use of Cable Television and Newspapers in a Midwestern Suburb," *Journalism Quarterly* (Summer, 1988) 65(2): 456-463. **[240]**

Finnegan, John R. Jr., K. Viswanath, Daniel Strickland, Peter Hannan and the Minnesota Heart Health Program Research Group. "Community Type and Exposure to Sources of Heart Disease Prevention Information in Six Upper Midwest Communities," paper presented to the Health Communication Division at the annual conference of the International Communication Association (ICA), Dublin, Ireland, June, 1990. [240]

Fishbein, Leslie. "From Sodom to Salvation: The Image of New York City in Films about Fallen Women, 1899-1934," *New York History* (April, 1989) 70(2): 171-190. **[367]**

Fishbein, Martin and I. Ajzen. *Belief, Attitude, Intention and Behavior: An Introduction to Theory and Research.* Reading, MA: Addison-Wesley, 1975. **[245]**

Fisher, B. Aubrey. *Perspectives on Human Communication.* New York: Macmillan Publishing Co., Inc., 1978. **[7, 8, 148, 325]**

Fisher, J., O.H. Gandy Jr. and N.Z. Janus. "The Role of Popular Media in Defining Sickness and Health," *Communication and Social Structure*, ed. E.G. McAnany et al. New York: Praeger Publishers, 1981, pp. 240-257. **[357]**

Fisher, James C. "Older Adult Readers and Nonreaders," *Educational Gerontology* (1988) 14: 57-67. **[192]**

Fishman, M. "Crime Waves as Ideology," *Justice and the Media: Issues and Research*, ed. R. Surette. Springfield, IL: Charles C. Thomas Publishers, 1984, pp. 159-180. **[138]**

Fishman, M. *Manufacturing the News.* Austin: University of Texas Press, 1980. **[20]**

Fishman, Mark. "News and Nonevents: Making the Visible Invisible," *Individuals in Mass Media Organizations*, eds. James S. Ettema and D. Charles Whitney. Beverly Hills, CA: Sage Publications, 1982, pp. 219-240. **[126]**

Fisk, S.T. and S.E. Taylor. *Social Cognitions.* New York: Random House, 1984. **[246]**

Fiske, Donald W. and Richard A. Shweder. *Metatheory in Social Science: Pluralisms and Subjectivities.* Chicago: University of Chicago Press, 1986. **[18]**

Fiske, J. "Popular Television and Commercial Culture: Beyond Political Economy," *Television Studies: Textual Analysis*, ed. G. Burns and R.J. Thompson. New York: Praeger, 1989, pp., 21-37. **[13]**

Fiske, J. *Television Culture.* New York: Methuen, 1987. **[20, 21]**

Fiske, John and John Hartley. *New Accents: Reading Television.* London: Methuen & Co., Ltd., 1978. **[360]**

Fiske, S.T. and P.W. Linville. "What Does the Concept Schema Buy Us?" *Personality and Social Psychology Bulletin* (1980) 6: 543-557. **[316]**

Fitzgerald, J. and D.L. Spiegel. "Enhancing Children's Reading Comprehension through Instruction in Narrative Structure," *Journal of Reading Behavior* (1983) 15: 1-17. **[316]**

Fitzgerald, J. "The Relationship between Reading Ability and Expectations for Story Structure," *Discourse Processes* (1984) 7: 21-41. **[316]**

Fleener, N. "'Breaking Down Buyer Resistance': Marketing the 1935 Pittsburgh 'Courier' to Mississippi Blacks," *Journalism History* (Autumn/Winter, 1986) 13(3/4): 78-84. **[71]**

Flocke, Elizabeth Lynne. "Coverage and Portrayal of Older Persons in Two Newspapers," paper presented to the Newspaper Division at the annual conference of the Association for Education in Journalism and Mass Communication, Minneapolis, August, 1990. **[347]**

Flournoy, Don, Debra Mason, Robert Nanney and Guido H. Stempel III. "Media Images of Canada: U.S. Media Coverage of Canadian Issues and U.S. Awareness of Those Issues," *The Ohio Journalism Monograph Series*, No. 3, Athena: Bush Research Center, Ohio University, August, 1992. **[371]**

Fogelson, S. "Music Distractor on Reading-Test Performance of Eighth Grade Students," *Perceptual and Motor Skills* (1973) 36: 1265-1266. **[227]**

Folkerts, Jean and Dwight L. Teeter Jr. *Voices of a Nation: A History of the Media in the United States*. New York: Macmillan Publishing Co., 1989. **[58]**

Foote, Joe S. "Women Correspondents' Visibility on the Network Evening News," *Mass Comm Review* (1992) 19(1/2): 36-40. **[351]**

Foote, Joe S. and Michael E. Steele. "Degree of Conformity in Lead Stories in Early Evening Network TV Newscasts," *Journalism Quarterly* (Spring, 1986) 63(1): 19-23. **[123]**

Foote, Joe S. and Ann C. Saunders. "Graphic Forms in Network Television News," *Journalism Quarterly* (Autumn, 1990) 67(3): 501-507. **[144, 363]**

Foote, Joe S. and Ann C. Saunders. "Graphic Forms in Network Television News," paper presented to the Visual Communication Division at the annual conference of the Association for Education in Journalism and Mass Communication (AEJMC), Minneapolis, Aug. 8-12, 1990. **[144]**

Fortner, Rosanne W. and Michele Wiggington. "Natural History Programming on Television: A Comparison of Markets," *Journal of Environmental Education* (Fall, 1989) 21(1): 15-18. **[371]**

Fournier, G.M. "The Determinants of Economic Rents in Television Broadcasting," *Antitrust Bulletin* (Winter, 1986) 31(4): 1045-1066. **[75]**

Fouts, Gregory T. "Television Use by the Elderly," *Canadian Psychology* (June/July, 1989) 39(3): 568-577. **[191, 259]**

Fowler, Gilbert L. and Tommy L. Mumert. "A Survey of Correction Policies of Arkansas Newspapers," *Journalism Quarterly* (Winter, 1988) 64(4): 853-858. **[110]**

Fowler, Gilbert L. and John Marlin Shipman. "Pennsylvania Editors' Perceptions of Communication in the Newsroom," *Journalism Quarterly* (Winter, 1984) 61(4): 822-826. **[154]**

Fowler, Gilbert Len Jr. "An Examination of Readership Changes: Does Altering Publication Time Affect the Reading Habit? *Newspaper Research Journal* (Fall, 1985) 7(1): 37-44. **[213]**

Foxall, Gordon. "The Meaning of Marketing and Leisure: Issues for Research and Development," *European Journal of Marketing* (1984) 18(2): 23-32. **[170]**

Francken, Dick A. and W. Fred van Raaij. "Satisfaction with Leisure Time Activities," *Journal of Leisure Research* (1981) 13: 337-352. **[230]**

Frank, Alan. *The Science Fiction and Fantasy Film Handbook*. Totowa, NJ: Barnes and Noble, 1982. **[331]**

Frank, Alan. *The Horror Film Handbook*. Totowa, NJ: Barnes and Noble, 1982. **[330]**

Frank, Ronald E. and Marshall G. Greenberg. *The Public's Use of Television: Who Watches and Why*. Beverly Hills: Sage Publications, 1980. **[273]**

Frank, Ronald E. and Marshall G. Greenberg, "Zooming in on TV Audiences," *Psychology Today* (October, 1979) 13(4): 92-103 +. **[270, 273]**

Franken, R.E. "Picture Recognition Memory as a Function of Picture Organization and Age," *Perceptual and Motor Skills* (1977) 44: 1151-1154. **[315]**

Frazer, Elizabeth. "Teenage Girls Reading 'Jackie,'" *Media, Culture and Society* (October, 1987) 9(4): 407-425. **[273]**

Fredin, Eric S. and Gerald M. Kosicki. "Cognitions and Attitudes about Community: Compensating for Media Images," *Journalism Quarterly* (Autumn, 1989) 66(3): 571-578. **[206]**

Freebody, Peter and Richard C. Anderson. "Effects of Vocabulary Difficulty, Text Cohesion, and Schema Availability on Reading Comprehension," *Reading Research Quarterly* (Spring, 1983) 18: 277-294. **[316]**

Freeman, Alan. "Some Dailies Adopt Lighter Paper, Trim Pages to Cut Newsprint Costs," *Wall Street Journal*, March 10, 1988, p. 26. **[71]**

Freeman, Lewis. "Social Mobility in Television Comedies," *Critical Studies in Mass Communication* (1992) 9: 400-406. **[368]**

Freimuth, Vicki S., Rachel H. Greenberg, Jean DeWitt, and Rose Mary Romano. "Covering Cancer: Newspapers and the Public Interest," *Journal of Communication* (Winter, 1984) 34(1):62-73. **[370]**

French, Warren (Ed.) *The South and Film.* Jackson: University Press of Mississippi, 1981. **[330]**

Frey, James H. and David R. Dickens. "Leisure as a Primary Institution," *Sociological Inquiry* (August, 1990) 60(3): 264-273. **[170]**

Frey-Vor, Gerlinde. "What Are Soap Operas and Telenovelas?" *Communication Research Trends* (1990) 10(1): 1-5. **[45]**

Fridriksson, L. "A Content Analysis of the 'Darts and Laurels' Column in 'Columbia Journalism Review,' *Mass Comm Review* (Fall, 1985) 11(3): 2-7. **[155]**

Friedman, Sharon M. "Two Decades of the Environmental Beat," *Gannett Center Journal* (Summer, 1990) 4(3): 12-23. **[134]**

Friedman, Sharon M., C.M. Gorney and B.P. Egolf. "Reporting on Radiation: A Content Analysis of Chernobyl Coverage," *Journal of Communication* (Summer, 1987) 37(3): 58-79. **[371]**

Friestad, Marian and Esther Thorson. "The Effects of Emotion on Episodic Memory for TV Commercials," paper presented at the annual conference of the International Communication Association, Honolulu, May, 1985. **[306, 319]**

Frijda, Nico H. "The Laws of Emotion," *American Psychologist* (May, 1988) 43(5): 349-358. **[246, 273]**

Frith, Katherine Toland and David Wesson. "A Comparison of Cultural Values in British and American Print Advertising: A Study of Magazines," *Journalism Quarterly* (Spring/Summer, 1991) 68(1/2): 216-223. **[359]**

Frith, Katherine Toland and Mohd. Adnan Bin Hashim. "Television Advertising in Malaysia," *Media Asia* (1988) 15(2): 81-86. **[47]**

Frith, U. and J.E. Robson. "Perceiving the Language of Film," *Perception* (1975) 4: 97-103. **[299]**

Fruth, Laurel and Allan Padderud. "Portrayals of Mental Illness in Daytime Television Serials," *Journalism Quarterly* (Summer, 1985) 62(2): 384-387, 449. **[370]**

Fry, Donald L. and Virginia H. Fry. "Some Structural Characteristics of Music Television Videos," *The Southern Speech Communication Journal* (Winter, 1987) 52: 151-164. **[336]**

Fryman, John E. and Benjamin J. Bates. "Bypassing the Gateways: International News on CNN WORLD REPORT," paper presented at the annual conference of the International Communication Association, Miami, May, 1992. **[363]**

Fulk, Janet, Charles W. Steinfield, Joseph Schmitz and J. Gerard Power. "A Social Information Processing Model of Media Use in Organizations," *Communication Research* (October, 1987) 14(5): 529-552. **[192]**

Fullerton, H.S. "Technology Collides with Relative Constancy: The Pattern of Adoption for a New Medium," *Journal of Media Economics* (Fall, 1988) 1(2): 75-84. **[42]**

Funkhouser, G. Ray and Eugene F. Shaw. "How Synthetic Experience Shapes Social Reality," *Journal of Communication* (Spring, 1990) 40(2): 75-87. **[14, 20]**

Furnham, Adrian and Barrie Gunter. "The Primacy of Print: Immediate Cued Recall of News as a Function of the Channel of Communication," *The Journal of General Psychology* (1989) 116(3): 305-310. **[310]**

Furnham, Adrian and Sandra Schofield. "Sex-Role Stereotyping in British Radio Advertisements," *British Journal of Social Psychology* (1986) 25(2): 165-171. **[367]**

Furnham, Adrian and Virginia Voli. "Gender Stereotypes in Italian Television Advertisements," *Journal of Broadcasting & Electronic Media* (Spring, 1989) 33(2): 175-185. **[367]**

Furno-Lamude, Diane and James Anderson. "The Uses and Gratifications of Rerun Viewing," *Journalism Quarterly* (Summer, 1992) 69(2): 362-372. **[251]**

Futch, E.J., S.A. Lisman and M.I. Geller. "An Analysis of Alcohol Portrayal on Prime-Time Television," *The International Journal of the Addictions* (1984) 19(4): 403-410. **[371]**

Gaddy, G.D. "The Power of the Religious Media: Religious Broadcast Use and the Role of Religious Organizations in Public Affairs," *Review of Religious Research* (June, 1984) 25(4): 289-302. **[270]**

Gaddy, G.D. and D. Pritchard. "When Watching Religious TV Is Like Attending Church," *Journal of Communication* (Winter, 1985) 35(1): 123-131. **[275]**

Gades, Amy. "A Study of Lifetime Newspaper Reading Patterns in 30- to 45-Year-Olds," master's thesis, University of Nebraska-Lincoln, 1988. **[261]**

Gagnard, A. "From Feast to Famine: Depiction of Ideal Body Type in Magazine Advertising: 1950-1984," *Proceedings of the 1986 Conference of the American Academy of Advertising*, ed. E.F. Larkin. Norman, OK: School of Journalism, University of Oklahoma, 1986, pp. R46-R50. **[354]**

Gagne, R.M. and W. Dick. "Instructional Psychology," *Annual Review of Psychology* (1983) 34: 261-295.

Galambos, James A., Robert P. Abelson and John B. Black (Eds.) *Knowledge Structures.* Hillsdale, NJ: Lawrence Erlbaum, 1986. **[317]**

Gale, J.L. and M.N. Wexler. "The Image of Business on Canadian-produced Television," *Canadian Journal of Communication* (Spring, 1983) 9(2): 15-36. **[356]**

Galician, M.L. "Perceptions of Good News and Bad News on Television," *Journalism Quarterly* (Autumn, 1986) 63(3): 611-616. **[193]**

Galician, M.L. and S. Pasternack. "Balancing Good News and Bad News: An Ethical Obligation?" *Journal of Mass Media Ethics* (Spring/Summer, 1987) 2(2): 82-92. **[217]**

Gallagher, M. *Employment and Positive Action for Women in the Television Organizations of the EEC Member States.* Luxembourg: Commission of the European Communities. Citied in Ferguson (1990). **[148, 164]**

Gallagher, Margaret. "Shifting Focus: Women and Broadcasting in the European Community," *Studies of Broadcasting* (1990) No. 26. Japan: NHK (Japan Broadcasting Corp.), pp. 61-82. **[148, 164]**

Gallagher, Margaret. "We've Come a Short Way, and Don't Call Me Baby," *Airwaves* (Quarterly journal of the Independent Broadcasting Authority), Summer, 1990, pp. 16-17. **[148]**

Gallup Polls.*The Gallup Report.* Report No. 253, October, 1986. Princeton, NJ: The Gallup Report. **[202]**

Galtung, Johan and Mari Holmboe Ruge. "The Structure of Foreign News," *Journal of Peace Research* (1965) 2: 64-91. **[120, 124]**

Gans, Herbert J. *Deciding What's News.* New York: Pantheon Books, 1979. **[20, 123]**

Gans, Herbert J. *Popular Culture and High Culture.* New York: Basic, 1974. **[117]**

Gantz, Walter. "Exploring the Role of Television in Married Life," *Journal of Broadcasting & Electronic Media* (Winter, 1985) 29(1): 65-78. **[197, 236]**

Gantz, Walter et al. "Gratifications and Expectations Associated with Pop Music Among Adolescents," *Popular Music & Society* (1978) 6(1): 81-89. **[278]**

Gantz, Walter and Susan Tyler Eastman. "Viewer Uses of Promotional Media to Find Out about Television Programs," *Journal of Broadcasting* (Summer, 1983) 27(3): 269-277. **[249]**

Gantz, Walter, Michael Fitzmaurice and Ed Fink. "Assessing the Active Component of Information-Seeking," *Journalism Quarterly* (Winter, 1991) 68(4): 630-643. **[244]**

Gantz, Walter and Jonathon Masland. "Television as Babysitter," *Journalism Quarterly* (Autumn, 1986) 63(3): 530-536. **[238, 270]**

Ganzert, Charles and Don M. Flournoy. "The Weekly 'World Report' on CNN, An Analysis," *Journalism Quarterly* (Spring, 1992) 69(1): 188-194. **[341]**

Gardner, Anthony. "The Media Under Gorbachev," *Journal of International Affairs* (Spring, 1989) 42(2): 357-362. **[59]**

Garfield, Brian. *Western Films: A Complete Guide.* New York: Rawson Associates, 1982. **[331]**

Garfield, Robert. "If You're Skeptical About Ads, You Have Plenty of Company," *USA Today,* May 15, 1985. **[219]**

Garnham, Nicholas. "Toward a Theory of Cultural Materialism," *Journal of Communication* (Summer, 1983) 33(3): 314-329. **[20]**

Garramone, Gina. "TV News and Adolescent Political Socialization," *Communication Yearbook 7,* ed. R. Bostrom. Beverly Hills, CA: Sage, 1983, pp. 651-671. **[305]**

Garrison, Bruce and Michael B. Salwen. "Professional Orientations of Sports Journalists: A Study of Associated Press Sports Editors," *Newspaper Research Journal* (Fall, 1989) 10(4): 77-83. **[166]**

Garrison, Bruce and Michael B. Salwen. "Magazines in Latin America, 1990: Changing Economic and Political Environments," paper presented to the Magazine Division of the Association for Education in Journalism and Mass Communication at the annual convention, Minneapolis, August, 1990. **[59]**

Gates, Henry Louis Jr. "TV Is Still Distorting Black Life," *Plain Dealer,* Jan. 28, 1990, p. 1H. New York Times dispatch. **[344]**

Gaunt, Philip. "The Training of Journalists in France, Britain and the U.S.," *Journalism Quarterly* (Fall, 1988) 65(3): 582-588. **[149]**

Gaziano, Cecilie. "Media Dependence for News: Some Neglected Groups," *Mass Comm Review* (1990) 17(3): 2-13, 43. **[182]**

Gaziano, Cecilie. "Chain Newspaper Homogeneity and Presidential Endorsements, 1972-1988," *Journalism Quarterly* (Winter, 1989) 66(4): 836-845. **[90]**

Gaziano, Cecilie. "How Credible Is the Credibility Crisis?" *Journalism Quarterly* (Summer, 1988) 65(2): 267-278. **[205]**

Gaziano, Cecilie. "News People's Ideology and the Credibility Debate," *Newspaper Research Journal* (Fall, 1987) 9(1): 1-18. **[203]**

Gaziano, Cecilie and David C. Coulson. "Effect of Newsroom Management Styles on Journalists: A Case Study," *Journalism Quarterly* (Winter, 1988) 65(4): 869-880. **[154]**

Gaziano, Cecilie and Kristin McGrath. "Segments of the Public Most Critical of Newspapers' Credibility: A Psychographic Analysis," *Newspaper Research Journal* (Summer, 1987) 8(4): 1-17. **[151, 203, 208]**

Gaziano, Cecilie and K. McGrath. "Newspaper Credibility and Relationships of Newspaper Journalists to Communities," *Journalism Quarterly* (Summer/Autumn, 1987) 64(2/3): 317-318. **[151]**

Gaziano, Cecilie and Kristin McGrath. "Measuring the Concept of Credibility," *Journalism Quarterly* (Autumn, 1986) 63(3): 451-462. **[207]**

Gaziano, Cecilie and Jean Ward. "Citizen-Developed Neighborhood Press," *Mass Com Review* (Spring, 1978) 5(2): 14-18. **[71]**

Geduld, Harry M. and Ronald Gottesman. *An Illustrated Glossary of Film Terms* (New York: Holt, Rinehart and Winston, 1973). **[329]**

Geertz, Clifford. "Blurred Genres," *American Scholar* (1980) 49:165-179. **[18]**

Gehring, Wes D. *Screwball Comedy: Defining a Film Genre.* Muncie, IN: Ball State University, 1983. **[331]**

Gentry, James W. and Mildred Doering. "Sex Role Orientation and Leisure," *Journal of Leisure Research* (Second Quarter, 1979) pp. 102-111. **[270]**

Gerard, Jeremy. "Minority Broadcasting Growing," *Plain Dealer*, Aug. 6, 1990, a New York Times dispatch. **[148]**

Gerbner, George. "Science on Television: How It Affects Public Conceptions," *Issues in Science and Industry* (1987) 3(3): 109-115. **[368]**

Gerbner, George, Larry Gross, Stewart Hoover, Michael Morgan and Nancy Signorielli. *Religion and Television*, Vol. 1 and 2. Philadelphia, PA: Annenberg School, 1984; also published under same title by the University of Pennsylvania Press, 1984. **[270]**

Gerbner, George, Larry Gross, Michael Morgan and Nancy Signorielli, "Political Correlates of Television Viewing," *Public Opinion Quarterly* (Spring, 1984) 48: 283-300. **[270]**

Gerbner, George, Larry Gross, Michael Morgan and Nancy Signorielli, "Charting the Mainstream: Television's Contributions to Political Contributions," *Journal of Communication* (Spring, 1982) 32(2): 100-127. **[204]**

Gerbner, George, Larry Gross, Michael Morgan and Nancy Signorielli. "Scientists on the TV Screen," *Society* (May/June, 1981) 18(4): 41-44. **[368]**

Gershon, Peter R. and Walter Gantz. "Music Videos and Television Commercials: A Comparison of Production Styles," paper presented to the Mass Communication Division at the annual conference of the International Communication Association, Miami, May, 1992. **[318]**

Gertner, Richard (ed.) *1985 International Television Almanac.* New York: Quigley Pub. Co., Inc., 1985. **[181]**

Gertner, Richard (ed) *International Motion Picture Almanac.* New York: Quigley Pub. Co., Inc., 1985. **[181]**

Ghiglione, Loren. "We Have a Lot to Learn about the Native American Press," *Minorities in the Newspaper Business* (May/June, 1987) 3(3): 4. **[72]**

Ghorpade, S. "Sources and Access: How Foreign Correspondents Rate Washington, D.C." *Journal of Communication* (Autumn, 1984) 34(4): 32-40. **[138]**

Giannetti, Louis. *Understanding Movies*, 4th ed. Englewood Cliffs, NJ: Prentice-Hall, 1987. **[58]**

Gibson, James J. *The Senses Considered as Perceptual Systems.* Boston: Houghton Mifflin, 1966. **[317]**

Gibson, James J. *The Ecological Approach to Visual Perception.* Boston: Houghton Mifflin, 1979. **[317]**

Gieber, W. "News Is What Newspapermen Make It," *People, Society and Mass Communications*, ed. L.A. Dexter and David Manning White. New York: Free Press, 1964. **[138]**

Giese, Thomas D. and T.M. Weisenberger. "The Perception and Use of Consumer Information Sources," *Journal of Education for Business* (October, 1985), pp. 38-43. **[276]**

Gilbert, Kathy and Joan Schleuder. "Effects of Color and Complexity in Still Photographs on Mental Effort and Memory," *Journalism Quarterly* (Winter, 1990) 67(4): 749-756. **[289, 290]**

Gilbert, Kathy and Joan Schleuder. "Effects of Color and Complexity in Still Photographs on Mental Effort and Memory," paper presented to the Theory and Methodology Division at the annual conference of the Association for Education in Journalism and Mass Communication, Portland, OR, 1988. **[289, 315]**

Gilbert, Kathy and Joan Schleuder. "Effects of Color and Complexity in Still Photographs on Mental Effort and Memory," *Journalism Quarterly* (Winter, 1990) 67(4): 749-756. **[290, 315]**

Giles, Dennis. "Television Reception," *Journal of Film and Video* (Summer, 1985) 38: 12-25. **[235]**

Giles, Dennis. "The Drive-In Economy: 1946-1981," paper presented at the Ohio University Film Conference, April, 1982. **[94]**

Gillet, J.W. and C. Temple. *Understanding Reading Problems: Assessment and Instruction.* Boston: Little, Brown, 1986. **[293, 316]**

Gilly, M.C. "Sex Roles in Advertising: A Comparison of Television Advertisements in Australia, Mexico, and the United States," *Journal of Marketing* (April, 1988) 52(2): 75-85. **[367]**

Ginsburg, Harvey J., Doug Bartels, Romana Kleingunther and Lisa Droege. "Cosmos Revisited: Just How Effective Are Special Effects for Instructional Communication?" *International Journal of Instructional Media* (1988) 15(4): 319-326. **[301]**

Gitlin, Todd. *The Whole World Is Watching: Mass Media in the Making and Unmaking of the New Left.* Berkeley: University of California Press, 1980. **[20, 126]**

Gitlin, Todd. *Inside Prime Time.* New York: Pantheon, 1983. **[113]**

Glaberson, William. "A Glimmer of Relief for Newspapers," *New York Times*, April 28, 1993, p. 18C. **[177]**

Gladney, George Albert. "Competition as a Predictor of Adoption of USA Today-Style Innovation," paper presented to the Media Management and Economics Division at the annual conference of the Association for Education in Journalism and Mass Communication, Montreal, August, 1992. **[91]**

Gladney, George A. "Newspaper Excellence: How Editors of Small and Large Papers Judge Quality," *Newspaper Research Journal* (Spring, 1990) 11(2): 58-69. **[110]**

Glasgow University Media Group. *Bad News.* London: Routledge and Kegan Paul, 1976. **[126]**

Glasgow University Media Group. *More Bad News.* London: Routledge and Kegan Paul, 1980. **[126]**

Glass, A.L. and D. Waterman. "Predictions of Movie Entertainment Value and the Representativeness Heuristic," *Applied Cognitive Psychology* (July-September, 1988) 2(3): 173-179. **[331]**

Glass, J.C. Jr. and J.L. Smith. "Television as an Educational and Outreach Medium for Older Adults," *Educational Gerontology* (1985) 11(4-6): 247-260. **[191]**

Glass, J.J. and D.N. Ammons. "Cable Television Refranchising Studies: An Important Role for Citizen Surveys," *International Journal of Public Administration* (1989) 12(5): 821-834. **[69]**

Glassner, Barry. "Fitness and the Postmodern Self," *Journal of Health and Social Behavior* (June, 1989) 30:180-191. **[18]**

Gluck, Mary. "Toward a Historical Definition of Modernism: Georg Luka'cs and the Avant-Garde," *Journal of Modern History* (December, 1986) 58: 845-882. **[18]**

Glynn, Carolyn J. "Science Reporters and Their Editors Judge 'Sensationalism,'" *Newspaper Research Journal* (Spring, 1985) 6(3): 69-74. **[157]**

Goban-Klas, Tomasz. "Gorbachev's Glasnost: A Concept in Need of Theory and Research," *European Journal of Communication* (1989) 4: 247-254. **[59]**

Goedkoop, R.J. "Elements of Genre in Television Situation Comedy," *Feedback* (Summer, 1983) 25(1):3-5. **[332]**

Golding, P. "The Missing Dimensions-News Media and the Management of Social Change," *Mass Media and Social Change*, ed. E. Katz and T. Szecko. Beverly Hills: Sage, 1981, pp. 63-82. **[20]**

Golding, Peter. "Communicating Capitalism: Resisting and Restructuring State Ideology--The Case of 'Thatcherism,'" *Media, Culture, & Society* (October, 1992) 14(4): 503-521. **[184]**

Golding, Peter and Philip Elliott. *Making the News.* London: Longman, 1979. **[364]**

Golding, Peter and Sue Middleton. *Images of Welfare.* Oxford: Martin Robertson, 1982. **[13]**

Goldman, Eric A. *Visions, Images, and Dreams: Yiddish Film Past and Present.* Ann Arbor: UMI Research Press, 1983. **[330]**

Goldman, Kevin. "FTC Won't Block Acquisition of FNN by Rival CNBC," *Wall Street Journal*, April 19, 1991, p. 4B. **[69]**

Goldman, Kevin. "NBC to Cut Pay to Affiliates 10% as Ratings Decline," *Wall Street Journal*, Aug. 22, 1990, p. 4B. **[67, 68]**

Goldman, Kevin. "Free-Form Radio Fights Static Formats," *Wall Street Journal*, May 18, 1990, p. 1B. **[67, 68, 328]**

Goldman, Kevin. "Radio Stations Luring Boomers with Old Songs," *Wall Street Journal*, April 24, 1990, p. 1B. **[67, 68, 361]**

Goldman, Kevin. "Fees Look Sad for Comedy Syndicators," *Wall Street Journal*, Jan. 12, 1990, p. 1B. **[67, 68]**

Goldman, S.L. "Images of Technology in Popular Films: Discussion and Film-ography," *Science, Technology and Human Values* (Summer, 1989) 14(3): 275-301. **[371]**

Gollin, A. "Are Sunday Newspapers Flowering While Weekday Readership Wilts? *Bulletin of the ASNE* (November/December, 1985) 682: 3-7. **[179]**

Gollin, Albert E. *An Assessment of Trends in U.S. Newspaper Circulation and Readership*. New York: Newspaper Advertising Bureau, December, 1991. **[177, 178, 183, 213, 230, 231, 232]**

Gollin, Albert E. "Soviets Express Views on Public Opinion," *AAPOR News* (newsletter of the American Association for Public Opinion Research) (Fall, 1990) 18(1): 3. **[59]**

Gollin, Albert E. "The Daily Diet of News: Patterns of Exposure to News in the Mass Media," New York: Newspaper Advertising Bureau, July, 1978. **[232]**

Goltz, Gene. "NY Tabs Make Own Headlines," *Presstime*, October, 1990, p. 48. **[154]**

Gomery, D. "Media Economics: Terms of Analysis," *Critical Studies in Mass Communication* (1989) 6: 43-60. **[20, 60, 80]**

Gomery, D. "Failed Opportunities: The Interaction of the U.S. Motion Picture and Television Industries," *Quarterly Review of Film Studies* (Summer, 1984) 9(3): 219-228. **[36]**

Gomery, Douglas. *Movie History*. Belmont, CA: Wadsworth, 1990. **[58]**

Gonzalez, Hernando. "The Evolution of Communication as a Field," *Communication Research* (June, 1988) 15(3): 302-308. **[12, 13]**

Gonzenbach, William J., M. David Arant and Robert L. Stevenson. "The World of U.S. Network Television News: Eighteen Years of International and Foreign News Coverage," *Gazette* (1992) 50: 53-72. **[364]**

Goodman, R. Irwin. "Television News Viewing by Older Adults," *Journalism Quarterly* (Spring, 1990) 67(1): 137-141. **[58, 259]**

Gormley, William T. Jr. *The Effects of Newspaper-Television Cross-Ownership on News Homogeneity*. Chapel Hill: University of North Carolina, Institute for Research in Social Science, 1976. **[90]**

Gorney, Carole. "Numbers versus Pictures: Did Network Television Sensationalize Chernobyl Coverage?" *Journalism Quarterly* (Summer, 1992) 69(2): 455-465. **[157]**

Gottschall, Edward M. *Typographic Communications Today*. Cambridge, MA: MIT Press, 1989. **[338]**

Gouldner, A. *The Rise of the Intellectuals and the Future of the New Class*. London: Macmillan, 1979. **[64]**

Gourley, J.W. "Discourse Structure: Expectations of Beginning Readers and Readability of Text," *Journal of Reading Behavior* (1984) 16: 169-188. **[316]**

Graber, Doris A. *News and Democracy: Are Their Paths Diverging?* Roy W. Howard Public Lecture in Journalism and Mass Communication Research, No. 3, School of Journalism, Indiana University, Bloomington, April 16, 1992. **[122, 145, 341, 363]**

Graber, Doris. "Seeing Is Remembering: How Visuals Contribute to Learning from Television News," *Journal of Communication* (1990) 40(3): 134-155. **[307]**

Graber, Doris A. *Processing the News*, 2nd ed. White Plains, NY: Longman, 1988/first edition, 1984. **[294, 313]**

Graber, Doris A. *Crime News and the Public*. New York: Praeger, 1980. **[371]**

Grady, L. and R. Baxter. "Attitudes about the Business Community as Expressed in the Popular Music of 1983," *Popular Music and Society* (1985) 10(1): 51-58. **[357]**

Grady, L. "How Voice Reports, Actualities Affect Recall of Radio News," *Journalism Quarterly* (Summer/Autumn, 1987) 64(2/3): 587-590. **[309]**

Graesser, A.C. and L.F. Clark. *Structures and Procedures of Implicit Knowledge*. Norwood, NJ: Ablex, 1985. **[314]**

Graesser, A.C. and G.V. Nakamura. "The Impact of a Schema on Comprehension and Memory," *The Psychology of Learning and Motivation*, ed. H. Bower (1982) 16: 59-109. **[293, 316]**

Gramsci, A. *The Modern Prince and Other Writings*. New York: International Publishers, 1983. **[126]**

Gramsci, A. *Selections from the Prison Notebooks*. London: Lawrence and Wishart, 1971. **[126]**

Gramsci, A. *Prison Notebooks*. New York: International Publishers, 1971. **[126]**

Gramsci, Antonio. *Selections from the Prison Notebooks*, trans., and ed. Quintin Hoare and Geoffrey Nowell Smith. New York: International, 1971 (written 1929-1935). **[126]**

Grandi, Roberto. "Italy," *International Handbook of Broadcasting Systems*, ed. Philip T. Rosen (1988). New York: Greenwood Press, pp. 163-172. **[48]**

Grannis, Chandler B. "Book Sales Statistics: Highlights from AAP Surveys, 1988 and 1989," *The Bowker Library and Book Trade Almanac 1990-91*, ed. Filomena Simora. New York: R.R. Bowker, 1990. **[28]**

Grant, Barry Keith. *Planks of Reason: Essays on the Horror Film*. Metuchen, NJ: Scarecrow, 1985. **[330]**

Greaney, V. "Factors Related to Amount and Type of Leisure Reading," *Reading Research Quarterly* (1980) 15: 337-357. **[181]**

Greatbatch, D. "A Turn-Taking System for British News Interviews," *Language in Society* (September, 1988) 17(3): 401-430. **[143]**

Greatbatch, D. "Aspects of Topical Organization in News Interviews: The Use of Agenda-Shifting Procedures by Interviewees," *Media, Culture and Society* (October, 1986) 8(4): 441-456. **[134]**

Greco, Albert N. "The Growth in Mergers and Acquisitions in the United States Publishing Industry: 1984-1988," paper presented at the annual conference of the International Communication Association, San Francisco, CA, May, 1989. **[88]**

Green, G.M. *Organization, Goals, and Comprehensibility in Narratives: News Writing, A Case Study*. Technical Report No. 132. Urbana, IL: University of Illinois, Center for the Study of Reading, 1979. (ERIC Document Reproduction Service No. ED 174 949). Cited in Durham (1990). **[294, 317]**

Green, Norma, Stephen Lacy and Jean Folkerts. "Journalists at the Turn of the Century: Chicago Journalists Compared to Their Rural Counterparts," paper presented to the History Division at the annual conference of the Association for Education in Journalism and Mass Communication, Portland, OR, July, 1988. **[164]**

Green, Stanley. *Encyclopedia of the Musical Film*. New York: Oxford University Press, 1981. **[331]**

Greenberg, Bradley S. "Changes in the Viewing Process over Time," *Cable-Viewing*, ed. Carrie Heeter and Bradley S. Greenberg. Norwood, NJ: Ablex, 1988, pp. 97-109. **[227]**

Greenberg, Bradley S. (ed.) *Life on Television: Content Analyses of U.S. TV Drama*. Norwood, NJ: Ablex, 1980. **[347, 348, 371]**

Greenberg, Bradley S. "Additional Data on Variables Related to Press Freedom," *Journalism Quarterly* (1961) 38: 76-78. **[60]**

Greenberg, Bradley S. et al. *Mexican-Americans and the Mass Media*. Norwood, NJ: Ablex Publishers, 1983. **[233, 346]**

Greenberg, Bradley S. and Charles K. Atkin. "The Portrayal of Driving on Television, 1975-1980," *Journal of Communication* (Spring, 1983) 33(2): 44-55. **[371]**

Greenberg, Bradley and Brenda Dervin. "Mass Communication among the Urban Poor," *Public Opinion Quarterly* (1970) 34: 224-235. **[278]**

Greenberg, Bradley and J. Dominick. "Racial and Social Class Differences in Teenagers' Use of Television," *Journal of Broadcasting* (Fall, 1969) 13: 331-334. **[278]**

Greenberg, Bradley S. and Carrie Heeter. "VCRs and Young People: The Picture at 39% Penetration," *American Behavioral Scientist* (May/June, 1987) 30(5): 509-521.

Greenberg, Bradley S., Carrie Heeter, David D'Alessio and Sherri Sipes. "Cable and Noncable Viewing Style Comparisons," *Cable-Viewing*, ed. Carrie Heeter and Bradley S. Greenberg. Norwood, NJ: Ablex, 1988, pp. 207-225. **[227, 269]**

Greenberg, Bradley S., Carrie Heeter, Judee K. Burgoon, Michael Burgoon and Felipe Korzenny. "Local Newspaper Coverage of Mexican Americans," *Journalism Quarterly* (Winter, 1983) 60(4): 671-676. **[346]**

Greenberg, Bradley S., Carrie Heeter, and Sherri Sipes. "Viewing Context and Style with Electronic Assessment of Viewing Behavior," *Cable-Viewing*, ed. Carrie Heeter and Bradley S. Greenberg. Norwood, NJ: Ablex, 1988, pp. 123-139. **[227]**

Greenberg, Bradley S. and Carolyn Lin. "Adolescents and the VCR Boom: Old, New, and Nonusers," *The VCR Age: Home Video and Mass Communication*, ed. M.R. Levy. Newbury Park, CA: Sage Publications, 1989, pp. 73-91. **[144, 176]**

Greenberg, Bradley S. and Kimberly A. Neuendorf. "Black Family Interactions on Television," *Life on Television*, ed. Bradley S. Greenberg. Norwood, NJ: Ablex, 1980, pp. 173-181. **[344]**

Greenberg, Bradley S. and Byron Reeves. "Children and the Perceived Reality of Television," *Journal of Social Issues* (Fall, 1976) 32: 86-97. **[215]**

Greenberg, Bradley S., Marcia Richards and Laura Henderson, "Trends in Sex-Role Portrayals on Television," *Life on Television*, ed. Bradley S. Greenberg. Norwood, NJ: Ablex, 1980, pp. 65-87. **[347, 366]**

Greenberg, Bradley S. and M.E. Roloff. "Mass Media Credibility: Research Results and Critical Issues," *News Research for Better Newspapers*, ed. Galen Rarick. Vol. 7. Washington, D.C.: American Newspaper Publishers Association Foundation, 1975. **[207]**

Greenberg, Marshall G. and Ronald E. Frank. "Leisure Lifestyles: Segmentation by Interests, Needs, Demographics, and Television Viewing," *American Behavioral Scientist* (March/April, 1983) 26(4): 439-458. **[266]**

Greenberg, Michael and Daniel Wartenberg. "Network Television Evening News Coverage of Infectious Disease Events," *Journalism Quarterly* (Spring, 1990) 67(1): 142-146. **[370]**

Greenberg, Michael R., David B. Sachsman, Peter M. Sandman and Kandice L. Salomone. "Risk, Drama and Geography in Coverage of Environmental Risk by Network TV," *Journalism Quarterly* (Summer, 1989) 66(2): 267-276. **[120, 144]**

Greenberg, Michael R., David B. Sachsman, Peter M. Sandman and Kandice L. Salomone. "Network Evening News Coverage of Environmental Risk," paper presented at the annual conference of the Association for Education in Journalism and Mass Communication, Portland, OR, July, 1988. **[156]**

Greenfield, Patricia. *Mind and Media*. Cambridge, MA: Harvard University Press, 1984. **[298, 317]**

Greenwald, Marilyn S. "Gender Representation in Newspaper Business Sections," *Newspaper Research Journal* (Winter, 1990) 11: 68-74. **[353]**

Griffin, Jeffrey L. and Robert L. Stevenson. "The Influence of Statistical Graphics on Newspaper Reader Knowledge Gain," paper presented to the Newspaper Division at the annual conference of the Association for Education in Journalism and Mass Communication, Montreal, August, 1992. **[289]**

Griffin, Jeffrey L. and Robert L. Stevenson. "The Influence of Text and Graphics in Increasing Understanding of the Context of Foreign News," paper presented to the Newspaper Division at the annual conference of the Association for Education in Journalism and Mass Communication, Boston, August, 1991. **[289]**

Griffiths, Thomas A. and R. Irwin Goodman. "Radio News Directors' Perception of Involvement in Advertising and Sales," *Journalism Quarterly* (Autumn, 1989) 66(3): 600-606. **[116]**

Grimes, Tom. "Encoding TV News Messages into Memory," *Journalism Quarterly* (Winter, 1990) 67(4): 757-766. **[309]**

Grimes, Tom. "The Consequence of 'Grabbing B-Roll' in Television News: Why Semantic Audio and Video Redundancy Is Crucial to Recognition," paper presented to the Radio-Television Division at the annual conference of the Association for Education in Journalism and Mass Communication, Washington, D.C., August, 1989. **[308, 320]**

Grimes, William. "What Debt Does Hollywood Owe to Truth?" *New York Times*, March 5, 1992, p. 1B. **[328]**

Griswold, W. "American Character and the American Novel," *American Journal of Sociology* (1981) 86: 740-765. **[20]**

Griswold, W.F. and R.L. Moore. "Factors Affecting Readership of News and Advertising in a Small Daily Newspaper," *Newspaper Research Journal* (Winter, 1989) 10(2): 55-66. **[270]**

Griswold, William F. Jr. "Support for 'Watchdog' and 'Consensus' Roles of the Press: The Influence of Education and Community Structure," paper presented to the Mass Communication and Society Division at the annual conference of the Association for Education in Journalism and Mass Communication, Portland, OR, July 2-5, 1988. **[166]**

Grossberg, L. "MTV: Swinging on the (Postmodern) Star," *Cultural Politics in Contemporary America*, ed. I. Angus and S. Jhally. New York: Routledge, 1989, pp. 254-268. **[16, 21]**

Grossberg, L. "'I'd Rather Feel Bad than Not Feel Anything at All': Rock and Roll, Pleasure and Power,'" *Enclitic* (1984) 8(1/2): 94-111. **[21]**

Grossberg, L. and P.A. Treichler. "Intersections of Power: Criticism, Television, Gender," *Communication* (1987) 9: 273-287. **[20]**

Grotta, Gerald L., Ernest F. Larkin, and Bob L. Carrell Jr., "News vs. Advertising: Does the Audience Perceive the Journalist Distinction?" *Journalism Quarterly* (Autumn, 1976) 53: 448-456. **[219]**

Grotta, Gerald L., Ernest F. Larkin and Barbara De Plois. "How Readers Perceive and Use a Small Daily Newspaper," *Journalism Quarterly* (Winter, 1975) 52: 711-715. **[277]**

Groves, D.L. "Sport and Leisure and Its Use in Television Programs and Commercials," *International Journal of Sports Psychology* (1986) 17(1): 71-81. **[275]**

Groves, D.L. "Sport and Leisure and Its Use in Television Programs and Commercials--A Model," *Psychology* (1987) 24(1/2): 13-21. **[275]**

Groves, D.L. "Sport and Leisure and Its Use in Television Programs and Commercials," *International Journal of Sports Psychology* (1986) 17(1): 71-81. **[275]**

Grunig, James E. "Time Budgets, Level of Involvement and Use of the Mass Media," *Journalism Quarterly* (Summer, 1979) 56(2): 248-261. **[249]**

Guback, Thomas. "Ownership and Control in the Motion Picture Industry," *Journal of Film and Video* (Winter, 1986) 38: 7-20. **[91]**

Guback, Thomas. "The Evolution of the Motion Picture Theater Business in the 1980s," *Journal of of Communication* (Spring, 1987) 37(2): 60-77. **[66, 81, 82]**

Guenther, Lea. "Four Categories of Change at the Weekly Newspaper," *Journalism Quarterly* (Winter, 1987) 64(4): 863-867. **[88]**

Gunter, B. *Poor Reception: Misunderstanding and Forgetting Broadcast News.* Hillsdale, NJ: Lawrence Erlbaum, 1987. **[310]**

Gunter, B. "Forgetting the News," *Intermedia* (September, 1981) 9(5): 41-43. **[307, 316]**

Gunter, B. "Remembering Television News: Effects of Picture Content," *Journal of General Psychology* (1980) 102: 127-133. **[316, 319]**

Gunter, B. "Remembering the Television News: Effects of Visual Format on Information Gain," *Journal of Educational Television* (1980) 6: 8-11. **[316, 319]**

Gunter, B., B.R. Clifford and C. Berry. "Release from Proactive Interference with Television News Items: Evidence for Encoding Dimensions within Televised News," *Journal of Experimental Psychology: Human Learning and Memory* (1980) 6: 216-223. **[307]**

Gunter, B., A. Furnham and G. Gietson. "Memory for the News as a Function of the Channel of Communication," *Human Learning* (1984) 3: 265-271. **[310]**

Gunter, B., A. Furnham and J. Jarrett. "Personality, Time of Day and Delayed Memory for TV News," *Personality and Individual Differences* (1984) 5(1): 35-39. **[307, 319]**

Gunter, B., J. Jarrett and A. Furnham. "Time of Day Effects on Immediate Memory for Television News," *Human Learning* (1983) 2: 261-267. **[307]**

Gunter, Barrie and Mark R. Levy. "Social Contexts of Video Use," *American Behavioral Scientist* (May/June, 1987) 30(5): 486-494. **[271]**

Gunter, Barrie and Mallory Wober. "The Uses and Impact of Home Video in Great Britain," *The VCR Age: Home Video and Mass Communication*, ed. Mark R. Levy. Newbury Park, CA: Sage Publications, 1989, pp. 50-69. **[212]**

Gunther, Albert and Dominic L. Lasorsa. "Issue Importance and Trust in Mass Media," *Journalism Quarterly* (Winter, 1986) 63(4): 844-848. **[209]**

Gunther, Albert. "Biases Press or Biased Public? Attitudes toward Media Coverage of Social Groups," *Public Opinion Quarterly* (Summer, 1992) 56(2): 147-167. **[208]**

Gunther, Albert. "Attitude Extremity and Trust in Media," *Journalism Quarterly* (Summer, 1988) 65(2): 279-287. **[206]**

Guy, Pat. "Winners, Losers in Circulation," *USA Today*, Nov. 4, 1988, p. 7B. **[97]**

Ha, Louisa. "Journalistic Excellence in Two Different Political Systems: A Comparative Study of American and Chinese News Reporting Awards," paper presented to the International Communication Division at the annual conference of the Association for Education in Journalism and Mass Communication, August, 1992. **[165]**

Haberlandt, Karl and G. Bingham. "Verbs Contribute to the Coherence of Brief Narratives: Reading Related and Unrelated Sentence Triplets," *Journal of Verbal Learning and Verbal Behavior* (1978) 17: 419-425. **[314]**

Haberlandt, Karl and Arthur C. Graesser. "Buffering New Information during Reading," *Discourse Processes* (1989) 12: 479-494. **[284, 314]**

Habermann, Peter, Lillian Lodge Kopenbauer and David L. Martinson. "Sequence Faculty Divided on PR Value, Status and News Orientation," *Journalism Quarterly* (Summer, 1988) 65(2): 490-496. **[161]**

Habermas, J. *The Theory of Communicative Action*. Cambridge: Polity Press, 1985. **[11]**

Hachten, William A. and Harva Hachten. *The World News Prism*. Ames: Iowa State University Press, 2nd ed., 1987. **[53, 54]**

Hachten, William A. "Media Development without Press Freedom: Lee Kuan Yew's Singapore," *Journalism Quarterly* (Winter, 1989) 66(4): 822-827. **[46, 59]**

Hackett, R.A. "Decline of a Paradigm? Bias and Objectivity in News Media Studies," *Critical Studies in Mass Communication* (September, 1984) 1(3): 229-259. **[159]**

Hackett, R.A. "The Depiction of Labor and Business on National Television News," *Canadian Journal of Communication* (Winter, 1983) 10(11: 5-50. **[356]**

Hackett, Robert A. "A Hierarchy of Access: Aspects of Source Bias in Canadian TV News," *Journalism Quarterly* (1985) 62: 256-265, 277. **[160, 161]**

Haefner, Margaret J., Sandra Metts and Ellen Wartella. "Siblings' Strategies for Resolving Conflict over Television Program Choice," *Communication Quarterly* (Summer, 1989) 37(3): 223-230. **[238]**

Haefner, Margaret J. and Ellen A. Wartella. "Effects of Sibling Coviewing on Children's Interpretations of Television Programs," *Journal of Broadcasting & Electronic Media* (Spring, 1987) 31(2): 153-168. **[238]**

Hage, George S., Everette E. Dennis, Arnold H. Ismach and Stephen Hartgen. *New Strategies for Public Affairs Reporting*. Englewood Cliffs, NJ: Prentice-Hall, Inc., 1983, 2nd ed. **[159]**

Hagen, Lutz, M. "The Consonant Witnesses: Bias in Newspaper Coverage on a Controversial Issue," paper presented at the annual conference of the International Communication Association, Miami, May, 1992. **[159]**

Hagner, Paul R. "Newspaper Competition: Isolating Related Market Characteristics," *Journalism Quarterly* (Summer, 1983) 60(2): 281-287. **[58]**

Hale, F. Dennis. "The Influence of Chain Ownership on News Service Subscribing," *Newspaper Research Journal* (Fall, 1991) 12(4): 34-46. **[98]**

Hale, F. Dennis. "Influence of Chain Ownership on Wire Service Usage," paper presented to the Newspaper Division at the annual conference of the Association for Education in Journalism and Mass Communication, Minneapolis, August, 1990. **[98]**

Hale, F.D. "Editorial Diversity and Concentration," *Press Concentration and Monopoly: New Perspectives on Newspaper Ownership and Operation*, ed. R.G. Picard et al. Norwood, NJ: Ablex, 1988, pp. 161-176. **[90]**

Hale, Gary A. and Richard C. Vincent. "Locally Produced Programming on Independent Television Stations," *Journalism Quarterly* (Autumn, 1986) 63(3): 562-567, 599. **[155, 335]**

Halfpenny, P. *Positivism and Sociology: Explaining Social Life.* London: Allen & Unwin, 1982. **[18]**

Hall, Claude and Barbara Hall. *The Business of Radio Programming.* New York: Billboard Pub., Inc. 1977. **[326]**

Hall, G.S. *Adolescence: Its Psychology and Its Relations to Physiology, Anthropology, Sociology, Sex, Crime, Religion and Education.* Vols. 1, 2. New York: Appleton-Century-Crofts, 1904. **[215]**

Hall, J.L., C. Miller and J. Hanson. "Music Television: A Perceptions Study of Two Age Groups," *Popular Music and Society* (1986) 10(4): 17-28. **[196]**

Hall, John R. "Epistemology and Sociohistorical Inquiry," *Annual Review of Sociology* (1990) 16:329-351). **[18]**

Hall, R. "A System Pathology of Organization: The Rise and Fall of the Old Saturday Evening Post," *Administrative Science Quarterly* (1976) 21(2): 185-211. **[80]**

Hall, Stuart. "Culture, the Media and the 'Ideological Effect,'" *Mass Communication and Society*, ed. James Curran, Michael Gurevitch and Janet Woollacott. Beverly Hills: Sage, 1977. **[20]**

Hall, Trish. "The Gift for Gab--We're All Getting It," *Plain Dealer*, Oct. 11, 1989, p. 13A. New York Times dispatch. **[96]**

Hall, William S. "Reading Comprehension," *American Psychologist* (February, 1989) 44(2): 157-161. **[96, 314]**

Hallin, D. "Hegemony: The American News Media from Vietnam to El Salvador: A Study of Ideological Change and Its Limits," *Political Communication Research*, ed. D. Paletz. Norwood, NJ: Ablex, 1987, pp. 3-25. **[126]**

Hallin, D.C. and P. Mancini. "Speaking of the President: Political Structure and Representational Form in U.S. and Italian Television News," *Theory and Society* (November, 1984) 13(6): 829-850. **[158]**

Hamilton, Neal F. and Alan M. Rubin. "The Influence of Religiosity on Television Viewing," *Journalism Quarterly* (Fall, 1992) 69(3): 667-678. **[270]**

Hamilton, Richard F. "Work and Leisure: On the Reporting of Poll Results," *Public Opinion Quarterly* (1991) 55: 347-356. **[211]**

Hammond, Robert A. and A. Douglas Melamed. "Antitrust in the Entertainment Industry," *Gannett Center Journal* (Summer, 1989) 3(3): 138-155. **[82, 83]**

Han, K.T. "Composition of Board of Directors of Major Media Corportions," *Journal of Media Economics* (Fall, 1988) 1(2): 85-102. **[80]**

Handberg, Roger and Milan D. Meeske. "Controversial Programming on Educational Television," *Mass Comm Review* (Winter, 1978) 5(1): 18-23. **[92]**

Hansen, Anne and David C. Coulson. "The Louisville Courier-Journal's News Content after Purchase by Gannett," paper presented to the Newspaper Division at the annual conference of the Association for Education in Journalism and Mass Communication, Montreal, August, 1992. **[90]**

Hansen, Elizabeth S. and Roy L. Moore. "Public Attitudes toward Libel: Do Newspaper Readers and Editors See Eye to Eye?" *Newspaper Research Journal* (Summer, 1992) 13(3): 2-12. **[219]**

Hansen, Kathleen A. "Source Diversity and Newspaper Enterprise Journalism," *Journalism Quarterly* (Fall, 1991) 68(3): 474-482. **[137]**

Hansen, Kathleen A. "Information Richness and Newspaper Pulitzer Prizes," *Journalism Quarterly* (Winter, 1990) 67(4): 930-935. **[137]**

Hansen, Elizabeth K. and Roy L. Moore. "'Chilling the Messenge': Impact of Libel on Community Newspapers," *Newspaper Research Journal* (Spring, 1990) 11(2): 86-95. **[146]**

Hansen, Kathleen A., Jean Ward and Doug M. McLeod. "Role of the Newspaper Library in the Production of News," *Journalism Quarterly* (Winter, 1987) 64(4): 714-720. **[161]**

Haque, S.M. Mazharul. "News Content Homogeneity in Elite Indian Dailies," *Journalism Quarterly* (Winter, 1986) 63(4): 827-832. **[124, 276]**

Hardenberg, N. "Promise vs. Performance: Four Public Access Channels in Connecticut, A Case Study," *Mass Comm Review* (1986) 13(1-3): 32-39. **[196]**

Hardy, Phil. *The Film Encyclopedia: The Western*. New York: Morrow, 1983. **[331]**

Harmetz, Aljean. "Independents Flood Market with Titles," *Plain Dealer*, Jan. 11, 1988, p. 5B. New York Times dispatch. **[65, 66]**

Harmetz, Aljean. "Where Movie Ticket Income Goes," *New York Times*, Jan. 28, 1987, p. 20. **[66, 94]**

Harmetz, Aljean. "Redford Production Deal," *New York Times*, Oct. 13, 1987, p. 24. **[66, 94]**

Harmon, Mark D. "Market Size and Local Television News Judgments," *Journal of Media Economics* (Spring, 1989) 2(1): 15-30. **[119, 134, 144, 156]**

Harmon, Mark D. "Mr. Gates Goes Electronic: The What and Why Questions in Local Television News," *Journalism Quarterly* (Winter, 1989) 66(4): 857-863. **[119, 134, 144, 156]**

Harmon, Mark D. "Featured Persons in Local Television News," paper presented to the Radio-Television Journalism Division at the annual conference of the Association for Education in Journalism and Mass Communication, Washington, D.C., August, 1989. **[119, 134, 144, 156]**

Harp, D.A., S.H. Harp and S.M. Stretch. "Apparel Impact on Viewer Responses to Television News Anchorwomen," *Southwestern Mass Communication Journal* (June, 1985) 1(1): 49-60. **[220]**

Harre, Rom. *Personal Being*. Oxford: Blackwell, 1983. **[20]**

Harrington, David E. "Economic News on Television: The Determinants of Coverage," *Public Opinion Quarterly* (Spring, 1989) 53(1): 17-40. **[157, 369]**

Harris, John Leonard. "The Portrayal of the Black Family on Prime-Time Network TV: A Look at Stereotypic Images and Disorganization of Family Structure," *Journal of Intergroup Relations* (Spring, 1992) 19(1): 44-58. **[343]**

Harris, M. *London Newspapers in the Age of Walpole: A Study of the Origins of the Modern English Press*. Cranbury, NJ: Fairleigh Dickinson University Press, 1987. **[58]**

Harris, Peter R. and Jonathan Stobart. "Sex-Role Stereotyping in British Television Advertisements at Different Times of the Day: An Extention and Refinement of Manstead & McCulloch (1981)," *British Journal of Social Psychology* (1986) 25: 155-164. **[367]**

Harris, R.J., T.M. Dubitsky and K.J. Bruno. "Psycholinguistic Studies of Misleading Advertising," *Information Processing Research in Advertising*, ed. R.J. Harris. Hillsdale, NJ: Lawrence Erlbaum Associates, 1983. **[320]**

Harrison, M. "A Window on the World?: Foreign Coverage by a British Radio Current Affairs Program," *Critical Studies in Mass Communication* (1986) 3: 409-428. **[127]**

Hartman, John K. "'USA Today' and Young-Adult Readers: Can a New-Style Newspaper Win Them Back?" *Newspaper Research Journal* (Winter, 1987) 8(2): 1-11. **[276]**

Hartman, Paul. "News and Public Perceptions of Industrial Relations," *Media, Culture and Society* (July, 1979) 1(3): 255-270. **[269]**

Hartung, B.W., A. Jacoby and D.M. Dozier. "Reader's Perceptions of Purpose of Newspaper Ombudsman Program," *Journalism Quarterly* (Winter, 1988) 65(4): 914-919. **[199]**

Harvey, Michael G. and James T. Rothe. "Video Cassette Recorders Impact on Viewers and Advertisers," *Journal of Advertising Research* (December, 1985/January, 1986) 25(6): 19-28. **[18, 213]**

Harwood, K. "Women in Broadcasting 1984-1990," Feedback (Spring, 1984) 25(4): 18-21. **[164]**

Hassan, Ihab. *The Literature of Silence: Henry Miller and Samuel Beckett.* New York, 1967. **[18]**

Hastings, Deborah. "Status of Women Behind the Scene in TV Still Fuzzy," *Plain Dealer*, Dec. 4, 1990, p. 7E. **[164]**

Hattori, Takaaki. "The Administration of Radio Waves for Broadcasting in Japan," *Studies of Broadcasting* (1989) 25: 54-75. **[59]**

Haviland, Susan E. and Herbert H. Clark. "What's New? Acquiring New Information as a Process in Comprehension," *Journal of Verbal Learning and Verbal Behavior* (October, 1974) 13(5): 512-521. **[314]**

Hawes, William. *American Television Drama: The Experimental Years.* University of Alabama Press, 1986. **[361]**

Hawkins, R.P. "The Dimensional Structure of Children's Perceptions of Television Reality," *Communication Research* (1977) 4(3): 299-320. **[14]**

Hawkins, Robert P., Nancy Reynolds and Suzanne Pingree. "In Search of Television Viewing Styles," paper presented at the annual conference of the International Communication Association, Dublin, Ireland, June, 1990. **[228]**

Haws, Dick. "Minorities in the Newsroom and Community: A Comparison," *Journalism Quarterly* (Winter, 1991) 68(4): 764-771.

Hay, J.C. "Optical Motions and Space Peception: An Extension of Gibson's Analysis," *Pshchological Review* (1966) 73: 550-565. **[318]**

Hayes, Dona and John D. Mitchell. "Criteria of Quality in Local Television Newscasts: News Directors' and Educators' Views," paper presented to the Radio-Television Journalism Division at the annual conference of the Association for Education in Journalism and Mass Communication, Washington, D.C., August, 1989. **[156, 162]**

Head, Sydney W. *World Broadcasting Systems.* Belmont, CA: Wadsworth Publishing Co., 1985. **[59]**

Head, Sydney W. and Christopher H. Sterling. *Broadcasting in America: A Survey of Electronic Media.* Boston: Houghton Mifflin Co., 6th ed., 1990. **[58]**

Healy, Alice F., William L. Oliver and Timothy P. McNamara. "Detecting Letters in Continuous Text: Effects of Display Size," *Journal of Experimental Psychology: Human Perception and Performance* (1987) 13(2): 279-290. **[288]**

Heeter, Carrie. "The Choice Process Model," *Cable-Viewing*, ed. Carrie Heeter and Bradley S. Greenberg. Norwood, NJ: Ablex, 1988, pp. 11-32. **[227, 228, 261]**

Heeter, Carrie. "New Fall Season Viewing," *Cable-Viewing*, ed. Carrie Heeter and Bradley S. Greenberg. Norwood, NJ: Ablex, 1988, pp. 74-88. **[227, 228, 261]**

Heeter, Carrie. "Program Selection with Abundance of Choice: A Process Model," *Human Communication Research* (Fall, 1985) 12(1): 126-152. **[213, 227]**

Heeter, Carrie and Thomas F. Baldwin. "Channel Types and Viewing Styles," *Cable-Viewing*, ed. Carrie Heeter and Bradley S. Greenberg. Norwood, NJ: Ablex, 1988, pp. 167-176. **[228]**

Heeter, Carrie and Ed Cohen. "Viewing Style Differences between Radio and Television," *Cable-Viewing*, ed. Carrie Heeter and Bradley S. Greenberg. Norwood, NJ: Ablex, 1988, pp. 113-122. **[228]**

Heeter, Carrie, Bradley S. Greenberg, Bradley E. Mendelson, Judee K. Burgoon, Michael Burgoon and Felipe Korzenny. "Cross Media Coverage of Local Hispanic American news," *Journal of Broadcasting* (Fall, 1983) 27(4): 395-402. **[346]**

Heft, Harry and Ragnar Blondal. "The Influence of Cutting Rate on the Evaluation of Affective Content of Film," *Empirical Studies of the Arts* (1987) 5(1): 1-14. **[303]**

Heisner, Beverly. *Hollywood Art: Art Direction in the Days of the Great Studios*. Jefferson, NC: McFarland & Co., Publishers, Inc., 1990. **[104]**

Helregel, Brenda K. and James B. Weaver. "Mood-Management during Pregnancy through Selective Exposure to Television," *Journal of Broadcasting & Electronic Media* (Winter, 1989) 33(1): 15-33. **[273]**

Henderson, Laura and Bradley S. Greenberg. "Sex-Typing of Common Behaviors on Television," *Life on Television*, ed. Bradley S. Greenberg. Norwood, NJ: Ablex, 1980, pp. 89-85. **[359]**

Henderson, Laura, Bradley S. Greenberg and Charles K. Atkin. "Sex Differences in Giving Orders, Making Plans, and Needing Support on Television," *Life on Television*. ed. Bradley S. Greenberg. Norwood, NJ: Ablex, 1980. **[366]**

Hendon, D.W. and W.F. Muhs. "Origin and Early Development of Outdoor Advertising in the United States," *Journal of Advertising History* (1986) 9(1): 7-17. **[40]**

Hendrickson, Laura. "Child Maltreatment: Press Frames in the 20th Century," paper presented to the Qualitative Studies Division at the annual conference of the Association for Education in Journalism and Mass Communication, Montreal, August, 1992. **[348]**

Henke, Lucy L. "Perceptions and Use of News Media by College Students," *Journal of Broadcasting and Electronic Media* (Fall, 1985) 29(4): 431-436. **[184, 231]**

Henke, Lucy L. and Thomas R. Donohue. "Functional Displacement of Traditional Television Viewing by VCR Owners," *Journal of Advertising Research* (April/May, 1989) 29(2): 18-23. **[213, 255]**

Henke, Lucy L. and Thomas R. Donohue. "Teletext Viewing Habits and Preferences," *Journalism Quarterly* (Autumn, 1986) 63(3): 542-545, 553. **[183]**

Henke, Lucy L., Thomas R. Donohue, Christopher Cook and Diane Cheung. "The Impact of Cable on Traditional TV News Viewing," *Journalism Quarterly* (Spring, 1984) 61(1): 174-178. **[212]**

Henningham, J.P. "Relations between Television News Gratifications and Content Preferences," *Gazette* (1985) 35(3): 197-207. **[252]**

Henningham, J.P. "Comparisons between Australian and U.S. Broadcast Journalists' Professional Values," *Journal of Broadcasting and Electronic Media* (Summer, 1984) 28(3): 323-331. **[165]**

Henningham, J.P. "Comparisons between Three Versions of the Professional Orientation Index," *Journalism Quarterly* (Summer, 1984) 61(2): 302-309. **[165]**

Henry, S. "Juggling the Frying Pan and the Fire: The Portrait of Employment and Family Life in Seven Women's Magazines, 1975-1982," *Social Science Journal* (October, 1984) 21(4): 87-107. **[350]**

Hepworth, M. and K. Robins. "Whose Information Society? A View from the Periphery," *Media, Culture and Society* (July, 1988) 10(3): 323-343. **[65]**

Hepworth, M.E., A.E. Green and A.E. Gillespie. "The Spatial Division of Information Labour in Great Britain," *Environment and Planning A* (1987) 19: 793-806. **[93]**

Hepworth, Mark. *Geography of the Information Economy*. New York: Guilford Press, 1990. **[93, 94]**

Herd, Denise. "Ideology, Melodrama, and the Changing Role of Alcohol Problems in American Films," *Contemporary Drug Problems* (Summer, 1986) 13: 213-247. **[371]**

Herman, Edward S. "Market Systen Constraints on Freedom of Expression," *Journal of Communication Inquiry* (Winter, 1991) 15(1): 45-53. **[90]**

Herman, Edward S. and Noam Chomsky. *Manufacturing Consent: The Political Economy of the Mass Media*. New York: Pantheon Books, 1988. **[163]**

Herzog, H. "Professor Quiz: A Gratification Study," *Radio Research, 1941*, ed. Paul F. Lazersfeld and F.N. Stanton. New York: Duell, Sloan & Pearce, 1942. **[272]**

Hertoz, James, John R. Finnegan Jr., Emily Kahn, David Fan, Michael Moen and Roy Nelson. "News Sources Quoted in Media Reporting about AIDS: Trends in a National Wire Service and a Local Daily Newspaper," paper presented to the Communication Theory and Methodology Division at the annual conference of the Association for Education in Journalism and Mass Communication, Montreal, August, 1992. [137]

Hess, S. *The Ultimate Insiders: U.S. Senators in the National Media.* Washington, D.C.: Brookings Institution, 1986. [161]

Hess, Beth B. "Stereotypes of the Aged," *Journal of Communication* (Autumn, 1974) 24:79. [278]

Hesterman, V. "Consumer Magazines and Ethical Guidelines," *Journal of Mass Media Ethics* (Spring/Summer, 1987) 2(2): 93-101. [163]

Hetherington, A. *News in the Regions: Plymouth Sound to Moray Firth.* London: Macmillan Press, Ltd., 1989. [120]

Heuvelman, Ard. "Cognitive Effects of Different Visual Formats in an Educaional Television-Programme," *Communication and Cognition* (1989) 22(1): 61-71. [303, 304]

Hewitt, John and Rick Houlberg. "Local Broadcast News Editors and Managers: A Multiple Station, Single Market Study," *Journalism Quarterly* (Winter, 1986) 63(4): 834-839. [162]

Heylighen, Francis. "A Cognitive-Systemic Reconstruction of Maslow's Theory of Self-Actualization," *Behavioral Science* (1992) 37: 39-58. [279]

Hiatt, Fred. "Giant Newspaper Guides Japan," *Plain Dealer*, Washington Post Report, Sept. 2, 1990, p. 21A. [43, 44]

Hiemstra, R. et al. "How Older Persons Are Portrayed in Television Advertising: Implications for Educators," *Educational Gerontology* (March-June, 1983) 9(2-3): 111-122. [365]

Hill, A.B. and R.E. Perkins. "Toward a Model of Boredom," *British Journal of Psychology* (1985) 76: 235-240. [250]

Hill, David B. "Qualitative Dimensions of Exposure to Political Television," *Social Science Quarterly* (September, 1983) 64(3): 614-623. [229]

Hill, Michael. "TV News Celebrities Cozy Up to the Rich," *Plain Dealer*, Feb. 4, 1988, p. 9F. [149]

Hilliard, Robert L. (Ed.). *Television Broadcasting: An Introduction.* New York: Hastings House, 1978. [162]

Hilliard, Robert D. "The 'Kept' Press? Swedish Newspapers Balance Subsidy, Editorial Independence," paper presented to the Newspaper Division at the annual conference of the Association for Education in Journalism and Mass Communication, Montreal, August, 1992. [92]

Hilliard, Robert L. (Ed.) *Radio Broadcasting.* New York: Longman, 3rd ed., 1985. [58]

Hilts, Philip J. "Photos Show Mind Recalling a Word: X-Ray Data Yield Surprises on Workings of Memory," *New York Times*, Dec. 11, 1991, p. 1. [288]

Himmelweit, Hilde and Betty Swift. "Continuities and Discontinuities in Media Usage and Taste: A Longitudinal Study," *Journal of Social Issues* (1976) 32(4): 133-155. [190, 270]

Hinds, H.E. Jr. and C. Tatum. "Images of Women in Mexican Comic Books," *Journal of Popular Culture* (Summer, 1984) 18(1): 146-162. [366]

Hinkle, Gerald and William R. Elliott. Science Coverage in Three Newspapers and Three Supermarket Tabloids" *Journalism Quarterly* (Summer, 1989) 66(2): 353-358. [368]

Hirose, Hidehiko. "International Comparison of Media Policies--Broadcasting and New Media Policies in the West," *Studies of Broadcasting* (1988) 24: 7-13. [48]

Hirschman, E.C. "The Ideology of Consumption: A Structural-Syntactical Analysis of 'Dallas' and 'Dynasty,'" *Journal of Consumer Research* (December, 1988) 15(3): 344-359. [372]

Hirschman, Elizabeth C. "Consumer Preferences in Literature, Motion Pictures, and Television Programs," *Empirical Studies of the Arts* (1987) 5(1): 31-46. [192]

Hirschman, Elizabeth C. "A Multidimensional Analysis of Content Preferences for Leisure-Time Media," *Journal of Leisure Research* (1985) 17(1): 14-28. [192, 193, 249, 274]

Hirst, William, Elizabeth S. Spelke, Cecilia C. Reaves, George Caharack and Ulric Neisser. "Dividing Attention without Alternation or Automaticity," *Journal of Experimental Psychology: General* (1980) 109(1): 98-117. **[320]**

Hobbs, Renee, Richard Frost, Arthur Davis and John Stauffer. "How First-Time Viewers Comprehend Editing Conventions," *Journal of Communication* (Autumn, 1988) 38(4): 50-60. **[297, 300, 302, 317]**

Hochberg, J. and V. Brooks. "The Perception of Motion Pictures," *Handbook of Perception*, ed. E.C. Carterette and M.P. Friedman. Vol. 10. *Perceptual Ecology*. New York: Academic Press, 1978, pp. 259-304. **[299]**

Hoffman-Riem, Wolfgang. "Federal Republic of Germany," *International Handbook of Broadcasting Systems*, ed. Philip T. Rosen. New York: Greenwood, 1988, pp. 91-103. **[48]**

Hoffner, Cynthia, Joanne Cantor and Esther Thorson. "Children's Understanding of a Televised Narrative: Developmental Differences in Processing Video and Audio Content," *Communication Research* (June, 1988) 15(3): 227-245. **[319]**

Hofstetter, C. Richard and David M. Dozier. "Useful News, Sensational News: Quality, Sensationalism and Local TV News," *Journalism Quarterly* (Winter, 1986) 63(4): 815-820, 853. **[121]**

Hohenberg, John. *The Professional Journalist*. 4th ed., New York: Holt, Rinehart and Winston, 1978. **[340]**

Hoijer, B. "Television-Evoked Thoughts and Their Relation to Comprehension," *Communication Research* (April, 1989) 16(2): 179-203. **[244]**

Holbrook, M.B. and D.R. Lehmann. "Allocating Discretionary Time: Complementarity Among Activities," *Journal of Consumer Research* (March, 1981) 7(4): 395-406. **[274]**

Hollander, Barry A. "Information Graphics and the Bandwagon Effect: Does the Visual Display of Opinion Aid in Persuasion?" paper presented to the Visual Communication Division at the annual conference of the Association for Education in Journalism and Mass Communication, Montreal, August, 1992. **[315]**

Hollstein, Milton. "Chinese TV: Better Broadcasting for the Billion," paper presented to the International Communication Division of the Association for Education in Journalism and Mass Communiction," Washington, D.C., Aug. 12, 1989. **[45, 46, 48, 193]**

Holstein, Lisa W. "The Revolutionary Power of the Press: Newspapers as a Shadow Political Arena in 1848 in France and 1917 in Russia," paper presented to the History Division at the annual conference of the Association for Education in Journalism and Mass Communication, Montreal, August, 1992. **[55]**

Holtzman, J.M. and H. Akiyama. "What Children See: The Aged on Television in Japan and the United States," *The Gerontologist* (February, 1985) 25(1): 62-68. **[347]**

Holub, Miroslav. "The Third Culture." The Unicorn. Cleveland State University, Department of English (March, 1987) No. 53, p. 1-2. **[19]**

Hong, Jae W., Aydin Muderrisogiu and George M. Zinkhan. "Cultural Differences and Advertising Expression: A Comparative Content Analysis of Japanese and U.S. Magazine Advertising," *Journal of Advertising* (1987) 16(1): 55-62. **[362]**

Hoover, N.L. *A Study of Story Schema Acquisition and Its Influence on Beginning Reading*. Doctoral Dissertation. Virginia Polytechnic Institute and State University, Blacksburg, VA., 1981. Cited in Durham (1990). **[293]**

Hoover, Stewart M. "The Religious Television Audience: A Matter of Significance, Or Size?" *Review of Religious Research* (December, 1987) 29(2): 135-151. **[196, 270]**

Hoover, Stewart M. *Mass Media Religion: The Social Sources of the Electronic Church*. Newbury Park: Sage, 1988. **[218]**

Hopkins, Nancy M. and Ann K. Mullis. "Family Perceptions of Television Viewing Habits," *Family Relations* (April, 1985) 34: 177-181. **[236, 261]**

Horn, John. "High Costs Have Movie Makers Reeling," *Plain Dealer*, April 1, 1991, p. 1E; Associated Press story. **[66]**

Horna, Jarmila L.A. "Leisure Studies in Czechoslovakia: Some East-West Parallels and Divergences," *Leisure Sciences* (1988) 10: 79-94. **[211]**

Hornig, Susanna, Lynne Walters and Julie Templin. "Voices in the News: Newspaper Coverage of Hurricane Hugo and the Loma Prieta Earthquake," *Newspaper Research Journal* (Summer, 1991) 12(3): 32-45. **[161]**

Horton, D. and R.R. Wohl. "Mass Communication and Para-Social Interaction," *Psychiatry* (1956) 19: 215-229. **[277]**

Houlberg, Rick. "Local Television News Audience and the Para-Social Interaction," *Journal of Broadcasting* (Fall, 1984) 28(4): 423-429. **[257]**

Housel, Thomas J. "Understanding and Recall of TV News," *Journalism Quarterly* (1984) 61(3): 505-508, 741. **[317]**

Howard, Herbert H. "Group and Cross-Media Ownership of TV Stations: A 1989 Update," *Journalism Quarterly* (Winter, 1989) 66(4): 785-792. **[83, 89]**

Howard, Herbert H. "An Update on Cable TV Ownership: 1985," *Journalism Quarterly* (Winter, 1986) 63(4): 706-709, 781. **[84]**

Howard, Herbert H. "An Update on TV Ownership Patterns," *Journalism Quarterly* (Fall, 1983) 60(3): 395-400. **[83]**

Howard, Howard H., Edward Blick and Jan P. Quarles. "Media Choices for Specialized News," *Journalism Quarterly* (Summer/Autumn, 1987) 64(2/3): 620-623. **[276]**

Howe, Christine Z. and Ann M. Rancourt. "The Importance of Definitions of Selected Concepts for Leisure Inquiry," *Leisure Sciences* (1990) 12: 395-406. **[170]**

Howe, Irving. *Decline of the New*. New York, 1970. **[18]**

Howenstine, Erick. "Environmental Reporting: Shift from 1970 to 1982," *Journalism Quarterly* (Winter, 1987) 64(4): 842-846. **[135, 371]**

Hoyer, Wayne E., R.K. Srivastava and Jacob Jacoby. "Examining the Sources of Advertising Miscomprehension," *Journal of Advertising* (1984) 13(2): 17-26. **[305]**

Hsia, H.J. "Redundancy: Is it the Lost Key to Better Communication?" *AV Communication Review* (1977) 25(1): 63-85. **[319]**

Hu, Yu-Wei and Yi-Chen Wu. "A Reconsideration of Some Sociological and Psychological Differences between Daily Newspaper Readers and Nonreaders. A Discriminant Analysis," paper presented at the annual conference of the Midwest Association of Public Opinion Research, Chicago, November, 1991. **[276]**

Hubbard, J.T.W. "Newspaper Business News Staffs Increase Markedly in Last Decade," *Journalism Quarterly* (Spring, 1987) 64(1): 171-177. **[134]**

Hubell, Richard W. *4000 Years of Television* New York: G.P. Putnam's Sons, 1942. **[38]**

Hudson, Heather E. and Louis Leung. "The Growth of the Information Sector," *Measuring the Information Society*, ed. Frederick Williams. Newbury Park, CA: Sage Publications, 1988, pp. 35-54. **[93]**

Hughes, Kathleen A. "IBM-Sears Computer-Services Venture Shows Promise, But a Lot of Kinks Remain," *Wall Street Journal*, Feb. 8, 1989, p. 1B. **[32, 74]**

Humphrey, C.S. "'Little Ado about Something': Philadelphia Newspapers and the Constitutional Convention," *American Journalism* (1988) 5(2): 63-80. **[29]**

Humphrey, C.S. "Producers of the 'Popular Engine': New England's Revolutionary Newspaper Printers," *American Journalism* (1987) 4(2): 97-117. **[29]**

Humphrey, Ronald and Howard Schuman. "The Portrayal of Blacks in Magazine Advertisements: 1950-1982," *Public Opinion Quarterly* (1984) 48: 551-563. **[364]**

Hunnicutt, Benjamin. "Historical Attitudes Toward the Increase of Free Time in the Twentieth Century: Time for Work, for Leisure, or as Unemployment," *Society and Leisure* (1980) 3(2): 195-215. Cited in Horna (1988). **[211]**

Hunt, Todd and Michael Cheney. "Content Comparison of Free and Paid Circulation Weeklies," *Journalism Quarterly* (Spring, 1982) 59(1): 134-137. **[337]**

Hur, K. Kyoon and Leo W. Jeffres, "Communication, Ethnicity, and Stratification: A Review for Research Directives, Hypotheses, and Generalizations," *Progress in Communiction Sciences*, Vol. 6, led. Brenda Dervin and Mel Voigt. Norwood, NJ: Ablex Publishing Co., 1985.

Husni, Samir A. "Influences on the Survival of New Consumer Magazines," *Journal of Media Economics* (Spring, 1988) 1(1) 39-49.

Husni, Samir A. "The Typical American Consumer Magazine of the 1980s," paper presented to the Magazine Division at the annual conference of the Association for Education in Journalism and Mass Communication, Gainesville, Florida, 1984. **[80]**

Huston, A.C., J.C. Wright, E. Wartella, M.L. Rice, B.A. Watkins, T. Campbell, and R. Potts. "Communicating More than Content: Formal Features of Children's Television," *Journal of Communication* (Summer, 1981) 31: 32-48. **[317]**

Huston, A.C. and J.C. Wright. "Children's Processing of Television: The Informative Functions of Formal Features," *Children's Understanding of Television*, ed. J. Bryant and D.R. Anderson. New York: Academic Press, 1983. **[300]**

Hutcheon, Linda. *The Politics of Postmodernism*. London: Routledge, 1989. **[18]**

Huttenlocher, J. and L.F. Kubicek. "The Source of Relatedness Effects on Naming Latency," *Journal of Experimental Psychology: Learning, Memory and Cognition* (1983) 9: 486-496. **[320]**

Hyden, C. and N.J. McCandless. "Men and Women as Portrayed in the Lyrics of Contemporary Music," *Popular Music & Society* (1983) 9(2): 19-26. **[366]**

Hynds, Ernest C. "Editorials, Opinion Pages Still Have Vital Roles at Most Newspapers," *Journalism Quarterly* (Autumn, 1984) 61(3): 634-639. **[338]**

Hynds, Ernest C. "Changes in Editorials: A Study of Three Newspapers, 1955-1985," *Journalism Quarterly* (Summer, 1990) 67(2): 302-312. **[136, 338]**

Hynds, Ernest C. "Editors Expect Editorial Pages to Remain Vital in the Year 2000," *Journalism Quarterly* (Summer, 1989) 66(2): 441-445. **[355]**

Hynes, Terry. "Magazine Portrayal of Women, 1911-1930," *Journalism Monographs* (May,1981), No.72. **[353]**

Idid, Syed Arabi. "Magazine use among Malaysian Youth: A Uses and Gratifications Perspective," *Media Asia* (1988) 15(1): 9-16.

Idsvoog, Karl A. and James L. Hoyt, "Professionalism and Performance of Television Journalists," *Journal of Broadcasting* (Winter, 1977) 21(1): 97-109. **[165]**

Incitti, Michael A. "Organizational Communication Deficits and Overloads: The Origins of Entropy in the News Room," paper presented to the Newspaper Division at the annual conference of the Association for Education in Journalism and Mass Communication, Montreal, August, 1992. **[154]**

Intintoli, M.J. *Taking Soaps Seriously: The World of Guiding Light*. New York: Praeger, 1984. **[20]**

Irwin, Barbara J. "Watching Seniors Watch 'Their Story': An Ethnographic Study of Soap Opera Viewing," paper presented to the Mass Communication Division at the annual conference of the International Communication Association, San Francisco, May 25-29, 1989. **[228]**

Ismach, Arnold H. and Everette E. Dennis. "A Profile of Newspaper and Television Reporters in a Metropolitan Setting," *Journalism Quarterly* (1978) 55: 739-743, 898. **[165]**

Iso-Ahola, S.E. "Basic Dimensions of Leisure," *Journal of Leisure Research* (1979) 11:15-27. **[211]**

Iso-Ahola, Seppo E. and Ellen Weissinger. "Perceptions of Boredom in Leisure: Conceptualization, Reliability and Validity of the Leisure Boredom Scale," *Journal of Leisure Research* (1990) 22(1): 1-17. **[250, 274]**

Ito, Youichi. "Mass Communication Theories from a Japanese Perspective," *Media, Culture and Society* (1990) 12: 423-464. **[124]**

Izard, R.S. "Public Confidence in the News Media," *Journalism Quarterly* (Summer, 1985) 62(2): 247-255. **[203, 209]**

Izcaray, F. and J.T. McNelly. "Selective Media Use by Venezuelans: The Passing of the Passive Audience in a Rapidly Developing Society," *Studies in Latin American Popular Culture*, ed. H.E. Hinds Jr. and C.M. Tatum. Vol. 6. Tucson, Ariz.: Department of Spanish and Portuguese, University of Arizona, 1987, pp. 27-41. **[274]**

Jackson, K.M. *Images of Children in American Film*. Metuchen, NJ: The Scarecrow Press, 1986. **[348]**

Jackson, Kenneth M. "Local Community Orientations of Suburban Newspaper Subscribers," *Newspaper Research Journal* (April, 1981) 2(3): 42-49. **[272]**

Jackson-Beeck, Marilyn. "The Nonviewers: Who Are They?" *Journal of Communication* (Summer, 1977) 27: 65-72. **[269]**

Jacobs, Sanford L. "Little Publisher Has Big Ideas on Where to Sell His Books," *Wall Street Journal*, March 19, 1987, p. 1. **[74]**

Jacobson, Thomas L. "Empirical Development Communication Research in the Wake of Positivism," paper presented in the Intercultural and Development Communication Division at the 1990 annual conference of the International Communication Association, Dublin, Ireland, June 24-29, 1990. **[19]**

Jacobson, Thomas L. "Use of Commercial Data Bases for Television News Reporting," paper presented in the Human Communication Technology Special Interest Group at the annual conference of the International Communication Association, May, 1989. **[167]**

Jacobson, Thomas L. and John Ullman. "Commercial Databases and Reporting: Opinions of Newspaper Journalists and Librarians," *Newspaper Research Journal* (Winter, 1989) 10(2): 15-25. **[14]**

Jacoby, J., W.D. Hoyer, and M.R. Zimmer. "To Read, View, or Listen? A Cross-Media Comparison of Comprehension," *Current Issues & Research in Advertising 1983*. ed. J.H. Leigh and C.R. Martin Jr. Ann Arbor: Graduate School of Business Administration, University of Michigan, 1983, pp. 201-213. **[311]**

Jacoby, Jacob and Wayne D. Hoyer. *The Comprehension and Miscomprehension of Print Communications: An Investigation of Mass Media Magazines.* New York: The Advertising Educational Foundation, Inc., 1987. **[285, 286, 287, 310, 314, 320]**

Jacoby, Jacob, Wayne D. Hoyer and D.A. Sheluga. *Miscomprehension of Televised Communications*. New York: American Association of Advertising Agencies, 1980. **[287, 297, 319]**

Jacoby, Jacob, T. Troutman and T. Whittler. "Viewer Miscomprehension of the 1980 Presidential Debate," *Political Psychology* (1986) 7(2): 297-308. **[297]**

Jaddou, L. and J.A. Williams. "A Theoretical Contribution to the Struggle Against the Dominant Representations of Women," *Media, Culture and Society* (April, 1981) 3(2): 105-124. **[360]**

Jakab, Zoltan. "On the Institutional Infrastructure of Glasnost: Centralization and Concentration of the Hungarian Press," *European Journal of Communication* (1989) 4: 255-265. **[59]**

Jakubowicz, Karol. "Polish Broadcasting Studies in Search of a Raison d'Etre," *European Journal of Broadcasting* (1989) 4: 267-285. **[59]**

Jakubowicz, Karol. "Musical Chairs? The Three Public Spheres of Poland," *Media, Culture and Society* (1990) 12: 195-212. **[59]**

Jameson, Fredric. "Postmodernism, or The Cultural Logic of Late Capitalism," *New Left Review* (1984) 146: 53-92. **[18]**

Janes, Barry T. "History and Structure of Public Access Television," *Journal of Film and Video* (Summer, 1987) 39: 14-23. **[361]**

Janowitz, Morris. "Professional Models in Journalism: the Gatekeeper and the Advocate," *Journalism Quarterly* (Winter, 1975) 52: 618-626 +. **[130]**

Janowitz, Morris. *The Community Press in an Urban Setting*. Chicago: Chicago University Press, 1952. **[201, 239]**

Jarvella, R. "Syntactic Processing of Connected Speech," *Journal of Verbal Learning and Verbal Behavior* (1975) 10: 409-416. **[312]**

Jarvella, R.J. "Immediate Memory and Discourse Processing," *The Psychology of Learning and Motivation: Advances in Research and Theory*, ed. G.H. Bower. Vol. 13. New York: Academic, 1979. **[314]**

Jarvie, I.E. *Movies and Society*. New York: Basic Books, Inc., 1970. **[331]**

Jeffres, Leo W, "Socialization for Mass Media Consumption," *Participation in Social and Political Activities*, ed. David Horton Smith, Jacqueline Macaulay and Associates. San Francisco: Jossey-Bass, Inc., 1980, pp. 244-256.

Jeffres, Leo W. "Cable TV and Viewer Selectivity," *Journal of Broadcasting* (Spring, 1978) 22(2): 167-177. **[272]**

Jeffres, Leo W. "Cable TV and Interest Maximization," *Journalism Quarterly* (Spring, 1978) 55(1): 149-154. **[272]**

Jeffres, Leo W. "Consequences of the Television of Abundance," paper presented to the Theory & Methodology Division of the Association for Education in Journalism, College Park, Maryland, August, 1976. **[274]**

Jeffres, Leo W. "Functions of Media Behaviors," *Communication Research* (April, 1975) 2(2): 137-161. **[249, 274]**

Jeffres, Leo W. "A Study of Similarities in the Use of Print Media by Fathers and Sons," Unpublished master's thesis, Department of Communication, University of Washington, 1968. **[279]**

Jeffres, Leo W. and Mildred Barnard. "Communication and the Persistence of Ethnicity," *CRC Monographs* (May, 1982) No. 5. Cleveland State University: Communication Research Center. **[234]**

Jeffres, Leo W., Jean Dobos and Jae-won Lee. "Media Use and Community Ties," *Journalism Quarterly* (Fall, 1988) 65(3): 575-581, 677.**[240]**

Jeffres, Leo W. and K. Kyoon Hur. "Communication and Perspectives on Ethnicity," paper presented at the Conference on Culture and Communication, Temple University, Philadelphia, PA., March 25, 1983. **[9]**

Jeffres, Leo W. and K. Kyoon Hur. "The Forgotten Media Consumer--The American Ethnic," *Journalism Quarterly* (Spring, 1980) 57(1): 10-17. **[234]**

Jeffres, Leo W. and K. Kyoon Hur. "White Ethnics and Their Media Images: Ethnic Studies in Black and White," *Journal of Communication* (Winter, 1979) 29(1): 1 16-122. **[220]**

Jeffres, Leo W., Kim Neuendorf, and Dennis Giles. "Film Genre: Matching Audience Expectations with Critical Assessments," paper presented at the annual conference of the Midwest Association for Public Opinion Research, Nov. 16, 1990, Chicago. **[329]**

Jen, Gish. "Challenging the Asian Illusion," *The New York Times*, Aug. 11, 1991, sec. 2, p. 1. **[346]**

Jenkins, Simon. "The More Things Change...Fleet Street's Half-Hearted Revolution," *Political Quarterly* (January-March, 1987) 58(1): 53-61. **[59]**

Jensen, K.B. "Qualitative Audience Research: Toward an Integrative Approach to Reception," *Critical Studies in Mass Communication* (1987) 4: 21-36. **[21]**

Jensen, K.B. "News as Ideology: Economic Statistics and Political Ritual in Television News," *Journal of Communication* (Winter, 1986) 37(1): 8-27. **[128]**

Jensen, Klaus Bruhn. "The Politics of Polysemy: Television News, Everyday Consciousness and Political Action," *Media, Culture and Society* (1990) 12: 57-77. **[230]**

Jensen, Klaus Bruhn. "Television Futures: A Social Action Methodology for Studying Interpretive Communities," *Critical Studies in Mass Communication* (1990) 7: 129-146. **[230, 275]**

Joas, Hans. "The Unhappy Marriage of Hermeneutics and Functionalism," *Praxis International* (April, 1988) 8(1): 34-51. **[11]**

Johansson, G., C. von Hofsten and G. Jansson. "Event Perception," *Annual Review of Psychology* (1980) 31: 23-67. **[301]**

Johns, Jerry L., Colleen Faye Brownlie and Rhoda L. Ramirez. "How Newspapers Cover Education in Three Countries," *Journalism Quarterly* (Spring, 1986) 63(1): 177-180. **[368]**

Johnson, Carolyn and Lynne Gross. "Mass Media Use by Women in Decision-Making Positions," *Journalism Quarterly* (1985) 62(4): 850-854, 950. **[258]**

Johnson, Elizabeth. "Credibility of Black and White Newscasters to a Black Audience," *Journal of Broadcasting* (Summer, 1984) 28(3): 365-368. **[233]**

Johnson, J. David and Omar S. Oliveira. "Program Ratings and Levels of Television Exposure in Belize," *Journalism Quarterly* (Summer, 1988) 65(2): 497-500. **[173]**

Johnson, O. V. "Unbridled Freedom: The Czech Press and Politics, 1918-1938," *Journalism History* (Autumn/Winter, 1986) 13(3/4): 96-103. **[52]**

Johnson, Owen V. "Media Research. Clio Among the Ethnic Media," *Ethnic Forum* (1988) 8(2): 40-51. **[72]**

Johnson, Sammye and William G. Christ. "Women through 'Time': Who Gets Covered?" *Journalism Quarterly* (Winter, 1988) 65(4): 889-897. **[354]**

Johnson, Thomas J. and Wayne Wanta. "Newspaper Competition and Message Diversity in an Urban Market," paper presented to the Media Management and Economics Division at the annual conference of the Association for Education in Journalism and Mass Communication, Montreal, August, 1992. **[91]**

Johstone, John W.C., Edward J. Slawski and William W. Bowman. *The News People: A Sociological Portrait of American Journalists and Their Work*. Urbana: University of Illinois Press, 1976. **[109, 147, 165]**

Johnstone, S.M. and R.C. Allen. "Functional Analysis of Soap-Opera Viewing: A Comparison of Two Populations," *Studies in Mass Communication and Technology*, ed. S. Thomas. Studies in Communication, Vol. 1. Norwood, NJ: Ablex Publishing Corp., 1984, pp. 220-228. **[275]**

Jolliffe, Lee B. "Comparing Gender Differentiation in the New York 'Times,' 1885 and 1985," *Journalism Quarterly* (Autumn, 1989) 66(3): 683-691. **[353]**

Jones, Alex S. "To Papers, Funnies Are No Joke," *New York Times*, April 8, 1991, p. 1C. **[193]**

Jones, Felecia G. "The Black Audience and the BET Channel," *Journal of Broadcasting & Electronic Media* (Fall, 1990) 34(4): 477-486. **[233]**

Jones, James T. IV. "Blacks, Whites: Different TV Worlds," *USA Today*, Aug. 12, 1988, p. 3D. **[270]**

Jones, T.S. "A Media Definition of Alcoholism," *Studies in Mass Communication and Technology*, ed. S. Thomas. Vol. 1. Norwood, NJ: Ablex Publishing Corp., 1984, pp. 130-139. **[371]**

Jordan, Amy B. "Social Class, Temporal Orientation, and Mass Media Use within the Family System," *Critical Studies in Mass Communication* (December, 1992) 9: 374-386. **[271]**

Joseph, Ted. "Daily Publishers' Preferences on Reporter Decision-Making," *Journalism Quarterly* (Winter, 1985) 62(4): 899-901. **[154]**

Joseph, Ted. "Reporters' and Editors' Preference Toward Reporter Decision Making," *Journalism Quarterly* (Summer, 1982) 59: 219-222. **[109]**

Just, Marcel Adam and Patricia A. Carpenter. "A Theory of Reading: From Eye Fixations to Comprehension," *Psychological Review* (1980) 87: 329-354. **[284]**

Juster, F. Thomas and Frank P. Stafford. "Comment," *Public Opinion Quarterly* (1991) 55: 357-359. **[211]**

Juster, Susan M. and Maris A. Vinovskis. "Changing Perspectives on the American Family in the Past," *Annual Review of Sociology* (1987) 13: 193-216. **[278]**

Kabanoff, Boris and Gordon E. O'Brien. "Stress and the Leisure Needs and Activities of Different Occupations," *Human Relations* (1986) 39(10): 903-916. **[265]**

Kaiser, S.B. and J.L. Chandler. "Older Consumers' Use of Media for Fashion Information," *Journal of Broadcasting & Electronic Media* (Spring, 1985) 29(2): 201-207. **[278]**

Kalisch, Philip A. and Beatrice J. Kalisch. "Sex-Role Stereotyping of Nurses and Physicians on Prime-Time Television: A Dichotomy of Occupational Portrayals," *Sex Roles* (April, 1984) 10(758): 533-553. **[368]**

Kalisch, Philip A., Beatrice J. Kalisch, and Margaret Scobey. *Images of Nurses on Television.* New York: Springer Pub. Co., 1983. **[368]**

Kam, Lock Yut and Victor T. Valbuena. "Mass Media and Teen Culture in Singapore: An Exploratory Study," *Media Asia* (1988) 15(1): 3-8. **[216]**

Kamerer, D.J., N. Mundorf, J.J. Wakshlag, and A.S. Bhatia. "Repeat Viewing of Daytime Television Programs," paper presented at the regional conference of the Association for Education in Journalism and Mass Communication, Bloomington, Indiana, 1986. **[174]**

Kamerer, David. "How Television Audiences Cumulate: An Examination of Reach and Frequency Using People Meters," paper presented in the Advertising Division at the annual conference of the Association for Education in Journalism and Mass Communication, Minneapolis, 1990. **[173]**

Kaminsky, Stuart M. with Jeffrey H. Mahan. *American Television Genres.* Chicago: Nelson-Hall, 1985. **[361]**

Kaminsky, Stuart M. *American Film Genres* (Chicago: Nelson-Hall), 2nd edition, 1985.

Kane, Kathryn R. *Visions of War: Hollywood Combat Films of World War II.* Ann Arbor: UMI Research Press, 1982. **[331]**

Kang, J.M. "Reporters and Their Professional and Occupational Commitment in a Developing Country," *Gazette* (1987) 40(1): 3-20. **[165]**

Kaniss, Phyllis. *Making Local News.* Chicago: University of Chicago Press, 1991. **[98]**

Kanso, Ali and Richard Alan Nelson. "Before 'Desert Storm': A Comparison of 1980 Iraq-Iran War Coverage in Four American and Arab Newspapers," paper presented to the International Communication Division at the annual conference of the Association for Education in Journalism and Mass Communication, Montreal, August, 1992. **[159]**

Kaplan, E.A. *Rocking Around the Clock: Music Television, Post Modernism, and Consumer Culture.* New York: Methuen, 1988. **[362]**

Kaplan, G.A. "Kinetic Disruption of Optical Texture: The Perception of Depth at an Edge," *Perception and Psychophysica* (1969) 6: 193-198. Cited in Kipper (1986). **[318]**

Kaplan, Peter W. "Women Upgrade Image on TV's Network Shows," *Plain Dealer*, Dec. 16, 1984, p. 15p. **[348, 366]**

Kapoor, Suraj. "Perception of and Conformity to Policy in Indian Newspapers," *Journalism Quarterly* (Summer, 1979) 56(2): 388-391. **[92]**

Kapoor, Suraj and Carl Botan. "Editors' Perceptions of the Letters to the Editor Column," paper presented at the annual conference of the International Communication Association, San Francisco, May, 1989. **[339]**

Kapoor, Suraj and John F. Cragan. "Conformity in the Newsroom--A Fresh Look," paper presented at the annual conference of the Association for Education in Journalism and Mass Communication, Washington, D.C., August, 1989. **[149]**

Kapoor, Suraj, John Cragan and Irene Cooper. "Publishers' and Opinion Page Editors Political Perceptions: A Comparative Analysis," paper presented to the Newspaper Division at the annual conference of the Association for Education in Journalism and Mass Communication, Minneapolis, August, 1990. **[136, 149, 156]**

Kapoor, Suraj, John Cragan and Jay Groves. "Political Diversity Is Alive in TV and Newspaper Rooms," *Communication Research Reports* (June, 1992) 9(1): 89-97. **[149]**

Karnick, K.B. "NBC and the Innovation of Television News, 1945-1953," *Journalism History* (Spring, 1988) 15(1): 26-34. **[143]**

Karp, Jonathan. "Decline? What Decline?" *Media Studies Journal* (Summer, 1992) 6(3): 45-53. **[73]**

Katz, Elihu, Hanna Adoni and Pnina Parness. "Remembering the News: What the Picture Adds to Recall," *Journalism Quarterly* (1977) 54: 231-239. **[319]**

Katz, Elihu, Michael Gurevitch and H. Haas. "On the Use of Mass Media for Important Things," *American Sociological Review* (1973) 38: 164-181. **[247, 273]**

Katz, H.E. and K.M. Lancaster. "How Leading Advertisers and Agencies Use Cable Television," *Journal of Advertising Research* (February/March, 1989) 29(1): 30-38. **[81]**

Katz, Helen. "The Future of Public Broadcasting in the US," *Media, Culture and Society* (1989) 11: 195-205. **[48, 89]**

Katz, J. "What Makes Crime 'News'?" *Media, Culture and Society* (January, 1987) 9(1): 47-75. **[128]**

Kaul, A.J. and J.P. McKerns. "The Dialectic Ecology of the Newspaper," *Critical Studies in Mass Communication* (September, 1985) 2(3): 217-233. **[58]**

Kaye, J. "Coming: Shows that Interact with Toys," *TV Guide* Feb. 7, 1987, p. 1A. **[177]**

Kebbel, Gary. "The Importance of Political Activity in Explaining Multiple News Media Use," *Journalism Quarterly* (Autumn, 1985) 62: 559-566. **[254]**

Keenan, J.M., S.D. Baillet and P. Brown. "The Effects of Causal Cohesion on Comprehension and Memory," *Journal of Verbal Learning and Verbal Behavior* (1984) 23: 115-126. **[314]**

Keirstead, Phillip O. and Sonia-Kay Keirstead. "The Many Faces of Community Radio," *International Communication Bulletin* (Spring, 1987) 22(1-2): 6-12. **[59]**

Kelley, P., B. Gunter, and L. Buckle. "'Reading' Television in the Classroom: More Results from the Television Literacy Project," *Journal of Educational Television* (1987) 13(1): 7-20. **[273]**

Kelly, J.R. "Socialization Toward Leisure: A Development Approach," *Journal of Leisure Research* (1974) 6: 181-193. **[274]**

Kelly, James D. "The Effects of Tabular and Graphical Display Formats on Time Spent Processing Statistics," paper presented to the Visual Communication Division at the annual conference of the Association for Education in Journalism and Mass Communication, Montreal, August, 1992. **[315]**

Kelly, James D. "The Graph Makers: A Survey of the Newspaper Editorial Workers Who Create Charts and Graphs," paper presented to the VisComm Division at the annual conference of the Association for Education in Journalism and Mass Communication, Minneapolis, Aug. 9, 1990. **[164]**

Kelly, James D. "Gender, Pay and Job Satisfaction of Faculty in Journalism," *Journalism Quarterly* (Summer, 1989) 66(2): 446-452. **[316]**

Kelly, James D. "The Data-Ink Ratio and Accuracy of Newspaper Graphs," *Journalism Quarterly* (Autumn, 1989) 66(3): 632-639. **[316]**

Kelly, John R. *Leisure Identities and Interactions*. London: George Allen & Unwin, 1983. **[170, 211]**

Kelly, John R. "Leisure Styles and Choices in Three Environments," *Pacific Sociological Review* (April, 1978) 21(2): 187-207. **[249, 259, 265]**

Kelly, John R., Marjorie W. Steinkamp and Janice R. Kelly. "Later-Life Satisfaction: Does Leisure Contribute?" *Leisure Sciences* (1987) 9(3): 189-199. **[191]**

Kelly, John R. and Jo-Ellen Ross. "Later-Life Leisure: Beginning a New Agenda," *Leisure Sciences* (1989) 11(1): 47-59. **[190]**

Kelly, Patricia R. "The Influence of Reading Content on Students' Perceptions of the Masculinity or Femininity of Reading," *Journal of Reading Behavior* (1986) 18(3): 243-256. **[187]**

Kenney, Keith, and Stephen Lacy. "Economic Forces behind Newspapers' Increasing Use of Color and Graphics," *Newspaper Research Journal* (Spring, 1987) 8(3): 33-41. **[91, 98]**

Kent, Kurt. "Freedom of the Press: An Empirical Analysis of One Aspect of the Concept," *Gazette* (1972) 18: 65-75. **[60]**

Kepplinger, Hans Mathias and Renate Kocher. "Professionalism in the Media World," *European Journal of Communication* (1990) 5: 285-311. **[158, 160]**

Kerr, J. and W.E. Niebauer Jr. "Use of Full Text, Database Retrieval Systems by Editorial Page Writers," *Newspaper Research Journal* (Spring, 1987) 8(3): 21-32. **[161]**

Kessler, L. "Women's Magazines' Coverage of Smoking Related Health Hazards," *Journalism Quarterly* (Summer, 1989) 66(2): 316-322. **[165, 371]**

Kessler, Lauren. "Sixties Survivors: The Persistence of Countercultural Values in the Lives of Underground Journalists," *Journalism History* (Spring/Summer, 1989) 16(1-2): 2-11. **[165, 371]**

Kielbowicz, Richard B. "Speeding the News by Postal Express, 1825-1861: The Public Policy of Privileges for the Press," *Social Science Journal* (January, 1985) 22(1): 50-63.

Kielbowicz, Richard B. "Newsgathering by Printers' Exchanges before the Telegraph," *Journalism History* (Summer, 1982) 9(2): 42-48. **[34]**

Kielbowicz, Richard B. and L. Lawson. "Protecting the Small-Town Press: Community, Social Policy and Postal Privileges, 1845-1970," *Canadian Review of American Studies* (Spring, 1988) 19(1): 23-45. **[30]**

Kieras, David E. "Topicalization Effects in Cued Recall of Technical Prose," *Memory and Cognition* (November, 1981) 9(6): 541-549. **[314]**

Kiesel, Diane, June Nicholson, John Henkel and Geri Fuller-Col. "Washington Neglected," *The Quill* (May, 1978), pp. 19-26. **[160]**

Kiger, Derrick M. "Effects of Music Information Load on a Reading Comprehension Task," *Perceptual and Motor Skills* (1989) 69: 531-534. **[226, 268]**

Kilbourne, Jean. "The Child as Sex Object: Images of Children in the Media," *Challenging Media Images of Women* (Summer, 1991) 3(3): 1-2. Reprinted from *The Educator's Guide to Preventing Sexual Abuse.* Santa Cruz, CA: Network Publishers, ETR Associates, 1986. **[348]**

Kim, Won Yong, Stanley J. Baran and Kimberly K. Massey. "Impact of the VCR on Control of Television Viewing," *Journal of Broadcasting & Electronic Media* (Summer, 1988) 32(3): 351-358. **[236]**

Kindem, Gorham. *The Moving Image: Production Principles and Practices.* Glenview, IL: Scott, Foresman, 1987. **[162]**

Kingsolver, P.S. and H.V. Cordry. "Gender and the Press: An Update," *Advances in Gender and Communication Research*, eds. L.B. Nadler, M.K. Nadler and W.R. Todd-Mancillas. Lanham, M.D.: University Press of America, 1988, pp. 307-315. **[139]**

Kintsch, Walter and T.A. van Dijk. "Toward a Model of Text Comprehension and Production," *Psychological Review* (1978) 85: 363-394. **[314, 321]**

Kippax, S. and J.P. Murray. "Using the Mass Media: Need Gratification and Perceived Utility," *Communication Research* (1980) 7: 335-360. **[273]**

Kipper, Philip. "Television Camera Movement as a Source of Perceptual Information," *Journal of Broadcasting & Electronic Media* (Summer, 1986) 30(3): 295-307. **[300, 301, 318]**

Kirsch, Irwin S. and John T. Guthrie. "Adult Reading Practices for Work and Leisure," *Adult Education Quarterly* (Summer, 1984) 34(4): 213-232. **[258]**

Kisielius, J. and B. Sternthal. "Detecting and Explaining Vividness Effects in Attitudinal Judgments," *Journal of Marketing Research* (1984) 21: 54-64. **[319]**

Kitchen, Philip J. and David A. Yorke. "Commercial Television Breaks, Consumer Behavior, and New Technology: An Initial Analysis," *European Journal of Marketing* (1986) 20(2): 40-53. **[237]**

Kleiman, Howard M. "Unshackled but Unwilling: Public Broadcasting and Editorializing," *Journalism Quarterly* (Winter, 1987) 64(4): 707-713. **[145]**

Klein, Howard A. "The Effect Three Testing Modes--Reading while Listening, Listening and Silent Reading--Have on Sixth Grade Boys and Girls," *Reading Improvement* (Winter, 1989) 26(4): 298-304. **[226, 320]**

Kleinfield, N.R. "Video News Releases Are Making Headway," *Plain Dealer*, Jan. 3, 1989, p. 12B; New York Times dispatch. **[161]**

Kleinnijenhuis, Jan. "News as Olds," *Gazette* (1989) 43: 205-228. **[120]**

Kliesch, Ralph E. "The U.S. Press Corps Abroad Rebounds: A 7th World Survey of Foreign Correspondents," *Newspaper Research Journal* (Winter, 1991) 12(1): 24-33. **[135]**

Klopfenstein, Bruce C. and David Sedman. "Technical Standards and the Marketplace: The Case of AM Stereo," *Journal of Broadcasting & Electronic Media* (Spring, 1990) 34(2): 171-194. **[75]**

Klopfenstein, Bruce C., Sara C. Spears and Douglas A. Ferguson. "VCR Attitudes and Behaviors by Length of Ownership," *Journal of Broadcasting & Electronic Media* (Fall, 1991) 35(4): 525-531. **[175, 199]**

Knapp, S. and B.L. Sherman. "Motion Picture Attendance: A Market Segmentation Approach," *Current Research in Film: Audiences, Economics and Law*, ed. B.A. Austin, Vol. 2. Norwood, NJ: Ablex Publishing Corp., 1986, pp. 35-46. **[232]**

Kneale, Dennis. "TV's Nielsen Ratings, Long Unquestioned, Face Tough Challenges," *Wall Street Journal*, July 19, 1990, p. 1. **[211]**

Knelman, Judith. "Subtly Sensational: A Study of Early Victorian Crime Reporting," paper presented to the History and International Divisions at the annual conference of the Association for Education in Journalism and Mass Communication, Minneapolis, August, 1990. **[135]**

Knowles, A.D. et al. "Television Or Not Television: The Impact of Two Weeks without Television," *Media Information Australia* (May, 1989) 52: 26-29. **[256]**

Knudson, Jerry W. "The Ultimate Weapon: Propaganda and the Spanish Civil War," *Journalism History* (Winter, 1988) 15(4): 102-111. **[55]**

Kobayashi, K. "Man and C&C: The Long Term View," *Intermedia*, 10(6), 1982, p. 23. **[177]**

Koch, Neal. "TV Independents Feel Pinch," *Plain Dealer*, Oct. 1, 1990, p. 4C. New York Times dispatch. **[67, 129]**

Koch, T. "The News as Myth: Fact and Context in Journalism," *Contributions to the Study of Mass Media and Communications*, No. 17. Westport, CT: Greenwood Press, 1990. **[67]**

Kocher, Renate. "Bloodhounds or Missionaries: Role Definitions of German and British Journalists," *European Journal of Communication* (1986) 1: 43-64. **[160]**

Kochersberger, R.G. Jr. "Survey of Suicide Photos Use by Newspapers in Three States," *Newspaper Research Journal* (Summer, 1988) 9(4): 1-10. **[157]**

Koek, Karin E. and Julie Winklepleck (eds.) *Gale Directory of Publications and Broadcast Media*. Vol. 1-3. Detroit: Gale Research, Inc., 1991. **[34]**

Koenig, F. and G. Lessan. "Viewers' Relationship to Television Personalities," *Psychological Reports* (August, 1985) 57(1): 263-266. **[258]**

Kohn, Melvin L., Atsushi Naoi, Carrie Schoenbach, Carmi Schooler and Kazimierz M. Slomczynski. "Position in the Class Structure and Psychological Functioning in the United States, Japan and Poland," *American Journal of Sociology*; (January, 1990) 95(4): 964-1008. **[269]**

Kojima, K. "Youth and Television in Contemporary Japan--Analytical Framework, Background, and Characteristics," *Gazette* (1986) 37(1/2): 87-102. **[216]**

Komatsubara, Hisao. "New Broadcasting Technologies and the Press in Japan," *Studies of Broadcasting* (1989) 25: 41-75. **[59]**

Kopenhaver, Lillian Lodge, David L. Martinson and Michael Ryan. "How Public Relations Practitioners and Editors in Florida View Each Other," *Journalism Quarterly* (Winter, 1984) 61: 860-865, 884. **[161]**

Korzenny, Felipe, Kimberly Neuendorf, Michael Burgoon, Judee K. Burgoon and Bradley S. Greenberg. "Cultural Identification as Predictor of Content Preferences of Hispanics," *Journalism Quarterly* (Winter, 1983) 60(4): 677-685. **[234]**

Kosicki, Gerald M. and Jack M. McLeod. "Learning from Political News: Effects of Media Images and Information-Processing Strategies," *Mass Communication and Political Information Processing*, ed. Sidney Kraus. Hillsdale, NJ: Lawrence Erlbaum Associates, Publishers, 1990, pp. 69-83. **[202]**

Koten, John. "A Once Tightly Knit Middle Class Finds Itself Divided and Uncertain," *Wall Street Journal*, March 9, 1987, p. 19. **[263]**

Kotlowitz, Alex. "Changes among Families Prompt a Vanishing Sense of Community," *Wall Street Journal*, March 11, 1987, p. 33. **[263]**

Kowalski, Tadeusz. "Evolution after Revolution: the Polish Press System in Transition," *Media, Culture and Society* (1988) 10: 183-196. **[49]**

Kraft, Robert N. "The Influence of Camera Angle on Comprehension and Retention of Pictorial Events," *Memory & Cognition* (1987) 15(4): 291-307. **[298, 299, 301, 317, 318]**

Kraft, Robert N. "Rules and Strategies of Visual Narratives," *Perceptual and Motor Skills* (1987) 64: 3-14. **[298, 299, 317, 318]**

Kramer, Hilton. *The Age of the Avant-Garde: An Art Chronicle of 1956-72.* New York, 1973. **[18]**

Kress, G. "Language in the Media: The Construction of the Domains of Public and Private," *Media, Culture and Society* (October, 1986) 8(4): 395-420. **[128]**

Krishnan, R. and Lawrence Soley. "Controlling Magazine Circulation," *Journal of Advertising Research* (August/September, 1987), pp. 17-22. **[80]**

Kristiansen, C.M. "The British Press's Coverage of Health: An Antagonistic Force," *Media Information Australia* (February, 1988) 47: 56-60. **[370]**

Kristiansen, Connie M. and Christina M. Harding. "Mobilization of Health Behavior by the Press in Britain," *Journalism Quarterly* (Summer, 1984) 61(2): 364-370, 398. **[126]**

Krugman, D.M. and R.T. Rust. "The Impact of Cable Penetration on Network Viewing," *Journal of Advertising Research* (October/November, 1987) 27(5): 9-13. **[81]**

Ku, Linlin, Kak Yoon and Bradley S. Greenberg. "Children and Adolescent Attitudes toward Advertising in China and the United States," paper presented to the Intercultural & Development Communication Division at the annual conference of the International Communication Association, Dublin, Ireland, 1991. **[200]**

Kubey, Robert W. "Television and the Quality of Family Life," *Communication Quarterly* (Fall, 1990) 38(4): 312-324. **[237, 267]**

Kubey, Robert W. "Television Use in Everyday Life: Coping with Unstructured Time," *Journal of Communication* (Summer, 1986) 36(3): 108-123. **[246, 258]**

Kubey, Robert W. and Mihaly Csikszentmihalyi. *Television and the Quality of Life: How Viewing Shapes Everyday Experiences.* Hinsdale, NJ: Lawrence Erlbaum Associates, 1990. **[246, 267]**

Kubey, Robert W. and Mihaly Csikszentmihalyi. "Television as Escape: Subjective Experience before an Evening of Heavy Viewing," *Communication Reports* (Summer, 1990) 3(2): 92-100. **[246, 267]**

Kubey, Robert and Reed Larson. "The Use and Experience of the New Video Media among Children and Young Adolescents," *Communication Research* (February, 1990) 17(1): 107-130. **[174, 235]**

Kuhn, Annette. "Women's Genres," *Screen* (January-February, 1984) 25: 18-28. **[331]**

Kuklinski, James H. and Lee Sigelman. "When Objectivity Is Not Objective: Network Television News Coverage of U.S. Senators and the 'Paradox of Objectivity,'" *Journal of Politics* (August, 1992) 54(3): 810-833. **[161]**

Kumar, K. *Prophecy and Progress: The Sociology of Industrial and Postindustrial Society.* Harmondsworth: Allen Lane, 1978. **[65]**

Kumar, Krishan. "Holding the Middle Ground: the BBC, the Public and the Professional Broadcaster," *Sociology* (1975) 9: 67-68. **[166]**

Kuo, E.C.Y. "Mass Media and Language Planning: Singapore's "Speak Mandarin' Campaign," *Journal of Communication* (Spring, 1984) 34(2): 24-35. **[46]**

Kurtz, Howard. "Media Jitters: Almost Anything Creates Uproar," *Plain Dealer*, Jan. 23, 1991, p. 5B; Washington Post dispatch. **[146]**

Labov, William. *Sociolinguistic Patterns.* Philadelphia: Labunski, R.E. and J.V. Pavlik. "The Legal Environment of Investigative Reporters: A Pilot Study," *Newspaper Research Bureau* (Spring, 1985) 6(3): 13-19. **[163]**

Labunski, R.E. and J.V. Pavlik. "The Legal Environment of Investigative Reporters: A Pilot Study," *Media Asia* (1986) 13(1): 43-45. **[163]**

Lacy, Stephen. "The Financial Commitment Approach to News Media Competition," *Journal of Media Economics* (Summer, 1992) 5(2): 5-21. **[91]**

Lacy, Stephen. "Effects of Group Ownership on Daily Newspaper Content," *Journal of Media Economics* (Spring, 1991) 4(1): 35-47.

Lacy, Stephen. "Newspaper Competition and Number of Press Services Carried: A Replication," *Journalism Quarterly* (Spring, 1990) 67(1): 79-82. **[91]**

Lacy, Stephen. "Effect of Intermedia Competition on Daily Newspaper Content," (Spring, 1988) 65(1): 95-99. **[88, 91]**

Lacy, Stephen. "Content of Joint Operation Newspapers," *Press Concentration and Monopoly: New Perspectives on Newspaper Ownership and Operation*, ed. R.G. Picard et al. Norwood, NJ: Ablex, 1988, pp. 147-160. **[88, 91]**

Lacy, Stephen. "The Impact of Intercity Competition on Daily Newspaper Content," *Journalism Quarterly* (Summer, 1988) 65(2): 399-406. **[88, 91]**

Lacy, Stephen. "The Effect of Growth of Radio on Newspaper Competition, 1929-1948," *Journalism Quarterly* (Winter, 1987) 64(4): 775-781. **[59, 97]**

Lacy, Stephen. "The Effects of Ownership and Competition on Daily Newspaper Content," Ph.D. dissertation, University of Texas-Austin, 1986. **[91]**

Lacy, Stephen. "Monopoly Metropolitan Dailies and Inter-City Competition," *Journalism Quarterly* (Autumn, 1985) 62(3): 640-647. **[87]**

Lacy, Stephen, Tony Atwater and Xinmin Qin. "Competition and the Allocation of Resources for Local Television News," *Journal of Media Economics* (Spring, 1989) 2(1): 3-12. **[91]**

Lacy, Stephen, Tony Atwater and Angela Powers. "Use of Satellite Technology in Local Television News," *Journalism Quarterly* (Winter, 1988) 65(4): 925-929, 966. **[143]**

Lacy, Stephen and James M. Bernstein. "The Impact of Competition and Market Size on the Assembly Cost of Local Television News," *Mass Comm Review* (1992) 19(1/2): 41-48. **[91]**

Lacy, Stephen and James M. Bernstein. "Daily Newspaper Content's Relationship to Publication Cycle and Circulation Size," *Newspaper Research Journal* (Winter, 1988) 9(2): 49-56. **[337]**

Lacy, Stephen and Shikha Dalmia. "The Relationship between Daily and Weekly Newspaper Penetration in Non-Metropolitan Areas," paper presented to the Media Management and Economics Division at the annual conference of the Association for Education in Journalism and Mass Communication, Montreal, August, 1992. **[87]**

Lacy, Stephen and Shikha Dalmia. "Michigan Newspaper Competition from 1980 to 1986: Expanding the Geographic Application of the Umbrella Model," paper presented to the Newspaper Division at the annual conference of the Association for Education in Journalism and Mass Communication, Boston, August, 1991. **[87]**

Lacy, Stephen and Frederick Fico. "The Link between Newspaper Content Quality and Circulation," *Newspaper Research Journal* (Spring, 1991) 12(2): 46-57. **[98]**

Lacy, Stephen and Frederick Fico. "Newspaper Quality & Ownership: Rating the Groups," *Newspaper Research Journal* (Spring, 1990) 11(2): 42-53. **[90]**

Lacy, Stephen, Frederick Fico and Todd F. Simon. "Fairness and Balance in the Prestige Press," *Journalism Quarterly* (Fall, 1991) 68(3): 363-370. **[132]**

Lacy, Stephen, Jean Folkerts and Stephen Dravis. "Market Forces and the Populist Press: Surviving when a Movement Ends," paper presented to the History Division at the annual conference of the Association for Education in Journalism and Mass Communication, Minneapolis, August, 1990. **[30]**

Lacy, Stephen and Robert G. Picard. "Interactive Monopoly Power in the Daily Newspaper Industry," *Journal of Media Economics* (Fall, 1990) 3(2): 27-38. **[85]**

Lacy, Stephen and David Matustik. "Dependence on Organization and Beat Sources for Story Ideas: A Case Study of Four Newspapers," *Newspaper Research Journal* (Winter, 1983) 5(2): 9-16. **[134]**

Lacy, Stephen and Ardyth B. Sohn. "Correlations of Newspaper Content with Circulation in the Suburbs: A Case Study," *Journalism Quarterly* (Winter, 1990) 67(4): 785-793. **[98]**

Lafky, S. "Economic Equity and the Journalistic Work Force," *Women in Mass Communication: Challenging Gender Values*, ed. P.J. Creedon. Sage Focus Editions, No. 106. Newbury Park, CA: Sage Publications, 1989, pp. 164-179. **[148]**

LaFollette, M.C. "Eyes on the Stars: Images of Women Scientists in Popular Magazines," *Science Technology and Human Values* (1988) 13(3/4): 262-275. **[354]**

Lain, L.B. "Steps toward a Comprehensive Model of Newspaper Readership," *Journalism Quarterly* (Spring, 1986) 63(1): 69-74. **[230, 239, 273, 276]**

Lain, L.B. "More Evidence on the Needs of Readers," *Newspaper Research Journal* (Summer, 1985) 6(4): 8-18. **[257]**

Lain, Laurence B. and Philip J. Harwood. "Mug Shots and Reader Attitudes toward People in the News," *Journalism Quarterly* (Summer, 1992) 69(2): 293-300. **[291]**

Laliberte, Raymond, "Concerning the Journalist and Various Powers," *Communication et Information* (Autumn, 1976) 3: 231-242. **[166]**

Lamude, Diane and Joseph Scudder. "The Influence of Gender and Age upon Favorite Program Selection and Motives for Adult Television Viewers," paper presented at the annual conference of the Speech Communication Association, New Orleans, La., Nov. 3-6, 1988. **[191]**

Lamude, Diane. "A Cultural Model of Nostalgia and Media Use," *World Communication* (1990) 19(2): 37-51. **[273]**

Landro, Laura and Daniel Akst. "Studios Rush to Add Theaters, Change Marketing of Oscar-Nominated Films," *Wall Street Journal*, Feb. 18, 1988, p. 28. **[66, 84]**

Landro, Laura. "Airing Grievances: As Cable-TV Industry Keeps Growing, Rivals Demand Regulation," *Wall Street Journal*, Sept. 17, 1987, p. 1. **[73, 84, 88]**

Landro, Laura. "Direct-Broadcast TV May Be Getting Off the Ground," *Wall Street Journal*, Feb. 21, 1990, p. 1B. **[74]**

Landro, Laura. "Book Industry Faces More Consolidation: Only a Handful of Big Publishers May Survive," *The Wall Street Journal*, March 13, 1987. **[73, 84, 88]**

Landro, Laura. "Market for Cable TV Systems Heats Up," *Wall Street Journal*, March 9, 1988, p. 4. **[84]**

Landro, Laura. "Film Magazine Tries to Tap Market Where Others Have Failed Before," *Wall Street Journal*, June 2, 1987, p. 33. **[73, 84, 88]**

Landrum, Larry N. "Recent Genre Work," *Journal of Popular Film and Television* (Fall, 1985) 13(3): 151-158. **[328]**

Landsberger, B.H. *Sex Differences in Factors Related to Early School Achievement*. N.P. ERIC ED 197 839, February, 1981. Cited in Patricia R. Kelly, "The Influence of Reading Content on Students' Perceptions of the Masculinity or Femininity of Reading," *Journal of Reading Behavior* (1986) 18(3): 243-256. **[187]**

Lang, Annie. "A Limited Capacity Theory of Television Viewing," paper presented to the Information Systems Division at the annual conference of the International Communication Association," Miami, May, 1992. **[318]**

Lang, Annie. "Effects of Chronological Presentation of Information on Processing and Memory for Broadcast News," *Journal of Broadcasting & Electronic Media* (Fall, 1989) 33(4): 441-452. **[305, 306, 307, 319]**

Lang, Annie, Melody Strickwerda, Janine Sumner, Mark Winters and Byron Reeves. "The Effects of Related and Unrelated Cuts on Viewers Memory for Television: A Limited Capacity Theory of Television Viewing," paper presented to the Communication Theory and Methodology Division at the annual conference of the Association for Education in Journalism and Mass Communication, Boston, August, 1991. **[302]**

Langford, Barry and Douglas Gomery. "Studio Geneologies," *Gannett Center Journal* (Summer, 1989) 3(3): 157-175. **[103]**

Lank, Nancy H., Connie E. Vickery, Nancy Cotugna and Daniel D. Shade. "Food Commercials during Television Soap Operas: What Is the Nutrition Message?" *Journal of Community Health* (December, 1992) 17(6): 377-384. **[370]**

Larkin, Ernest F. and Gerald L. Grotta. "A Market Segmentation Approach to Daily Newspaper Audience Studies," *Journalism Quarterly* (Spring, 1979) 56(1) 31-37 +. **[253]**

LaRose, Robert and David Atkin. "Attributes of Movie Distribution Channels and Consumer Choice," *Journal of Media Economics* (Spring, 1991) 4(1): 3-17. **[246]**

LaRose, Robert and David Atkin. "Satisfaction, Demographic, and Media Environment Predictors of Cable Subscription," *Journal of Broadcasting & Electronic Media* (Fall, 1988) 32(4): 403-413. **[234, 246, 255]**

LaRose, Robert and David Atkin. "Understanding Cable Subscribership as Telecommunications Behavior," *Telematics and Infomatics* (Winter, 1988) 5: 377-388. **[234, 246, 255]**

Larson, James F. *Television's Window on the World: International Affairs Coverage on the U. S. Networks.* Norwood, NJ: Ablex Pub. Co., 1984. **[340, 364]**

Larson, James F., Emile G. McAnany and J. Douglas Storey. "News of Latin America on Network Television, 1972-1981: A Northern Perspective on the Southern Hemisphere," *Critical Studies in Mass Communication* (1986) 3: 169-183. **[121]**

Larson, Mary. "Sibling Interactions in 1950s Versus 1980s Sitcoms: A Comparison," *Journalism Quarterly* (Fall, 1991) 68(3): 381-387. **[349]**

Larson, Mary S. "Health-Related Messages Embedded in Prime-Time Television Entertainment," *Health Communication* (1991) 3(3): 175-184. **[370]**

Larson, Mary S. "Interaction between Siblings in Primetime Television Families," *Journal of Broadcasting & Electronic Media* (Summer, 1989) 33(3): 305-315. **[349]**

Larson, Stephanie Greco. "Television's Mixed Messages: Sexual Content on 'All My Children,'" *Communication Quarterly* (Spring, 1991) 39(2): 156-163. **[350]**

Larson, Timothy L. "The U.S. Television Industry: Concentration and the Question of Network Divestiture of Owned and Operated Television Stations," *Communication Research* (January, 1980) 7(1): 23-44. **[83]**

Lashley, Marilyn E. "Even in Public Television, Ownership Changes Matter," *Communication Research* (December, 1992) 19(6): 770-786. **[92]**

Lassiter, G. Daniel and Audrey A. Irvine. "Videotaped Confessions: The Impact of Camera Point of View on Judgments of Coercion," *Journal of Applied Social Psychology* (1986) 16(3): 268-276. **[303]**

Lasswell, H. "The Structure and Function of Communications in Society," *The Communication of Ideas*, ed. L. Bryson. New York: Harper, 1948. **[272]**

Lau, Tuen-Yu. "Market Analysis of the Chinese-Language Newspapers in the U.S." *Gazette* (1989) 43: 77-92. **[72]**

Lavine, John M. and Daniel B. Wackman. *Managing Media Organizations: Effective Leadership of the Media.* New York: Longman, 1988. **[109]**

Lavrakas, Paul J. and Jack K. Holley. "Images of Daily Newspapers in Their Local Markets," *Newspaper Research Journal* (Spring, 1989) 10(3): 51-59. **[109, 148]**

Lavrakas, Paul J. "The Extent and Nature of Readership of Chicago Dailies," paper presented at the annual conference of the Midwest Association for Public Opinion Research, Chicago, Nov. 17, 1990. **[232]**

Lavrakas, Paul J. and Jack K. Holley. "Surveying Media Executives about Management Training," paper presented at the annual conference of the Midwest Association for Public Opinion Research, Chicago, Nov. 17, 1989.   Elaborated in full report, "Medill Media Executives Management Curriculum Survey," by Jack K. Holley and Paul J. Lavrakas, 1989. **[109, 148, 199]**

Lawrence, F.C. et al. "Adolescents' Time Spent Viewing Television," *Adolescence* (Summer, 1986) 21(82): 431-436. **[238]**

Lawrence, Patricia A. and Philip C. Palmgreen. "Arousal Needs and Gratifications Sought from Theatrical Films," paper presented to the Mass Communication Division at the annual conference of the International Communication Association, Chicago, 1991. **[257]**

Lay, Yun-Ju and John C. Schweitzer. "Advertising in Taiwan Newspapers Since the Lifting of the Bans," *Journalism Quarterly* (Spring, 1990) 67(1): 201-206. **[49]**

Le Duc, Don R. "French and German New Media Policies: Variations on a Familiar Theme," *Journal of Broadcasting & Electronic Media* (Fall, 1987) 31(4): 427-447. **[48, 59, 212]**

Leach, Jim. "The Screwball Comedy," in Barry K. Grant, ed. *Film Genre: Theory and Criticism* (Metuchen, NJ: The Scarecrow Press, Inc.), pp. 75-89, 1977. **[331]**

Ledden S. and F. Fejes. "Female Gender Role Patterns in Japanese Comic Magazines," *Journal of Popular Culture* (Summer, 1987) 21(1): 155-176. **[366]**

Lee, B. "Prosocial Content on Prime-Time Television," *Television as a Social Issue*, ed. S. Oskamp. Newbury Park, CA: Sage, 1988, pp. 238-246. **[359]**

Lee, Chang Seek and Ely D. Gomez. "The Contribution of the Information Sector to the Industrial Growth of Korea," *Media Asia* (1992) 19(3): 156-164. **[65, 275]**

Lee, Chin-Chuan. "The United States as Seen Through the People's Daily," *Journal of Communication* (Autumn, 1981) 31(4): 92-101. **[371]**

Lee, Jae-won (Ed.) *Seoul Olympics and the Global Community.* Seoul, Korea: Seoul Olympics Memorial Association, 1992. **[275]**

Lee, J.W. and H.D. Kang. "Professional Socialization of Newspeople: A Test of Dependency through Comparative News-Value Judgments," *The Third Channel* (December, 1986) 2(2): 541-560. **[125]**

Lees, Francis A. and Charles Yneu Yang. "The Redistributional Effect of Television Advertising," *The Economic Journal* (June, 1966) 76(302): 328-336. **[77]**

Lehrer, Adrienne. "Between Quotation Marks," *Journalism Quarterly* (Winter, 1989) 66(4): 902-906, 941. **[144]**

Lemert, James B. "News Content and the Elimination of Mobilizing Information: An Experiment," *Journalism Quarterly* (Summer, 1984) 61(2): 243-249. **[162]**

Lemert, James B. and Marguerite Gemson Ashman. "Extent of Mobilizing Information in Opinion and News Magazines," *Journalism Quarterly* (Winter, 1983) 60(4): 657-662. **[162]**

Lemish, D. "Viewers in Diapers: The Early Development of Television Viewing," *Natural Audiences: Qualitative Research of Media Uses and Effects*, ed. T.R. Lindlof. Norwood, NJ: Ablex, 1987, pp. 33-57.

Lemish, D. "Soap Opera Viewing in College: A Naturalistic Inquiry," *Journal of Broadcasting & Electronic Media* (Summer, 1985) 29(3): 275-293. **[275]**

Lemish, D. and M.L. Rice. "Television as a Talking Picture Book: A Prop for Language Acquisition," *Journal of Child Language* (June, 1986) 13(2): 251-274. **[238]**

Lemon, B.W., V. Bengston and J. Peterson. "An Exploration of the Activity Theory of Aging: Activity Types and Life Satisfaction among In-Movers to a Retirement Community," *Journal of Gerontology* (1972) 27(4): 511-523. **[259]**

Lennon, Sharron J. "Bondage in Women's Clothing as Reflected in Television," *Empirical Studies of the Arts* (1990) 8(1): 77-83. **[366]**

Lent, J.A. "Women and Mass Communications: The Asian Literature," *Gazette* (1985) 35(2): 125-142. **[148, 366]**

Lent, John A. "Mass Communication in Asia and the Pacific: Recent Trends and Developments," *Media Asia* (1989) 16(1): 16-24. **[59]**

Leslie, Michael and William Barlow. "Illusion and Reality on Commercial Television: A Comparison of Brazil and the U.S.," paper presented at the annual conference of the International Communication Association, Chicago, May, 1991. **[344]**

Lester, Paul. "Use of Visual Elements on Newspaper Front Pages," *Journalism Quarterly* (Fall, 1988) 65(3): 760-763. **[340]**

Lester, Paul. "Front Page Mug Shots: A Content Analysis of Five U.S. Newspapers in 1986," *Newspaper Research Bureau* (Spring, 1988) 9(3): 1-9. **[340]**

Lester, Paul and Ron Smith. "African-American Photo Coverage in Life, Newsweek and Time, 1937-1988," *Journalism Quarterly* (Spring, 1990) 67(1): 128-136. **[365]**

Lester, Paul and Ron Smith. "African-American Picture Coverage in Life, Newsweek and Time, 1937-1988," paper presented to the Minorities and Communication Division at the annual conference of the Association for Education in Journalism and Mass Communication, Washington, D.C., August, 1989. **[365]**

Leung, Kenneth W.Y. "Radio Listening and Social Participation in Hong Kong," *The Third Channel* (December, 1986) 2(2): 519-535. **[213]**

Levie, W.H. and R. Lentz. "Effects of Text Illustrations: A Review of Research," *Educational Communication and Technology Journal* (1982) 30: 195-232. **[316]**

Levin, H.J. "Program Duplication, Diversity and Effective Viewer Choices: Some Empirical Findings," *American Economic Review* (1971) 61(2): 81-82. **[97]**

Levin, Harry. *Refractions: Essays in Comparative Literature.* New York, 1966. **[18]**

Levin, J.R. "On Functions of Pictures in Prose," *Neuropsychological and Cognitive Processes in Reading,* ed. F.J. Pirozzolo and M.C. Wittrock. New York: Academic Press, 1981. **[291, 316]**

Levin, J.R. and A.M. Lesgold. "On Pictures in Prose,"*Educational Communication and Technology Journal* (1978) 26: 233-243. **[316]**

Levin, Jack, Amita Mody-Desbareau and Arnold Arluke. "The Gossip Tabloid as Agent of Social Control," *Journalism Quarterly* (Summer, 1988) 65(2): 514-517. **[339]**

Levine, D.N. "Cultural Integration," *International Encyclopedia of the Social Sciences,* ed. D.L. Sills, Vol. 7, pp. 372-380. New York: Macmillan & Free Press, 1968. **[263]**

Levine, Grace Ferrari. "Learned Helplessness in Local TV News," *Journalism Quarterly* (Spring, 1986) 63(1): 12-18, 23. **[128]**

Levinson, Daniel J. "A Conception of Adult Development," *American Psychologist* (January, 1986) 41(1): 3-13. **[190]**

Levy, D.A. "Social Support and the Media: Analysis of Responses by Radio Psychology Talk Show Hosts," *Professional Psychology: Research and Practice* (April, 1989) 20(2): 73-78. **[116]**

Levy, Emanuel. "Stage, Sex and Suffering: Images of Women in American Films," *Empirical Studies of the Arts* (1990) 8(1): 53-76. **[352]**

Levy, Leonard W. *Emergence of a Free Press.* Cambridge: Oxford University Press, 1985. **[56]**

Levy, Mark R. (Ed.). *The VCR Age: Home Video and Mass Communication.* Newbury Park, CA: Sage Publications, 1989. **[116, 212]**

Levy, Mark R. "TV News Research Is More than Cognitive Psychology," *American Behavioral Scientist* (November/December, 1989) 33(2): 203-205. **[116, 212]**

Levy, Mark R. "VCR Use and the Concept of Audience Activity," *Communication Quarterly* (Summer, 1987) 35(3): 267-275. **[245]**

Levy, Mark R. "The Time-Shifting Use of Home Video Recorders," *Journal of Broadcasting* (Summer, 1983) 27(3): 263-268. **[174]**

Levy, Mark R. "Experiencing Television News," *Journal of Communication* (1977) 27(4): 112-117. **[273]**

Levy, Mark R. and Edward L. Fink. "Home Video Recorders and the Transience of Television Broadcasts," *Journal of Communication* (Spring, 1984) 34(2): 56-71. **[174]**

Levy, Mark R. and S. Windahl. "Audience Activity and Gratifications: A Conceptual Clarification and Exploration," *Communication Research* (1984) 11: 51-78. **[229, 246, 273]**

Lewenstein, Marion and James N. Rosse. "Joint Operating Agreements: Can the First Amendment and Profits Both Survive?" *Gannett Center Journal* (Winter, 1988) 2(1): 107-118. **[90]**

Lewis, C. *The TV Director/Interpreter.* New York: Hastings House, 1968. **[300]**

Lewis, Charles. "Negotiation and Socialization in the Family Room: Television and American Domestic Life," paper presented to the Qualitative Studies Division at the annual conference of the Association for Education in Journalism and Mass Communication, Minneapolis, August 11, 1990. **[271]**

Lewis, Russell. *The New Service Society*. London: Longman, 1973. **[264]**

Lewis, W.H. "Witness for the Prosecution," *TV Guide*, Nov. 30, 1974, pp. 5-7. **[369]**

Lichtenberg, Judith. "Foundations and Limits of Freedom of the Press," *Philosophy & Public Affairs* (Fall, 1987) 16(4): 329-355. **[56]**

Lichtenstein, Alien and Lawrence Rosenfeld. "Normative Expectations and Individual Decisions Concerning Media Gratification Choices," *Communication Research* (July, 1984) 11(3): 393-413. **[242]**

Lichter, Linda S. and S. Robert Lichter. *Prime Time Crime*. Washington, D.C.: The Media Institute, 1983. **[371]**

Lichter, S. Robert, Stanley Rothman and Linda S. Lichter. *The Media Elite: America's New Powerbrokers*. Bethesda, Maryland: Adler & Adler, 1986. **[148, 149, 164]**

Lichter, S. Robert, Linda S. Lichter, Stanley Rothman and Daniel Amundson. "Prime-Time Prejudice: TV's Images of Blacks and Hispanics," *Public Opinion*, July/August, 1987, p. 13-16. **[343]**

Liebler, Carol M. "Beyond Kerner: Ethnic Diversity and Minority Journalists," *Mass Comm Review* (1988) 15(2 & 3): 32-43. **[148]**

Liebler, Carol M. "Beyond Kerner: Ethnic Diversity and Minority Journalists," paper presented to the Mass Communication & Society Division at the annual conference of the Association for Education in Journalism and Mass Communication, Portland, OR, July, 1988. **[148]**

Liebman, NC "Mini-Series/Maxi-Messages: Ideology and the Interaction between 'Peter the Great,' AETNA, AT&T and Ford," *Journal of Film and Video* (Spring, 1987) 39(2): 5-18. **[372]**

Likert, Rensis. *The Human Organization*. New York: McGraw-Hill, 1967. **[154]**

Likert, Rensis. *New Patterns of Management*. New York: McGraw-Hill, 1961. **[154]**

Likert, Rensis. "Conversations with Rensis Likert," *Organizational Dynamics* (1973) 2: 32-49. **[154]**

Lill, D., C. Gross and R. Peterson. "The Inclusion of Social Responsibility Themes by Magazine Advertisers: A Longitudinal Study," *Journal of Advertising* (1986) 15(2): 35-41. **[336]**

Lillienstein, Maxwell J. "The Consolidation of the Book Industry," *American Bookseller*, April, 1987, p. 50. **[88]**

Limbacher, James L. *Sexuality in World Cinema*. Metuchen, NJ: Scarecrow, 1983. **[330]**

Lin, Carolyn A. "Audience Selectivity of Local Television Newscasts," *Journalism Quarterly* (Summer, 1992) 69(2): 373-382. **[252]**

Lin, Carolyn A. "The Functions of the VCR in the Home Leisure Environment," *Journal of Broadcasting & Electronic Media* (Summer, 1992) 36(3): 345-351. **[252]**

Lin, Carolyn A. "Exploring the Role of VCR Use in the Emerging Home Entertainment Culture," paper presented at the annual conference of the Midwest Association for Public Opinion Research, Chicago, November, 1991. **[251]**

Lin, Carolyn A. "Household Communication Patterns in the Home Video Culture," paper presented at the annual conference of the Midwest Association for Public Opinion Research (MAPOR), Chicago, IL., 1989. **[236]**

Lin, Carolyn A. "Relations among Audience Activity, Exposure and Satisfaction," paper presented at the annual conference of the Midwest Association for Public Opinion Research, Chicago, Nov. 18-19, 1988. **[268]**

Lin, Carolyn. "A Quantitative Analysis of World Wide VCR Penetration," *Communications* (1987) 13(3): 131-159. **[212]**

Lin, Carolyn A. and David J. Atkin. "Parental Mediation and Rulemaking for Adolescent Use of Television and VCRs," *Journal of Broadcasting & Electronic Media* (Winter, 1989) 33(1): 53-67. **[236]**

Lin, Carolyn and Michael B. Salwen. "Three Press Systems View Sino-U.S. Normalization," *Journalism Quarterly* (Summer, 1986) 63(2): 360-362. **[127]**

Lin, Nan. *The Study of Human Communication.* Indianapolis: Bobbs-Merrill Co., Inc., 1973. **[14]**

Lindlof, Thomas R. "Media Audiences as Interpretive Communitives," *Communication Yearbook*, Vol. 11, pp. 81-107. Newbury Park, CA: Sage, 1988. **[20, 21]**

Lindlof, Thomas R. (Ed.). *Natural Audiences: Qualitative Research of Media Uses and Effects.* Norwood, NJ: Ablex, 1987. **[271]**

Lindlof, Thomas R. "Social and Structural Constraints on Media Use in Incarceration," *Journal of Broadcasting & Electronic Media* (Summer, 1986) 30(3): 341-355. **[270, 278]**

Lindstrom, P.B. "Home Video: The Consumer Impact," *The VCR Age: Home Video and Mass Communication*, ed. M.R. Levy. Newbury Park, CA: Sage Publications, 1989, pp. 40-49. **[197]**

Lipman, Joanne. "Hurt by Ad Downturn, More Magazines Use Favorable Articles to Woo Sponsors," *Wall Street Journal*, July 30, 1991, p. 1B. **[67, 154]**

Lipman, Joanne. "Fall's Prime-Time TV Ad Prices Decline," *Wall Street Journal*, May 28, 1991, p. 4B. **[67, 154]**

Lipman, Joanne. "Media Business Is in Recession, But Very Few Dare to Admit It," *Wall Street Journal*, April 26, 1990, p. 7B. **[72, 94, 95]**

Lipman, Joanne and Kathleen A. Hughes. "Disney Prohibits Ads in Theaters Showing Its Movies," *Wall Street Journal*, Feb. 9, 1990, p. 1B. **[94, 95]**

Lipman, Joanne. "Network TV Provides Good Way for Advertisers to Reach Blacks," *Wall Street Journal*, May 25, 1989, p. 6B. **[233, 270]**

Lipschultz, Jeremy Harris. "A Comparison of Trial Lawyer and News Reporter Attitudes about Courthouse Communication," *Journalism Quarterly* (Winter, 1991) 68(4): 750-763. **[161]**

Lipschultz, Jeremy Harris. "The Nonreader Problem: A Closer Look at Avoiding the Newspaper," *Newspaper Research Journal* (Summer, 1987) 8(4): 59-69. **[276]**

Lipschultz, Jeremy Harris and Michael L. Hilt. "Political and Social Views of Broadcast General Managers and News Directors in the United States," paper presented to the Radio-Television Journalism Division at the annual conference of the Association for Education in Journalism and Mass Communication, Montreal, August, 1992. **[149]**

Lipset, S.M. and W.S. Schneider. *The Confidence Gap: Business, Labor, and Government.* New York: Free Press, 1983. **[208]**

Lipstadt, Deborah E. *Beyond Belief: The American Press and the Coming of the Holocaust 1933-1945.* New York: Free Press, 1986. **[371]**

Lipstein, B. "Theories of Advertising and Measurement Systems," *Attitude Research Enters the 80's.* Chicago: American Marketing Association, 1980. Cited in Jacoby and Hoyer, 1987. **[297]**

Lisby, Gregory C. "Commentary: Death Watch for America's Sister Newspapers," *Newspaper Research Journal* (Spring, 1986) 7(3): 27-33. **[97, 98]**

Lisenby, F. "American Women in Magazine Cartoons," *American Journalism* (1985) 2(2): 130-134. **[367]**

List, Karen K. "Magazine Portrayals of Women's Role in the New Republic," *Journalism History* (Summer, 1986) 13(2): 64-70. **[367]**

Litman, Barry R. "The Economics of the Television Market for Theatrical Movies," *Journal of Communication* (Autumn, 1979) 29(4): 20-33. **[68]**

Litman, Barry R. "Is Network Ownership in the Public Interest?" *Journal of Communication* (Spring, 1978) 28(2): 51-59. **[92]**

Litman, Barry R. and Elizabeth Bain. "The Viewership of Religious Television Programming: A Multidisciplinary Analysis of Televangelism," *Review of Religious Research* (June, 1989) 30(4): 329-343. **[270]**

Litman, Barry R. and Janet Bridges. "An Economic Analysis of Daily Newspaper Performance," *Newspaper Research Journal* (Spring, 1986) 7(3): 9-26. **[154]**

Litman, Barry R. and Linda S. Kohl. "Predicting Financial Success of Motion Pictures: The '80s Experience," *Journal of Media Economics* (Fall, 1989) 2(2): 35-48. **[67, 106]**

Litman, Barry R. and Linda S. Kohl. "Network Rerun Viewing in the Age of New Programming Services," *Journalism Quarterly* (Summer, 1992) 69(2): 383-391. **[217]**

Litman, Barry R., Linda S. Kohl and Gary Pizante. "Network Rerun Viewing in the Age of New Programming Services," paper presented to the Mass Communication Division at the annual conference of the Association for Education in Journalism, Minneapolis, Aug. 10, 1989. **[251]**

Litman, Barry. "Microeconomic Foundations," *Press Concentration and Monopoly: New Perspectives on Newspaper Ownership and Operation*, ed. Robert G. Picard, James P. Winter, Maxwell E. McCombs, and Stephen Lacy. Norwood, NJ: Ablex, 1988, pp. 3-34. **[98]**

Litman, G.K. "Women, Alcohol and Cultural Stereotyping: Updating the Myth," *Women's Studies International Quarterly* (1980) 3(4): 347-354. **[371]**

Little, Rod. "USA Snapshoots, World View of Sports on TV," *USA Today*, June 16, 1992, p. 1C. **[362]**

Littlejohn S.W. and D.M. Jabusch. *Persuasive Transactions*. Glenview, IL: Scott, Foresman and Co., 1987. **[257]**

Livant, B. "The Audience Commodity: On the Blindspot Debate," *Canadian Journal of Political & Social Theory* (1979) 3(1): 91-106. **[20]**

Livingstone, S.M. "Why People Watch Soap Operas: An Analysis of the Explanations of British Viewers," *European Journal of Communication* (March, 1988) 3(1): 55-80. **[256]**

Livingstone, S.M. "The Implicit Representation of Characters in 'Dallas'" A Multidimensional Scaling Approach," *Human Communication Research* (Spring, 1987) 13(3): 399-420. **[313]**

Livingstone, Sonia and Gloria Green. "Television Advertisements and the Portrayal of Gender," *British Journal of Social Psychology* (1986) 25: 149-154. **[367]**

Lloyd, Ronald. *American Film Directors*. New York: Franklin Watts, 1976. **[103]**

Lochte, Robert H. and John Warren. "A Channel Repertoire for TVRO Satellite Viewers," *Journal of Broadcasting & Electronic Media* (Winter, 1989) 33(1): 91-95. **[176]**

Loevinger, Lee. "Media Concentration: Myth and Reality," *The Antitrust Bulletin* (Fall, 1979), pp. 479-498. **[89]**

Loftus, G.R. and H.J. Kallman. "Encoding and Use of Detail Information in Picture Recognition," *Journal of Experimental Psychology: Human Learning and Memory* (1979) 5: 197-211. **[316]**

Loftus, Geoffrey and Susan Bell. "Two Types of Information in Picture Memory," *Journal of Experimental Psychology-Human Learning and Meaning* (1975) 104(2): 103-113. **[290]**

Logan, Robert and Bruce Garrison. "Factors Affecting News Coverage: Two Florida Papers and the Mariel Refugee Influx," *Newspaper Research Journal* (Fall, 1983) 5(1): 43-52.

Lometti, Guy E. and Tori Addington. "Testing Opposing Views of the Audience: How the Active Television Viewer Selects Programs," paper presented at the annual conference of the Association for Education in Journalism and Mass Communication, Montreal, August, 1992. **[244]**

Lometti, Guy E., Larry Hyams and Kangcong Zhang. "The Dynamics of Television Program Audience Accumulation," paper presented at the annual conference of the Association for Education in Journalism and Mass Communication, Montreal, August, 1992. **[272]**

Lometti, Guy E., Byron Reeves and Carl R. Bybee. "Investigating the Assumptions of Uses and Gratifications Research," *Communication Research* (July, 1977) 4(3): 321-338. **[278]**

Long, Marilee, Jocelyn Steinke, John Kalter, Amy Schwaab, Andrew Savagian, Nazima Jaffer, Jae Shim and Wayne Wenzel. "Explanation in Newspaper Science Section News Articles," paper presented to the Magazine Division at the annual conference of the Association for Education in Journalism and Mass Communication, Boston, August, 1991. **[162]**

Long, Marilee. "Explanation in Media Science Stories and the Influence of Production-Based Variables and Journalistic Conventions on Its Inclusion," paper presented to the Science Communication Section of the Magazine Division at the annual conference of the Association for Education in Journalism and Mass Communication, Montreal, August, 1992. **[162]**

Long, S.L. "Technological Change and Institutional Response: The Creation of American Broadcasting," *Journal of Economic Issues* (June, 1987) 21(2): 743-763. **[37, 58]**

Loov, Thomas and Fredrik Miegel. "The Notion of Lifestyle: Some Theoretical Contributions," *Nordicom Review* (1990) No. 1, pp. 21-31. **[279]**

Loughlin, Beverly. "The Women's Magazine Short-Story Heroine," *Journalism Quarterly* (Spring, 1983) 60(1): 138-142. **[354]**

Lounsbury, John W. and Linda L. Hoopes. "Five-Year Stability of Leisure Activity and Motivation Factors," *Journal of Leisure Research* (1988) 20(2): 118-134. **[216]**

Lowenstein, Ralph L. "Press Freedom as a Parameter of Political Democracy," *International and Intercultural Communications*, ed. Heinz-Dietrich Fischer and John C. Merrill. New York: Hastings House, 1970, pp. 129-140. **[60]**

Lowry, D.T. "Establishing Construct Validity of the Hayakawa-Lowry News Bias Categories," *Journalism Quarterly* (Autumn, 1986) 63(3): 573-580. **[208]**

Lowry, Dennis T. and David E. Towles. "Prime Time TV Portrayals of Sex, Contraception and Venereal Diseases," *Journalism Quarterly* (Summer, 1989) 66(2): 347-352. **[358]**

Lowry, Dennis T. and David E. Towles. "Soap Opera Portrayals of Sex, Contraception, and Sexually Transmitted Diseases," *Journal of Communication* (Spring, 1989) 39(2): 76-83. **[358]**

Luebke, B.F. "News about Women on the A Wire," *Journalism Quarterly* (Summer, 1985) 62(2): 329-333. **[367]**

Luebke, Barbara F. "Out of Focus: Images of Women and Men in Newspaper Photographs," *Sex Roles* (1989) 20(3/4): 121-133. **[353]**

Lukacs, *Studies in European Realism*. trans. Edith Bone. London, 1950. **[18]**

Luke, Carmen "Luther and the Foundations of Literacy, Secular Schooling and Educational Administration," *The Journal of Educational Thought* (August, 1989) 23(2): 120-140. **[26]**

Lull, James. *Inside Family Viewing: Ethnographic Research on Television's Audiences*. London: Routledge, 1990. **[236, 237, 239]**

Lull, James (Ed.). *World Families Watch Television*. Newbury Park, CA: Sage Publications, 1988. **[235, 271]**

Lull, James. "Constructing Rituals of Extension through Family Television Viewing," *World Families Watch Television*, ed. James Lull. Newbury Park, CA: Sage Publications, 1988, pp. 237-259. **[235, 271]**

Lull, James. "The Family and Television in World Cultures," *World Families Watch Television*, ed. James Lull. Newbury Park, CA: Sage Publications, 1988, pp. 9-21. **[235, 271]**

Lull, James T., Lawrence M. Johnson and Carol E. Sweeny. "Audiences for Contemporary Radio Formats," *Journal of Broadcasting* (Fall, 1978) 22: 439-453. **[270]**

Lull, James and Se-Wen Sun. "Agent of Modernization: Television and Urban Chinese Families," *World Families Watch Television*, ed. James Lull. Newbury Park, CA: Sage Publications, 1988, pp. 193-236. **[195, 235, 237]**

Lund, S. and A. Rolland. "Faith in the Media--An Unmixed Good?" *Nordicom Review* (1987) 1:1-8. **[209, 220]**

Lundy, K. "Cultural Identity as Basis for Community Television," *Nordicom Review of Nordic Mass Communication Research* (1988) 2: 24-30. **[239]**

Luttbeg, Norman R. "News Consensus: Do U.S. Newspapers Mirror Society's Happenings?" *Journalism Quarterly* (Autumn, 1983) 60(3): 484-488, 578. **[156]**

Luyken, G.M. "The VCR Explosion and Its Impact on Television Broadcasting in Europe," *Columbia Journal of World Business* (Fall, 1987) 22(3): 65-70.

Lyle, Jack and H.R. Hoffman. "Children's Use of Television and Other Media," *Television and Social Behavior* Vol. 4, *Television in Day-to-Day Life: Patterns of Use*, ed. E.A. Rubinstein, G.A. Comstock and J.P. Murray. Washington, D.C.: National Institute of Mental Health, 1971, pp. 129-256. **[261]**

Lynn, Michael, Sharon Shavitt and Thomas Ostrom. "Effects of Pictures on the Organization and Recall of Social Information," *Journal of Personality and Social Psychology* (1985) 49(5): 1160-1168. **[291, 316]**

Lyon, David. "Information Technology and Information Society: A Response to Fincham," *Sociology* (August, 1987) 21(3): 467-468. **[94]**

Lyon, David. "From 'Post-Industrialism' to 'Information Society': A New Social Transformation?" *Sociology* (November, 1986) 20(4): 577-588. **[64, 65, 94]**

Lysonski, S. "Female and Male Portrayals in Magazine Advertisements: A Re-examination," *Akron Business and Economic Review* (Summer, 1983) 14(2): 45-50. **[354]**

MacDonald, J. Fred. *Blacks and White TV*. Chicago: Nelson-Hall, Publishers, 1983. **[343]**

Mace, W.M. and R. Shaw. "Simple Kinetic Information for Transparent Depth," *Perception and Psychophysics* (1974) 15: 201-209. **[318]**

Machlup, Fritz. *The Production and Distribution of Knowledge in the United States*. Princeton, NJ: Princeton University Press, 1962. **[64]**

Maddox, L.M. and E.J. Zanot. "The Image of the Advertising Practitioner as Presented in the Mass Media, 1900-1972," *American Journalism* (1985) 2(2): 117-129. **[369]**

Madge, Timothy S. "Great Britain," *International Handbook of Broadcasting Systems*, ed. Philip T. Rosen. New York: Greenwood Press, 1988, pp. 105-117. **[48]**

Madigan, S. "Picture Memory," *Imagery, Memory and Cognition*, ed. J.C. Yuille. Hillsdale, NJ: Erlbaum, 1983, pp. 65-89. **[316]**

Makita, Tetsuo and Yasuko Muramatsu. "Changing Themes and Gender Images in Japanese TV Dramas, 1974-1984," *Studies of Broadcasting* (March, 1987) No. 23, pp. 51-72. Tokyo: NHK Theoretical Research Center. **[366]**

Manaev, Oleg. "A Vicious Circle in Soviet Media--Audience Relations," *European Journal of Communication* (1989) 4: 287-305. **[59]**

Mandler, J.M. "A Code in the Node: The Use of Story Schema in Retrieval," *Discourse Processes* (1978) 1: 14-35. **[316]**

Mandler, Jean M. and N.S. Johnson. "Remembrances of Things Parsed: Story Structures and Recall," *Cognitive Psychology* (1977) 9: 111-151. **[293, 312, 316]**

Mann, Michael (ed.) *The International Encyclopedia of Sociology*. New York: Continuum, 1984. **[269]**

Mannell, Roger C. and William Bradley. "Does Greater Freedom Always Lead to Greater Leisure? Testing a Person X Environment Model of Freedom and Leisure," *Journal of Leisure Research* (1986) 18(4): 215-230. **[211]**

Markus, M. Lynne. "Toward a 'Critical Mass' Theory of Interactive Media: Universal Access, Interdependence and Diffusion," *Communication Research* (October, 1987) 14(5): 491-511. **[42]**

Marshall, N. and M. Glock. "Comprehension of Connected Discourse," *Reading Research Quarterly* (1979) 16: 10-56. **[316]**

Martin, L. John and Anju Grover Chaudhary. *Comparative Mass Media Systems*. New York: Longman, 1983. **[59]**

Martin, Ralph R., Garrett J. O'Keefe, and Oguz B. Nayman. "Opinion Agreement and Accuracy Between Editors and Their Readers," *Journalism Quarterly* (Autumn, 1972) 49:460-468. **[132]**

Martin, Shannon Rossi. "Proximity of Event as Factor in Selection of News Sources," *Journalism Quarterly* (Winter, 1988) 65(4): 986-989, 1043. **[156]**

Martindale, Carolyn. "Coverage of Black Americans in Five Newspapers since 1950," *Journalism Quarterly* (Summer, 1985) 62(2): 321-328, 436. **[345]**

Martindale, Carolyn. *The White Press and Black America*. New York: Greenwood Press, 1986. **[345]**

Martindale, Carolyn. "Coverage of Black Americans in Four Major Newspapers, 1950-1989," *Newspaper Research Journal* (Summer, 1990) 11(3): 96-112. **[345]**

Maslin, Janet. "If It's in the Book, It Doesn't Mean It's in the Movie," *New York Times*, Feb. 28, 1992, p. 1B. **[153]**

Masterton, M. "Mass Media in the South Pacific," *Media Information Australia* (May, 1989) 52: 46-49. **[150]**

Matelski, M.J. *The Soap Opera Evolution: America's Enduring Romance with Daytime Drama.* Jefferson, NC: McFarland & Co., 1988. **[335]**

Matelski, Marilyn J. "Image and Influence: Women in Public Television," *Journalism Quarterly* (Spring, 1985) 62(1): 147-150. **[366]**

Mathewson, William. "Postscripts," *Wall Street Journal*, Aug. 3, 1990, p. 8A. **[59]**

May, W.F. "Professional Ethics, the University, and the Journalist," *Journal of Mass Media Ethics* (Spring/Summer, 1986) 1(2): 20-31. **[166]**

Mayer, Jane. "Washington Press Corps, in Iran-Contra Affair, Raises Questions on Its Handling of Tough Stories," *The Wall Street Journal*, May 1, 1987, p. 42. **[138]**

Mayerle, Judine and David Rarick. "The Image of Education in Primetime Network Television Series 1948-1988," *Journal of Broadcasting & Electronic Media* (Spring, 1989) 33(2): 139-157. **[368]**

Mazingo, Sherrie. "An Exploratory Analysis of the Impact of VCR Movie Cassette Use and Pay-TV Movie Subscription on Movie Theater Attendance," *Mass Comm Review* (1987) 14(3): 30-35. **[277]**

Mazur, Janet. "The Exodus from Fleet Street," *Editor and Publisher* (1987) Sept. 26, pp. 14-15, 44. **[59]**

McAdams, Katherine C. "Readability Reconsidered: A Study of Reader Reactions to Differences in Fog Indexes," paper presented at the annual conference of the Association for Education in Journalism and Mass Communication, Boston, August, 1991. **[292]**

McAdams, Katherine C. "Non-Monetary Conflicts of Interest for Newspaper Journalists," *Journalism Quarterly* (Winter, 1986) 63(4): 700-705, 727. **[110, 155]**

McArthur, Colin. "The Iconography of the Gangster Film," in Barry K. Grant, ed. *Film Genre: Theory and Criticism* (Metuchen, NJ: The Scarecrow Press, Inc.), pp. 118-123, 1977. **[330]**

McCain, Thomas, Joseph Chilberg and Jacob Wakshlag. "The Effects of Camera Angle on Source Credibility and Attraction," *Journal of Broadcasting* (1977) 21: 35-46. **[220, 301]**

McCain, Thomas A. and G. Ferrell Lowe. "Localism in Western European Radio Broadcasting: Untangling the Wireless," *Journal of Communication* (Winter, 1990) 40(1): 86-101. **[45, 49, 59]**

McCain, Tom. "The Invisible Influence: European Audience Research," *InterMedia* (July-September, 1985) 13(4/5): 74-78. **[173]**

McCall, R.B. "Exploratory Manipulation and Play in the Human Infant," *Monographs of the Society for Research in Child Development* (1974) 39 (No. 155).Cited in Iso-Ahola and Weissinger (1990). **[274]**

McCall, Robert B. "Science and the Press: Like Oil and Water? *American Psychologist* (February, 1988) 43(2): 87-94. **[163]**

McCarthy, Michael J. "Viewers Will Get to Place Orders for News Stories," *Wall Street Journal*, July 13, 1990, p. 3B. **[74]**

McCartney, Hunter P. "Applying Fiction Conflict Situations to Analysis of News Stories," *Journalism Quarterly* (Spring, 1987) 64(1): 163-170. **[156]**

McChesney, Robert W. "Labor and the Markeplace of Ideas," *Journalism Monographs* (August, 1992) No. 134. **[37]**

McChesney, Robert W. "Toward a Reinterpretation of the American Press-Radio War of the 1930s," paper presented to the History Division at the annual conference of the Association for Education in Journalism and Mass Communication, Minneapolis, August, 1990. **[58]**

McChesney, Robert W. "The Battle for the U.S. Airwaves, 1928-1935," *Journal of Communication* (Autumn, 1990) 40(4): 29-57. **[37, 58]**

McChesney, Robert W. "Crusade Against Mammon: Father Harney, WLWL and the Debate Over Radio in the 1930s," *Journalism History* (Winter, 1987) 14(4): 118-130. **[37]**

McCleneghan, J. Sean. "Sportswriters Talk about Themselves: An Attitude Study," *Journalism Quarterly* (Spring, 1990) 67(1): 114-118. **[160]**

McCombs, Maxwell E. "Testing the Myths: A Statistical Review 1967-86," *Gannett Center Journal* (Spring, 1988) 2(2): 101-108. **[147, 148, 164]**

McCombs, Maxwell. "Effect of Monopoly in Cleveland on Diversity of Newspaper Content," *Journalism Quarterly* (Winter, 1987) 64(4): 740-744. **[91]**

McCombs, Maxwell E. "Mass Media in the Marketplace," *Journalism Monographs*, No. 24 (1972). **[42, 59, 169]**

McCombs, Maxwell E. and Chaim Eyal. "Spending on Mass Media," *Journal of Communication* (Winter, 1980) 30: 153-158. **[59]**

McCombs, Maxwell E. and J.B. Mauro. "Predicting Newspaper Readership from Content Characteristics," *Journalism Quarterly* (1977) 54: 3-7. **[296]**

McCombs, Maxwell E., John B. Mauro and Jinok Son. "Predicting Newspaper Readership from Content Characteristics: A Replication," *Newspaper Research Journal* (Fall, 1988) 10(1): 25-29. **[296]**

McCombs, Maxwell and Jack Nolan. "The Relative Constancy Approach to Consumer Spending for Media," *Journal of Media Economics* (Summer, 1992) 5(2): 43-52. **[59]**

McCombs, Maxwell E. and Donald I. Shaw. "Structuring the 'Unseen Envionment,'" *Journal of Communication* (Spring, 1976) 26(2): 18-22. **[161]**

McCombs, Maxwell E. and J.M. Smith. "The Graphics of Prose," *Journalism Quarterly* (1971) 48: 134-136. **[290]**

McCombs, Maxwell E. and Jinok Son. "Patterns of Economic Support for Mass Media during a Decade of Electronic Innovation, paper presented at the annual conference of the Association for Education in Journalism and Mass Communication, Norman, Okla., 1986. **[42]**

McCombs, Maxwell E., Jinok Son and Hae-Kyong Bang. "Impact of Journalism Genres on Readership," paper presented to the Communication Theory and Methodology Division at the annual conference of the Association for Education in Journalism and Mass Communication, Portland, OR, July, 1988. **[147, 340]**

McConkey, K.M., S.M. Roche and P.W. Sheehan. "Television Reports of Forensic Hypnosis: What's on the News?" *Australian Journal of Social Issues* (February, 1989) 24(1): 44-53. **[371]**

McConkie, George W., N. Roderick Underwood, David Zola and G.S. Wolverton. "Some Temporal Characteristics of Processing during Reading," *Journal of Experimental Psychology: Human Perception and Performance* (1985) 11(2): 168-186. **[313]**

McCracken, Kevin W.J. "Australia and Australians: View from New York 'Times,'" *Journalism Quarterly* (Spring, 1987) 64(1): 183-187. **[371]**

McCusker, John J. "The Business Press in England before 1775," *The Library* (September, 1986) Sixth Series, 8(3): 14-231. **[28]**

McDonald, Daniel G. "Media Orientation and Television News Viewing," *Journalism Quarterly* (Spring, 1990) 67(1): 11-19. **[276]**

McDonald, Daniel G. "Generational Aspects of Television Coviewing," *Journal of Broadcasting & Electronic Media* (Winter, 1986) 30(1): 75-85. **[238]**

McDonald, Daniel G. and Carroll J. Glynn. "The Stability of Media Gratifications," *Journalism Quarterly* (Autumn, 1984) 61(3): 542-549, 741. **[248, 274]**

McDonald, Daniel G. and Stephen D. Reese. "Television News and Audience Selectivity," *Journalism Quarterly* (Winter, 1987) 64(4): 763-768. **[245]**

McDonald, Daniel G. and Russell Schechter. "Audience Role in the Evolution of Fictional Television Content," *Journal of Broadcasting & Electronic Media* (Winter, 1988) 32(1): 61-71. **[334]**

McGee, L. "Awareness of Text Structure: Effects of Children's Recall of Expository Text," *Reading Research Quarterly* (1982) 17: 581-590. **[316]**

McGee, Vikki A. and Andrew M. Weaver. "Economic News Literacy as Defined by the Economic Vocabulary of Television Newswriters," *International Journal of Instructional Media* (1988) 15(3): 258-270. **[369]**

McGill, Lawrence T. "The Twilight Zone Beat," *Gannett Center Journal* (Winter, 1991) 5(1): 11-23. **[134, 341]**

McGrath, Kristin and Cecilie Gaziano. "Dimensions of Media Credibility: Highlights of the 1985 ASNE Survey," *Newspaper Research Bureau* (Winter, 1986) 7(2): 55-67. **[205]**

McGregor, Donald and Paul Slovic. "Graphic Representation of Judgmental Information," *Human-Computer Interaction* (1986) 3: 179-200. **[290]**

McIntyre, J.S. "Repositioning a Landmark: The Hutchins Commission and Freedom of the Press," *Critical Studies in Mass Communication* (June, 1987) 4(2): 136-160. **[26, 51]**

McKean, Michael L. and Vernon A. Stone. "Deregulation and Competition: Explaining the Absence of Local Broadcast News Operations," *Journalism Quarterly* (Fall, 1992) 69(3): 713-723. **[68]**

McKechnie, G.E. "The Psychological Structure of Leisure: Past Behavior," *Journal of Leisure Research* (1974) 6: 27-45. **[274]**

McKenzie, Robert. "Comparing the Use of Media by Americans in Britain and Britons in the United States for Accessing 'Home Country' Information," paper presented at the annual conference of the Speech Communication Association, New Orleans, La., Nov. 3-6, 1988. **[277]**

McLean, Polly E. "State-Press Relations in Grenada, 1955-1983," *Howard Journal of Communications* (Fall, 1990) 2(4): 333-348. **[49]**

McLeod, Jack M., C.K. Atkin and S.H. Chaffee. "Adolescents, Parents and Television Use: Self-Report and Other-Report Measures from the Wisconsin Sample," *Television and Social Behavior*, ed. G.A. Comstock and E.A. Rubinstein. Washington, D.C.: U.S. Government Printing Office, 1972. **[271]**

McLeod, Jack M. and Lee B. Becker. "Testing the Validity of Gratification Measures through Political Effects Analysis," *The Uses of Mass Communications: Current Perspectives on Gratifications Research*, ed. Jay G. Blumler and Elihu Katz. Beverly Hills: Sage Publications, 1974, pp. 137-164. **[273]**

McLeod, Jack M., C.R. Bybee and J.A. Durall. "Evaluating Media Performance by Gratifications Sought and Received," *Journalism Quarterly* (1982) 59: 3-12, 59. **[246, 273]**

McLeod, Jack and S. Hawley Jr. "Professionalism among Newsmen," *Journalism Quarterly* (Autumn, 1964) 41: 529-538. **[165]**

McLeod, Jack M. and P.G. McDonald. "Beyond Simple Exposure: Media Orientations and Their Impact on the Political Process," *Communication Research* (1985) 12: 3-33. **[273]**

McLeod, Jack M. and Garrett J. O'Keefe Jr. "The Socialization Perspective and Communication Behavior," *Current Perspectives in Mass Communication Research*, ed. F. Gerald Kline and Phillip J. Tichenor. Beverly Hills, Sage, 1972, pp. 121-168. **[261]**

McLeod, Jack M. and Byron Reeves. "On the Nature of Mass Media Effects," *Television and Social Behavior: Beyond Violence and Children*, ed. S.B. Withey and R.P. Abeles. Hillsdale, NJ: Lawrence Erlbaum, 1980. **[298]**

McLuhan, Marshall. "The Role of New Media in Social Change," *Marshall McLuhan: The Man and His message*, ed. G. Sanderson and F. Macdonald. Goldon, CO: Fulcrum, Inc., 1989, pp. 34-40. **[310]**

McMane, Aralynn Abare. "A Comparative Study of Journalism and Gender in France," paper presented to the Commission on the Status of Women at the annual conference of the Association for Education in Journalism and Mass Communication, Montreal, August, 1992. **[148, 164]**

McManus, John. "An Economic Theory of News Selection," paper presented to the Mass Communication and Society Division at the annual conference of the Association for Education in Journalism and Mass Communication, Portland, OR, July, 1988. **[145]**

McManus, John. "How Local Television Learns What Is News," *Journalism Quarterly* (Winter, 1990) 67(4): 672-683. **[145]**

McManus, John. "How Objective Is Local Television News?" paper presented to the Mass Communication Division at the annual conference of the International Communication Association, Chicago, May, 1991. **[129, 145, 159]**

McManus, John. "How Objective Is Local Television News?" *Mass Comm Review* (1991) 18(3): 21-30. **[129, 145, 159]**

McNair, Brian. "Glasnost and Restructuring in the Soviet Media," *Media, Culture and Society* (1989) 11: 327-349. **[59]**

McNelly, J.T. and F. Izcaray. "International News Exposure and Images of Nations," *Journalism Quarterly* (Autumn, 1986) 63(3): 546-553. **[121]**

McQuail, D. "From Bias to Objectivity and Back: Competing Paradigms for News Analysis and a Pluralistic Alternative," *Studies in Communication: News and Knowledge*, ed. Thelma McCormack, vol.3. Greenwich, CT: JAI Press, 1986, pp. 1-36.

McQuail, Denis. "Communication Research Past, Present and Future: American Roots and European Branches," *Public Communication: The New Imperatives*, ed. M. Ferguson. Newbury Park, CA: Sage Publications, 1990, pp. 135-151. **[44]**

McQuail, Denis, Jay G. Blumler and J.R. Brown. "The Television Audience: A Revised Perspective," *Sociology of Mass Communications*, ed. Denis McQuail. Harmondsworth: Penguin, 1972. **[241, 247]**

McQuail, Denis and the Euromedia Research Group. "Caging the Beast: Constructing a Framework for the Analysis of Media Change in Western Europe," *European Journal of Communication* (1990) 5: 313-331.

Meadow, H.L. and M.J. Sirgy (Ed.). *Quality-of-Life Studies in Marketing & Management.* Blacksburg, VA: Virginia Polytechnic Institute & State University, 1990. **[279]**

Meadowcroft, Jeanne M. and Dolf Zillmann. "Women's Comedy Preferences during the Menstrual Cycle," *Communication Research* (April, 1987) 14(2): 204-218. **[273]**

Meehan, E. "Conceptualizing Culture as a Commodity: The Problem of Television," *Critical Studies in Mass Communication* (1986) 3: 448-457. **[20]**

Meeske, Milan D. and Mohamad Hamid Javaheri. "Network Television Coverage of the Iranian Hostage Crisis," *Journalism Quarterly* (Winter, 1982) 59(4): 641-645. **[371]**

Mehrabian, Albert. *Public Places and Private Spaces.* New York: Basic Books, 1976. **[268]**

Mele, Alfred R. "Intention, Belief, and Intentional Action," *American Philosophical Quarterly* (January, 1989) 26(1): 19-30. **[272]**

Melton, G.W. and M.L. Galician. "A Sociological Approach to the Pop Music Phenomenon: Radio and Music Video Utilization for Expectation, Motivation and Satisfaction," *Popular Music and Society* (Fall, 1987) 11(3): 35-46. **[184]**

Melton, G.W. and G.L. Fowler. "Female Roles in Radio Advertising," *Journalism Quarterly* (Spring, 1987) 64(1): 145-149. **[353]**

Melwani, G. "Impression Formation and the Media: A Social Cognitive Exploration," paper presented to the Information Systems Division at the annual conference of the International Communication Association, San Francisco, May, 1989. **[310, 311]**

Mencher, Melvin. *News Reporting and Writing*. 2nd ed. Dubuque, Iowa: William C. Brtown Co., 1981. **[292]**

Menneer, P. "Audience Appreciation--A Different Story from Audience Numbers," *Journal of the Market Research Society* (July, 1987) 29(3): 241-264. **[195]**

Merrill, John C. *Global Journalism: Survey of International Communication*. New York: Longman, 2nd ed., 1991. **[59]**

Merrill, John C. "How Inclined Are Nations to Control the Press?" paper presented at the annual convention of the International Communication Association, New Orleans, May 29-June 2, 1988. **[60]**

Merrill, John C. "Inclination of Nations to Control Press and Attitudes on Professionalism," *Journalism Quarterly* (1988) 65(4): 839-844. **[60]**

Merrill, John C. "Governments and Press Control: Global Attitudes on Journalistic Matters," *Political Communication and Persuasion* (1987) 4(4): 223-262. **[57]**

Merrill, John C. "Professionalization: Danger to Press Freedom and Pluralism," *Journal of Mass Media Ethics* (Spring/Summer, 1986) 1(2): 56-60. **[151]**

Merrill, John C. *The Imperative of Freedom*. New York: Hastlngs House, Publishers, 1974. **[56, 129, 165]**

Merrill, John C. and Ralph L. Lowenstein. *Media, Messages and Men*. New York: David McKay Co., Inc., 1971. **[53]**

Merton, Robert. "Patterns of Influence: A Study of Interpersonal Influences and of Communication Behaviors in a Local Community," *Communication Research, 1948-49*, ed. Paul Lazarsfeld and W. Stanton. New York: Harper & Co., 1950. **[239]**

Messaris, Paul. "To What Extent Does One Have to Learn to Interpret Movies?" *Film/Culture*, ed. S. Thomas. Metuchen, NJ: Scarecrow Press, 1982. **[302]**

Messaris, Paul. "The Role of Visual 'Literacy' in Film Communication," paper presented at the annual conference of the Speech Communication Association, Boston, MA, Nov. 6, 1987. **[302]**

Metzger, G.D. "Cable Television Audiences," *Journal of Advertising Research* (August/September, 1983) 23(4): 41-49. **[279]**

Meunier, F. and M. Volle. "The Effect of the New Communications Media on Employment," *Information Economics and Policy* (September, 1986) 2(3): 195-210.**[65]**

Meyer, B.J.F. "What Is Remembered from Prose: A Function of Passage Structure," *Discourse Production and Comprehension Vol. 1*, ed. R.O. Freedle, 1977, Norwood, NJ: Ablex, pp. 307-336. **[316]**

Meyer, B.J.F. *The Organization of Prose and Its Effects on Memory*. Amsterdam: North Holland Publishing, 1975. **[316]**

Meyer, B.J.F., D.M. Brandt and G.J. Bluth. "Use of Top-Level Structure in Text: Key for Reading Comprehension in Ninth-Grade Students," *Reading Research Quarterly* (1980) 16: 72-103. **[316]**

Meyer, B.J.F. and R.O. Freedle. *The Effects of Different Discourse Types on Recall*. Princeton, NJ; Educational Testing Service, 1979. **[316]**

Meyer, David F. and Roger W. Schvaneveldt. "Facilitation in Recognizing Pairs of Words: Evidence of a Dependence between Retrieval Operations," *Journal of Experimental Psychology* (1971) 90: 227-234. **[313]**

Meyer, P. "Defining and Measuring Credibility of Newspapers: Developing an Index," *Journalism Quarterly* (Fall, 1988) 65(3): 567-574. **[207]**

Meyer, Philip and Stanley T. Wearden. "The Effects of Public Ownership on Newspaper Companies: A Preliminary Inquiry," *Public Opinion Quarterly* (Fall, 1984) 48: 564-577. **[98]**

Meyers, Marian. "Creating Diversity in the News: Reporters and Their Jobs," paper presented in the Mass Communication and Society Division at the annual conference of the Association for Education in Journalism and Mass Communication, Minneapolis, August, 1990. **[159]**

Meyrowitz, Joshua. *No Sense of Place: The Impact of Electronic Media on Social Behavior.* New York: Oxford University Press, 1985. **[7]**

Michaelson, Judith. "Independent Producers Get Boost," *Plain Dealer*, Nov. 18, 1988, p. 13B. Los Angeles Times dispatch. **[155]**

Mickiewicz, Ellen. *Split Signals: Television and Politics in the Soviet Union.* New York: Oxford University Press, 1988. **[59]**

Miege, B. "The Logics at Work in the New Cultural Industries," *Media, Culture and Society* (July, 1987) 9(3): 291-300. **[63]**

Milavsky, J. Ronald. "How Good Is the A.C. Nielsen People-Meter System: A Review of the Report by the Committee on Nationwide Television Audience Measurement," *Public Opinion Quarterly* (Spring, 1992) 56: 102-115. **[171]**

Millar, Frank E. and L. Edna Rogers. "A Relational Approach to Interpersonal Communication," *Explorations in Interpersonal Communication*, ed. Gerald R. Miller. Beverly Hills: Sage Publications, 1976, pp. 87-103. **[9]**

Miller, Carolyn Boulger. "An Analysis of Competition for Listeners and Advertisers between New England Areas of Dominant Influence," paper presented to the Media Management and Economics Division at the annual conference of the Association for Education in Journalism and Mass Communication, Montreal, August, 1992. **[98]**

Miller, G.A. (Ed.). *Linguistic Communication: Perspectives for Research.* Newark, DE: International Reading Association, 1973. Cited in Hall (1989). **[314]**

Miller, George A. "Some Preliminaries to Psycholinguistics," *American Psychologist* (1965) 20: 15-20. **[314]**

Miller, George A. "The Magical Number Seven, Plus or Minus Two: Some Limits on Our Capacity for Processing Information," *Psychology Review* (1956) 63: 81-97. **[314]**

Miller, Gerald R. and Michael J. Sunnafrank. "All Is for One But One Is Not for All: A Conceptual Perspective of Interpersonal Communication," *Human Communication Theory*, ed. Frank E.X. Dance. New York: Harper & Row, 1982, pp. 220-242. **[127]**

Miller, J. "Divided Attention: Evidence for Coactivation with Redundant Signals," *Cognitive Psychology* (1982) 14: 247-279. **[319]**

Miller, James R. and Walter Kintsch. "Readability and Recall of Short Prose Passages: A Theoretical Analysis," *Journal of Experimental Psychology: Human Learning and Memory* (1980) 6(4): 335-354. **[284, 314]**

Miller, Laurence. "How Many Films Noirs Are There?: How Statistics Can Help Answer this Question," *Empirical Studies of the Arts* (1989) 7(1): 51-55. **[330]**

Miller, M. and S. Reese. "Media Dependency as Interaction: Effects of Exposure and Reliance on Political Activity and Efficacy," *Communication Research* (1982) 2: 227-248. **[305, 306]**

Miller, M. Mark, Julie L. Andsager and Robert O. Wyatt. "How Gender and Select Demographics Relate to Support for Expressive Rights," paper presented to the Communication Theory & Methodology Division at the annual conference of the Association for Education in Journalism and Mass Communication, Montreal, August, 1992. **[204]**

Miller, M.M., S.-L. Chen, and S.E. Everett. "Trading Places; Reader Reactions to the Knoxville Newspaper Switch," *Newspaper Research Journal* (Winter, 1988) 9(2): 49-58. **[213]**

Miller, Michael W. "High-Tech Alteration of Sights and Sounds Divides the Art World," *Wall Street Journal*, Sept. 1, 1987, p. 1. **[329]**

Miller, Ralph R., Wesley J. Kasprow and Todd R. Schachtman. "Retrieval Variability: Sources and Consequences," *American Journal of Psychology* (1986) 99(2): 145-218. **[313]**

Miller, Steven (Ed.) *America's Watching: 30th Anniversary 1959-1989.* The 1989 TIO/Roper Report. New York: Television Information Office. (Roper Organization). **[173, 184, 202, 218, 219]**

Miller, Susan. "America's Dailies and the Drive to Capture Lost Readers," *Gannett Center Journal* (Spring, 1987) 1(1): 56-68. **[177]**

Miller, Susan Heilmann. "Reporters and Congressmen: Living in Symbiosis," *Journalism Monographs* (1978) 53: 25. **[161]**

Mills, Kay. *A Place in the News: From the Women's Pages to the Front Page.* New York: Dodd, Mead & Co., 1988. **[148]**

Minsky, M. "Frame-System Theory," *Theoretical Issues in Natural Language Processing*, ed. R.C. Shank and B. Nash-Webber. Cambridge, MA: MIT, 1975. **[320]**

Miraldi, R. *Muckraking and Objectivity: Journalism's Colliding Traditions.* Contributions to the Study of Mass Media and Communications, No. 18. Westport, Conn.: Greenwood Press, 1990. **[33]**

Miraldi, Robert. "Scaring Off the Muckrakers with the Threat of Libel," *Journalism Quarterly* (Fall, 1988) 65(3): 609-614. **[163]**

Mitchell, A.A. "Cognitive Processes Initiated by Exposure to Advertising," *Information Processing Research in Advertising*, ed. R.J. Harris. Hillsdale, NJ: Lawrence Erlbaum Associates, 1983, pp. 13-42. **[263]**

Miyo, Y. "The Knowledge-Gap Hypothesis and Media Depedency," *Communication Yearbook 7*, ed. R. Bostom. Beverly Hills, CA: Sage, 1983, pp. 626-650. **[305, 306]**

Mobley, G.M. "The Political Influence of Television Ministers," *Review of Religious Research* (June, 1984) 25(4): 314-320. **[231]**

Mohr, Phillip J. "Parental Guidance of Children's Viewing of Evening Television Programs," *Journal of Broadcasting* (Spring, 1979) 23(2): 213-228. **[261]**

Molitor, Fred. "How Accurate Is the Science News We Receive from the Mass Media?" paper presented to the Mass Communication Division at the annual conference of the International Communication Association, Chicago, May, 1991. **[163]**

Monk, Abraham. "Aging, Loneliness and Communications," *American Behavioral Scientist* (May/June, 1988) 31(5): 532-563. **[278]**

Monmonier, Mark. *Maps with the News: The Development of American Journalistic Cartography.* Chicago: University of Chicago Press, 1989. **[339]**

Monmonier, Mark and Val Pipps. "Weather Maps and Newspaper Design: Response to 'USA Today'?" *Newspaper Research Journal* (Summer, 1987) 8(4): 31-42.

Montgomery, Kathryn C. *Target: Prime Time - Advocacy Groups and the Struggle over Entertainment Television.* New York: Oxford University Press, 1989. **[117]**

Montgomery, Louise F. "Criticism of Government Officials in the Mexican Press, 1951-1980," *Journalism Quarterly* (Winter, 1985) 62(4): 763-769. **[59]**

Monti, Daniel J. "Biased and Unbiased News: Reporting Racial Controversies in the New York Times. 1960-1964," *The Sociological Quarterly* (Summer, 1979) 20: 399-409. **[132]**

Moore, Barbara and Michael Singletary. "Scientific Sources' Perceptions of Network News Accuracy," *Journalism Quarterly* (Winter, 1985) 62(4): 816-823. **[144, 163]**

Moore, Barbara A., Herbert H. Howard and George C. Johnson. "TV News Viewing and the Decline of the Afternoon Newspaper," *Newspaper Research Journal* (Fall, 1988) 10(1): 15-22. **[184]**

Moore, Brian C.J. *An Introduction to the Psychology of Hearing.* London: Academic Press, 1982. **[309]**

Moore, R., G. Moschis and L. Stephens. "Mass Media and Interpersonal Influences on the Acquisition of Consumer Competencies," paper presented at the annual conference of the International Communication Association, Chicago, 1978. **[278]**

Moore, Wayne S., David R. Bowers and Theodore A. Granovsky. "What Are Magazines Telling Us about Insects?" *Journalism Quarterly* (Autumn, 1982) 59(3): 464-467. **[371]**

Moores, S. "'The Box on the Dresser': Memories of Early Radio and Everyday Life," *Media, Culture and Society* (January, 1988) 10(1): 23-40. **[235]**

Morais, Richard C. "The Whole Thing Is Breaking Up," *Forbes* (May 18, 1987) pp. 148-153. **[59]**

Morgan, Michael. "Heavy Television Viewing and Perceived Quality of Life," *Journalism Quarterly* (Autumn, 1984) 61(3): 499-504, 740. **[246]**

Morgan, Michael, Alison Alexander, James Shanahan and Cheryl Harris. "Adolescents, VCRs, and the Family Environment," *Communication Research* (February, 1990) 17(1): 83-106. **[250, 271, 277]**

Morgenstern, Stephanie. "The Epistemic Autonomy of Mass Media Audiences," *Critical Studies in Mass Communication* (September, 1992) 9: 293-310. **[21]**

MORI Research, Inc. *Newspaper Credibility: Building Reader Trust*, commissioned by the American Society of Newspaper Editors, Minneapolis, April, 1985. **[199]**

Moriarty, Sandra Ernst. "A Search for the Optimum Line Length," *Journalism Quarterly* (Summer, 1986) 63(2): 337-340, 435. **[288]**

Moriarty, Sandra Ernst. "Trends in Advertising Typography," *Journalism Quarterly* (Summer, 1982) 59(2): 290-294. **[339]**

Morley, D. *The 'Nationwide' Audience: Structure and Decoding.* London: British Film Institute, 1980. **[20]**

Morley, David. "Domestic Relations: The Framework of Family Viewing in Great Britain," *World Families Watch Television*, ed. James Lull. Newbury Park, CA: Sage Publications, 1988, pp. 22-48. **[236, 237]**

Morley, David. *Family Television: Cultural Power and Domestic Leisure.* Comedia Series No. 37. London: Comedia Publishing Group, 1986. **[271]**

Morre, T.E. and L. Cadeau. "The Representation of Women, the Elderly and Minorities in Canadian Television Commercials," *Canadian Journal of Behavioral Science* (July, 1985) 17(3): 215-225. **[367]**

Morris, Jon D. "A Review of Literature on the Effects of Production Techniques in Instructional Television," *International Journal of Instructional Media* (1988) 15(1): 41-47. **[300]**

Morris, Jon D. "The Use of Television Production Techniques to Facilitate the Learning Process: An Experiment," *International Journal of Instructional Media* (1988) 15(3): 244-256. **[300]**

Moslem, Shima. "Women and the Media in Bangladesh: A Case Study," *Media Asia* (1989) 16(3): 148-153. **[367]**

Mott, Frank Luther. *A History of American Magazines.* Vol. 2, 1850-1865; Vol. 3, 1865-1885; Vol. 4, 1885-1905; Vol. 5, 1905-1930. Cambridge, MA: Harvard University Press, 1968. **[58]**

Mukerji, Chandra and Michael Schudson. "Popular Culture," *Annual Review of Sociology* (1986) 12:47-66. **[13, 51]**

Mulcahy, P.I. and S.J. Samuels. "Problem-Solving Schemata for Text Types: A Comparison of Narrative and Expository Text Structures," *Reading Psychology* (1987) 8: 247-256. **[316]**

Mulgan, G.J. *Communication and Control.* New York: Guilford Press, 1991. **[57]**

Multer, Paul and Candace Mayson. "Role of Graphics in Item Selection from Menus," *Behavior and Information Technology* (1986) 5(1): 89-95. **[289]**

Muramatsu, Yasuko. "Of Women by Women for Women?: Japanese Media Today," *Studies of Broadcasting* (1990) No. 26. Japan: NHK (Japan Broadcasting Corp.), pp. 83-104. **[148, 366]**

Murdock, G. "Blindspots about Western Marxism: A Reply to Dallas Smythe," *Canadian Journal of Political & Social Theory* (1978) 2(2): 109-119. **[20]**

Murdock, Graham and Peter Golding. "Capitalism, Communication and Class Relations," *Mass Communication and Society.* ed. James Curran, Michael Gurevitch and Janet Woolacott. London: Edward Arnold Publishers, Ltd., in association with The Open University Press, 1977, pp. 12-43. **[20]**

Murphy, James E. and Donald R. Avery. "A Comparison of Alaskan Native and Non-Native Newspaper Content," *Journalism Quarterly* (Summer, 1983) 60(2): 316-322. **[346]**

Murphy, James E. and Donald R. Avery. "A Study of Favorability Toward Natives in Alaskan Newspapers," *Newspaper Research Journal* (Fall, 1982) 4(1): 39-45. **[346]**

Murray, M.D. "The St. Louis Post-Dispatch Campaign Against Radio's Middle Commercials," *American Journalism* (1989) 6(1): 30-40. **[40]**

Murray, M.J. and S.E. White. "VCR Owners' Use of Pay Cable Services," *Journalism Quarterly* (Spring, 1987) 64(1): 193-195. **[213]**

Nace, T. "Lighting a Path to the Future," *Macworld* (February, 1986) 3: 100-106. **[177]**

Naficy, Hamid. "Television Intertextuality and the Discourse of the Nuclear Family," *Journal of Film and Video* (Winter, 1989) 41(4). **[116]**

Nakasa, Hideo. "Scandal vs. Social Responsibility: The Growing Criticism of Journalism in Japan," *Studies of Broadcasting* (1987) No. 23, pp. 27-49. **[220]**

Naremore, Games. *Acting in the Cinema.* Berkeley: University of California Press, 1988. **[104]**

National Conference on Visual Information Processing. Report to the National Institute of Education, Washington, D.C., 1974. Cited in Hobbs, Frost, Davis and Stauffer (1988). **[317]**

Nayman, Oguz, Blaine K. McKee, and Dan L. Lattimore, "PR Personnel and Print Journalists: A Comparison of Professionalism," *Journalism Quarterly* (1977) 54(3): 492-497. **[164]**

Near, Janet P. and Mary Deane Sorcinelli. "Work and Life Away from Work: Predictors of Faculty Satisfaction," *Research in Higher Education* (1986) 25(4): 377-394. **[280]**

Negrine, Ralph and Andre Goodfriend. "Public Perceptions of the New Media: A Survey of British Attitudes," *Media, Culture and Society* (July, 1988) 10(3): 303-321. **[218]**

Nelson, Dean E. "Business and Economic Reporting: U.S. Daily Newspaper Coverage 1970 to 1990," *Ohio Journalism Monograph Series*, No. 2, Athens: Bush Research Center, E.W. Scripps School of Journalism, Ohio University, April, 1992. **[356]**

Nerone, John C. "Violence Against the Press in U.S. History," *Journal of Communication* (Summer, 1990) 40(3): 6-33. **[58, 60]**

Nerone, John. "The Problem of Teaching Journalism History," *Journalism Educator* (Autumn, 1990) 45(3): 16-24. **[58, 60]**

Neuendorf, Kim and Robert Abelman. "An Interactional Analysis of Religious Television Programming," *Review of Religious Research* (December, 1987) 29(2): 175-198. **[357]**

Neuendorf, Kimberly A., James E. Brentar and James Porco. "Media Exposure and Its Variance across Media: Differences in Cognitive Patterns," paper presented to the Information Systems Division at the annual conference of the International Communication Association, Dublin, Ireland, June, 1990. **[310]**

Neuendorf, Kimberly A. and Glenn G. Sparks. "Predicting Emotional Responses to Horror Films from Cue-Specific Affect," *Communication Quarterly* (1988) 36: 16-27. **[107]**

Neuendorf, Kimberly A. and Tom Fennell. "A Social Facilitation View of the Generation of Humor and Mirth Reactions: Effects of a Laugh Track," *Central States Speech Journal* (Spring, 1988) 39(1): 37-48. **[303]**

Neuman, Susan B. "The Home Environment and Fifth-Grade Students' Leisure Reading," *The Elementary School Journal* (1986) 86(3): 335-343. **[182, 214]**

Neuman, W.R. "Patterns of Recall among Television News Viewers," *Public Opinion Quarterly* (1976) 40: 115-123. **[316]**

Neurath, Paul. "One-Publisher Communities: Factors Influencing Trend," *Journalism Quarterly* (September, 1944) 21: 230-242. **[97]**

Neuwirth, Kurt, Carol M. Liebler, Sharon Dunwoody and Jennifer Riddle. "The Effect of 'Electronic' News Sources on Selection and Editing of News," *Journalism Quarterly* (Spring, 1988) 65(1): 85-94. **[161]**

Neuwirth, Kurt, Charles T. Salmon and M. Neff. "Community Orientation and Media Use," *Journalism Quarterly* (Spring, 1989) 66(1): 31-39. **[239]**

Newcomb, Horace. "One Night of Prime Time: An Analysis of Television's Multiple Voices," *Media, Myths and Narrative: Television and the Press*, ed. J.W. Carey. Newbury Park, CA: Sage, 1988. **[20]**

Newcomb, Horace. "On the Dialogic Aspects of Mass Communication," *Critical Studies in Mass Communication* (1984) 1: 34-50. **[20]**

Newcomb, Horace M. and Robert S. Alley. "The Producer as Artist: Commercial Television," *Individuals in Mass Media Organizations: Creativity and Constraint*, eds. James S. Ettema and D. Charles Whitney. Beverly Hills, CA: Sage Publications, 1982, pp. 69-89. **[114]**

Newcomb, Horace and P. Hirsch. "Television as a Cultural Forum," *Interpreting Television: Current Research Perspectives*, eds. W. Rowland and B. Watkins. Beverly Hills, CA: Sage Publications, 1984, pp. 58-73. **[20, 127]**

Newell, A. "Reasoning, Problem Solving and Decision Processes: The Problem Space as a Fundamental Category," *Attention and Performance*, ed. R. Nickerson. Hillsdale, NJ: Lawrence Erlbaum, 1981. **[321]**

Newhagen, J.E. "The Evening's Bad News: The Effects of Compelling Negative Television News Images on Memory," *Journal of Communication* (Spring, 1992) 42(2): 25-41. **[304]**

Newhagen, John and Clifford Nass. "Differential Criteria for Evaluating Credibility of Newspapers and TV News," *Journalism Quarterly* (Summer, 1989) 66(2): 277-284. **[205]**

Newhagen, John and Byron Reeves. "This Evening's Bad News: Effects of Compelling Negative Television News Images on Memory," paper presented to the Information Systems Division at the annual conference of the International Communication Association, Chicago, June, 1991. **[304, 307]**

Newman, Jay. *The Journalist in Plato's Cave*. Rutherford, NJ: Fairleigh Dickinson University Press, 1990. **[152]**

Newsom, D. and J.A. Wollert. *Media Writing: Preparing Information for the Mass Media.* 2nd ed. Belmont, CA: Wadsworth Pub. Co., 1988. **[316]**

Newtson, D. and G. Enquist. "The Perceptual Organization of Ongoing Behavior," *Journal of Experimental Social Psychology* (1976) 12: 436-450. **[321]**

Nichols, Peter M. "Drop in Video Rentals Signals Need for Broader Selection," *Plain Dealer*, May 15, 1990, p. 16B. New York Times dispatch. **[175]**

Nicolini, P. "Puerto Rican Leaders' Views of English-Language Media," *Journalism Quarterly* (Summer/Autumn, 1987) 64(2/3): 597-601. **[365]**

Nicolini, P. "Philadelphia Puerto Rican Community Leaders' Perceptions of Spanish-Language Media," *Mass Comm Review* (1986) 13(1-3): 11-17. **[365]**

Niebauer, Walter E. Jr., Stephen Lacy, James M. Bernstein and Tuen-yu Lau. "Central City Market Structure's Impact on Suburban Newspaper Circulation," *Journalism Quarterly* (Fall, 1988) 65(3): 726-732. **[58]**

Niekamp, Raymond A. "Satellite Newsgathering and Its Effect on Network-Affiliate Relations," paper presented to the Radio-Television Journalism Division at the annual conference of the Association for Education in Journalism and Mass Communication, Minneapolis, August, 1990. **[75]**

Nielsen, M.C. "Labor Power and Organization in the Early U.S. Motion Picture Industry," *Film History* (1988) 2(2): 121-132. **[35]**

Nixon, Raymond B. "Trends in Daily Newspaper Ownership: Concentration with Competition," *Gazette* (1968) 14: 181-193. **[97]**

Nixon, Raymond B. "Factors Related to Press Freedom in National Press Systems," *Journalism Quarterly* (1960) 37: 13-28. **[60]**

Nixon, Raymond B. and Jean Ward. "Trends in Newspaper Ownership and Inter-Media Competition," *Journalism Quarterly* (Winter, 1961) 38: 3-14. **[85]**

Nmungwun, A.F. *Video Recording Technology: Its Impact on Media and Home Entertainment.* Hillsdale, NJ: Lawrence Erlbaum Associates, 1989. **[58]**

Noam, E.M. "Broadcasting in Italy: An Overview," *Columbia Journal of World Business* (Fall, 1987) 22(2): 19-25. **[48]**

Noble, G. "The Social Significance of VCR Technology: Television or Not Television?" *The Information Society* (1987/1988) 5(3): 133-146. **[212]**

Nolan, J.C. *Chronological and Inverted Pyramid News Forms: Impacts on Readers and Writers*. Doctoral dissertation, Unviersity of Texas at Austin, 1989. **[317]**

Nolan, John C. "Chronological and Inverted Pyramid News Forms: Impacts on Readers and Writers," paper presented at the annual conference of the International Communication Association, June 24-29, 1990, Dublin, Ireland. **[292, 293, 294, 295]**

Nord, D.P. "The Business Values of American Newspapers: The 19th Century Watershed in Chicago," *Journalism Quarterly* (Summer, 1984) 61(2): 265-273. **[26, 356]**

Nord, David Paul. "Working-Class Readers: Family, Community, and Reading in Late Nineteenth-Century America," *Communication Research* (April, 1986) 13(2): 156-181.

Nord, David Paul. "A Plea for 'Journalism' History," *Journalism History* (Spring, 1988) 15(1): 8-15. **[58]**

Nordberg, J. and B. Nordstrom. "Media Consumption and Other Cultural Activities in Sweden," *Communications: The European Journal of Communication* (1986) 12(2): 103-118. **[214]**

Norman, D.A. and D.B. Bobrow. "On Data-Limited and Resource-Limited Processes," *Cognitive Psychology* (1975) 7: 44-64. **[314]**

Norris, Vincent P. "Consumer Valuation of National Ads," *Journalism Quarterly* (Summer, 1983) 60(2): 262-268. **[219]**

Norton, S.F. "Tea Time on the 'Telly': British and Australian Soap Opera," *Journal of Popular Culture* (Winter, 1985) 19(3): 3-20. **[372]**

Norton, Seth W. and Will Norton Jr. "Economies of Scale and the New Technology of Daily Newspapers: A Survivor Analysis," *Quarterly Review of Economics and Business* (Summer, 1986) 26(2): 66-83.

Norton, Will Jr., John W. Windhauser and Allyn Boone. "Agreement between Reporters and Editors in Mississippi," *Journalism Quarterly* (Autumn, 1985) 62(3): 633-636. **[158]**

Norton, Will Jr., John W. Windhauser and Susan Langdon Norton. "Two Comparisons of Rural Public Television Viewers and Non-Viewers in Northern Mississippi," *Journalism Quarterly* (Fall, 1992) 69(3): 691-701. **[218]**

Nugent, G.C. "Pictures, Audio and Print: Symbolic Representation and Effect on Learning," *Educational Communication and Technology Journal* (1982) 30(3): 163-174. **[319]**

Nwankwo, Robert L. "Community Information Source Usage and Community Opinion," *Mass Comm Review* (Spring/Fall, 1982) 9(2/3): 17-22. **[206]**

O'Connor, Alan. "The Alternative Press in Bolivia and Ecuador: The Examples of 'Aqui' and 'Punto de Vista,'" *Howard Journal of Communication* (Fall, 1990) 2(4): 349-356. **[59]**

O'Guinn, T.C. and T.P Meyer. "Segmenting the Hispanic Market: The Use of Spanish-Language Radio," *Journal of Advertising Research* (December, 1983/January, 1984) 23(6): 9-18. **[233]**

O'Keefe, Garrett J., Jeanne Burull and Kathaleen Reid. "The Uses of Newspapers by Elderly Audiences," paper presented to the Newspaper Division at the annual conference of the Association for Education in Journalism and Mass Communication, Minneapolis, August, 1990. **[225, 254, 259]**

O'Keefe, Garrett J., Jeanne Burull and Kathaleen Reid. "Urban vs. Rural Perspectives on Media Use among Elderly Persons," paper presented to the Mass Communication Division at the annual conference of the International Communication Association, Dublin, Ireland, June, 1990. **[225, 254, 259]**

O'Keefe, Garrett J. and Barbara K. Sulanowski. "More than Just Talk: Uses, Gratifications and the Telephone," paper presented to the Communication Theory and Methodology Division at the annual conference of the Association for Education in Journalism and Mass Communication, Montreal, August, 1992. **[275]**

O'Rourke, J.S. IV. "The Development of Color Television: A Study in the Free Market Process," *Journalism History* (Autumn/Winter, 1982-83) 9(3/4): 78-85. **[58]**

Ogan, Christine. "The Audience for Foreign Film in the United States," *Journal of Communication* (Autumn, 1990) 40(4): 58-77. **[214]**

Ogan, Christine. "The Worldwide Cultural and Economic Impact of Video," *The VCR Age: Home Video and Mass Communication*, ed. Mark R. Levy. Newbury Park, CA: Sage Publications, 1989, pp. 230-251. **[212]**

Ogan, Christine L. "Mass Media Use Factors in a Turkish Squatter Settlement: A 23-Year Panel Study," *Gazette* (1987) 40(3): 145-166. **[256]**

Ogan, Christine L. "Life at the Top for Men and Women Newspaper Managers: A Five-Year Update of Their Characteristics," *Newspaper Research Journal* (Winter, 1983) 5(2):57-68. **[148]**

Okigbo, C. "Media Use by Foreign Students," *Journalism Quarterly* (Winter, 1985) 62(4): 901-904. **[270]**

Olasky, M.N. "When World Views Collide: Journalists and the Great Monkey Trial," *American Journalism* (1986) 4(3): 133-146. **[124]**

Oldham, J. "Law Reporting in the London Newspapers 1756-1786," *American Journal of Legal History* (July, 1987) 31(3): 177-206. **[58]**

Olhausen, M.M. and C.M. Roller. "The Operation of Text Structure and Content Schemata in Isolation and in Interaction," *Reading Research Quarterly* (1988) 23: 70-88. **[58, 295, 316]**

Olien, Clarice N., Phillip J. Tichenor, and George A. Donohue. "Editor Views of Press Role in U.S. and Europe: Differences Across Cultures, or Differences Within?" paper presented to the International Division at the annual conference of the Association for Education in Journalism and Mass Communication, Washington, D.C., Aug. 10, 1989. **[147]**

Olien, Clarice N., Phillip J. Tichenor and George A. Donohue. "Relation between Corporate Ownership and Editor Attitudes about Business," *Journalism Quarterly* (Summer, 1988) 65: 259-266. **[90, 92]**

Olien, Clarice N., Phillip J. Tichenor, George A. Donohue, K.L. Sandstrom and D.M. McLeod. "Community Structure and Editor Opinions about Planning," *Journalism Quarterly* (Spring, 1990) 67(1): 119-127. **[146]**

Olson, Laury D. (Masher). "Job Satisfaction of Journalists and PR Personnel." *Public Relations Review* (Winter, 1989) 15(4): 37-45. **[150]**

Olson, Scott R. "An Evolution of Mass Communication Models: New Formulations for Converging Technologies," paper presented at the annual conference of the International Communication Association, Nov. 1, 1988. **[177]**

Olszewska, A. and K. Roberts. *Leisure and Life-Style: A Comparative Analysis of Free Time.* Newbury Park, CA: Sage, 1989. **[211]**

Omori, Yukio. "Broadcasting Legislation in Japan--Its Historical Process, Current Status and Future Tasks," *Studies of Broadcasting* (1989) 25: 7-40. **[59]**

Orman, J. "Covering the American Presidency: Valenced Reporting in the Periodical Press, 1900-1982," *Presidential Studies Quarterly* (Summer, 1984) 14(3): 381-390. **[369]**

Ortizano, Giacomo L. "Visibility of Blacks and Whites in Magazine Photographs," *Journalism Quarterly* (Autumn, 1989) 66(3): 718-721. **[345]**

Ortony, Andrew. "Remembering, Understanding, and Representation," *Cognitive Science* (1978) 2: 53-69. **[306, 319]**

Osborn, Suzanne. "Gender Depictions in Television Advertisements: 1988," paper presented at the annual conference of the International Communication Association, San Francisco, May, 1989. **[352]**

Osgood, C.E. "The Representational Model and Relevant Research Methods," *Trends in Content Analysis*, ed. I. de Sola Pool. Urbana: University of Illinois Press, 1959. **[314]**

Osiel, Mark J. "The Professionalization of Journalism: Impetus or Impediment to a 'Watchdog' Press," *Sociological Inquiry* (Spring, 1986) 56(2): 163-189. **[165]**

Ostbye, Helge. "Norwegian Media in the 1980s: Structural Changes, Stable Consumption," *The Nordicom Review of Nordic Mass Communication Research* (1991) No. 2: 19-35. **[48]**

Ostman, Ronald E. and Dennis W. Jeffers. "Life Stage and Motives for Television Use," *International Journal of Aging and Human Development* (1983) 17(4): 315-321. **[258]**

Ostman, Ronald E. and Jill L. Parker. "A Public's Environmental Information Sources and Evaluations of Mass Media," *Journal of Environmental Education* (Winter, 1986-1987) 18(2): 9-17. **[231, 254]**

Oumano, Ellen. *Film Forum: Thirty Five Top Filmmakers Discuss Their Craft.* New York: St. Martin's Press, 1985. **[105]**

Overbeck, Wayne. "A Free-Marketplace Myth: The New 'Must Carry' Rule, A/B Switches and Deed Restrictions," *Mass Comm Review* (1987) 14(1/2): 54-60. **[268]**

Owen, Bruce M. "The Economic View of Programming," *Journal of Communication* (Spring, 1978) 28(2): 43-47. **[78]**

Owens, Alfred W. and Dominic A. Infante. "Television Director Communication as Perceived by Production Personnel," *Journal of Broadcasting & Electronic Media* (Fall, 1988) 32(4): 429-440. **[162]**

Paap, K.R., S.L. Newsome and R.W. Noel. "Word Shape's in Poor Shape for the Race to the Lexicon," *Journal of Experimental Psychology: Human Perception and Performance* (1984) 10(3): 413-428. **[288]**

Paglin, M.D. (Ed.) *A Legislative History of the Communications Act of 1934.* New York: Oxford University Press, 1990. **[58]**

Paivio, Allan. *Imagery and Verbal Processes.* Hillsdale, NJ: Erlbaum, 1979. **[316]**

Paivio, Allan, T.B. Rogers and P.C. Smythe. "Why Are Pictures Easier to Recall than Words?" *Psyhchonomic Science* (1968) 11: 137-138. **[315]**

Palmer, P. "New Methods, New Reasons: Television and Children's Leisure Time," *Media Information Australia* (August, 1985) 37: 55-58. **[269]**

Palmgreen, Philip. "Uses and Gratifications: A Theoretical Perspective," *Communication Yearbook 8,* eds. R.N. Bostrom and B.H. Westley. Beverly Hills, CA: Sage Publications, 1984, pp. 20-55. **[272]**

Palmgreen, Philip, P.L. Cook, J. Harvill and D. Helm. "The Motivational Framework of Movie Going: Uses and Avoidances of Theatrical Films," *Current Research in Film: Audiences, Economics and Law,* ed. B.A. Austin. Vol. 4. Norwood, NJ: Ablex, 1988, pp. 1-23. **[252]**

Palmgreen, Philip and J.D. Rayburn II. "An Expectancy-Value Approach to Media Gratifications," *Media Gratifications Research: Current Perspectives,* ed. K.E. Rosengren, L.A. Wenner and P. Palmgreen. Beverly Hills, CA: Sage Publications, 1985, pp. 61-72. **[245]**

Palmgreen, Philip and J.D. Rayburn II. "Uses and Gratifications and Exposure to Public Television: A Discrepancy Approach," *Communication Research* (April, 1979) 6(2): 155-180. **[258]**

Palmgreen, Philip, L.A. Wenner and J.D. Rayburn II. "Relations between Gratifications Sought and Obtained: A Study of Television News," *Communication Research* (1980) 7: 161-192. **[246, 273]**

Palmgreen, Philip, L.A. Wenner and K.E. Rosengren. "Uses and Gratifications Research: The Past Ten Years," *Media Gratifications Research: Current Perspectives.* eds. K.E. Rosengren, L.A. Wenner and P. Palmgreen. Beverly Hills, CA: Sage Publications, 1985, pp. 11-37. **[272]**

Paper, Lewis J. *Empire: William S. Paley and the Making of CBS.* New York: St. Martin's Press, 1987. **[58]**

Paraschos, Manny. "Constitutional Press Provisions on the Press: A World View," paper presented to the International Communication Division at the annual conference of the Association for Education in Journalism and Mass Communication, Washington, D.C., August, 1989. **[56]**

Parenti, Michael. *Inventing Reality: The Politics of Mass Media.* New York: St. Martin's Press, 1986. **[127]**

Parisot, Laurence. "Attitudes about the Media: A Five Country Comparison," *Public Opinion* (January/February, 1988), pp. 18-19, 60. **[201]**

Park, Robert E. "News as a Form of Knowledge," *American Journal of Sociology* (March, 1940) 45: 667-686. **[132]**

Park, Robert E. "Urbanization as Measured by Newspaper Circulation," *American Journal of Sociology* (1929) 34: 60-79. **[272]**

Parker, S. and M. Smith. "Work and Leisure," *Handbook of Workbook Organization and Society*, ed. R. Dubin. Chicago: Rand McNally, 1976, pp. 37-64. **[280]**

Parsigian, Elise Keoleian. "News Reporting: Method in the Midst of Chaos," *Journalism Quarterly* (Winter, 1987) 64(4): 721-730. **[133]**

Parsons, Talcott. *The Social System.* Glencoe, IL: Free Press, 1957. **[165]**

Pasadeos, Yorgo. "Sources in Television Coverage of Automotive Strikes," *Journal of Broadcasting & Electronic Media* (Winter, 1990) 34(1): 77-84. **[137]**

Pasadeos, Yorgo. "Application of Measures of Sensationalism to a Murdoch-Owned Daily in the San Antonio Market," *Newspaper Research Journal* (Summer, 1984) 5(4): 9-17. **[157]**

Pasadeos, Yorgo and P. Renfro. "Rupert Murdoch's Style: The 'New York Post,'" *Newspaper Research Journal* (Summer, 1988) 9(4): 25-34. **[90]**

Pasadeos, Yorgo, Barbara Shoemake, and Suzanne Campbell. "The Information Content of Radio Advertisements," *Journal of Broadcasting & Electronic Media* (Summer, 1992) 36(3): 337-343. **[362]**

Pasternack, Steve. "The Open Forum: A Study of Letters to the Editor and the People Who Write Them," paper presented to the Newspaper Division at the annual conference of the Association for Education in Journalism and Mass Communication, Portland, OR, August, 1988. **[363]**

Pasternack, Steve and Sandra H. Utt. "Reader Use & Understanding of Newspaper Infographics," *Newspaper Research Journal* (Spring, 1990) 11(2): 28-41. **[289, 290]**

Pasternack, Steve and Sandra H. Utt. "Newspapers' Policies on Rejection of Ads for Products and Services," *Journalism Quarterly* (Fall, 1988) 65(3): 695-701. **[110]**

Pasternack, Steve and Sandra H. Utt. "Subject Perception of Newspaper Characteristics Based on Front Page Design," *Newspaper Research Journal* (Fall, 1986) 8(1): 29-36. **[199]**

Patner, Andrew. "Papers Take Alternative Path to Success," *Wall Street Journal*, June 19, 1990, p. 1B.**[71]**

Paugh, Ronald. "Music Video Viewers," *Cable-Viewing.* ed. Carrie Heeter and Bradley Greenberg. Norwood, NJ: Ablex, 1989. **[270]**

Payne, Gregg A., Jessica J.H. Severn and David M. Dozier. "Uses and Gratifications Motives as Indicators of Magazine Readership," *Journalism Quarterly* (Winter, 1988) 65(4): 909-913, 959. **[253]**

Pearson, Larry. "When Newspapers Aren't There: Getting Information in a Media-Poor Environment," paper presented to the Theory and Methodology Division at the annual conference of the Association for Education in Journalism and Mass Communication, Minneapolis, Aug. 9, 1990. **[260]**

Pearson, P. David, Jane Hansen and Christine Gordon. "The Effects of Background Knowledge on Young Children's Comprehension of Explicit and Implicit Information," *Journal of Reading Behavior* (1979) 11: 201-209. **[316]**

Pearson, P.E. and K. Camperell. "Comprehension of Text Structure," *Theoretical Models and Processes of Reading*, ed. H. Singer and R.B. Ruddell. 3rd ed. Newark, DE: International Reading Association, 1985, pp. 323-342. **[316]**

Pease, Edward C. "Minority News Coverage in the 'Columbus Dispatch,'" *Newspaper Research Journal* (Spring, 1989) 10(3): 17-33. **[148, 365]**

Pease, Ted and Guido H. Stempel III. "Surviving to the Top: Views of Minority Newspaper Executives," *Newspaper Research Journal* (Summer, 1990) 11(3): 64-79. **[148]**

Pease, Ted. "Cornerstone for Growth: How Minorities Are Vital to the Future of Newspapers," *Newspaper Research Journal* (Fall, 1989) 10(4): 1-12. **[148]**

Pease, Ted. "Race, Gender and Job Satisfaction in Newspaper Newsrooms," *Readings in Media Management*, ed. Stephen Lacy, Ardyth B. Sohn and Robert H. Giles. Columbia, S.C.: Media Management and Economics Division, Association for Education in Journalism and Mass Communication, 1992, pp. 97-122. **[148]**

Peel, E.A. "Generalizing Through the Verbal Medium," *British Journal of Educational Psychology* (February, 1978) pp. 36-46, cited in Pasternack and Utt (1991). **[290]**

Penman, Robyn. "Communication Reconstructed," *Journal for the Theory of Social Behavior* (December, 1988) 18:4:391-410. **[11, 20]**

Perfetti, Charles A., Sylvia Beverly, Laura Bell, Kimberly Rodgers and Robert Faux. "Comprehending Newspaper Headlines," *Journal of Memory and Language* (1987) 26: 692-713. **[291]**

Perkins, R.E. and A.B. Hill. "Cognitive and Affective Aspects of Boredom," *British Journal of Psychology* (1985) 76: 221-234. **[250]**

Perlmutter, Ruch and Archie Perlmutter. "Eastern European Films after Glasnost," *Eastern European Quarterly* (March, 1990) 24(1): 101-112. **[59]**

Perse, Elizabeth M. "Predicting Attention to Local Television News: Need for Cognition and Motives for Viewing," *Communication Reports* (Winter, 1992) 5(1): 40-49. **[275]**

Perse, Elizabeth M. "Media Involvement and Local News Effects," *Journal of Broadcasting & Electronic Media* (Winter, 1990) 34(1): 17-36. **[244, 278]**

Perse, Elizabeth M. "Audience Selectivity and Involvement in the Newer Media Environment," *Communication Research* (October, 1990) 17(5): 675-697. **[244, 278]**

Perse, Elizabeth M. and Alan M. Rubin. "Chronic Loneliness and Television Use," *Journal of Broadcasting & Electronic Media* (Winter, 1990) 34(1): 37-53. **[257]**

Perse, Elizabeth M. and Alan M. Rubin. "Audience Activity and Satisfaction with Favorite Television Soap Opera," *Journalism Quarterly* (Summer, 1988) 65(2): 368-374. **[244, 246]**

Perse, Elizabeth M. and Rebecca B. Rubin. "Attribution in Social and Parasocial Relationships," *Communication Research* (February, 1989) 16(1): 59-77. **[258]**

Peters, Anne K. and Muriel G. Cantor. "Screen Acting As Work," *Individuals in Mass Media Organizations: Creativity and Constraint*, eds. James S. Ettema and D. Charles Whitney. Beverly Hills, CA: Sage Publications, 1982, pp. 53-68. **[104, 155]**

Petersen, Barbara K. "The Managerial Benefits of Understanding Organizational Culture," *Readings in Media Management*, ed. Stephen Lacy, Ardyth B. Sohn and Robert H. Giles. Columbia, S.C.: Media Management and Economics Division, Association for Education in Journalism and Mass Communication, 1992, pp. 123-151. **[109]**

Peterson, Anne C. "Adolescent Development," *Annual Review of Psychology* (1988) 39: 583-607. **[215]**

Peterson, Beck K. "Tables and Graphs Improve Reader Performance and Reader Reaction," *Journal of Business Communication* (Spring, 1983) pp. 47-55. **[289]**

Peterson, R.A. and R.B. Davis Jr. "The Contemporary American Radio Audience," *Popular Music & Society* (1978)6(2): 169-183. **[231]**

Peterson, Richard A. "Revitalizing the Culture Concept," *Annual Review of Sociology*, ed. Alex Inkeles (1979) 5: 137-166. **[120, 360]**

Peterson, Sophia. "Foreign News Gatekeepers and Criteria of Newsworthiness," *Journalism Quarterly* (Spring, 1979) 56(1): 116-125. **[120]**

Peterson, Theodore. *Magazines in the Twentieth Century*. Urbana: University of Illinois Press, 1964, 2nd ed. **[58]**

Petrescu, Camil. "Newspaper Tests 'New' Romania's Freedom," *Wall Street Journal*, June 7, 1990, p. 16A. **[59]**

Petro, Patrice. "Mass Culture and the Feminine: The 'Place' of Television in Film Studies," *Cinema Journal* (Spring, 1986) 25(3): 5-21. **[18]**

Petty, Richard and J. Cacioppo. *Communication and Persuasion: Central and Peripheral Routes to Attitude Change.* New York: Springer-Verlag, 1986. **[321]**

Pfau, Michael. "A Channel Approach to Television Influence," *Journal of Broadcasting & Electronic Media* (Spring, 1990) 34(2): 195-214. **[14]**

Pfetsch, B. and A. Kutteroff. "The Short-Term Impact of Cable Television in West Germany: Preliminary Findings from a Quasi-Experimental Study," *European Journal of Communication* (September, 1988) 3(3): 323-343. **[175]**

Phillips, T. Mark, Thomas A. Griffiths and Norman C. Tarbox. "Public Television Efficiency Versus Diversity," *Journal of Media Economics* (Spring, 1991) 4(1): 19-33. **[77]**

Picard, Robert G. "Pricing Behavior of Newspapers," *Press Concentration and Monopoly: New Perspectives on Newspaper Ownership and Operation*, ed. R.G. Picard et al., Norwood, NJ: Ablex, 1988, pp. 61-70. **[97]**

Picard, Robert G. "Regression Analysis of State Role in Press Economics," *Journalism Quarterly* (Winter, 1987) 64(4): 848-850. **[54, 57]**

Picard, Robert. *The Press and the Decline of Democracy.* Westport, CT: Greenwood Press, 1985. **[54]**

Picard, Robert G. "Revisions of the "Four Theories of the Press' Model," *Mass Comm Review* (Winter/Spring, 1982/1983) 10(1,2): 25-28. **[54]**

Picard, Robert G. and P.D. Adams. "Characterizations of Acts and Perpetrators of Political Violence in Three Elite U.S. Daily Newspapers," *Political Communication and Persuasion* (1987) 4(1): 1-10. **[137]**

Picard, Robert G. and Stephen Lacy. "Interactive Monopoly Power: A Concept for Analyzing the Daily Newspaper Industry," paper presented to the Media Management and Economics Division at the annual conference of the Association for Education in Journalism and Mass Communication, Minneapolis, August, 1990. **[85]**

Picard, Robert G., James P. Winter, Maxwell E. McCombs, and Stephen Lacy. *Press Concentration and Monopoly: New Perspectives on Newspaper Ownership and Operation.* Norwood, NJ: Ablex, 1988. **[97]**

Pierce, J.C., L. Lee-Sammons, and N.P. Lovrich Jr. "U.S. and Japanese Source Reliance for Environmental Information," *Journalism Quarterly* (Winter, 1988) 65(4): 902-908. **[254]**

Pierce, R.C. "Dimensions of Leisure I: Satisfactions," *Journal of Leisure Research* (1980) 12: 5-19. **[274]**

Pierce, Thurman. "New Values in Print," *Marketing & Media Decisions* (March, 1983) pp. 121-132. **[85]**

Pingree, Suzanne, Robert P. Hawkins, Ulla Johnsson-Smaragdl, Karl Erik Rosengren and Nancy Reynolds. "Patterns of Television Viewing Behaviors: A Swedish-American Comparison," paper presented to the Intercultural and Development Division at the annual conference of the International Communication Association, Dublin, Ireland, June 29, 1990. **[224, 268]**

Pittatore, Oddina. "The Image of Italy in Ads in Five U.S. Magazines," *Journalism Quarterly* (Winter, 1983) 60(4): 728-730. **[371]**

Pitts, Beverly. "Model Provides Description of News Writing Process," *Journalism Educator* (1989) 44: 12-19, 59. **[139]**

Pitts, Beverly J. "The News Selection Process of Student and Professional Journalists," *Newspaper Research Journal* (Fall, 1987) 9(1): 41-47. **[139]**

Pitts, Beverly J. "Protocol Analysis and the Newswriting Process," *Newspaper Research Journal* (1982) 4: 12-21. **[139]**

Poggioli, Renato. *The Theory of the Avant-Garde.* Cambridge, MA, 1968. **[18]**

Polivka, Jirina S. "Is America Aging Successfully? A Message from Media Cartoons," *Communication and Cognition* (1988) 21(1): 97-106. **[365]**

Pollard, G. "Profile of Canadian Radio Newsworkers," *Journalism Quarterly* (Spring, 1989) 66(1): 80-86. **[148]**

Pollard, G. "The Effects of Profession and Organization on Decision Acceptance among Radio Newsworkers," *Gazette* (1988) 41(3): 185-199. **[151]**

Pollard, G. "Professionalism among Canadian News Workers: A Cross Media Analysis," *Gazette* (1985) 36(1): 21-38. **[165]**

Pollay, R.W. "Twentieth-Century Magazine Advertising: Determinants of Informativeness," *Written Communication* (January, 1984) 1(1): 56-77. **[336]**

Pollay, R.W. "The Subsiding Sizzle: A Descriptive History of Print Advertising, 1900-1980," *Journal of Marketing* (Summer, 1985) 49(3): 24-37. **[336]**

Poole, Millicent E. and George H. Cooney. "Work and Leisure Relationships: An Exploration of Life Possibilities During Adolescence," *Journal of Youth and Adolescence* (1986) 15(6): 475-486. **[280]**

Poore, Chris. "Just the Fax, Ma'am' Come by Phone," *Plain Dealer*, Oct. 29, 1989, p. 5A. **[74]**

Popkin, Jeremy. "International Gazettes and Politics of Europe in the Revolutionary Period," *Journalism Quarterly* (Autumn, 1985) 62(3): 482-488. **[29]**

Popkin, Jeremy. "Pamphlet Journalism at the End of the Old Regime," *Eighteenth Century Studies* (Spring, 1989) 22(3): 351-367. **[29]**

Popper, K.R. *Objective Knowledge: An Evolutionary Approach.* Oxford: Clarendon. Rev. ed., 1979 (1972). **[18]**

Porat, M. *The Information Economy: Definition and Measurement.* Special Publication 77-12(1), Office of Telecommunications, U.S. Department of Commerce, Washington, 1977. Cited in Hepworth (1990). **[93]**

Porter, Gregory S. and Mark J. Banks. "Cable Public Access as a Public Forum," *Journalism Quarterly* (Spring, 1988) 65(1): 39-45. **[196]**

Porter, Michael J. "A Comparative Analysis of Directing Styles in 'Hill Street Blues,'" *Journal of Broadcasting & Electronic Media* (Summer, 1987) 31(3): 323-334. **[116]**

Porter, Vincent. "The Re-Regulation of Television: Pluralism, Constitutionality and the Free Market in the USA, West Germany, France and the UK," *Media, Culture and Society* (1989) 11: 5-27. **[59]**

Porter, William C. and Flint Stephens. "Estimating Readability: A Study of Utah Editors' Abilities," *Newspaper Research Journal* (Winter, 1989) 10(2): 87-96. **[292]**

Posner, M.I., M.J. Nissen and R.M. Klein. "Visual Dominance: An Information-Processing Account of Its Origins and Significance," *Psychological Review* (1976) 83(2): 157-171. **[320]**

Potter, W. James. "How Do Adolescents' Perceptions of Television Reality Change Over Time?" *Journalism Quarterly* (Summer, 1992) 69(2): 392-405. **[188]**

Potter, W. James. "Perceived Reality in Television Effects Research," *Journal of Broadcasting & Electronic Media* (Winter, 1988) 32(1): 23-41. **[15]**

Potter, W. James. "Gender Representation in Elite Newspapers," *Journalism Quarterly* (Autumn, 1986) 62(3): 636-640. **[353]**

Powell, Lawrence A. and John B. Williamson. "The Mass Media and the Aged," *Social Policy* (Summer, 1985) 16(1): 38-49. **[20, 347]**

Powell, Walter W. "From Craft to Corporation: The Impact of Outside Ownership on Book Publishing," *Individuals in Mass Media Organizations: Creativity and Constraint,* eds. James S. Ettema and D. Charles Whitney. Beverly Hills, CA: Sage Publications, 1982, pp. 33-52. **[73]**

Power, R.P. "Hypotheses in Perception: Their Development about Unambiguous Stimuli in the Environment," *Perception* (1978) 7: 105-111. **[315]**

Powers, Angela. "Financial Commitment and Performance in Local Television News: Applying the Industrial Organizational Model," paper presented to the Management and Economics Division at the annual conference of the Association for Education in Journalism and Mass Communication, Montreal, August, 1992. **[91]**

Powers, Angela. "The Effect of Leadership Behavior on Job Satisfaction and Goal Agreement and Attainment in Local TV News," *Journalism Quarterly* (Winter, 1991) 68(4): 772-780. **[142]**

Powers, Angela. "The Changing Market Structure of Local Television News," *Journal of Media Economics* (Spring, 1990) 3(1): 37-55. **[67, 68]**

Powers, Angela and Stephen Lacy. "A Model of Job Satisfaction in Local Television Newsrooms," *Readings in Media Management*, ed. Stephen Lacy, Ardyth B. Sohn and Robert H. Giles. Columbia, S.C.: Media Management and Economics Division, Association for Education in Journalism and Mass Communication, 1992, pp. 5-20. **[150]**

Powers, Angela and Stephen Lacy. "A Model of Job Satisfaction in Local Television Newsrooms," paper presented to the Radio-Television Journalism Division at the annual conference of the Association for Education in Journalism and Mass Communication, Boston, August, 1991. **[150]**

Prince, Paul. "Rental of Feature Films on Videocassette: Changes in Industry Structure and Consumer Behavior from the Perspective of the Rental Stores," paper presented at the annual conference of the Association for Education in Journalism and Mass Communication, Montreal, August, 1992. **[66]**

Prior-Miller, Marcia R. "An Analysis of 'Magazine Type': Toward an Empirically Based Typology of Magazines and Non-Newspaper Periodicals," paper presented to the Magazine Division at the annual conference of the Association for Education in Journalism and Mass Communication, Montreal, August, 1992. **[95]**

Prisuta, Robert H. "The Adolescent and Television News: A Viewer Profile," *Journalism Quarterly* (Summer, 1979) 56(2): 277-282.

Pritchard, David. "Race, Homicide and Newspapers," *Journalism Quarterly* (Autumn, 1985) 62(3): 500-507. **[135, 345]**

Pritchard, David and Dan Berkowitz. "How Readers' Letters May Influence Editors and News Emphasis: A Content Analysis of 10 Newspapers, 1948-1978," *Journalism Quarterly* (Fall, 1991) 68(3): 388-395. **[163]**

Pritchard, David and Madelyn Peroni Morgan. "Impact of Ethics Codes on Judgments by Journalists: A National Experiment," *Journalism Quarterly* (Winter, 1989) 66(4): 934-941. **[159]**

Priyadarsini, S. "Crime News in Newspapers: A Case Study in Tamil Nadu, India," *Deviant Behavior* (1984) 5(4): 313-326. **[124]**

Pronovost, Gilles. "The Sociology of Time," *Current Sociology* (Winter, 1989) 37(3): 37-62. **[170]**

Propp, V. *The Morphology of the Folktale*. Austin: University of Texas Press, 1968. **[312]**

Puig, Claudia. "Female Foot in TV, Film's Big Doors," *Plain Dealer*, Aug. 14, 1991. Los Angeles Times dispatch. Based on study "The Employment of Executive Women in Film and Television: 1991," for Women in Film. **[164]**

Putnam, Hilary. *Realism and Reason: Philosophical Papers. Volume 3*. New York: Cambridge University Press, 1983. **[19]**

Quarantelli, E.L. "Realities and Mythologies in Disaster Films," *Communications: The European Journal of Communication* (1985) 11(1): 31-44. **[330]**

Quine, Willard V. *Ontological Relativity and Other Essays*. New York: Columbia University Press, 1969. **[19]**

Radway, J.A. "Interpretive Communitive and Variable Literacies: The Functions of Romance Reading," *Daedulus* (1984) 113(3): 44-73. **[20, 21]**

Ragheb, M. and J. Beard. "Measuring Leisure Attitude," *Journal of Leisure Research* (1982) 14: 155-167. **[211]**

Rahtz, Don R., M. Joseph Sirgy and H. Lee Meadow. "The Elderly Audience: Correlates of Television Orientation," *Journal of Advertising* (1989) 18(3): 9-20. **[191, 259]**

Rak, Diana S. and Linda M. McMullen. "Sex-Role Stereotyping in Television Commercials: A Verbal Response Mode and Content Analysis," *Canadian Journal of Behavioral Science* (1987) 19(1): 25-39. **[367]**

Rakow, Lana F. and Kimberlie Kranich. "Woman as Sign in Television News," *Journal of Communication* (Winter, 1991) 41(1): 8-23. **[351]**

Ramaprasad, Jyotika. "Content, Geography and Source Consonance among the U.S. Networks in Foreign News Coverage," paper presented to the International Division at the annual conference of the Association for Education in Journalism and Mass Communication, Boston, August, 1991. **[123, 160, 315]**

Ramaprasad, Jyotika. "Informational Graphics in Newspapers," *Newspaper Research Bureau* (Summer, 1991) 12(3): 92-103. **[123, 160, 315]**

Ramaprasad, Jyotika and Kazumi Hasegawa. "Informational Content of American and Japanese Television Commercials," *Journalism Quarterly* (Fall, 1992) 69(3): 612-622. **[362]**

Rambo, C. David. "Shoppers: A Successful Tool for Market Saturation," *Presstime* (October, 1980), pp. 5-8. **[72]**

Randall, D.M., L. Lee-Sammons, and P.R. Hagner. "Common Versus Elite Crime Coverage in Network News," *Social Science Quarterly* (December, 1988) 69(4): 910-929. **[156]**

Randall, Donna M. "The Portrayal of Corporate Crime in Network Television Newscasts," *Journalism Quarterly* (Spring, 1987) 64(1): 150-153, 250. **[356]**

Randall, Donna and R. DeFillipi. "Media Coverage of Corporate Malfeasance in the Oil Industry," *Social Science Journal* (1987) 24(1): 31-42. **[356]**

Randall, Donna. "The Portrayal of Business Malfeasance in the Elite and General Public Media," *Social Science Quarterly* (June, 1987) 68(2): 281-293. **[356]**

Rao, Leela. "Woman in Indian Films--A Paradigm of Continuity and Change," *Media, Culture and Society* (1989) 11: 443-458.**[47]**

Raphael, David E. "The Information Industry: A New Portrait," *Business Economics* (July, 1989), pp. 28-33. **[64]**

Rarick, Galen. "Differences Between Daily Newspaper Subscribers and Non-Subscribers," *Journalism Quarterly* (1973) 50: 265-270. **[272]**

Rarick, Galen R. and James B. Lemert. "Subscriber Behavior and Attitudes One Year After PM-AM Conversion," *Newspaper Research Journal* (Spring, 1988) 9(3): 21-30. **[255]**

Raub, P. "The 'National Geographic' Magazine's Portrayal of Urban Ethnicity: The Celebration of Cultural Pluralism and the Promise of Social Mobility," *Journal of Urban History* (May, 1988) 14(3): 346-371. **[365]**

Rayburn, J.D. II and P. Palmgreen. "Merging Uses and Gratifications and Expectancy-Value Theory," *Communication Research* (October, 1984) 11(4): 537-562. **[245]**

Rayner, K. "The Perceptual Span and Peripheral Cues in Reading," *Cognitive Psychology* (1975) 7: 65-81. **[313]**

Read, Herbert. *The Philosophy of Modern Art.* New York, 1953. **[18]**

Reagan, Joey. "Effects of Cable Television on News Use," *Journalism Quarterly* (Summer, 1984) 61(1): 317-324. **[212]**

Reagan, Joey and Janay Collins. "Sources for Health Care Information in Two Small Communities," *Journalism Quarterly* (Summer/Autumn, 1987) 64(2/3): 560-563, 676. **[276]**

Reagan, Joey, Richard V. Ducey and James Bernstein. "Local Predictors of Basic and Pay Cable Subscribership," *Journalism Quarterly* (Summer, 1985) 62(2): 397-400. **[191]**

Reagan, Joey. "New Technologies and News Use: Adopters vs. Nonadopters," *Journalism Quarterly* (Winter, 1989) 66(4): 871-875, 887. **[183]**

Reardon, Kathleen K. and Everett M. Rogers. "Interpersonal Versus Mass Media Communication: A False Dichotomy," *Human Communication Research* (Winter, 1988) 15(2): 284-303.

Reber, Bryan H. "How Two Kansas Newspapers Cover Higher Education," paper presented at the annual conference of the Association for Education in Journalism and Mass Communication, Minneapolis, August, 1990. **[368]**

Reed, Edward S. *James J. Gibson and the Psychology of Perception*. New Haven: Yale University Press, 1988. **[317]**

Reep, D.C. and F.H. Dambrot. "Television's Professional Women: Working with Men in the 1980s," *Journalism Quarterly* (Summer/Autumn, 1987) 64(2/3): 376-381. **[366]**

Reese, Stephen D. "The News Paradigm and the Ideology of Objectivity: A Socialist at the Wall Street Journal," *Critical Studies in Mass Communication* (December, 1990) 7(4): 390-409. **[129, 159]**

Reese, Stephen D., John A. Daly and Andrew P. Hardy. "Economic News on Network Television," *Journalism Quarterly* (Spring, 1987) 64(1): 137-144. **[340, 369]**

Reese, Stephen D., Pamela J. Shoemaker, and Wayne A. Danielson. "Social Correlates of Public Attitudes Toward the New Communication Technologies," paper presented at the 10th annual conference of the Midwest Association for Public Opinion Research, Chicago, Ill., 1984. **[198]**

Reeves, Byron, Steven Chaffee and Al Tims. "Social Cognition and Mass Communication," *Social Cognition and Communication*, ed. M. Roloff and C. Berger. Newbury Park, CA: Sage Publications, 1982. **[321]**

Reeves, Byron and Esther Thorson. "Watching Television: Experiments on the Viewing Process," *Communication Research* (July, 1986) 13(3): 343-361. **[274, 298, 299, 301, 320]**

Regan, Trace and Hochang Shin. "Minority Journalists in Ohio: A Study of Their Job Satisfaction," paper presented to the Minorities and Communication Division at the annual conference of the Association for Education in Journalism and Mass Communication, Portland, OR, July 3, 1988. **[148]**

Reid, D.J., M. Beveridge and P. Wakefield. "The Effect of Ability, Colour and Form on Children's Perceptions of Biological Pictures," *Educational Psychology* (1986) 6: 9-18. **[315]**

Reilly, Patrick M. "Gannett Tests Formula to Lure Readers," *Wall Street Journal*, Dec. 6, 1991, p. 1B. **[157]**

Reilly, Patrick M. "Ingersoll Closes Down St. Louis Sun After Seven Months," *Wall Street Journal*, April 26, 1990, p. 1B. **[71, 98]**

Reilly, Patrick M. "Sun Publications' New Newspaper Seeks to Defy Odds," *Wall Street Journal*, May 10, 1990, p. 5B. **[71, 98]**

Reilly, Patrick M. "New York Papers Face a Daily Struggle," *Wall Street Journal*, Sept. 10, 1990, p. 1B. **[71, 98]**

Reilly, Patrick M. "Magazine Firms, Despite Woes, Plan Plenty of New Publications," *Wall Street Journal*, Oct. 24, 1989, p. 7B. **[72]**

Reinstein, P.G. "Sex Roles in Recent Picture Books," *Journal of Popular Culture* (Spring, 1984) 17(4): 116-123. **[368]**

Reisner, Ann E. "Between the Sheets: Determining the Professional Codes Editors Use to Arrange Stories on Newspaper Pages (A Case Study)," paper presented at the annual conference of the Association for Education in Journalism and Mass Communication, Washington, D.C., 1989. **[123, 124]**

Rentner, Terry Lynn and James H. Bissland. "Job Satisfaction: A Nationwide Survey of Public Relations Practitioners," paper presented to the Public Relations Special Interest Group at the annual conference of the International Communication Association, May 28, 1989. **[150]**

Reynolds, Nancy. "Instantiating Stereotypes: How Program Creators Use Cues to Guide Audience Impressions of Television Characters," paper presented at the annual conference of the International Communication Association, Chicago, May, 1991. **[107]**

Rice, G. Elizabeth, Bonnie J.F. Meyer and David C. Miller. "Relation of Everyday Activities of Adults to their Prose Recall Performance," *Educational Gerontology (1988) 14: 147-158*. **[268]**

Rice, Mabel, Aletha Huston and John C. Wright. "The Forms and Codes of Television: Effects on Children's Attention, Comprehension and Social Behavior," *Television and Behavior: Ten Years of Scientific Progress and Implications for the Eighties*, ed. David Pearl, Lorraine Bouthilet and Joyce Lazar. Vol. 2. Rockville, MD: National Institute of Mental Health, 1982. **[300, 317]**

Rich, Tom, David Owens and Irving Ellenbogen. "What Canadians Dislike About TV Commercials," *Journal of Advertising Research* (December, 1978) 18(6): 37-44. **[219]**

Richards, David A.J. "Toleration and Free Speech," *Philosophy and Public Affairs* (Fall, 1988) 17(4): 323-336.

Richards J. *Classroom Language: What Sorts?* London: Allen & Unwin, 1978. **[316]**

Richardson, Laurel. "The Collective Story: Postmodernism and the Writing of Sociology," *Sociological Focus* (August, 1988) 21(3): 199-208. **[18]**

Richardson-Klavehn, Alan and Robert A. Bjork. "Measures of Memory," *Annual Review of Psychology* (1988) 39: 475-543. **[309, 320]**

Riddick, Carol Cutler. "Leisure Satisfaction Precursors," *Journal of Leisure Research* (1986) 18(4): 259-265. **[190, 211]**

Riddle, Charles. "A Profile of Namibian Media: The Censored Debate," *Gazette* (1989) 44: 45-55. **[26, 53]**

Riffe, Daniel, Brenda Ellis, Momo K. Rogers, Roger L. Van Ommeren and Kieran A. Woodman. "Gatekeeping and the Network News Mix," *Journalism Quarterly* (Summer, 1986) 63(2): 315-321. **[144, 156]**

Riffe, Daniel, Donald Sneed and Roger Van Ommeren. "How Editorial Page Editors and Cartoonists See Issues," *Journalism Quarterly* (Winter, 1985) 62(4): 896-899. **[164]**

Riffe, Daniel and Eugene F. Shaw. "Ownership, Operating, Staffing and Content Characteristics of 'News Radio' Stations," *Journalism Quarterly* (Winter, 1990) 67(4): 684-691. **[90]**

Riffe, Daniel, Helene Goldson, Kelly Saxton and Yang-Chou Yu. "Females and Minorities in Television Advertisements in 1987 Saturday Children's Programs," *Journalism Quarterly* (Spring, 1989) 66(1): 129-136. **[364]**

Riffe, Daniel, Don Sneed, and Roger Van Ommeren. "Black Elected Officeholders find White Press Coverage Insensitive, Incomplete, and Inappropriate," *The Howard Journal of Communications* (Fall, 1990) 2(4): 397-406. **[206]**

Riley, Sam G. and Gary Selnow. "Southern Magazine Publishing, 1764-1984," *Journalism Quarterly* (Winter, 1988) 65(4): 898-901. **[58, 73]**

Riley, Sam G. and Gary W. Selnow. "U.S. Regional Interest Magazines, 1950-1988: A Statistical Overview," paper delivered to the Magazine Division at the annual convention of the Association for Education in Journalism and Mass Communication, Washington, D.C., August, 1989.

Rimmer, Tony and David Weaver. "Different Questions, Different Answers? Media Use and Media Credibility," *Journalism Quarterly* (Spring, 1987) 64(1): 28-36, 44. **[206]**

Ritchey, Gary H. "Pictorial Detail and Recall in Adults and Children," *Journal of Experimental Psychology: Learning, Memory & Cognition* (1982) 8: 139-141. **[290]**

Rivet, Jacques. "Writing and the Journalist--from "Opinion-Event' to "Opinion-Document'," *Communication et Information* (Winter, 1976) 1(2): 75-96. **[131]**

Roberts, Johnnie L. "Trintex, Hayes Microcomputer to Offer Package Combining Videotex, Hardware," *Wall Street Journal*, Feb. 29, 1988, p. 24. **[74]**

Roberts, Robert E. Lee. "Those Who Do Not Watch Television," *Sociology and Social Research* (January, 1987) 71(2): 105-107. **[191, 215, 230, 231, 269, 270]**

Robertson, Douglas S. "The Information Revolution," *Communication Research* (April, 1990) 17(2): 235-254. **[65, 94]**

Robinson, D.O., M. Abbamonte and S.H. Evans. "Why Serifs Are Important: The Perception of Small Print," *Visible Language* (1971) 4: 353-359. **[287]**

Robinson, John P. "Quitting Time," *American Demographics*, May, 1991, pp. 34-36. **[232]**

Robinson, John P. "I Love My TV," *American Demographics*, September, 1990, pp. 24-27. **[170, 171, 230, 232, 234]**

Robinson, John P. "Time's Up," *American Demographics*, July, 1989, pp. 33-35. **[170]**

Robinson, John P. "Television and Leisure Time: A New Scenario," *Journal of Communication* (Winter, 1981) 31(1): 120-130. **[183]**

Robinson, John P. *How Americans Use Time: A Social- Psychological Analysis of Everyday Behavior.* New York: Praeger, 1977. **[170, 216]**

Robinson, John P. *Changes in Americans' Use of Time- 1965-1975. A Progress Report.* Cleveland, Ohio: Communication Research Center, Cleveland State University, August, 1977. **[170, 216]**

Robinson, John P., Vladimir G. Andreyenkov and Vasily D. Patrushev. *The Rhythm of Everyday Life: How Soviet and American Citizens Use Time.* Boulder, Colo.: Westview Press, 1989. **[171, 172]**

Robinson, John P. and Leo W. Jeffres. "The Great Age Readership Mystery," *Journalism Quarterly* (Summer, 1981) 58(2): 219-224, 231. **[213]**

Robinson, John P. and Leo W. Jeffres. "The Changing Role of Newspapers in the Age of Television," *Journalism Monographs* (September, 1979) No. 63. **[182, 213, 215]**

Robinson, John P. and Haluk Sahin. "Beyond the Realm of Necessity: Television and the Colonization of Leisure," *Media, Culture and Society* (January, 1981) 3(1): 85-95. **[250]**

Robinson, Michael J. and Andrew Kohut. "Believability and the Press," *Public Opinion Quarterly* (1988) 52: 174-189. **[205, 208]**

Robinson, John P. and Mark R. Levy with Dennis K. Davis, in association with W. Gill Woodall, Michael Gurevitch and Haluk Sahin. *The Main Source: Learning from Television News.* Beverly Hills, CA: Sage Publications, 1986. **[297, 310, 319]**

Roch, I. "Journalism as Storytelling: Coverage as Narrative," *American Behavioral Scientist* (November/December, 1989) 33(2): 162-168. **[162]**

Roe, K. and U. Johnsson-Smaragdi. "The Swedish 'Media Scape' in the 1980s," *European Journal of Communication* (September, 1987) 2(3): 357-370. **[169]**

Roe, K. "Swedish Youth and Music: Listening Patterns and Motivations," *Communication Research* (July, 1985) 12(3): 353-362. **[196, 278]**

Roe, Keith. "Adolescents' Video Use," *American Behavioral Scientist* (May/June, 1987) 30(5): 522-532. **[212]**

Roeh, Itzak and Peter Dahlgren. "Stories Nations Tell Themselves: The Global Newsroom Project," *The Nordicom Review* (1991) 1: 48-52. **[363]**

Rogers, Everett and Steven H. Chaffee. "Communication as an Academic Discipline: A Dialogue," *Journal of Communication* (1983) 33: 18-30. **[297]**

Rogers, Rosemarie. "Language Policy and Language Power: The Case of Soviet Publishing," *Language Problems and Language Planning* (Spring, 1987) 11(1): 82-103. **[46]**

Rogge, Jan-Uwe and Klaus Jensen. "Everyday Life and Television in West Germany: An Empathic-Interpretive Perspective on the Family as a System," *World Families Watch Television,* ed. James Lull. Newbury Park, CA: Sage Publications, 1988, pp. 80-115. **[237]**

Rollin, Roger B. "Triple-X: Erotic Movies and their Audiences," *Journal of Popular Film and Television* (Spring, 1982) 10(1): 2-21. **[330]**

Rollings, J. "Mass Communications and the American Worker," *The Critical Communications Review,* ed. V. Mosco and J. Wasko. Vol. 1. Norwood, NJ: Ablex Publishers, 1983, pp. 131-152. **[356]**

Romanow, Walter I. and Walter C. Soderlund. "Thomson Newspapers' Acquisition of 'The Globe and Mail': A Case Study of Content Change," *Gazette* (1988) 41: 5-17. **[90]**

Romanow, Walter I. and Walter C. Soderlund, "The Southam Press Acquisition of the Windsor Star: A Canadian Case Study of Change," *Gazette* (1978) 24(4): 255-270. **[98]**

Rondina, M.L., Mary Cassata and Thomas Skill. "Placing a 'Lid' on Television Serial Drama: An Analysis of the Lifestyles, Interpersonal Management Skills, and Demography of Daytime's Fictional Population," *Life on Daytime Television: Tuning In American Serial Drama,* ed. Mary Cassata and Thomas Skill. Norwood, NJ: Ablex Publishers, 1983, pp. 3-21. **[368]**

Room, Robin. "Alcoholism and Alcoholics Anonymous in U.S. Films, 1945-1962: The Party Ends for the 'Wet Generations,'" *Journal of Studies on Alcohol* (1989) 50(4): 368-383. **[371]**

Roper Organization, Inc. *Public Attitudes Toward Television and Other Media in a Time of Change.* New York: Television Information Office, May, 1985. **[206]**

Roper Organization, Inc. The 1980 Virginia Slims American Women's Opinion Poll. 1980. **[211, 236]**

Rorty, R. *Philosophy and the Mirror of Nature.* Princeton, NJ: Princeton University Press, 1979. **[18]**

Rosenberg, Howard. "Irony Served as TV Newswomen Cover the Gulf," *Plain Dealer*, Jan. 17, 1991, p. 11E. Los Angeles Times dispatch. **[148]**

Rosengren, Karl Erik and Sven Windahl. *Media Matter: TV Use in Childhood and Adolescence.* Norwood, NJ: Ablex, 1989. **[188]**

Roshco, Bernard. *Newsmaking.* Chicago: University of Chicago Press, 1975. **[121, 160]**

Rositi, Franco. "Televised Information: The Cutting and Recomposition of the Image of Society: A Study of the News Broadcasts of Four European Networks," *Studies of Radio- Television* (November, 1977) 24: 123-148. **[126]**

Ross, Andrew (ed.).   *Universal Abandon?: The Politics of Postmodernism.*   Edinburgh: Edinburgh University Press, 1989. **[18]**

Ross, Bonnie Lou. "Education Reporting in the Los Angeles Times," *Journalism Quarterly* (Summer, 1983) 60(2): 348-352. **[368]**

Rosse, James N. "Economic Limits of Press Responsibility," Discussion Paper.   Stanford University: Studies in Industry Economics, No. 56, 1975; discussed in Devey, 1989, and Compaine, 1979. **[98]**

Rossow, Marshel D. and Sharon Dunwoody. "Inclusion of 'Useful' Detail in Newspaper Coverage of a High-Level Nuclear Waste Siting Controversy," *Journalism Quarterly* (Spring/Summer, 1991) 68(1/2): 87-100. **[162]**

Rota, Josep and Denise Tremmel. "Rural-Urban Differences in Television Uses, Functions and Gratifications among Mexican Children," paper presented to the Intercultural and Development Communication Division at the annual conference of the International Communication Association, Chicago, May, 1991. **[259]**

Rothenberg, Randall, "Slower Rise in Costs of Commercials," *New York Times*, May 4, 1990, p. 17C. **[211]**

Rothenbuhler, E.W. "The Living Room Celebration of the Olympic Games," *Journal of Communication* (Autumn, 1988) 38(4): 61-81. **[275]**

Rothenbuhler, Eric W. "Programming Decision Making in Popular Music Radio," *Communication Research* (April, 1985) 12(2): 209-232.**[116, 166]**

Rothschild, Michael L., Esther Thorson, Byron Reeves, Judith E. Hirsch and Robert Goldstein. "EEG Activity and the Processing of Television Commercials," *Communication Research* (April, 1986) 13(2): 182-220. **[274]**

Routt, Edd, James B. McGrath and Frederic A. Weiss. *The Radio Format Conundrum.* New York: Hastings House, 1978. **[326, 328]**

Rowe, John Carlos. "From Documentary to Docudrama: Vietnam on Television in the 1980s," *Genre* (Winter, 1988) 21: 451-477. **[331]**

Rubin, Alan M. "Ritualized and Instrumental Television Viewing," *Journal of Communication* (1987) 14: 58-84.

Rubin, Alan M. "Age and Family Control Influences on Children's Television Viewing," *The Southern Speech Communication Journal* (Fall, 1986) 52: 35-51. **[186, 278]**

Rubin, Alan M. "Media Gratifications through the Life Cycle," *Media Gratifications Research: Current Perspectives*, ed. K.E. Rosengren, L.A. Wenner and P. Palmgreen. Beverly Hills, CA: Sage Publications, 1985, pp. 195-208. **[259, 275]**

Rubin, Alan M. "Uses of Daytime Television Soap Operas by College Students," *Journal of Broadcasting & Electronic Media* (Summer, 1985) 29(3): 241-258. **[259, 275]**

Rubin, Alan M. "Ritualized and Instrumental Television Viewing," *Journal of Communication* (Summer, 1984) 34(3): 67-77. **[273]**

Rubin, Alan M. "Television Uses and Gratifications: The Interactions of Viewing Patterns and Motivations," *Journal of Broadcasting* (Winter, 1983) 27(1): 37-51. **[251, 273]**

Rubin, Alan M. "Television Uses and Gratifications: The Interactions of Viewing Patterns and Motivations," *Journal of Broadcasting* (1983) 27: 37-51. **[251, 273]**

Rubin, Alan M. "A Multivariate Analysis of '60 Minutes' Viewing Motivations," *Journalism Quarterly* (1981) 58: 529-534. **[273]**

Rubin, Alan M. "Television Usage, Attitudes and Viewing Behaviors of Children and Adolescents," *Journal of Broadcasting* (Summer, 1977) 21(3): 355-369. **[278]**

Rubin, Alan M. and Charles R. Bantz. "Utility of Videocassette Recorders," *American Behavioral Scientist* (May/June, 1987) 30(5): 471-485. **[251]**

Rubin, Alan M. and E.M. Perse. "Audience Activity and Television News Gratifications," *Communication Research* (1987) 14: 58-84. **[244, 273]**

Rubin, Alan M., Elizabeth M. Perse and R.A. Powell. "Loneliness, Parasocial Interaction, and Local Television Viewing," *Human Communication Research* (Winter, 1985) 12(2): 155-180. **[273, 277]**

Rubin, Alan M. and Rebecca B. Rubin. "Social and Psychological Antecedents of VCR Use," *The VCR Age: Home Video and Mass Communication*, ed. M.R. Levy. Newbury Park, CA: Sage publications, 1989, pp. 92-111. **[255]**

Rubin, Alan M. and Sven Windahl. "The Uses and Dependency Model of Mass Communication," *Critical Studies in Mass Communication* (1986) 3(2): 184-199. **[226, 244, 256]**

Rubin, M.R. and M.T. Huber. *The Knowledge Industry in the United States 1960-1980.* Princeton University Press, 1986. **[93]**

Rubin, Rebecca B. and M.P. McHugh. "Development of Parasocial Interaction Relationships," *Journal of Broadcasting & Electronic Media* (Summer, 1987) 31(3): 279-292. **[278]**

Rubin, Rebecca B., Alan M. Rubin, Elizabeth M. Perse, Cameron Armstrong, Michael McHugh and Noreen Faix. "Media Use and Meaning of Music Video," *Journalism Quarterly* (Summer, 1986) 63(2): 353-359. **[305, 309]**

Rubin, Steven Jay. *Combat Films: American Realism, 1945-1970.* Jefferson, NC: McFarland, 1981. **[331]**

Ruddell, R.B. and R. Speaker. "The Interactive Reading Process: A Model," *Theoretical Models and Processes of Reading*, ed. H. Singer and R.B. Ruddell. 3rd ed. Newark, DE: International Reading Association, 1985, pp. 751-793. **[316]**

Ruggerio, J.A. and L.C. Weston. "Work Options for Women in Women's Magazines: The Medium and the Message," *Sex Roles* (March, 1985) 12(5/6): 535-548. **[367]**

Rumelhart, D.E. "Toward an Interactive Model of Reading," *Theoretical Models and Processes of Reading*, ed. H. Singer and R.B. Ruddell, 3rd ed. Newark, DE: International Reading Association, 1985, pp. 722-750. **[316]**

Rumelhart, D.E. "Understanding and Summarizing Brief Stories," *Basic Processes in Reading: Perception and Comprehension*, ed. D. LaBerge and S.J. Samuels. Hillsdale, NJ: Lawrence Erlbaum, 1977, pp. 265-303; technical report with same title, cited in Nolan (1990). **[312, 314, 316]**

Rumelhart, D.E. *Introduction to Human Information Processing.* New York: Wiley, 1977. **[312, 314, 316]**

Rumelhart, D.E. "Notes on a Schema for Stories," *Representation and Understanding: Studies in Cognitive Science*, ed. D.G. Bobrow and A.M. Collins. New York: Academic Press, 1975, pp. 211-236. **[316]**

Ruofolo, A. "Professional Orientation among Journalists in Three Latin American Countries," *Gazette* (1987) 40(2): 131-142. **[165]**

Ruotolo, A. Carlos. "A Typology of Newspaper Readers," *Journalism Quarterly* (Spring, 1988) 65(1): 126-130. **[253]**

Rust, L. "Using Attention and Intention to Predict At-Home Program Choice," *Journal of Advertising Research* (April/May, 1987) 27(2): 25-30. **[242]**

Rust, Roland T. and Naras V. Eechambadi. "Scheduling Network Television Programs: A Heuristic Audience Flow Approach to Maximizing Audience Share," *Journal of Advertising* (1989) 18(2): 11-18. **[268]**

Ryan, John and Richard A. Peterson. "The Product Image: The Fate of Creativity in Country Music Songwriting," *Individuals in Mass Media Organizations: Creativity and Constraint*, eds. James Ettema and D. Charles Whitney. Beverly Hills, CA: Sage Publications, Vol. 10, Sage Annual Reviews of Communication Research, 1982, pp. 11-32. **[63]**

Ryan, John and Deborah A. Sim. "When Art Becomes News: Portrayals of Art and Artists on Network Television News," *Social Forces* (March, 1990) 68(3): 869-889. **[369]**

Ryan, Michael and David L. Martinson. "Journalists and Public Relations Practitioners: Why the Antagonism?" *Journalism Quarterly* (Spring, 1988) 65(1): 131-140. **[59, 138]**

Ryan, Timothy. "Living Dangerously--Changing Press Law in India," paper presented at the annual conference of the Association for Education in Journalism and Mass Communication, Portland, OR, 1988. **[49]**

Saddler, Jeanne. "Newest TV Stations Are Low in Power, High in Local Color," *Wall Street Journal*, Oct. 23, 1984, p. 1. **[68]**

Salmon, C.T. and J.S. Lee. "Perceptions of Newspaper Fairness: A Structural Approach," *Journalism Quarterly* (Winter, 1983) 60(4): 663-670. **[207]**

Salmon, Charles T. "Message Discrimination and the Information Environment," *Communication Research* (July, 1986) 13(3): 363-372.

Salomon, Gavriel. "Television Is 'Easy' and Print Is 'Tough,'" *Journal of Educational Psychology* (1984) 76: 647-658. **[311]**

Salomon, Gavriel. "Television Watching and Mental Effort: A Social Psychological View," *Children's Understanding of Television*, ed. J. Bryant and D.R. Anderson. New York: Academic Press, 1983, pp. 181-198. **[311]**

Salomon, Gavriel. *Communication and Education*. Beverly Hills, CA: Sage, 1981. **[311]**

Salomon, Gavriel. "Introducing AIME: The Assessment of Children's Mental Involvement with Television," *Children and the Worlds of Television*, ed. H. Gardner and H. Kelly. San Francisco: Jossey-Bass, 1981. **[311]**

Salomon, Gavriel. *Interaction of Media, Cognition and Learning*. San Francisco: Jossey-Bass, 1979. **[297, 317]**

Salomon, Gavriel and Akiba A. Cohen. "On the Meaning and Validity of Television Viewing," *Human Communication Research* (Spring, 1978) 4: 265-270. **[229]**

Salomon, Gavriel and T. Leigh. "Predispositions about Learning from Print and Television," *Journal of Communication* (1984) 34: 119-135. **[311]**

Salomone, Kandice, Michael R. Greenberg, Peter M. Sandman and David B. Sachsman, "A Question of Quality: How Journalists and News Sources Evaluate Coverage of Environmental Rick," *Journal of Communication* (Autumn, 1990) 40(4): 117-130. **[163]**

Salt, Barry. *Film Style and Technology: History and Analysis*. London: Starword, 1983. **[106, 107]**

Salvaggio, Jerry L. (ed.) *The Information Society: Economic, Social and Structural Issues*. Hillsdale, NJ: Lawrence Erlbaum Associates, 1989. **[94]**

Salwen, M.B. "Credibility of Newspaper Opinion Polls: Source, Source Intent and Precision," *Journalism Quarterly* (Winter, 1987) 64(4): 813-819. **[205]**

Salwen, Michael B. and James M. Bernstein. "Coverage of Aftermath of 1984 World Series," *Journalism Quarterly* (Summer, 1986) 63(2): 385-389. **[159]**

Salzmann, Z. "Portrayal of Gender Relations in Contemporary Czech Mass Media," *East European Quarterly* (January, 1990) 23(4): 399-407. **[366]**

Sampson, Edward E. "The Challenge of Social Change for Psychology: Globalization and Psychology's Theory of the Person," *American Psychologist* (June, 1989) 44(6): 914-921. **[18]**

Sandage, C.H., Arnold M. Barban and James E. Haefner, "How Farmers View Advertising," *Journalism Quarterly* (Summer, 1976) 53: 303-308. **[219]**

Sapolsky, Barry S. and Joseph O. Tabarlet. "Sex in Primetime Television: 1979 Versus 1989," *Journal of Broadcasting & Electronic Media* (Fall, 1991) 35(4): 505-516. **[350]**

Sarf, Wayne Michael. *God Bless You, Buffalo Bill: A Layman's Guide to History and the Western Film.* Rutherford, NJ: Fairleigh Dickinson University Press, 1983. **[331]**

Sarlo, G., L.A. Jason and C. Lonak. "Parents' Strategies for Limiting Children's Television Watching," *Psychological Reports* (1988) 63(3): 435-438. **[271]**

Saunders, C.S. and B.A. Stead. "Women's Adoption of a Business Uniform: A Content Analysis of Magazine Advertisements," *Sex Roles* (1986) 15(3/4): 197-205. **[368]**

Sayre, Nora. "Winning the Weepstakes: The Problems of American Sports Movies," *Film Genre: Theory and Criticism*, ed. Barry K. Grant. Metuchen, NJ: The Scarecrow Press, Inc., pp. 182-194, 1977. **[331]**

Scanlon, T.J. "Viewer Perceptions on Color, Black and White TV: An Experiment," *Journalism Quarterly* (1970) 47: 366-368. **[315]**

Scanlon, T.J. "Color Television: New Language?" *Journalism Quarterly* (1967) 44: 225-230. **[315]**

Scardino, Albert. "Newspaper Guild Drifts as Its Industry Surges," *New York Times*, Aug. 15, 1988, p. 21. **[150]**

Schaefer, David J. and David Atkin. "An Analysis of Policy Options for High Definition Television," paper presented to the Communication Technology Committee at the annual conference of the Association for Education in Journalism and Mass Communication," Minneapolis, 1990. **[75]**

Schank, R.C., and R. Abelson. *Scripts, Plans, Goals and Understanding.* Hillsdale, NJ: Lawrence Erlbaum Associates, 1977. **[312, 316]**

Scharlott, Bradford W. "The Hoosier Journalist and the Hooded Order: Indiana Press Reaction to the Ku Klux Klan in the 1920s," *Journalism History* (Winter, 1988) 15(4): 122-131. **[60]**

Scharlott, Bradford W. "Influence of Telegraph on Wisconsin Newspaper Growth," *Journalism Quarterly* (Autumn, 1989) 66(3): 710-715. **[26]**

Schatz, Thomas. *Hollywood Genres.* Philadelphia, Pa: Temple University Press, 1981. **[329]**

Schement, J.R. and L. Lievrouw. "A Behavioral Measure of Information Work," *Telecommunications Policy* (December, 1984) 8(4): 321-328. **[93]**

Schement, Jorge Reina. "The Origins of the Information Society in the United States: Competing Visions," *The Information Society: Economic, Social and Structural Issues.* Hillsdale, NJ: Lawrence Erlbaum Associates, 1989. **[94]**

Scherer, Clifford W. "The Videocassette Recorder and Information Inequity," *Journal of Communication* (Summer, 1989) 39(3): 94-103. **[182, 230, 231, 272]**

Scheurer, Timothy E. "The Aesthetics of Form and Convention in the Movie Musical," *Film Genre: Theory and Criticism*, ed. Barry K. Grant. Metuchen, NJ: The Scarecrow Press, Inc., pp. 145-160, 1977. **[331]**

Schibeci, R.A. "Patterns of Media Use in Perth, Western Australia," *Media Information Australia* (May, 1989) 52: 50-52. **[215]**

Schickel, Richard. "The Crisis in Movie Narrative," *Gannett Center Journal* (Summer, 1989) 3(3): 1-15. **[103, 105]**

Schiff, Frederick. "The Dominant Ideology in the Press: A Test of Competing Theories in Ohio Newspapers," paper presented at the annual conference of the Association for Education in Journalism and Mass Communication, Boston, August, 1991. **[127, 159]**

Schiller, Dan. *Objectivity and the News: The Public and the Rise of Commercial Journalism.* Philadelphia, PA: Temple University Press, 1981. **[65, 130]**

Schiller, Herbert I. "Whose New International Economic Information Order?" *Communication* (1980) 5(2): 299-314. **[198]**

Schiller, H. *Who Knows: Information in the Age of the Fortune 500.* Norwood, NJ: Ablex, 1981. **[65, 129]**

Schleuder, J., E. Thorson and B. Reeves. "Effects of Complexity and Scene Reordering on Attention to Television Messages," paper presented at the annual meeting of the International Communication Association, Montreal, May, 1987. **[316]**

Schleuder, J., E. Thorson and B. Reeves. "Effects of Time Compression and Complexity on Attention to Television Commercials," paper presented at the annual conference of the International Communication Association, New Orleans, May, 1988. **[316]**

Schneider, Walter and Richard M. Shiffrin. "Controlled and Automatic Human Information Processing: Detection, Search and Attention," *Psychological Review* (1977) 84: 1-66. **[308, 320]**

Schneider, W. and I.A. Lewis. "Views on the News," *Public Opinion* (August/September, 1985) 8(4): 6-11. **[149, 231]**

Schoenbach, Klaus and Josef Hackforth. "Video in West German Households: Attitudinal and Behavioral Differences," *American Behavioral Scientist* (May/June, 1987) 30(5): 533-543. **[198, 255]**

Schrag, Robert L. and Lawrence B. Rosenfeld. "Assessing the Soap Opera Frame: Audience Perceptions of Value Structures in Soap Operas and Prime-Time Serial Dramas," *The Southern Speech Communication Journal* (Summer, 1987) 52: 362-376. **[275, 361]**

Schramm, Wilbur. *The Story of Human Communication: Cave Painting to Microchip.* New York: Harper & Row, Publishers, 1988. **[25, 28]**

Schramm, Wilbur. *Men, Messages and Media.* New York: Harper & Row, Publishers, 1973. **[56, 229]**

Schramm, Wilbur. "Channels and Audience," *Handbook of Communication,* ed. Ithiel de Sola Pool and Wilbur Schramm. Chicago: Rand McNally, 1973, pp. 116-140.

Schudson, M. "Why News Is the Way It Is," *Raritan* (1983) 2: 109-125. **[20]**

Schudson, Michael. "The Sociology of News Production," *Media, Culture and Society* (1989) 11: 263-282. **[161]**

Schultz, Ernie. "Toward the Year 2000: The Challenge of Change," *RTNDA Communicator,* January, 1988, p. 91. **[164]**

Schumacher, G.M. et al. "Cognitive Processes in Journalistic Genres: Extending Writing Models," *Written Communication* (July, 1989) 6(3): 390-407. **[139]**

Schwarzlose, Richard A. "The Marketplace of Ideas: A Measure of Free Expression," *Journalism Monographs* (December, 1989) No. 118. **[54, 78, 79]**

Schweitzer, John C. "Personal Computers and Media Use," *Journalism Quarterly* (Winter, 1991) 68(4): 689-697. **[177]**

Schwenk, Nancy E. "Household Expenditures for Education and Reading," *Family Economics Review* (1988) 1(3): 6-8. **[71, 95]**

Schwichtenberg, C. "Articulating the People's Politics: Manhood and Right-Wing Populism in 'The A-Team,'" *Communication* (1987) 9(3): 379-398. **[372]**

Scott, David and Fern K. Willits. "Adolescent and Adult Leisure Patterns: A 37-Year Follow-Up Study," *Leisure Sciences* (1989) 11: 323-335. **[190]**

Scott, David K. and Robert H. Gobetz. "Hard News/Soft News Content of the National Broadcast Networks, 1972-1987," *Journalism Quarterly* (Summer, 1992) 69(2): 406-412. **[340, 363]**

Seaton, J. "The BBC and the Holocaust," *European Journal of Communication* (March, 1987) 2(1): 53-80. **[371]**

Seggar, John F., Jeffrey K. Hafen, and Helena Hannonen-Gladen. "Television's Portrayals of Minorities and Women in Drama and Comedy Drama, 1971-80," *Journal of Broadcasting* (Summer, 1981) 25(3): 277-288. **[364]**

Seidman, Steve. *Comedian Comedy: A Tradition in Hollywood Film*. Ann Arbor: UMI Research Press, 1981. **[331]**

Self, Charles C. "The Flight from Fleet Street: Causes and Consequences," *Gazette* (1990) 45: 49-64. **[43, 59]**

Self, Charles C. "Recent Developments in Communication Technology in the Japanese Newspaper Industry," *International Communication Bulletin* (Spring, 1990) 25(1-2): 17-21. **[43, 90]**

Self, Charles C. "Perceived Task of News Report as a Predictor of Media Choice," *Journalism Quarterly* (Spring, 1988) 65(1): 119-125. **[149]**

Self, Charles C. "A Study of News Credibility and Task Perception among Journalists in the United States and England," *International Communication Bulletin* (Spring, 1988) 23(1-2): 16-21. **[149, 165]**

Selnow, Gary W. "Values on Prime-Time Television," *Journal of Communication* (Spring, 1990) 40(2): 64-74. **[359]**

Selnow, Gary W. "Solving Problems on Prime-Time Television," *Journal of Communication* (Spring, 1986) 36(2): 63-72. **[359]**

Selnow, Gary W. and Hal Reynolds. "Some Opportunity Costs of Television Viewing," *Journal of Broadcasting and Electronic Media* (Summer, 1984) 28(3): 315-322. **[186, 188, 256]**

Senat, Tracy C. "How Management Training Relates to Newspaper Editors' Professional Commitment," paper presented to the Media Management and Economics Division at the annual conference of the Association for Education in Journalism and Mass Communication, Montreal, August, 1992. **[109]**

Sengupta, Subir. "Role Portrayals of Women in Magazine Advertisements," *Media Asia* (1992) 19(3): 145-149, 155. **[367]**

Sentman, Mary Alice. "When the Newspaper Closes: A Case Study of What Advertisers Do," *Journalism Quarterly* (Winter, 1986) 63(4): 757-762. **[85]**

Sentman, Mary Alice. "Black and White: Disparity in Coverage by Life Magazine from 1937 to 1972," *Journalism Quarterly* (Fall, 1983) 60(3): 501-508. **[364]**

Seo, Sae Kyung. "Source-Television Journalist Relationship: Coverage of News Sources in Network Evening Newscast," paper presented at the annual conference of the Association for Education in Journalism and Mass Communication, Washington, D.C., August, 1989. **[134, 137, 161]**

Servaes, Jan. "European Press Coverage of the Grenada Crisis," *Journal of Communication* (Autumn, 1991) 41(4): 28-41. **[158]**

Servaes, Jan. "Concentration of Ownership in the Belgian Daily Press," *Journalism Quarterly* (Summer, 1989) 66(2): 367-372. **[44, 48, 49, 59, 98]**

Shaffer, Garnett Stokes. "Patterns of Work and Nonwork Satisfaction," *Journal of Applied Psychology* (1987) 72(1): 115-124. **[280]**

Shagrin, C. "On the Trail of the Elusive 90's Viewer," *Nielsen Newscast* (Spring, 1990), cited in Ferguson (1991). **[228]**

Shaheen, J.G. "Perspectives on the Television Arab," *Image Ethics: The Moral Rights of Subjects in Photographs, Film and Television*, ed. L. Gross, J.S. Katz and J. Ruby. New York: Oxford University Press, 1988. **[346]**

Shamir, Jacob. "Israeli Elite Journalists: Views on Freedom and Responsibility," *Journalism Quarterly* (Fall, 1988) 65(3): 589-594, 647. **[165]**

Shanks, Bob. *The Cool Fire: How to Make It in Television*. New York: Vintage Books, 1976. **[112]**

Shapiro, Eben. "New Marketing Specialists Tap Collegiate Consumers," *New York Times*, Feb. 27, 1992, p. 16C. **[174]**

Shapiro, Michael A. "The Effect of Headlines on Attitude Activation and Agenda Setting," paper presented to the Information Systems Division at the annual conference of the International Communication Association, Chicago, Ill., May, 1991. **[296]**

Shapiro, Mitchell E. and Lemuel B. Schofield. "How Proximity, Circulation and Geographical Distribution Influences Coverage of Miami's Overtown Disturbance," *Newspaper Research Journal* (Summer, 1986) 7(4): 55-61. [156]

Shapiro, Mitchell and Wenmouth Williams Jr. "Civil Disturbance in Miami: Proximity and Conflict in Newspaper Coverage," *Newspaper Research Journal* (Spring, 1984) 5(3): 61-69. [156]

Sharbutt, Jay. "Cable Television Has Big Plans to Branch Out Despite Clouded Picture," *Plain Dealer*, Jan. 26, 1991, p. 6E. Associated Press story. [69]

Sharf, Barbara F. "Send in the Clowns: The Image of Psychiatry during the Hinckley Trial," *Journal of Communication* (Autumn, 1986) 36(4): 80-93. [369]

Sharkey, Joe. "Weekly Newspapers Challenge the Dailies," *Wall Street Journal*, April 13, 1989, p. 7B. [72]

Sharp, E.B. "Consequences of Local Government Under the Klieg Lights," *Communication Research* (October, 1984) 11(4): 497-517. [196]

Shaw, D.L. and J.W. Slater. "In the Eye of the Beholder? Sensationalism in American Press News, 1820-1860," *Journalism History* (Autumn/Winter, 1985) 12(3/4): 86-91. [58]

Shaw, David. "A Handfull of Opinion-Makers Lead Pack Journalists," *Plain Dealer*, Sept. 10, 1989, p. 7C, Los Angeles dispatch. [138]

Shaw, Donald Lewis. "News About Slavery from 1820-1860 in Newspapers of South, North and West," *Journalism Quarterly* (Autumn, 1984) 61(3): 483-492. [363]

Shaw, Donald Lewis. "At the Crossroads: Change and Continuity in American Press News, 1820-1860," *Journalism History* (Summer, 1981) 8(2): 38-50. [363]

Shaw, Donald Lewis and Sylvia L. Zack. "Rethinking Journalism History: How Some Recent Studies Support One Approach," *Journalism History* (Winter, 1987) 14(4): 111-117. [58]

Shaw, Punch. "Generic Refinement on the Fringe: The Game Show," *The Southern Speech Communication Journal* (Summer, 1987) 52: 403-410. [335, 362]

Shaw, Susan M. "The Meaning of Leisure in Everyday Life," *Leisure Sciences* (1985) 7(1): 1-24. [211]

Sherer, Michael. "Assaults on Photojournalists," *Newspaper Research Journal* (Spring, 1991) 12(2): 82-91. [60]

Sherman, B.L. "News from Home: The Media Needs of Canadians in the USA," *Canadian Journal of Communication* (Spring, 1985) 11(2): 181-192. [277]

Sherman, Barry L. and Joseph R. Dominick. "Perceptions of Colorization," *Journalism Quarterly* (Winter, 1988) 65(4): 976-980. [197]

Shevelow, K. *Women and Print Culture: The Construction of Femininity in the Early Periodical.* New York: Routledge, Chapman and Hall, 1989. [34]

Shields, Steven and Sharon Dunwoody. "The Social World of the Statehouse Pressroom," *Newspaper Research Journal* (Fall, 1986) 8(1): 43-51. [138, 161]

Shields, Steven O. "Creativity and Creative Control in the Work of American Music Radio Announcers," paper presented to the Mass Communication and Society Division at the annual conference of the Association for Education in Journalism and Mass Communication, Minneapolis, August, 1990. [155]

Shimizu, Shinichi. "The Challenges to Public Service Broadcasting--How NHK Prepares for the Future," paper prepared for The Aspen Institute Conference, Berlin, 1986; cited in Helen Katz, 1989. [59]

Shlapentokh, Vladimir. "Public Opinion in Gorbachev's USSR: Consensus and Polarization," *Media, Culture and Society* (1990) 12: 153-174. [59]

Shoaf, Linda R., Powell D. McClellan and Kimberly A. Birskovich. "Nutrition Knowledge, Interests, and Information Sources of Male Athletes," *Journal of Nutrition Education* (1986) 18(6): 243-245. [276]

Shoben, E., K. Wescourt and E. Smith. "Sentence Verification, Sentence Recognition and the Semantic-Episodic Distinction," *Journal of Experimental Psychology* (1978) 4: 304-317. [319]

Shoebridge, A. "Alcohol on Television," *Media Information Australia* (May, 1988) 48: 6-10. **[371]**

Shoemaker, D.H. "An Analysis of the Effects of Three Vertical Camera Angles and Three Lighting Ratios on the Connotative Judgments of Photographs of Three Human Models," Ph.D. dissertation, Indiana University, 1964. *Dissertation Abstracts International*, 25, 5650.

Shoemaker, Pamela J. "Predicting Media Uses," *Measuring the Information Society*, ed. F. Williams. Newbury Park, CA: Sage Focus Editions, No. 97, Sage Publications, 1989, pp. 229-242. **[231]**

Shoemaker, Pamela J. "The Communication of Deviance," *Progress in Communication Sciences*, eds. Brenda Dervin and M.J. Voigt. Vol. 8. Norwood, NJ: Ablex, 1987, pp. 151-175. **[156]**

Shoemaker, Pamela J. "Media Treatment of Deviant Political Groups," *Journalism Quarterly* (Spring, 1984) 61(1): 66-75, 82. **[132, 156, 318]**

Shoemaker, Pamela J. et al. "Ethnic Concentration as Predictor of Media Use," *Journalism Quarterly* (Summer/Autumn, 1987) 64(2/3): 593-596. **[156, 270]**

Shoemaker, Pamela J., Lucig H. Danielian and Nancy Brendlinger. "Deviant Acts, Risky Business and U.S. Interests: The Newsworthiness of World Events," *Journalism Quarterly* (Winter, 1991) 68(4): 781-795. **[156]**

Shoemaker, Pam J. and E.K. Mayfield, "Building a Theory of News Content," *Journalism Monographs*, No. 103, June, 1987. **[145]**

Shoemaker, Pamela J. and Stephen D. Reese. *Mediating the Message: Theories of Influence on Mass Media Content*. New York: Longman, 1991. **[153]**

Shout, John D. "The Film Musical and the Legacy of Show Business," *Journal of Popular Film and Television* (Spring, 1982) 10(1): 23-26. **[331]**

Siebert, Fred S,, Theodore Peterson and Wilbur Schramm. *Four Theories of the Press*. Urbana: University of Illinois Press, 1956, 1963. **[50]**

Siemicki, Michele, David Atkin, Bradley Greenberg and Thomas Baldwin. "Nationally Distributed Children's Shows: What Cable TV Contributes," *Journalism Quarterly* (Winter, 1986) 63(4): 710-718, 734. **[361]**

Sigal, Leon V. *Reporters and Officials: The Organization and Politics of Newsmaking*. Lexington, MA: D.C. Heath & Co., 1973. **[134, 151, 161]**

Signitzer, Benno and Kurt Luger. "Austria," *International Handbook of Broadcasting Systems*, ed. Philip T. Rosen (1988), pp. 15-24. **[49]**

Signorielli, Nancy. "Television and Conceptions about Sex Roles: Maintaining Conventionality and the Status Quo," *Sex Roles* (1989) 21(5/6): 341-360. **[350]**

Signorielli, Nancy. "The Stigma of Mental Illness on Television," *Journal of Broadcasting & Electronic Media* (Summer, 1989) 33(3): 325-331. **[370]**

Signorielli, Nancy. "Selective Television Viewing: A Limited Possibility," *Journal of Communication* (Summer, 1986) 36(3): 64-76. **[268, 333, 351]**

Signorielli, Nancy. "The Demography of the Television World," *Proceedings from the Tenth Annual Telecommunications Policy Research Conference*, ed. O.H. Gandy Jr., P. Espinosa and J.R. Ordover. Norwood, NJ: Ablex Publishers, 1983, pp. 53-73. **[342]**

Silva, Indra de. "Foreign Movies on American Screens: An Empirical Study," paper presented at the annual conference of the International Communication Association, Miami, May 23, 1992. **[197, 361]**

Silver, Diane. "A Comparison of Newspaper Coverage of Male and Female Officials in Michigan," *Journalism Quarterly* (Spring, 1986) 63(1): 144-149. **[137]**

Simon, Julian L., Walter J. Primeaux Jr., and Edward Rice. "The Price Effects of Monopolistic Ownership in Newspapers," *The Antitrust Bulletin* (Spring, 1986) 31(1): 113-131. **[85]**

Simon, Rita J. *Public Opinion and the Immigrant: Print Media Coverage, 1880-1980*. Lexington, MA: Lexington Books, 1985. **[346]**

Simon, Todd F., Frederick Fico and Stephen Lacy. "Covering Conflict and Controversy: Measuring Balance, Fairness, Defamation," *Journalism Quarterly* (Summer, 1989) 66(2): 427-434. **[135, 156]**

Sims, Jonathan B. "VCR Viewing Patterns: An Electronic and Passive Investigation," *Journal of Advertising Research* (April/May, 1989) 29(2): 11-17. **[176]**

Singal, Daniel Joseph. "Towards a Definition of American Modernism," *American Quarterly* (Spring-Summer, 1987) 39:7-26. **[18]**

Singer, Benjamin D. "Minorities and the Media: A Content Analysis of Native Canadians in the Daily Press," *Canadian Review of Sociology and Anthropology* (August, 1982) 19(3): 348-359. **[346]**

Singer, E. and P. Endreny. "Reporting Hazards: Their Benefits and Costs," *Journal of Communication* (Summer, 1987) 37(3): 10-26. **[156]**

Singer, Eleanor, Phyllis Endreny and Marc B. Glassman. "Media Coverage of Disasters: Effect of Geographic Location," *Journalism Quarterly* (Spring/Summer, 1991) 68(1/2): 48-58. **[119, 156]**

Singer, Eleanor. "A Question of Accuracy: How Journalists and Scientists Report Research on Hazards," *Journal of Communication* (1990) 4(4): 102-116. **[163]**

Singer, J.L. "The Power and Limitations of Television: A Cognitive-Affective Analysis," *The Entertainment Functions of Television*, ed. P.H. Tannenbaum. Hillsdale, NJ: Lawrence Erlbaum, 1980, pp. 31-65. **[311]**

Singhal, Arvind, J.K. Doshi, Everett M. Rogers, and S. Adnan Rahman. "The Diffusion of Television in India," *Media Asia* (1988) 15(4): 222-229). **[27]**

Singletary, Michael W. "Reliability of Immediate Reward and Delayed Reward Categories," *Journalism Quarterly* (Spring, 1985) 62(1): 116-120. **[254]**

Singletary, Michael W. "Components of Credibility of a Favorable News Source," *Journalism Quarterly* (Summer, 1976) 53: 316-319. **[205]**

Singletary, Michael W., Susan Caudill, Edward Caudill and Allen White. "Motives for Ethical Decision-Making," *Journalism Quarterly* (Winter, 1990) 67(4): 964-972. **[155]**

Singeltary, Michael W. and Richard Lipsky. "Accuracy in Local TV News," *Journalism Quarterly* (Summer, 1977) 54: 362-364. **[144]**

Singleton, Jerome F., Wayne Mitic, and Jane Farquharson. "Activity Profile of Retired Individuals," *Activities, Adaptation & Aging* (Fall, 1989) 9(1): 17-24. **[191]**

Sipchen, Bob. "The Good, the Bad and the Ludicrous," *Los Angeles Times*, Dec. 27, 1990, p. 1E. **[73]**

Sirgy, M. Joseph, H. Lee Meadow, Don R. Rahtz and A.C. Samli (Eds.) *Developments in Quality-of-Life Studies in Marketing*. Vol. 4, 1992. Proceedings of the Academy of Marketing Science's Fourth Quality-of-Life/Marketing Conference. Washington, D.C., November, 1992. **[279]**

Sissors, Jack Z. "Some New Concepts of Newspaper Design," *Journalism Quarterly* (1965) 42: 236-242. **[338]**

Skeikh, Mughees-Ud-Din. "New Tendencies of Electronic Media in Iran after the Revolution," *Media Asia* (1988) 15(2): 87-89. **[47]**

Skelly, Gerald U. and William J. Lundstrom. "Male Sex Roles in Magazine Advertising, 1959-1979," *Journal of Communication* (Fall, 1981) 31(4): 52-56. **[354]**

Skill, Thomas, James D. Robinson and Samuel P. Wallace. "Portrayal of Families on Prime-Time Television: Structure, Type and Frequency," *Journalism Quarterly* (Summer/Autumn, 1987) 64(2/3): 360-367, 398. **[348]**

Skill, Thomas and Sam Wallace. "Family Interactions on Primetime Television: A Descriptive Analysis of Assertive Power Interactions," *Journal of Broadcasting & Electronic Media* (Summer, 1990) 34(3): 243-262. **[349]**

Slade, Joseph W. and Leonard J. Barchak. "Public Broadcasting in Finland: Inventing a National Television Programming Policy," paper presented at the annual conference of the International Communication Association, San Francisco, May 25-29, 1989. **[46]**

Slater, D. and T.L. Thompson. "Attitudes of Parents concerning Televised Warning Statements," *Journalism Quarterly* (Winter, 1984) 61(4): 853-859. **[239]**

Sloan, De Villo. "The Decline of American Postmodernism," *Substance* (1987) 16(3): 29-43. **[18]**

Sloan, W.D. "The Party Press and Freedom of the Press, 1798-1988," *American Journalism* (1987) 4(2): 82-96. **[59]**

Sloan, W.D. "Scurrility and the Party Press, 1789-1816," *American Journalism* (1988) 5(2): 97-112. **[29]**

Sloat, Bill. "Residents Accuse Television Crews of Insensitivity," *Plain Dealer*, June 19, 1990, p. 3A. **[156]**

Slusser, George E. and Eric S. Rabkin (Eds.) *Shadows of the Magic Lamp: Fantasy and Science Fiction in Film.* Carbondale: Southern Illinois University Press, 1985. **[331]**

Smith, Carol and Carolyn Stewart Dyer. "Taking Stock, Placing Orders: A Historiographic Essay on the Business History of the Newspaper," *Journalism Monographs* (April, 1992) No. 132. **[58]**

Smith, Conrad and Lee B. Becker. "Television Reporters and Producers as Journalists," paper presented to the Radio-TV Division at the annual conference of the Association for Education in Journalism and Mass Communication, Portland, OR, August, 1988. **[149]**

Smith, Conrad, Eric S. Fredin and Carroll Ann Ferguson. "Sex Discrimination in Earnings and Story Assignments among TV Reporters," *Journalism Quarterly* (Spring, 1988) 65(1): 3-11, 19. **[148]**

Smith, Conrad and Lee B. Becker. "Comparison of Journalistic Values of Television Reporters and Producers," *Journalism Quarterly* (Winter, 1989) 66(4): 793-800. **[143]**

Smith, Conrad, "Reporters, News Sources, Accuracy, and the Yellowstone Forest Fires," paper presented at the annual conference of the International Communication Association, San Francisco, May, 1989. **[56, 145, 289]**

Smith, Conrad. "News Critics, Newsworkers and Local Television News," *Journalism Quarterly* (Summer, 1988) 65(2): 341-346. **[29, 56, 142, 156]**

Smith, Craig R. *Freedom of Expression and Partisan Politics.* Columbia: University of South Carolina Press, 1989. **[56, 145]**

Smith, David M. "Some Patterns of Reported Leisure Behavior of Young People: A Longitudinal Study," *Youth & Society* (March, 1987) 18(3): 255-281. **[119, 146, 188]**

Smith, Edward J. and Donna J. Hajash. "Informational Graphics in 30 Daily Newspapers," *Journalism Quarterly* (Fall, 1988) 65(3): 714-718.**[339]**

Smith, Kim A. "Effects of Coverage on Neighborhood and Community Concerns," *Newspaper Research Journal* (Summer, 1988) 9(4): 35-48. **[29, 56, 142, 156]**

Smith, Kim A. "Growth and Conflict Reporting in One Community from 1945 to 1985," *Journalism Quarterly* (Winter, 1987) 64(4): 820-825, 833. **[119, 146]**

Smith, Kim A. "Community Perceptions of Media Impressions," *Journalism Quarterly* (Spring, 1984) 61(1): 164-168. **[201]**

Smith, Kim A. "Perceived Influence of Media on What Goes on in a Community," *Journalism Quarterly* (Summer, 1984) 61(2): 260-264, 338. **[201]**

Smith, Kim A. and Douglas A. Ferguson. "The Portrayal and Influence of the Personal and Professional Behavior of Prime-Time Television Characters," paper presented to the Mass Communication and Society Division at the annual conference of the Association for Education in Journalism and Mass Communication, August, 1990. **[355]**

Smith, Marilyn Chapnik and Lochlan E. Magee. "Tracing the Time Course of Picture-Word Processing," *Journal of Experimental Psychology: General* (December, 1980) 109(4): 373-392. **[320]**

Smith, R.F. and P. Voelz. "Newspaper Stylistic Codes: A Hindrance to Understanding?" *Journalism Quarterly* (1983) 60: 641-646, 662. **[296]**

Smith, R.L. and S. Kapoor. "'So Who's Complaining?'--Negative Feedback and Local Television," *Television Quarterly* (1985) 21(3): 53-59. **[162]**

Smith, Richard, Judyth Sachs, David Chant and Brian Carss. "Use of Information Technology by Young People in Australia and Sweden," *Nordicom Review* (1988) 2: 37-39. **[216]**

Smith, Ron F. "How Design & Color Affect Reader Judgment of Newspapers," *Newspaper Research Journal* (Winter, 1989) 10(2): 75-85. **[56, 145, 199, 289]**

Smith, Ron F., Sherlyn-Ann Tumlin and Volker Henning. "A Gatekeeping Study of Gannett's All-Local Newspaper Experiment," *Journalism Quarterly* (Fall, 1988) 65(3): 740-744. **[98]**

Smith, Ron F. and Peter Voelz. "Newspaper Stylistic Codes: A Hindrance to Understanding?" *Journalism Quarterly* (Winter, 1983) 60(4): 641-646. **[317]**

Smith, Sharon P. and V. Kerry Smith. "Successful Movies: A Preliminary Empirical Analysis," *Applied Economics* (1986) 18: 501-507. **[153]**

Smith, William Edward. "The Shrinking Sound Bite: Two Decades of Stylistic Evolution in Television News," paper presented at the annual conference of the Association for Education in Journalism and Mass Communication, Washington, D.C., Aug. 13, 1989. **[56, 145, 289, 340]**

Smythe, D. "Communications: Blindspot of Western Marxism," *Canadian Journal of Political & Social Theory* (1977) 1(3): 1-27. **[20]**

Smythe, D.W., P.B. Lusk and C.A. Lewis. "Portrait of an Art-Theater Audience," *Quarterly of Film, Radio and Television* (Fall, 1953) 8(1): 28-50. **[214]**

Sneegas, Janice J. "Components of Life Satisfaction in Middle and Later Life Adults: Perceived Social Competence, Leisure Participation, and Leisure Satisfaction," *Journal of Leisure Research* (1986) 18(4): 248-258. **[211, 257]**

Snider, Paul. "Mr. Gates' Revisited: A 1966 Version of the 1949 Case Study," *Journalism Quarterly* (1967) 44: 419-427. **[161]**

Snyder, Robert J. "Research from Beginning to End: Linking Local Television News Practices to the Audience via Information Processing Theory: A Three Station Case Study," paper presented to the Radio-Television Division at the annual conference of the Association for Education in Journalism and Mass Communication, Minneapolis, August, 1990. **[142, 162]**

So, C.Y.K. "The Summit as War: How Journalists Use Metaphors," *Journalism Quarterly* (Summer/Autumn, 1987) 64(2/3): 623-626. **[139]**

Sobchack, Thomas. "Genre Film: A Classical Experience," *Film Genre: Theory and Criticism,* ed. Barry K. Grant. Metuchen, NJ: The Scarecrow Press, Inc., pp. 39-52, 1977. **[330, 331]**

Sobel, Michael E. "Lifestyle Expenditures in Contemporary America," *American Behavioral Scientist* (March/April, 1983) 26(4): 521-533. **[263, 279]**

Soderlund, Walter C. and Carmen Schmitt. "El Salvador's Civil War as Seen in North and South American Press," *Journalism Quarterly* (Summer, 1986) 63(2): 268-274. **[158]**

Soderlund, Walter C., Stuart H. Surlin, and Walter I. Romanow. "Gender in Canadian Local Television News: Anchors and Reporters," *Journal of Broadcasting & Electronic Media* (Spring, 1989) 33(2): 187-196. **[366]**

Sofalvi, A.J. and J.C. Drolet. "Health-Related Content of Selected Sunday Comic Strips," *Journal of School Health* (May, 1986) 56(5): 184-187. **[370]**

Soley, Lawrence C. "The News Shapers," paper presented at the annual conference of the Association for Education in Journalism and Mass Communication, Minneapolis, August, 1990. **[137, 161]**

Soley, Lawrence C. "Does Advertising Lower the Prices of Newspapers to Consumers?" *Journalism Quarterly* (Winter, 1989) 66(4): 801-806. **[77]**

Soley, Lawrence C. and R. Krishnan. "Does Advertising Subsidize Consumer Magazine Prices?" *Journal of Advertising* (1987) 16(2): 4-9. **[77]**

Soley, Lawrence C. and Sheila J. O'Brien. "Clandestine Broadcasting in the Southeast Asian Peninsula," *International Communication Bulletin* (Spring, 1987) 22(1-2): 13-10. **[45]**

Soley, Lawrence C. and Robert L. Craig. "Advertising Pressures on Newspapers: A Survey," *Journal of Advertising* (December, 1992) 21(4): 1-9. **[146]**

Soley, Lawrence C. and Leonard N. Reid. "Taking It Off: Are Models in Magazine Advertisements Wearing Less?" *Journalism Quarterly* (Winter, 1988) 65(4): 960-966. **[354]**

Soley, Lawrence C. and Leonard N. Reid. "What Audience Data Do Newspapers Provide Advertisers? *Newspaper Research Journal* (Summer, 1985) 6(4): 1-7. **[71]**

Soley, Lawrence C. and Leonard N. Reid. "Satisfaction with the Informational Value of Magazine and Television Advertising," *Journal of Advertising* (1983) 12(3): 27-31. **[219]**

Solomon, William S. "News Frames and Media Packages: Covering El Salvador," *Critical Studies in Mass Communication* (1992) 9: 56-74. **[158]**

Soloski, John. "Sources and Channels of Local News," *Journalism Quarterly* (Winter, 1989) 66(4): 864-870. **[134, 137, 151, 161]**

Soloski, John. "News Reporting and Professionalism: Some Constraints on the Reporting of the News," *Media, Culture and Society* (1989) 11: 207-228. **[134, 137, 151, 161]**

Soloski, John. "Economics and Management: The Real Influence of Newspaper Groups," *Newspaper Reserch Journal* (1979) 1(1): 19-29. **[92]**

Soong, Roland. "The Statistical Reliability of People Meter Ratings," *Journal of Advertising Research* (February/March, 1988) 28: 50-56. **[171, 212]**

Sosanie, Arlene K. and George J. Szybillo. "Working Wives: Their General Television Viewing and Magazine Readership Behavior," *Journal of Advertising* (1978) 7(2): 5-13. **[270]**

Spangler, L.C. "A Historical Overview of Female Friendships on Prime-Time Television," *Journal of Popular Culture* (Spring, 1989) 22(4): 13-23. **[351]**

Sparkes, Vernone M. "The Impact of Cable TV on Public Television: A Three Year Perspective," paper presented at the annual conference of the Midwest Association for Public Opinion Research, Chicago, November, 1989. **[218]**

Sparkes, Vernone M. "Public Perception of and Reaction to Multi-Channel Cable Television Service," *Journal of Broadcasting* (Spring, 1983) 27(2): 163-175. **[241]**

Sparkes, Vernone M. and Namjun Kang. "Public Reactions to Cable Television: Time in the Diffusion Process," *Journal of Broadcasting & Electronic Media* (Spring, 1986) 30(2): 213-229. **[199]**

Sparks, C. "The Readership of the British Quality Press," *Media, Culture and Society* (October, 1987) 9(4): 427-455. **[270]**

Sparks, Colin and Slavko Splichal. "Journalistic Education and Professional Socialization," *Gazette* (1989) 43: 31-52. **[147]**

Sparks, Colin. "The Press, the Market, and Democracy," *Journal of Communication* (Winter, 1992) 42(1): 36-51. **[49]**

Sparks, Glen and Chris L. Fehlner. "Faces in the News: Gender Comparisons of Magazine Photographs," *Journal of Communication* (Autumn, 1986) 36(4): 70-79. **[368]**

Sparks, Glenn G. and Melissa M. Spirek. "Individual Differences in Coping with Stressful Mass Media: An Activation-Arousal View," *Human Communication Research* (Winter, 1988) 15(2): 195-216. **[257]**

Sperber, Dan and Dierdre Wilson. *Relevance: Communication and Cognition.* Cambridge, MA: Harvard University Press, 1986. **[285]**

Spiegel, D.L. and J. Fitzgerald. "Improving Reading Comprehension through Instruction about Story Parts," *The Reading Teacher* (1985) 7: 676-682. **[316]**

Spirek, Melissa M. "Sex Roles in Frightening Film Newspaper Advertisements: An Overview of the Past 50 Years," paper presented to the Advertising Division at the annual conference of the Association for Education in Journalism and Mass Communication, Montreal, August, 1992. **[352]**

Spreitzer, Elmer and Eldon E. Snyder. "Educational-Occupational Fit and Leisure Orientation as Related to Life Satisfaction," *Journal of Leisure Research* (1987) 19(2): 149-158. **[265]**

Squire, Peverill. "Who Gets National News Coverage in the U.S. Senate?" *American Politics Quarterly* (April, 1988) 16(2): 139-156. **[119, 161]**

Staab, Joachim Friedrich. "The Role of News Factors in News Selection: A Theoretical Reconsideration," *European Journal of Communication* (1990) 5: 423-443. **[160]**

Stahl, S.R. and M.G. Jacobson. "Vocabulary Difficulty, Prior Knowledge, and Text Comprehension," *Journal of Reading Behavior* (1986) 18: 309-323. **[316]**

Stamm, Keith. *Newspaper Use and Community Ties: Toward a Dynamic Theory.* Norwood, NJ: Ablex, 1985. **[240]**

Stamm, Keith and Lisa Fortini-Campbell. "The Relationship of Community Ties to Newspaper Use," *Journalism Monographs* (August, 1983) No. 84. **[272]**

Stamm, Keith R. and Avery M. Guest. "Communication and Community Integration: An Analysis of the Communication Behavior of Newcomers," *Journalism Quarterly* (Winter, 1991) 68(4): 644-656. **[272]**

Stamm, Keith R., Avery M. Guest and Judith Fiedler. "Communication and Community Integration: An Analysis of the Communication Behavior of Newcomers," paper presented to the Communication Theory & Methodology Division at the annual conference of the Association for Education in Journalism and Mass Communication, Minneapolis, August, 1990. **[240]**

Stamps, Spurgeon M. Jr. and Miriam B. Stamps. "Race, Class and Leisure Activities of Urban Residents," *Journal of Leisure Research* (1985) 17(1): 40-56. **[234, 270]**

Standing, L. "Learning 10,000 Pictures," *Quarterly Journal of Experimental Psychology* (1973) 9: 207-222. **[290]**

Stanfield, D.W. and J.B. Lemert. "Alternative Newspapers and Mobilizing Information," *Journalism Quarterly* (Summer/Autumn, 1987) 64(2/3): 604-607. **[162]**

Stanford, Serena Wade. "Predicting Favorite TV Program Gratifications from General Orientations," *Communication Research* (1984) 11(4): 519-536. **[242, 245]**

Stanley, Linda R. and Marty Tharp. "Trends in Daily Newspaper Costs and Revenues 1978-1990," paper presented to the Media Management and Economics Division at the annual conference of the Association for Education in Journalism and Mass Communication, Montreal, August, 1992. **[71]**

Stapler, Harry. "The One-Sentence/Long-Sentence Habit of Writing Leads and How It Hurts Readership," *Newspaper Research Bureau* (Fall, 1985) 7(1): 17-27. **[292]**

Starck, Kenneth and John Soloski. "Effect of Reporter Predisposition in Covering Controversial Story," *Journalism Quarterly* (Spring, 1977) 54: 120-125. **[132]**

Starck, Kenneth and Xu Yu. "Loud Thunder, Small Raindrops: The Reform Movement and the Press in China," *Gazette* (1988) 42: 143-159. **[124]**

Stark, John. *The Literature of Exhaustion: Borges, Nabokov and Barth.* Durham, NC, 1974. **[18]**

Stark, Pegie M. and Barry A. Hollander. "Information Graphics: Do They Help Readers Understand News Events?" paper presented to the Visual Communication Division at the annual conference of the Association for Education in Journalism and Mass Communication, Minneapolis, August, 1990. **[289]**

Stauffer, J., R. Frost and W. Rybolt. "The Attention Factor in Recalling Network Television News," *Journal of Communication* (1983) 33(1): 29-36. **[305]**

Stegall, Sandra Kruger and Keith P. Sanders. "Coorientation of PR Practitioners and News Personnel in Education News," *Journalism Quarterly* (Summer, 1986) 63(2): 341-347. **[138]**

Stein, Harry H. "American Muckraking of Technology since 1900," *Journalism Quarterly* (Summer, 1990) 67(2): 401-409. **[58]**

Stein, N.L. and C.G. Glenn. "An Analysis of Story Comprehension in Elementary School Children," *Advances in Discourse Processes: New Directions in Discourse Processing Vol. II,* ed. R.O. Freedle. Norwood, NJ: Ablex, 1979, pp. 53-120. **[316]**

Stein, N.L. and T. Nezworski. "The Effects of Organization and Instructional Set on Story Memory," *Discourse Processes* (1978) 1: 177-193. **[316]**

Steiner, George. *Language and Silence.* New York, 1967. **[18]**

Steinke, Jocelyn. "The Science Newswriting Process: A Study of Science Writers' Cognitive Processing of Information," paper presented to the Magazine Division at the annual conference of the Association for Education in Journalism and Mass Communication, Montreal, August, 1992. **[139]**

Stempel, Guido H. III. "Public Attitudes about the First Amendment," paper presented to the Law and Communication Theory & Methodology divisions at the annual conference of the Association for Education in Journalism and Mass Communication, Boston, August, 1991. **[204]**

Stempel, Guido H. III. "Topic and Story Choice of Five Network Newscasts," *Journalism Quarterly* (Fall, 1988) 65(3): 750-752. **[103, 341]**

Stempel, Guido H. III "Gatekeeping: The Mix of Topics and the Selection of Stories," *Journalism Quarterly* (Winter, 1985) 62(4): 791-796. **[122, 139]**

Stempel, Guido H. III "Content Patterns of Small and Metropolitan Dailies," *Journalism Quarterly* (1962) 39: 88-91. **[161]**

Stempel, Guido H. III and Hugh M. Culbertson. "The Prominence and Dominance of News Services in Newspaper Medical Coverage," *Journalism Quarterly* (Autumn, 1984) 61(3): 671-676. **[137]**

Stempel, Guido H. III and John W. Windhauser. "The Prestige Press Revisited: Coverage of the 1980 Presidential Campaign," *Journalism Quarterly* (Spring, 1984) 61(1): 49-55. **[369]**

Stempel, Tom. *Framework: A History of Screenwriting in the American Film.* New York: Continuum, 1988. **[104]**

Stensaas, Harlan S. "Development of the Objectivity Ethic in U.S. Daily Newspapers," *Journal of Mass Media Ethics* (Fall/Winter, 1986/1987) 2(1): 50-60. **[130]**

Stephens, Mitchell. *Broadcast News.* 2nd ed., New York: Harcourt Brace, 1986. **[306, 319]**

Stephens, Mitchell. *A History of News: From the Drum to the Satellite.* New York: Viking Penguin, Inc., 1988. **[58]**

Sterling, Anna Kate. *Cinematographers on the Art and Craft of Cinematography.* Metuchen, NJ: Scarecrow Press, 1987. **[103]**

Sterling, Christopher H. "Trends in Daily Newspaper and Broadcast Ownership, 1922-1970," *Journalism Quarterly* (Summer, 1975) 52(2): 247-256. **[65, 80]**

Sterling, Christopher and John Kittross. *Stay Tuned: A Concise History of American Broadcasting.* Belmont, CA: Wadsworth, 1978. **[58]**

Steuer, Jonathan. "Defining Virtual Reality: Dimensions Determining Telepresence," *Journal of Communication* (Autumn, 1992) 42(4): 73-93. **[20]**

Stevens, John D. "Sensationalism in Perspective." *Journalism History* (Winter-Autumn, 1985) 12(3-4): 78-79. **[32]**

Stevens, John D. "Sensationalism and the New York Press," Columbia: Freedom Forum Media Studies Center, 1991. **[32, 121]**

Stevens, S.S. *Psychophysics: Introduction to Its Perceptual, Neural and Social Prospects.* New York: Wiley, 1975. **[290]**

Stevens, Summer E. and Owen V. Johnson. "From Black Politics to Black Community: Harry C. Smith and the Cleveland Gazette," *Journalism Quarterly* (Winter, 1990) 67(4): 1090-1102. **[58]**

Stevenson, Richard W. "A Financial Battle to Make TV Series," *New York Times*, April 27, 1987, p. 23. **[67]**

Stevenson, Robert L. and Donald Lewis Shaw (Ed.). *Foreign News and the New World Information Order.* Ames: Iowa State University Press, 1984. **[364]**

Stevenson, Robert L. and Dulcie M. Straughan. "The World at Home: Geographic Proximity as a Factor in Reading Interest," paper presented to the International Communication Division at the annual conference of the Association for Education in Journalism and Mass Communication, Boston, August, 1991. **[121]**

Steward, Robert K. "Jacksonians Discipline a Party Editor: Economic Leverage and Political Exile," *Journalism Quarterly* (Autumn, 1989) 66(3): 591-599. **[30]**

Stinnett, Lee (ed.) *The Changing Face of the Newsroom.* Washington, D.C.: American Society of Newspaper Editors, Human Resources Committee Report, May, 1989. **[110, 148, 154, 164]**

Stipp, Horst. "Children's Knowledge of and Taste in Popular Music," *Popular Music and Society* (1985) 10(2): 1-15. **[216]**

Stocking, S. Holly and Nancy LaMarca. "How Journalists Describe Their Stories: Hypotheses and Assumptions in Newsmaking," *Journalism Quarterly* (Fall, 1990) 67(2): 295-301. **[133, 157]**

Stocking, S. Holly. "Effect of Public Relations Efforts on Media Visibility of Organizations," *Journalism Quarterly* (Summer, 1985) 62(2): 358-366, 450. **[161]**

Stokes, Jane C. "Mapping the Domain of the Cinema: Applying Multidimensional Scaling to How Potential Movie-Goers Conceptualize Films," paper presented to the Mass Communication Division at the annual conference of the International Communication Association, Miami, Fla., May, 1992. **[218]**

Stone, Gerald. "Do Dual Subscribers Differ from Single Subscribers," *Newspaper Research Journal* (Spring, 1988) 9(3): 31-47. **[164, 177, 182, 279]**

Stone, Gerald. "Measuring Adult Readership Potential of the Newspaper in Education Program," *Newspaper Research Journal* (Winter, 1988) 9(2): 77-86. **[164, 177, 182, 215, 279]**

Stone, Gerald. "Community Commitment: A Predictive Theory of Daily Newspaper Circulation," *Journalism Quarterly* (1977) 54: 509-514. **[272]**

Stone, Gerald C. and Elinor Grusin. "Network TV as the Bad News Bearer," *Journalism Quarterly* (Autumn, 1984) 61(3): 517-523, 592. **[342]**

Stone, Gerald, Barbara Hartung and Dwight Jensen. "Local TV News and the Good-Bad Dyad," *Journalism Quarterly* (Spring, 1987) 64(1): 37-44. **[128, 342]**

Stone, Gerald and John Lee. "Portrayal of Journalists on Prime Time Television," *Journalism Quarterly* (Winter, 1990) 67(4): 697-707. **[355]**

Stone, Vernon A. "Trends in the Status of Minorities and Women in Broadcast News," *Journalism Quarterly* (Summer, 1988) 65(2): 288-293.

Stone, Vernon A. "Pipelines and Dead Ends: Jobs Held by Minorities and Women in Broadcast News," *Mass Comm Review* (1988) 15(2 & 3): 10-19.

Stone, Vernon A. "Changing Profiles of News Directors of Radio and TV Stations, 1972-1986," *Journalism Quarterly* (Winter, 1987) 64(4): 745-749. **[164]**

Stover, Ronald G. and Albeno P. Garbin. "Explanations of Leisure Behavior: An Analysis," *Journal of Leisure Research* (1982) 14: 91-99. **[234]**

Strange, J.J. and J.B. Black. "Imagined Point of View, Causal Inference and Mental Models of Narrative Events," paper presented to the Information Systems Division at the annual conference of the International Communication Association, San Francisco, May, 1989. **[321]**

Straughan, D.M. "An Experiment on the Relation between News Values and Reader Interest," *Gazette* (1989) 43(2): 93-107. **[119, 124]**

Streckfuss, Richard. "Objectivity in Journalism: A Search and a Reassessment," *Journalism Quarterly* (Winter, 1990) 67(4): 973-983. **[130]**

Strickland, D.E., T.A. Finn and M.D. Lambert. "A Content Analysis of Beverage Alcohol Advertising," *Journal of Studies on Alcohol* (1982) 43(7): 655-682. **[371]**

Stroman, Carolyn A., Bishetta D. Merritt and Paula W. Matabane. "Twenty Years after Kerner: The Portrayal of African-Americans on Prime-Time Television," *Howard Journal of Communications* (Winter, 1989-1990) 2(1): 44-56. **[344, 364]**

Strover, Sharon. "Urban Policy and Telecommunications," *Journal of Urban Affairs* (1988) 10(4): 341-356. **[65, 93]**

Stutts, M.A., J. Eure and G.G. Hunnicutt. "Survey of the Incidence of Television Zapping among College Students," *Proceedings of the 1985 Conference of the American Academy of Advertising,* ed. N. Stephens. Provo, UT: American Academy of Advertising, 1985, pp. 86-90. **[228]**

Sullivan, Denis F. "Comprehensiveness of Press Coverage of a Food Irradiation Proposal," *Journalism Quarterly* (Winter, 1985) 62(4): 832-837. **[371]**

Sullivan, G.L. and P.J. O'Connor. "Women's Role Portrayals in Magazine Advertising: 1958-1983," *Sex Roles* (1988) 18(3/4): 181-188. **[368]**

Suls, J. and J.W. Gastoff. "The Incidence of Sex Discrimination, Sexual Contents and Hostility in Television Humor," *Journal of Applied Communication Research* (Spring, 1981) 9(1): 42-49. **[351]**

Summers, Harrison B. (Ed.) *A Thirty-Year History of Programs Carried on National Radio Networks in the United States 1926-1956.* New York: Arno Press and the New York Times, 1971 reprint edition (first published, January, 1958). **[360]**

Sumner, David E. "Winners and Losers: Making It in the Magazine Marketplace 1986-90," paper presented at the annual conference of the Association for Education in Journalism and Mass Communication, Montreal, August, 1992. **[80]**

Sundar, S.S., J.W. Perkins and D. Zillmann. "Perception of an Issue as a Function of Infographics," paper presented at the annual conference of the Association for Education in Journalism and Mass Communication, Boston, August, 1991. **[289, 315]**

Surlin, Stuart. "Uses of Jamaican Talk Radio," *Journal of Broadcasting & Electronic Media* (Fall, 1986) 30(4): 459-466. **[253]**

Surlin, Stuart H. and Hermann H. Kosak. "The Effect of Graphic Design in Advertising on Reader Ratings," *Journalism Quarterly* (Winter, 1975) 52: 685-691. **[270]**

Swank, C. "Media Uses and Gratifications: Need Salience and Source Dependence in a Sample of the Elderly," *American Behavioral Scientist* (September/October, 1979) 23(1): 95-117. **[278]**

Swann, W.B. and L.C. Miller. "Why Never Forgetting a Face Matters: Visual Imagery and Social Memory," *Journal of Personality and Social Psychology* (1982) 43: 475-480. **[291, 316]**

Swanson, David L. (Ed.) "The Uses and Gratifications Approach to Mass Communications Research," *Communication Research* (January, 1979) 6(1) (issue devoted to uses and gratifications research). **[260]**

Swartz, T.A. and L. Meyer. "News Versus Entertainment TV Viewers," *Journal of Advertising Research* (December, 1985/January, 1986) 25(6): 9-18. **[275]**

Swayne, L.E. and A.J. Greco. "The Portrayal of Older Americans in Television Commercials," *Journal of Advertising* (1987) 16(1): 47-54. **[347]**

Sylvester, Charles D. "The Ethics of Play, Leisure, and Recreation in the Twentieth Century, 1900-1983," *Leisure Sciences* (1987) 9: 173-188. **[211]**

Sylvie, George. "Study of a Riot: The Effect of News Values and Competition on Coverage by Two Competing Daily Newspapers," paper presented in the Newspaper Division at the annual conference of the Association for Education in Journalism and Mass Communication, Washington, D.C., Aug. 13, 1989.

Szekfu, A. "Intruders Welcome? The Beginnings of Satellite Television in Hungary," *European Journal of Communication* (June, 1989) 4(2): 161-171. **[59]**

Tadayon, M. "The Image of Iran in the New York Times," *Gazette* (1980) 26(4): 217-233. **[371]**

Talabi, J.K. "The Television Viewing Behavior of Families in Kwara State, Nigeria," *Journal of Educational Technology* (1989) 20(2): 135-139. **[173]**

Talbot, Mary N. "Households with Expenditures for Entertainment Services," *Family Economics Review* (1989) 2(4): 21-24. **[231]**

Talbott, Albert D. "Journalists in the Movies: How Journalists Are Perceived to be Portrayed in Feature Films," paper presented to the Mass Communication and Society and Media Management and Economics divisions at the annual conference of the Association for Education in Journalism and Mass Communication, Minneapolis, Minn.: August, 1990. **[355]**

Tamborini, Ron and James Stiff. "Predictors of Horror Film Attendance and Appeal: An Analysis of the Audience for Frightening Films," *Communication Research* (August, 1987) 14(4): 415-436. **[252]**

Tamura, Minoru. "The Information Environment Around the Japanese People," *Studies of Broadcasting* (1987) 23: 7-25. **[59, 173, 180, 181, 213, 342, 362]**

Tan, Alexis S. "Why TV Is Missed: A Functional Analysis," *Journal of Broadcasting* (Summer, 1977) 21(3): 371-380. **[277]**

Tangney, J.P. and S. Feshbach. "Children's Television-Viewing Frequency: Individual Differences and Demographic Correlates," *Personality and Social Psychology Bulletin* (March, 1988) 14(1): 145-158. **[188, 270]**

Tankard, J.W. Jr. "Effects of Chartoons and Three-Dimensional Graphs on Interest and Information Gain," *Newspaper Research Journal* (Spring, 1989) 10(3): 91-103. **[290]**

Tannenbaum, P.H. and J.A. Fosdick. "The Effect of Lighting Angle on the Judgment of Photographed Subjects," *Audio-Visual Communication Review* (1960) 8: 253-262. **[318]**

Tanney, J.B. and S.D. Johnson. "Religious Television in Middletown," *Review of Religious Research* (June, 1984) 25(4): 303-313. **[270]**

Tannsjo, Torbjorn. "Against Freedom of Expression," *Political Studies* (1985) 33: 547-559.

Tarr, Joel A., Thomas Finholt and David Goodman. "The City and the Telegraph: Urban Telecommunications in the Pre-Telephone Era," *Journal of Urban History* (November, 1987) 14(1): 38-80.

Tarratt, Margaret. "Monsters from the Id," *Film Genre: Theory and Criticism*, ed. Barry K. Grant. Metuchen, NJ: The Scarecrow Press, Inc., pp. 161-181, 1977. **[331]**

Taylor, B.M. and S.J. Samuels. "Children's Use of Text Structure in the Recall of Expository Material," *American Educational Research Journal* (1983) 20: 517-528. **[316]**

Taylor, Barbara M. "Children's Memory for Expository Text after Reading," *Reading Research Quarterly* (1980) 15: 399-411. **[316]**

Taylor, S. and S. Fisk. "Salience, Attention and Attribution: Top of the Head Phenomena," *Advances in Experimental Social Psychology*, ed. L. Berkowitz. Vol. 11. New York: Academic Press, 1978, pp. 250-287. **[321]**

Tempest, A.C. "Advertising--A Viable Source of Revenue for Electronic Publishing?" *International Journal of Information Management* (June, 1987) 7(2): 77-84. **[74]**

Tesser, A., Karen Millar and Cheng-Huan Wu. "On the Perceived Functions of Movies," *Journal of Psychology* (September, 1988) 122(5): 441-449. **[252]**

Thaber, B.J. "Gender Stereotyping in Comic Strips," *Communication, Gender and Sex Roles in Diverse Interaction Contexts*, ed. L.P. Stewart and S. Ting-Toomey. Norwood, NJ: Ablex, 1987, pp. 189-199. **[367]**

Tharp, Marty and Linda R. Stanley. "A Time Series Analysis of Newspaper Profitability by Circulation Size," *Journal of Media Economics* (Spring, 1992) 5(1): 3-12. **[71]**

Tharp, Marty and Linda R. Stanley. "Trends in Profitability of Daily U.S. Newspapers by Circulation Size 1978-1988," paper presented in the Media Management and Economics Division at the annual conference of the Association for Education in Journalism and Mass Communication, Minneapolis, August, 1990. **[71]**

Tharp, Marty. "Turnover and Mobility at Small Daily Newspapers," *Newspaper Research Journal* (Winter, 1991) 12(1): 76-91. **[149]**

Thibodeau, Ruth. "From Racism to Tokenism: The Changing Face of Blacks in 'New Yorker' Cartoons," *Public Opinion Quarterly* (Winter, 1989) 53(4): 482-494. **[345]**

Thomas, Larry W. and Laslo V. Boyd. "Television News Coverage of Six Federal Regulatory Agencies," *Journalism Quarterly* (Spring, 1984) 61(1): 160-164. **[135, 369]**

Thomas, Sari and Steven V. LeShay. "Bad Business? A Reexamination of Television's Portrayal of Businesspersons," *Journal of Communication* (Winter, 1992) 42(1): 95-105. **[356]**

Thomason, Tommy and Paul LaRocque. "Television and Crime Coverage: A Comparison of the Attitudes of News Directors and Victim Advocates," paper presented to the Radio-TV Journalism Division at the annual conference of the Association for Education in Journalism and Mass Communication, Boston, Aug. 7, 1991. **[160]**

Thomason, Tommy and Paul LaRocque. "Newspaper Identification of Crime Victims: Editors Change Address Policies," paper presented in the Newspaper Division at the annual conference of the Association for Education in Journalism and Mass Communication, August, 1990. **[160]**

Thompson, John B. *Ideology and Modern Culture: Critical Social Theory in the Era of Mass Communication.* Stanford: Stanford University Press, 1990. **[7]**

Thompson, Margaret E. "Cognitive Activity and Patterns of Involvement among Television Viewers," paper presented to the Information Systems Division at the annual conference of the International Communication Association, Miami, May, 1992. **[321]**

Thompson, R.B. II, C. Olsen and J.R. Dietrich. "Attributes of News about Firms: An Analysis of Firm-Specific News Reported in the 'Wall Street Journal Index,'" *Journal of Accounting Research* (Autumn, 1987) 25(2): 245-274. **[369]**

Thompson, R.S. "Structure and Conduct in Local Advertising Markets: The Case of Irish Provincial Newspapers," *The Journal of Industrial Economics* (December, 1984) 33(2): 241-249. **[97]**

Thorn, J. Dale. "Television in the Lives of the Class of 1980," *LSU School of Journalism Research Bulletin* (1978) 2(1): 1-8. **[279]**

Thorndyke, Perry W. "Knowledge Acquisition from Newspaper Stories," *Discourse Processes* (1977) 2: 95-112. **[295, 312, 316, 317]**

Thorndyke, Perry W. "Cognitive Structures in Comprehension and Memory of Narrative Discourse," *Cognitive Psychology* (1977) 9: 77-110. **[312, 316]**

Thornton, James E. and John B. Collins. "Patterns of Leisure and Physical Activities among Older Adults," *Activities, Adaptation and Aging* (March, 1986) 8(2): 5-27. **[190]**

Thorson, E. and Annie Lang. "The Effects of Television Videographics and Lecture Familiarity in Adult Cardiac Orienting Responses and Memory," 1989, unpublished manuscript cited in Edwardson, Kent, Engstrom and Hofman (1991). **[307]**

Thorson, E. and B. Reeves. "Effects of Over-Time Measures of Viewer Liking and Activity during Programs and Commercials on Memory for Commercials," *Advances in Consumer Research*, (1986) Vol. 13. **[305]**

Thorson, E., B. Reeves and J. Schleuder. "Message Complexity and Attention to Television," *Communication Research* (1985) 12: 427-454. **[316]**

Thorson, E., B. Reeves and J. Schleuder. "Attention to Local and Global Complexity in Television Messages," *Communication Yearbook 10*, ed. M.L. McLaughlin. Newbury Park, CA: Sage Publications, 1986, pp. 366-383. **[316]**

Thrift, Ralph R. Jr. "How Chain Ownership Affects Editorial Vigor of Newspapers," *Journalism Quarterly* (1977) 54: 327-331. **[90]**

Tichenor, Phillip J., George A. Donohue and Clarice N. Olien. "American and European Editor Views of Press Role: One Western World of Community Journalism?" paper presented at the annual conference of the Midwest Association for Public Opinion Research, Chicago, Ill., Nov. 18, 1988. **[166]**

Tichenor, Phillip, George A. Donohue and Clarice N. Olien, *Community Conflict and the Press*. Beverly Hills, CA: Sage Publications, 1980. **[13, 146, 201]**

Tiedge, James T. and Kenneth J. Ksobiech. "The Sandwich Programming Strategy: A Case of Audience Flow," *Journalism Quarterly* (Summer, 1988) 65(2): 376-383. **[224, 268]**

Tiedge, James T. and Kenneth J. Ksobiech. "Counter-Programming Primetime Network Television," *Journal of Broadcasting and Electronic Media* (Winter, 1987) 31(1): 41-55. **[224]**

Tiedge, James T. and Kenneth J. Ksobiech. "The 'Lead-In' Strategy for Prime-Time TV: Does It Increase the Audience?" *Journal of Communication* (Summer, 1986) 36(3): 51-63. **[224]**

Tillinghast, D.S. "Limits of Competition," *Press Concentration and Monopoly: New Perspectives on Newspaper Ownership and Operation*, ed. R.G. Picard et al. Norwood, NJ: Ablex, 1988, pp. 71-87. **[87]**

Tillinghast, William A. "Changes in Bias Perceptions: A Case Study of the San Jose Mercury and News after the Knight-Ridder Merger," paper presented to the Mass Communication and Society Division at the annual conference of the Association for Education in Journalism and Mass Communication, Corvallis, OR, August, 1983. **[220]**

Timberg, Bernard. "Television Talk and Ritual Space: Carson and Letterman," *The Southern Speech Communication Journal* (Summer, 1987) 52: 390-402. **[335, 372]**

Tinsley, H.E.A. and Tinsley, D.J. "A Holistic Model of Leisure Counseling," *Journal of Leisure Research* (1982) 14: 100-116. **[170]**

Tinsley, Howard E.A. and Thomas L. Johnson. "A Preliminary Taxonomy of Leisure Activities," *Journal of Leisure Research* (1984) 16(3): 234-244. **[247]**

Toffler, Alvin. *Future Shock*. New York: Bantam Books, 1971. **[89]**

Tomaselli, Keyan G. "Community and the Progressive Press: A Case Study in Finding Our Way," *Journal of Communication Inquiry* (Winter, 1988) 12(1): 26-44. **[26]**

Tomlinson, Timothy C. "Sweden," *International Handbook of Broadcasting Systems*, ed. Philip T. Rosen (1988). New York: Greenwood Press, pp. 269-281. **[59]**

Tomovic, Vladislav A. (Ed.) *Definitions in Sociology: Convergence, Conflict and Alternative Vocabularies*. St. Catharines, Ontario, Canada: Diliton Publications, Inc., 1979. **[269]**

Toplin, Robert Brent. "The Filmmaker as Historian," *American Historical Review* (October-December, 1988) 93(5): 1210-1227. **[328]**

Tourangeau, R. "Cognitive Sciences and Survey Methods," *Cognitive Aspects of Survey Methodology: Building a Bridge between Disciplines*, ed. T.B. Jabine et al. Washington, D.C.: National Academy Press, 1984, pp. 73-100. **[285]**

Towers, W.M. "Uses and Gratifications of Magazine Readers: A Cross-Media Comparison," *Mass Comm Review* (1986) 13(1-3): 44-51. **[275, 276]**

Towers, Wayne M. "Replication of a Study on Uses and Gratifications for Weekday and Sunday Readers," *Newspaper Research Journal* (Spring, 1986) 7(3): 61-68. **[275, 276]**

Towers, Wayne M. "Weekday and Sunday Readership Seen Through Uses and Gratifications," *Newspaper Research Journal* (Spring, 1985) 6(3): 20-32. **[276]**

Trahant, Mark N. "Publisher Says Politics, Not Finances, Closed Navajo Daily," *Minorities in the Newspaper Business* (May/June, 1987) 3(3): 3. **[72]**

Tramer, Harriet and Leo W. Jeffres. "Talk Radio--Forum and Companion," *Journal of Broadcasting* (Summer, 1983) 27(3): 297-300. **[116, 156]**

Traudt, Paul J., James A. Anderson and Timothy P. Meyer. "Phenomenology, Empiricism, and Media Experience," *Critical Studies in Mass Communication* (1987) 4:301-324. **[10, 19]**

Traudt, Paul J. and C. Lont. "Media-Logic-In-Use: The Family as Locus of Study," *Natural Audiences: Qualitative Research of Media Uses and Effects*, ed. T. Lindlof. Norwood, NJ: Ablex, 1987, pp. 139-160. **[271]**

Travis, Leroy D. and Claudio Violato. "Experience, Mass Media Use and Beliefs about Youth: A Comparative Study," *The Alberta Journal of Educational Research* (June, 1985) 31(2): 99-112. **[202]**

Trayes, Edward J. "Managing Editors and Their Newsrooms: A Survey of 208 APME members," *Journalism Quarterly* (Winter, 1978) 55(4): 744-749. **[154]**

Treisman, A. "Features and Objects: The Fourteenth Bartlett Memorial Lecture," *Quarterly Journal of Experimental Psychology* (1988) 40A: 201-237. **[315]**

Treisman, A.M. "Focused Attention in the Perception and Retrieval of Multidimensional Stimuli," *Perception and Psychophysics* (1977) 22: 1-11. **[315]**

Treisman, A.M. "Strategies and Models of Selective Attention," *Psychological Review* (1968) 76: 282-299. **[320]**

Treisman, A.M. and G. Gelade. "A Feature-Integration Theory of Attention," *Cognitive Psychology* (1980) 12: 97-136. **[315]**

References and Author Index **489**

Treisman, A.M., M. Sykes and G. Gelade. "Selective Attention and Stimulus Integration," *Attention and Performance VI*, ed. S. Dornic. Hillsdale, NJ: Lawrence Erlbaum, 1977, pp. 333-361. **[315]**

Trilling, Lionel. "Teaching Modern Literature," *Beyond Culture: Essays on Literature and Learning*. New York, 1965. **[18]**

Trujillo, N. and L.R. Ekdom. "A 40-year Portrait of the Portrayal of Industry on Prime-Time Television," *Journalism Quarterly* (1987) 64(2/3): 368-373. **[369]**

Tsuchiya, Ken. "A Semiological Analysis of Japanese and German Versions of a Co-Produced Television Series," *Studies of Broadcasting* (1988) No. 24, pp. 75-97. **[116]**

Tuchman, Gaye. "Culture as Resource: Actions Defining the Victorian Novel," *Media, Culture and Society* (1982) 4: 3-18. **[20]**

Tuchman, Gaye. "The News Net," *Social Research* (Summer, 1978) 45(2): 253-276. **[118, 125, 134]**

Tuchman, Gaye. "Professionalism as an Agent of Legitimation: Social Research on Broadcasting," *Journal of Broadcasting* (1978) 28(2): 106-113. **[118, 125, 134]**

Tuchman, Gay. "Women's Depiction by the Mass Media," *Signs* (1979) 4: 528-542.

Tuchman, Gay. *Making News*. New York: Free Press, 1978. **[118, 125, 134]**

Tuchman, Gaye. "Objectivity as Strategic Ritual: An Examination of Newsmen's Notions of Objectivity," *American Journal of Sociology* (1972) 77:660-679. **[20, 132]**

Tudor, Andrew. "Genre," *Film Genre: Theory and Criticism*, ed. Barry K. Grant. Metuchen, NJ: The Scarecrow Press, Inc., pp. 16-23, 1977. **[329, 330, 331]**

Tudor, B.A. "Retail Trade Advertising in the 'Leicester Journal' and the 'Leicester Chronicle' 1855-1871," *European Journal of Marketing* (1986) 20(9): 41-56. **[39]**

Tufte, Edward R. *The Visual Display of Quantitative Information*. Cheshire, Conn.: Graphics Press, 1983. **[290, 315, 316]**

Tulving, Endel and W. Donaldson. *Organization of Memory*. New York: Academic Press, 1972. **[319]**

Tulving, Endel. "Episodic and Semantic Memory," *Organization and Memory*, ed. E. Tulving and W. Donaldson. New York: Academic Press, 1972. **[319]**

Turk, Judy VanSlyke, Jim Richstad, Robert L. Bryson Jr. and Sammye Johnson. "Hispanic Americans in the News: A Minority Group Comes of Age in Two Southwestern Cities," paper presented to the Minorities and Communication Division at the annual conference of the Association for Education in Journalism and Mass Communication, Portland, OR, July, 1988. **[346]**

Turk, Judy VanSlyke, Jim Richstad, Robert L. Bryson Jr. and Sammye Johnson. "Hispanic Americans in the News in Two Southwestern Cities," *Journalism Quarterly* (Spring, 1989) 66(1): 107-113. **[346]**

Turk, Judy V. "Information Subsidies and Influences," *Public Relations Review* (Fall, 1985) 11(3): 10-25. **[161]**

Turner, Ralph H. "Role Change," *Annual Review of Sociology* (1990) 16: 87-110. **[153, 166]**

Turner, Richard and Pauline Yoshihashi. "Herald Examiner in Los Angeles to Publish Its Last Issue Today," *Wall Street Journal*, Nov. 2, 1989, p. 4B. **[97]**

Turner, Richard. "How Larry Gordon Got His $100 Million Movie Deal," *Wall Street Journal*, Aug. 23, 1989, p. 1B. **[103]**

Turow, Joseph. "The Organizational Underpinnings of Contemporary Media Conglomerates," *Communication Research* (December, 1992) 19(6): 682-704. **[89]**

Turow, Joseph. *Playing Doctor: Television, Storytelling, and Medical Power*. Communication and Society Series. New York: Oxford University Press, 1989. **[89, 156]**

Turow, Joseph. "Hospital and Healthcare Executives on TV: Image Problems for the Profession," *Hospital and Health Services Administration* (November/December, 1985) 30(6): 96-105. **[357]**

Turow, Joseph. *Media Industries: The Production of News and Entertainment*. New York: Longman, 1984. **[20, 156]**

Turow, Joseph. "Pressure Groups and Television Entertainment: A Framework for Analysis," *Interpreting Television: Current Research Perspectives*, eds. W.D. Rowland Jr. and B. Watkins. Beverly Hills, CA: Sage Publications, 1984, pp. 142-162. [20, 156]

Turow, Joseph. "Local Television: Producing Soft News," *Journal of Communication* (Spring, 1983) 33(2): 111-123. [340]

Turow, Joseph. "Unconventional Programs on Commercial Television: An Organizational Perspective," *Individuals in Mass Media Organizations: Creativity and Constraint*, eds., James S. Ettema and D. Charles Whitney. Beverly Hills, CA: Sage Publications, 1982, pp. 107-129. [113]

Turow, Joseph and Lisa Coe. "Curing Television's Ills: The Portrayal of Health Care," *Journal of Communication* (Autumn, 1985) 35(4): 36-51. [370]

Udell, Jon G. "Recent and Future Economic Status of U.S. Newspapers," *Journalism Quarterly* (Summer, 1990) 67(2): 331-339. [70]

Ugboajah, F.O. "Media Habits of Rural and Semirural (Slum) Kenya," *Gazette* (1985) 36(3): 155-174.

Umphrey, Don. "A Comparison of Cable Disconnecters and Subscribers," *Journalism Quarterly* (Autumn, 1989) 66(3): 628-631, 779. [275]

Umphrey, Don. "Segmenting the Cable Audience by Reason for Subscribing," *Journalism Quarterly* (Winter, 1988) 65(4): 972-975. [251]

Underwood, Doug and Keith Stamm. "Balancing Business with Journalism: Newsroom Policies at 12 West Coast Newspapers," *Journalism Quarterly* (Summer, 1992) 69(2): 301-317. [111]

Utt, Sandra H. and Steve Pasternack. "How They Look: An Updated Study of American Newspaper Front Pages," *Journalism Quarterly* (Autumn, 1989) 66(3): 621-627. [338, 339, 362]

Utt, Sandra H. and Steve Pasternack. "Use of Graphic Devices in a Competitive Situation: A Case Study of 10 Cities," *Newspaper Research Journal* (Fall, 1985) 7(1): 7-16. [91]

Utt, Sandra H. and Steve Pasternack. "Front Pages of U.S. Daily Newspapers," *Journalism Quarterly* (1984) 61: 879-884. [362]

Valette-Florence, P. and A. Jolibert. "Social Values, A.I.O., and Consumption Patterns," *Journal of Business Research* (1990) 20: 109-122. [266]

van Dijk, T.A. *News as Discourse*. Hillsdale, NJ: Lawrence Erlbaum Associates, Publishers, 1988. [312, 316]

van Dijk, T.A. "Discourse Analysis: Its Development and Application to the Structure of News," *Journal of Communication* (1983) 33: 20-43. [316]

van Dijk, T.A. and W. Kintsch. *Strategies of Discourse Comprehension*. New York: Academic Press, 1983. [316]

van Driel, Barend, and James T. Richardson. "Print Media Coverage of New Religious Movements: A Longitudinal Study," *Journal of Communication* (Summer, 1988) 38(3): 37-61. [156, 357]

van Dyke, Vernon. "The Individual, the State, and Ethnic Communities in Political Theory," *World Politics* (April, 1977) 29(3): 343-369. [343]

van Wyk, K. "The Press and South Africa's Foreign Relations: An Events Analysis," *Communicare* (November, 1989) 8(2): 5-14. [46]

Van der Voort, Tom H.A. and Jan E. Van Lil. "Does Television Reduce Children's Leisure Time Reading?" paper presented to the Mass Communication Division at the annual conference of the International Communication Association, San Francisco, May 25-29, 1989. [187]

Vande Berg, Leah R. and Diane Streckfuss. "Prime-Time Television's Portrayal of Women and the World of Work: A Demographic Profile," *Journal of Broadcasting & Electronic Media* (Spring, 1992) 36(2): 195-208. [350]

Vande Berg, Leah R. and Nick Trujillo. *Organizational Life on Television*. Norwood, NJ: Ablex Publishing Co., 1989. [355, 356]

VanderMeer, A.W. "Color vs. Black-and-White in Instructional Films," *Audio-Visual Communication Review* (1954) 3: 121-134. [315]

Vanneman, Reeve and Lynn Weber Cannon. *The American Perception of Class*. Philadelphia: Temple University Press, 1987. **[230]**

Vaughn, Stephen and Bruce Evensen. "Democracy's Guardians: Hollywood's Portrait of Reporters, 1930-1945," *Journalism Quarterly* (Winter, 1991) 68(4): 829-838. **[355, 369]**

Verer, A.M. and L.R. Knupka. "Over-the-Counter Drug Advertising in Gender Oriented Popular Magazines," *Journal of Drug Education* (1986) 16(4): 367-382. **[362]**

Vilanilam, John. "Television Advertising and the Indian Poor," *Media, Culture and Society* (1989) 11: 485-497. **[47]**

Villani, Kathryn E.A. "Personality/Life Style and Television Viewing Behavior," *Journal of Marketing Research* (November, 1975) 12: 432-439. **[266]**

Vincent, R.C., B.K. Crow and D.K. Davis. "When Technology Fails: The Dramas of Airline Crashes in Network Television News," *Journalism Monographs* (1989) No. 117. **[128]**

Vincent, Richard C., Dennis K. Davis and Lilly Ann Boruszkowski. "Sexism on MTV: The Portrayal of Women in Rock Videos," *Journalism Quarterly* (Winter, 1987) 64(4): 750-755. **[351]**

Viswanath, Kasisomayajula. "International News in U.S. Media: Perceptions of Foreign Students," *Journalism Quarterly* (Winter, 1988) 65(4): 952-959. **[220]**

Viswanath, Kasisomayajula, John R. Finnegan Jr. and John Potter. "Community Ties and Use of Newspapers and Cable TV in a Rural Midwest Community," paper presented to the annual conference of the Midwest Association for Public Opinion Research, Chicago, Ill., November, 1989. **[240]**

Viswanath, Kasisomayajula, John R. Finnegan Jr., Brenda Rooney and John Potter. "Community Ties in a Rural Midwest Community and Use of Newspapers and Cable Television," *Journalism Quarterly* (Winter, 1990) 67(4): 899-911. **[240]**

Voakes, Paul S. "Unpopular, Maybe--But Not Illegitimate," paper presented to the Mass Communication and Society Division at the annual conference of the Association for Education in Journalism and Mass Communication, Montreal, August, 1992. **[204]**

Von Feilitizen, C. "The Functions Served by the Media," *Children and Television*, ed. R. Brown. Beverly Hills: Sage, 1976, pp. 90-115. **[216]**

Wackman, Daniel B., Donald M. Gillmor, Cecilie Gaziano and Everett E. Dennis, "Chain Newspaper Autonomy as Reflected in Presidential Campaign Endorsements," *Journalism Quarterly* (1975) 52: 411-420. **[90]**

Wade, E. "The Miners and the Media: Themes of Newspaper Reporting," *Journal of Law and Society* (Winter, 1985) 12(3): 273-284. **[369]**

Wade, Serena E. "Interpersonal Discussion: A Critical Predictor of Leisure Activity," *Journal of Communication* (December, 1973) 23(4): 426-445. **[278]**

Wafai, Mohamed. "Senators' Television Visibility and Political Legitimacy," *Journalism Quarterly* (Summer, 1989) 66(2): 323-331, 390. **[119]**

Wagenberg, Ronald H. and Walter C. Soderlund. "The Effects of Chain Ownership on Editorial Coverage: The Case of the 1974 Canadian Federal Election," *Canadian Journal of Political Science* (December, 1976) 9(4): 682-689. **[98]**

Wahl, Otto F. "Mass Media Images of Mental Illness: A Review of the Literature," *Journal of Community Psychology* (October, 1992) 20: 343-352. **[358]**

Wakshlag, Jacob and William Jenson Adams. "Trends in Program Variety and the Prime Time Access Rule," *Journal of Broadcasting & Electronic Media* (Winter, 1985) 29(1): 23-34. **[333]**

Wakshlag, Jacob J. and Bradley S. Greenberg. "Programming Strategies and the Popularity of Television Programs for Children," *Human Communication Research* (Fall, 1979) 6: 58-68. **[186]**

Wakshlag, Jacob, Virginia Vial and Ronald Tamborini. "Selecting Crime Drama and Apprehension about Crime," *Human Communication Research* (Winter, 1983) 10(2): 227-242. **[330]**

Waldman, Diane. "'At Last I Can Tell It to Someone!' Feminine Point of View and Subjectivity in the Gothic Romance Film of the 1940s," *Cinema Journal* (1984) 2: 29-40. **[331]**

Waldman, Peter. "Silver Screens Lose Some of Their Luster," *Wall Street Journal*, Feb. 9, 1989, p. 1B. **[87]**

Waldrop, Judith. "Spending by Degree," *American Demographics*, February, 1990, pp. 23-26. **[230, 269]**

Walker C.H. and F.R. Yekovich. "Script-Based Inferences: Effects of Text and Knowledge Variables on Recognition Memory," *Journal of Verbal Learning and Verbal Behavior* (1984) 23: 357-370. **[317]**

Walker, C.H. and B.J.F. Meyer. "Integrating Different Types of Information in Text," *Journal of Verbal Learning and Verbal Behavior* (1980) 19: 263-275. **[296, 317]**

Walker, Doug. "Predictors of Professionalism: An International Study of First Year Journalism Students," paper presented to the Intercultural/Development Communication Division at the annual conference of the International Communication Association, Chicago, May 26, 1991. **[159, 163]**

Walker, J.R. "The Context of MTV: Adolescent Entertainment Media Use and Music Television," *Popular Music and Society* (Fall, 1987) 11(3): 1-9. **[275]**

Walker, James R. "Inheritance Effects in the New Media Environment," *Journal of Broadcasting & Electronic Media* (Fall, 1988) 32(4): 391-401. **[268]**

Walker, James R. and Robert V. Bellamy Jr. "Gratifications Derived from Remote Control Devices: A Survey of Adult RCD Use," paper presented to the Communication and Technology Division at the annual conference of the International Communication Association, Miami, May, 1992. **[251]**

Walker, James R. and Robert V. Bellamy Jr. "Gratifications of Grazing: An Exploratory Study of Remote Control Use," *Journalism Quarterly* (Fall, 1991) 68(3): 422-431. **[251]**

Walker, M. *Powers of the Press: Twelve of the World's Influential Newspapers*. New York: The Pilgrim Press, 1983. **[362]**

Wallach, H. and D.N. O'Connell. "The Kinetic Depth Effect," *Journal of Experimental Psychology* (1953) 45: 205-217. **[318]**

Wallack, Lawrence, Warren Breed and John Cruz. "Alcohol on Prime-Time Television," *Journal of Studies on Alcohol* (1987) 48(1): 33-38. **[371]**

Waller, Robert and Peter Whalley. "The Processing of Graphically Organized Prose," paper presented at the annual conference of the American Educational Research Association, New Orleans, La., 1984. Cited in Pasternack and Utt, 1990). **[289]**

Wang, Georgette. "Information Utility as a Predictor of Newspaper Readership," *Journalism Quarterly* (1977) 54(4): 791-794. **[258]**

Wanta, W. and D. Leggett. "Gender Stereotypes in Wire Service Sports Photos," *Newspaper Research Journal* (Spring, 1989) 10(3): 105-114. **[367]**

Wanta, Wayne. "The Effects of Competition on the Content of the St. Louis Post-Dispatch," paper presented to the Newspaper Division at the annual conference of the Association for Education in Journalism and Mass Communication, Minneapolis, August, 1990. **[91]**

Ward, Douglas B. "The Effectiveness of Sidebar Graphics," *Journalism Quarterly* (Summer, 1992) 69(2): 318-319. **[289]**

Ward, Jean and Kathleen A. Hansen. "Commentary: Information Age Methods in a New Reporting Model," *Newspaper Research Journal* (Spring, 1986) 7(3): 51-59. **[161]**

Ward, Jean and Kathleen A. Hansen. "Journalist and Librarian Roles, Information Technologies and Newsmaking," *Journalism Quarterly* (Fall, 1991) 68(3): 491-498. **[161]**

Ward, Jean. "Attacking the King's English: Implications for Journalism in the Feminist Critique," *Journalism Quarterly* (Winter, 1975) 52(4): 699-705. **[139]**

Ward, Scott. "Consumer Behavior," *Handbook of Communication Science*, ed. Charles R. Berger and Steven H. Chaffee. Newbury Park, CA: Sage Publications, 1987, 651-674. **[313]**

Ward, Scott, Daniel B. Wackman and Ellen Wartella. *How Children Learn to Buy*. Beverly Hills: Sage Publications, 1977. **[215]**

Ward, Steven A. and Rick Seifert. "The Importance of Mechanics in Journalistic Writing: A Study of Reporters and Editors," *Journalism Quarterly* (Spring, 1990) 67(1): 104-113. **[139]**

Ware, M.C. and M.F. Stuck. "Sex-Role Messages vis-a-vis Microcomputer Use: A Look at the Pictures," *Sex Roles* (1985) 13(3/4): 205-214. **[368]**

Wartella, Ellen (Ed.) *Children Communicating: Media and Development of Thought, Speech. Understanding.* Beverly Hills: Sage Publications, 1979. **[215]**

Wartella, Ellen, Katharine Elizabeth Heintz, Amy Joan Aidman and Sharon Rose Mazzarella. "Television and Beyond: Children's Video Media in One Community," *Communication Research* (February, 1990) 17(1): 45-64. **[186]**

Wartella, Ellen and Byron Reeves. "Communication and Children," *Handbook of Communication Science*, ed. Charles R. Berger and Steven H. Chaffee. Newbury Park, CA: Sage Publications, 1987, pp. 619-650. **[310, 311, 313]**

Waterman, David. "A New Look at Mass Media Chains and Groups, 1977-1987," paper presented at the annual conference of the International Communication Association, San Francisco, May, 1989. **[80, 82, 98]**

Waterman, David. "World TV Menus: The Economic Effects of New Technology and Privatization," paper presented at the annual conference of the International Communication Association, New Orleans, 1988. **[89]**

Waterman, David. "The Failure of Cultural Programming on Cable TV: An Economic Interpretation," *Journal of Communication* (Summer, 1986) 36(3): 92-107. **[195, 335]**

Watzlawick, P., J. Beavin and D.D. Jackson. *Pragmatics of Human Communication.* New York: Norton, 1967.

Way, W.L. "Using Content Analysis to Examine Consumer Behaviors Portrayed on Television: A Pilot Study in a Consumer Education Context," *Journal of Consumer Affairs* (Summer, 1984) 18(1): 79-91. **[18, 371]**

Weaver, David H. "The Press and Government Restrictions: A Cross-National Study Over Time," *Gazette* (1977) 23: 152-170. **[57, 60]**

Weaver, David H. and J.M. Budeenbaum. "Newspapers and Television: A Review of Research on Uses and Effects," *ANPA News Research Report* (April 20, 1979) No. 19. Washington, D.C.: ANPA. **[254]**

Weaver, David H., J.M. Buddenbaum and J.F. Fair. "Press Freedom, Media, and Development, 1950-1979: A Study of 134 Nations," *Journal of Communication* (Spring, 1985) 35(2): 104-117.

Weaver, David and LeAnne Daniels. "Public Opinion on Investigative Reporting in the 1980s," *Journalism Quarterly* (Spring, 1992) 69(1): 146-155. **[203]**

Weaver, David, Dan Drew and G. Cleveland Wilhoit. "U.S. Television, Radio and Daily Newspaper Journalists," *Journalism Quarterly* (Winter, 1987) 64: 683-692. **[57, 164]**

Weaver, David and Virginia Dodge Fielder. "Civic Attitudes and Newspaper Readership in Chicago," *Newspaper Research Journal* (Summer, 1983) 4(4): 11-18.

Weaver, David H. and John B. Mauro. "Newspaper Readership Patterns," *Journalism Quarterly* (Spring, 1978) 55: 84-91, 134. **[270]**

Weaver, James B., Christopher J. Porter and Margaret E. Evans. "Patterns in Foreign News Coverage on U.S. Network TV: A 10-Year Analysis," *Journalism Quarterly* (Summer, 1984) 61(2): 356-363. **[364]**

Weaver, David and G. Cleveland Wilhoit. *A Profile of JMC Educators: Traits, Attitudes, Values.* Bloomington, Indiana: School of Journalism, 1989. Also reported in *Journalism Educator* (Summer, 1988) 43(2): 4-41. **[164]**

Weaver, David H. and G. Cleveland Wilhoit. *The American Journalist: A Portrait of U.S. News People and Their Work.* Bloomington: Indiana University Press, 1986. **[147, 148, 149, 150, 164, 165]**

Weaver, David, G. Cleveland Wilhoit, and H. De Bock. "Personal Needs and Media Use in the Netherlands and the United States," *Gazette* (1980) 26: 171-194. **[273]**

Weaver, David H., G. Cleveland Wilhoit and P. Riede. "Personal Needs and Media Use," *ANPA News Research Report* (July 20, 1979) No. 21. Washington, D.C.: American Newspaper Publishers Association. **[277]**

Weber, Larry J. and Dan B. Fleming. "Media Use and Student Knowledge of Current Events," *Journalism Quarterly* (Summer, 1983) 60(2): 356-358. **[216]**

Webster, J.G. "Program Audience Duplication: A Study of Television Inheritance Effects," *Journal of Broadcasting & Electronic Media* (Spring, 1985) 29(2): 121-133. **[268]**

Webster, James G. "Audience Behavior in the New Media Environment," *Journal of Communication* (1986) 36(3): 77-91. **[17, 270]**

Webster, James G. "Cable Television's Impact on Audience for Local News," *Journalism Quarterly* (Summer, 1984) 61(2): 419-422. **[212]**

Webster, James G, and Jacob J. Wakshlag. "A Theory of Television Program Choice," *Communication Research* (October, 1983) 10(4): 430-446. **[268]**

Webster, James G. and Ting-Yu Wang. "Structural Determinants of Exposure to Television: The Case of Repeat Viewing," *Journal of Broadcasting & Electronic Media* (Spring, 1992) 36(2): 125-136. **[224]**

Webster, James G. and Gregory D. Newton. "Structural Determinants of the Television News Audience," *Journal of Broadcasting & Electronic Media* (Fall, 1988) 32(4): 381-389. **[223, 224]**

Weibbecker, Helga. "Die Veranderung der Themenschwerpunkte in den Horfunk-Nachrichten des HR von 1955 bis 1985," master's thesis, Mainz, 1989, cited in Kepplinger and Kocher (1990).

Weibull, Lennart and Magnus Anshelm. "Signs of Change: Swedish Media in Transition," *The Nordicom Review of Nordic Mass Communication Research* (1991) No. 2: 37-61. **[59]**

Weigel, Russell H. and James W. Loomis. "Televised Models of Female Achievement Revisited: Some Progress," *Journal of Applied Social Psychology* (January/February, 1981) 11(1): 58-63. **[366]**

Weimann, Gabriel, Hans-Bernd Brosius and Mallory Wober. "TV Diets: Towards a Typology of TV Viewership," *European Journal of Communication* (1992) 7: 491-515. **[218]**

Weis, W.L. and C. Burke. "Media Content and Tobacco Advertising: An Unhealthy Addition," *Journal of Communication* (1986) 36: 59-69. **[163]**

Weiss, C. "Media Report Card for Social Science," *Society* (March/April, 1985) 22(3): 39-47. **[163]**

Weiss, C.H. and E. Singer. *Reporting of Social Science in the National Media.* New York: Russell Sage Foundation, 1988. **[368]**

Welch, A.J. and J.H. Watt Jr. "Visual Complexity and Young Children's Learning from Television," *Human Communication Research* (1982) 8: 133-145. **[310]**

Welch, Edward. "News Sharing: TV and Newspapers," paper presented at the annual conference of the Association for Education in Journalism and Mass Communication, Boston, August, 1991. **[122]**

Weldon, M.S. and H.L. Roediger III. "Altering Retrieval Demands Reverses the Picture Superiority Effect," *Memory and Cognition* (July, 1987) 15(4): 269-280. **[290]**

Wellman, Bill. "Freedom Makes ADN A News Agency: Professionalism Replaces Propaganda as the Guidepost for East German Journalists," *Presstime*, October, 1990, p. 14-15. **[49]**

Wells, A. "Women in Popular Music: Changing Fortunes from 1955 to 1984," *Popular Music and Society* (1986) 10(4): 73-85. **[366]**

Wells, Alan and Ernest A. Hakanen. "The Emotional Use of Popular Music by Adolescents," *Journalism Quarterly* (Fall, 1991) 68(3): 445-454. **[275]**

Wember, B. "Wie Informiert das Fernsehen?" *Ein Indizienbeweis.* Munich: List Verlag, 1976. Cited in Heuvelman (1989). **[319]**

Wenner, L.A. "Gratifications Sought and Obtained in Program Dependency: A Study of Network Evening News Programs and 60 Minutes," *Communication Research* (1982) 9: 539-560. **[273]**

Wenner, L.A. "The Nature of News Gratifications," *Media Gratifications Research: Current Perspectives*, ed. K.E. Rosengren, L.A. Wenner and P. Palmgreen. Beverly Hills, CA: Sage Publications, 1985, pp. 171-194. **[254]**

Wenner, L.A. "Model Specification and Theoretical Development in Gratifications Sought and Obtained Research: A Comparison of Discrepancy and Transactional Approaches," *Communication Monographs* (1986) 53: 160-179. **[273]**

Werner, Anita. "Mass Media Expenditures in Norway: The Principle of Relative Constancy Revisited," *Communication Yearbook 9*, ed. M.L. McLaughlin. Beverly Hills, CA: Sage, 1986, pp. 251-260. **[59, 211]**

Westerstahl, Jorgen. "Objective News Reporting: General Premises," *Communication Research* (July, 1983) 10(3): 403-424. **[129]**

Westerstahl, Jorgen and Folke Johansson. "News Ideologies as Moulders of Domestic News," *European Journal of Communication* (1986) 1(2): 133-149. **[158]**

Westley, Bruce H. *News Editing*. 2nd ed., Boston: Houghton Mifflin, 1980. **[292]**

Whaley, J.F. "Story Grammars and Reading Instruction," *Reading Teacher* (1981) 34: 762-771. **[316]**

Whaley, J.F. "Readers' Expectations of Story Structures," *Reading Research Quarterly* (1981) 17: 90-114. **[316]**

Whitby, Gary L. "Horns of a Dilemma: The 'Sun,' Abolition, and the 1833-34 New York Riots," *Journalism Quarterly* (Summer, 1990) 67(2): 410-419. **[31]**

White, D.L. "The Poetics of Horror: More than Meets the Eye," *Film Genre: Theory and Criticism*, ed. Barry K. Grant. Metuchen, NJ: The Scarecrow Press, Inc., pp. 124-144, 1977. **[330]**

White, David Manning. "The Gatekeeper: A Case Study in the Selection of News," *Journalism Quarterly* (Fall, 1950) 27: 383-390. **[138, 161]**

White, H. Allen and Julie L. Andsager. "Winning Newspaper Pulitzer Prizes: The (Possible) Advantage of Being a Competitive Paper," *Journalism Quarterly* (Winter, 1990) 67(4): 912-919. **[91]**

White, Mimi. "Television Genres: Intertextuality," *Journal of Film and Video* (Summer, 1985) 38: 41-47. **[332]**

White, Robert A. "Mass Communication and Culture: Transition to a New Paradigm," *Journal of Communication* (Summer, 1983) 33(3): 279-301. **[20]**

White, Stephen. "Our Public Television Experiment," *Public Interest* (Summer, 1987) No. 88, pp. 79-93. **[75]**

White, Sylvia E. "VCR Owners' Use of Pay Cable Services," *Journalism Quarterly* (Spring, 1987) 64(1): 193-195. **[75, 213]**

Whitenead, F., A.C. Capey, W. Maddren and A. Wellings. *Children and Their Books*. London: Macmillan, 1977. **[214]**

Whitney, D. Charles and Lee B. Becker. "Keeping the Gates' for Gatekeepers: The Effects of Wire News," *Journalism Quarterly* (1982) 59: 60-65. **[139]**

Whitney, D. Charles. "Current Research on American Mass Communicators: Expanding the Margins," *Mass Comm Review* (1991) 18(3): 3-8. **[102]**

Whitney, D. Charles, Marilyn Fritzler, Steven Jones, Sharon Mazzarella and Lana Rakow. "Geographic and Source Biases in Network Television News 1982-1984," *Journal of Broadcasting & Electronic Media* (Spring, 1989) 33(2): 159-174. **[121, 136, 157, 341]**

Whitney, D.C. *The Media and the People: Soundings from Two Communities*. New York: Gannett Center for Media Studies, Columbia University, 1985. **[203, 205, 208]**

Whitney, D.C. *The Media and the People: America's Experience with the News Media--A Fifty-Year Review*. New York: Gannett Center for Media Studies, Columbia University, 1985. **[203, 205, 208]**

Wicke, Jennifer (Ed.) *Advertising Functions: Literature, Advertisement and Social Reading*. New York: Columbia University Press, 1988. **[58]**

Wicker, F.W. "Photographs, Drawings and Nouns as Stimuli in Paired-Associate Learning," *Psychonomic Science* (1970) 18(4): 205-206. **[315]**

Wickham, Kathleen Woodruff. "The Generation of Story Ideas: An Exploratory Study of Gatekeeping in Local Television News," paper presented to the Radio-Television Journalism Division at the annual conference of the Association for Education in Journalism and Mass communication," Washington, D.C., Aug. 11, 1989. **[162]**

Wicks, Robert H. "Segmenting Broadcast News Audiences in the New Media Environment," *Journalism Quarterly* (Summer, 1989) 66(2): 383-390. **[251]**

Wigand, R.T. and E.H. Craft. "Television as a Socializing Agent and Need Gratifier in Mature Adults," *Communications: European Journal of Communication* (1985) 11(1): 9-30. **[278]**

Wiggins, W.H. "Boxing's Sambo Twins: Racial Stereotypes in Jack Johnson and Joe Louis Newspaper Cartoons, 1908 to 1938," *Journal of Sport History* (Winter, 1988) 15(3): 242-252. **[365]**

Wilhoit, G. Cleveland and Dan G. Drew. "Editorial Writers on American Daily Newspapers: A 20 Year Portrait," *Journalism Monographs*, October, 1991, No. 129. **[149, 164]**

Wilhoit, G. Cleveland and Dan G. Drew. "Politics, Professional Values, and Social Profile of Editorial Writers: A Twenty-Year Portrait," paper presented to the Newspaper Division at the annual conference of the Association for Education in Journalism and Mass Communication, Washington, D.C., Aug. 10-13, 1989. **[161, 164]**

Wilke, J. "The Changing World of Media Reality," *Gazette* (1984) 34(3): 175-190. **[124]**

Wilkes, Robert E. and Humberto Valencia. "Hispanics and Blacks in Television Commercials," *Journal of Advertising* (1989) 18(1): 19-25. **[364]**

Wilkins, Lee and Philip Patterson. "Risk Analysis and the Construction of News," *Journal of Communication* (Summer, 1987) 37(3): 80-92. **[126]**

Wilkins, L. "Television and Newspaper Coverage of a Blizzard: Is the Message Helplessness?" *Newspaper Research Journal* (Summer, 1985) 6(4): 51-65. **[119]**

Willett, John. *The New Sobriety, 1917-1933: Art and Politics in the Weimar Period.* Over Wallop, Hampshire, 1978. **[18]**

Williams, D.M. "A New Medium for Advertising: The Postcard, 1900-1920," *European Journal of Marketing* (1988) 22(8): 17-33. **[40, 64, 65]**

Williams, F. (ed.) *Measuring the Information Society.* Newbury Park, CA: Sage Publications, 1988. **[40, 64, 65]**

Williams, F., A.F. Phillips, and P. Lum. "Gratifications Associated with New Communication Technologies," *Media Gratifications Research: Current Perspectives*, ed. K.E. Rosengren, L.A. Wenner and P. Palmgreen. Beverly Hills, CA: Sage Publications, 1985, pp. 241-252. **[250]**

Williams, Frederick. "The Information Society as an Object of Study," *Measuring the Information Society*, ed. Frederick Williams. Newbury Park, CA: Sage Publications, 1988, pp. 13-31. **[64]**

Williams, J.A. Jr. et al. "Sex Role Socialization in Picture Books: An Update," *Social Science Quarterly* (March, 1987) 68(1): 148-156. **[368]**

Williams, L.G. "The Effect of Target Specifications on Objects Fixated During Visual Search," *Perception & Psychophysics* (1966) 1: 315-318. **[288]**

Williams, Raymond. *Television: Technology and Cultural Form.* New York: Schocken, 1974. **[116]**

Williams, Raymond. *Culture.* London: Fontana, 1981. **[116]**

Williams, Wenmouth Jr. and Mitchell E. Shapiro. "A Study of the Effects In-Home Entertainment Alternatives Have on Film Attendance," *Current Research in Film: Audiences, Economics, and Law*, ed. Bruce A. Austin. Norwood, NJ: Ablex, 1985, pp. 93-100. **[180]**

Wilson, John. "Sociology of Leisure," *Annual Review of Sociology* (1980) 6: 21-40. **[265]**

Windahl, Sven, Ingrid Hojerback and Elias Hedinsson. "Adolescents without Television: A Study in Media Deprivation," *Journal of Broadcasting & Electronic Media* (Winter, 1986) 30(1): 47-63. **[248, 255]**

Winick, C. and M.P. Winick. "Courtroom Drama on Television," *Journal of Communication* (1974) 24(3): 67-73. **[369]**

Winick, C. "The Functions of Television: Life without the Big Box," *Television as a Social Issue*, ed. S. Oskamp. Newbury Park, CA: Sage Publications, 1988, pp. 217-237. **[248]**

Winter, J.P. "Interlocking Directorships and Economic Power," *Press Concentration and Monopoly: New Perspectives on Newspaper Ownership and Operation*. Norwood, NJ: Ablex, 1988, pp. 105-116. **[80]**

Wirth, M.O. "Economic Barriers to Entering Media Industries in the United States," *Communication Yearbook 9*, ed. M.L. McLaughlin. Beverly Hills, CA: Sage, 1985, pp. 423-442. **[98]**

Wirth, Michael O. "Cable's Economic Impact on Over-the-Air Broadcasting," *Journal of Media Economics* (Fall, 1990) 3(2): 39-53. **[70]**

Wirth, Michael O. "The Economic Impact of Cable on Broadcasting," paper presented to the Mass Communication Division at the annual conference of the International Communication Association, San Francisco, May, 1989. **[84]**

Witt, P.A. "Factor Structure of Leisure Behavior for High School Age Youth in Three Communities," *Journal of Leisure Research* (1971) 4: 213-219.

Woal, M. "Program Interests of NPR Subaudiences," *Journalism Quarterly* (Summer, 1986) 63(2): 348-352.

Wober, J. Mallory and Barrie Gunter. "Television Audience Research at Britain's Independent Broadcasting Authority, 1974-1984," *Journal of Broadcasting & Electronic Media* (Winter, 1986) 30(1): 15-31. **[257]**

Wolf, R. T. Thomason and P. LaRocque. "The Right to Know Vs. the Right of Privacy: Newspaper Identification of Crime Victims," *Journalism Quarterly* (Summer/Autumn, 1987) 64(2/3): 503-507. **[160]**

Wolfe, D. "The Effect of Interruptions and Continuous Music on Bodily Movement and Task Performance of Third Grade Students," *Journal of Music Therapy* (1982) 19: 82-83. **[227]**

Wolfe, Tom. *The Painted Word*. New York, 1975. **[18]**

Wolseley, Roland E. *The Changing Magazine*. New York: Hastings House, 1973. **[58]**

Wolverton, David and D. Vance. "Newspaper Coverage of Proposals for Rate Increases by Electric Utility," *Journalism Quarterly* (Summer/Autumn, 1987) 64(2/3): 551-584. **[120]**

Wonsek, Pamela L. "College Basketball on Television: A Study of Racism in the Media," *Media, Culture and Society* (1992) 14: 449-461. **[364]**

Wood, James Playsted. *Magazines in the United States*. New York: Ronald, 1956, 2nd ed. **[58]**

Wood, W.C. "Consumer Spending on the Mass Media: The Principle of Relative Constancy Reconsidered," *Journal of Communication* (Spring, 1986) 36(2): 39-51. **[59]**

Wood, William C. and Sharon L. O'Hare. "Paying for the Video Revolution: Consumer Spending on the Mass Media," *Journal of Communication* (Winter, 1991) 41: 24-30. **[59]**

Wood, William C. "Consumer Spending on the Mass Media: The Principle of Relative Constancy Reconsidered," *Journal of Communication* (Spring, 1986) 36: 39-51. **[211]**

Woodall, W. Gill, Dennis K. Davis and Haluk Sahin. "From the Boob Tube to the Black Box: Television News Comprehension from an Information Processing Perspective," *Journal of Broadcasting* (1983) 27: 1-23. **[294, 305, 320]**

Woodard, Michael D. "Class, Regionality, and Leisure Among Urban Black Americans: The Post-Civil Rights Era," *Journal of Leisure Research* (1988) 20(2): 87-105. **[234, 270]**

Woolf, Virginia. "Mr. Bennett and Mrs. Brown," *Collected Essays*. New York: 1967, pp. 320-321. **[18]**

Worth, Sol and John Adair. "Navajo Filmmakers," *American Anthropologist* (1972) 74: 9-34. **[318]**

Worth, Sol. *Studying Visual Communication*. Philadelphia: University of Pennsylvania Press, 1981. **[318]**

498   References and Author Index

Wright, Erik Olin. "The Comparative Project on Class Structure and Class Consciousness: An Overview," *Acta Sociologica* (1989) 32(1): 3-22. **[269]**

Wright, John S, and John E. Mertes. *Advertising's Role in Society*, St. Paul, Minn.: West, 1974. **[58]**

Wright, John W. II and Lawrence A. Hosman. "Listener Perceptions of Radio News," *Journalism Quarterly* (Winter, 1986) 63(4): 802-814. **[196]**

Wulfemeyer, K. Tim. "Defining Ethics in Electronic Journalism: Perceptions of News Directors," *Journalism Quarterly* (Winter, 1990) 67(4): 984-991. **[142]**

Wulfemeyer, K. Tim. "How and Why Anonymous Attribution Is Used by 'Time' and 'Newsweek,'" *Journalism Quarterly* (Spring, 1985) 62(1): 81-86. **[132]**

Wulfemeyer, K. Tim. "Perceptions of Viewer Interests by Local TV Journalists," *Journalism Quarterly* (Summer, 1984) 61(2): 432-435. **[120]**

Wulfemeyer, K. Tim. "A Content Analysis of Local Television Newscasts: Answering the Critics," *Journal of Broadcasting* (Winter, 1982) 26(1): 481-486. **[340]**

Wulfemeyer, K. Tim and Lori L. McFadden. "Anonymous Attribution in Network News," *Journalism Quarterly* (Autumn, 1986) 63(3): 468-471. **[132]**

Wuliger, Gregory T. "The Moral Universes of Libertarian Press Theory," *Critical Studies in Mass Communication* (1991) 8: 152-167. **[53]**

Wuthnow, R. "The Social Significance of Religious Television," *Review of Religious Research* (December, 1987) 29(2): 125-134. **[196]**

Wyatt, R.O. and D.P. Badger. "What Newspaper Film Critics Value in Film and Film Criticism: A National Survey," *Current Research on Film: Audiences, Economics and Law*, ed. B.A. Austin. Vol. 4. Norwood, NJ: Ablex, 1988, pp. 54-71. **[164]**

Wyatt, Robert O. and Geoffrey P. Hull. "The Music Critic in the American Press: A Nationwide Survey of Newspapers and Magazines," *Mass Com Review* (1990) 17(3): 38-43. **[164]**

Wyatt, Robert O. and David P. Badger. "Toward a New Typology of Journalistic Genres," paper presented at the annual conference of the International Communication Association, Dublin, Ireland, June, 1990. **[340]**

Wyatt, Robert O. *Free Expression and the American Public: A Survey Commemorating the 200th Anniversary of the First Amendment*. Murfreesboro, Tenn.: Middle Tennessee State University, 1991. **[204]**

Wyer, R. and S. Gordon. "The Cognitive Representation of Social Information," *Handbook of Social Cognition*, ed. R. Wyer and T. Srull. Vol. 2 Hillsdale, NJ: Lawrence Erlbaum, 1984. **[321]**

Wynter, Leon E. "Black TV Viewers Have Big Impact on Shows' Ratings," *Wall Street Journal*, Sept. 1, 1989, p. 4B. **[233]**

Yacowar, Maurice. "The Bug in the Rug: Notes on the Disaster Genre," *Film Genre: Theory and Criticism*, ed. Barry K. Grant. Metuchen, NJ: The Scarecrow Press, Inc., pp. 90-107, 1977. **[330]**

Yadava, J.S. "Press System in India," *Media Asia* (1991) 18(3): 132-136, 142. **[43]**

Yadava, J.S. and Usha V. Reddi. "In the Midst of Diversity: Television in Urban Indian Homes," *World Families Watch Television*, ed. James Lull. Newbury Park, CA: Sage Publications, 1988, pp. 116-135. **[235]**

Yanclay, F. and B. Metcalf. "Alternative Lifestyle Magazines: An Analysis of Readers," *Media Information Australia* (May, 1985) 36: 49-55. **[280]**

Yang, Tai-en, John C. Schweitzer and Mark D. Harmon. "How Three U.S. Newsmagazines Covered Gorbachev and Deng," paper presented to the Magazine Division at the annual conference of the Association for Education in Journalism and Mass Communication, Montreal, August, 1992. **[127]**

Yankelovich, Skelly and White, Inc. "Tracking the Attitudes of the Public Towards the Newspaper Business," *ANPA News Research Report* (April 20, 1979) No. 19. Washington, D.C. **[206]**

Yarborough, D.B. and E.D. Gagne. "Metaphor and the Free Recall of Technical Text," *Discourse Processes* (January-March, 1987) 10(1): 81-91. **[296]**

Yasuko, Muramatsu. "For Wives on Friday: Women's Roles in TV Dramas," *Japan Quarterly* (April-June, 1986) 33(2): 159-163. **[366]**

Yoshida, Jun. "Development of Television and Changes in TV Viewing Habits in Japan," *Studies of Broadcasting* (1986) 22: 127-154. Japan: Nippon Hoso Kyokai (NHK).**[224, 255]**

Yoshida, Roland K., Lynn Wasilewski and Douglas L. Friedman. "Recent Newspaper Coverage about Persons with Disabilities," *Exceptional Children* (February, 1990) 56(5): 418-423. **[370]**

Youm, K.H. "Press Law in the Republic of Korea," *New York Law School Journal of International and Comparative Law* (Spring, 1986) 6(3): 667-702. **[26]**

Young, C. "Ethnic Media and Ethnic Groups," *Media Information Australia* (May, 1986) 40: 49-55. **[270]**

Yu, Yang-Chou and Daniel Riffe. "Chiang and Mao in U.S. News Magazines," *Journalism Quarterly* (Winter, 1989) 66(4): 913-919. **[121]**

Zablocki, Benjamin D. and Rosabeth Moss Kanter. "The Differentiation of Life-Styles," *Annual Review of Sociology* (1976) 2: 269-298. **[263, 264]**

Zaharopoulos, Thimios. "The Image of Greece in the U.S. Press," *Journalism Quarterly* (Winter, 1984) 61(4): 901-905. **[371]**

Zaharopoulos, Thimios. "The Image of the U.S. in the Greek Press," *Journalism Quarterly* (Spring, 1989) 66(1): 188-192. **[371]**

Zahn, Susan B. and Stanley J. Baran. "It's All in the Family: Siblings and Program Choice Conflict," *Journalism Quarterly* (Winter, 1984) 61(4): 847-852. **[239]**

Zanot, E.J. "Public Attitudes Toward Advertising: The American Experience," *International Journal of Advertising* (1984) 3(1): 3-15. **[200]**

Zehr, Leonard. "Screen Giant: Garth Drabinsky Jars Movie-House Industry, Sets New Standards," *Wall Street Journal*, March 16, 1987. **[66]**

Zeki, S.M. "The Functional Organization of Projections from Striate to Prestriate Visual Cortex in the Rhesus Monkey," *Cold Spring Harbor Symposia on Quantitative Biology* (1976) 15: 591-600. Cited in Gilbert and Schleuder (1988). **[288]**

Zelizer, Barbie. "Achieving Journalistic Authority through Narrative," *Critical Studies in Mass Communication* (1990) 7: 366-376. **[157, 159]**

Zerbinos, Eugenia. "Information Seeking and Information Processing: Newspapers Versus Videotext," *Journalism Quarterly* (Winter, 1990) 67(4): 920-929. **[311, 320]**

Zettl, H. *Sight, Sound, Motion: Applied Media Aesthetics*. Belmont, CA: Wadsworth, 1973. **[300]**

Zhou, He. "Changes in the Soviet Concept of News--To What Extent and Why?" *Gazette* (1988) 42: 193-211. **[59, 177]**

Zhu, Jian-Hua and David Weaver. "Newspaper Subscribing: A Dynamic Analysis," *Journalism Quarterly* (Summer, 1989) 66(2): 285-294, 337. **[276]**

Zhu, Jian-Hua. "Recent Trends in Adversarial Attitudes among American Newspaper Journalists: A Cohort Analysis," *Journalism Quarterly* (Winter, 1990) 67(4): 992-1004. **[152]**

Zhu, Jian-Hua. "Dropping Vs. Restarting: A Dynamic Analysis of Two Newspaper Subscribing Behaviors," paper presented to the Communication Theory & Methodology Division at the annual conference of the Association for Education in Journalism and Mass Communication, Portland, OR, July 2, 1988.

Ziegler, Dhyana and Alisa White. "Women and Minorities on Network Television News: An Examination of Correspondents and Newsmakers," *Journal of Broadcasting & Electronic Media* (Spring, 1990) 34(2): 215-223. **[364]**

Zillmann, Dolf. "Mood Management through Communication Choices," *American Behavioral Scientist* (1988) 31(3): 327-340.

Zillmann, Dolf and Norbert Mundorf. "Image Effects in the Appreciation of Video Rock," *Communication Research* (June, 1987) 14(3): 316-334. **[196, 275]**

Zinkhan, George M., William J. Qualls, and Abhijit Biswas. "The Use of Blacks in Magazine and Television Advertising: 1946 to 1986," *Journalism Quarterly* (Autumn, 1990) 67(3): 547-553. **[364]**

Zinkhan, George M., Keith K. Cox and Jae W. Hong. "Changes in Stereotypes: Blacks and Whites in Magazine Advertisements," *Journalism Quarterly* (Autumn, 1986) 63(3): 568-572. **[344, 365]**

Ziporyn, T. "Disease in the Popular American Press: The Case of Diptheria, Typhoid Fever and Syphilis, 1870-1920," *Contributions in Medical Studies*, No. 24. Westport, CT: Greenwood Press, 1988. **[370]**

Zohoori, A.R. "A Cross-Cultural Analysis of Children's Television Use," *Journal of Broadcasting & Electronic Media* (Winter, 1988) 32(1): 105-113. **[255, 258]**

Zohoori, Ali R. "Children, Traditional Media, and Modern Media: The Displacement Hypothesis Revisited," paper presented at the annual conference of the Speech Communication Association, New Orleans, Nov. 3-6, 1988. **[255, 258]**

Zola, Irving Kenneth. "Depictions of Disability--Metaphor, Message, and Medium in the Media: A Research and Political Agenda," *The Social Science Journal* (October, 1985) 22(4): 5-17. **[370]**

Zolf, Dorothy and Paul W. Taylor. "Redressing the Balance in Canadian Broadcasting: A History of Religious Broadcasting Policy in Canada," *Studies in Religion* (1989 18(2): 153-170. **[96]**

Topic Index

501